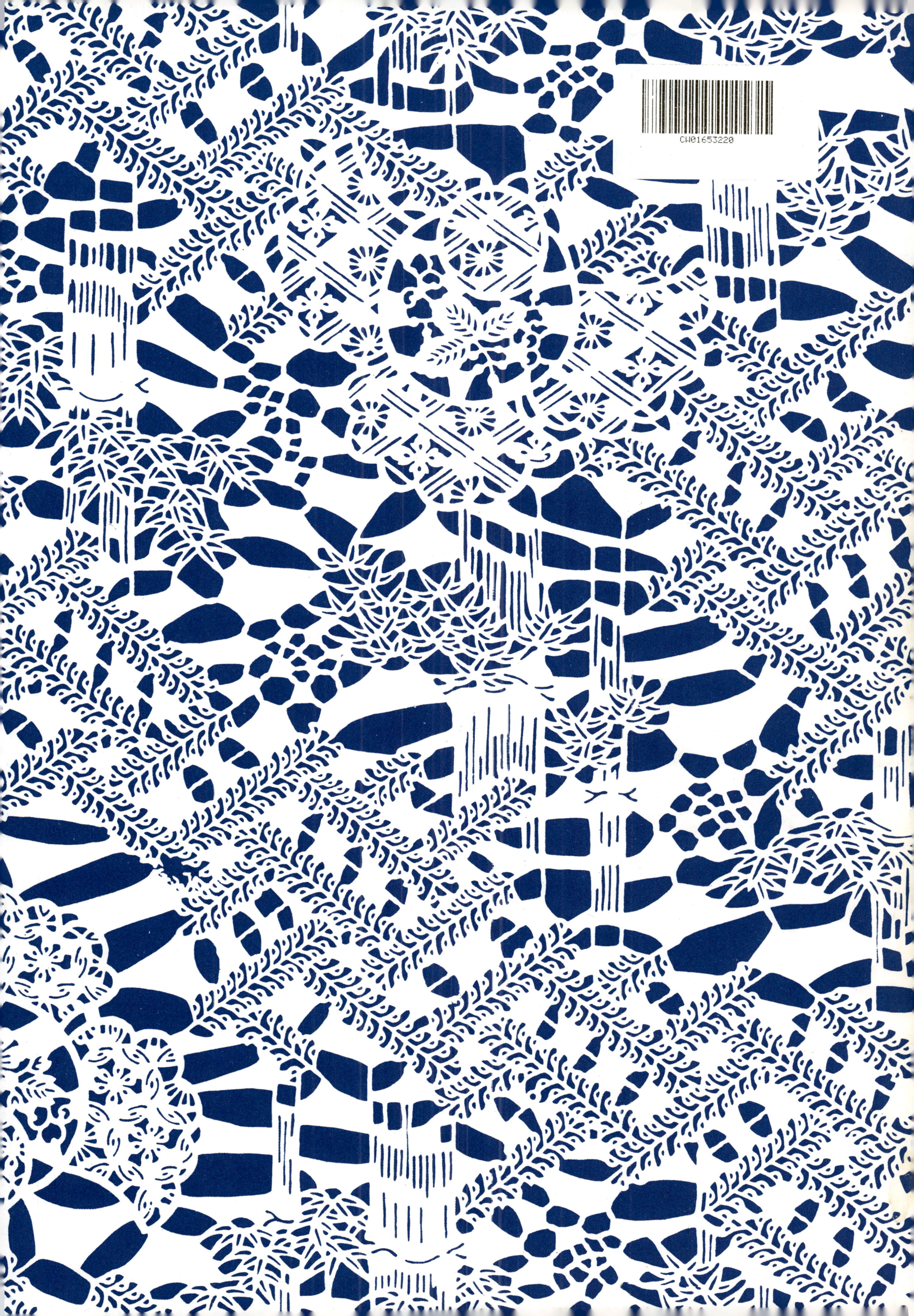

Ukiyo-e to Shin hanga

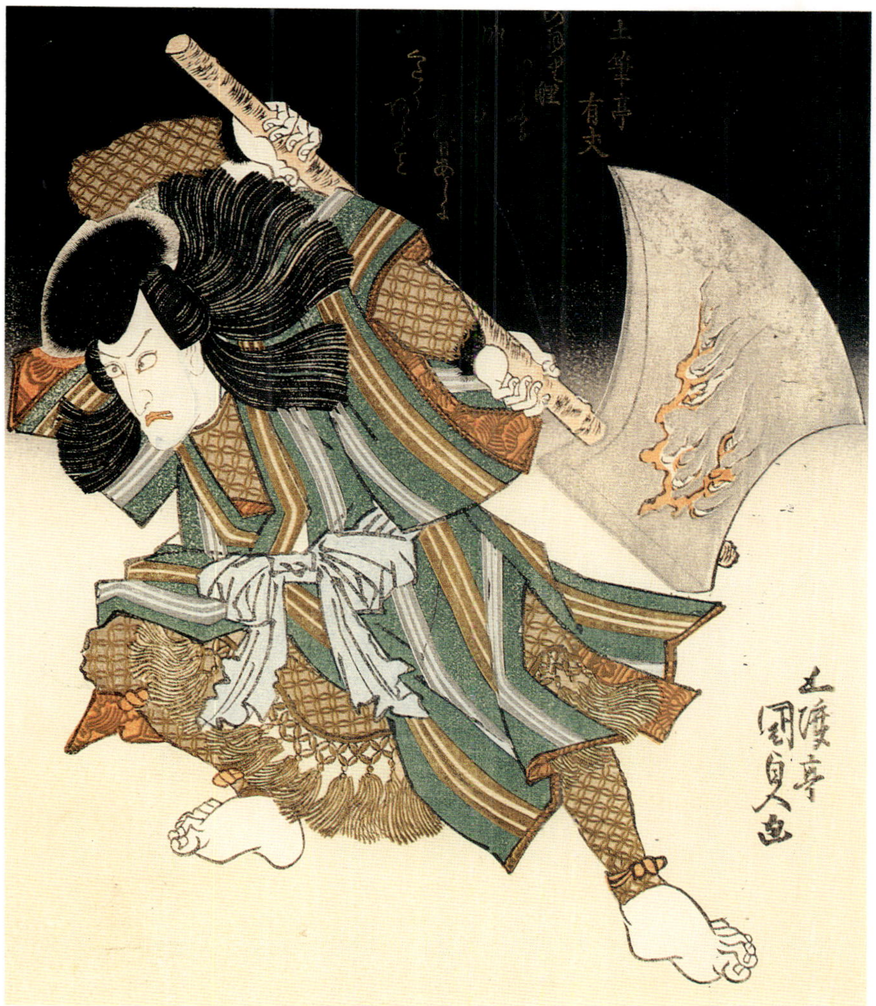

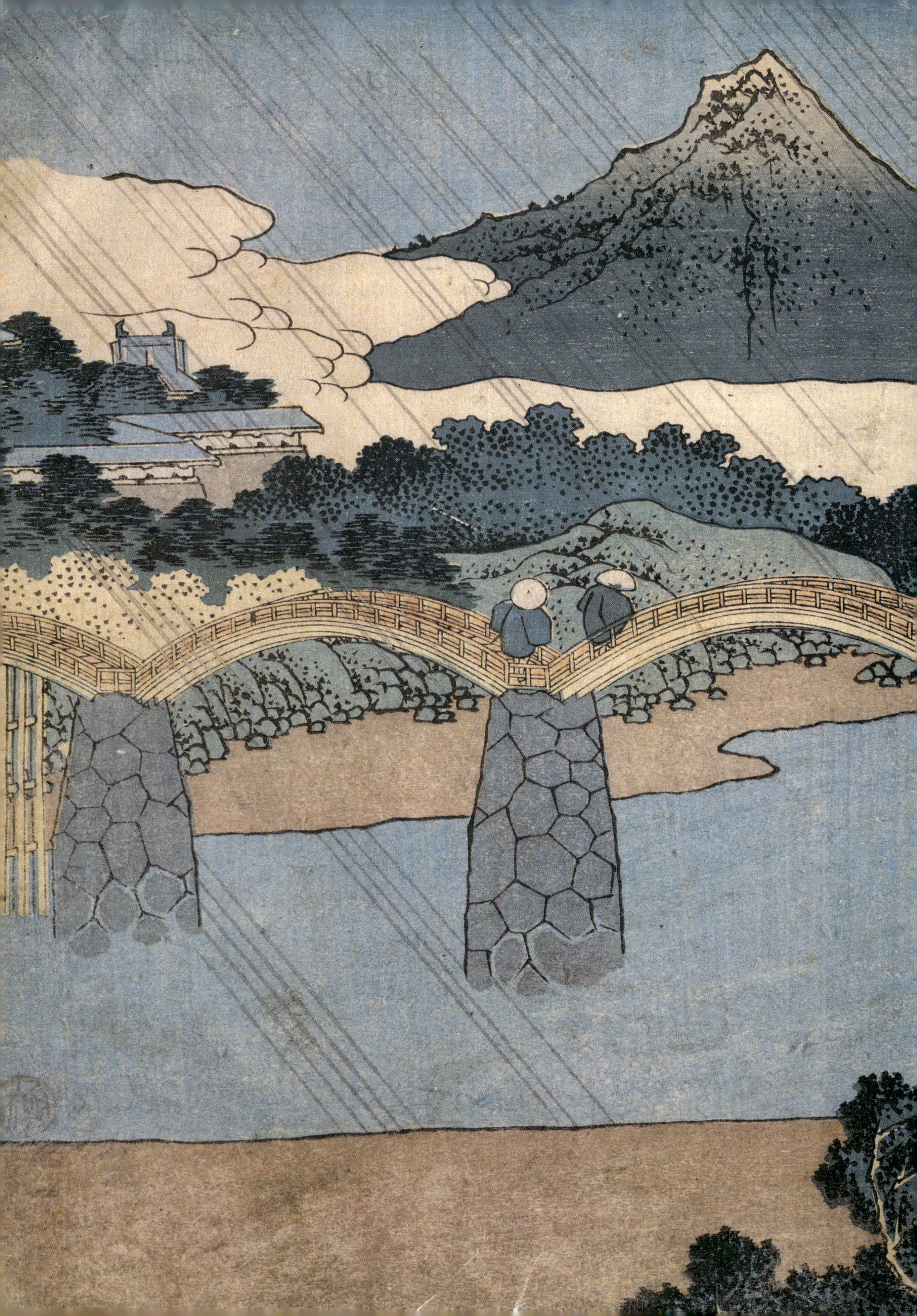

Ukiyo-e to Shin hanga

The Art of Japanese Woodblock Prints

Consulting Editors: AMY NEWLAND and CHRIS UHLENBECK

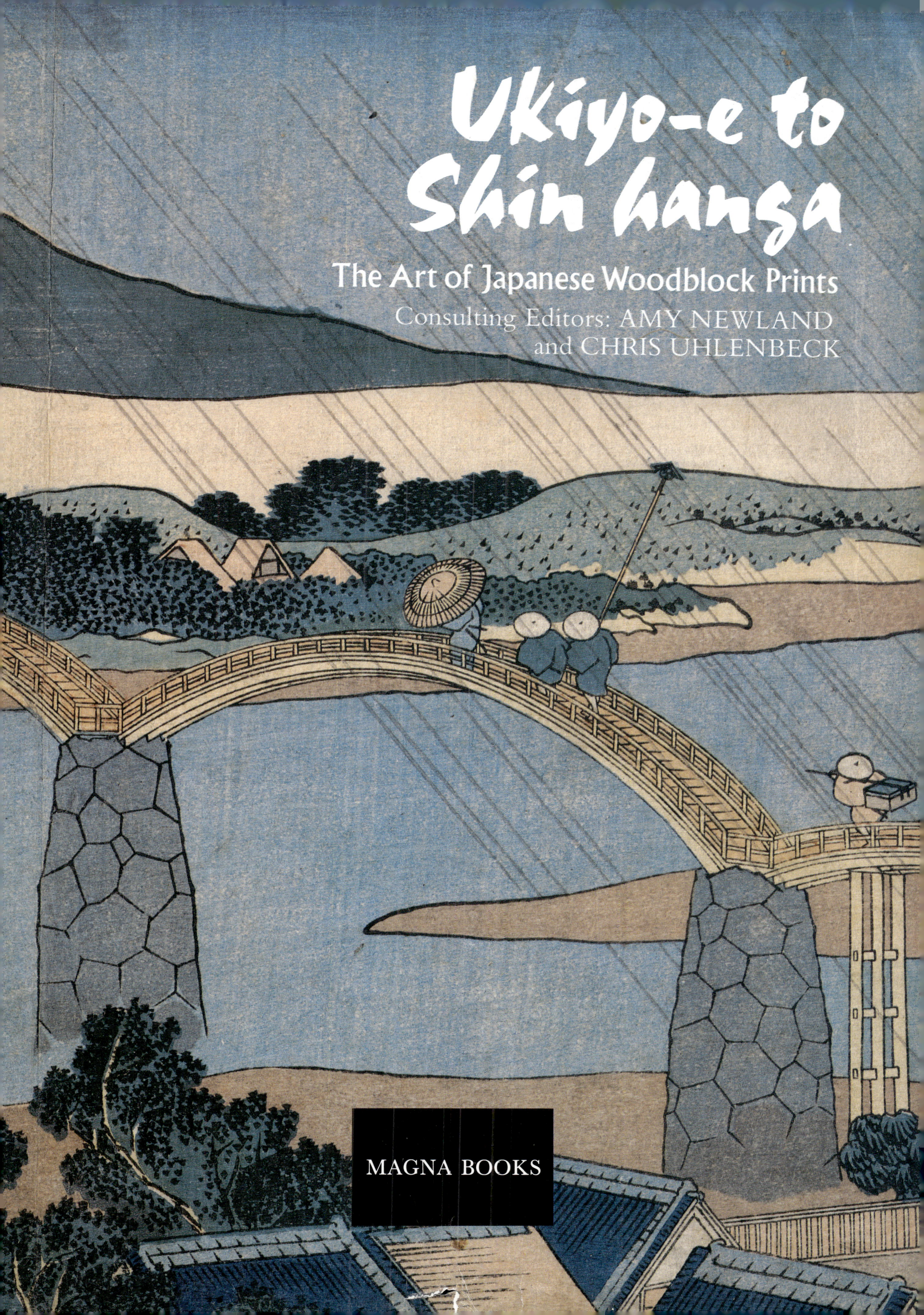

MAGNA BOOKS

Published by Magna Books
Magna Road
Wigston
Leicester LE8 2ZH

Produced by Bison Books Ltd
Kimbolton House
117A Fulham Road
London SW3 6RL

ISBN 1-85422-039-X

Printed in Hong Kong

Page 1: Utagawa Kunisada (1786-1865) 'Scene from *Sukeroku*' (detail), c. 1835, *surimono* triptych (see page 136).

Page 2-3: Katsushika Hokusai (1760-1849) 'Kintai Bridge, Suō Province' (*Suō no kuni, Kintai-bashi*; detail), 1831-32 (see pages 152-53).

CONTRIBUTORS

Jonathan Bennett read English at Trinity Hall, Cambridge. He worked in the Chinese Department of Sotheby's, London, for eight years before leaving to become an independent antique dealer based in London and Manchester.

Lawrence Bickford, a retired IBM research physicist, spent two years on assignment in Tokyo (1963-65). Becoming interested in *ukiyo-e* woodblock prints, he received instruction in classical printmaking techniques from Toshi Yoshida, and settled upon *sumo* prints as a collection speciality and research subject. He has published several articles in *Andon* and *Impressions*.

Julia Hutt studied Chinese Art and Archaeology at the School of Oriental and African Studies, University of London and currently works as a curator in the Far Eastern Collections of the Victoria and Albert Museum, London. She has written articles in various journals and a book, *Understanding Far Eastern Art* (1987).

Dr Richard Illing lives in Warwickshire, England. He has been a collector and student of Japanese prints for over 25 years and has published several popular books on the history and collecting of *ukiyo-e*.

Richard Kruml has been a London-based dealer in Japanese prints, paintings, and books for the past 23 years. He has always held *surimono* in high regard.

Haruo Matsuoka has been promoting Japanese prints through dealing, organizing exhibitions, and publishing catalogues for many years. He is Director of the *Ukiyo-e* Dealers' Association of Japan and Chairman of the Association for the Study of Prints.

Amy Newland was educated at the University of Washington, Seattle, and is presently engaged on doctoral studies at the University of Kansas, Lawrence. Ms Newland's area of interest is the illustrated books of the Edo period, particularly those of the impressionistic Maruyama/Shijō school. She is currently area editor for Japanese Art at Macmillan Publishers' *Dictionary of Art*.

Charlotte van Rappard-Boon is an art historian who works at the Netherlands Office for Fine Arts as Inspector of Cultural Heritage. She has published on Japanese prints and on Japonisme.

Chris Uhlenbeck was born in 1954 and graduated from Leiden University in 1980 with a master's degree in African anthropology. Since 1982 he has dealt in Japanese prints from his shop in Leiden, to which he added in 1988 a bookshop with reference materials on Japanese prints and drawings. He has published on *surimono* and has acted as an editor on the Japanese art journal, *Andon*.

David Waterhouse, a native of Yorkshire, is Professor of East Asian Studies at the University of Toronto. He has published widely on Japanese and other Asian art and music. His other professional interests include Highland bagpipes and judo.

Contents

Introduction

CHRIS UHLENBECK

Being exposed for the first time to a collection of Japanese prints one is startled by the strength of these images. The enormous variety of colors, styles and genres, all unmistakably Japanese, make one wonder about the complexities of the Japanese print. Questions regarding the history, the artists, the techniques of production and the social context cry out to be answered in order to deepen the appreciation of these works of art.

This book endeavors to provide a first set of answers to the most basic questions. The structure is chronological. The seven chapters span the history of Japanese printmaking from its inception to the *sōsaku* and *shin hanga* movements of the twentieth century. As well as covering the high points of Japanese prints history, there are also four thematic excursions: one into the techniques of print production, one into the genre of *surimono*, one into the fascinating world of the wrestler prints and one into Osaka printmaking traditions. The contribution of each chapter by different scholars lends a varied interpretation of this multi-faceted tradition.

HISTORICAL DEVELOPMENT AND SOCIAL CONTEXT

The technique of woodblock printing is said to have originated in China in the fourth century AD. It was introduced to Japan in the wake of the arrival of Chinese and Korean Buddhist missionaries in the sixth century. Woodblock printing came into use primarily for the reproduction of the written word and it was only in the late sixteenth century that woodblock printed illustrations were added to text. The production of illustrated books received an enormous stimulus from the Tokugawa shogunate in the Edo period (1600-1868). Ieyasu (1542-1616), the first Tokugawa shogun and architect of the political structure of Edo Japan which lasted until the Meiji Restoration of 1868, personally encouraged the development of book production. He helped the Rinpa artist Hon'ami Kōetsu (1558-1637) and the calligrapher Suminokura Sōan (1571-1632) set up a center for the Arts and Crafts at Kōetsumura. Kōetsu and Sōan have been credited with first essays into the production of illustrated books where illustration and text form an integrated artistic whole.

Initially illustrations were only in black and white, but gradually, in the middle seventeenth century, books with woodblock-printed coloring appeared. By the late seventeenth century, however, the first independent prints were made. One of the first designers whose identity is firmly established is Hishikawa Moronobu (c. 1618-94). He was known as a book illustrator, but he also designed several, principally erotic, *ōban* (15×10¼ inches [c.38×26cm]) prints. They were initially made only in black and white, with color sometimes added by hand.

Moronobu established a school of painting and illustration which was inspired by the 'floating world,' or *ukiyo*. The 'floating world' can perhaps best be

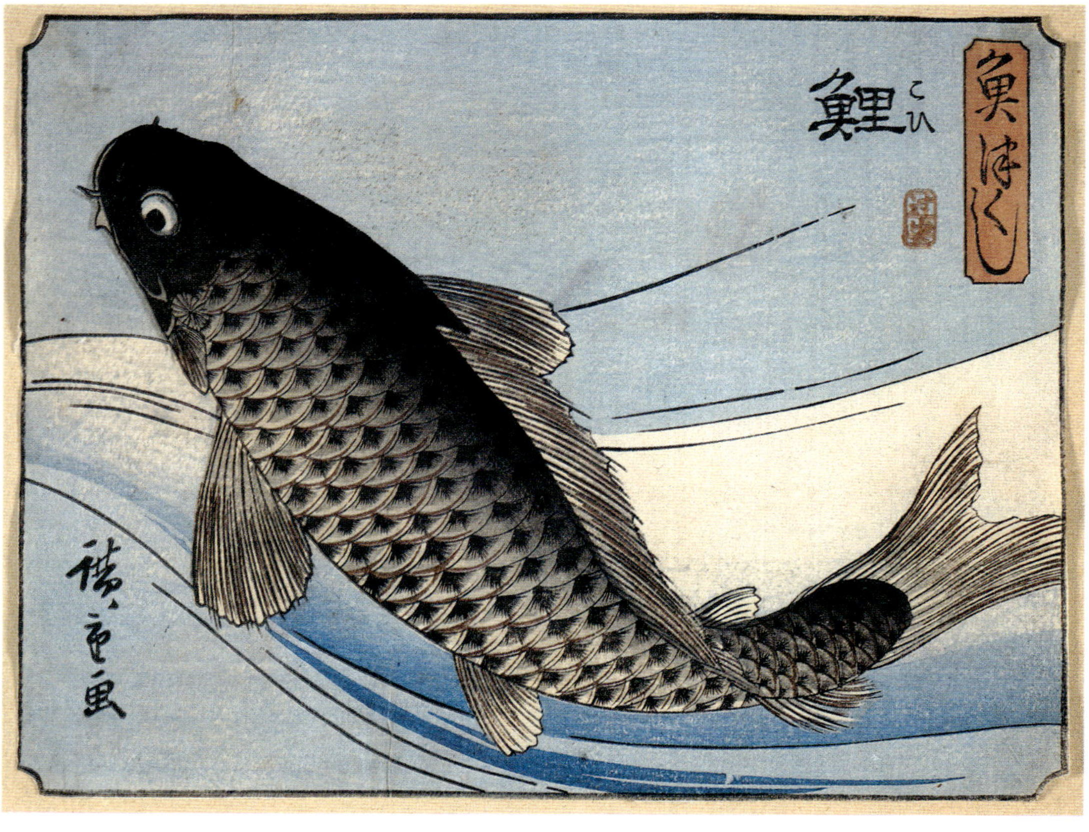

Left: Utagawa Hiroshige (1797-1858) 'A Carp,' from the series 'Small Fishes,' c. 1832. Courtesy, the Whitworth Art Gallery, University of Manchester.

Right: Katsushika Hokusai (1760-1849) 'Amida Falls,' from the series 'A Journey along the Waterfalls of all the Provinces,' (*Shokoku taki meguri*), c. 1831. Signed *Zen Hokusai Iitsu hitsu*. Published by Nishimuraya Yohachi. Collection Hotei, Netherlands.

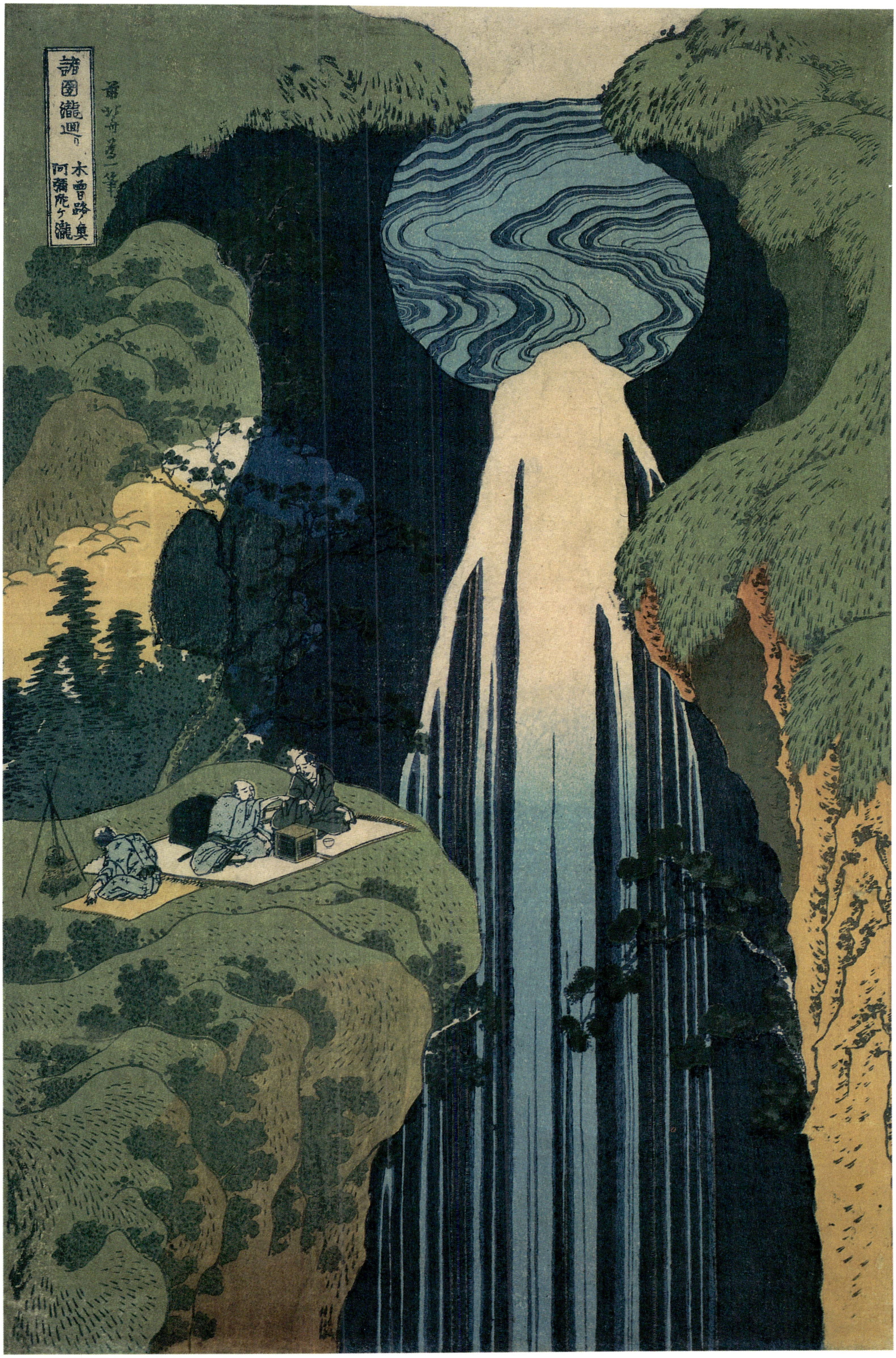
諸國瀧廻リ
木曾路ノ奥
阿彌陀ヶ瀧
前北斎為一筆

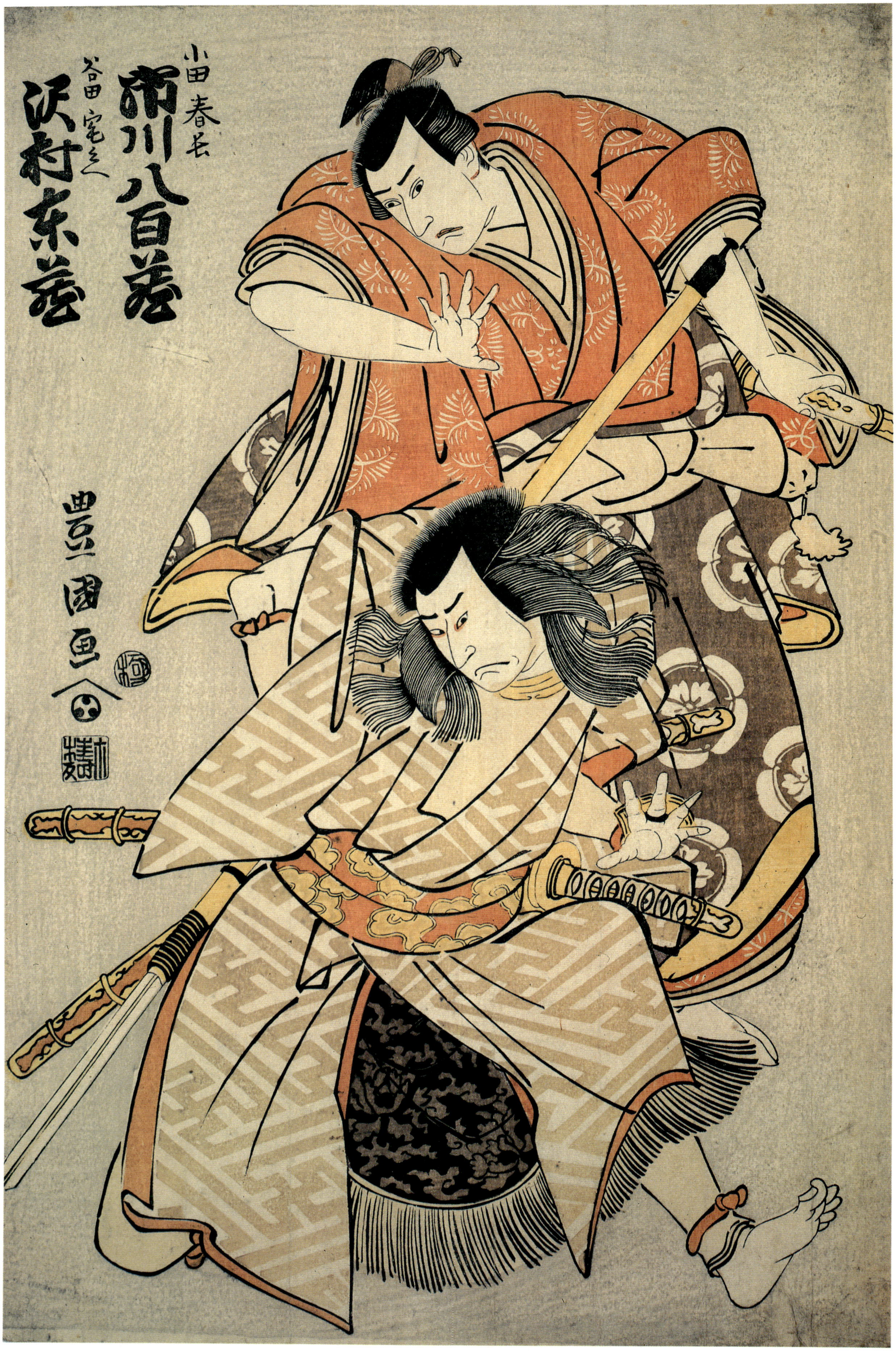
市川八百蔵
沢村東蔵
豊国画

Left: Utagawa Toyokuni (1769-1825) 'The Actors Ichikawa Yaozō III and Sawamura Tōzō in the Roles of Oda Harunaga and Yata Takumie,' c. 1798. Signed *Toyokuni ga.* Published by Nishimuraya Yohachi. A classic double portrait showing actors in a *mie* pose. Note the neutral gray background, characteristic of the actor portraits of the eighteenth century. Collection R. Schaap, Netherlands.

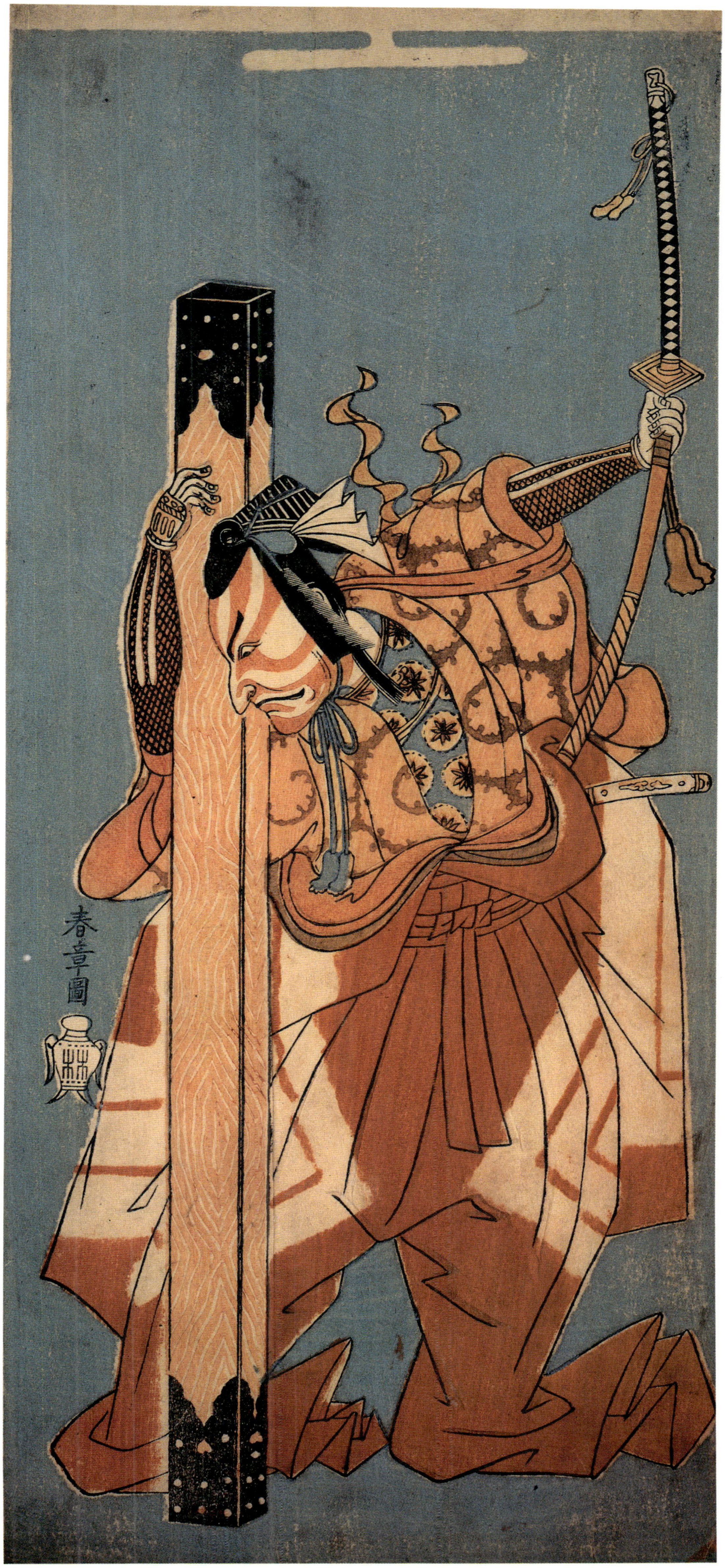

Right: Katsukawa Shunshō (1726-92) 'The Actor Ichikawa Danjūrō IV in a Role in the *kaomise* Play *Sakae hachinoki*, performed in 1769,' *hosoban*. Collection R. Schaap, Netherlands.

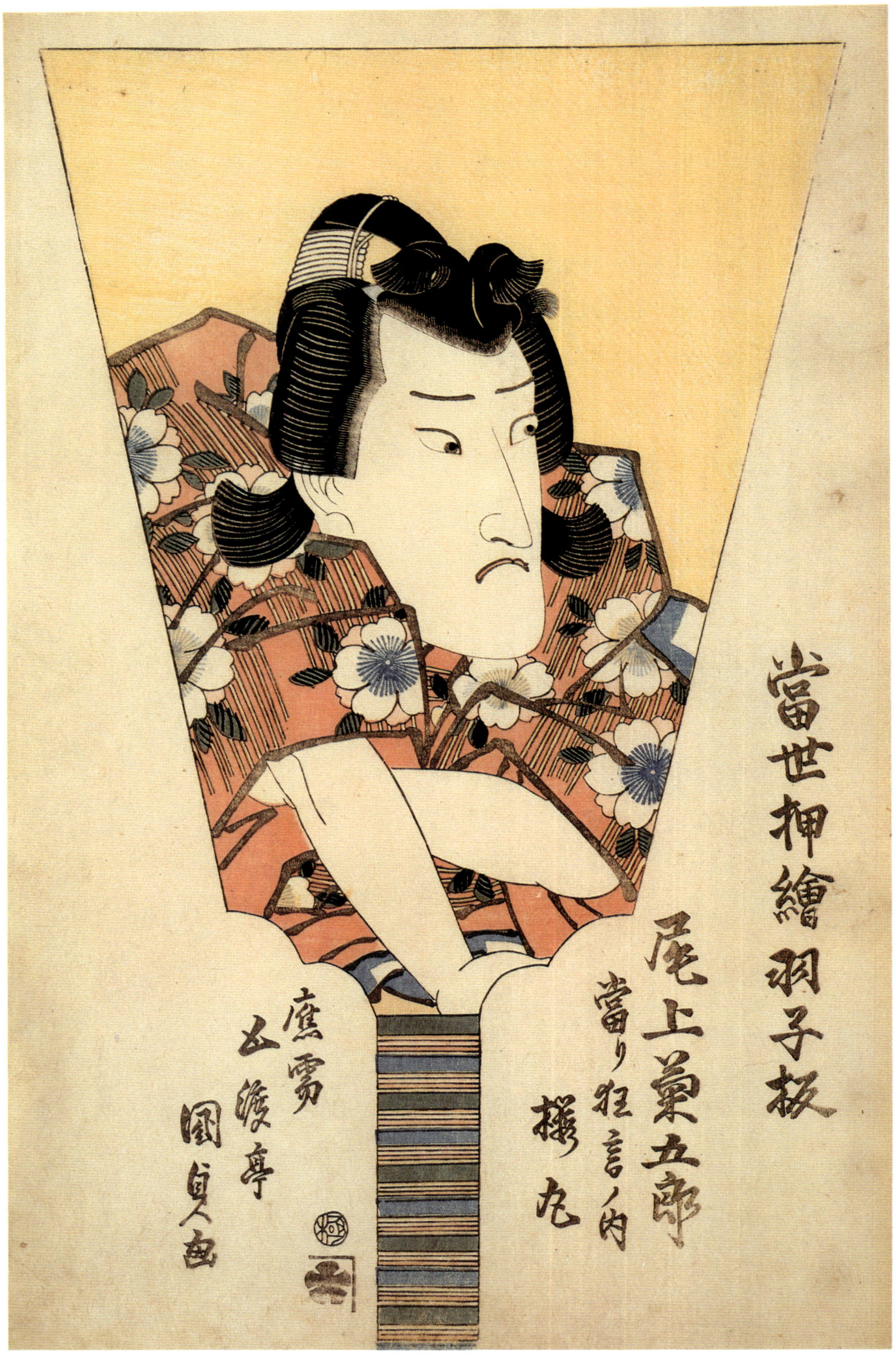

Left and right: Utagawa Kunisada (1786-1865), from the series 'Modern-day Portrayals of Shuttlecocks,' (*Tōsei oshi-e hagoita*), 1822. Signed *Ojū Gototei Kunisada ga*. Published by Asuyama Daisuke. On the left an actor in the role of Soga no Jūrō Sukenari in the play *Sangano-sho Soga no shimadai*, on the right the actor Seki Sanjūrō in the role of Soga no Gorō Tokimune in the same play.

described as an atmosphere of transience and was the unique product of the socio-economic changes that occurred in the Edo period. Moronobu's work and that of his contemporaries is dealt with by Richard Illing in 'The Primitives to Harunobu.' This is followed by David Waterhouse's 'Suzuki Harunobu, Isoda Koryūsai and the Early Katsukawa School, 1760-80.'

UKIYO: THE FLOATING WORLD

Tokugawa Ieyasu, then later his son Hidetada (1579-1623) and his grandson Iemitsu (1608-51), reconstructed the political constellation of sixteenth and seventeenth-century Japan. Their main concern was to contain the segmentary tendencies of the feudal society which had been the cause of 150 years of incessant strife.

Their office was conferred upon them by the Emperor from whom their legitimacy as Shogun was derived. At the same time the Emperor and his followers, however, were isolated from any polticial activity, so as not to become party to any form of power struggle. The seat of Tokugawa power was the Castle in Edo (present-day Tokyo). Around them they allocated land to loyal vassals (*fudai daimyō*). To prevent these vassals from trying their luck in the power game, Iemitsu created the system of 'alternate attendance at the court (*sankin kōtai*). The *sankin kōtai* structure demanded that each daimyo spend six months a year in Edo. During the rest of the year, when he was looking after his domains and securing his income, he was forced to leave his wife and children behind in Edo as 'hostages.'

This system of alternate attendance had far-reaching consequences: Edo became a rapidly growing urban center. The congregation of large numbers of daimyo and their followings created mercantile opportunities. The merchant classes took over in a financial sense. The samurai consumed more than they could afford and the lowly ranked townsmen became the creditors to the formal bearers of power. It was in this rapidly urbanized mercantile world of seventeenth-century Edo, that *ukiyo*, a sub-culture of the non-samurai classes, whereby the unique,

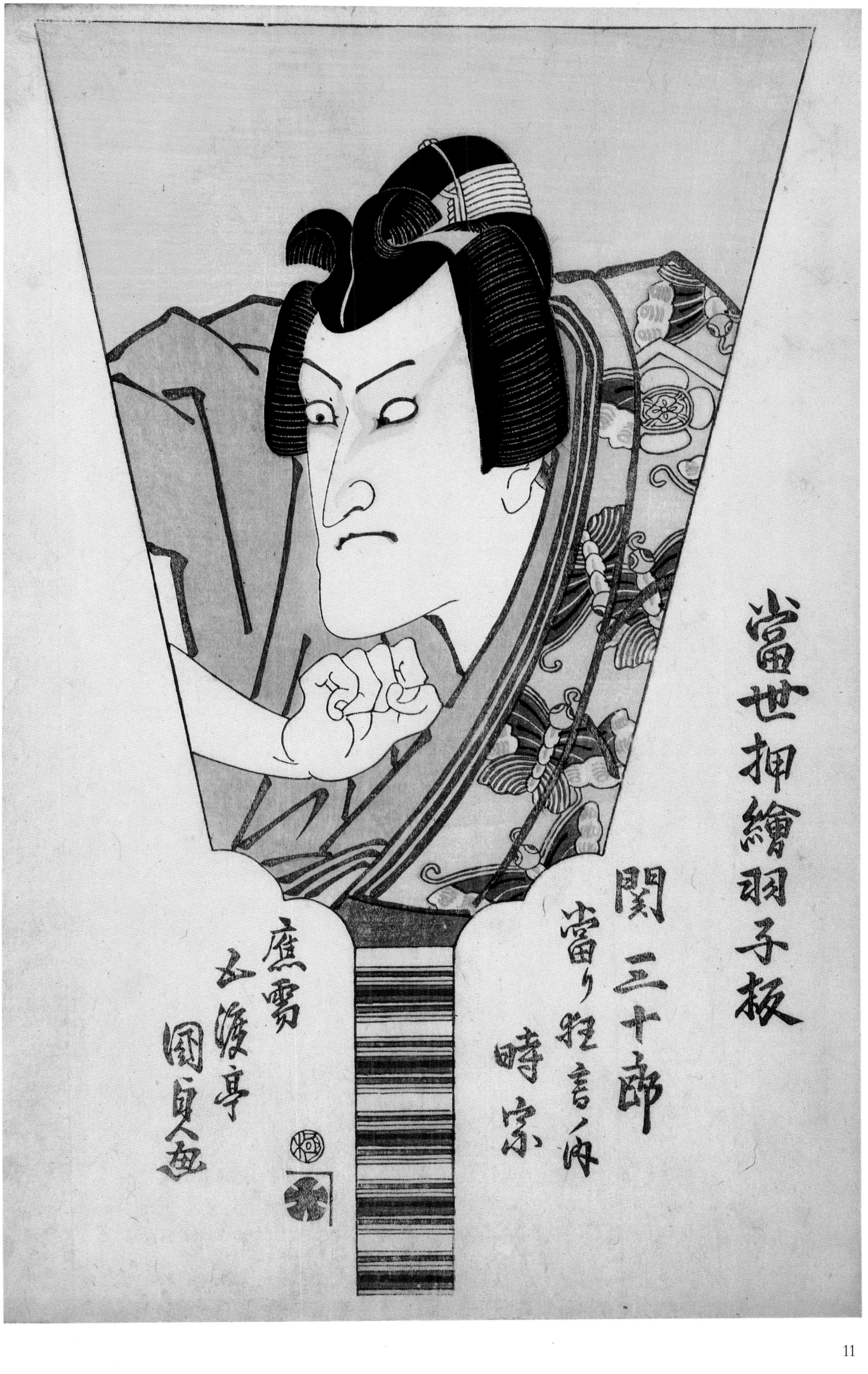
當世押繪羽子板
関三十郎
當り狂言ノ内
時宗
應需
五渡亭
國貞画

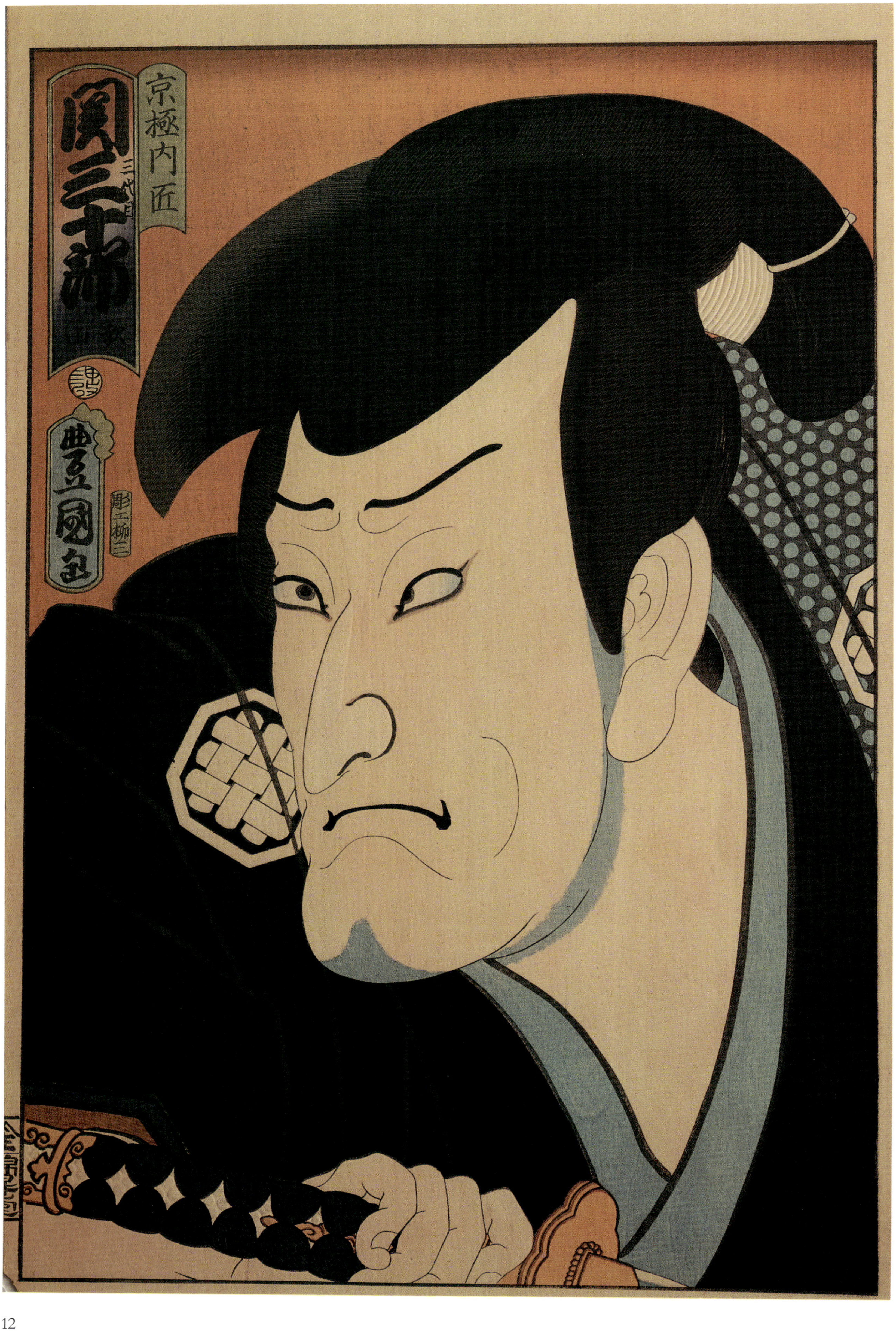
京極内匠
三代目
関三十郎
豊国画
彫工柳三

transient, fleeting moment of pleasure stands central, developed. *Ukiyo* encompasses the idea of pleasure in its widest sense: the merchants were active patrons of the literary and pictorial arts, of the theater, and, of course, of the world of 'female entertainment.' The images with which artists have tried to capture this atmosphere are called *'ukiyo-e'* (pictures of the floating world).

Ukiyo-e printmakers derived their inspiration from the various forms of entertainment available to the urbanized population of Edo. The prints fulfilled the same 'needs' as our current pin-ups or photographs of our idols from the world of music, film and entertainment.

THE KABUKI THEATER

The roots of the Kabuki theater can be found in the rather loose song and dance performances held in the sixteenth century. The actress Okuni is generally considered the founder or originator of the entirely female song and dance acts (*onna kabuki*) held in Kyoto in the last decade of the sixteenth century. The imitation of her highly popular routines by other female groups and the increasingly sexual overtones led the shogunate to ban these groups and the women from the stage in 1629. Young men were banned from the stage in 1652 and subsequently all roles were assumed by older men. The performances became displays of male physical virtues and homosexual relations. This development prompted the Government to intervene against explicit male love on the stage: the actors (*onnagata*) playing female roles were forced to cover their forelocks with a cloth. Again the world of Kabuki found an answer in a gradual development towards a fully fledged medium of dramatic expression.

Kabuki was staged in a large theater, where men and women would sit through many hours of drama. The actors hailed from families that worked within the Kabuki world. Some families would have developed specific specialities: for example, the Danjūrō family has always been known for their fierce male roles. The playwrights derived their stories either from history and mythology, or from the everyday life of Edo. Depending on the nature of the play, a specific style of acting would be called for. On prints one often encounters the extremely aggressive and rough style of acting (*aragoto*) represented or the closely related *mie*-style, whereby, as a climax to a certain scene, a pose is held for a short while (page 8). The often-encountered print of an extremely cross-eyed actor is a example of such moment.

It should be stressed that this entertainment was entirely for the non-samurai Edoites: in fact, samurai were not even allowed within the theater. The Government tried at various moments to curtail the Kabuki theater and also the related output of prints. Non-productive spending on luxury goods and entertainment was worrying in an apparently overheated economy during the 1830s and 1840s. It can safely be said that all measures proved counterproductive. The restriction of theaters within one area following the example of the Yoshiwara (the licensed area of legitimate sexual entertainment) only strengthened the world of Kabuki. Similarly the prohibition to produce prints of actors stimulated the creativity of artists and publishers to find ways of circumventing this censorship. This is seen in the work of such artists as Utagawa Kunisada (1786-1865) and Kuniyoshi (1798-1861) which are treated in Jonathan Bennett's 'The Nineteenth Century until the Meiji Restoration.'

Prints of actors first developed in the hands of the Torii masters, who, from the seventeenth century held the rights to produce the theater-programs. They

Left: Utagawa Kunisada (1786-1865) 'The Actor Seki Sanjurō in the Role of Kiogoku Takumi,' 1860. Signed *Toyokuni ga*. Published by Ebisuya Shōshichi. An example from one of Kunisada's greatest series, from the last years of his life. It is printed on a deluxe heavy paper, with gauffrage (blindprinting) employed as well as burnishing. Collection Hotei, Netherlands.

Below: Chōkyōsai Eiri (c. 1790s) 'Streetwalkers of the Yoshiwara,' triptych, c. 1790s. This is an extreme representation of the contemporary fashion for elongation. Courtesy Christie's, New York.

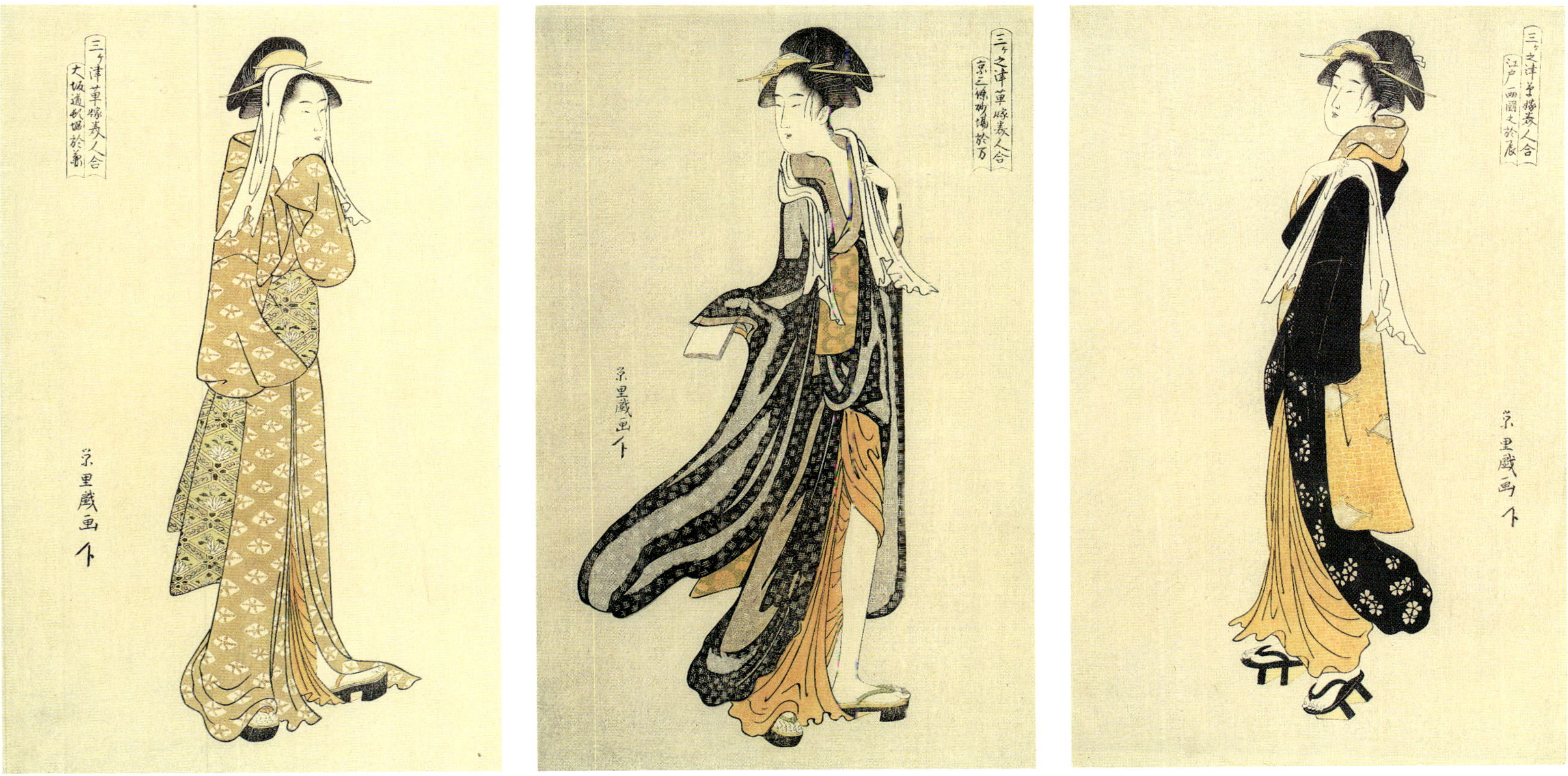

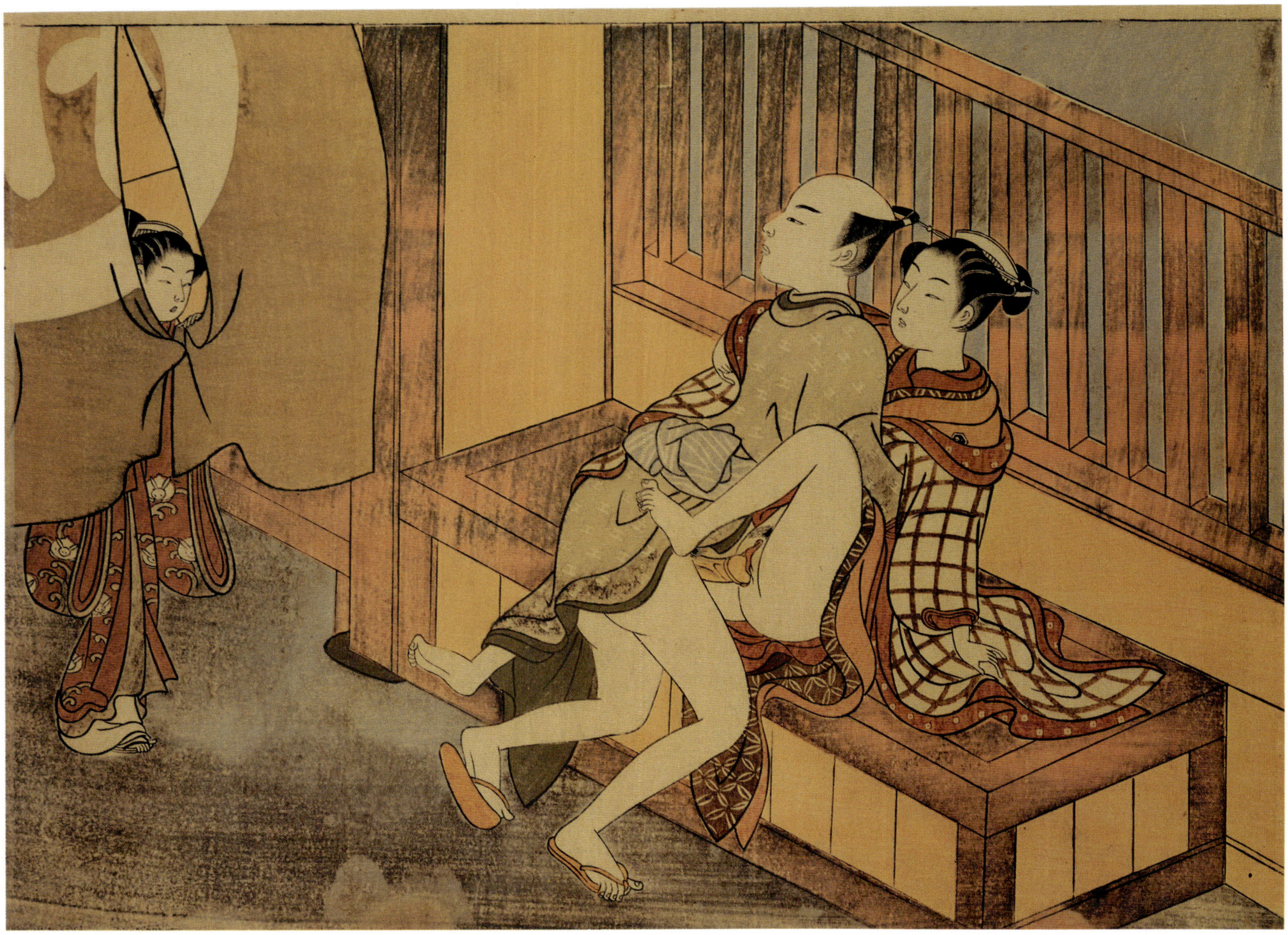

Above: Suzuki Harunobu (1725?-70) A *chūban yoko-e shunga* print, c. 1770. Unsigned. Collection Hotei, Netherlands.

dominated the output in the days before the full-color print. From the 1760s the Katsukawa school, founded by Katsukawa Shunshō (1723-92) took over. In the last decade of the eighteenth century Utagawa Toyokuni (1769-1825) became the leading Kabuki printmaker, only occasionally being rivalled by such enigmatic figures as Tōshūsai Sharaku (*fl* 1795-95), by his own brilliant pupil Kunimasa (1773-1810) and by the last great masters of the Katsukawa school, Shun'ei (1762-1819) and Shunkō (1743-1812). The many pupils of Utagawa Toyokuni dominated the Kabuki print scene in the nineteenth century, led by the most prolific of artists, Utagawa Kunisada. Following his death and the Meiji Restoration four years later, the Kabuki print lost its prominence as an *ukiyo-e* subject. The insert on Osaka printmakers briefly discusses another center of actor prints, Osaka.

THE YOSHIWARA

A second subject which proved a fertile source for print publishers and artists was derived from the 'female services' provided in the Yoshiwara, the most famous licensed pleasure quarter in the Edo period. In 1618, in an attempt to curtail widespread prostitution, the Government decided to concentrate the life of pleasure within one district. Here within its gates teahouses, restaurants and brothels provided the setting for the 'floating world.'

Within this quarter, a 'nightless city' developed, with its own extensive set of rules. Brothels and courtesans were ranked, access was by no means easy and immediate, and for the most desired courtesans of high rank, an extensive period of courtship was required. Preliminary visits, go-betweens and above all large amounts of money were needed finally to gain access. The prints generally depict the most famous of the courtesans. They provided idolized images of female beauty and contemporary fashion. In prints current trends and attitudes towards posture, dress and hairstyle were presented, and if one compares the *bijin* (beautiful women) as portrayed over a period of a hundred years, one can immediately see the changes over time.

Right: Natori Shunsen (1886-1960) 'The Actor Nakamura Ganjirō in the role of Kamiya Jihei,' 1916. R O Müller Collection.

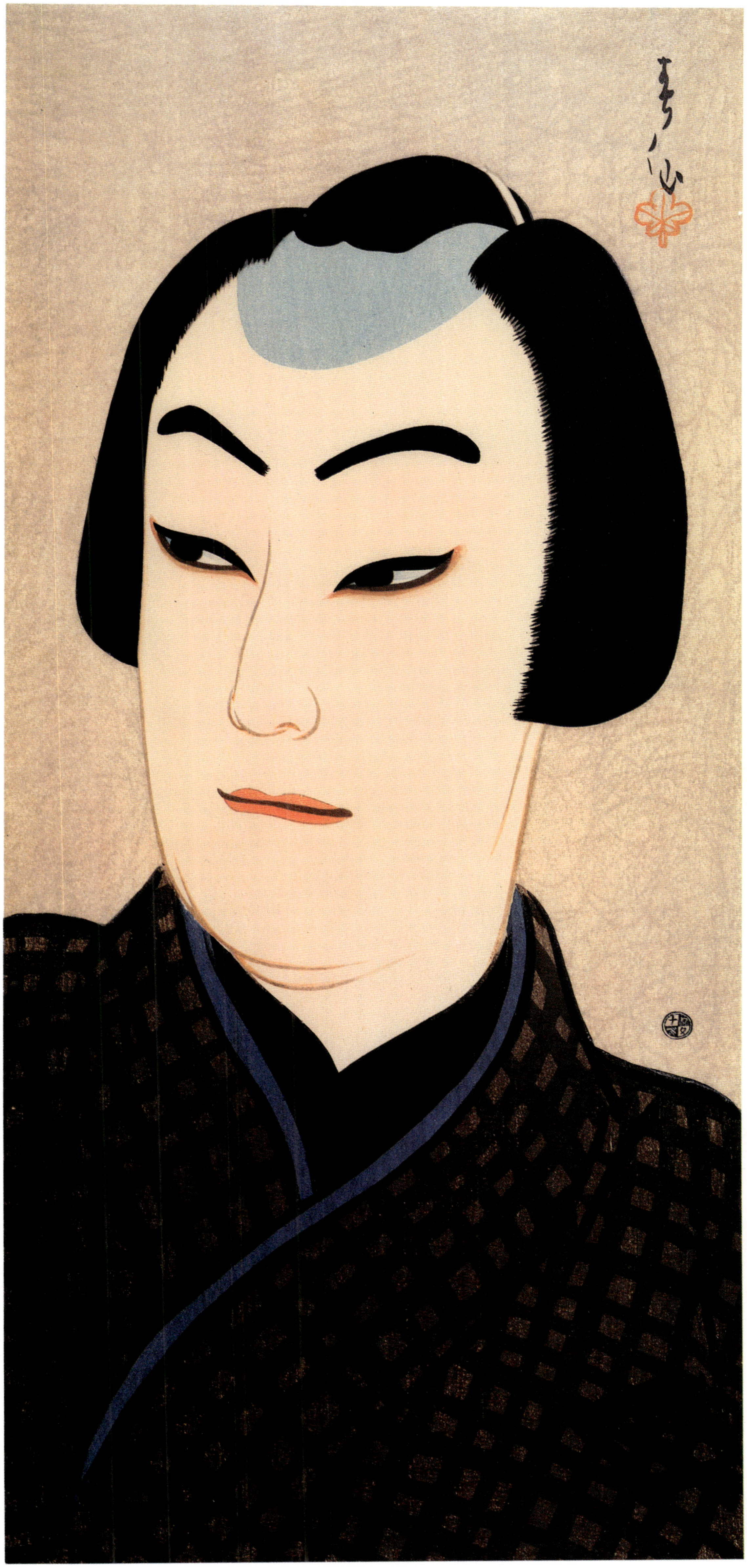

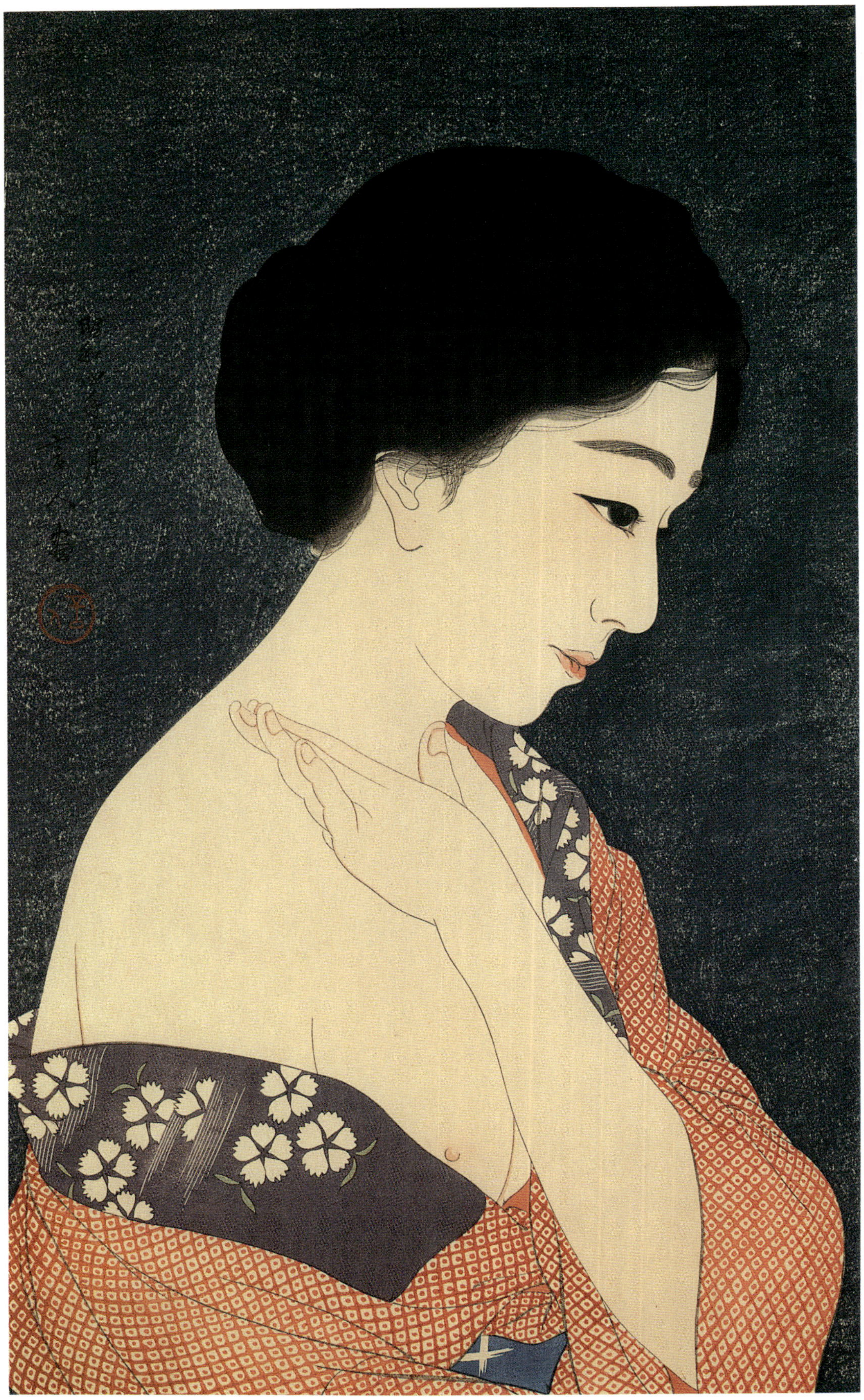

Above: Torii Kotondo (1900-76) 'Beauty Combing her Hair.' Collection Hotei, Netherlands.

Right: Keisai Eisen (1790-1848) 'The Prostitute Hanaoka Holding a Poem,' from the series 'Prostitutes from the New Yoshiwara Compared to the Nine Episodes in the Life of Onono Komachi (*Shin Yoshiwara yukun nana Komachi*).

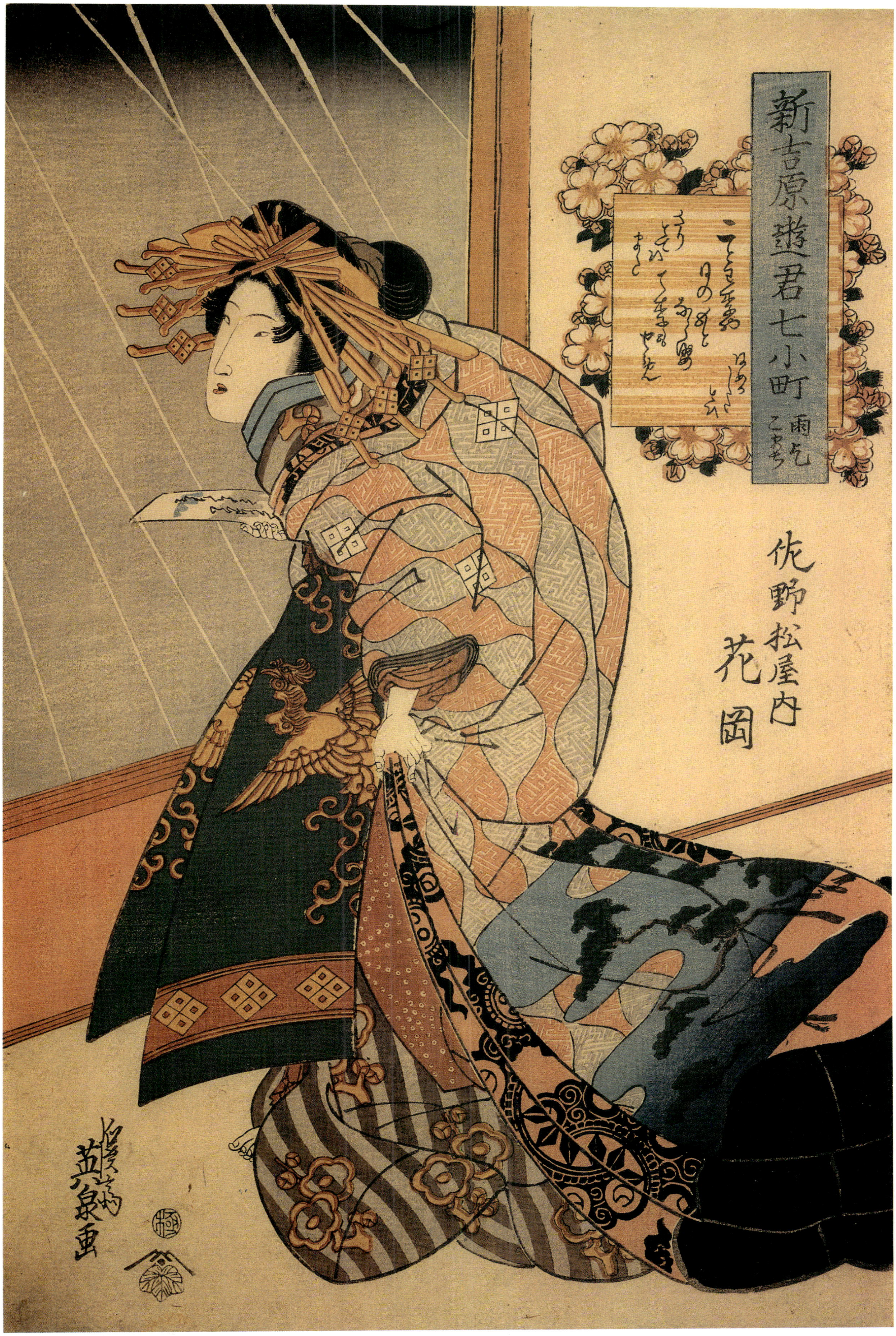
新吉原遊君七小町
雨乞
こまち
佐野松屋内
花岡
英泉画

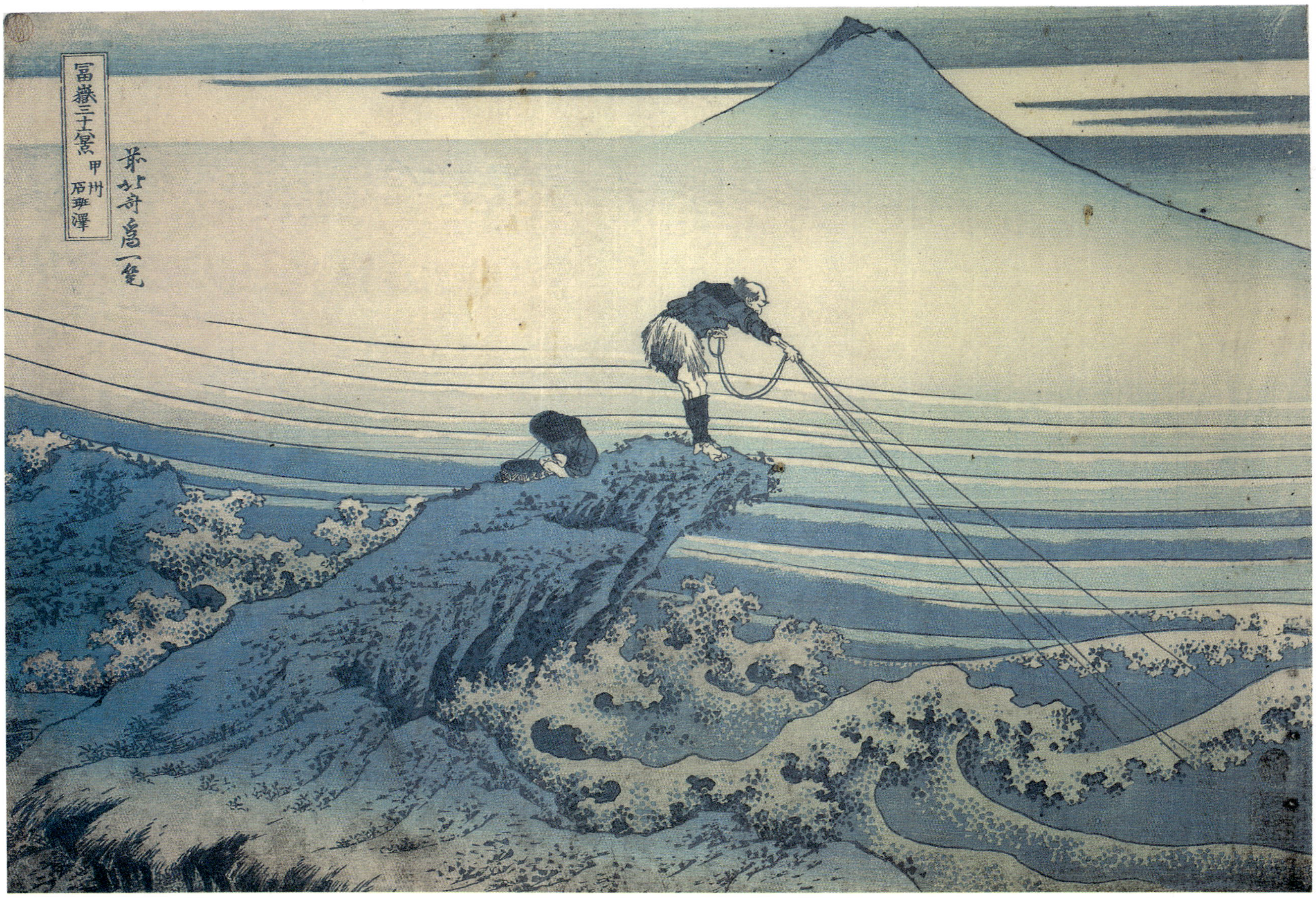

Above: Katsushika Hokusai (1760-1849) 'A Fisherman Standing on a Rocky Promontory at Kajikazawa in Kai Provence,' (*Kōshu Kajikazawa*), from the series '36 Views of Mt Fuji' (*Fugaku sanjūrokkei*), c. 1830-31. Signed *Zen Hokusai litsu no fudc.* Published by Nishimuraya Yohachi. The so-called *aizuri-e* impression, generally considered to be the earliest state. Formerly Collection Hotei, Netherlands.

Above right: Hasegawa Sadanobu (1809-79) 'Rain Over Tōgano,' from the series 'Famous Views of Kyoto,' (*Miyako meisho no zu*), c. 1855. A print from one of the rare Osaka landscape series. Unlike Edo, Osaka never developed a diversified print tradition. 95% of the output consisted of actor prints. Collection P. Beeten, Netherlands.

The most provocative of sheets were of course the *shunga*, overtly erotic works, in the form of single prints or illustrated books. The Government did not approve of erotica and again their suppression was counterproductive. It did cause most prints to be unsigned, and without publishers' marks. *Shunga* were often produced in series of 12 prints, bound into albums and truly 'used' as stimulating erotica.

The prints of beauties have existed ever since single print production came into being. Its heyday was the last two decades of the eighteenth century, when Torii Kiyonaga, Hosoda Eishi, Katsukawa Shunchō, Kitagawa Utamaro, Toyokuni and many others excelled in this genre. Julia Hutt covers this period in 'The Golden Age, 1780-1810.' Parallel to the decline in popularity of the Kabuki print ran the downward course of *bijinga* (pictures of beautiful women). Two revivals after 1868 can be recognized: one in the Meiji period, with artists such as Toyohara Chikanobu, his pupil Kunichika and Torii Kiyochika and later in the fabulous work of Hashiguchi Goyō, Torii Kotondo and Itō Shinsui in the 1910s and 1920s. Meiji printmakers are highlighted in Charlotte van Rappard-Boon's chapter on latter day *ukiyo-e* artists, and Taisho artists in Haruo Matsuoka's piece, 'The Artistic Legacy of Shin hanga.'

LANDSCAPES

Although the Kabuki theater and the 'world of pleasure' were the main suppliers of subject matter to the publishers

Right: Utagawa Hiroshige (1797-1858) 'Fall Moon at Seba,' from the series 'From the 69 Stations of the Kisokaido', (*Kisokaidō rokujūkyū tsugi no uchi*) late 1830s. Published by Hoeido and Kinjudo. Courtesy of the Trustees of the British Museum, London.

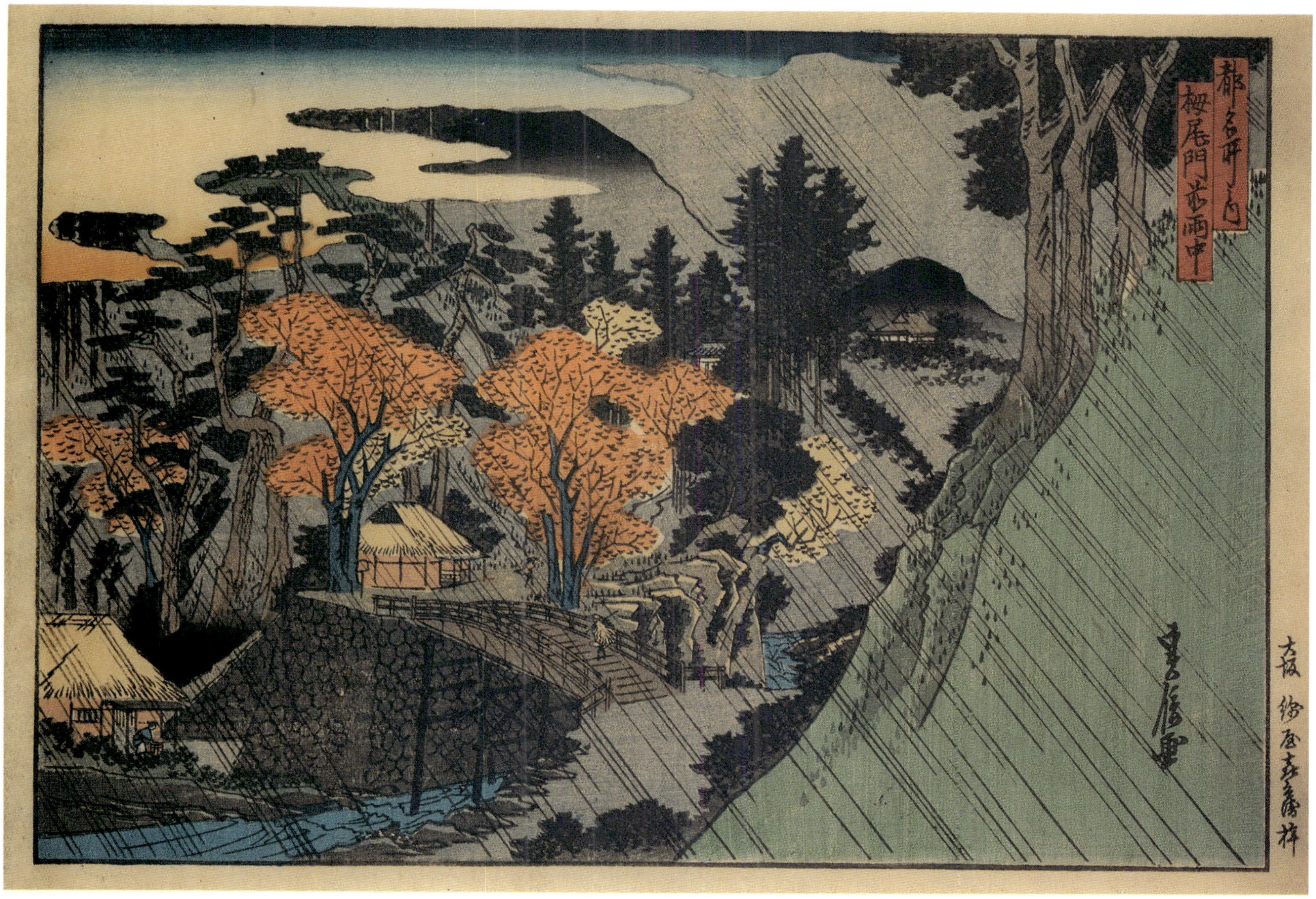

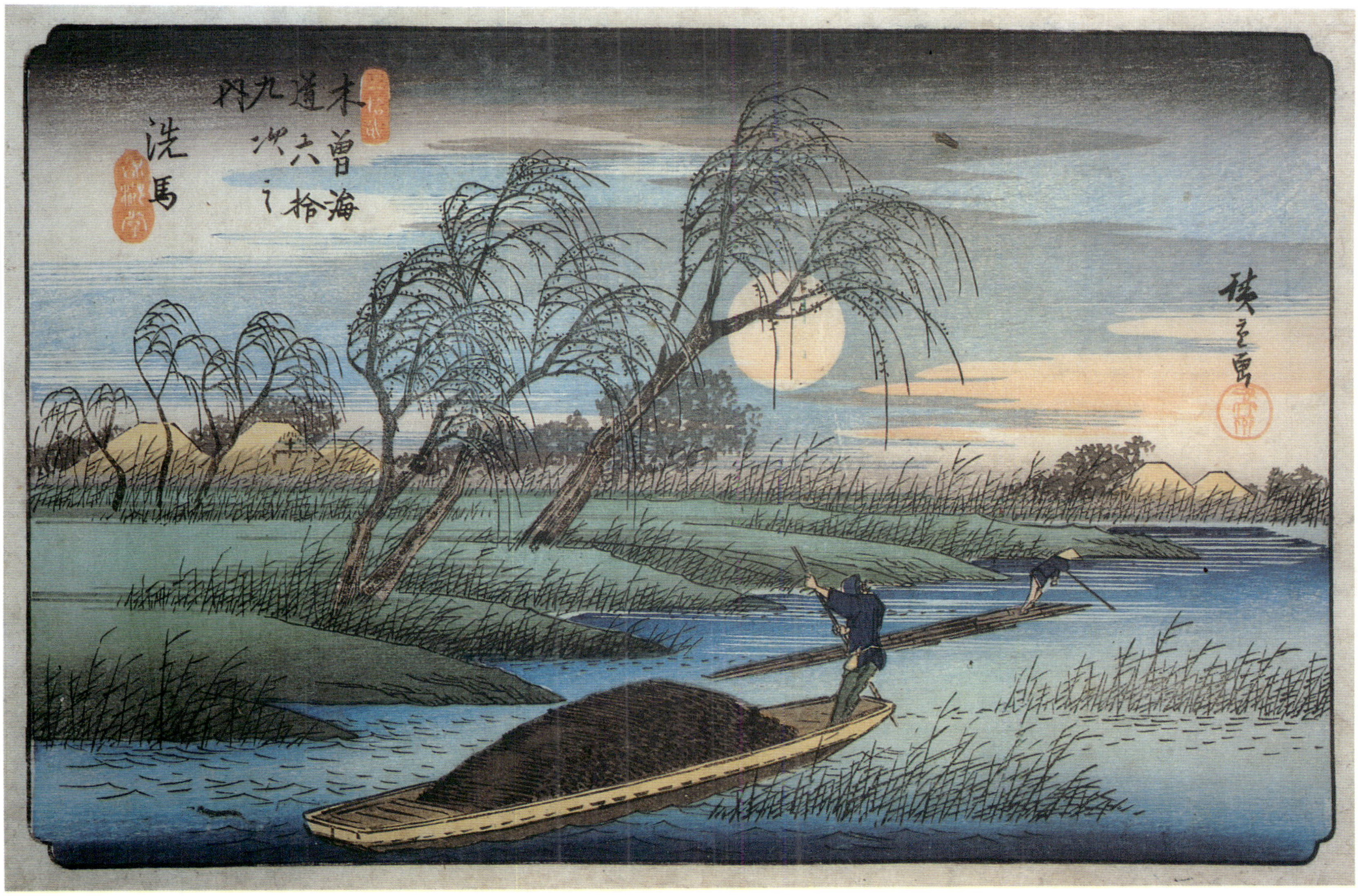
木曽海道六拾九次之内
洗馬

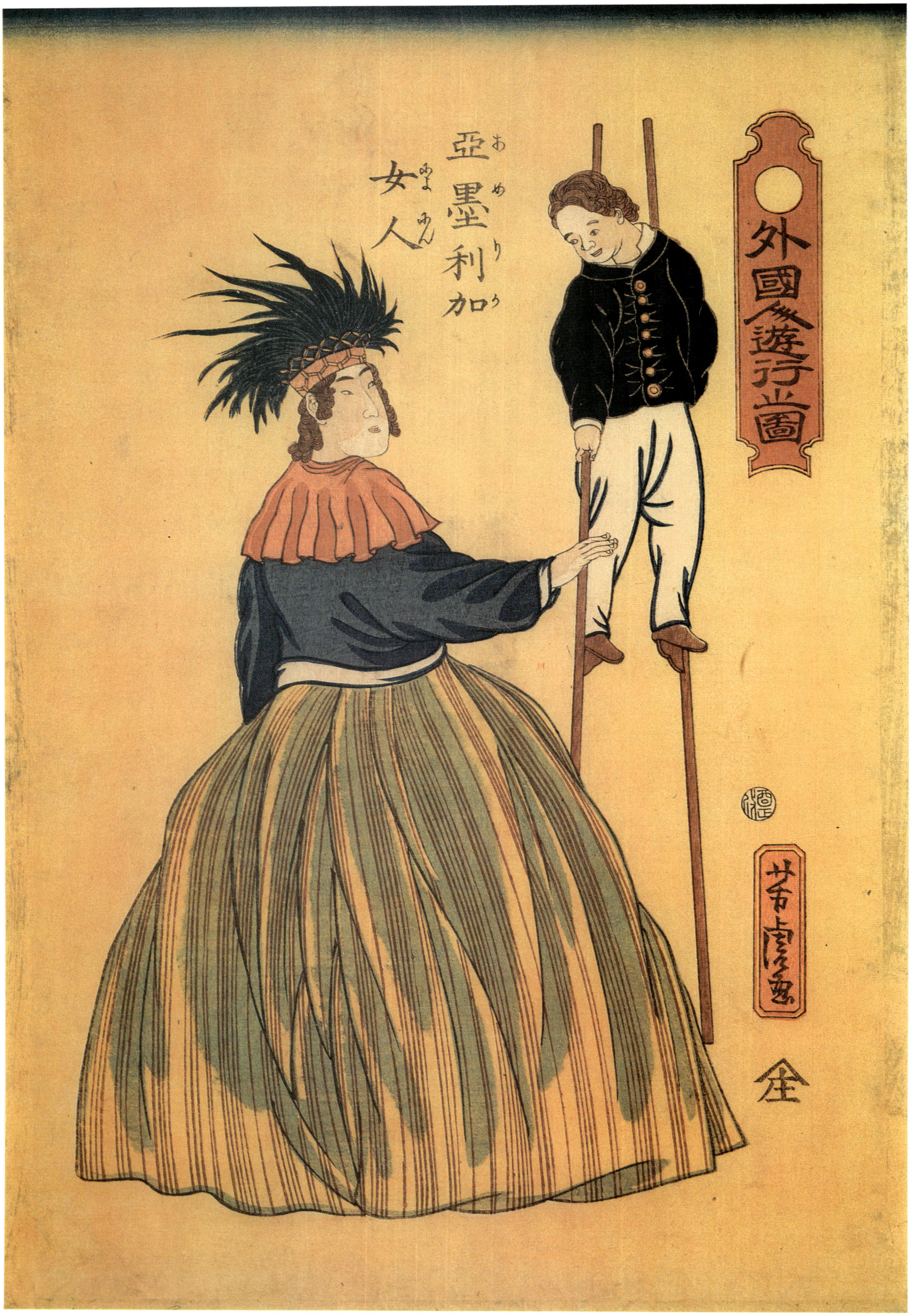
亞墨利加
女人
芳虎画

Left: Utagawa Yoshitora (*fl* 1850s-70s) A *Yokohama-e* showing an American woman and her child walking on stilts. An example of a typical print produced in the 1860s depicting foreigners. The genre of the *Yokohama-e* was dominated by Yoshikazu, Sadahide and Yoshitora. Around eight hundred designs of this type have been identified. The print quality was generally mediocre. Collection Hotei, Netherlands.

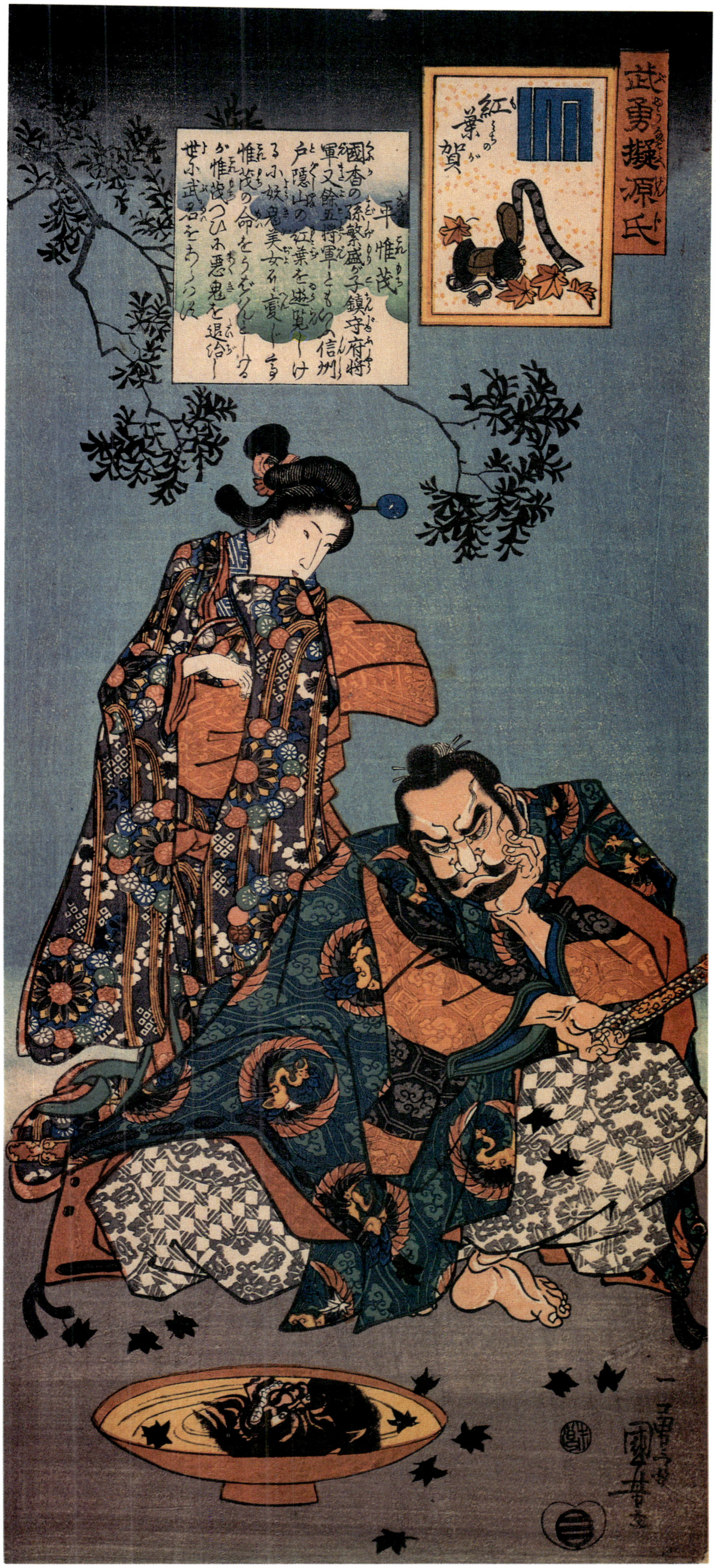

Right: Utagawa Kuniyoshi (1797-1861) 'Taira no Koremochi Waking up from a Drunken Sleep,' from the series 'Heroic Comparisons for the Chapters of Genji,' (*Buyū nazorae Genji*) 1843. The lady's face is reflected as a demon in her sake cup. Signed *Ichiyūsai Kuniyoshi*. Published by Ibaya Sensaburō. Collection J. Asselbergs, Netherlands.

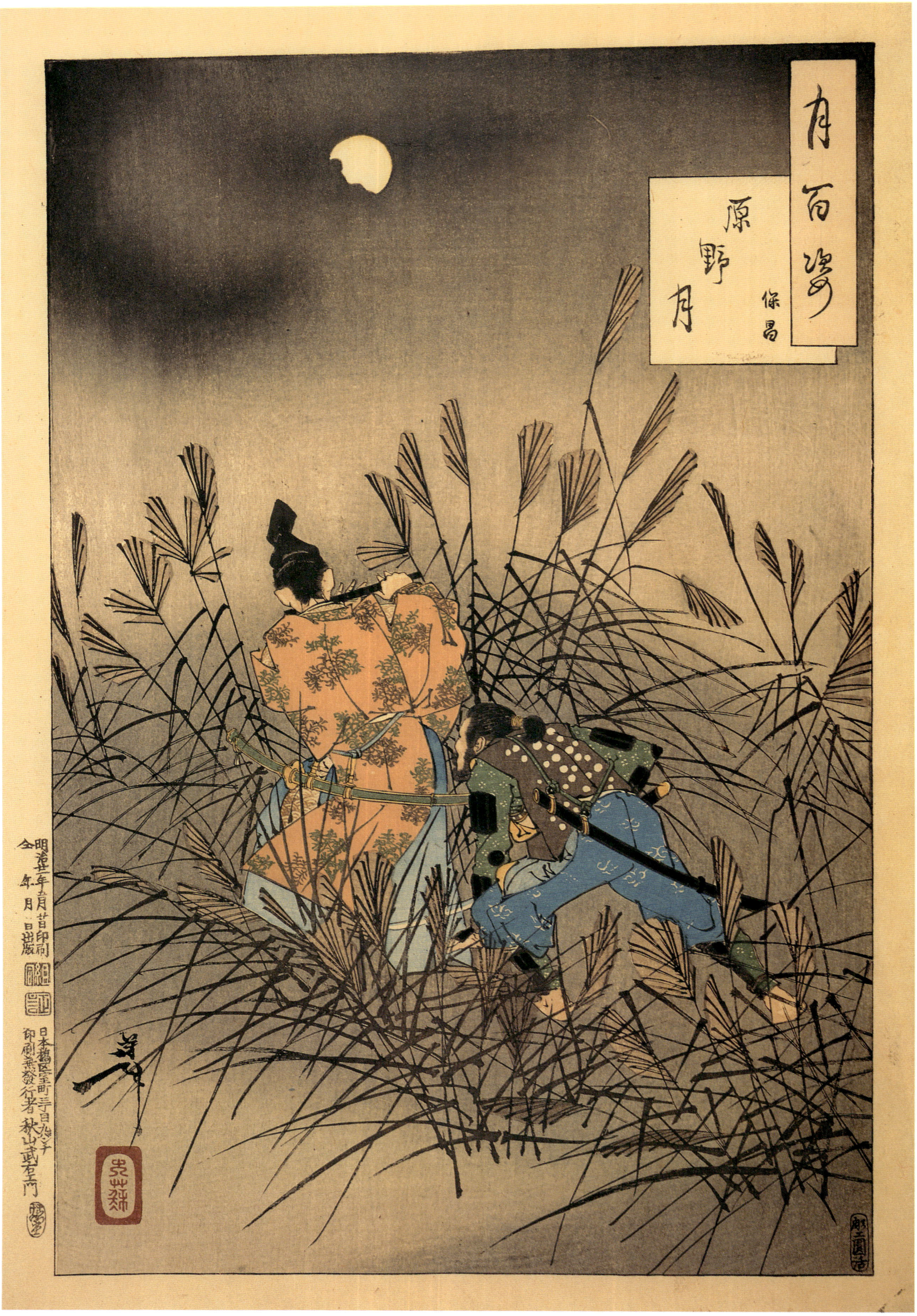
月百姿
原野月
保昌

Left: Tsukioka Yoshitoshi (1839-1892) 'The God of the Sumiyoshi Shrine Appearing to the Poet Fujiwara Teika in the Moonlight,' from the series 'One hundred aspects of the Moon' (*Tsuki hyakushi*), 1807. Published by Akiyama Buemon. Collection R. Schaap, Netherlands.

Right: Ohara Koson (1877-1945) 'Ducks and Reeds,' c. 1910. Collection Hotei, Netherlands.

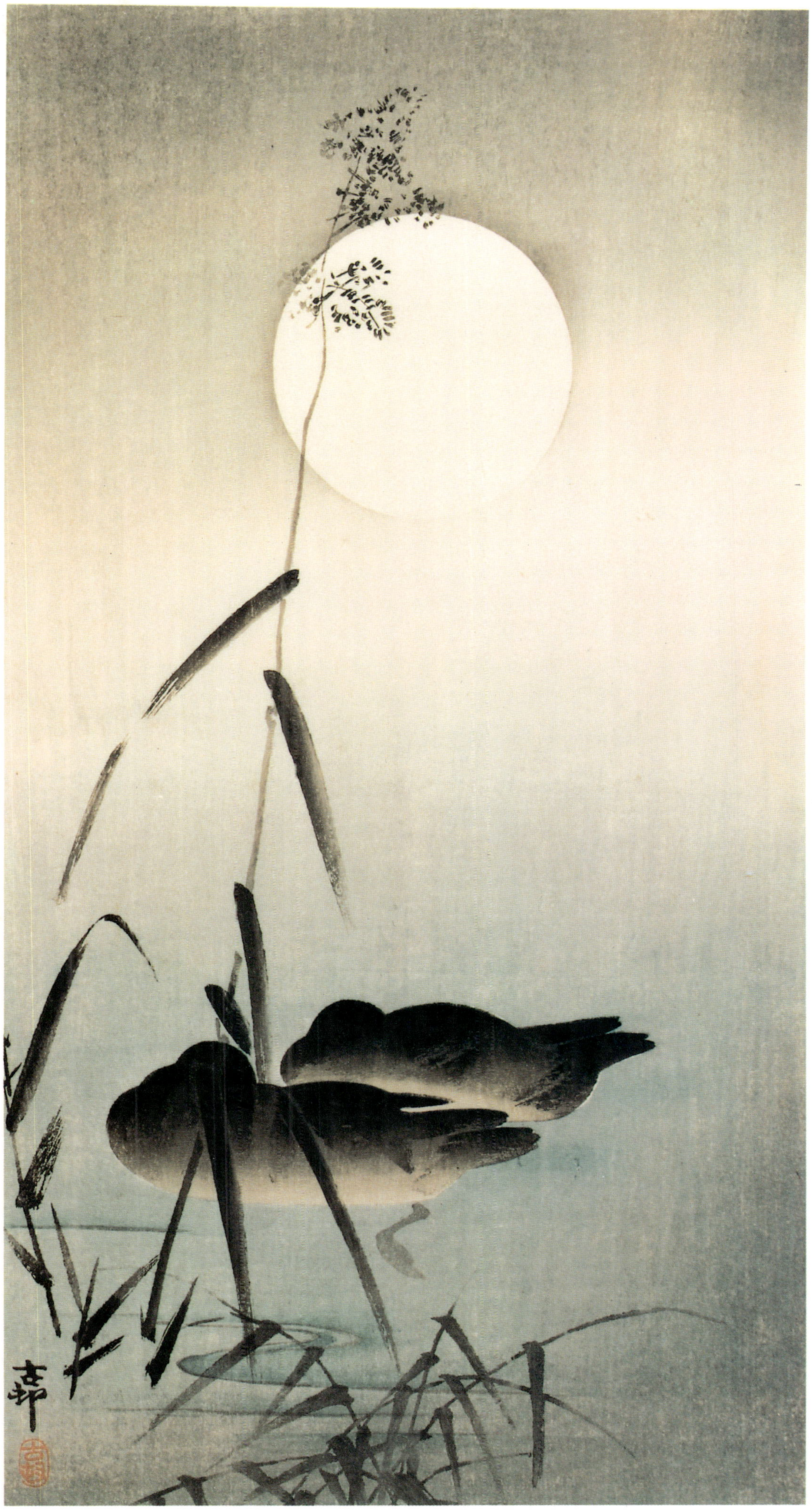

and the artists, they were by no means the only ones. Two other important genres stand out: landscape and historical/mythical prints.

Prints of scenery within or outside the city can be considered a very recent addition to the repertoire of the woodblock-print artist. In the eighteenth century landscapes only figured as a backdrop to courtesans on parade, and apart from Mt Fuji the scenery was rarely identifiable. The only extant eighteenth-century landscape prints were experiments with perspective (*uki-e*), occasionally imitations of European engravings. It was only when travel restrictions were lifted in the 1820s, that a market was truly created. Then Utagawa Hiroshige (1797-1858) and Katsushika Hokusai (1760-1849) stunned the audience with their pictorial surveys of landmarks of Japan: '36 Views of Mt Fuji,' '53 Stations on the Tokaido,' 'Famous Places in Edo,' and 'Famous Places in the Provinces' were typical titles of their print series. This genre also declined gradually after their deaths. There was a short revival when the opening up of Japan and the growth of the port city of Yokohama created a market for prints of foreigners, *Yokohama-e*. Later this is also seen in the work of one superior artist, Kobayashi Kiyochika, who laid the foundations for the twentieth-century landscape greats, Kawase Hasui and Yoshida Hiroshi.

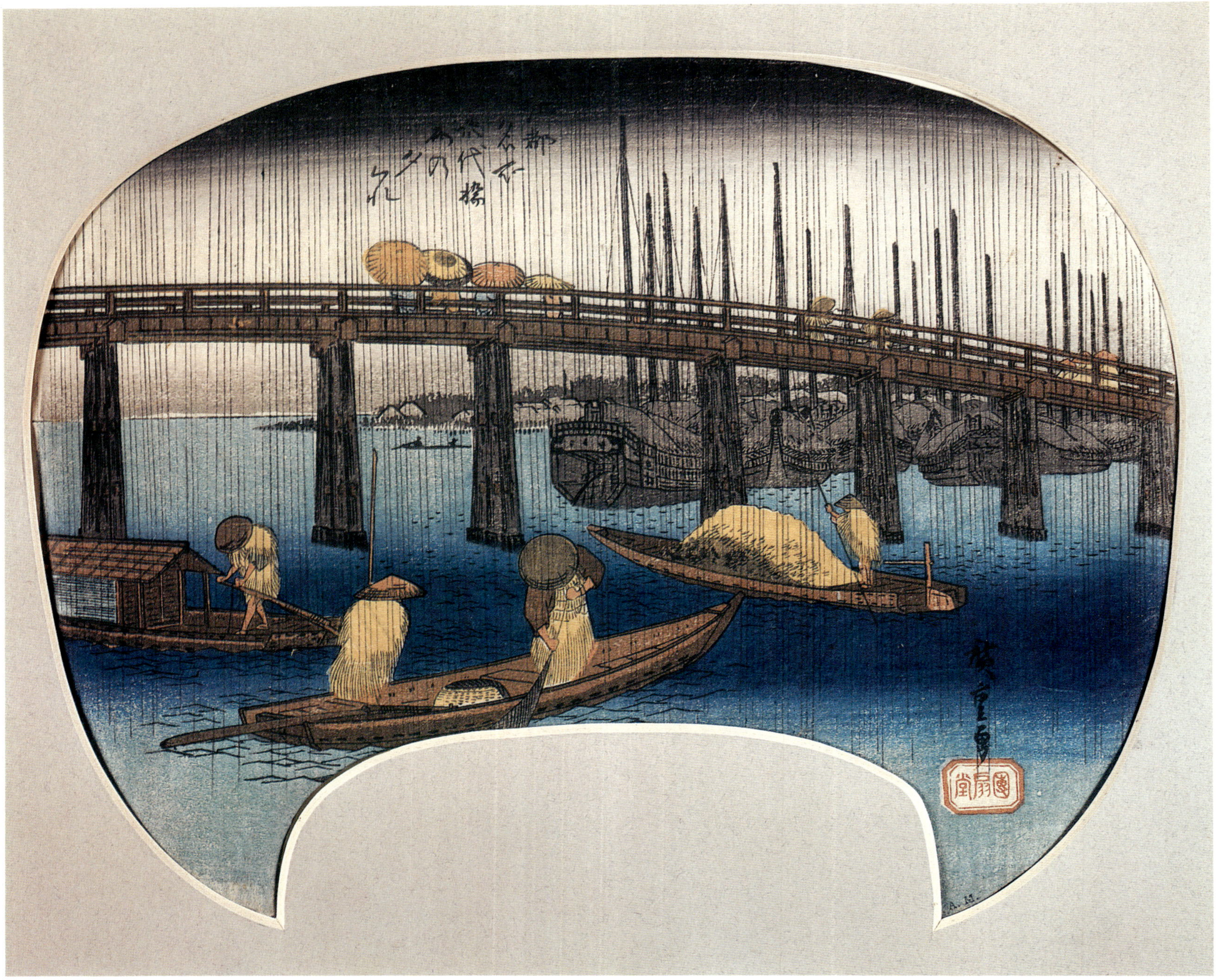

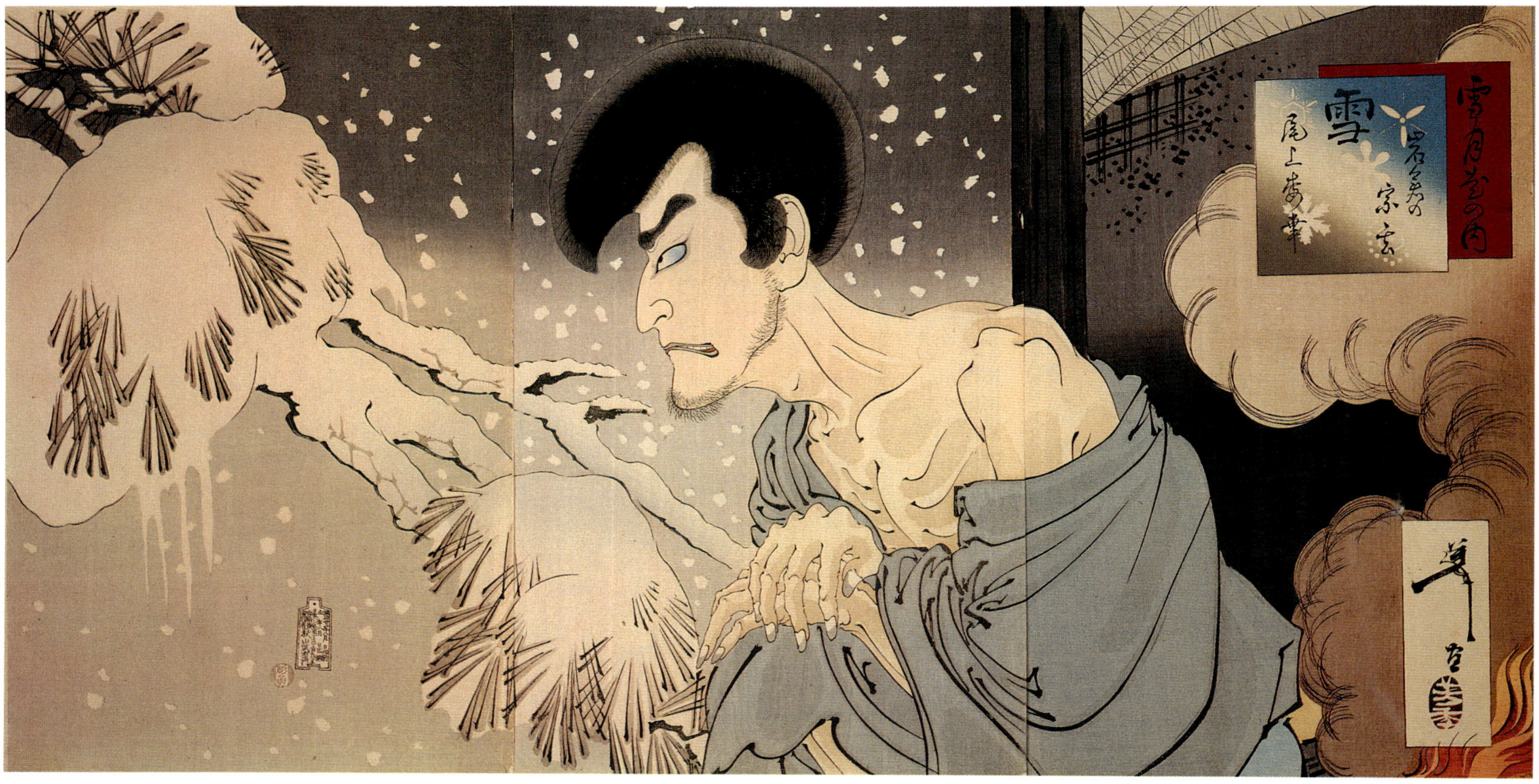
雪

Left: Utagawa Hiroshige (1797-1858) 'Evening Rain at Eitai Bridge,' from the series 'Famous Places in Edo' (*Edo meisho*), c. 1840, fan print. Signed *Hiroshige ga*. Published by Ibaya Sensaburō. Courtesy of the Trustees of the Victoria and Albert Museum, London.

Below left: Tsukioka Yoshitoshi (1839-92) 'Onoe Baikō as Iwakura Sōgen,' from the triptych series 'Snow, Moon and Flowers,' (*Setsugekka no uchi*), 1890. The print shows the priest Sōgen expelled from the priesthood for breaking the vows of celibacy having been tempted by the courtesan Orikotohime. Signed and sealed *Yoshitoshi*. Published by Akiyama Takeemon. Collection R. Schaap, Netherlands.

HISTORICAL AND MYTHICAL PRINTS

The genre of historical prints, like that of landscape, was slow to develop. It was Kuniyoshi who from the late 1820s brought to fruition this type of print. Perhaps it can be explained by the potentially political nature of historic and mythical prints. The government was sensitive to hidden political messages in prints. Kuniyoshi was himself arrested over a satirical print presumed to portray the Shogun. History and pseudo-history became favorite subjects in the Meiji period. In the hands of Kuniyoshi's best pupils, Yoshitoshi (1839-92) and Yoshiiku, it became a stunning genre, often showing extreme violence and garishness.

Although about 85% of all prints treat one of the four subjects mentioned above, the reader will encounter in this book prints of nature (*kachōga*), prints of the wrestling world (sumo) and prints which are different not in subject matter but in shape or size. For example, prints were designed to be pasted on fans; *surimono* will also be dealt with in detail.

THE JAPANESE PRINT: THE FORMAL FEATURES

Having briefly introduced the history, the socio-cultural context and the subject matter of prints, we should now address

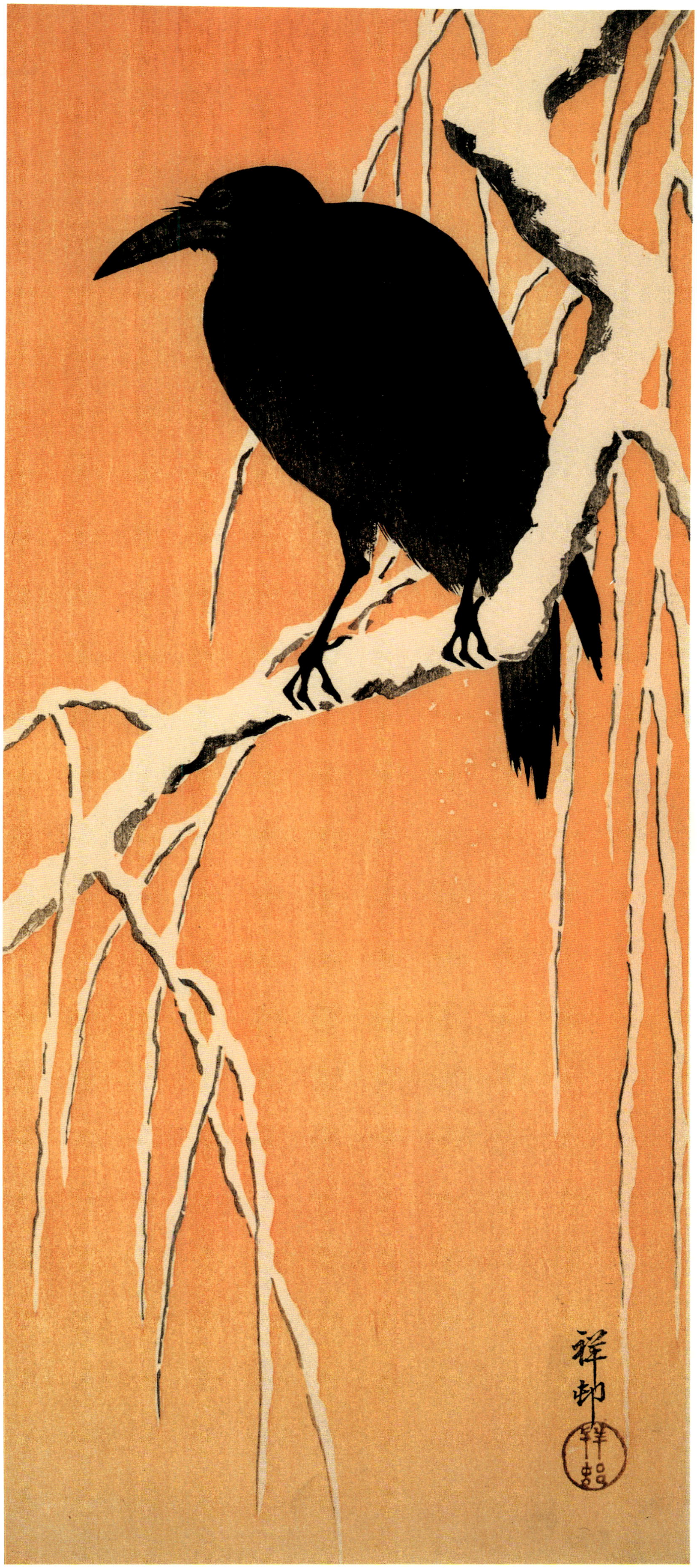

Right: Ohara Koson (1877-1945) 'A Crow on a Branch Against the Setting Sun,' from a series of *tanzaku*-sized nature prints. No date or publisher's mark, but c.1915. Signed and sealed *Shōson*. Collection R. Schaap, Netherlands.

the question of the formal characteristics of a print. How big is it? What is the paper like? How is it made? Who made it and what else, apart from the image, does one encounter on the print?

The initiative to produce a print was often taken by a publisher. He would see commercial opportunities for a specific type of design and he would approach an artist to make the design. The artist would do a rough sketch and would then discuss with the publisher such elements as the choice of colors or the special effects to be employed. The publisher subsequently supervised the production and employed the engravers and printers. The role of the artist during the production process was negligible. The refined techniques of the actual printing are discussed in detail in Richard Kruml's essay, 'The Techniques of Japanese Printmaking.' Once the print was finished it was distributed through retail shops, which sold the prints from their shops to the general public.

PRINT SIZES

The sizes of prints have of course been limited by the constraints deriving from the use of the woodblock. The basic size is the *ōban* and the vast majority of prints are executed in this format. Larger compositions would be created by using multiple sheets: *ōban*-triptychs, pentaptychs and even septaptychs are regularly encountered. Variations occur because of varying degrees of sizing and trimming since their production. Other formats like the *chūban* (10×7½ inches [26×19 cm]) and the *aiban* (13½×8¾ inches [34×22 cm]) are mathematically derived from the *ōban*.

Far right: Utagawa Kuniyoshi (1798-1861). This print contains the full range of formal features found on Japanese prints.
1. Signature: in red cartouche in lower left corner, reading Ichiyūsai Kuniyoshi ga. The last character, *ga*, is an easily recognizable feature in the majority of signatures. Sometimes one finds the character *hitsu* (see chapter 4 for one of Utamaro's).
2. Series title: top right, in the shape of a *tsuba* (sword guard).
3. Top middle/left: allusive cartouche by a daughter of Kuniyoshi, with poem.
4. Bottom left-hand corner: elongated small black and white cartouche, the name of the publisher: Iseya Isaburō.
5. Bottom left-hand corner: a round and slightly oval seal: a censorship-seal reading *aratame*, and a date seal, consisting of an abbreviated form of zodiacal sign (in this case the snake) and below it a numeral indicating the month within the snake year.
6. In lozenge-shaped cartouche: an *iroha* syllable, a system for numbering the prints within the series.
The presence of all these elements is characteristic of the mid-nineteenth century. On earlier prints one will encounter only two or three of these formal features.

SIGNATURES

Virtually all prints, with the exception of *shunga*, have a signature. An artist's signature is cut with the key block and is generally found on the left or right hand side of the lower part of the print. A typical signature consists of a *gō* which is a personally chosen artist's first name, and a second name which was allotted to him when he entered an artist's studio as an apprentice. For example, *Kuni*sada became a pupil in 1801 of Toyo*kuni* and was given the name Kunisada. He used more than 10 personal first names – for example Gototei, Ichiyūsai, Kōchōrō – during the remaining 63 years of his career. His formal first name was *Utagawa* which refers to the name of the school to which he belonged. Often one will encounter the addition of the characters *ga* or *hitsu* (picture or brush of) to the signature. The presence of these characters facilitates the separation of the signature from other textual information on the print.

In the left or right top corners, one often finds the series title or, in the case of single prints, the print-title, sometimes accompanied by subtitles. In the case of actor-prints of the eighteenth and early nineteenth centuries one will find the names of the actors and the role they are performing on the print.

PUBLISHERS' MARKS

With the exception of *shunga* and *surimono*, publishers' marks are usually present, generally near the signature. They are simplified forms of the publisher's personal or shop-name. Roughly speaking the marks have tended towards simplification during the last decade of the Edo period. In the Meiji period the publisher was required to provide his full name and address on the print as well as the full date of publication. This information was then provided in the left or right margin of the print, outside the image.

CENSORSHIP AND DATE-SEALS

From 1790 onwards a formal system of censorship was instituted. Until 1874 each print, except private publications such as *surimono* and *shunga*, carried a seal of government approval. During some periods they were combined with date-seals. In the chart (right) one finds the basic forms of the censorship-seals and the periods in which they were used. After 1874 information regarding the date of publication was included in the margin of the print above the name of the publisher.

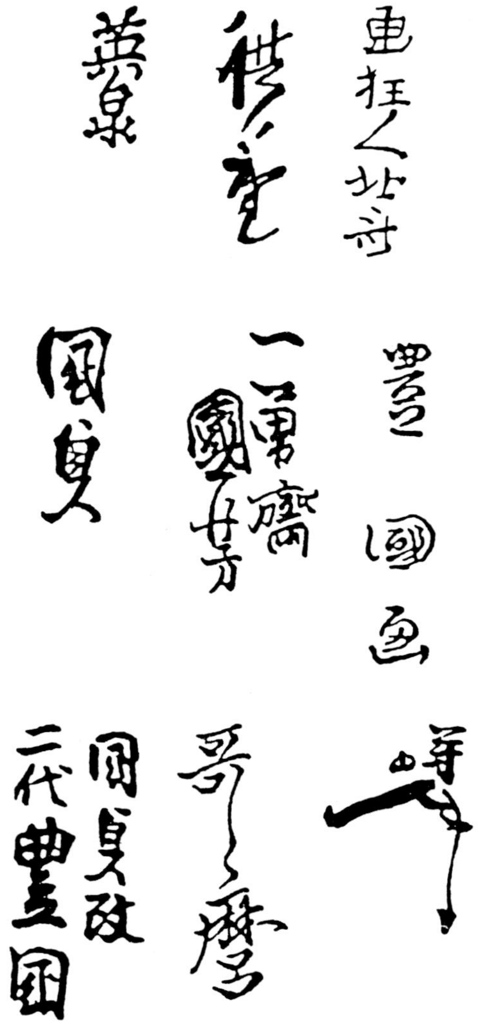

Nishimuraya

Tsutaya Jusaburō

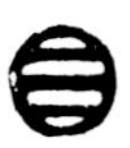
Ibaya Sensaburō

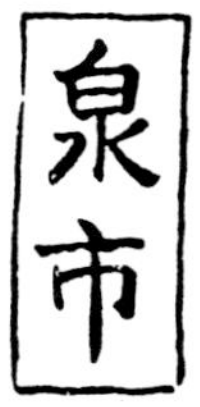
Izumiya Ichibei

Above, from the top: Signatures of the artists Eisen, Hiroshige, Hokusai, Kunisada, Kuniyoshi, Toyokuni (twice), Utamaro, and Yoshitoshi; publishers' seals; and date seals.

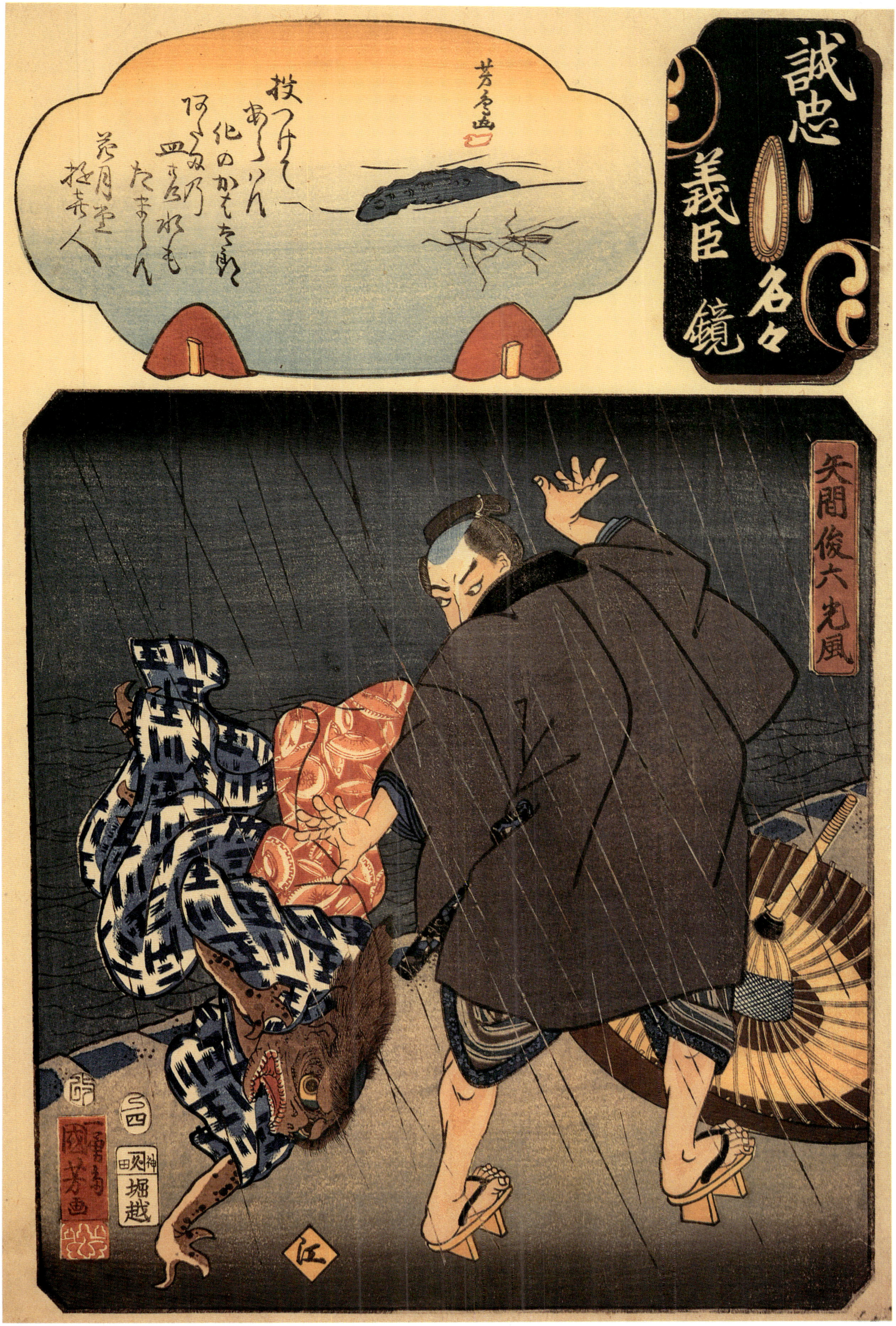
誠忠義臣名々鏡
矢間俊六光風
一勇斎国芳画
堀越

I
The Techniques of Japanese Printmaking

RICHARD KRUML

The history of *ukiyo-e* is one marked by the development and assimilation of technical innovations in the printmaking process as well as the adaptation of the numerous regulations imposed by the Tokugawa *bakufu* (shogunate) as a result of the economic climate of the Edo period (1600–1868). Mismanagement of the economy by the government and weak Shoguns led to the issuing intermittently of regulatory edicts in an attempt to raise funds, to cut spending and to encourage thrift. These decrees were also frequently aimed at raising moral standards, and as *ukiyo-e* – related as it was to the less-esteemed merchant class – prospered, it became one of the prime targets of the government. The *bakufu* viewed the widespread appeal and production of *ukiyo-e* as a barometer of the excesses of the period, and also as a potential instrument which could be used to satirize the establishment. Prohibitions were placed on paper quality, pigments, the number of blocks to be used, as well as subject matter. These statutes were, at certain times, vigorously applied, but depending on prevailing economic conditions, short-lived. Nonetheless resourceful publishers, and perhaps artists and artisans, were quick to find ways of evading them. In this way *ukiyo-e* periodically underwent change, usually resuming its original form after the relaxation of the edicts but having added further techniques and imagery to its repertoire. Two examples are the *benigirai-e* (red-hating pictures) and *aizuri-e* (prints produced almost entirely in blue) which were the outcome of edicts limiting colors on prints and books. *Benigirai-e* published during a period of austerity in the mid 1780s, are among the most subtle and attractive representations of Edo life, printed in delicate shades of gray and

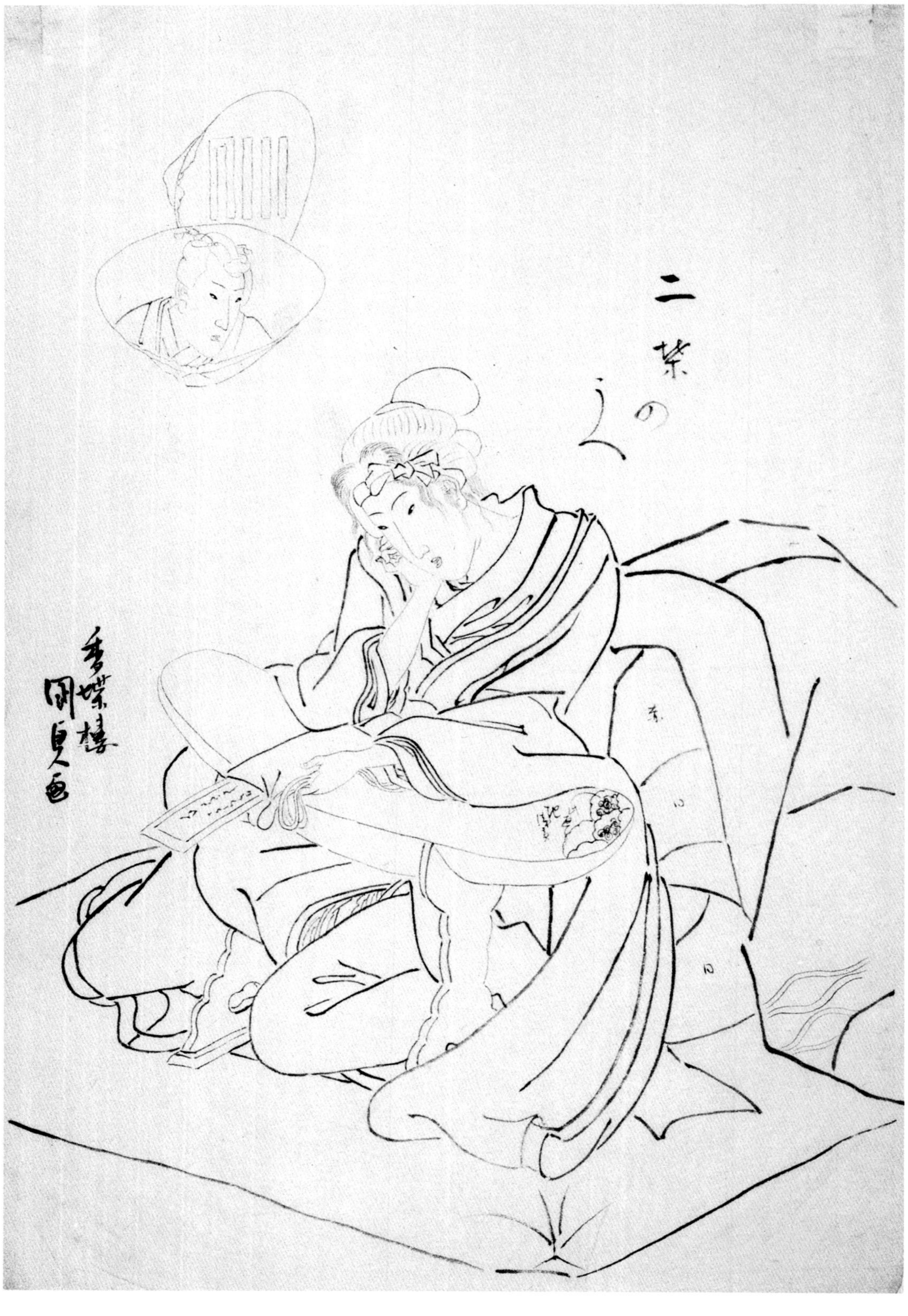

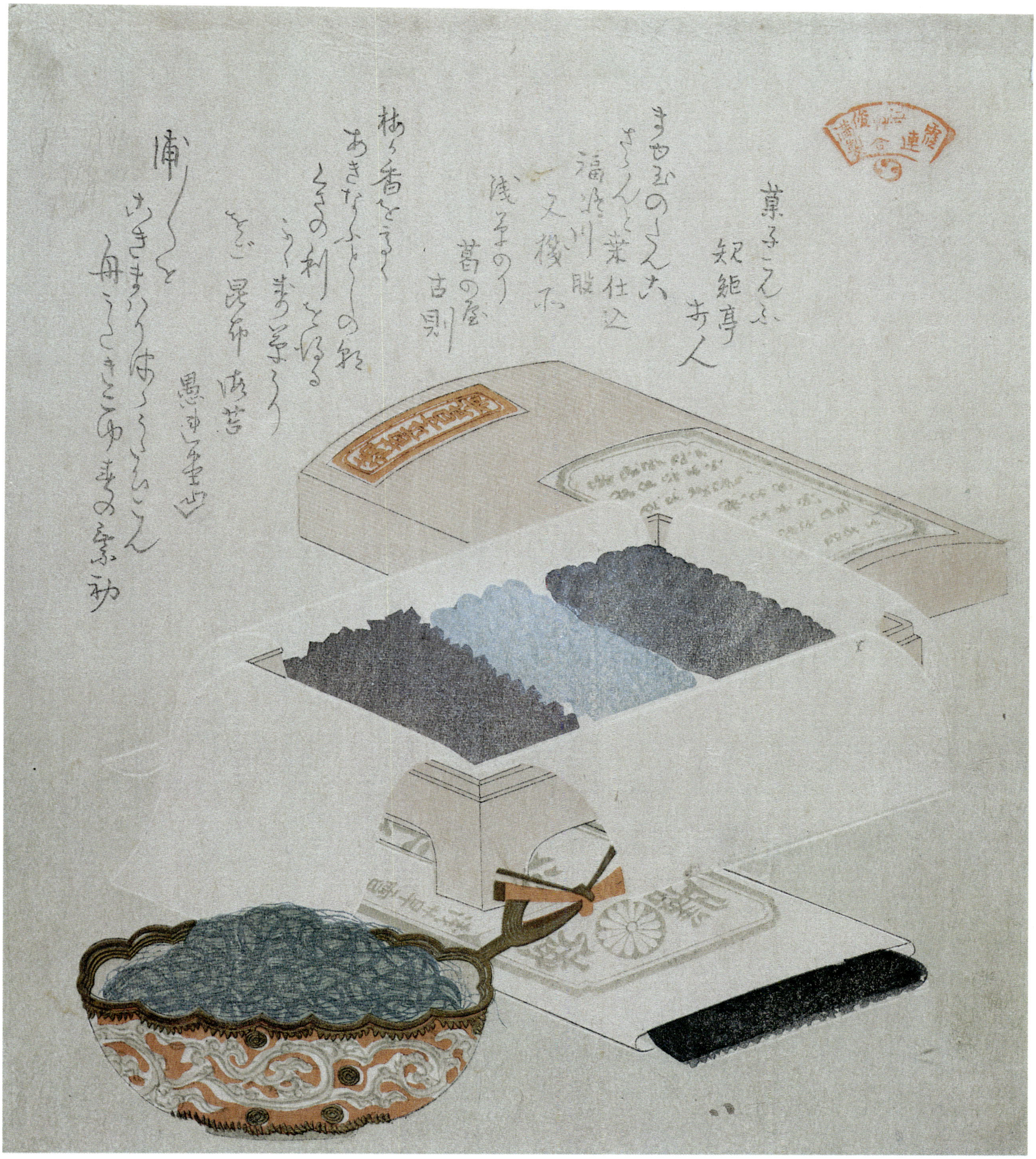

Above: Kubo Shunman (1757-1820) 'Pickled Seaweed' from 'A Series of Seaweeds for the Kasumi Group' *Kasumiren kaisō awase*, late 1810s. Poems by Kankutei Uchibito, Katsunoya Furunori, and Gurendō Nakakubo; signed *Shunman sei*. Kruml Collection.

Left: Utagawa Kunisada (1786-1865). Preparatory sketch for Genji series; this image is taken from chapter 9, *Aoi*, signed *Kōchōrō Kunisada ga*. The notes on the drawing specify the various colors. Kruml Collection.

with only the lightest touches of pale violet or green. *Aizuri-e* were issued in response to the Tempō Reforms of the early 1840s (Tempō era, 1830–44), and reached, in some cases, a high degree of sophistication, using as many as five blocks with varying hues of blue and only the smallest area of, usually, red. The Tempō reforms were also the inspiration behind Utagawa Hiroshige's (1797-1858) publishers experimenting with overprinting to obtain a fuller palette. There was also a profusion of sets at this time extolling virtuous occupations with titles such as *Stories of Chaste and Virtuous Women* and *Mirror of the Twenty-four Paragons of Filial Piety*; these were published in response to the government's exhortations to publishers to issue prints illustrating only moralistic subject-matter. Actor prints were likewise restricted at this time. However they slowly resurfaced in 1847. At this time, though, the actors were superficially and cleverly 'disguised' as historical folk-heroes of high moral standing to avoid censure.

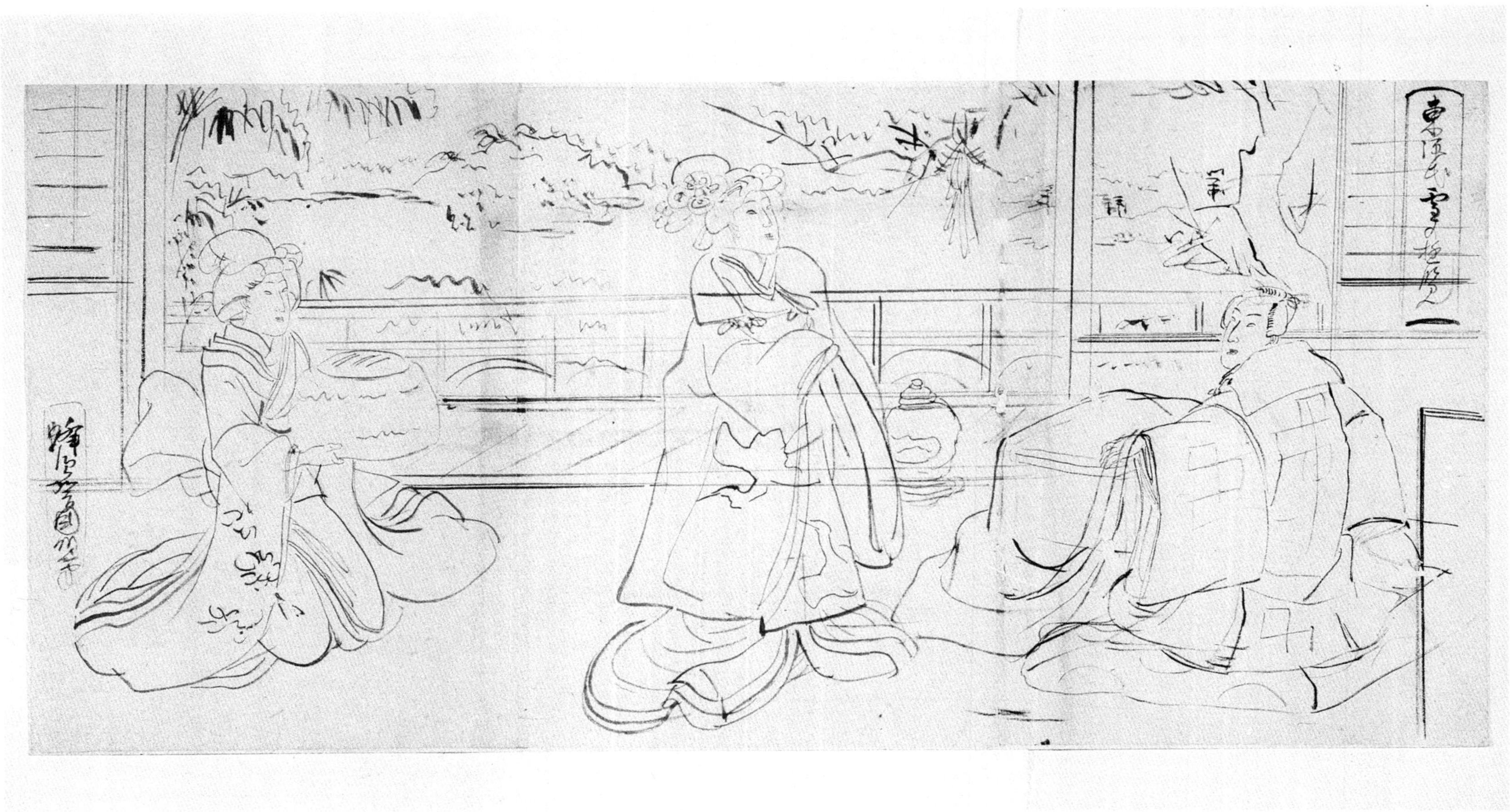

The materials used to create the various elements of a print – woodblock, paper, and pigments – were readily available in Japan (except for certain pigments), and were produced by studios of skilled artisans. However, not all stages of print production necessarily took place under one roof and the supervision of the publisher. Specialist studios were employed to cut blocks, for example, and work was farmed out to other studios. Each studio developed its own process of print production, with details or essentials varying from workshop to workshop. An operation satisfactorily solved one way would have been strictly adhered to regardless of what others were doing. There were also ateliers which concentrated on *surimono* – of which Kubo Shunman's (1757-1820) is the best-known example. It is now generally accepted that he supervised or directly cut and printed his and other artists' *surimono* when the word *sei* follows his name (page 29). (This may also be true of certain *surimono* by Gakutei and Hokkei.) Some publishers might also print *surimono* seasonally, i.e. during the summer when the work load was lighter and humidity problems made the smaller formats easier to handle. (The larger, more conventional sizes were, pro rata, more susceptible to any movement of wood or paper).

Whether resulting from a commission to an acknowledged artist (such as Totoya Hokkei [1780-1850], Yashima Gakutei [c. 1786-1868], Kubo Shunman, or Katsushika Hokusai [1760-1849] in the

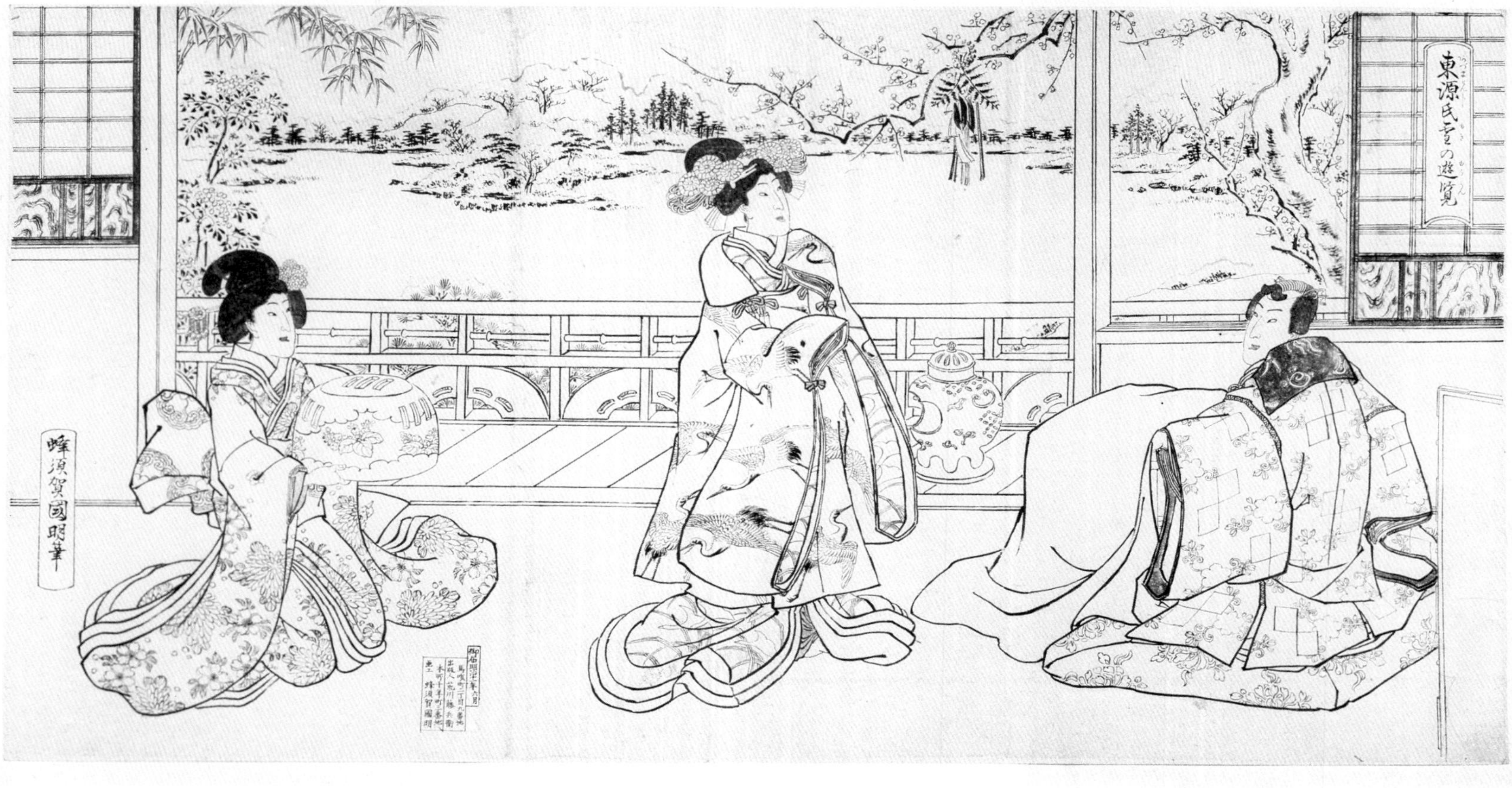

Left and below left: Hachisuka Kuniaki II (1835–88), preparatory sketch for a triptych dealing with the Azuma Genji series, 1879, and signed *Hachisuka Kuniaki hitsu*. The title is in upper right and signature in lower right; publishing details in lower center. Kruml Collection.

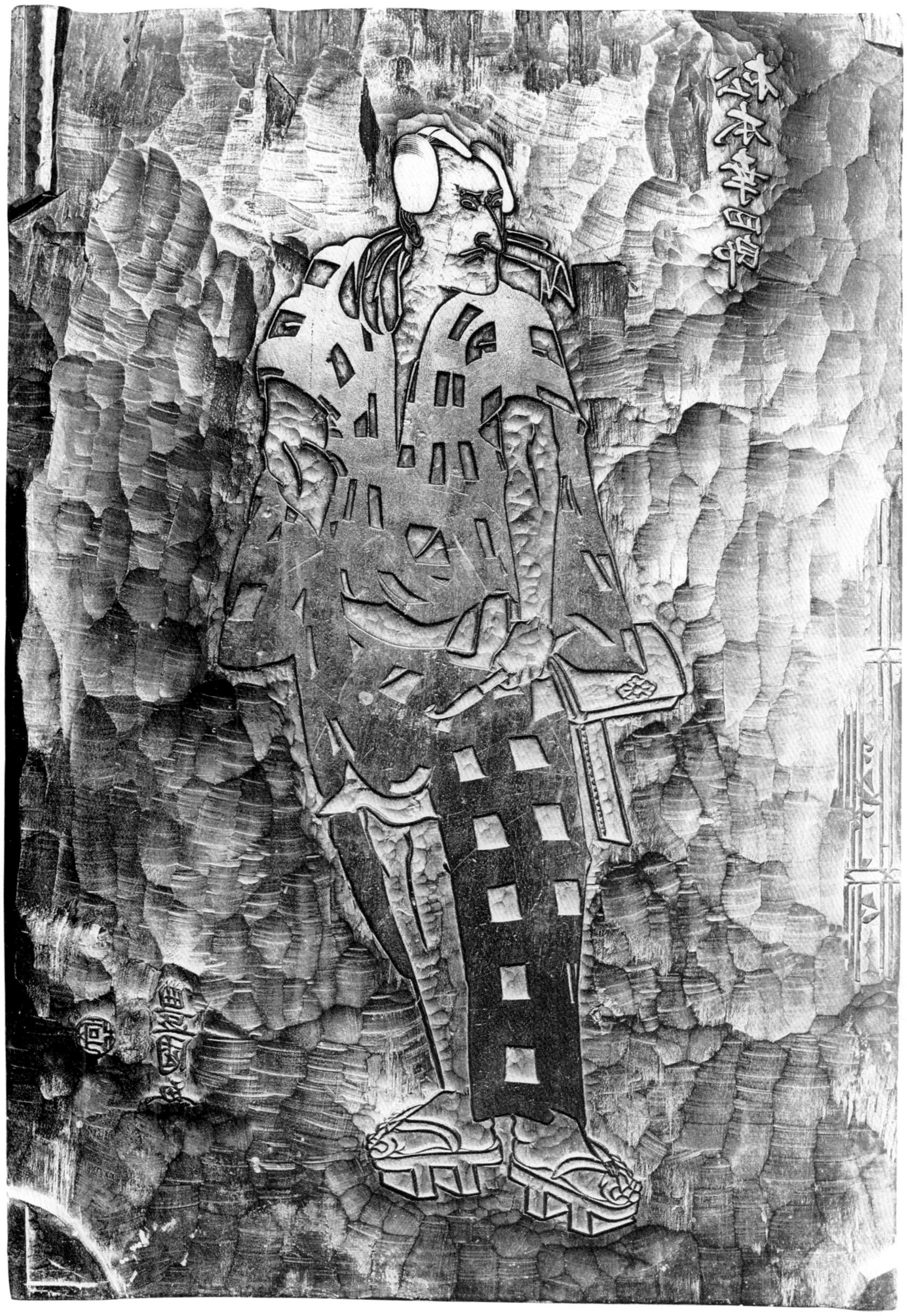

Right: Utagawa Toyokuni I (1769–1825). Portrait of the Actor Matsumoto Kōshirō. Signature in lower left. Original keyblock. Note the *kentō* marks cut on the lower and upper left-hand side. Small raised areas were also provided at the other corners so the paper would not drop on to the block and possibly smudge the ink. Kruml Collection.

case of *surimono*), or a design by an amateur artist/poet, a preparatory sketch (*gakō*) had to be drawn using a deer's fur brush and *sumi* on high-quality *mino-gami* paper. Alterations and corrections were made by gluing fresh paper over the relevant areas. Judging from extant drawings, prolific artists, such as Utagawa Kunisada (1786–1865), made very rough sketches, most attention being paid to the face, and with annotations for the sketches to be worked up by his or the publisher's studio (page 28). The *gakō* was given to a block-copyist who elaborated and produced a detailed drawing (*hanshita-e*) for the woodblock (page 30, left and below left). This drawing was presented to official censors. (*Gyogi* or *e-nanushi* – members of the Wholesale Publishers' Guild for the later part of the eighteenth century. In Edo from 1790 to 1842 they affixed a *kiwame* [passed] seal, a censorship seal, on designs sanctioned by them.) The *hanshita-e* was then pasted face downward using rice-starch paste (*himenori*) on to a block of single-petaled white mountain cherry (*shiro-yamasakura* or *Prunus mutabilis*). Other woods were available for *surimono* such as *tokachiyanagi* (Japanese willow); cross-sections or end-grain of *tsuge* (box-wood, *Buxus Japonica*); and *tsubaki* (camellia, *Camellia Japonica*). In order to render the drawing easily visible for the block-cutter, a thin layer was peeled off using the flat of the finger, or hempseed oil was rubbed in to make the paper transparent and the drawing visible. This first block, called the keyblock (above) or *sumi*-block, provided the black outline of the finished print and provided reversed or mirror-images of itself which would furnish, by the same process, the color blocks. The keyblock, besides delineating the imagery of a print and acting as a guide for the color blocks, could also, when it was necessary to align more than one block, indicate areas which were intended to be reversed-out (print white) by removing them from the color blocks. These areas on the key block were finally cut away after the color blocks had been completed (see keyblock above). To align the various color images accurately the keyblock had raised notches (key marks or registration marks [*kentō*]) cut at one corner and along the adjacent side (above). These were printed with the rest of the design and consequently cut in exactly the same position in relation to the image on each color block. The paper for printing was placed against these *kentō* marks and permitted colors to be regis-

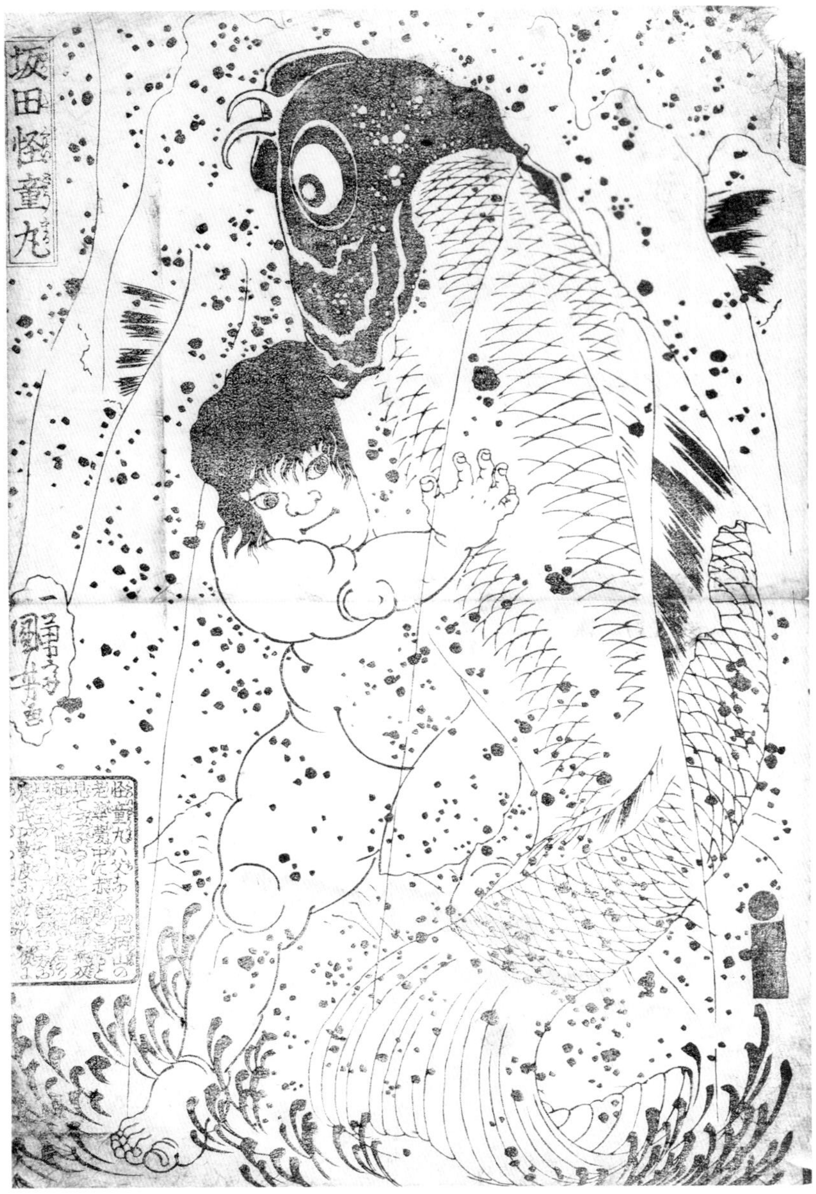

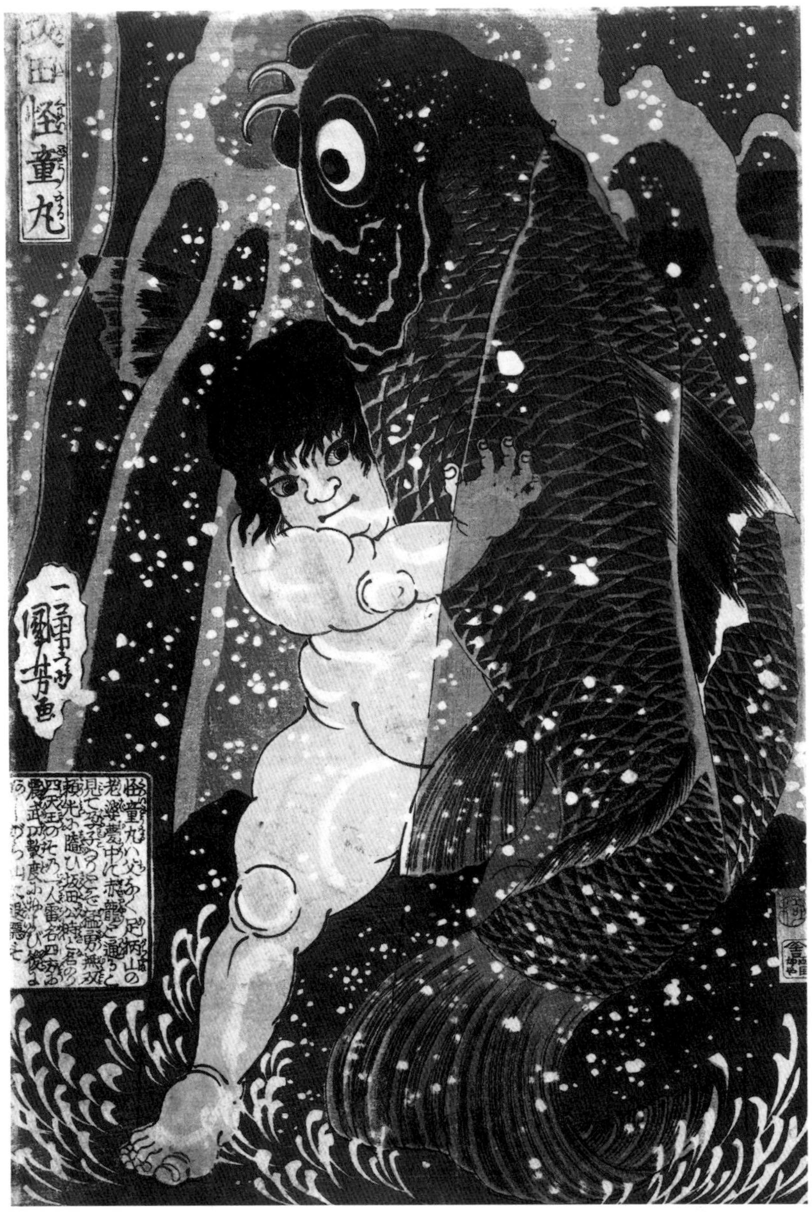

tered very accurately side by side or one on top of another. Discrepancies due to expanding or contracting of the wood or paper were counteracted by plugging the block with slivers of cherry wood next to the *kentō*.

A set of 'proofs' (*kyōgō*) was pulled from the key-block (above left and right), and there may have been as many as 20 or more, depending on the number of color blocks required. Certainly in the nineteenth century, both sides of the blocks were utilized because of the expense, although they were not necessarily related to the same design: surviving key-blocks invariably have disparate sides, often by different artists. The cutting of an average set of blocks, together with any alterations, could be completed in two or three days (and even complicated sets were finished within 20 days). Although the cutter had a large choice of chisels and knives at his disposal, he invariably used only a few basic tools, which can be divided into four groups: the *kagatana* or *tō* (knife) for cutting the lines; the *aisuke* (digging chisel) to clear superfluous wood between the carved lines, the blade of which was arc-shaped when viewed from above; the *marunomi* (gouge or round chisel) with a shape corresponding to a tube split down the middle, and the *nomi* (chisel), the cutting edge being arc-shaped in cross-section, and used in conjunction with the *kizuchi* mallet. The wood-cutter sat cross-legged at a low stand; the block was placed on pads on the stand to counteract any movement. The block slanted slightly toward him and was positioned with the top to the right (*tate-e* format). During the Edo period outlines were cut following the direction of the brush strokes of the original drawing. The knife was drawn toward the block-cutter and the lines were cut with slightly angled sides to prevent chipping. In Japan wood was cut with the grain; this method is fundamentally similar to Western chiaroscuro woodcuts, hence the operation is one of relief printing as opposed to intaglio. The impression from the grain of the woodblock was transferred to the paper during printing and should be visible on early impressions. As no two blocks have identical patterns (page 33), the appearance of the wood grain on the print was one reliable method of testing for authenticity, the exception being designs where blocks, for whatever reason, have been replaced. Sometimes the woodblock's grain was used deliberately to convey, for example, flowing water or raked sand (*mokumezuri*) (page 34). *Itame-mokuhan*,, *'imitation' wood-grain, is frequently found on actor prints where wood is incorporated into the design, for example the copying of wooden votive tablets (ema).* The appearance of wood was replicated by choosing a tight, highly figured block which had minimum preparation, or may have been treated with steam or water to raise the grain. After application of the pigment with a pad, every small pore of the wood was duplicated (page 34, below left).

Alterations or additions to the cut blocks were made by plugging areas with new pieces of wood. It is not uncommon to see these skillfully inserted corrections, when the names of actors or titles were often changed and especially on the hands and heads of *bijin* (beautiful women) which were the most demanding areas to cut, with their delicate face outlines and detailed hair (page 35, right and below). These sections were consequently cut by an accomplished master carver (*atama-bori*, or head carver). The remainder of the design was left to a trainee (*dō-bori* or body carver). Because of the often intricate patterns and fine lines on *surimono*, only the more experienced wood-cutters were employed to carve designs. The poems on *surimono* were copied by specialist calligraphers and cut on seperate blocks.

Left and far left: Utagawa Kuniyoshi (1797-1861). 'Kintarō Wrestling with the Giant Carp' (Sakata Kaidōmaru), from the *Suikoden* series, c. 1830-35. Published by Kagaya Kichiemon. Far left is the key-block proof (*kyōgō*) and left the finished print. Both signed *Ichiyūsai Kuniyoshi ga* in lower left. Note the *kentō* mark showing top right on the proof. Rijksmuseum, Amsterdam.

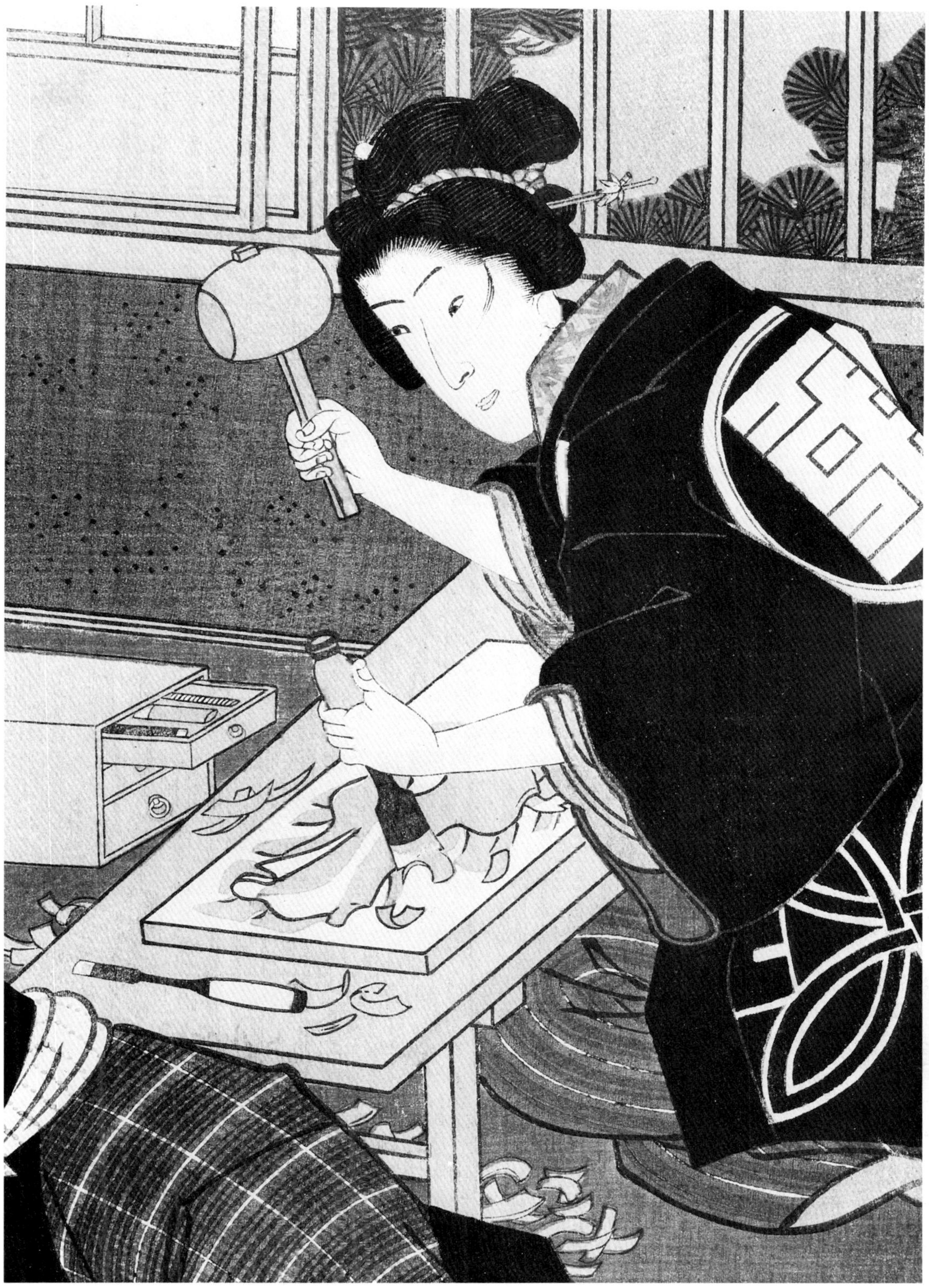

Right: Detail of Kunisada print on page 36, showing a blockcutter at work.

Below: Sakai Hōtsu (1761-1828) '*A Book of Paintings by Ōson*' (*Ōson gafu*), 1817. Illustration of one page from the book. This depiction of an iris reveals the wood grain of the block. Kruml Collection.

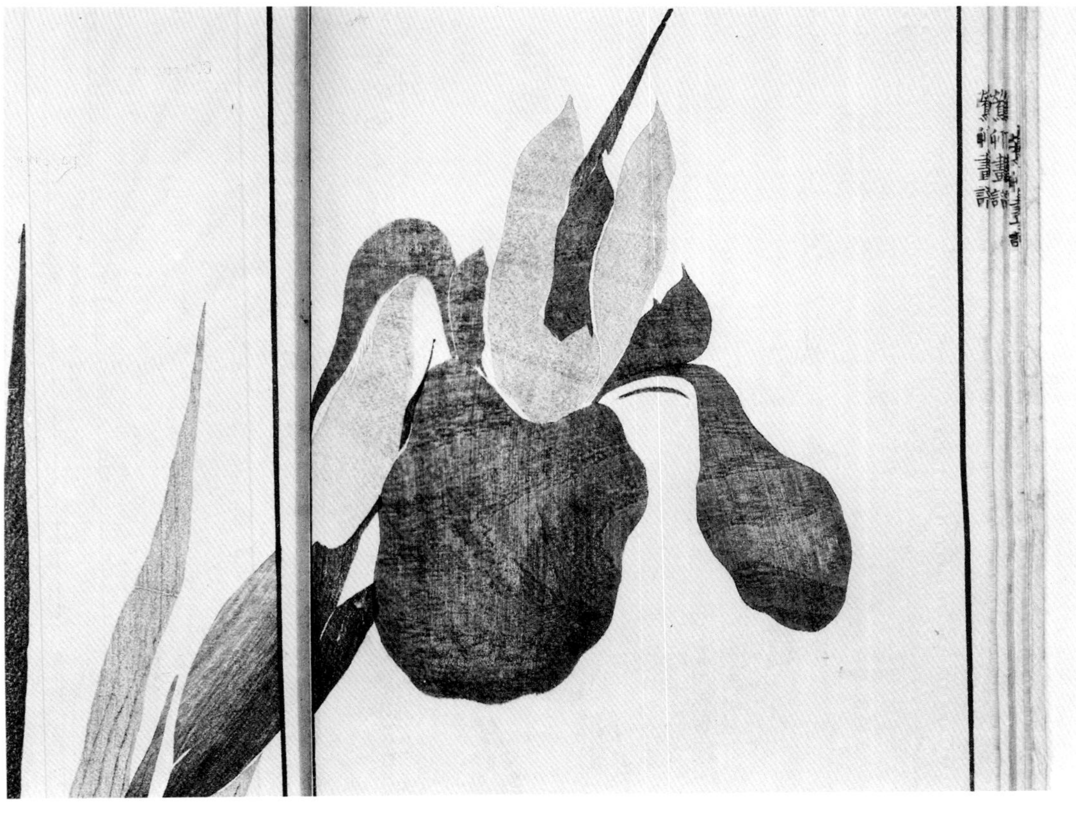

The finished set of blocks was marked to indicate the colors: *ai* (indigo), *kusa*, (green) etc, and other *kyōgō* were printed with detailed instructions on each as to how the printer was to grade the pigments. The hierarchy of the printer's studio was similar to that of the blockcutter's, with the technically demanding tasks performed by the more skilled printers: the *nishiki-e* printers looked down on those printers who worked in *sumi*. The latter were referred to as *dobu*-workers, a derogatory term meaning 'sewer' or 'drain' which derived from the fact that pickled *sumi* emitted an unsavory smell when prepared. The grinding and making of pigments called for a considerable amount of skill and was one of the jobs a trainee had to master. Each color was placed in its own porcelain bowl and before they were used the correct consistency was reached by adding several drops of water (page 36, left). With the

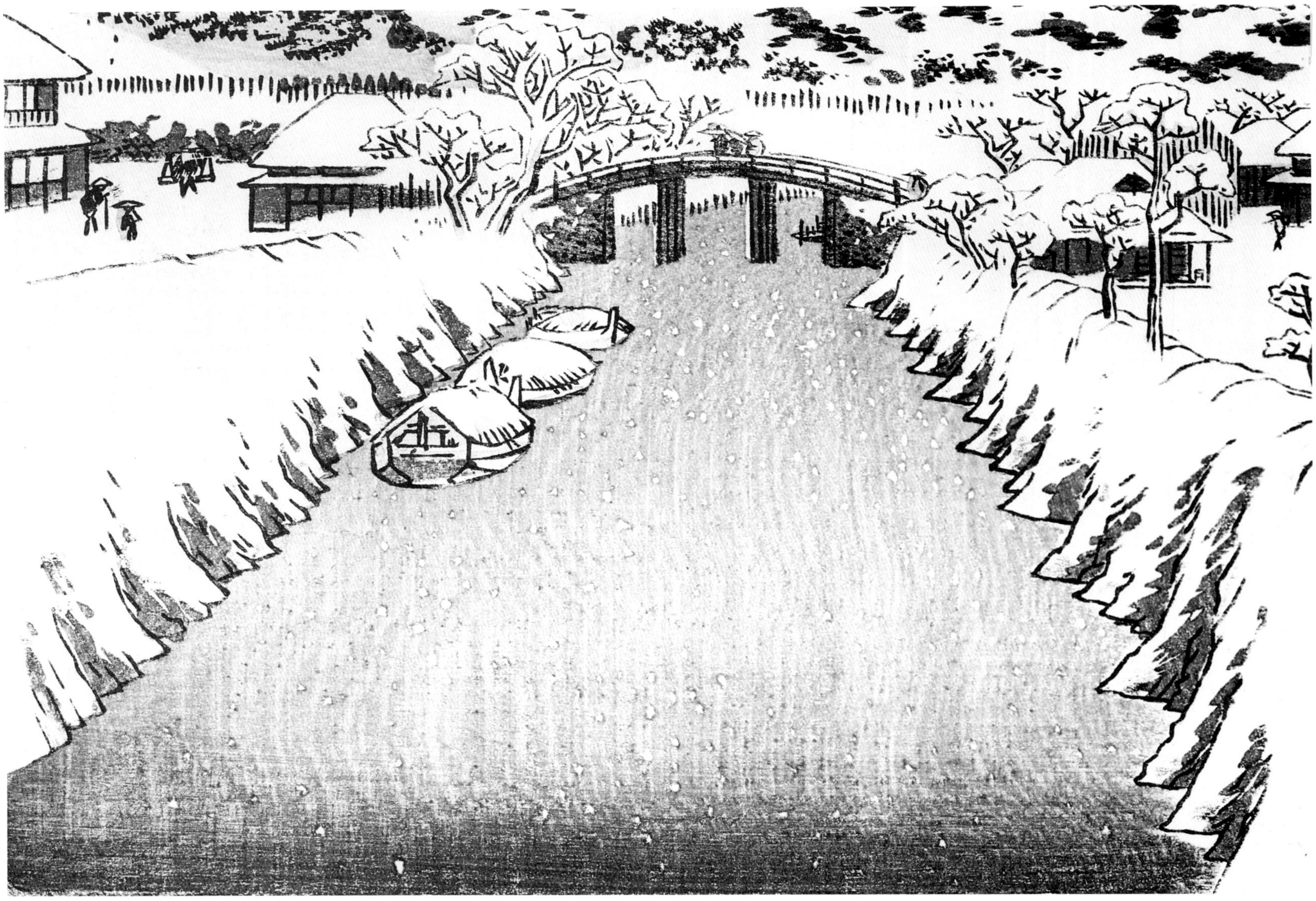

primary exception of *surimono* where block-cutters/printers are often acknowledged with hand-stamped seals (page 37), the recognition on prints of these printers and block-cutters is limited. In contemporary literature the block-cutter is mentioned more than the printer who has often been relegated to obscurity. The printer sat as the block-cutter, but with the block angled slightly away from him and with the top to the left (*tate-e* format) (page 38). Pigment was applied with brushes (*hake*) (page 38, left) made from the horse's mane. To give extra depth, thickness and better adhesion, rice-starch paste was dropped on the block and mixed with the color. Added sparkle was sometimes given by dusting the blocks with dry rice-flour after the application of pigment. Generally speaking, a set printing sequence would be observed, with the soft-hued colors such as *beni* (saf-flower) applied first, then yellow, gray, blue and purple; followed by any colored grounds and dense blacks that needed several printings. The process finished with mica grounds or surface polishing when the prints were dry. A common fallacy is that the *sumi*-block always took precedence so as to give a guide for subsequent colors; however, this was unnecessary if register was accurate. Careful inspection of prints proves that the reverse case can be true, with the key-block being printed over areas of color. Indeed, it is easy to see that any dark colors could easily obliterate the *sumi* outline if printed later.

Paper sized with a mixture of alum and a glue extracted from deer antler, bone, or skin cooked in hot water (*dosa*) was stacked, slightly dampened, ready for use. Most Japanese prints were made from two types of *kōzo* paper (mulberry, *Broussonetia*): *masa* and *hōsho*. Prior to true *nishiki-e*, *masa-gami* (masa paper) was used for prints. It was reintroduced after 1842 when the Tempō Reforms banned *hōsho* because of its luxurious nature and cost. The Reforms, however, did not affect *surimono* which continued to use *hōsho* as its high quality was needed to

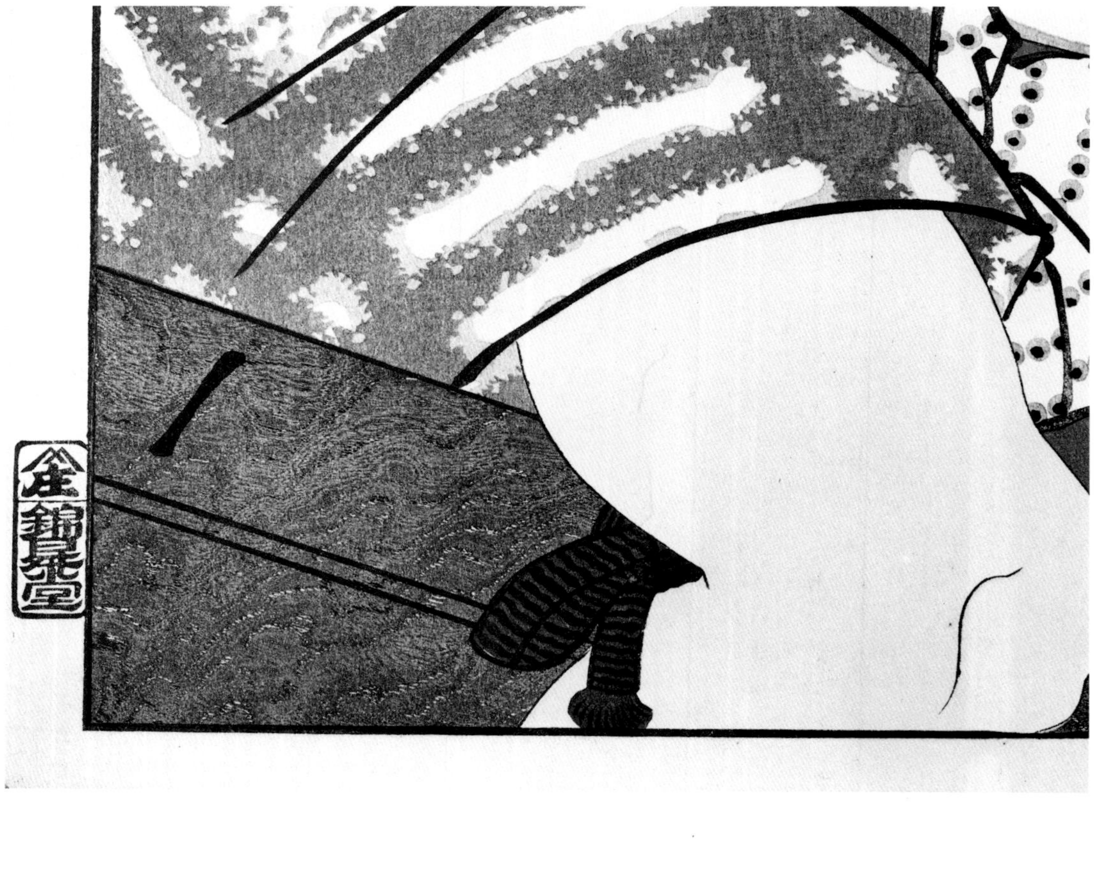

Left: Utagawa Hiroshige (1797-1858). 'Zōjōji, Akabane, Shiba,' from the series *Tōto meisho* ('Famous Places of the Eastern Capital'). Published by Sanoki, late 1830s. Here the grain of the wood is used to depict water. Kruml Collection.

Below left: Utagawa Kunisada (1786-1865). Replicated wood grain from a portion of a print from a set of actor bust portraits, 1863. Publisher: Ebisuya Kinshōdo. Kruml Collection.

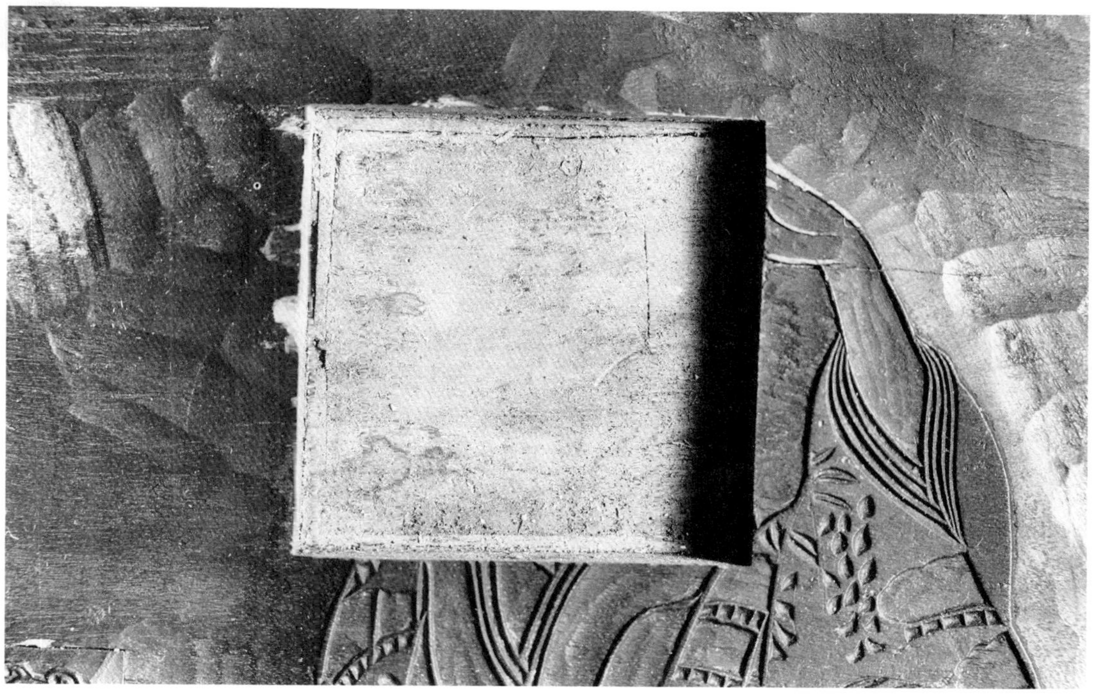

Right and below: woodblocks showing (right) carved out square awaiting to be inserted and (below) block with an inserted recarved portion in the block. Kruml Collection.

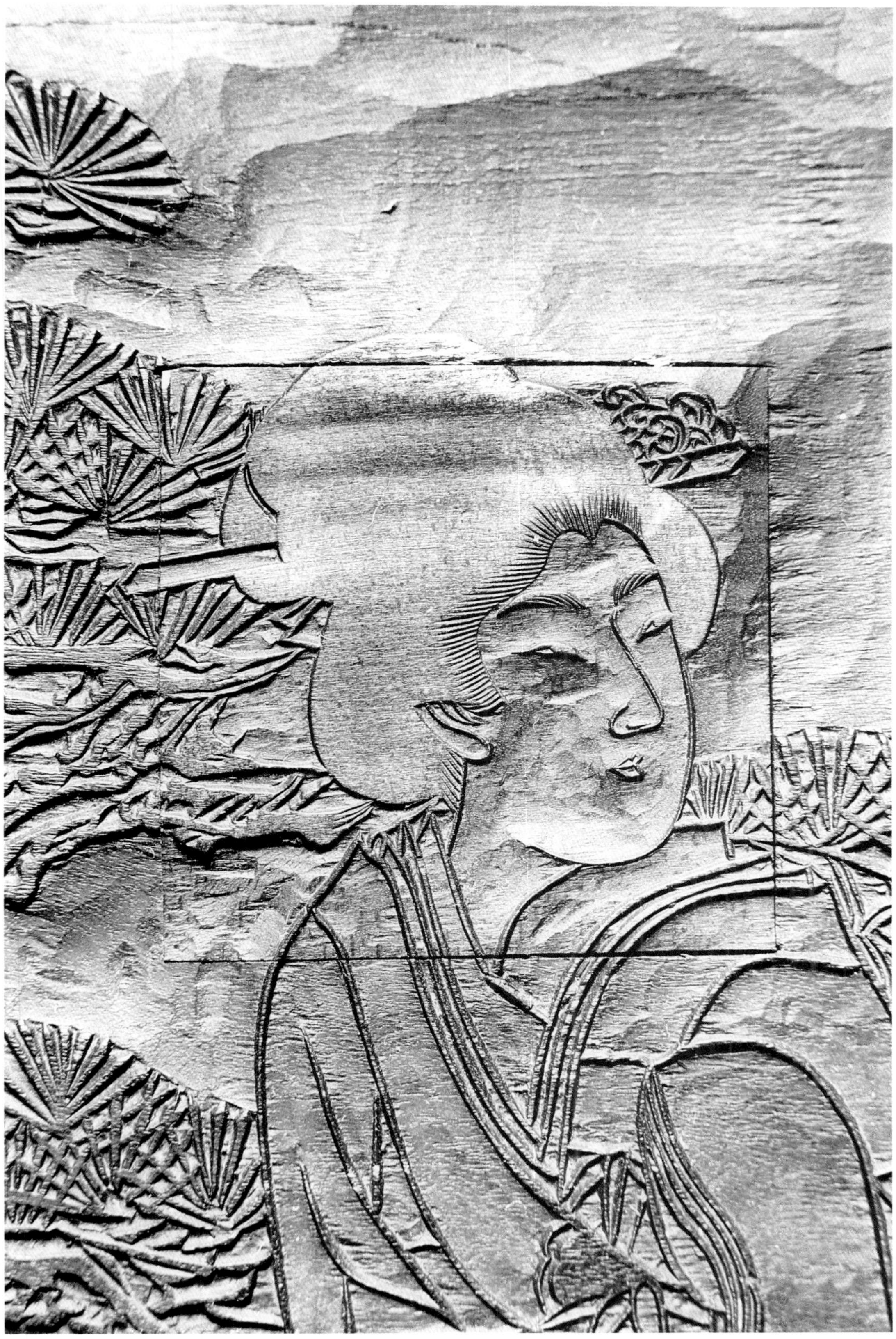

display adequately the frequently used technique of blind-printing.

Single-sheet print proportions were governed by the size the paper was couched in; the width across the grain of available wood; regulatory edicts; and the problems in keying larger designs. *Surimono* formats derive from their early *chūban* origins, with the square shape coming to dominate from the early 1800s to the mid-1830s. The natural outcome of these factors, together with the standardization of paper sizes in the late 1770s, resulted in the *ōban* (15×10¼ inches [38×26 cm]) becoming the standard format at the beginning of the 1780s. Multiple formats such as diptychs, triptychs, etc, were the publisher's solution to increasing the size of prints and avoiding prohibitions. The concept of multiple-linked images was familiar in Japan and most printed books, certainly those of the Edo period, open out to form diptychs in the form of double-page illustrations within borders; and the triptych theme had been used to link *kakemono* (hanging scrolls) by Kanō painters. The handicap imposed by size restrictions created, as with Torii Kiyonaga's (1752-1815) designs, separate panels which could stand and be viewed in isolation, but which when joined with other sheets, produced a new, enlarged and completely harmonious composition. Eventually the art of linking designs became an end in itself, with even *surimono* being executed in triptych and pentaptych formats.

The image was printed from the woodblock by forcefully impressing the back of the paper with a *baren* using rhythmical circular or semi-circular movements. Apart from the *kentō*, the baren was the most important development towards the perfection of *nishiki-e*. It was composed of a flat disk, approximately 5 inches (13 cm) wide, of twisted and knotted bamboo cord held within a

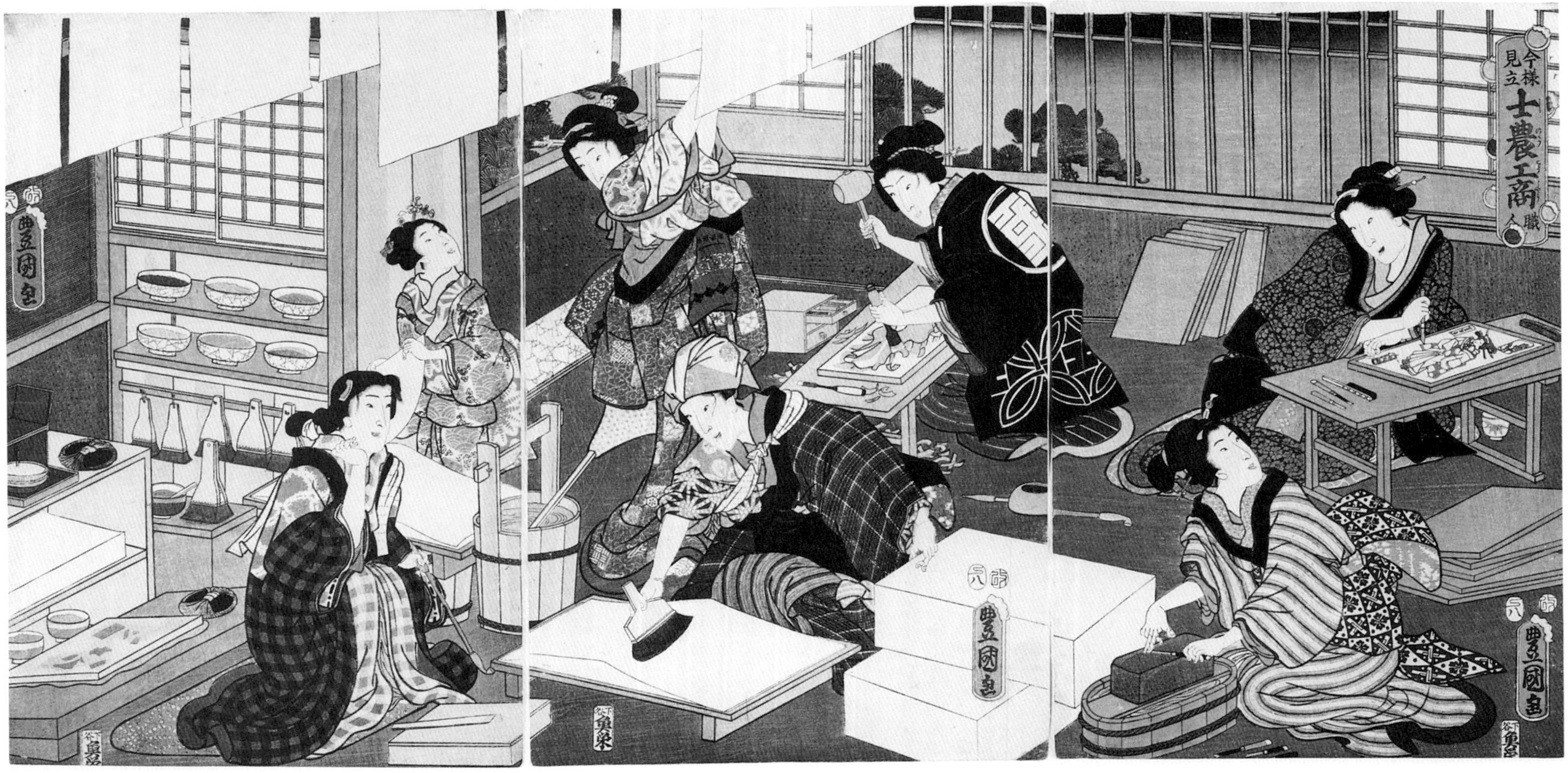

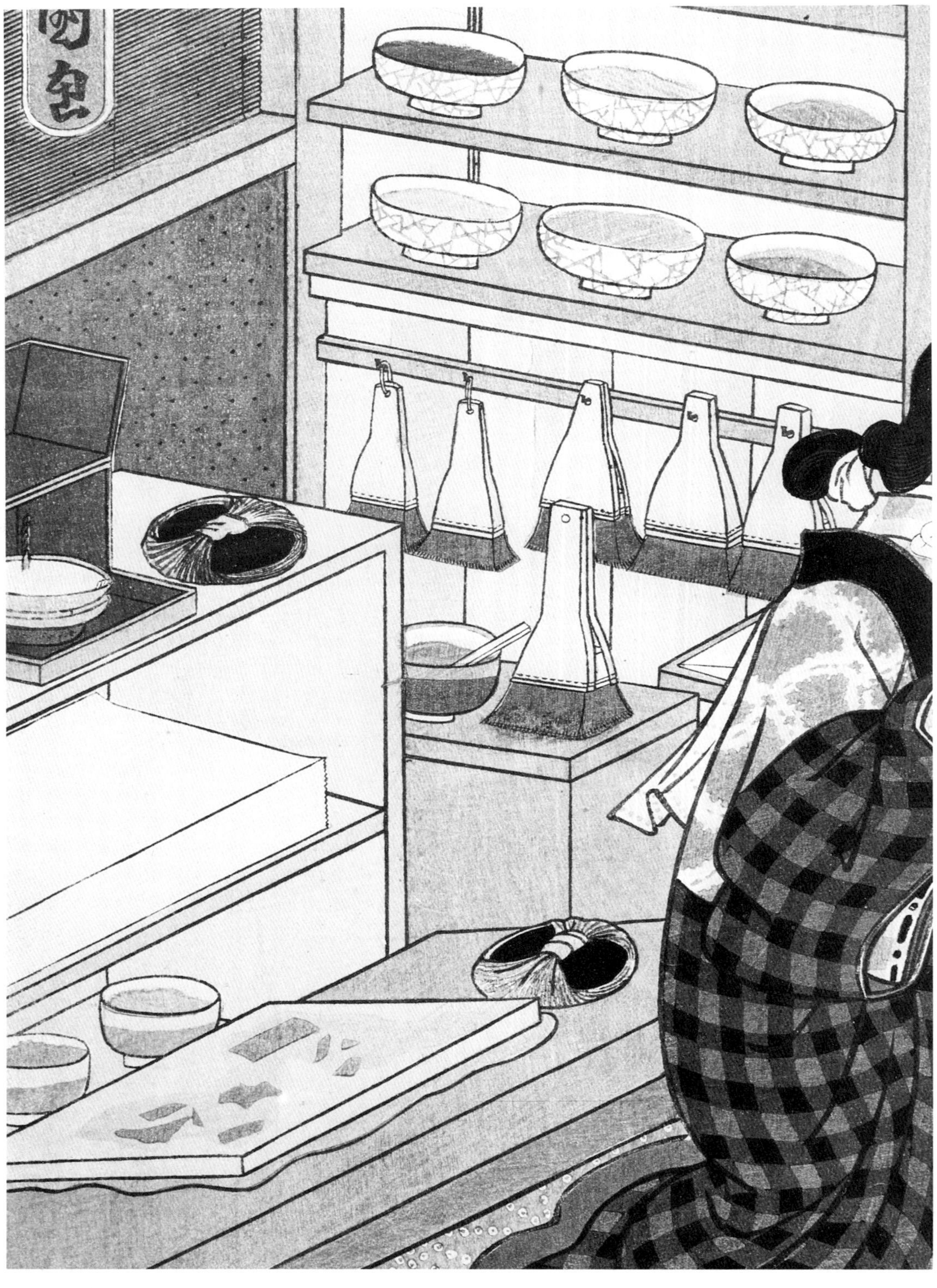

lacquered cover that was covered with bamboo leaf (page 39, below center and right). The coiled circle of bamboo fiber was twisted into cords (page 39, below left), a two-strand cord being doubled once, twice of three times to make from four up to sixteen strands, although eight was the norm during the Edo period. The strands were knotted together creating an uneven surface which facilitated in pressing the pigment into the paper. The *baren* marks are usually visible on the reverse side of prints (page 40, above), yet during the Edo period it was considered bad technique to have them showing on the front. However, some prints around the time of the Utagawa Toyokuni I's (1769-1825) series, 'Portraits of Actors on Stage' (*Yakusha butai no sugata-e*), 1794-9), with black or gray grounds, seem deliberately to emphasize and utilize the *baren* marks to give a patterned background. The *shin hanga* artist Itō Shinsui (1898-1972) exploited the lines of the *baren* to give a spontaneous and unique appearance to some of his designs. In Nagasaki the *baren* was covered with horsehair and used to rub the paper in straight parallel lines, a technique adopted from China where *tōshi* (Chinese paper) would not have withstood excessive hard rubbing. This is also the reason Nagasaki prints have a softer appearance.

Not all impressions were taken from the woodblock at the same time: the general view is that editions (*ippai*) of around 200 prints were pulled at one time. The number increased (sometimes to many thousands) depending on the popularity of the design. Running editions of this size allowed the blocks to 'rest' between printings as too many impressions taken at the same time caused

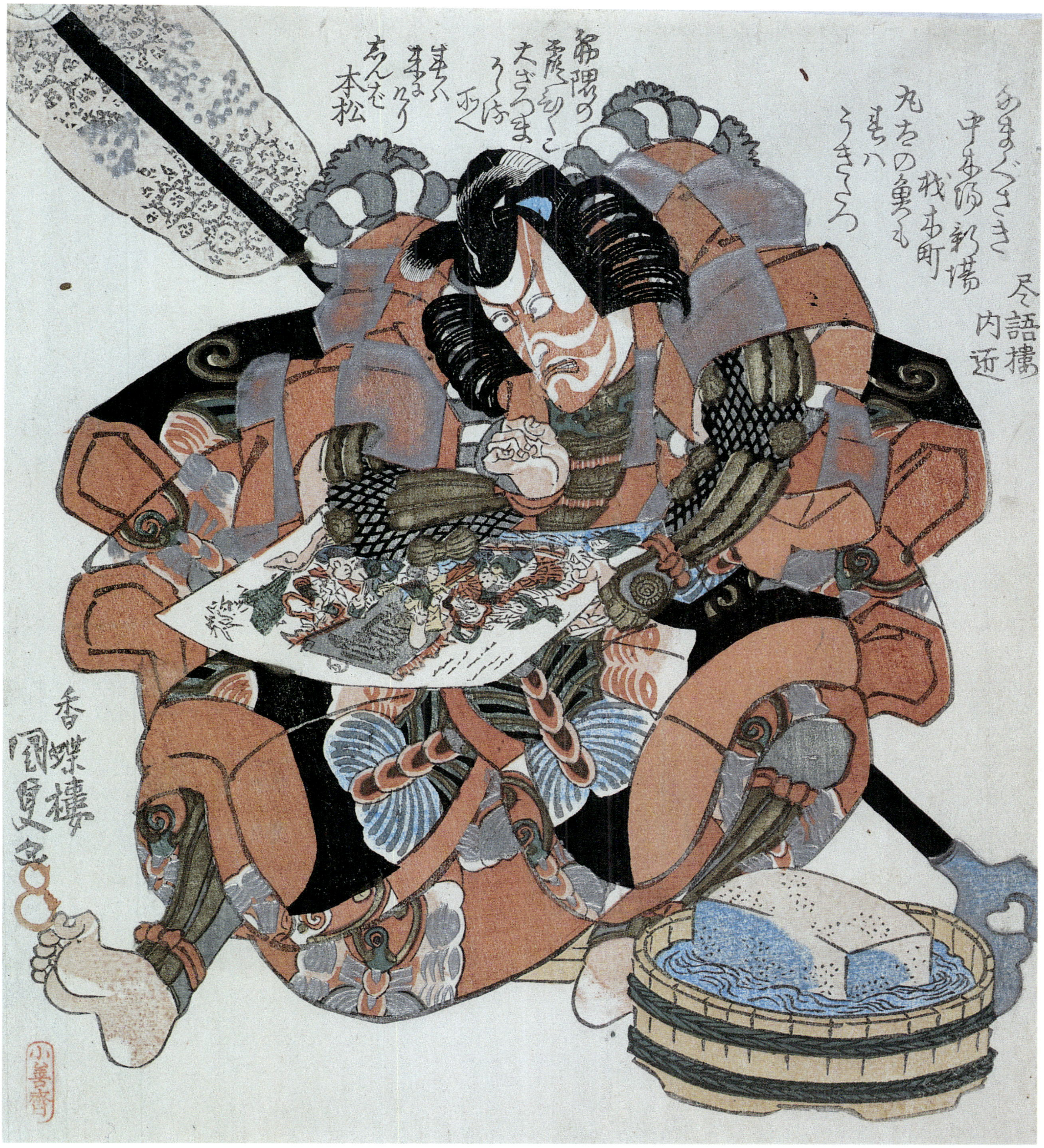

Above left: Utagawa Kunisada (1786-1865). Although this is a fanciful depiction of printmaking, as women were not employed to carve or print blocks, the various stages are still faithfully reproduced. Kruml Collection.

Left: Detail of the same print as above left. This shows the *baren* used for rubbing the back of the print while it is on the block; brushes for applying colors; and bowls of color.

Above: Utagawa Kunisada (1786-1865). 'The Actor Ichikawa Danjūrō VII as Soga no Gorō.' Signed and sealed *Kōchōrō Kunisada ga*. Printer's seal bottom left, *Kozensai*. Kruml Collection.

greater wear and tear on the wood and the blocks to become saturated with pigment and sluggish and erratic in relinquishing the color evenly. Although the production of Japanese prints is discussed in terms of editions, Japanese prints until the early twentieth century were not numbered or limited through cancellation of the blocks. With the exception of *surimono*, market demand governed the numbers printed and if the blocks became excessively worn they could be recut. Contrary to the accepted view that the normal edition comprised 200 impressions, it is the writer's opinion that printings in excess of 4000 were perfectly feasible before the blocks exhibited any signs of wear, and that printings of more than 20,000 were probable for popular Hiroshige sets. Verse *surimono*, due to their specialized nature, had, according to print historian Roger Keyes, probable editions of around 75 to 100 impressions.

The printer's technique of gradating pigments on the block enabled him to produce results which confuse many laymen into thinking Japanese prints are directly hand-colored. Gradation of

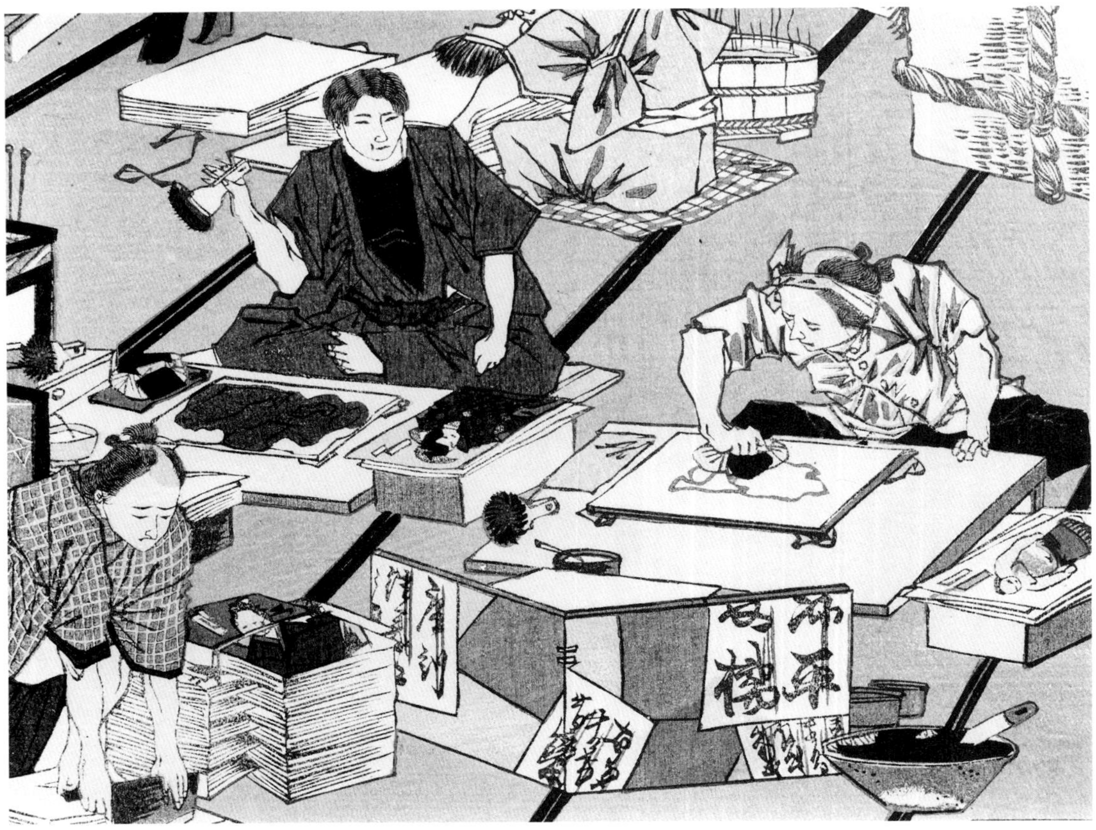

Left: Detail of the print below showing (left) application of ink to the block; (right) printing using the *baren*; and (below) trimming completed prints.

Below: Hosogi Toshikazo (*fl* late eighteenth century). 'Picture of Nishiki-e Production' (*Nishiki-e seizō no zu*), from the series 'A Comparison of Various Crafts' (*Shokō shokugyō kurabe*), 1879. Series title in rectangular cartouche in upper right. signed and sealed in lower left. Kruml Collection.

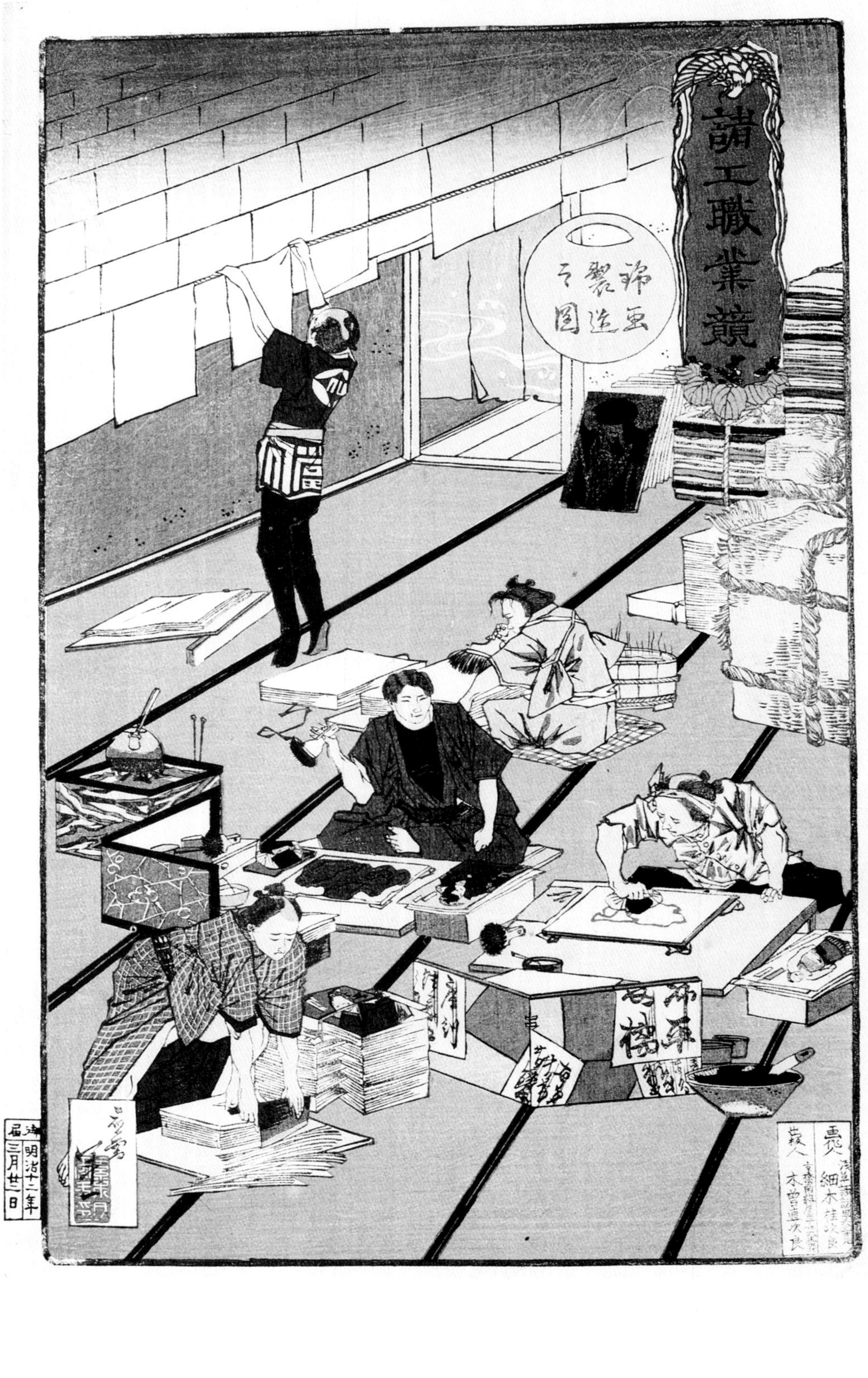

colors was achieved by various *bokashi* techniques (shading, or gradation) which used brushes partly loaded with pigment drawn across dampened areas, or by wiping with a cotton cloth or pad (page 40, below). Sophisticated results were possible in the hands of an experienced printer, giving form, depth or atmosphere to a subject, and also ensuring that no two impressions were identical. The block-cutter was also able to create color-gradation, called *ita-bokashi*, (edge gradation), by gradually 'lowering' the wood so that an edge printed with no definable line. This is generally only seen on key-blocks and illustrated books. Printers were able to pull color prints in around 15 to 25 seconds and key-blocks in about 9 seconds. In the late nineteenth century Mr Tokuno, chief of the Bureau of Engraving and Printing of the Japanese Ministry of Finance, states that 3000 sheets could be pulled in an approximately eight-hour day from the key-block, 1200 to 1800 from a straightforward color block, while a color block needing gradation yielded only 600 to 700.

Apart from these shading techniques, there were a number of other unique methods of enriching designs. The most important were *karazuri, tsuya-zuri, kiri-fuki* (*fukibokashi* or *fukibotan*); mica and metal powders; pigments and crêping. *Karazuri*, variously known as blind-printing, gauffrage, embossing or goffering, is a technique which produced a reversed braille outline seen best with a raked light (page 41, above). *Karazuri* did not utilize pigment; instead a specific block was cut and the paper lightly dampened. The image was formed by rubbing with a piece of ivory – usually the canine tooth of the wild boar, although the *baren* would also create shallow blind-printing, as would the tip of the printer's elbow rocked backward and forward. Before the Meiji period the heel was also used to extract deep gauffrage, but the more usual method of making deep outlines (*kimekomi*) was by gently tapping with a gutta percha hammer. Gutta percha hammers were made with the tough grayish-black gum from the Percha tree, common to the Malayan archipelago. Entire outlines of objects or animals could be 'printed' in this way, usually with a boxwood block; many *surimono* show rolls of paper or cloth, live or snow rabbits, and white cockerels and mice. It was also ideal for depicting white against white such as, for example, a white egret against a snowy embankment. Apart from *surimono*, this technique is exemplified on the *chūban* prints of Suzuki Harunobu (1725-70) and Isoda Koryūsai (*fl* c 1764-88), some of which are *shunga* prints where naked bodies are outlined by blind-printing. More sophisticated gauffraging effects were produced by gluing textured gauzes to the blocks, or randomly spreading particles, perhaps of sand, which would pit the paper when impressed. Glued muslin was also used to print a fine net pattern (*nunomezuri*). Otherwise mesh patterns were made by cutting two blocks which printed at right-angles or diagonally to each other.

With *tsuya-zuri* (surface polishing or burnishing) (page 40, below left), shiny areas meant to resemble, perhaps, silk or lacquer were given to prints by rubbing the surface vigorously with a round piece of porcelain or ivory. There is also mention of spoons being used in the Meiji period. A block was cut from a proof print taken from the desired region, which was pasted face up onto the wood. Similar results were obtained by painting with glue, especially over animals' or demons' eyes (page 41, below), and could also convincingly depict blood when applied to red pigments. A number of sets, primarily by Utagawa Kuniyoshi (1797-1861) and Utagawa Yoshiiku (1833-1904), had a sheen over the entire printed surface. These western-style series attempt to emulate the oil paintings and book illustrations that were known in Japan in the nineteenth century. In one series by Yoshiiku, entitled *A Photographic Picture* (or *Mirror*) the glazing of the surface was probably aided by the application of hard wax before the rubbing. Ogura Ryūson (*fl* 1880-90) had a rare set of moonlight landscapes published which were heavily coated by

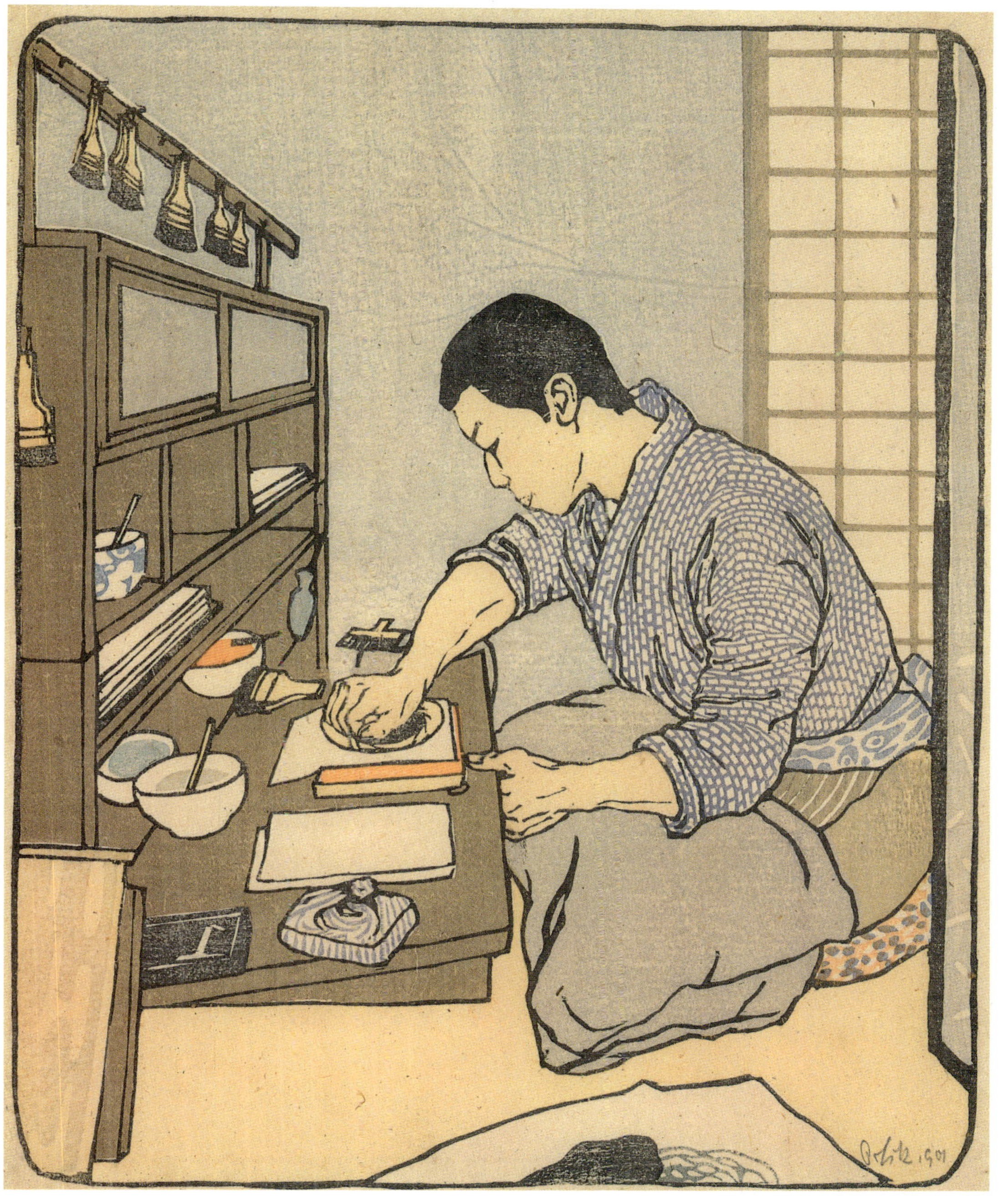

Above: Emil Orlik (1870-1935). Image of printer at work, 1901. Orlik was a Czech artist who visited Japan and studied and practiced printmaking techniques. Rijksmuseum, Amsterdam.

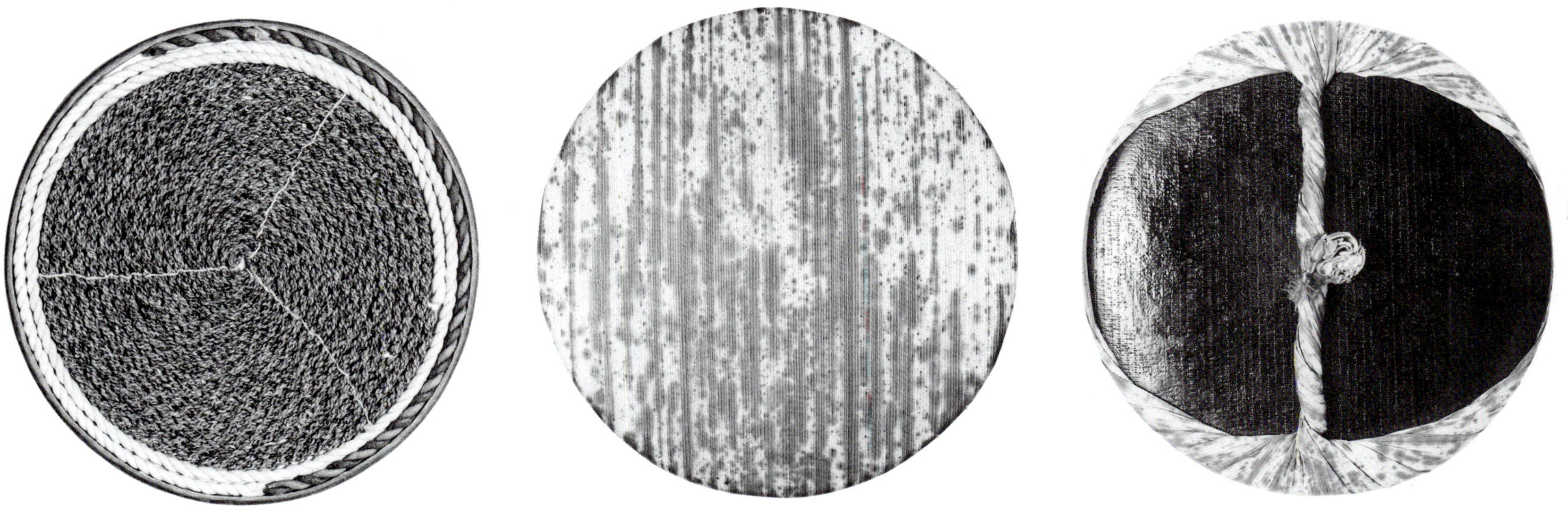

Below: Three views of a *baren*. At left is the inside with rolled fiber; at center is the completed *baren* seen from below; at right is the completed *baren* seen from above, with the bamboo leaf covering woven together to form a handle.

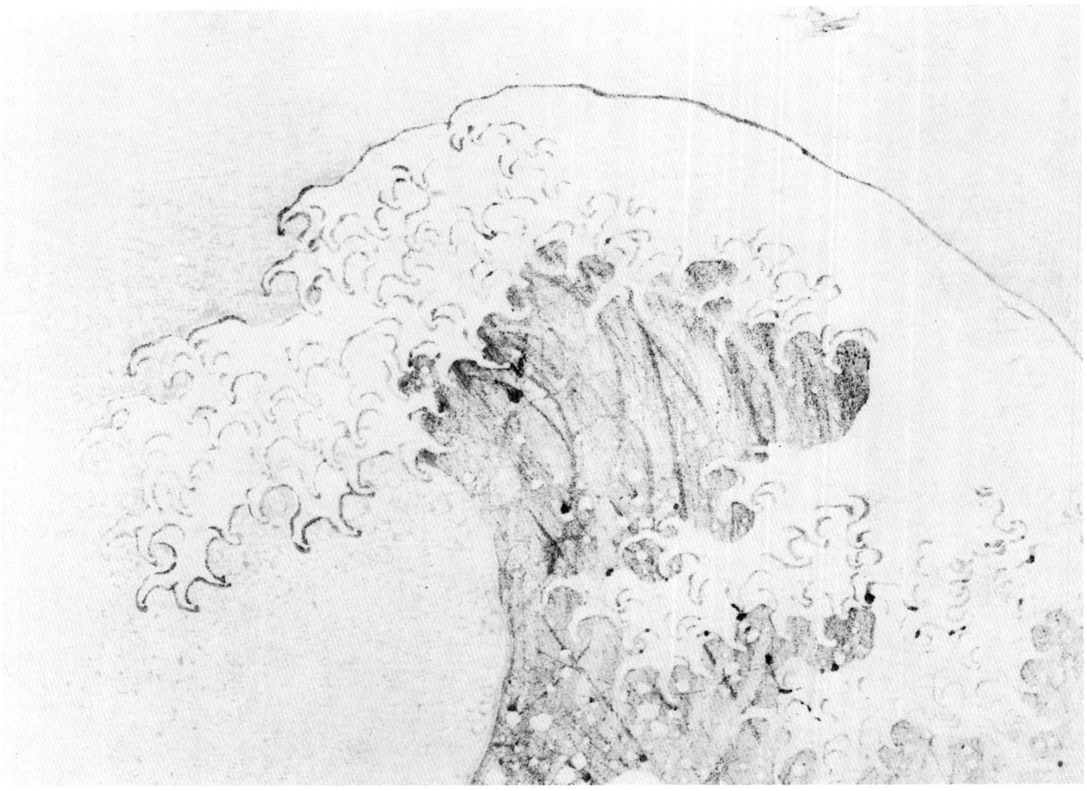

hand with a gluey varnish (*nisu-biki*), and a few landscapes of Kobayashi Kiyochika (1847-1915) from the same period were given the same treatment. Dense blacks were made by overprinting *sumi* on *sumi*, usually by having a separate block cut, and by using best-quality undiluted *sumi*. A lustrous black was formed by mixing in rice-paste on the block, or a *dosa* medium was added. A rich black derived from the best-quality ink sticks heated in a mortar and overprinted on *sumi* and gray areas to produce a rich sheen on hair. In order to represent fully the opulence of the courtesans' ornate coiffures and the actors' theatrical wigs, a technique developed of cutting and printing with two or three blocks, to achieve the required textural effect and depth of black. Starting a basic gray ground, which also delineated the edge of fine hair, the next block was printed further in and slightly to the side to give an alternating pattern. The option remained to have a second printing from this block, or a third variant block (page 42, right).

In *kirifuki, fukibokashi* or *fukibotan* (spray technique), pigment was splashed or sprayed onto prints by shaking a brush or sharply drawing the thumb across the brush's bristles (left). Alternatively, it has been suggested that printers could load their mouths with pigment and blow spray. Fine soufflé spray effects were applied with an atomizer consisting of a right-angle bamboo or metal tube, one end dipped into the pigment, the other being blown down causing a capillary action at the vertex, where a gap in the tube allowed the pigment to rise and be distributed on to the surface. The technique was used to represent steam, spray, dust, mist, and especially snow where *gofun* (powdered white chalk, kaolin or pulverized roasted bones mixed with glue or size and water) was used. Although Henri de Toulouse-Lautrec (1864-1901) stated in a letter to his mother that he had invented this process (called *crachis* in French), and that it would make him a lot of money, the process was already being employed by Henri-Gabriel Ibels (1867-1936), who had borrowed it from the Japanese prints he had seen.

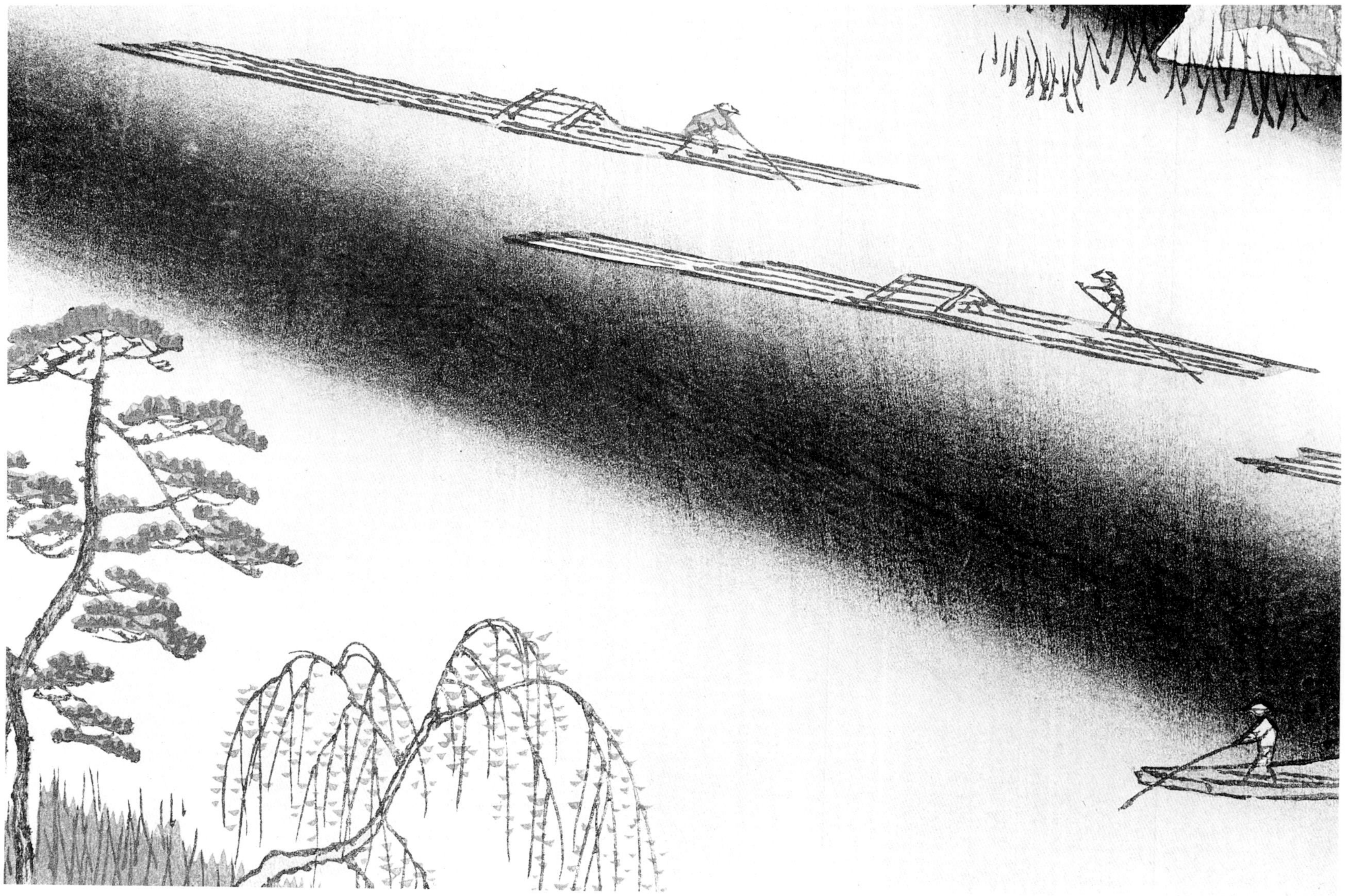

Left: Katsushika Hokusai (1760-1849). A detail of the 'The Great Wave' (*Kanagawa oki nami ura*) from the series 'The Thirty Six Views of Mount Fuji' (*Fugaku sanjū rokkei*), 1829-30. View from verso showing *baren* marks. Kruml Collection.

Below left: Utagawa Hiroshige (1797-1858). 'Kawaguchi Ferries, Zenkōji,' from the series 'One Hundred Famous Views of Edo' (*Meisho Edo hyakkei*, 1856-9). 1857. Example of the *bokashi* technique. Kruml Collection.

Right: Detail of crane's feathers showing deep gauffraging in a *surimono* of the Maruyama/Shijō school.

Below: Tsukioka Yoshitoshi (1839-92). 'Thirty-two Aspects of Women' (*Fūzoku sanjūni-sō*), 1888. Date of printing and publication details in large cartouche; artist's seal to left. Burnishing is apparent on the collar of the kimono. Kruml Collection.

Below right: Yoshitsuya Ichieisai (1822-66). Glue is applied to the eyes of the *shutendōji* demon. Detail from a triptych, 1858. Kruml Collection.

Another technique employed towards the end of the eighteenth century involved applied decoration used mica (*kira*) and metal powders. Large expanses of crushed mica were reserved for the backgrounds of *bijin* and actor prints. These costly, privately used and deluxe publications still command the highest prices today. Smaller areas of mica are found elsewhere in both books and prints, often as semi-transparent overlays. Pigments were either mixed with mica or mica was overlaid on printed color grounds so that in addition to the basic silvery-gray sheen, pink, yellow, brown, black and gray were also possible. Mica was made to adhere to the surface by using the white of an egg or rice-paste. Extensive areas were laid by printing the egg-white or rice-paste from a separate block, then sprinkling and brushing the mica on with a very soft brush using a stencil technique. Apart from this mineral, a number of other metal powders provided metallic lusters to prints, especially on *surimono*: powdered brass to simulate gold (*kiri*) (below right); powdered tin to imitate silver (*gin*), and pure copper powder (*akegane*). The use of brass was problematic because

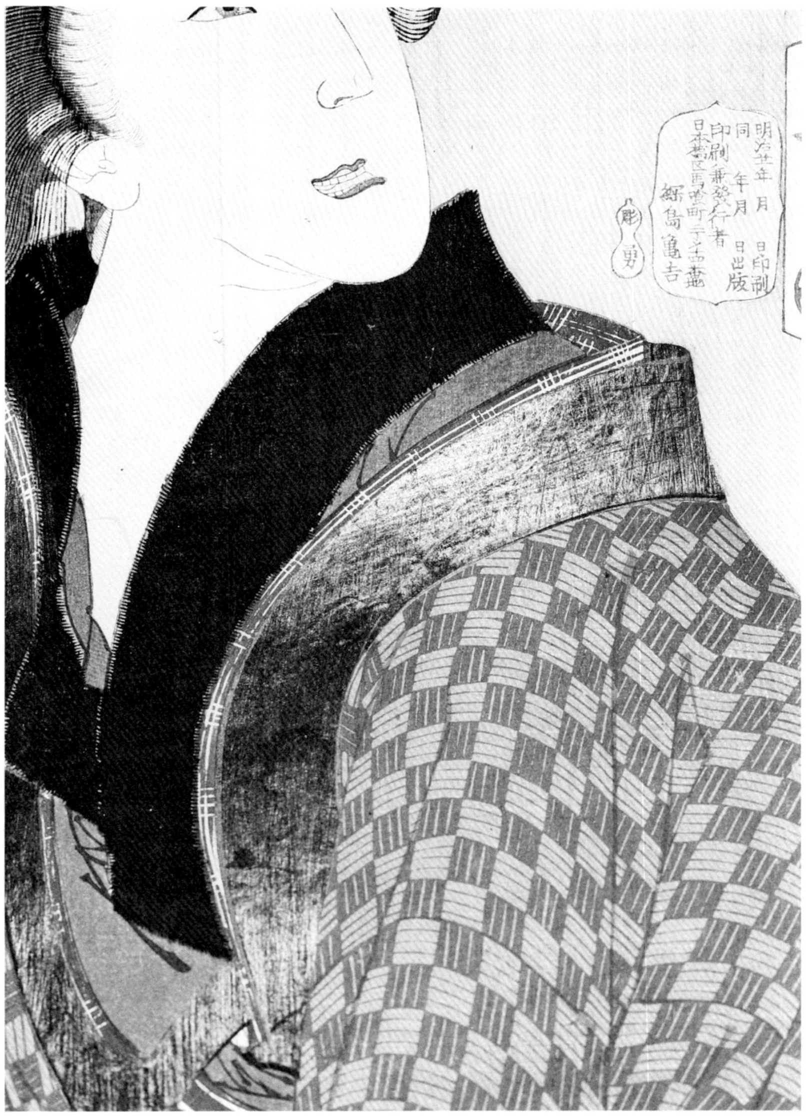

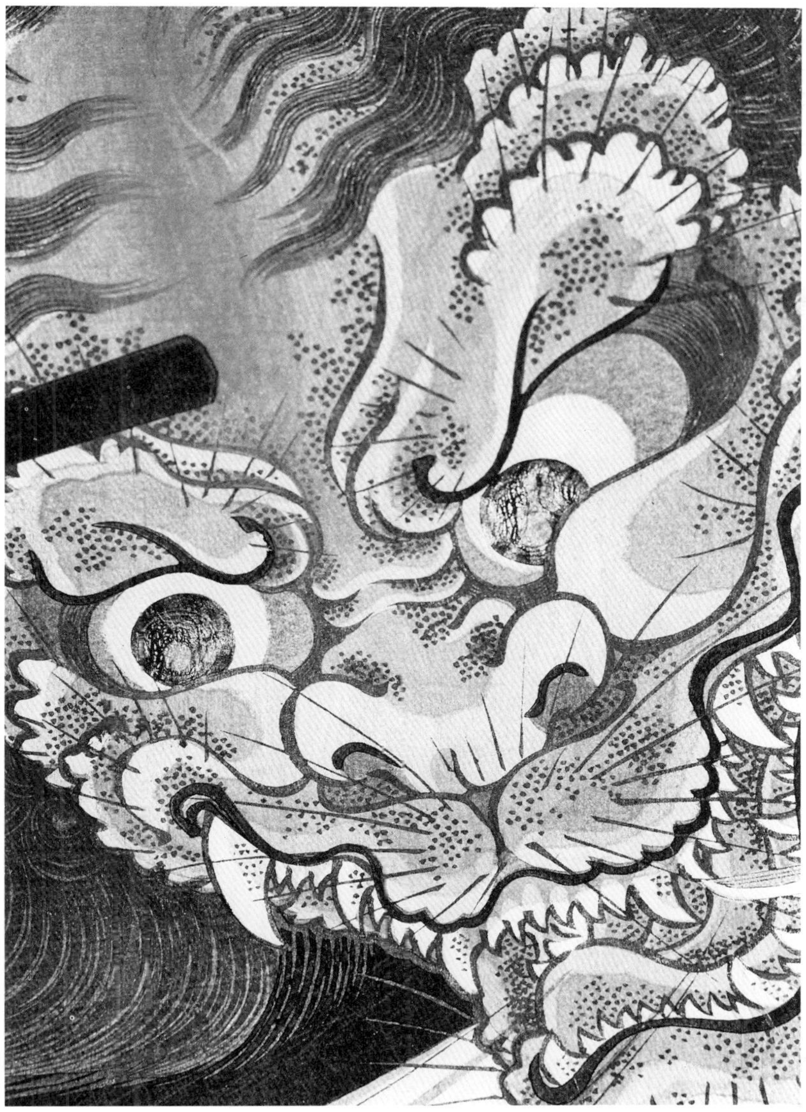

Right: Tsukioka Yoshitoshi (1839-92). 'Thirty-two Aspects of Women' (*Fūzoku sanjūnisō*), 1888. This shows the use of fine cutting to represent hair. Kruml Collection.

Far right: Utagawa Kuniyoshi (1797-1861). A detail of a print from the series 'Mirror of the Loyal Retainers,' (*Seichū gishin meimei kagami*), 1859, showing the technique of *kirifuki* of blowing or spraying ink on to the print. Kruml Collection.

Below: Yashima Gakutei (c.1786-1868). 'The Courtesan Hyōgo,' from the set 'Framed Paintings of Women for the Katsushika Circle' (*Katsushikaren gakumen fujin awase*), c. 1822. This print shows the decorative effects of applying gold powders. Kruml Collection.

Below right: Diagram of a *momi-dai* press for producing miniaturized prints.

Below, far right: Totoya Hokkei (1780-1850). 'Bamboo' from the *surimono* set 'A Series of Pine, Bamboo and Plum Warriors' (*Musha shōchikubai banzoku*). Plum, pine and bamboo were placed in the decorative alcove (*tokonoma*) at New Year. Kruml Collection.

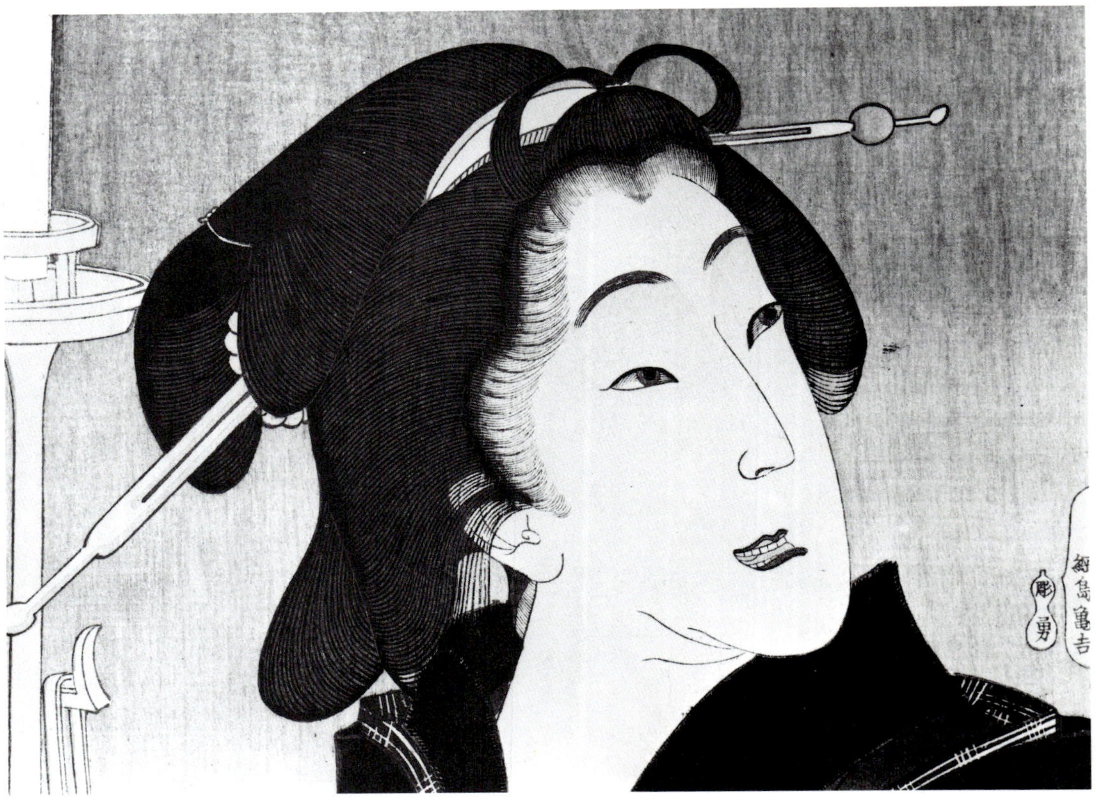

one of its constituent parts, copper, reacts with sulphur and moisture in the atmosphere to form the familiar green copper sulphate which 'burns' through paper. It was applied successfully to *surimono* as the thicker *hōsho* paper acted as a buffer, whereas degraded and fractured areas are common when the metal has been printed on paper of normal thickness. *Shunga* are a typical example. The powders were added to the blocks with small toothbrushes, *haku-hake*, and stuck to the paper where a previously made paste print (*nori-zuri*) had been printed.

Besides these special techniques, a wide range of organic and inorganic pigments was available. Many in the eighteenth century were extractions from plants, flowers, bark, grasses and mineral earths, providing delicate yet fugitive hues which have, unfortunately, left us with a vast number of faded prints. Because of their expense, some pigments were reserved for *surimono*, such as the yellow from *Garcinia morella*, the best quality *shio* (gamboge) and crimson, *komachi-beni*, the best *beni*. Other pigments more commonly used were: vermilion (*shu*), azurite (*gunjō*), red lead (*tan*), indigo (*ai*), orpiment (*kio*) and dayflower (*aobana*). The black key-block outline was printed with *sumi* which was produced from lamp-soot or lamp-black (*yuen*) made by burning oil obtained from the nuts of the *yama-giri* (*Elaecocca cordata*), or wood-oil from the *kin* paulownia tree (*Paulownia imperialis*). *Sumi* is pure carbon and therefore is one pigment that never fades. In the early 1800s pigments became progressively brighter and harsher, this being particularly noticeable in the reds and purples, while, for the most part, *surimono* retained the eighteenth-century palette. However, in the late 1820s and 1830s some *surimono* adopted a more saturated color range. In 1829 Prussian blue, *bero-ai*, was introduced and embraced by Utagawa Hiroshige (1797-1858) and Katsushika Hokusai for their landscapes. Around 1864 synthetic aniline dyes were imported and, while initially expensive and applied sparingly, they soon became cheap enough to be utilized even for the

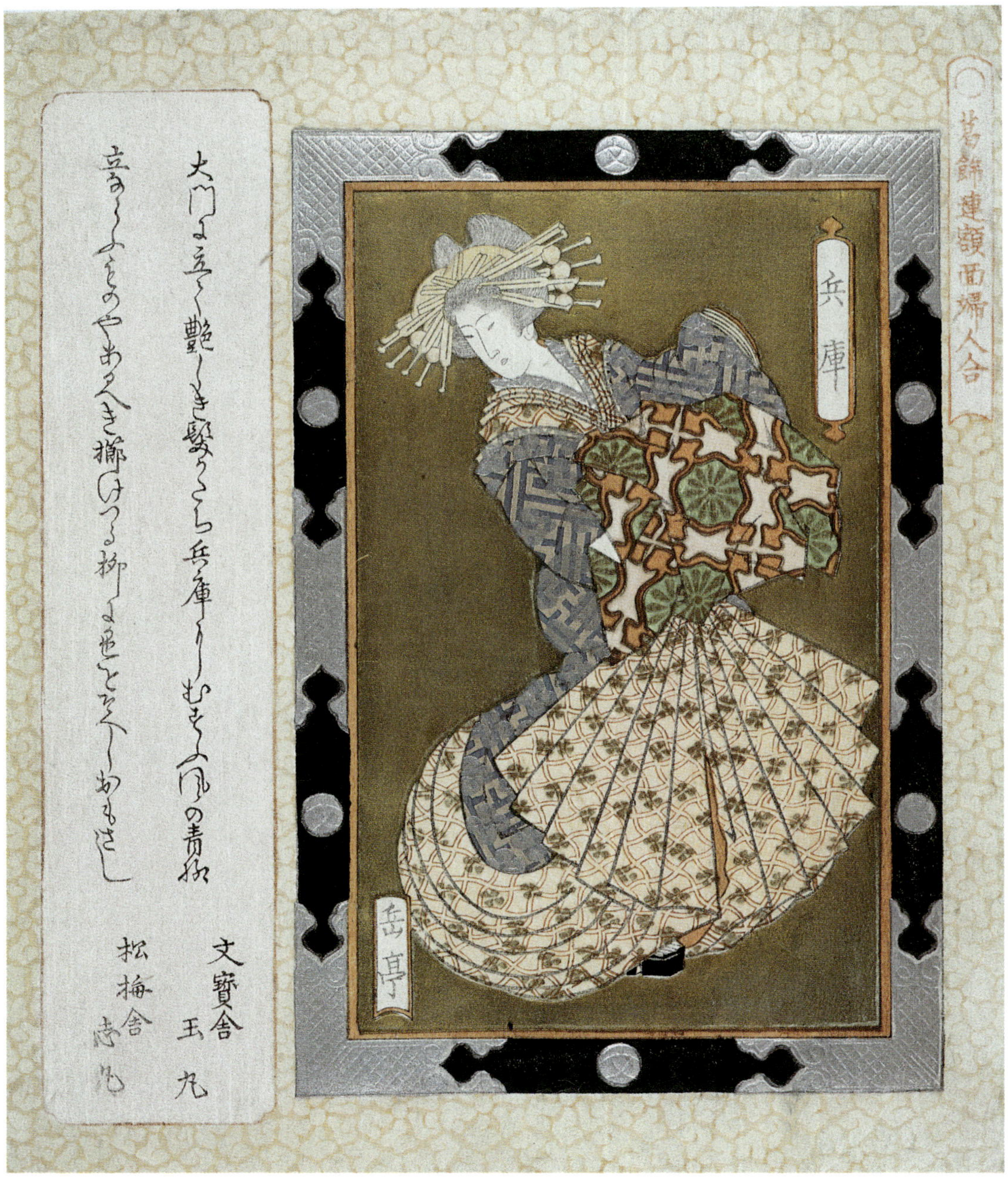

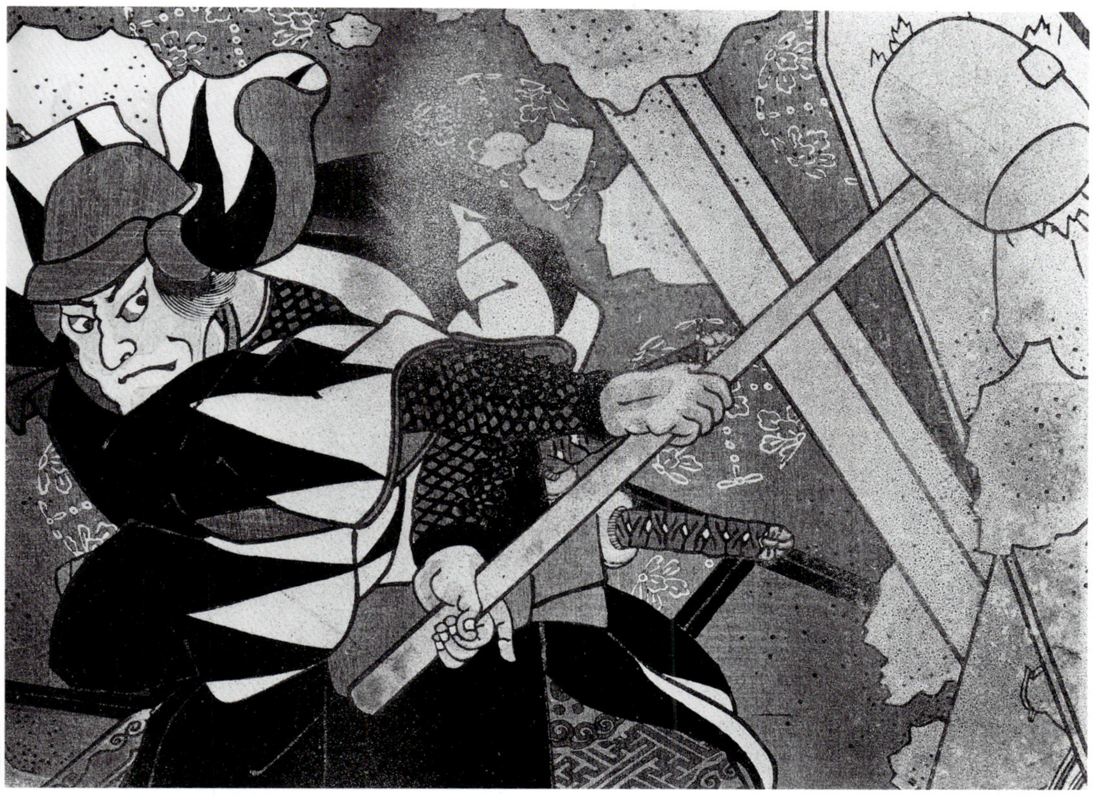

cheapest prints and with less and less discretion. At the end of the century some publishers, in order to compete with the mechanical reproductive systems becoming available, revived the more harmonious color schemes and introduced a fine shallow cutting technique, with an emphasis on color gradation.

One technique which was a closely guarded secret was crêping (*chirimen-gami*) which miniaturized prints (and books) and gave them a limp, cloth-like feel. There are numerous inaccurate reports on how crêping was done, but, to my knowledge, there exists only one accurate description of in English (Rein). In fact, it was a relatively simple operation. A press, *momi-dai*, of *kashi* or some other hard wood was used (below left). This consisted of a heavy base through which two perforated posts were fastened at one end. A tenon or dowling passed through one pair of these perforations to act as the fulcrum of a wooden board or lever, 2.5 to 3 meters (8 to 9½ feet) in length. This board was pierced by an elliptical hole through which passed a narrow cylinder rising from the baseboard. The height at which the tenon was fixed could be varied and determined the final size of the crêped prints. In the first stage of the process *kata* sheets – what we would call matrix sheets – were made by laying moistened thick sheets of old *kozo* paper on to a wooden board, which had parallel or crossed grooves cut into it. The paper was beaten into the grooves with hard brushes, and then painted over with *shibu* to make them firm and durable. The end result was a *kata* that showed considerable elasticity due to its concertina-like appearance. The prints to be crêped were dampened by piling them up in alternate layers with wet paste-boards and left for an hour under mild pressure. A *kata* was laid on a wooden board and two moistened prints were placed facing each other with a sheet of *hanshi* paper between them. This was repeated ten or more times finishing with another *kata*. The assemblage was rolled upon the narrow cylinder in the middle of the *momi-dai* press, making it about 5 inches (12 cm) in diameter, and wound round with a long strip of hemp canvas. The lever was then lowered and jerked down with considerable force from six to ten times. The roll was taken off the press, unrolled, and the prints relaid in different positions within the *katas*. After the seventh arrangement the *hanshi* was removed and the two prints were laid together and pressed twice more. The result was a considerably reduced and strongly crinkled print.

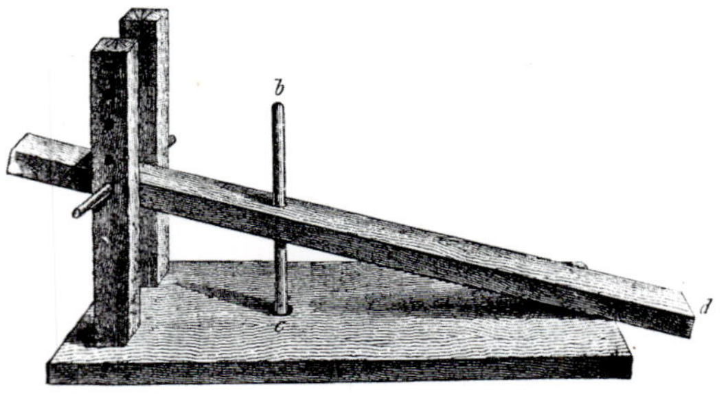

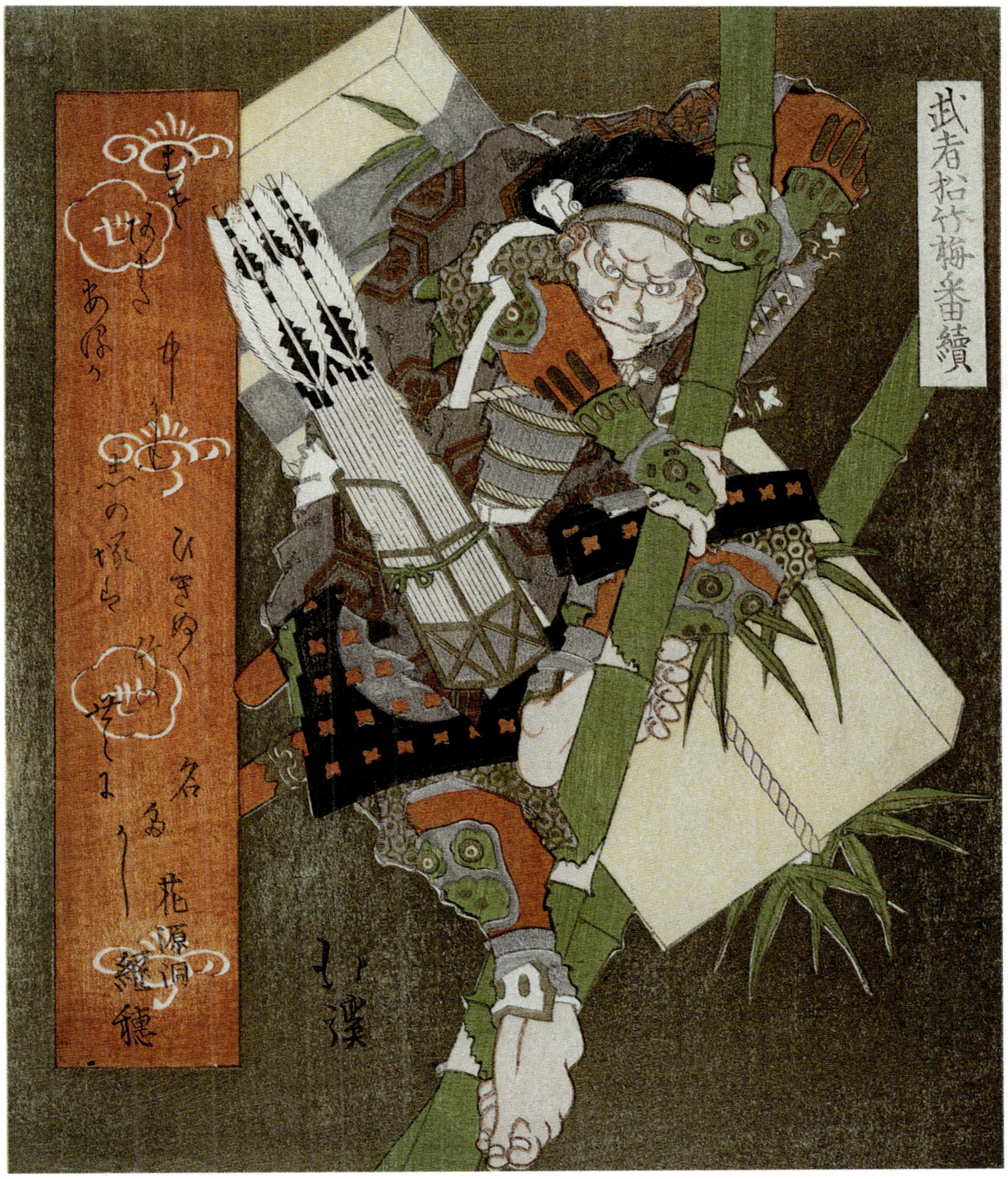

Surimono RICHARD KRUML

The printmaking process of *ukiyo-e* involved the use of numerous technical devices and embellishments; the most sophisticated use is seen in *surimono*. The technical perfection of *surimono* surpasses all other forms of *ukiyo-e*, only matched by certain deluxe *ōkubi-e ōban* and Osaka prints. This was facilitated by their being non-commercial ventures, thereby avoiding the numerous restrictions and bans passed on luxury items over a considerable time by the government.

Surimono literally means 'printed matter,' a prosaic term which belies the care and attention given to these small prints (the basic *shikishiban* format being 8×7¼ inches [20.5×18.5 cm]), and their restricted output. They expressed the taste of an artistic cognoscenti who demanded – and were willing to pay for – the best in technique and materials, and who often hired the leading artists of the day to design images comparable with the finest *ukiyo-e*. Many of these literati were well versed in Japanese and Chinese classics, and were lovers of the theater, painting, and, above all, of poetry. The poetry clubs they formed commissioned many of the *surimono* to celebrate the New Year, and also rewarded winners of poetry contests with *surimono* designed to accompany their poems. *Surimono*

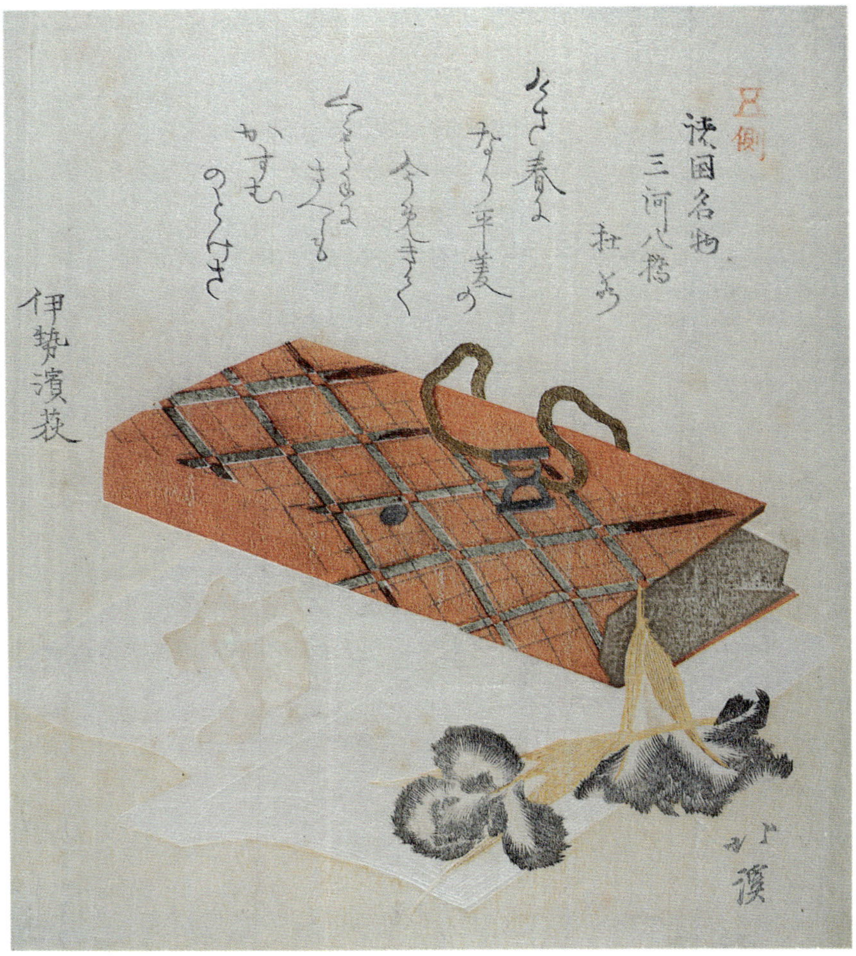

Above: Totoya Hokkei (1780-1850) 'The Irises of Yatsubashi in Mikawa' (*Mikawa yatsubashi kabitsubata*) from the set 'Famous Products of the Provinces' (*Shokoku meibutsu*). Printed late 1810s for Gogawa whose seal appears in top right and on the clasp of the pouch. Poem by Kise Hamahagi; signed *Hokkei*. Kruml Collection.

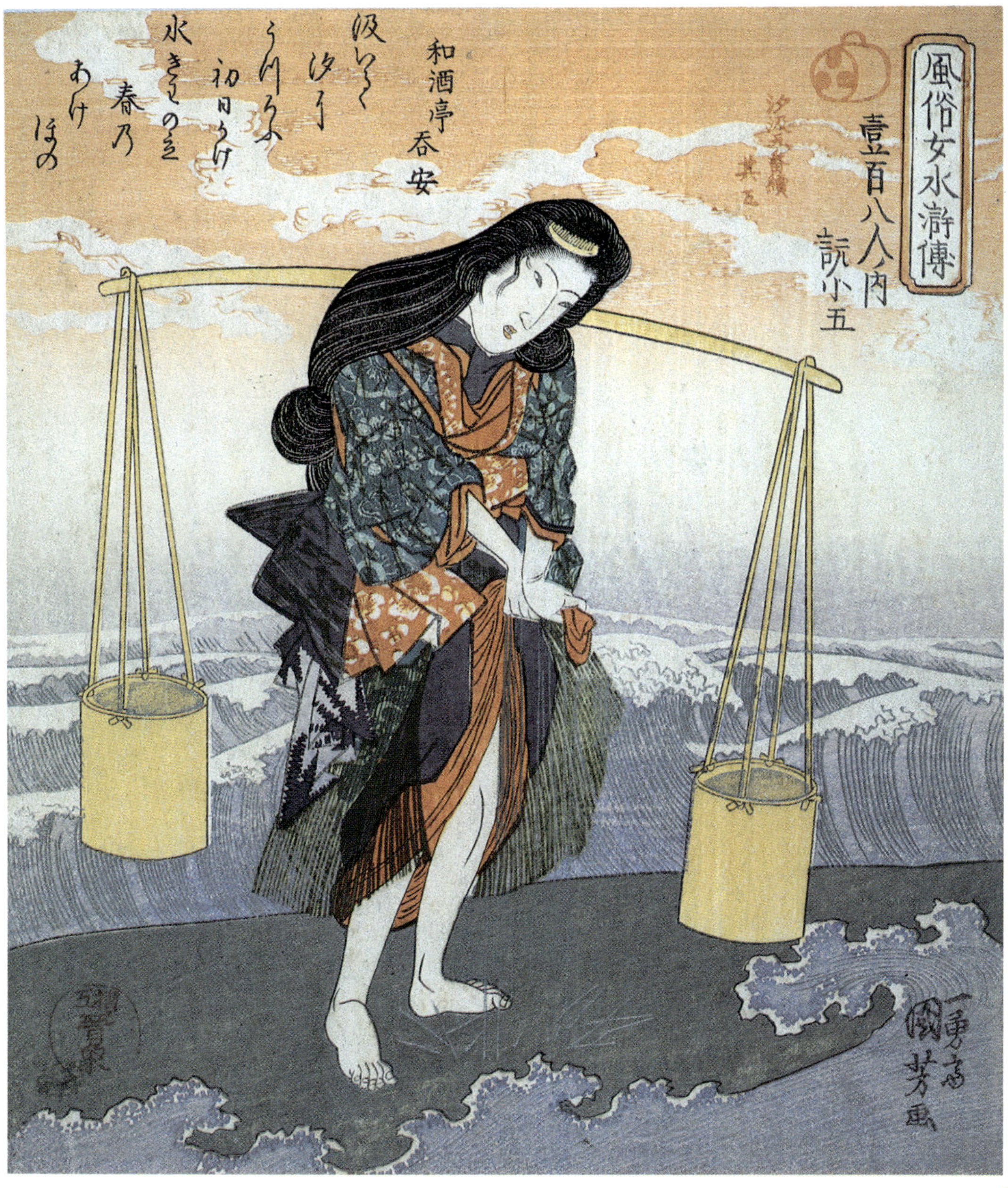

Left: Utagawa Kuniyoshi (1797-1861). 'A woman salt-gatherer on Akaishi Beach' from the *surimono* set 'Modern Women as the One Hundred and Eight Heroes of the Suikoden' (*Fūzoku onna suikoden hyakuhachiban no uchi*). The last design of a pentaptych. Commissioned by the poetry club, Taikogawa. Poem by Washutei Nomiyasu; signed and sealed *Ichiyūsai Kuniyoshi ga* with the printer's seal Surikō Shinzō. Kruml Collection.

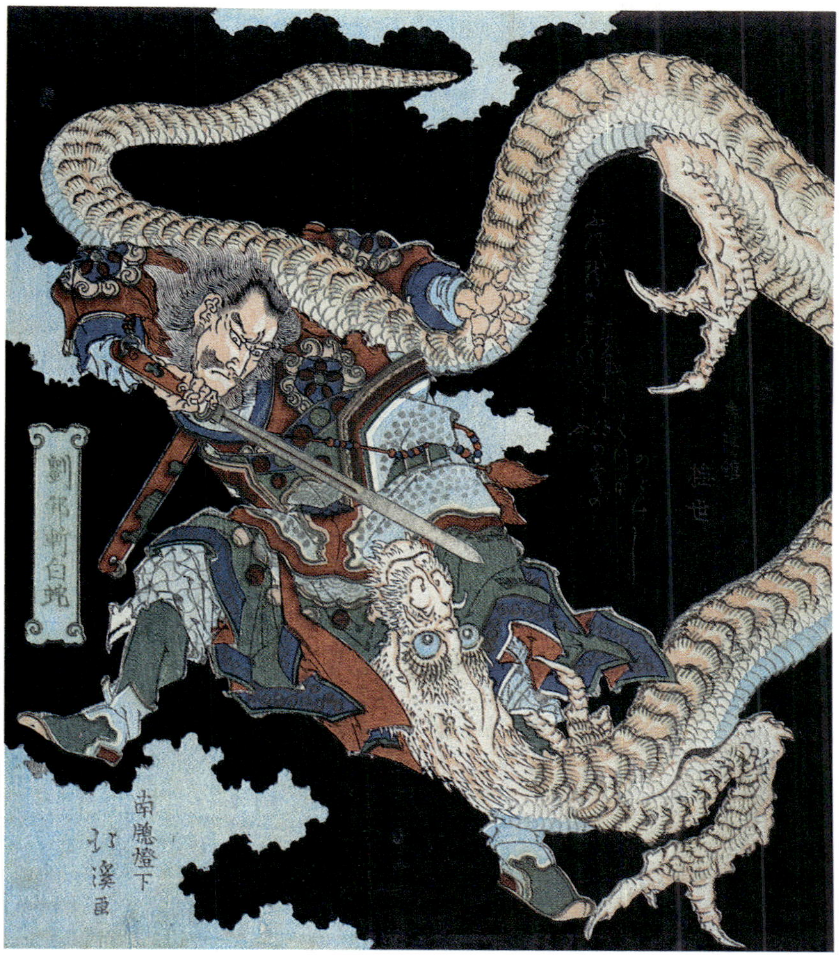

Above: Totoya Hokkei (1780-1850). 'Ryūhō Kills a White Serpent.' *Ryūhō hakuja o kiru* (in Chinese, Liu Bang) founded the Han dynasty. This surimono is most probably for the Dragon Year 1832. Poem by Seiyōkan Umeyo; signed *Nansō tōka Hokkei ga*. Kruml Collection.

Right: Utagawa Kunisada (1786-1865). 'Kugutsune Kanejo (Okane) Halting a Runaway Horse with Her Geta. 'Okane was a prostitute and reknowned as a strong woman. The legend in which she stops the runaway horse takes place while she is doing her washing on the shores of Lake Biwa. Probably for the Horse Year 1834. Poems by Madonoya and Somanoya. Signed *Kōchōrō Kunisada ga*. Kruml Collection.

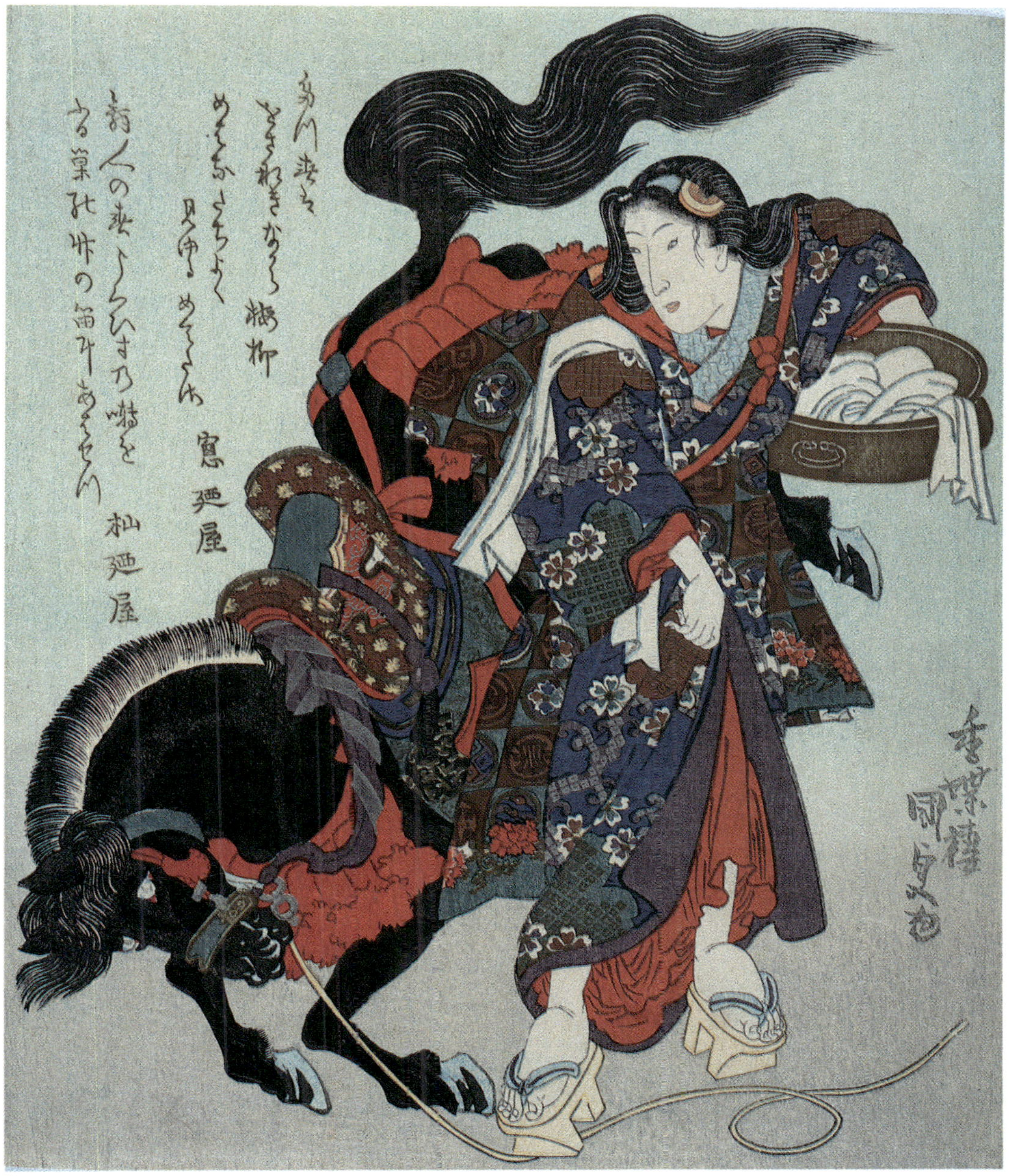

were also issued to commemorate events, such as musical evenings, anniversaries, or to announce a poet's or actor's change of name. Sometimes they were the product of an actor's fan club, and in some cases were issued by the actor himself for his patrons and fans. Poetry clubs devised logos which were usually appended to the top of the *surimono*,, and sometimes incorporated elsewhere into the design (pages below left). Although in the West we might only respond to the images, it must be remembered that they were an accompaniment to the poem(s) or the announcement, and that this was as, or more, important to an Edo-period Japanese. As a result *surimono* can be frustratingly enigmatic, even for the initiated, as the poems often prove difficult to translate. The Japanese reveled in witty *métaboles*, either in the rather staid 17-syllable haiku, but more often in the 31-syllable *kyōka* (mad poems) which predominate on post 1800 *surimono*.

Surimono were primarily celebrations of the New Year, and as such animals representing the 12 signs of the zodiac – *jūnishi*, were frequently incorporated into the design (below). The animal might be alluded to in the poem or poems; an object could reveal the year, directly or indirectly, by having a name which gave, as an alternative meaning, one of the animals of the zodiac. Some *surimono* indicate the year by inserting the long, the short or both months into the design. These *e-goyomi*, 'picture calendar,' of *daisho*, 'long-short' *surimono*, point to the origins of *surimono* which had evolved out of the early eighteenth-century verse sheets and musical announcements, via the picture calendars of Suzuki Harunobu (1725?-70) and Kikurensha Kyosen (*fl* mid-eighteenth century) that were privately published in 1765 – *surimono* inherited the innovative technical excellence of these works. Their hey-day occurred in the first quarter of the nineteenth century.

2
The Primitives to Harunobu

RICHARD ILLING

The history of *ukiyo-e* spans about 300 years, and during the first hundred years, from the mid-seventeenth century up to the mid 1760s, great achievements were made that established a graphic art-form that is still appreciated today.

Woodblock printing in Japan has enjoyed a long history. Woodblock-printed Buddhist texts appeared as early as the eleventh century in the *kansūbon* (scroll) format, and by the thirteenth century printed illustrations accompanying these were produced as *orihon* (accordion or concertina book). Therefore, by the Edo period (1600-1868), with the advent of the single-sheet print, the tradition of woodblock printing was already one that was well established.

Not long after the founding of the new seat of government in Edo (present-day Tokyo) by the Tokugawa shogunate, printing and publishing, which had hitherto been monopolized by Buddhist temples, became the province of commercial publishers. The rise of commercial publishing corresponded to the rise of an increasingly literate populace. These publishers commissioned designs from artists, employed block-cutters and printers, owned retail outlets and supplied publications to primitive lending libraries and itinerant peddlers who further distributed their products. Throughout the history of Japanese prints the influence exerted by these publishers was considerable. The first center of publishing was the Kamigata (Kyoto and Osaka area). The Kamigata remained the leader until the late seventeenth century, at which time the publishing center shifted from the Kamigata to Edo.

The illustrations of classical fiction (*kana-zōshi*, *otogi-zōshi*, etc.) in the mid-seventeenth century, while sometimes crudely done, were initially executed in *sumizuri* (black and white). Many were embellished with a rough hand-coloring, usually with *tan* (red lead), and *roku* (mineral green), although yellow and purple were also used. These books were known as *tanroku-bon* (page 47). The uniformity and style of the hand-coloring suggests that this was organized by the publisher before sale rather than being added later. The popularity of *tanroku-bon* was fairly short-lived, however, and they disappeared about 1650. They are prized now more for their rarity than for their artistic merit.

The second half of the seventeenth century saw a move away from the publication of traditional classical tales and a rise in the popularity of contemporary fiction and semi-literary genres of writing. Of these forms the most germane to the advancement of *ukiyo-e* were the semi-literate *meisho-ki* (chronicles of famous places) and *oraimono* (books on etiquette) and particularly with the publication of Ihara Saikaku's (1642-92) *Kōshoku ichidai otoko* (The Man Who Loved Love, 1682), the genre known as *ukiyo-zōshi*. The term *ukiyo* (*uki*, floating; *yo*, world), originally a Buddhist concept which denoted the ephemeral, transient nature of life, came to represent the bustling, urban culture of the Edo-period townsman and the transience of fleeting pleasures and a feeling that, if time is passing, now is the moment to enjoy it. The courtesans and revelry of the Yoshiwara quarter; the spectacular entertainments of the Kabuki theaters; the sumo wrestling bouts; boating on the river; festivals and fireworks – in short, the attitude of eat, drink and be merry – this was the underlying message of the Edo-period 'floating world.' The literature found in the *ukiyo-zōshi* portrayed every aspect of this rather hedonistic culture. It was witty, fast-moving and often salacious. By the Genroku era (1688-1704) the term *ukiyo* had come to be used to describe anything that was new, trendy and erotic.

Features of this exciting and seemingly glamorous world were portrayed by contemporary artists. Their paintings and prints became known as *ukiyo-e*, (pictures of the floating world). It must be noted that while *ukiyo-e* would find its most popular expression in the print medium, before the second half of the seventeenth century the history of *ukiyo-e* should be seen through that of *ukiyo-e* painting (*nikuhitsu ukiyo-e*). Historians of Japanese art have often found it convenient to refer to an *ukiyo-e* school of artists in an effort to distinguish the various groups who designed such pictures from the more traditional and academic schools of Japanese painting such as *Yamato-e*, Tosa and Kanō. In reality *ukiyo-e*, while sharing a common approach to subject matter and, in the prints at least, being forced into a similar mold by the technical and commercial limitations affecting the publishers, exhibit a wide variety of artistic styles and mannerisms.

Before 1700 almost all printed graphic art with *ukiyo-e* elements was in the form of illustrated books and albums. The early genre illustrators of *ukiyo-e* were generally anonymous but during the last quarter of the seventeenth century acknowledged artists such as Hinaya Ryūho

Right: Anonymous. Scenes from the *Soga monogatari*, 1696. Book plate; 8¼×5⅝ inches (21×14.2 cm). *Tanroku-bon*. Published by Sagamiya. Private Collection. The story of the Soga brothers was the basis for many wildly popular Kabuki plays and features strongly the ideas of filial piety and revenge. In 1190, when the two brothers, Jūrō and Gorō, were small children, their father was killed in a quarrel with the daimyo Kudō Suketsune. As adults they take leave of their mother (shown here) and ride off to seek revenge. They are successful in avenging their father's death; however, one brother dies in the attempt and the other is captured and later beheaded.

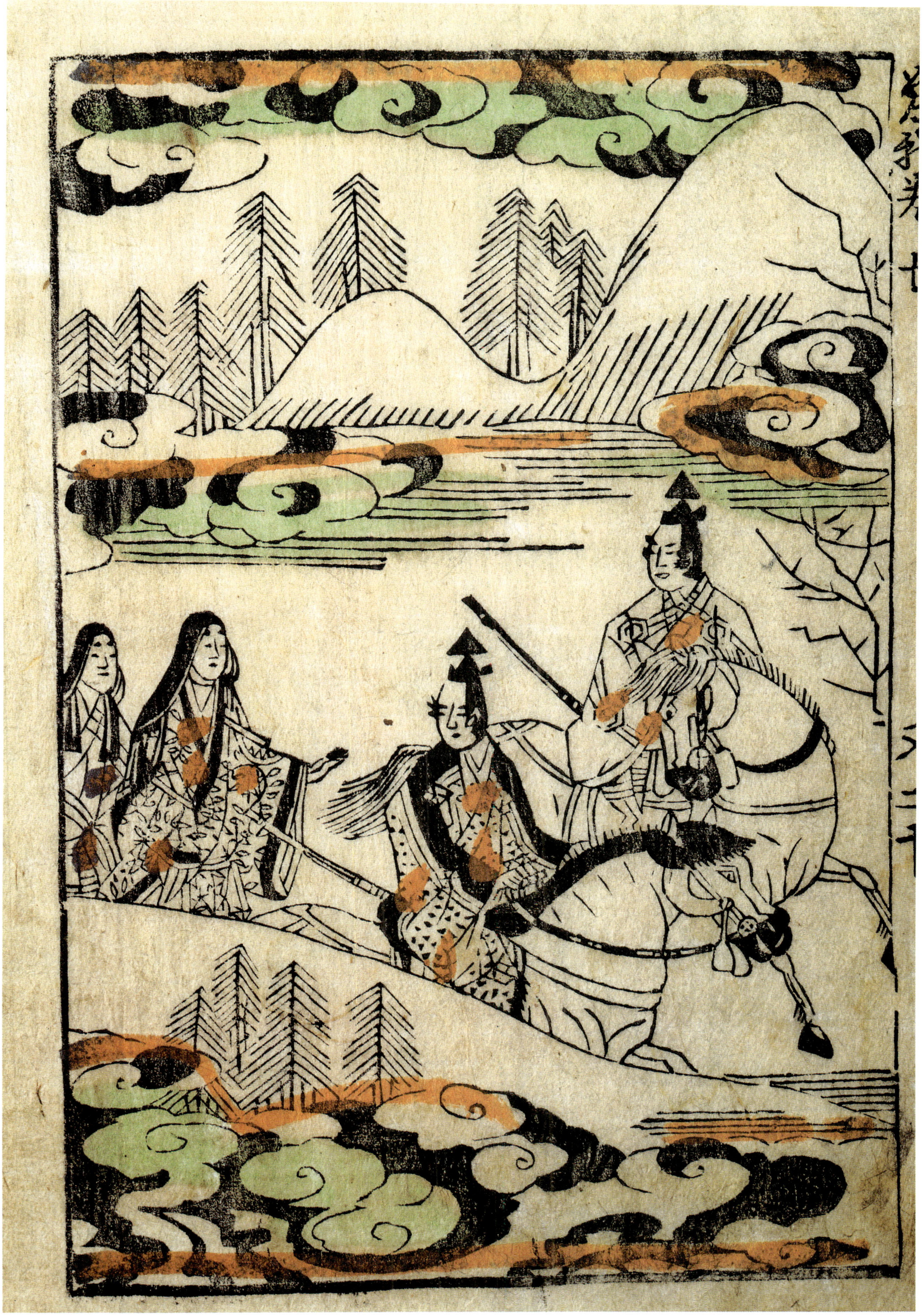

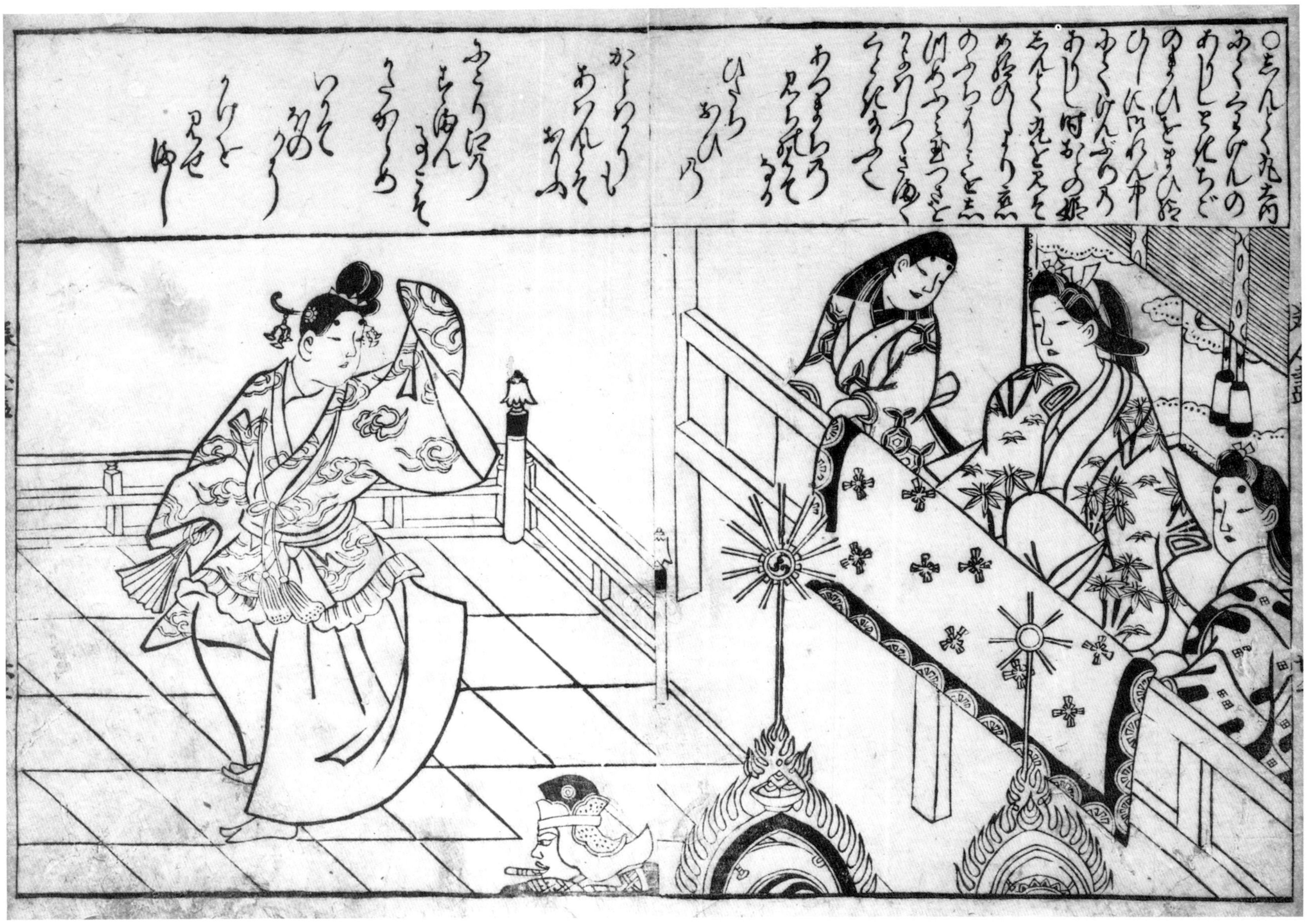

Above: Hishikawa Moronobu (c. 1618-94). Scene from *Bijin ezukushi* (Pictures of Beautiful Women), 8⅞×13 inches (22.6×33.1 cm). *Sumizuri-e*. Private Collection. Rendered in a style reminiscent of the traditional school of Tosa paintings, the famous court beauty, Otone Hime and two of her attendants are seated to the right viewing the Nō dance, *Shanto Kumaru* which is being performed on the stage at left.

(1595-1669) and Yoshida Hanbei (*fl* 1615-88) in Kyoto, and Hishikawa Moronobu and Jihei Sugimura in Edo were emerging. While Kyoto artists were influential in the sphere of book illustration, it was Moronobu and his follower Sugimura who can be credited with taking the art-form further and consolidating the various components of a so-called *ukiyo-e* style.

Hishikawa Moronobu (c. 1618-94) after early training first under a Tosa master in Kyoto, and later in a traditional painting style, under a Kanō school master in Edo. He illustrated approximately 130 books and albums between 1658 and his death in 1694. They included *meisho-ki, oraimono* and *ehon*. His most noteworthy contribution, however, was to the *ehon* (page 48). *Ehon* (picture book) existed before Moronobu's day only as copies or adaptations from Chinese books. They grew in popularity during the Edo period to meet the demands by a semi-literate readership for illustrated books and not books of text with scattered illustrations. The *ehon* would have been a natural step from the *meisho-ki*, which combined text with illustrations, as it focused on the pictorial aspect of the subject, relying on the figures and events of the *ukiyo* such as the pleasure-quarters of the Yoshiwara. Moronobu also initiated albums of larger pictures, some showing everyday scenes, others erotica. The latter were often published as sets of 12 images leading the viewer from romantic assignations (*abuna-e*) through gentle foreplay to the most explicit sexual scenes of love-making. To the traditional Japanese, sex was untinged with any concept of sinfulness. It was seen as an emotionally and physically enjoyable act and, therefore, was viewed as a normal subject for the Japanese artist. Erotica or *shunga* (spring pictures, the term for erotic paintings, prints and illustrations) was not a new subject. Evidence suggests that the first *shunga* were executed by Buddhist artists and artisans. In fact, a rather amateur sketch has been discovered at the base of the oldest extant temple in Japan, Hōryūji. The earliest *shunga* scroll cited in literature, however, was by the abbot Toba Sōjō (1053-1140) entitled 'The Phallic Contest' (*Yōbutsu kurabe*) which depicts the above-named contest at the Imperial court.[1] With the Edo period, however, the appreciation of *shunga* spread to the urban population as well, no longer being the sole domain of the samurai and aristocratic classes. In addition to the obvious enhancement through *shunga* imagery of the sexual encounter, it also appears to have played a didactic role,

Right: Hishikawa Moronobu (c.1618-94). 'Couple Making Love,' early 1680s, *ōban* plate from untitled album; 26.2×35.2 cm. *Sumizuri-e*. Private Collection.

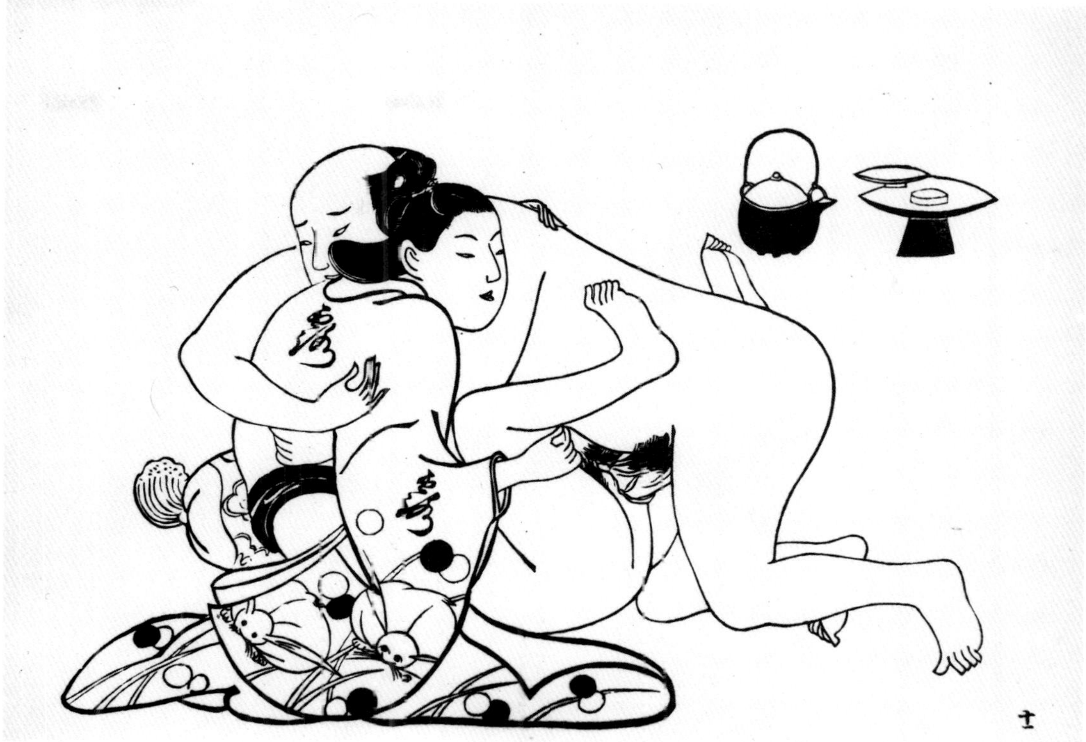

demonstrating the different techniques and positions whereby couples could give each other pleasure, rather than as pornographic stimulation for the sexually deprived. Emphasis was often placed on creating a subtle ambiance and clothing. The nude body was sufficiently commonplace and the presence of third parties, either as a voyeur, participant or jealous onlooker, often gave added piquancy to the events depicted (page 50). *Shunga* were produced by many *ukiyo-e* artists such as Moronobu and later by masters like Suzuki Harunobu (1725?-70) Kitagawa Utamaro (1753-1806), and Katsushika Hokusai (1760-1849). Although estimates vary, possibly a third or more of the total output of Japanese prints may have dealt with this theme. Until only a few years ago it was exceptional for any general book on the subject to include any but the most innocuous examples, which created an unbalanced view of the genre.

Although a master of erotica, Moronobu established a tradition of print design in the *ukiyo-e* style that covered many areas. Apart from the *ehon*, for which he is best-known, and illustrated albums, he and his followers began designing prints, primarily in the *ōban* format, in *sumizuri-e*. During the 1680s his pupils, most notably Hishikawa Moroshige (*fl.* 1678-98), Hishikawa Morofusa (*fl.* 1685-1703) and Ishikawa Tomonobu (*fl.* 1687-1713), worked in a similar style. Moroshige also had his own pupils and the most recognized is Furuyama Moromasa (c.1712-72), who created some interesting work in the 1740s. However, it was largely the followers of other ateliers who after 1700

Right: Torii Kiyonobu (1664-1729) 'Couple Making Love, with Sake Kettle,' c. 1703, *aiban* album print, 8¾×12½ inches (22.1×31.5 cm). *Sumizuri-e*. Private Collection. Kiyonobu produced several notable *shunga* albums in the early years of the century. This seems to be the eleventh from that provisionally listed by Shibui as Kiyonbu Series E. Okumura Masanobu was trying to make his mark on the Edo public at about the same time and seems to have shamelessly plagiarized some of Kiyonobu's work.

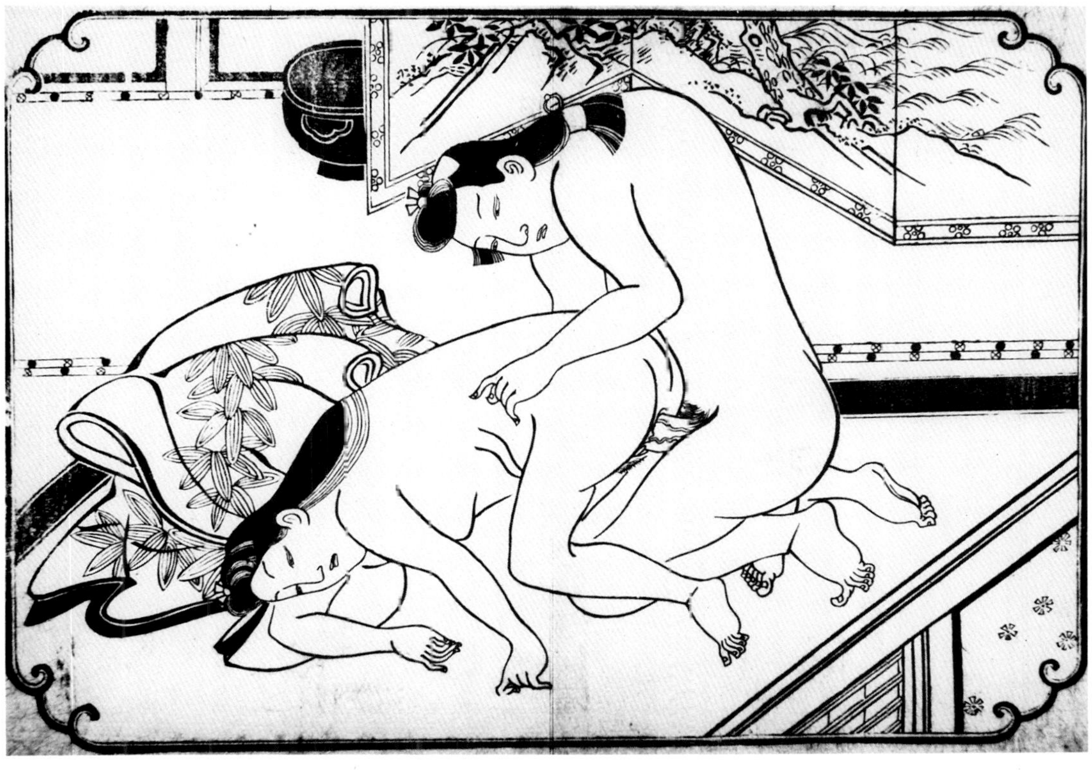

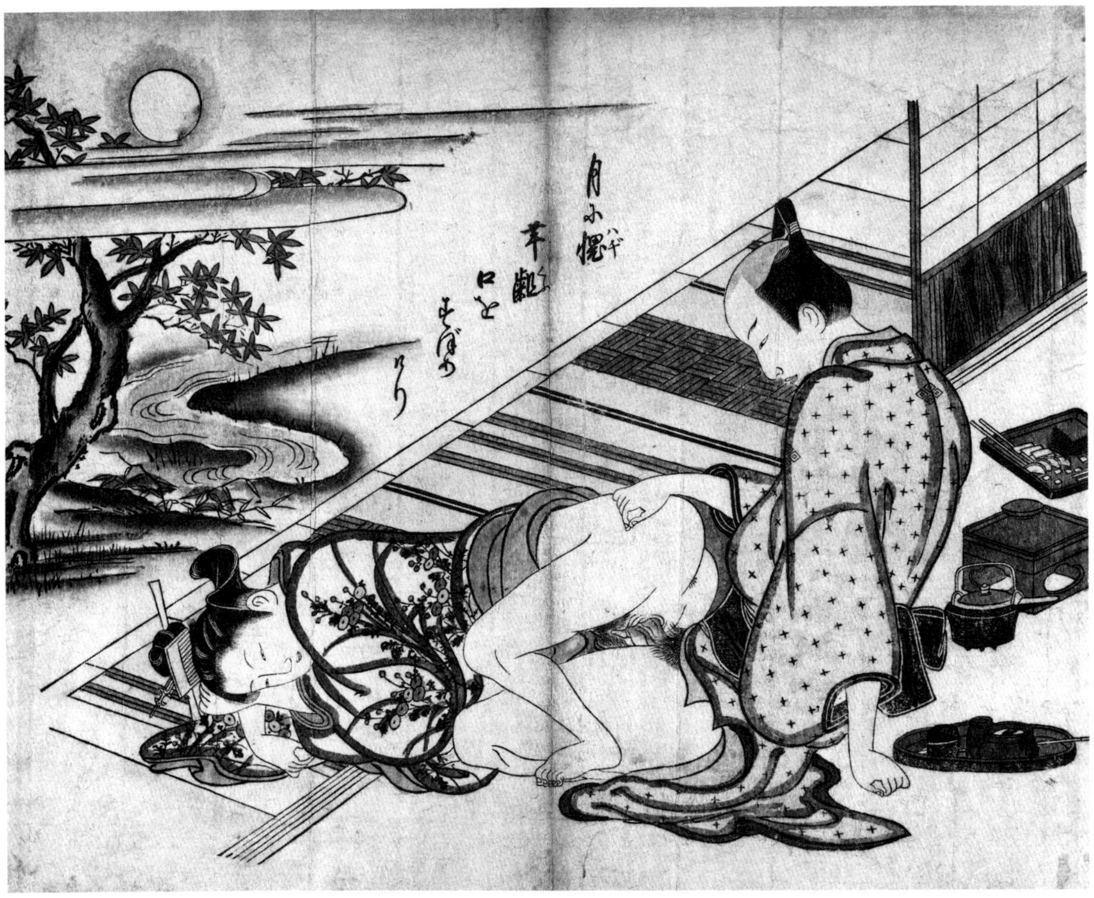

Left: Okumura Masanobu (1686-1764). 'Couple Making Love,' from the *shunga* album *Someiro no yama neya no hinagata* (Models of the Bedchamber), late 1730s, *ōban* 9$\frac{5}{8}$×14$\frac{1}{4}$ inches (24.4×36.3 cm). Hand-colored *urushi-e*. Courtesy of the Trustees of the British Museum, London. Like many of his contemporaries Masanobu produced many *shunga* prints. This example is the tenth (out of twelve) from one of his most famous sets, which is especially notable for the fine hand-coloring.

broadened the scope of the *ukiyo-e* print.

Sugimura Jihei (*fl* c 1680-98) produced albums and *ōban* sets in a style so close to that of Moronobu that until earlier in this century many of his works were attributed to Moronobu. Jihei designed more single-sheet prints than Moronobu and a number of *kakemono-e* (hanging scroll picture), yet his reputation rests on his illustration of *ukiyo-zōshi* which depict, as mentioned above, the lives and amorous exploits of the Edo-period townsmen. His work was rarely signed, yet he occasionally incorporated elements of his name into the design, which has helped identify his prints. His first signed work appears to be the picture book *Ukiyo raku-asobi* (pleasures of the floating world) of 1681. Nearly half of Sugimura's work consisted of *shunga* and, while he might at times have lacked the breadth of vision and capacity for innovation that seemingly characterizes the work of Moronobu, his *shunga* designs show a flair, verve and masterful composition that reveal his tremendous talent.

It is difficult today, with the ready availability of mass media, to fully understand the thrill that the colorful and extravagant spectacle of the Kabuki theater must have generated for an urban population whose outlets for entertainment were relatively limited. Kabuki evolved during the seventeenth century and by the eighteenth century there were four established theaters in Edo: Nakamura-za; Ichimura-za; Bando-za, later Morita-za; and Yamamura-za. The latter was closed down in 1714 after a scandalous affair involving a handsome actor and a lady of the court. Each theater billed up to six seasons of performances a year, each lasting as long as it was profitable. Performances continued from sunrise to sunset (artificial lighting being banned after several disastrous fires), with intervals between the plays. The plays themselves were divided into different categories with historical dramas (*jidaimono*) and domestic tales (*sewamono*) providing the main fare, while comic

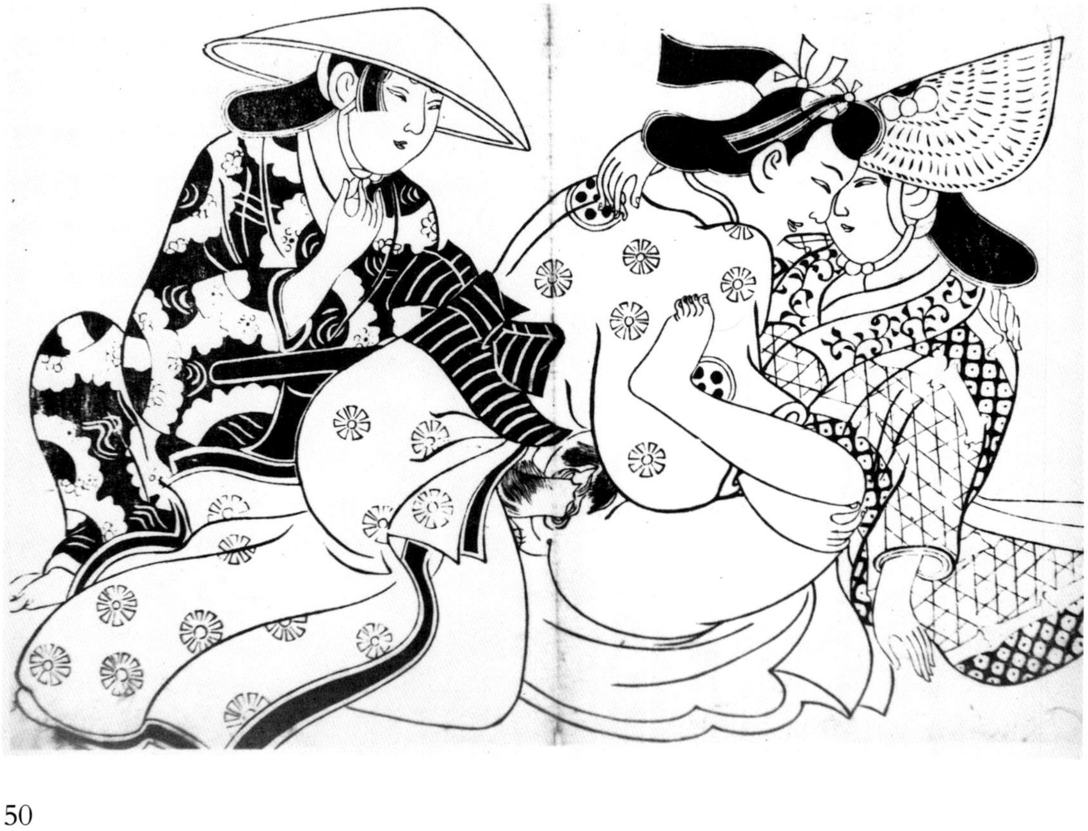

Left: Sugimura Jihei (*fl* 1680-98). 'Couple Making Love with Onlooker,' mid 1680s. *Ōban* plate from untitled album, 9$\frac{3}{8}$×13$\frac{5}{8}$ inches (23.8×34.7 cm), *Sumizuri-e*. Private Collection. There is no background setting in this *shunga* to set the scene or distract the eye. The eager young man and both young women are dressed for outdoors in the height of fashion. It is characteristic of Jihei's *shunga* that he stimulates the imagination beyond the immediate moment.

Right: Torii Kiyonobu (1664-1729) 'The Actors Nakamura Denkurō I and Bandō Matakurō as Yakko Performing a Spear Dance,' c. 1710. *Kakemono-e,* 21×17½ inches (53.2×31.6 cm). *Tan-e*, hand-colored in red, yellow and browns. Collectors seals: Tadamasa Hayashi. Rijksmuseum, Amsterdam. The *Yari-odori* 'spear dance' was an extravagant exhibition dance which was introduced to the Edo kabuki audiences in 1691 by a Kyoto actor and which became an instant hit. The 'spears' were the plumed ornamental staffs carried by servants in a daimyo's procession.

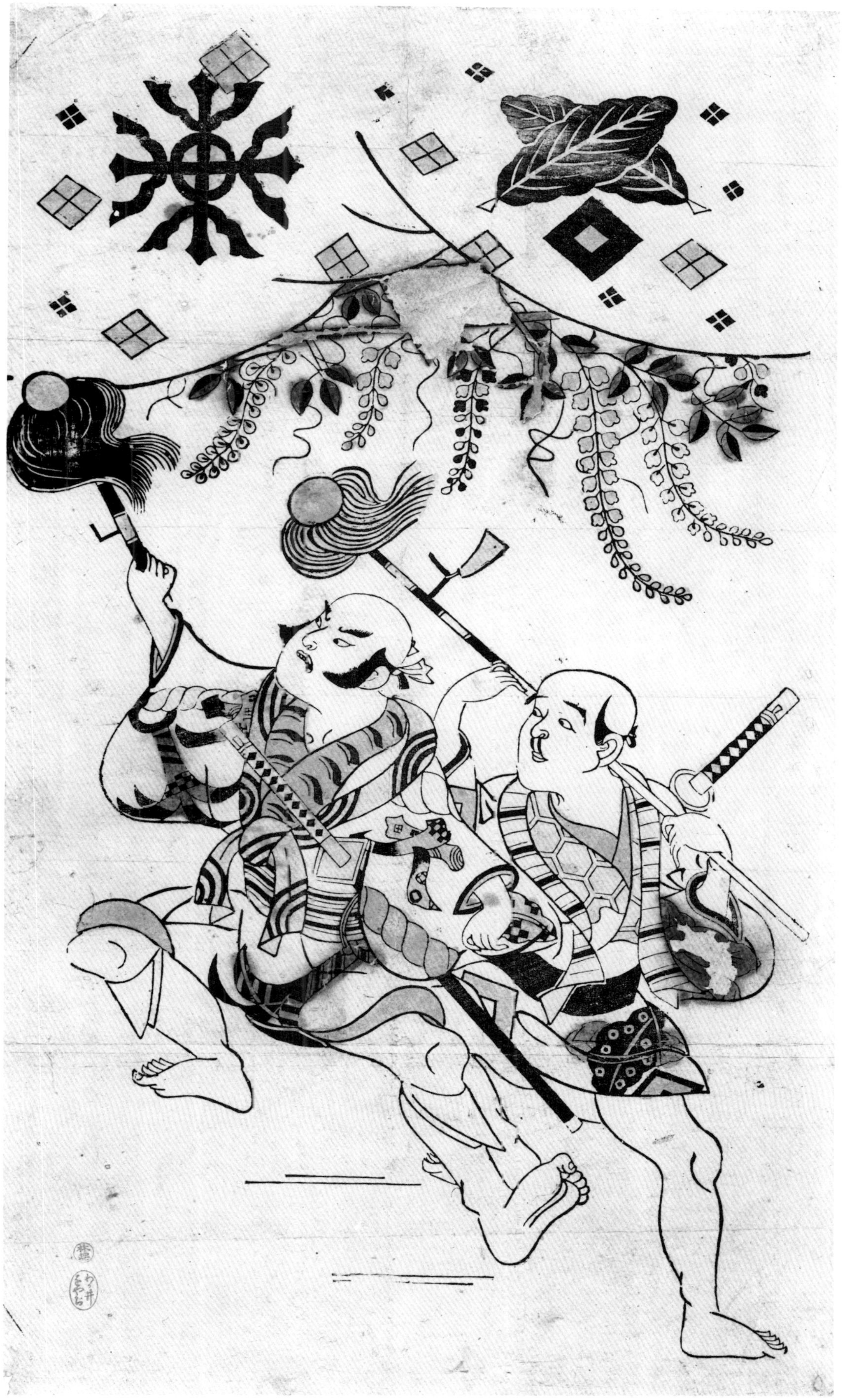

interludes or displays of dancing (*shosagoto*) (page 51) might be interspersed. The dramas, integrating elements of the prevailing Tokugawa society, were often based on conflicts between personal desires – the problems of love and affection–and Confucian ideals such as filial piety and social obligation. Women were forbidden to appear on stage after 1629 and in 1652 *wakashu kabuki* (young men's Kabuki) was also banned. Consequently, mature male actors assumed all roles and those playing female roles (*onnagata*) covered their shaven forelocks with a cloth. Actors were organized into strict hierarchical guilds and each actor remained in his assigned title until he was able to advance, undergoing a *shūmei* (name-assuming ceremony). The names of the actors who achieved fame would be passed on to worthy successors in the family.

Prints of actors in their roles began to be produced around 1700 and continued almost without interruption until a censorship ban in 1842. This is significant for both the historian of Kabuki and of prints as most prints identify the actors, either by name or by the display of their crest (*mon*). Often the name of the role being played is given. Identification of the play and reference to preserved theatrical records sometimes allows definite dates to be assigned to the prints. These references are often the only reliable method of following the development of the Japanese print during the eighteenth century, particularly since contemporary records regarding them or their artists are scant. The exception to this is the information sometimes gleaned from the colophons of illustrated books. Know-

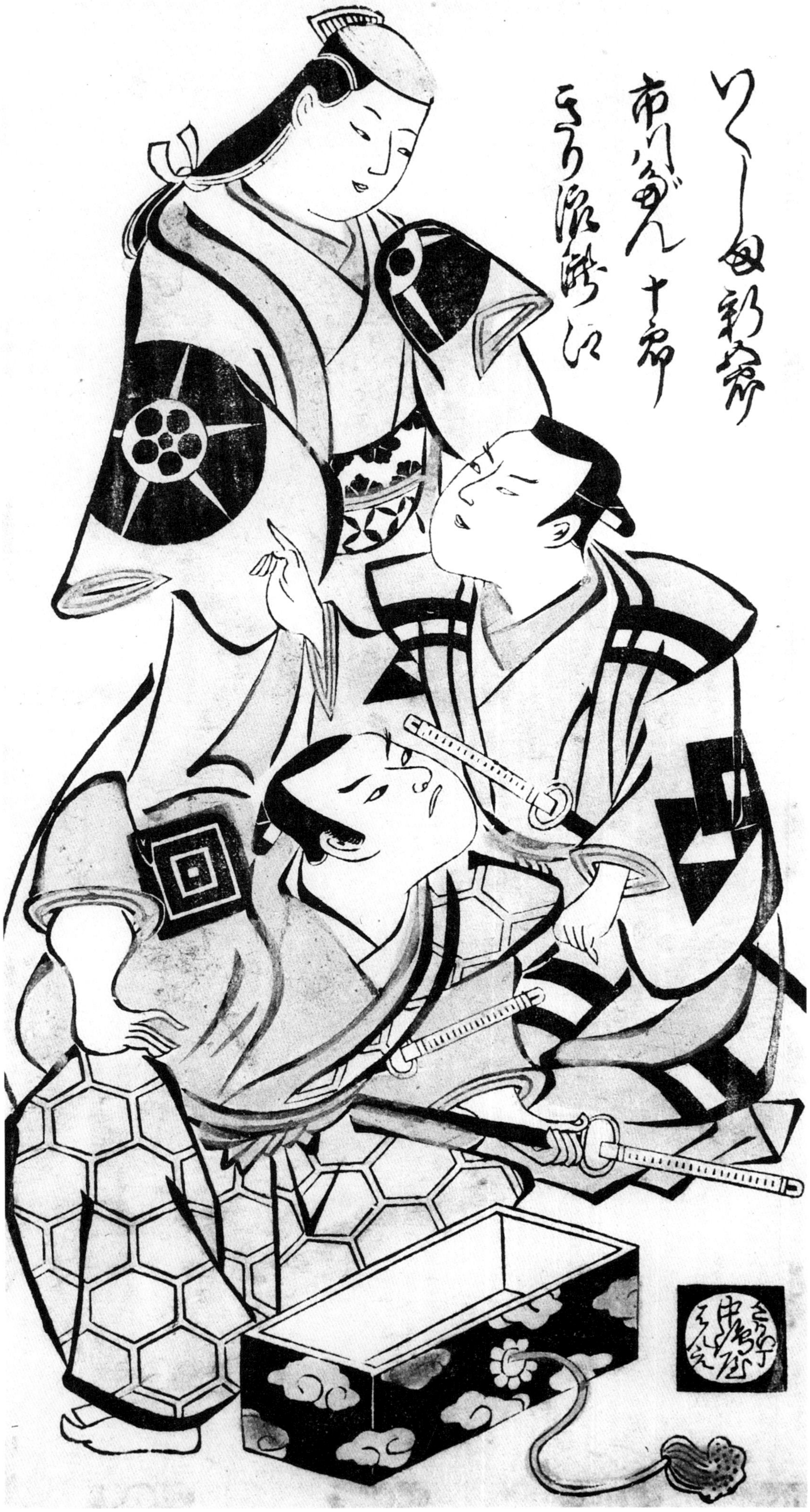

Left: Anonymous. Kinnami Takie as Takigudu's younger sister; Ikushima Shingorō as Yorimasa and Ichikawa Danjūrō II as Hayata, 1712, *hosoban*, 12×6⅛ inches (30.4×15.6 cm). *Tan-e*. Honolulu Academy of Arts, The James A. Mitchener Collection. The actors appeared together in the play *Shida Kiniro no Unoko*, which was put on at the Yamamura-za theater in 1711. This unsigned print has been assigned by different experts to both Kiyomasu I and Kiyonobu I.

ledge of the plays, the more popular of which were reworked repeatedly, is also helpful in deciphering the iconography of theatrical *ukiyo-e* as is the knowledge of the relationships between the characters in understanding them.

By 1700 depictions of actors (*yakusha-e*) had become a standard theme of the *ukiyo-e* repertoire. However, it was the Torii school of print designers that developed a style of theatrical prints that would lead to their monopoly of theatrical commissions in Edo for several decades. The first generation of Torii masters, Kiyonobu (1664-1729) and Kiyomasu (*fl.* 1696-1716), expressed the triumphs of the stage in graphic form. During the first quarter of the eighteenth century, they poured out prints, showing the pathos of the *nureba* ('wet-scene' or tear-jerker), the rambunctious vigor of the *aragoto* (rough stuff) style, and every variation in between. The best Torii school prints were in the *kakemono-e* format, either as *sumizuri-e* or *tan-e*, as in one print (page 52) which depicts a dramatic moment from the play *Shida Kiniro no Unoko*. The two actors in the foreground confront each other over a lacquer box which has just been opened in the presence of the Imperial envoy (top) and found to be empty of the treasured item it was meant to contain. Hand-coloring during this period was executed, with relative care, in two or three colors. *Tan* (red lead) was almost invariably present and often predominated. Such prints are called *tan-e*. The print is unsigned and on stylistic grounds could be attributed to either Kiyonobu or Kiyomasu (dates unrecorded), both of whom were active at this time. Although they share the Torii family name, their exact relationship to one another is not known. Both worked from the late 1690s to the mid-1720s, although even this is vague since, there was at least one other artist, working later in the same style, who signed himself Kiyonobu and probably more than one other signing Kiyomasu. At present it is generally accepted that, where a print can be dated, those signed Kiyonobu after 1729 are assigned to Kiyonobu II and likewise those signed Kiyomasu from the mid-1720s up to 1763 (after which no prints signed by either have been found) are designated Kiyomasu II.

The Kabuki theater, while wildly popular with the fun-loving Edo-period townsmen, seems to have been especially patronized by women. For men an alternative outlet for entertainment were the licensed pleasure quarters. The most famous was the Yoshiwara in Edo, although urban centers such as Kyoto and Osaka had their own pleasure quarters, the Shimbara and Shinmachi, respectively. Licensed pleasure districts were established by the Tokugawa shogunate in an attempt to regulate society further. The Yoshiwara was set up in 1617 on a filled-in swampy (*yoshi*) plain (*wara*). It was moved after the Great Meireki fire (1657) and until 1958 was located in the Taitō ward of Tokyo. Half a mile square, the Yoshiwara was entered through a single main gate (the *ōmon*, below), around which willow trees were planted (a Chinese symbol of prostitution). This opened on to the *naka-no-chō* (central street) which was planted with a row of flowering cherry trees. There were about 150 brothels (*jorōya*) classified into six grades, and possibly twice that number of tea-houses (*hikite jaya*) where guests could request an assignation. There were over 2000 prostitutes with the *tayū* being the highest ranking, as well as a host of

Below: Okumura Masanobu (1686-1764) 'Large Perspective Picture of Naka-no-chō seen through the Great Gate of the New Yoshiwara' (*Shin Yoshiwara ōmon-guchi naka-no-chō o-uki-e*), c. 1730, 17⅕×26⅛ inches (43.7×66.4 cm). Hand-colored print. Published by Okumuraya Genroku. Courtesy of the Royal Ontario Museum, Toronto, Canada. Here we see the entrance to the pleasure quarter, where visitors had to deposit their swords. Basket hats could be hired by those wishing to remain incognito.

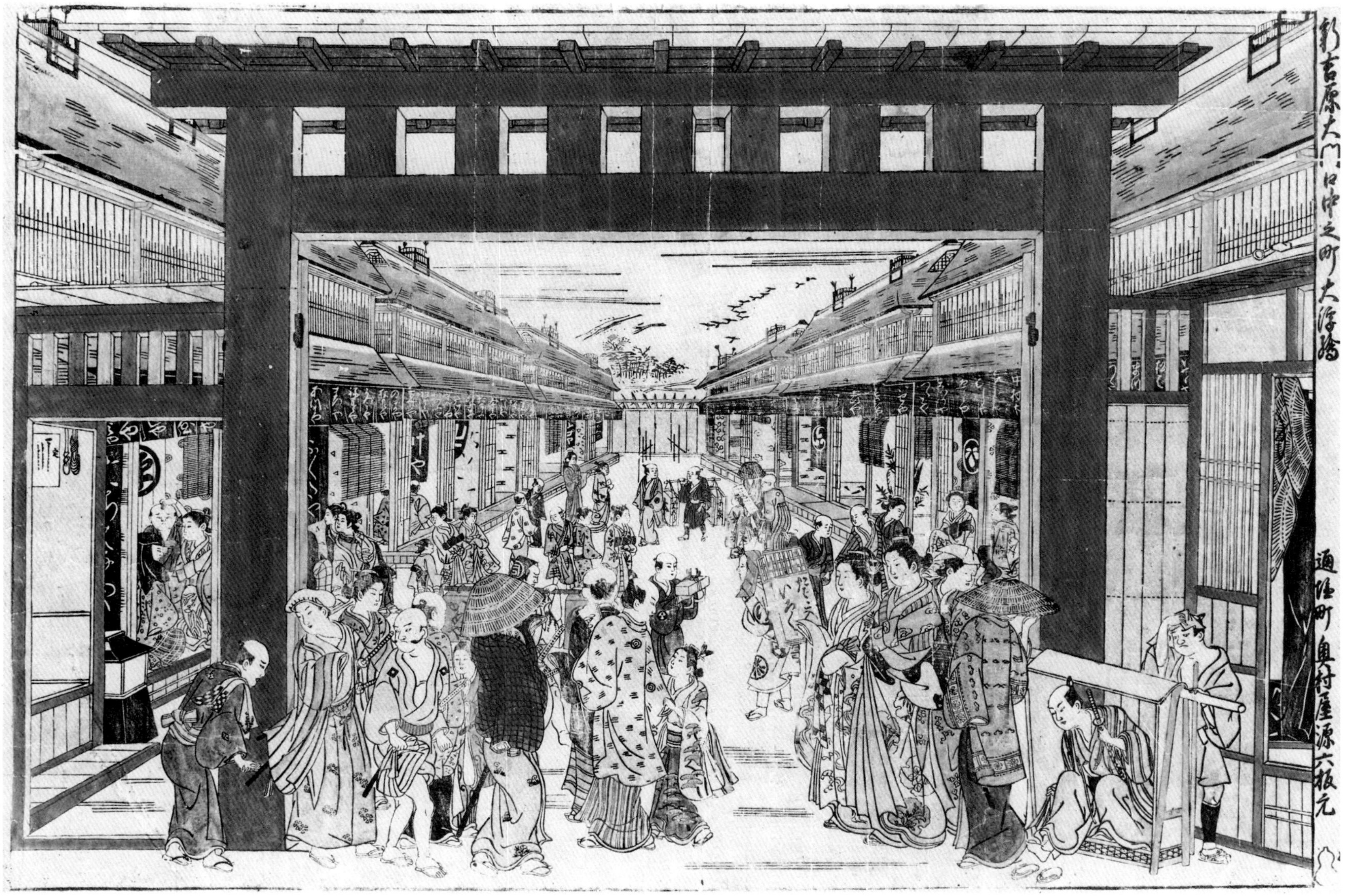

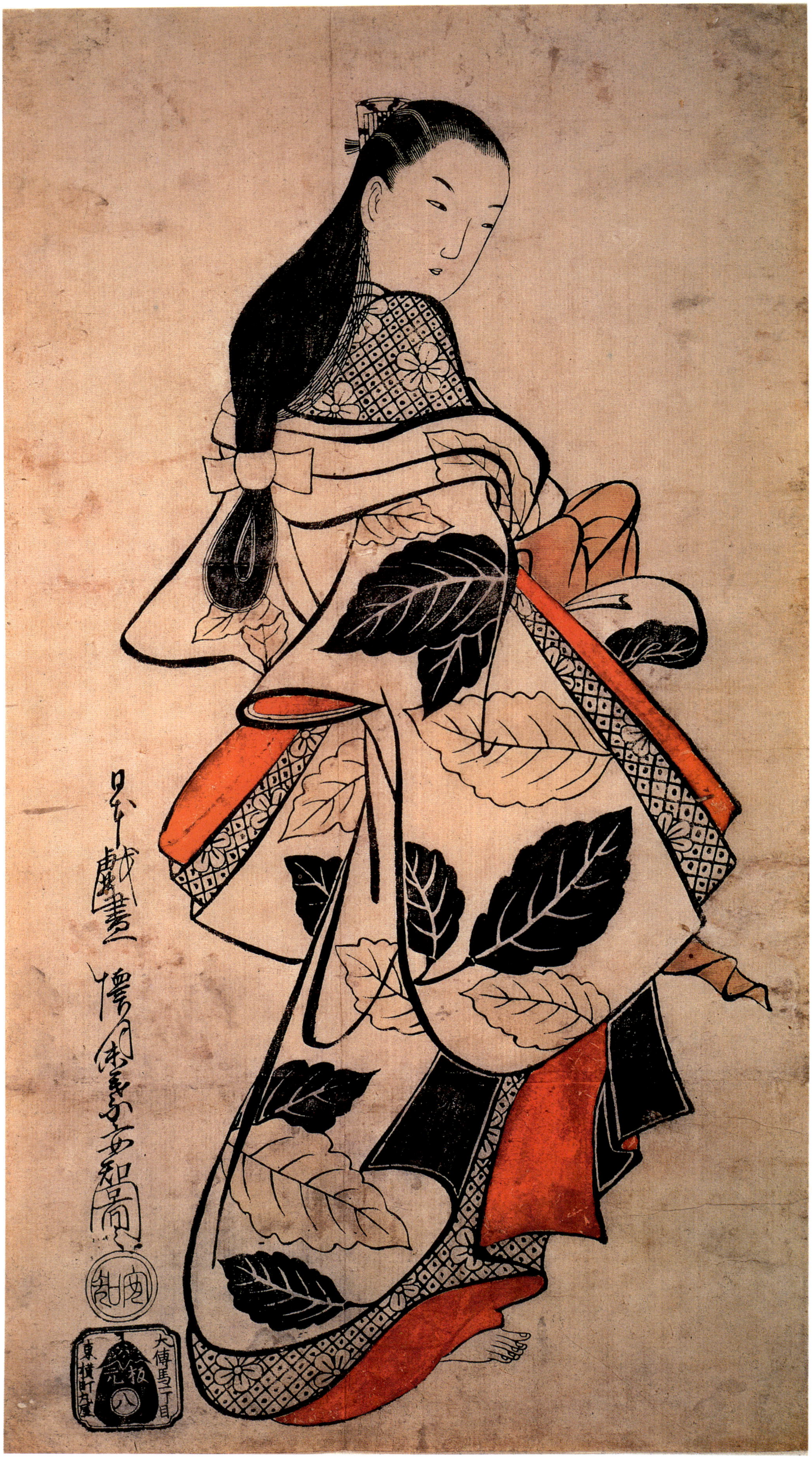

Left: Kaigetsudō Anchi (1671-1743) 'A Standing Courtesan,' c. 1715, 21½×12¼ inches (54.6×31.1 cm). Hand-colored *kakemono-e*. Private Collection. Such majestic large prints, although extremely rare, have come to represent one of the pinnacles of early *ukiyo-e* prints.

attendants, cooks, musicians and entertainers of all kinds, who lived permanently in this 'nightless city.' Some visitors would come by horse or walking along the embankment through the swampy fields, or by boat on the Sumida River, simply to meet their friends in convivial surroundings free from social repression. Many would spend the night with one of the young women – the more highly qualified the more expensive and, by all accounts, the most expensive were very highly qualified, not just in refinements of sexual athleticism but in wit, culture and beauty. Their beauty was enhanced by their garments and the top-grade courtesans became the purveyers of fashion. The highest class beauties were frequent subjects for the *ukiyo-e* artist.

Generations of print publishers and artists made their living by illustrating not just the young women in their sumptuous kimono but every minute detail of their world. In the early 1700s there was a vogue for large prints, almost small posters, showing the women of the pleasure quarters. Sometimes printed in *sumizuri-e*, or sometimes hand-colored *tan-e*, these prints are now exceedingly rare. As it states in the *Ukiyo ruikō*: 'There was a publisher's shop called Emiya in front of the Shinmei Temple in Shiba. Until 30 years ago it used to hand out old single-sheet *tan-e* as sun blinds. Now their woodblocks are prized possessions, and there are no more bamboo blinds or sun-blinds.' Examples of these large prints exist by Torii Kiyonobu, Kiyomasu and a group of artists of the Kaigetsudō school.

The Kaigetsudō artists are known exclusively for their paintings and prints of courtesans, which were produced and sold from a wayside studio on the road between Edo and the Yoshiwara. Most of the Kaigetsudō designs portray anonymous courtesans in statuesque poses set against plain backgrounds (page 54); their work was especially popular in the first two decades of the eighteenth century. One print by Kaigetsudō is interesting as it incorporates in the design an example of early advertising. The box on which the beauty sits playing with a kitten carries the name and address of the cake-maker Masaruya and illustrates his trademark of a crouching monkey, a device found on several other prints produced around 1710.

The first half of the eighteenth century saw the emergence of a number of talented print artists who were to be influential in promoting a widespread interest in Japanese prints. While the Torii school was forging a strong and enduring link between *ukiyo-e* and the Kabuki, others were continuing to expand the repertoire of styles and subjects. The most influential of the new men were Nishikawa Sukenobu, Nishimura Shigenaga,

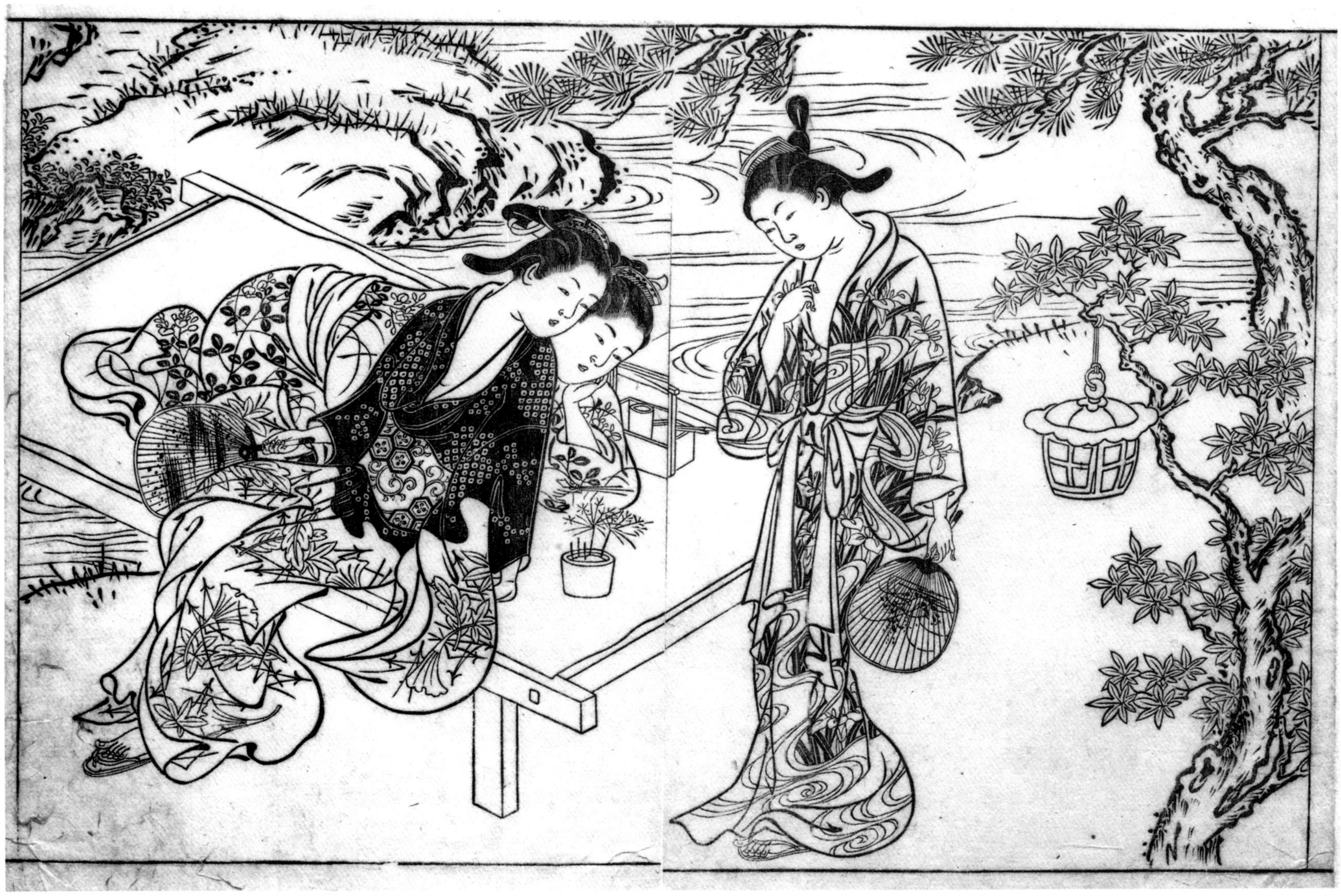

Below: Nishikawa Sukenobu. Bookplate from 'The Picture Book of Evergreens' (*Ehon Tokiwagusa*), 1731, 8¼×12⅞ inches (21×32.7 cm). *Sumizuri-e*. Private Collection. The three girls are amusing themselves letting off sparkling fireworks on a calm fall evening. The quiet gracefulness that pervades his work is typical of the style of *ukiyo-e* that was coming out of the artistic world beyond Edo from Osaka and Kyoto.

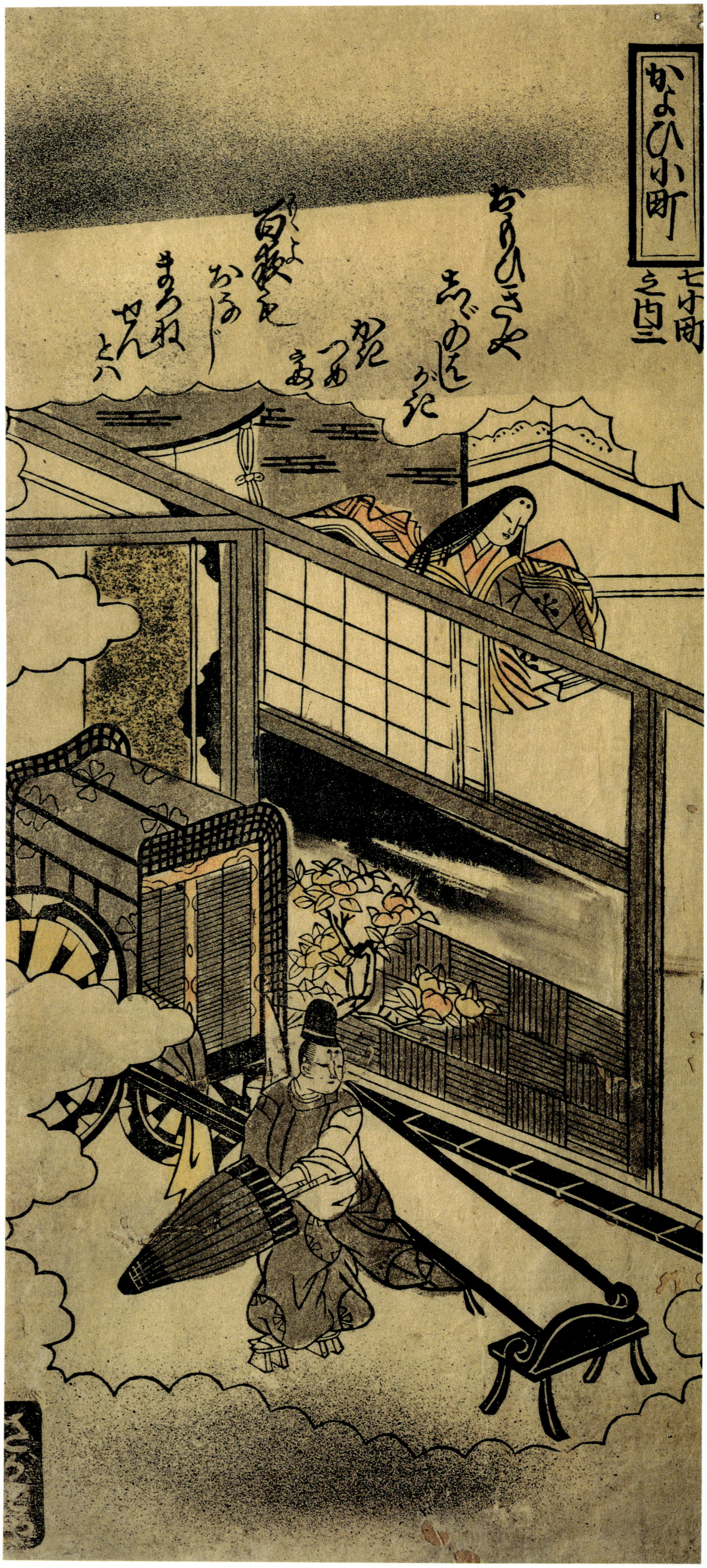

Left: Nishimura Shigenaga (1697?–1756) 'Komachi and her Suitor,' c. 1730, *hosoban*, 11½×5⅝ inches (29×14.2 cm). *Ushuri-e*. Private Collection. The life and loves of the semi-legendary ninth-century court poet Ono no Komachi were codified in a set of seven fourteenth-century Nō plays. This print, stylistically recalling classical court painting, alludes to the courtship of her suitor Fukakasa, who kept vigil outside her house for 99 nights. He failed to appear on the 100th night and was, as a result, rejected by her. The inscribed poem reads: 'I should have realized, having scored up all those marks on your mounting block, the 100th night is the same; I see I must sleep alone.' (Translated by David Waterhouse.)

Right: Okumura Masanobu (1686–1764). 'A "first night" at the Nakamura-za,' 1745. *Ōban*, 17¼×25⅝ inches (43.8×65 cm). *Tan-e*. Published by Okumuraya Genroku. (Masanobu imprints.) Courtesy of the Trustess of the British Museum, London. This large print gives an interesting view of the interior of a Kabuki theater, with the audience engaged in conversation; the atmosphere conveyed is one of general merriment. On the overhanging lanterns are the names of the actors who would be performing on this night, although this print might only suggest the 'first night' (occurring at the beginning of the season) is the 11th month.

Okumura Masanobu and their imitators and followers.

Sukenobu (1671-1751) stands as the most noteworthy artist working outside Edo: initially in Kyoto and, after 1730, in Osaka. He has been relatively neglected since, apart from paintings, his graphic work was almost entirely confined to *ehon*. He studied both Kanō and Tosa school painting (under Kanō Einō and Tosa Mitsusuke respectively). His prolific output of *ehon*, primarily between 1716 and 1741, included over a hundred illustrated books, mostly in three-volume sets, each of which contains, on average, a dozen double-page pictures. Initially influenced by Moronobu, Sukenobu was to forge an individualistic style and he designed some notable erotica and a series of books on the history and legends of old Japan. His forte, however, was the charming and idealized depiction of young women. Sukenobu portrayed them in a wide variety of situations and his talent was such that his designs were used as templates by many of his more famous contemporaries and successors such as Suzuki Harunobu. The influence of his style was felt up to the 1770s when a new ideal of feminine beauty was introduced by artists such as Isoda Koryūsai (*fl* 1764-88) and Kitao Shigemasa (1739-1820). The *Ehon Tokiwagusa* (The Picture Book of Evergreens, 1731) (page 55) consists of three volumes and was supposedly an instruction manual for amateur painters, devoted to pictures of the activities of young women. The first volume shows the past ladies of the Imperial court either fictional or factional; the second the commoners, the trendy 'girl-next-door'; and the third the courtesans of the gay quarters.

From about 1720 Nishimura Shigenaga (c.1697-1756) used and popularized a variety of styles and subject matter not previously common in prints. More sophisticated hand-coloring was being introduced. The vivid but effective coloring of the *tan-e* was supplanted about 1718 (when the large *kakemono-e* appear to have been banned) by a more delicate and precise tinting in which the attractive rose-pink *beni* dye (derived from the safflower, *Carthamus tinctorius*) often predominated. From 1720 to about 1740 such prints were often further embellished, by mixing glues with black pigments to produce a lustrous gleaming 'lacquer' effect. These *urushi-e* (lacquer pictures) were often also further decorated by sprinkling powdered bronze or brass dust onto glue to give a golden sparkle or flakes of mica to give a silvery sheen. A print by Shigenaga (page 58) shows an additional technique, *fukibokashi*, where by blowing pigment on to the paper through a small hinged tube, with or without stencil masking, a stippled effect is produced. This print also demonstrates a trend that Shigenaga helped to create that consisted of sets of prints of traditional groups of subjects, as seen for example, in his *Eight Views of Lake Omi* or, as here, the Seven Komachi, drawn in a style harking back to the conventions of the classical *Yamato-e* and Tosa schools of painting. Shigenaga was important as a teacher and some of his pupils, especially Ishikawa Toyonobu (1711-85) and Suzuki Harunobu went on to be leaders in *bijinga* (pictures of beautiful women).

The artist who, more than any other, was important in introducing and refining new styles, subjects and techniques in the first half of the eighteenth century was Okumura Masanobu (1686-1764). At a time when Moronobu's flair seemed to have few worthy successors, when the pupils of the first Torii masters appeared set to reproduce Kabuki scenes to stock patterns, and when even Sukenobu's delightful women were in danger of becoming repetitive, *ukiyo-e* was in need of a revitalizing force. James Michener wrote in his book, *The Floating World*, that what was needed was not eclecticism but explosive genius, some man of colossal self-assurance who will leap into the middle of a stagnant art, stir it up wildly, revitalize some of the old forms, kick others out and set up a whole new gener-

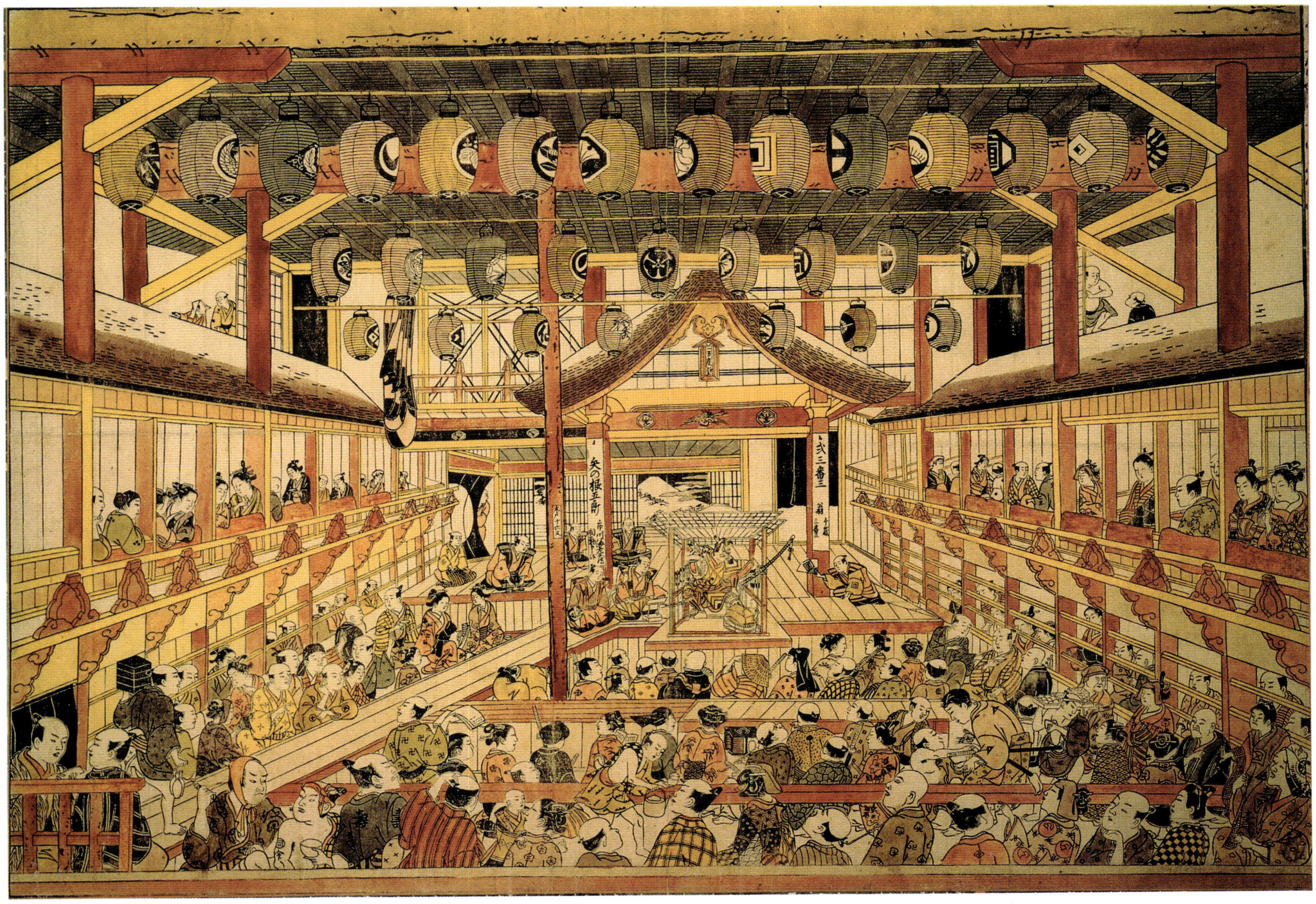

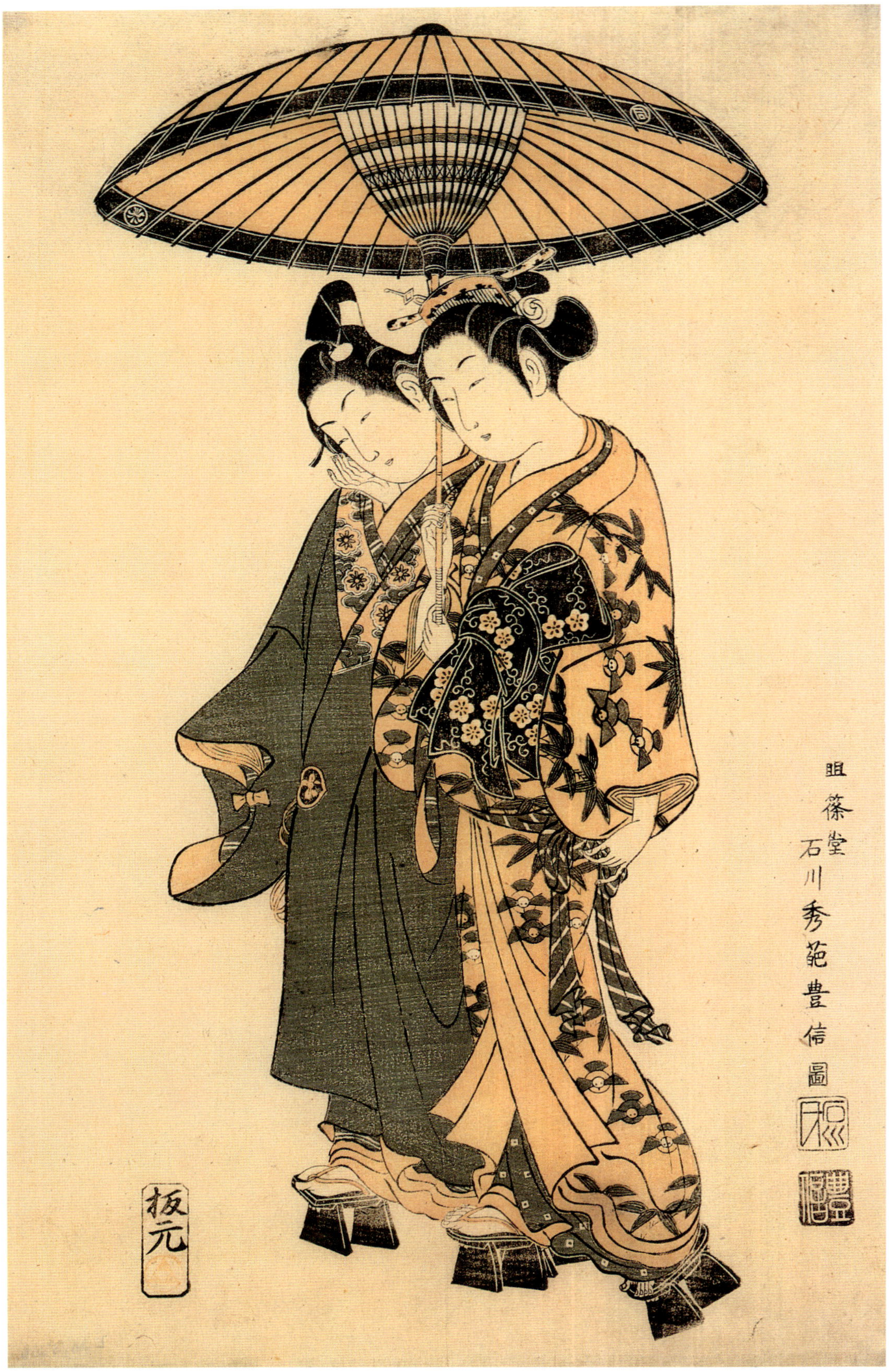

Left: Ishikawa Toyonobu (1711-85). 'The Actors Sanokawa Ichimatsu and Segawa Kikunojo as Lovers,' mid 1740s, *ōban*, 17⅙×11 inches (43.6×28.1 cm). Two-color *benizuri-e*. Signed *Meijodo Ishikawa Shuen Toyonobu* and sealed. Published by Urokogataya Magobei. Honolulu Academy of Arts, The James A. Michener Collection. A couple sharing an umbrella is a convenient shorthand implying that they are in love. The roles here are not given and this design has been variously linked to plays performed in 1747 and 1752.

Right: Torii Kiyohiro (*fl* 1757-76). 'The Letter in the Wind' c.1751-64, *hosoban*, 11⅝×5¼ inches (29.5×13.4 cm). Three-color *benizuri-e*. Signed *Torii Kiyohiro*. Oscar Raphael Bequest. Courtesy of the Trustees of the British Museum, London. This delightful print shows the freshness and vivacity that Kiyohiro brought to his work. Gusts of wind have not only blown away some compromising love letters but have also caught the young woman's skirts, revealing her legs. This type of print, which illustrates parts of the female body not normally seen, is called *abuna-e* (dangerous pictures). They were popular in the mid 1800s.

Far right: Torii Kiyomitsu (1735-85). 'The Actor Onoe Kikugorō I, early 1760s, *hosoban*, 11⅞×5⅝ inches (30.2×14.3 cm). Four-color *benizuri-e*. Signed *Torii Kiyomitsu hitsu*. Published by Urokogataya Magobei. Private Collection. Prints such as this must have served as souvenirs of a trip to the theater or handouts to members of the fan-clubs of the current stage stars, the Onoe family of actors were well-known for their portrayals of realistic and military characters. In this print the poem is signed 'Baikō,' which was Kikugorō's nom de plume.

ation into vigorous movement. Such a man was Okumura Masanobu. Michener described him as 'this vainglorious, avaricious, mendacious and vastly gifted little man . . . generally been credited with at least thirteen technical innovations that saved *ukiyo-e*.' While Michener's evidence for these comments was almost entirely circumstantial, it remains true that throughout Masanobu's long career – during part of which he was a publisher as well as a print designer – he was associated with a number of the exciting technical developments at the time, such as *urushi-e*. He was also a versatile print designer who worked in a variety subjects. Masanobu took the smaller *hosoban* format which appeared around 1715 and expanded upon it, by designing triptychs of three thematically, linked *hosoban* and by devising the pillar-prints, *hashira-e*, which were in vogue in the 1740s. He experimented with reviving the ancient Chinese style of ink-rubbings taken from incised stone, called *ishizuri-e* using, however, woodblocks, instead of stone. This produced strange prints on which the design comes out as white line against a black ground. Around 1740 *uki-e* (perspective prints; pages 53 and 57) became fashionable and they demonstrate that, if Japanese artists have tended to eschew the techniques of perspective, this was from choice rather than ignorance.

Shortly after 1740 commercially produced color prints began to appear. The process of hand-coloring, especially in *urushi-e*, was expensive to produce in terms of labor and materials and by this time the possibilities for further novelty with the technique were declining. Kruml[3] has argued cogently that such factors probably determined the advent of the first prints colored by overprinting the keyblock design with separate blocks for each color. Color printing had been in use on occasion in books, especially in diagrams in mathematical and scientific works. The earliest authenticated Japanese book with color illustrations was the mathematical treatise *Jinkō-ki* which was published in an edition with color-printed illustration in 1631[4], 1634 and 1641. In addition, there were anthologies of haiku poetry known from the 1720s and 1730s with color printing using between two and four blocks. The technical problem of effecting good register was accomplished by incorporating guide marks, *kentō*, on the keyblock. These consisted of an L-shaped ridge in one of the lower corners and a horizontal ridge at the lower margin. Keyblock proofs having been struck, these were in turn pasted on to fresh woodblocks and the areas to be colored engraved, with a new block for each color. Initially two color blocks were added, usually *beni*, and green. These *benizuri-e* (pink-printed pictures) became immensely popular and, although they did not immediately supplant hand-coloring, which continued to be used with increasing sophistication for a few years, it was soon apparent that color printing had come to stay. The earliest *benizuri-e* for which a date is assignable is a calendar print by Okumura Masanobu produced for the New Year. The design incorporates the sequence of long and short months of the year 1742[5].

The pink and green, executed skilfully use black outlines and white background, allowed the production of a number of beautiful prints. A good example of this (page 56) is by Shigenaga's pupil Toyonobu, who during the 1750s designed *benizuri-e* in a style much influenced by Masanobu. The size of the prints started to become larger again with the *ōban* format re-emerging.

Some of the variations in print format and decoration seem to have been in response to edicts issued by the government, then headed by the eighth shogun Yoshimune (1684–1751). From 1718 to the early 1740s repeated attempts at economic reform were accompanied by regulations designed to restrain ostentatious displays of wealth. The output of the Edo publishing houses was but a small part of the general prohibitions and such edicts

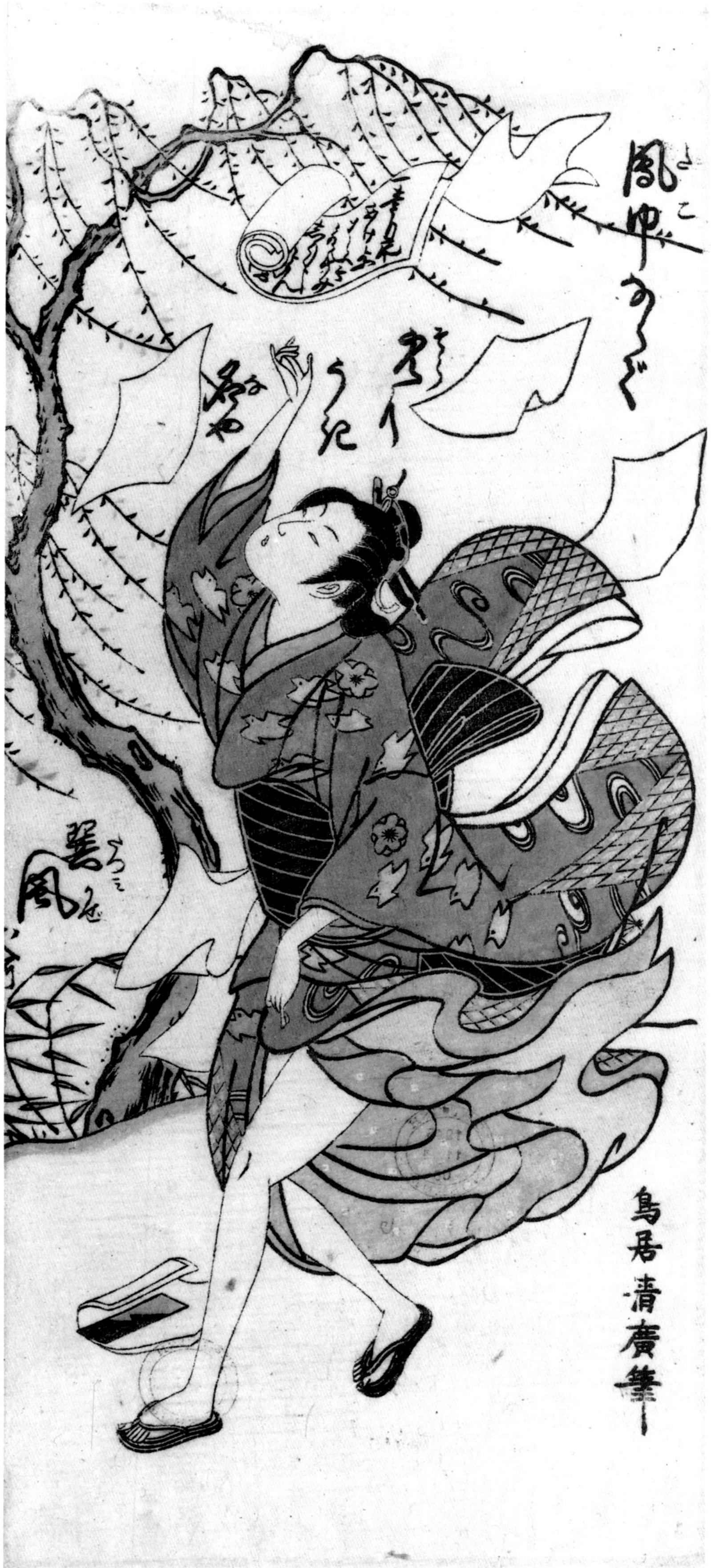

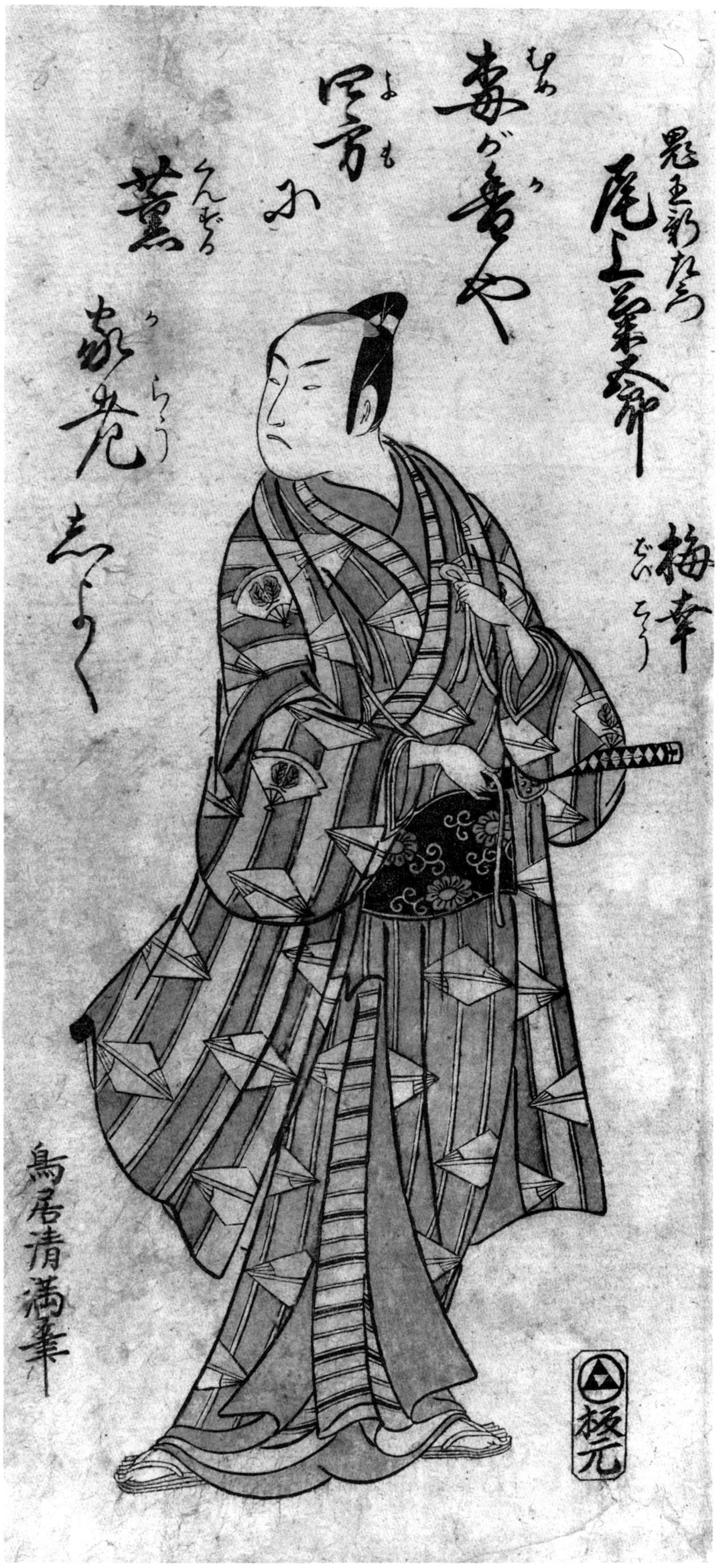

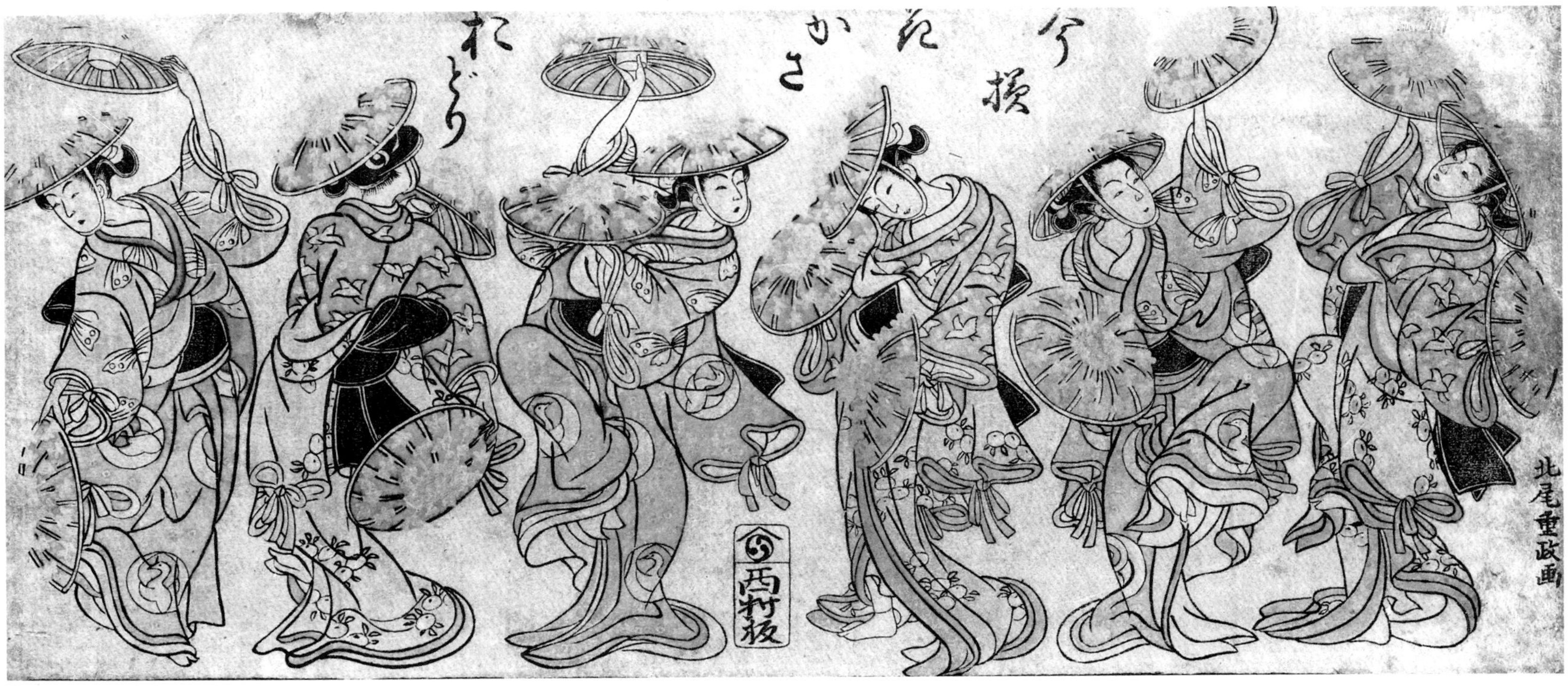

Above: Kitao Shigemasa (1739-1820) 'Spring Festival Dancers,' mid to late 1760s. Horizontal *hosoban*, 5⅓×12⅛ inches (13.5×30.8 cm). Four-color *benizuri-e*. Private Collection. The young women have all the winsome gracefulness of Sukenobu's designs of a generation before but are here not enclosed in a black and white Kyoto book-plate but are leaping into the colored Edo prints around the time that Harunobu's *nishiki-e* are about to take the town by storm.

seem frequently to have been ignored or circumvented. Their influence during the 1720s and 1730s, when restrictions were placed on the complexity, size, color and expense of the prints, should not, however, be totally discounted and later efforts at control in 1790 and 1842 had quite far-reaching effects.

As these changes took place they show up also in the continuing output of theatrical prints. As already mentioned the Torii school of print artists remained pre-eminent in this field. Working mostly in the smaller *hosoban* format, the verve of these prints has been toned down in the more vigorous scenes, and the pathos of the 'tear-jerker' sometimes appears a little forced. Howard Link[6] lists at least half a dozen Torii artists producing *beni-e* and *urushi-e* during the 1720s and 1730s, the most notable being Kiyotomo (*fl* 1720-40), Kiyoshige (*fl* 1720-60) and Kiyotada (*fl* 1720-50), who also experimented with *uki-e*.

By the 1750s the next generation of Torii artists was coming to the fore. While the older Kiyonobu II (1706-63), - Kiyomasu II (1706-63) and Kiyoshige worked on up to about 1760. The titular head of the school became Kiyomitsu (1735-85), who designed billboards and playbills for the theaters as well as a host of *benizuri-e* prints during the 1750s and 1760s. With him in the Torii atelier were Kiyotsune (*fl* 1757-79), Kiyohiro (*fl* 1757-76), Kiyohide and Kiyoharu (*fl* 1700-80). Kiyohiro stands apart from other members of the school by being less dependent on the Kabuki scenes and, perhaps under the influence of Toyonobu, designed some attractive two-color prints of a mildly suggestive nature (page 59).

A watershed in the history of Japanese prints occurred with the advent of full-color printing, first recorded for the calendar prints in 1765. These first prints were seemingly privately commissioned, but soon full-color printing became the norm. These full-color prints (*nishiki-e*, brocade pictures), which used up to nine color blocks in addition to the black key block (*kyōgō*) were preceded by prints using three or four blocks (blue and yellow were added to the pink and green of *benizuri-e*; pages 59, 60 and 61). The arrival of the *nishiki-e*, as will be seen in the works by the master Suzuki Harunobu, clearly marked the end of an era in Japanese printmaking.

NOTES

1 Lane, Richard *Erotic Art of the East*, ed. Philip Rawson, New York, 1968, pp. 301-03

2 Michener, James A *The Floating World: The Story of Japanese Prints*, New York, 1954, p. 73

3 Kruml, Richard 'The Birth of the Kentō,' *Andon*. 31, 1988, pp 140-43

4 Waterhouse, David B: *Harunobu and His Age: The Development of Color Printing in Japan*, London, 1964, pp. 18-19

5 Waterhouse, David B *Images of Eighteenth-Century Japan*, Toronto, 1975, p. 72

6 Link, Howard A *The Theatrical Prints of the Torii Masters*, Honolulu and Tokyo, 1977, p. 32

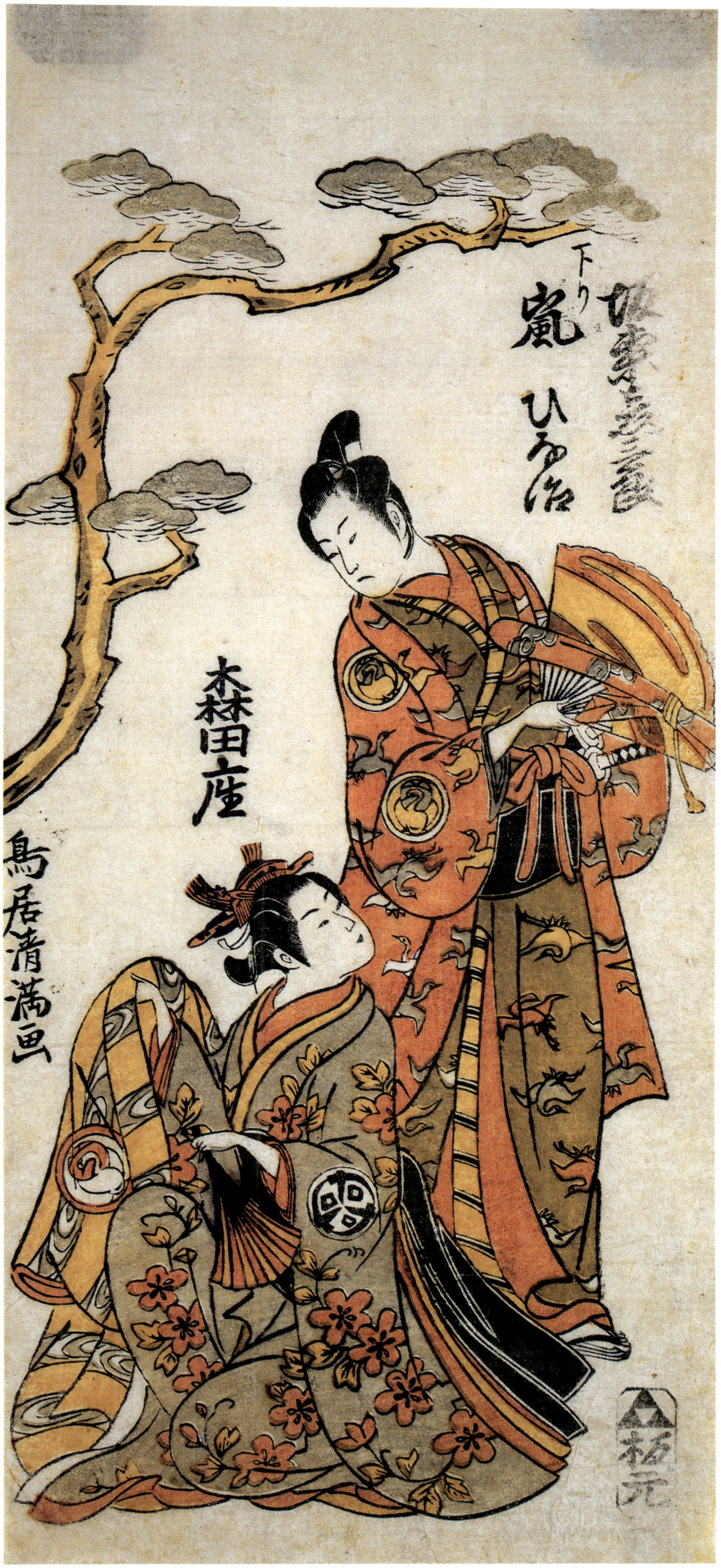

Right: Torii Kiyomitsu (*fl* 1696-1716). 'The Actors Bandō Hikasaburō and Arashi Hinaji,' mid-1760s. *Hosoban*; 11⅛×5½ inches (30×14 cm). Five-color *benizuri-e*; signed Torii Kiyomitsu; Published by Urokogataya Magobei. The Chester Beatty Library, Dublin. This five-color print is typical of the *benizuri-e* issued just before the advent of the full-color *nishiki-e*, which began to be commercially produced in 1766. A few such prints continued for a year or so after 1766 but the new full-color style soon replaced the old.

3
Suzuki Harunobu, Isoda Koryūsai and the early Katsukawa School, 1760-80

DAVID WATERHOUSE

HARUNOBU AND THE ADVENT OF FULL-COLOR PRINTING

The decade from 1760 to 1770 saw dramatic changes in the techniques, artistic sophistication and marketing of *ukiyo-e* prints. These developments were due to the work of one man above all, the print designer Suzuki Harunobu (1725?-70). Although little is known about him as an individual, there is no doubt about the impact of his work, which launched the full-color woodblock print in Japan and created a new image of feminine beauty for the townspeople of Edo. After Harunobu, it would have been unthinkable to continue producing single-sheet prints in the old way, in black-and-white, with hand-coloring or with two or three color blocks at most. To understand the psychology behind this, it is only necessary to consider the impact of technicolor film in our own day, or of color television. Although they are frequently charming and even beautiful, the *beni-e* and *benizuri-e* of the preceding decades must appear as transitional and technically crude as early color photography does to us today.

Harunobu's single-sheet prints typically used six to nine printed pigments, in addition to the black outline of the key block (*kyōgō*). For economic reasons, black-and-white continued to be used for most book illustrations; but, starting with Harunobu himself, some notable albums were printed in full color during the last 30 years of the eighteenth century. After 1770, although the basic technique of *ukiyo-e* woodcuts remained unchanged, the number of pigments used (and color blocks) gradually increased, until by the time of Utagawa Hiroshige

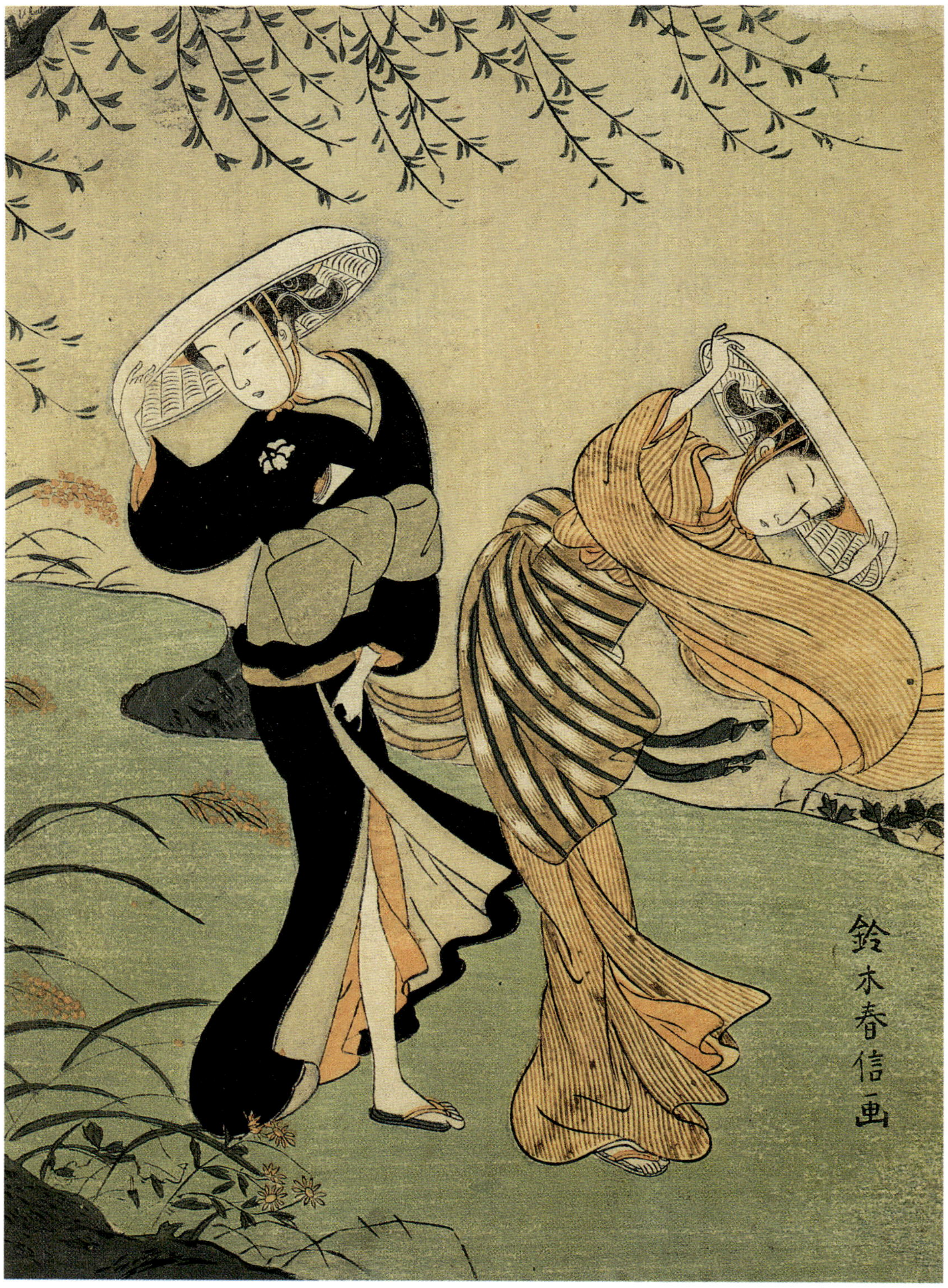

(1797-1858) more than twenty might be used. Special effects of printing, shading and fine block-cutting also came into regular use. These tendencies can also be observed in the work of Harunobu. Thus he used not only such obvious effects as over-printing (to obtain a third color), or *urushi* (lacquer stiffening, to make the color denser), but also occasionally a dusting with mica (*unmo, kirara*) or fine metallic particles; and in particular he liked to use varieties of *karazuri*, 'empty printing,' to bring out the folds of drapery, or to suggest the damask pattern of a silk fabric. The *karazuri* effects were made possible by use of the heavier *hōsho* paper, in place of the thin, semi-transparent sheets which were usual for *benizuri-e*. The result, usually in the new *chūban* 'medium print' format, was a clearly superior product, which might cost twenty times as much as one of the old prints. *Hōsho* (edict paper), was a fine-textured creamy paper, traditionally used for inscribing edicts, and made above all in the town of Takefu, in Echizen province (modern Fukui Prefecture).

The new techniques enabled Harunobu to display his gifts as a graphic artist and designer, and to convey his distinctive vision of women. Often he took artistic ideas from his earlier contemporaries: the *ukiyo-e* print artists Okumura Masanobu (1686-1764), Torii Kiyohiro (*fl* 1757-76), Torii Kiyonobu (1664-1729) and Ishikawa Toyonobu (1711-85) (page 62), who had all worked in Edo; from the Kyōto book illustrator Nishikawa Sukenobu (1671-1751); and from other, more obscure sources. However, even when borrowing entire figures from another artist, or sometimes from himself, Harunobu would both re-draw the heads and faces, and design a new background, usually simpler and always well adapted to the new palette of colors. His genius as a designer shows most clearly when he is compared with his sources: he abhors clutter in the same way as did Tawaraya Sōtatsu (d 1643?), whose great screen of court dancers isolates, like rocks in a Zen garden, figures lifted directly from a stereotyped tradition of the classical Japanese painting style, *Yamato-e*. In both cases, the result is a new whole, fresh and surprisingly modern in its simplicity. The parallel is not so far-fetched as it appears at first sight, since Harunobu, like Okumura Masanobu before him, actually described himself as a *Yamato-eshi*, a master *Yamato-e*.

In less obvious ways, Harunobu also extended greatly the range of subject matter available to *ukiyo-e* artists. Because of his classical predilections, and because he evidently moved in educated circles, his prints abound in literary allusions. Many of them quote classical Japanese poems, from one of the old imperial anthologies (above); others make direct or indirect reference to Nō plays, to medieval romances (page 64), or to Chinese literature. Often these prints are *mitate*, light-hearted parodies which reflect the fun-loving urban culture of old Edo. At that time *senryū* verse, a 17-syllable form less strict and less metaphysical than *haiku*, was all the rage, and Harunobu's friends included practitioners of this and other kinds of light verse. The term *mitate* literally means 'witnessing with one's own eyes.' Thus it could be used of making judgments or choices, of seeing off a traveler, or of making comparisons. In the last sense it became a technical term in linked-verse composition (*renga*), when a following verse (*tsuke-ai*) would give a new twist to the meaning of the first one. This usage helped to inspire the creation of *mitate* designs by *ukiyo-e* artists, although they also drew on the tradition of *manga* (cartoons) in Japanese painting, and on the Japanese sense of fun.

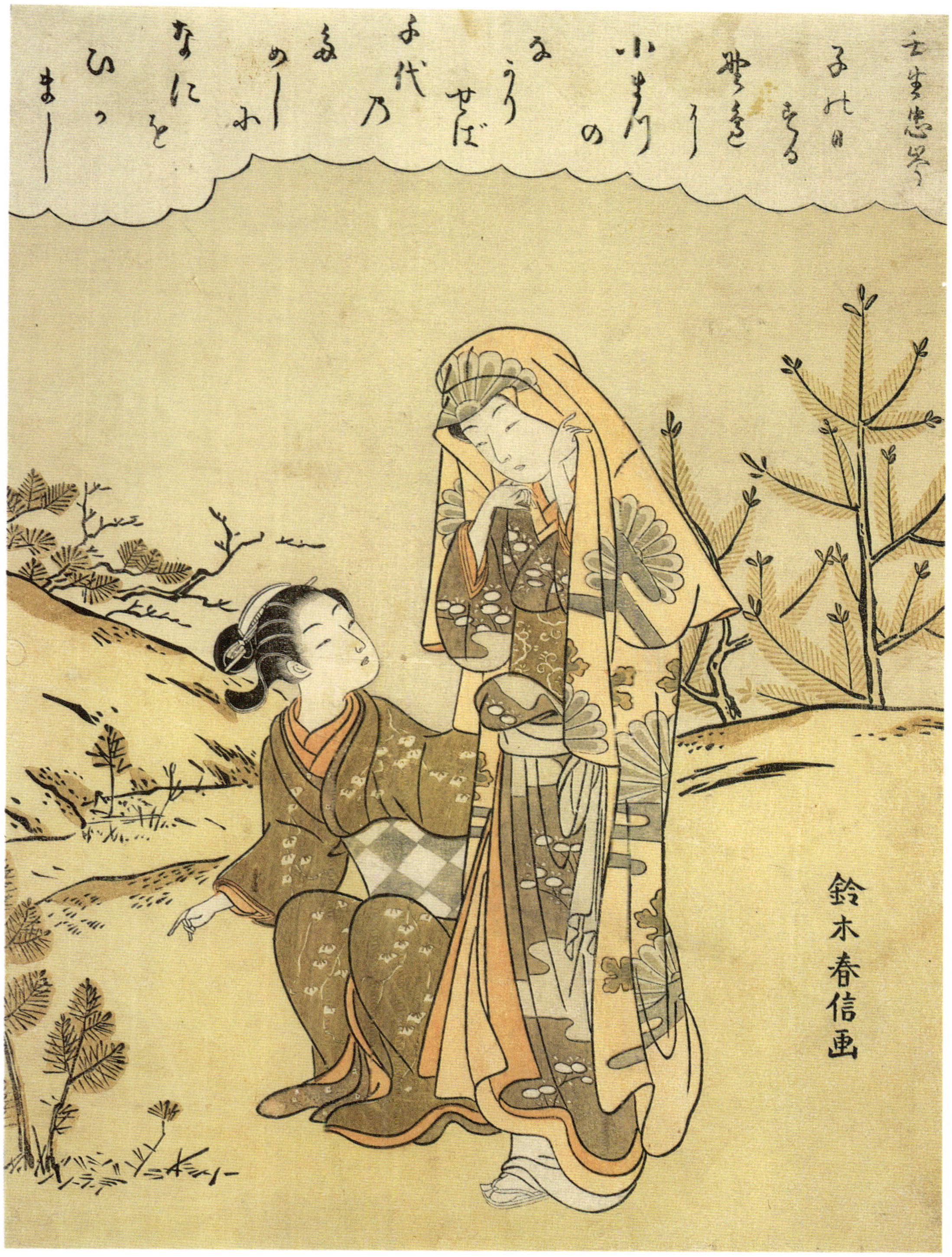

Above: Suzuki Harunobu, *'Mibu no Tadamine,'*. No. 20 from *Sanjūrokkasen* (36 Immortal Poets) series, 1767-68, *chūban*, 10⅝×8⅕ inches (27.2×20.8 cm). Museum of Fine Arts, Boston. 35 of Harunobu's designs for this series have now been identified, some of them surviving in unique impressions. The poem on the present print, by Mibu no Tadamine (d 965), reads:

ne no hi suru	If there were no pine
nobe ni komatsu no	shoots on the heath when we went
nakariseba	out on the Rat day
chiyo no tameshi no	what could I pluck for tokens
nani o hikamashi	to wish you a thousand years?

Left: Suzuki Harunobu, 'Two Girls Walking Out on a Windy Day,' 1768-69, *chūban*, 10¾×8 inches (27.3×20.3 cm). Minneapolis Institute of Arts. The figure of the right-hand girl is borrowed from Toyonobu's *Ehon Suetsumuhana* (1757); was first used by Harunobu in his own book *Ehon kagami-gusa* (1761); and used again by Harunobu's disciple Mitsunobu, in a print of the early 1770s. The context of these other illustrations, as well as details of the present print, make it clear that the season which is depicted is fall.

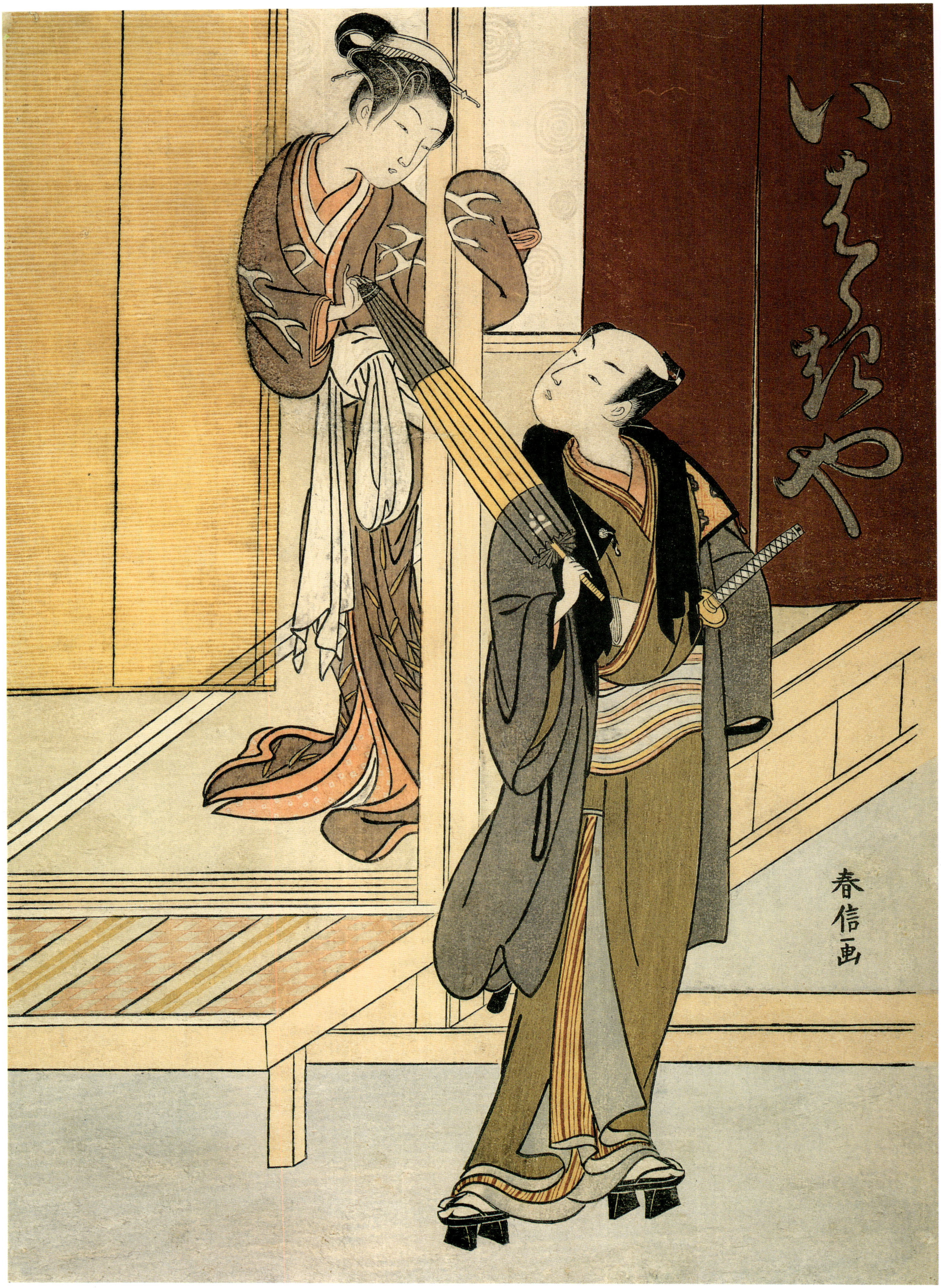
春信画

Left: Suzuki Harunobu, 'Parody of Watanabe no Tsuna and Ibaraki,' state 1, 1767-68, *chūban*, $10^{7}/_{16}$×8 inches (27.5×20.3 cm), Museum of Fine Arts, Boston. Harunobu probably borrowed the idea for this print in the first instance from Torii Kiyohiro (*fl* 1737-76). The allusion is to the medieval story of Watanabe no Tsuna and his struggle at the Rashōmon gate of Kyoto with the demon Ibaraki, whose arm he cut off. Hence one arm of Harunobu's courtesan is hidden inside her kimono, as she attempts to detain a potential client.

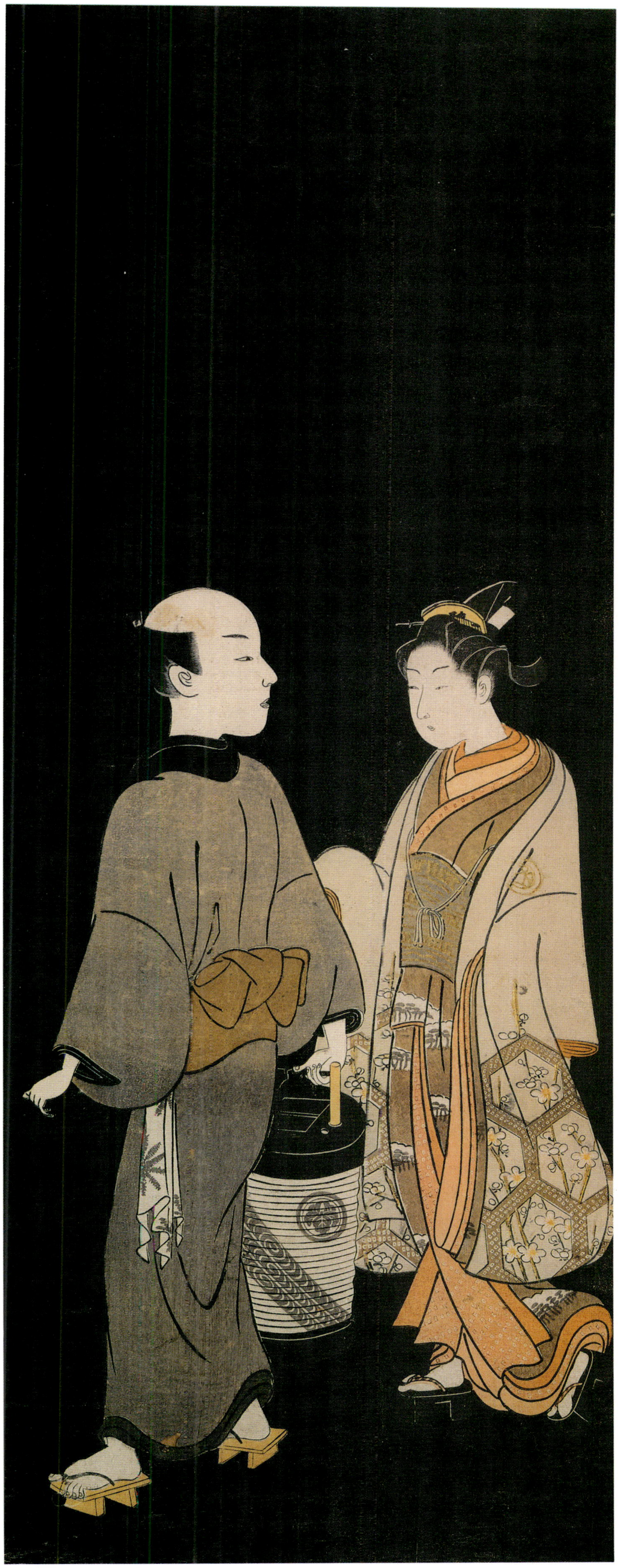

Right: Suzuki Harunobu (attr.), 'The Actor Yoshizawa Sakinosuke III, Preceded by a Manservant with a Lantern,' 1768-69. Large *hashira-e*, $20^{1}/_{2}$×$8^{1}/_{7}$ inches (52.2×20.7 cm), Museum of Fine Arts, Boston. This magnificent print can be identified, from the slanting motif and crest-badge on the lantern, as a portrait of Yoshizawa Sakinosuke III (1737-92). This actor's career can be followed from contemporary sources, and he is also listed in a guide to homosexual brothels compiled in 1768 by Harunobu's friend Hiraga Gennai.

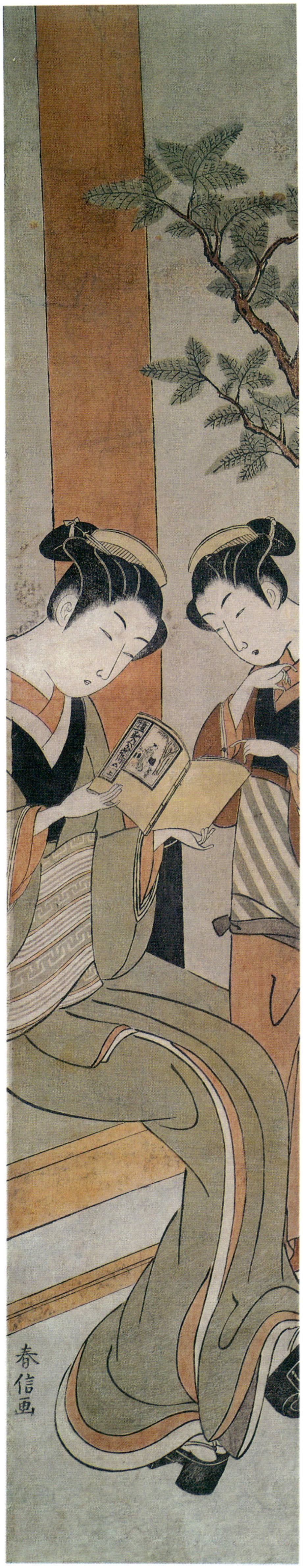

Left: Suzuki Harunobu, 'The Tea-stall Girl Kagiya Osen and Her Assistant Reading a Novelette,' 1769-70, *hashira-e*, $26\frac{5}{8}\times5\frac{1}{8}$ inches (67.6×13.0 cm). Museum of Fine Arts, Boston. The cover of Osen's book bears an illustration which is credited to Kitao Shigemasa (1739-1820), though the title of the book has not been traced. Behind the two girls rises a pillar of the *torii* gateway at the Kasamori Inari shrine, and a branch of a sacred cedar tree.

Right: Bunchō: *Niken chaya no bosetsu*, (Evening Snow at the Teahouse of the Two Eaves) from the series: *Azuma hakkei* (Eight Views in the East [Edo]), c. 1770, *chūban* $10\frac{5}{16}\times7\frac{11}{16}$ inches (26.2×19.5 cm). Art Institute of Chicago. A geisha stands with her maid outside the Yamamotoya, which was then part of the well-known Niken Chaya, 'Teahouse of the Double Bays [or Two Eaves],' within the precincts of the Hachiman Shrine at Fukagawa. The maid holds a wooden box containing the geisha's *shamisen* (three-stringed long lute).

Apart from doing prints which make literary or historical allusions, Harunobu often showed street-scenes or scenes of domestic life in Edo. At first sight even the street-scenes appear generic, and they seldom bear any identifying label, but careful research will sometimes prove or at least suggest that he had a particular location or person in mind. A case in point is a unique large print in Boston (page 65), which turns out to be a portrait of the Kabuki actor Yoshizawa Sakinosuke III (1737-92). A number of other prints are easily recognizable as depictions of the beautiful tea-stall girl Kagiya Osen (left). Osen became an instant celebrity in 1768 at the age of 18: there was a play about her, images of her were offered up at shrines, her likeness appeared on hand-cloths and backgammon boards, story-books and other publications alluded to her. She was portrayed by several other artists, including Ippitsusai Bunchō (*fl* c. 1765-92). Early in 1770 she married a well-placed samurai, and probably gave up her tea-stall. Most of Harunobu's prints of her are datable to 1769. As a result of the Osen craze, prints of other stall-girls appeared, such as Ofuji, who had a toothpick and cosmetic stall at Asakusa; Osode and Oyoshi, who had tea-stalls nearby; and Ofude, whose stall was at Ueno. Harunobu depicted all these girls, and therefore it is easy to confuse them.

Another place, depicted not only by Harunobu but also by Bunchō (page 67) and Katsukawa Shunshō (1726-92), was the Niken Chaya, 'Tea-house of the Two Eaves,' which was in the Fukagawa district, and was one of the earliest geisha houses in the city. Its parent house, in Kyoto, was famous for a special kind of fried bean-curd, and this was served at a short-lived branch restaurant in Asakusa, the Eiraku-an, depicted also by Harunobu (several times) and by Bunchō. Harunobu was probably the first artist to depict geisha, who started to become popular in his day, mainly in the Fukagawa and Yoshiwara districts. They replaced the older institutions of *odoriko* (dancing girls) and *geiko* (*shamisen* players accompanying singers or dancers); and their main role as entertainers was to play the *shamisen* (three-stringed long lute) and to sing popular *ko-uta* (short songs).

The direct impact of Harunobu on his contemporaries and successors in *ukiyo-e* was thus twofold: more than anyone else, he exploited the new technical possibilities of multi-color printing; and he offered a new range of subject matter, together with a more sophisticated style of depiction for figure prints above all. These two developments dominated *ukiyo-e* down to the end of the eighteenth century and beyond.

A third way in which Harunobu in-

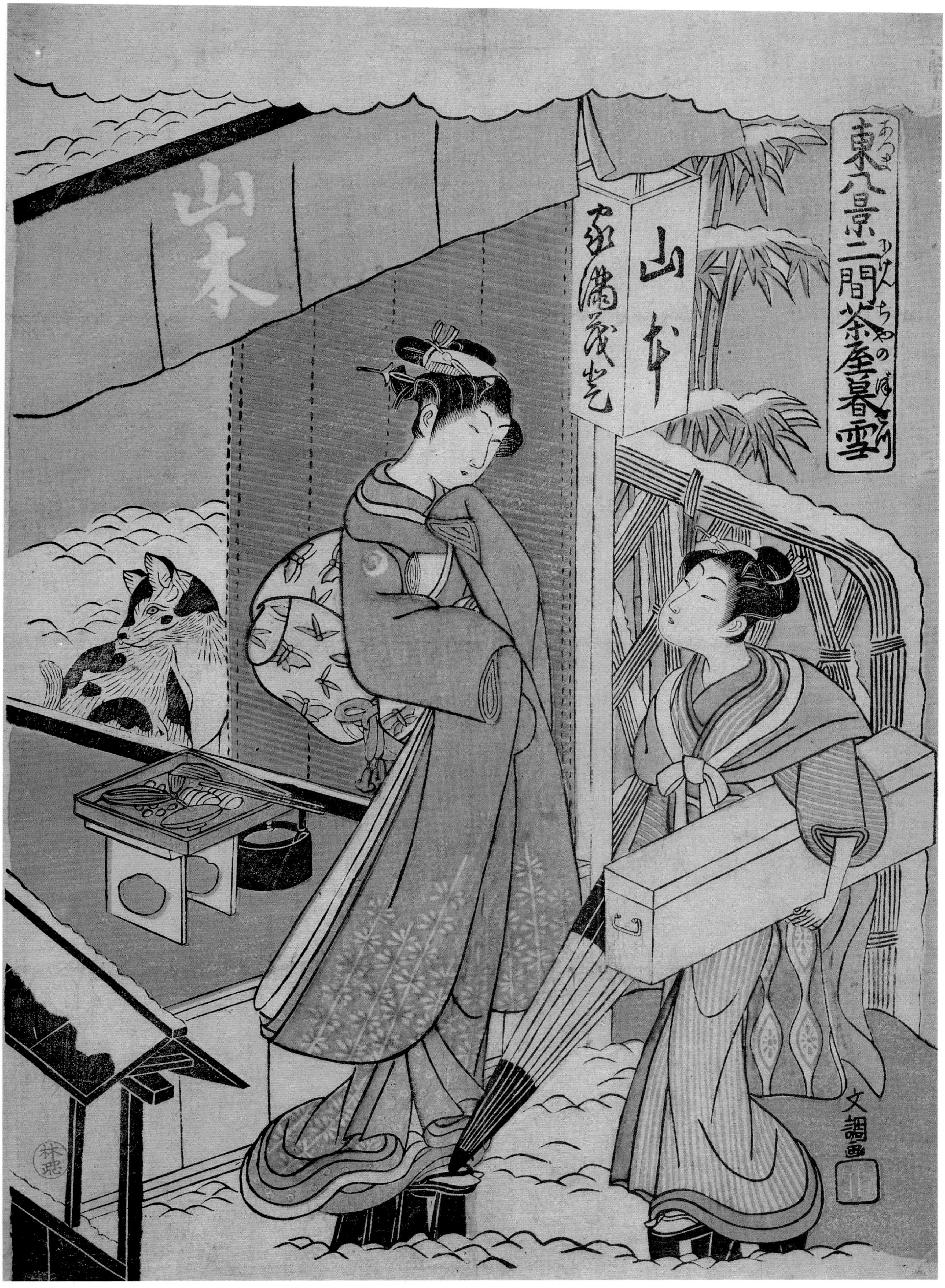
東八景二間茶屋暮雪
山本
山本
文調画

Below and right: Komatsuken (attr.): Illustration of Hangonkō, 'Spirit-Reflection Incense,' 1765 (calendar print), *chūban* vertical diptych, 10⅞×7¾ inches (27.6×19.7 cm) each. Art Institute of Chicago. The Western Han Emperor Xiao Wu Di (r. 141-87 BC), having lost his consort Lady Li, was burning incense in memory of her, and saw a vision of her appearing to him through the smoke. The story became well-known in Japan through a poem of Bo Juyi (772-846). There were Kabuki adaptations of it, and several *ukiyo-e* artists, including Harunobu, illustrated the theme. Here, calendrical markings for 1765 are concealed on the incense burner and on the costumes.

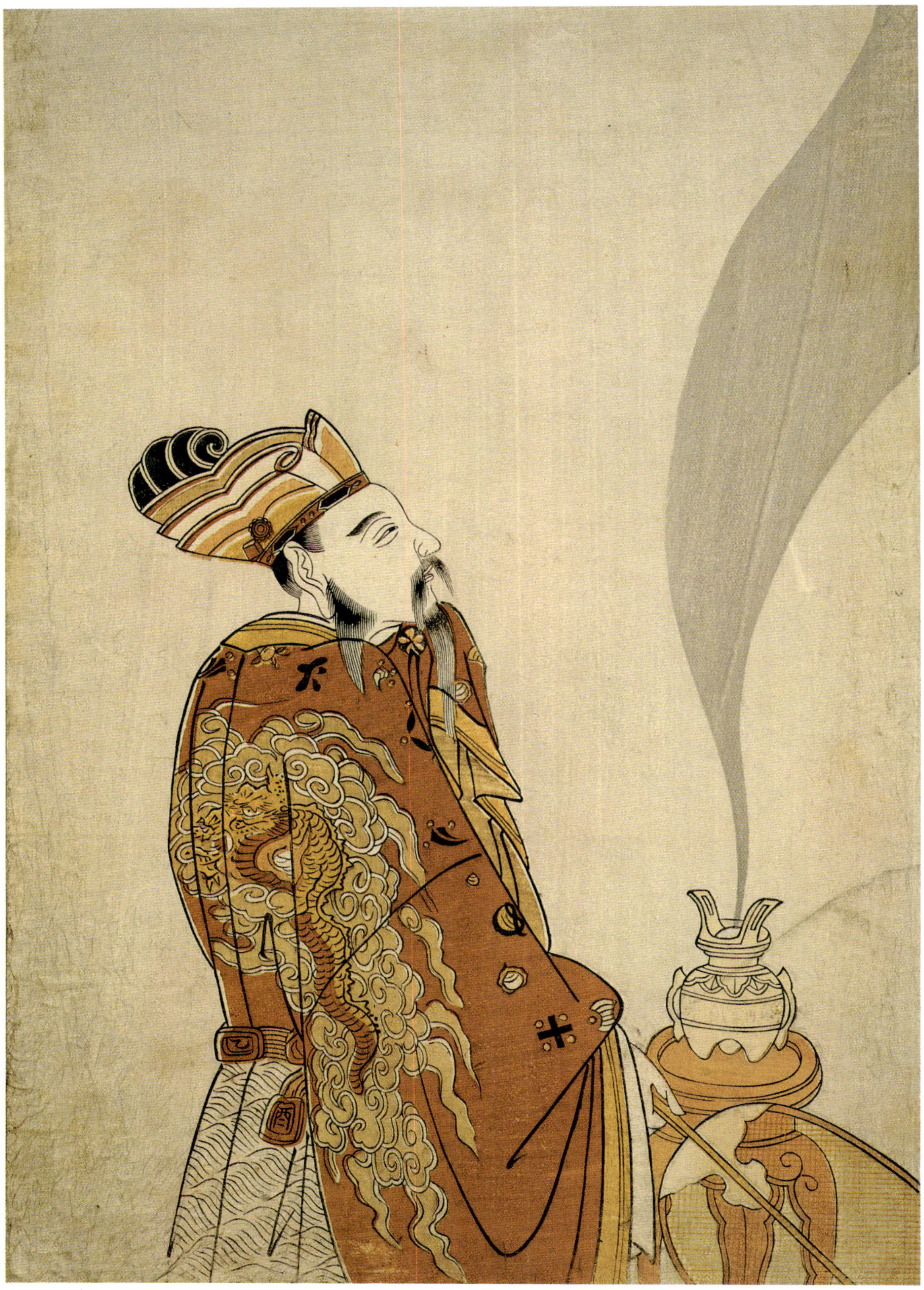

fluenced the course of *ukiyo-e* is harder to credit to him personally, because so little is known of his life, but he was probably responsible in part for new developments in the marketing and distribution of *ukiyo-e*. It used to be thought that the term *nishiki-e* (brocade pictures, or, more literally, pictures resembling cloth woven in colors), was first applied to Japanese color prints by Ōta Nampo (1749-1823), who as a young man had met Harunobu and some of his companions. In fact, the word *nishiki* appears in the title of one of Harunobu's own books, the early *Ehon shogei no nishiki* (1763), and the word for gold brocade (*kinran*) was used in another book of his, *Ehon kokinran*, published the same year. Both these contain only black-and-white illustrations, but they show that Harunobu was already alive to the analogy. Moreover, the character used for *nishiki* is found in the titles of several earlier Chinese albums printed in colors; and it is clear from texts that *nishiki-e* was the regular name for the new color prints even in Harunobu's lifetime.

He and his publishers must have been well organized to respond quickly to the demand for *nishiki-e*; but we know little about the system by which they were produced and sold at the time. Later, there was a guild of color-print wholesalers (*nishiki-e tonya*); but the earlier system was probably more informal, and less subject to government intervention. Nevertheless, it is possible to piece together the circumstances in which *nishiki-e* first came to be made, for private distribution among small groups of connoisseurs of *kyōka* (mad poem, a form of light verse in 31 syllables). The official promulgation of the calendar for 1765 happened to coincide with the opening of a new state observatory at Waradana, in the Ushigome district of Edo, and these events took place not at the beginning of the year, as one might expect, but in the sixth month. They were marked by parties at which specially designed color prints were exchanged. These prints, often bearing the pen-name of one of the connoisseurs, contain wittily concealed calendrical markings, usually the name of the year (Meiwa 2), and the sequence of long and short months chosen for it under the old Japanese system.

In the calendar prints and other privately commissioned *nishiki-e* of this early period, the role of the artist was sometimes to make a completely original design; but more often, it seems, it was to work up a crude sketch supplied by the connoisseur himself. In these cases it may be hard to attribute the final product to a single individual, not least because in *ukiyo-e* the block-cutting and printing were handled by other specialized craftsmen. Some calendar prints, in fact, bear the names of all four men: the connoisseur, the artist, the block-cutter and the printer. The best of the unsigned prints were clearly done by Harunobu himself, working especially for the *Kyosen-ren*, a group led by 'Kyosen,' or by Komatsuken, who worked for another group, the *Sakei-gumi*, led by 'Sakei.' Kyosen can be identified as the *haiku* pen-name of a bannerman (*hatamoto*) called Ōkubo Tadanobu, whose father and grandfather had been Commissioners of Finance (*kanjō-bugyō*), with the sizeable stipend of 1600 *koku*. Besides inheriting this, Kyosen had served in the Edo Castle guard until 1763. Sakei was also a bannerman, one Abe Hachinojō, for whom the artist Komatsuken (pages 68-9) worked. By profession, Komatsuken was actually a druggist, called Komatsuya Sanemon Hyakki. These men, and others in their circle, who apparently enjoyed some high connections in the government,

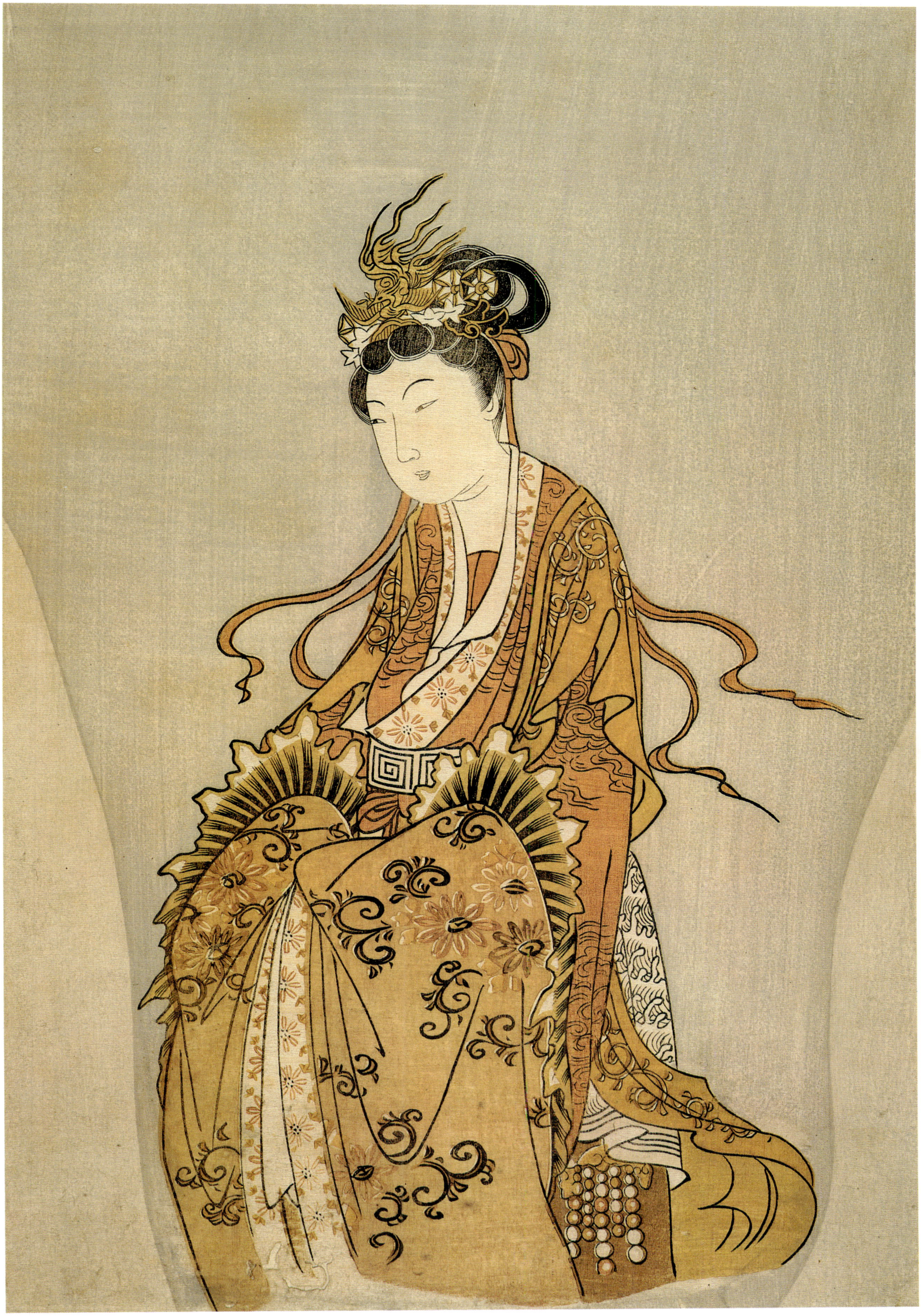

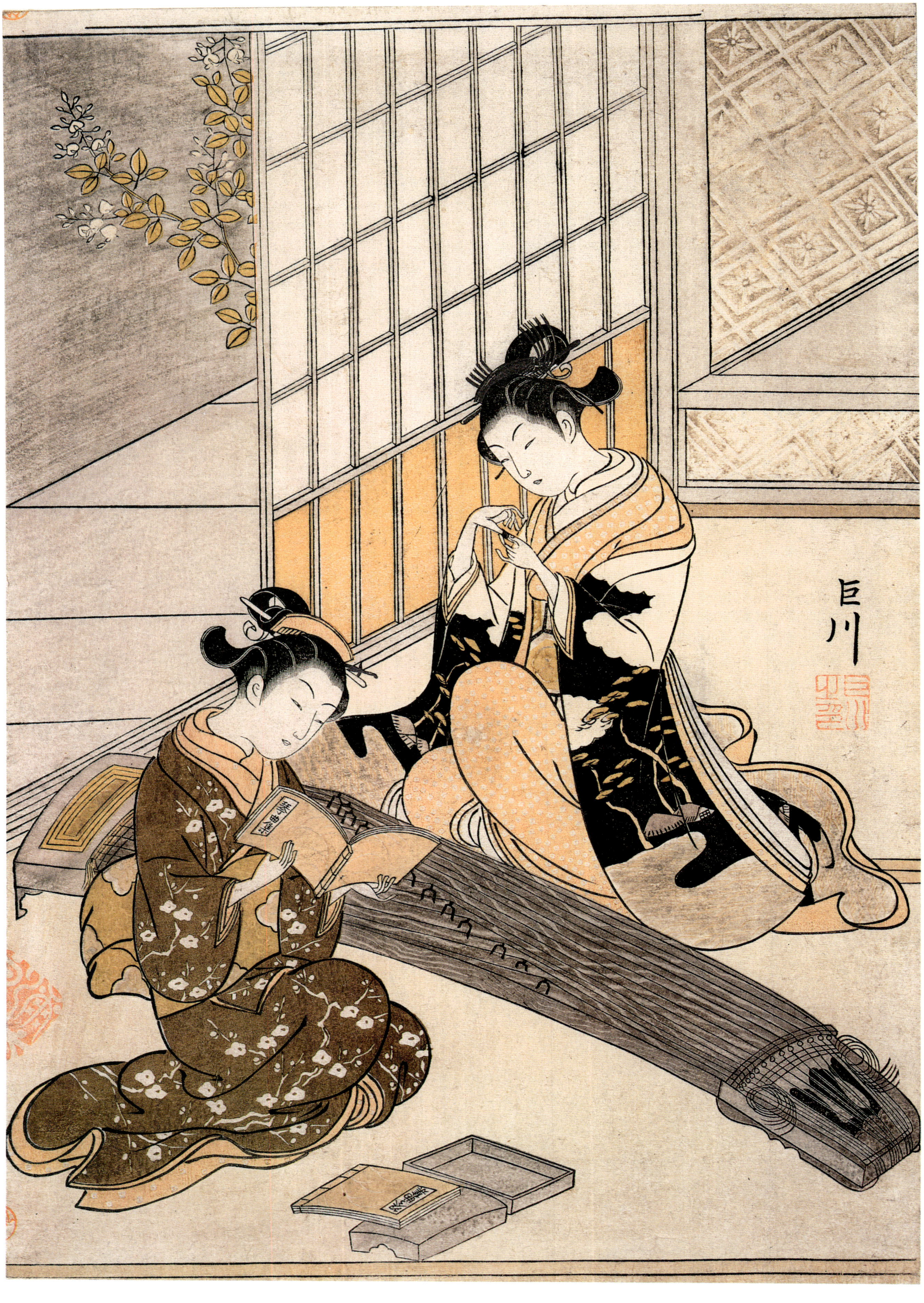
巨川

lived in or near the Ushigome district, and dabbled both in art and in various lighter forms of literature.

In 1765 more than 100 calendar prints were prepared, all by or with the aid of Harunobu. In 1766 about half this number appeared, Harunobu again being the main artist. The fashion then passed but already in 1766 *nishiki-e* had come to be available commercially. Harunobu immediately established himself as the leading artist in this movement, and some of the prints marketed in this way were reissues of calendars or other privately sponsored designs (pages 70 and 71).

Harunobu's work was an immediate success with the public; and by the time of his sudden death (on the 14th or 15th day, 6th month, 1770) he had produced over 1000 single-sheet designs, in addition to some 25 illustrated books, most of them in several volumes, and including two in full color. He also had many imitators, and some direct disciples, of whom Isoda Koryūsai (*fl* c. 1764-88; pages 72, 74, 75, and 76) went on to become a major artist in his own right.

ISODA KORYŪSAI AND THE SECOND PHASE OF THE FULL-COLOR PRINT

During the last year of Harunobu's life, his style had been developing some new characteristics. His faces became stronger and more elongated, and his bodies were more massive and powerful; he chose simple backgrounds, as in some of his earlier work; and the figures dominate the composition. This is particularly evident in his prints in the *ōban* (large print) format, a larger size which was made by cutting sheets of *hōsho* paper in half, rather than into four, as for *chūban*. In Harunobu's day these two sizes were called *ō-nishiki* and *ai-nishiki* respectively. (A third size occasionally used by Harunobu was the *koban* 'small print,' made by cutting a *hōsho* sheet into eight, and known at the time as *mago-nishiki*.)

The general effect of the late prints is heavier and even coarser, but it is idle to speculate if Harunobu was played out as an artist, or what he might have done if he had lived longer. In the hands of his successors the preferred figure type continued to change in the same way, perhaps reflecting to some extent changes in contemporary feminine fashion, or the admired female type. On the 29th day, 2nd month, 1772, a terrible fire swept through Edo, destroying most of the city. This must have temporarily darkened the optimism of both ordinary townspeople and their samurai masters. In retrospect, however, the 1770s in Edo appear as a period of relaxed and innocent hedonism, compared to the two succeeding decades, when a series of natural disasters and stern sumptuary edicts made life far less comfortable. The consequences of such public events for *ukiyo-e* are hard to gauge, or even to discern: it always created something of a fantasy world, and the artists themselves knew that they could not with impunity venture into social and political satire. Nevertheless, in addition to the myriad literary and historical allusions in *ukiyo-e*, we continue to find not only topical and topographical references, but also more subtle reflections of the ambient Kulturkreis, itself only a little less fluid. Thus prints of the 1770s particularly exhibit the qualities of *sui* and *tsū*, untranslatable terms that epitomize a casual elegance that was being cultivated by the contemporary man about town.

The sudden death of Harunobu must have caught his publishers off guard; but, as in 1765-66, they responded to the challenge quickly, and in several ways. The next few years saw re-issues of some of his prints, and of several of his illustrated

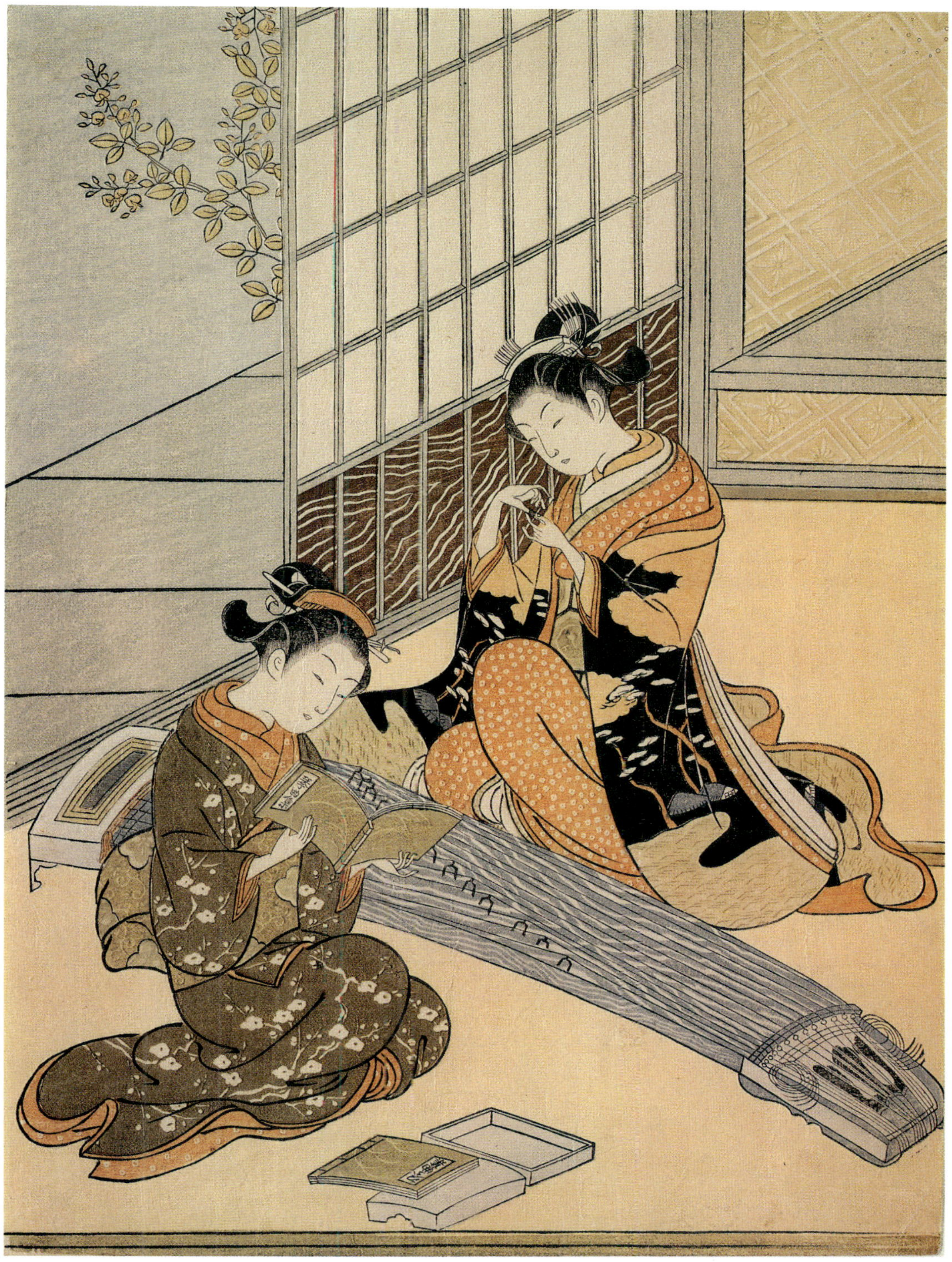

Above: Suzuki Harunobu (attr.), 'Homing Geese of the *koto* Bridges' (*Kotoji no rakugan*), State 2, c. 1766 *Zashiki hakkei* series, *chūban*. Worcester Art Museum, Worcester, MA.

Left: Suzuki Harunobu (attr.), 'Homing Geese of the *koto* Bridges' (*Kotoji no rakugan*), State 1a. *Zashiki hakkei* series, c. 1766, *chūban*, 11¼×8⅕ inches (28.5×20.8 cm). Museum of Fine Arts, Boston. This print belongs to a set of 'Eight Views in the Parlor,' which was evidently commissioned by Kyosen from Harunobu, and in its first state bears the name of Kyosen. There are variant first states of three of the designs, including *Kotoji no rakugan*, which itself exists in three variant first states. In the second state (above), for public circulation, Kyosen's name is removed. There is also a third state of this design, with the signature of Harunobu.

The 'Eight Views,' a conventional theme in Chinese and Japanese painting, are often treated lightly in *ukiyo-e*. The *Zashiki hakkei* prints take their titles from a series of poems composed in 1725. Here, the bridges of the *koto* are imagined as a flight of homing geese, and the grain of its top plank suggests rippling water.

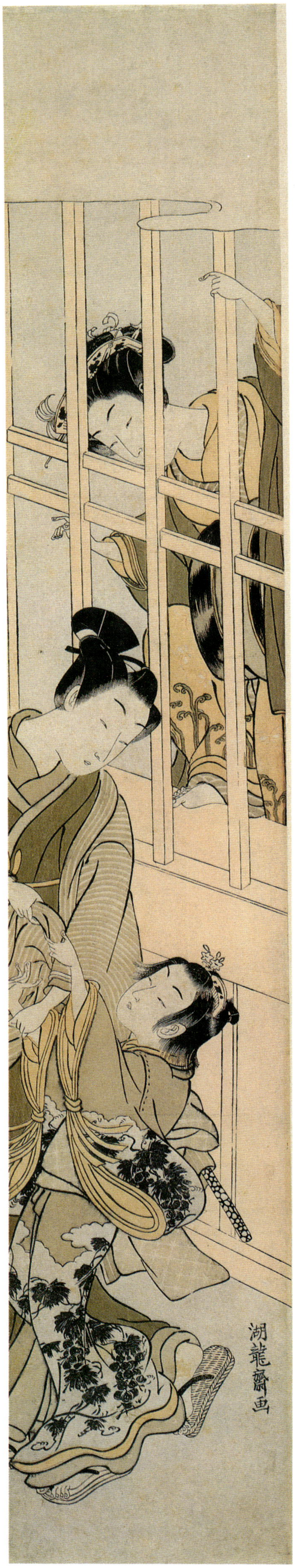

Left: Isoda Koryūsai, '*Kamuro* Soliciting a Client,' *hashira-e*, earlier 1770s, 28$\frac{3}{8}$×5$\frac{3}{16}$ inches (72.1×13.1 cm). Rijksmuseum, Amsterdam. The young attendant (*kamuro*) of a courtesan tugs at the sleeve of a handsome young samurai, while her mistress encourages her from behind the bars of the *mise* (display room) of her house in the Yoshiwara.

Right: Komai Yoshinobu, 'Two Courtesans with a Love Letter, late 1760s, *chūban*, 10$\frac{1}{3}$×7$\frac{7}{8}$ inches (26.2×19.9 cm). Museum of Fine Arts, Boston. The poem is by a distinguished Tendai monk, Shinkaku Hōshi (d 1182), and reads:

koi sureba	When we are in love
ukimi sae koso	torments of the flesh may make
oshimarure	us rue it – not least
onaji yo dani	when we reflect that this world
suman to omoeba	we live in is still the same

books. Further, there were new designs by artists who had been or could claim to have been his pupils, and who used in their brush-names the elements *Haru-* or *-nobu*. There were also several other prints, indeed series of prints, which were made in small editions, and bore the signature *Harunobu ga* (painted by Harunobu). But these works by the scholar of Dutch studies and printmaker Shiba Kōkan (1747-1818) are stylistically distinct from those of the master himself, even in his late work, and they are artistically inferior. For this purpose Kōkan is designated as Harunobu II – even if he does not really deserve the title. It has long been known that he did such imitations of Harunobu, but it has only recently become clear, as a result of close study of the period, just which prints they were. After a year or two Kōkan changed his signature to *Harushige ga* (occasionally *Suzuki Harushige ga*); and he adopted also a more personal style, of which receding perspective in the Dutch manner is a conspicuous feature. Some time in the early 1770s, however, he abandoned *ukiyo-e* altogether, in favor of other pursuits.

Other pupils or followers who had short-lived careers as *ukiyo-e* artists include Yamamoto Fujinobu (*fl* 1750-70); Suzuki Haruji (*fl* 1760-70), Kikugawa Hidenobu (*fl* c. 1764-81), Masunobu, Mitsunobu (*fl* c. 1730-60), Naonobu and Komai Yoshinobu (*fl* 1765-70). Yoshinobu is known for an attractive small group of prints in the manner of Harunobu (page 73), the others for no more than one or two designs each.

Other artists who came under the influence of Harunobu, but are not known to have studied with him, include such contemporaries as Ishikawa Toyonobu, Kitao Shigemasa and Katsukawa Shunshō; but his main artistic heir was Isoda Koryūsai, who does seem to have been a pupil.

A unique pillar print in the Museum of Fine Arts, Boston, bears an inscription by Koryūsai, which states:

> The woodblock for this picture left by the late Suzuki Harunobu had already been cut, and somebody has given it to me to color. I have some familiarity with painting and could not bear to see it as it was: and although I do not know Shunshi's [ie Harunobu's] own way I have finished it off by adding my own clumsy brushwork.

A poem follows:

> Even violet
> is not a color which will rob
> his black ink of its luster!

Apart from this direct evidence of an artistic relationship between the two men, we have some early prints which bear the signature *Koryūsai Haruhiro*. It is

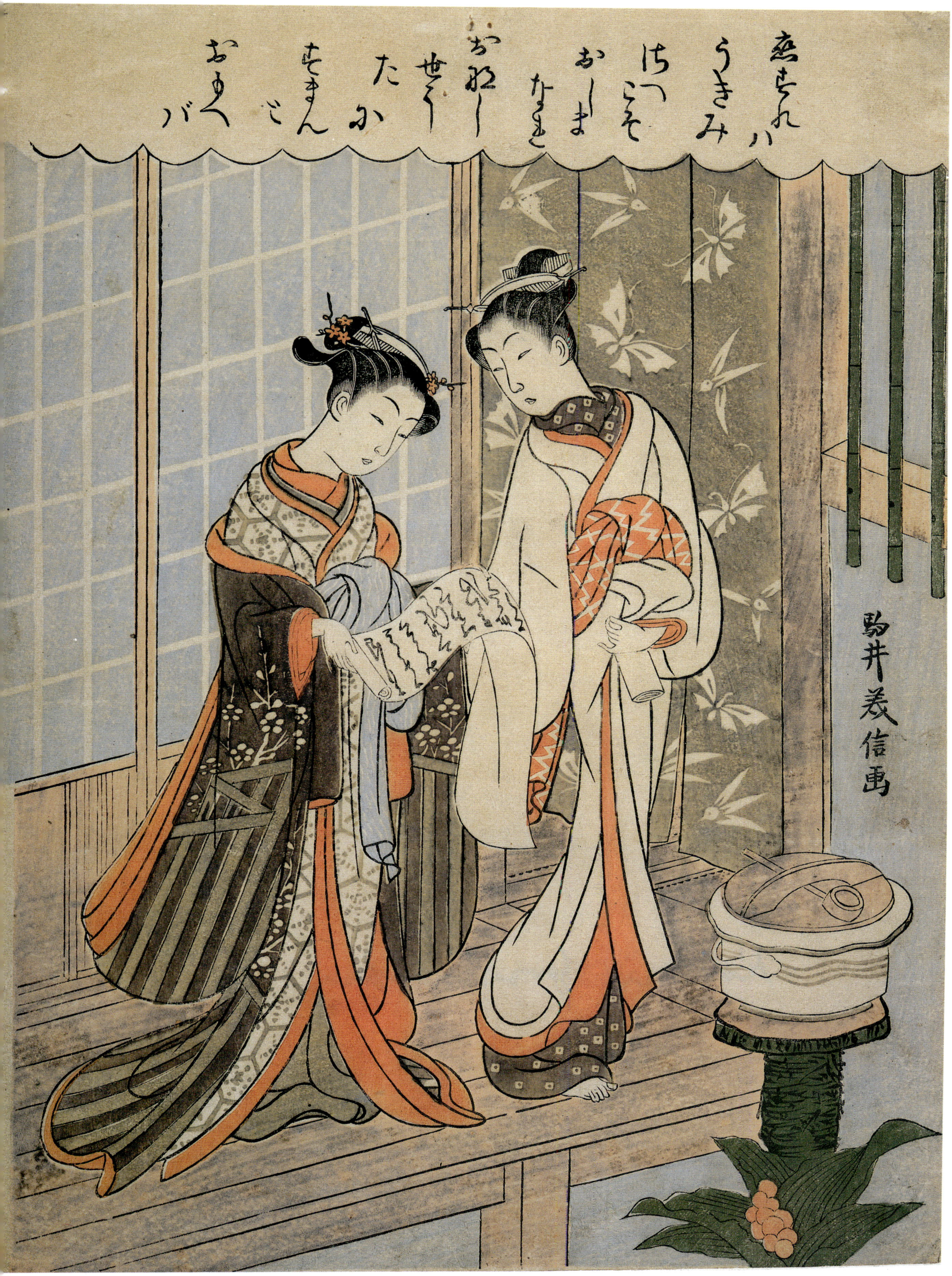
駒井美信画

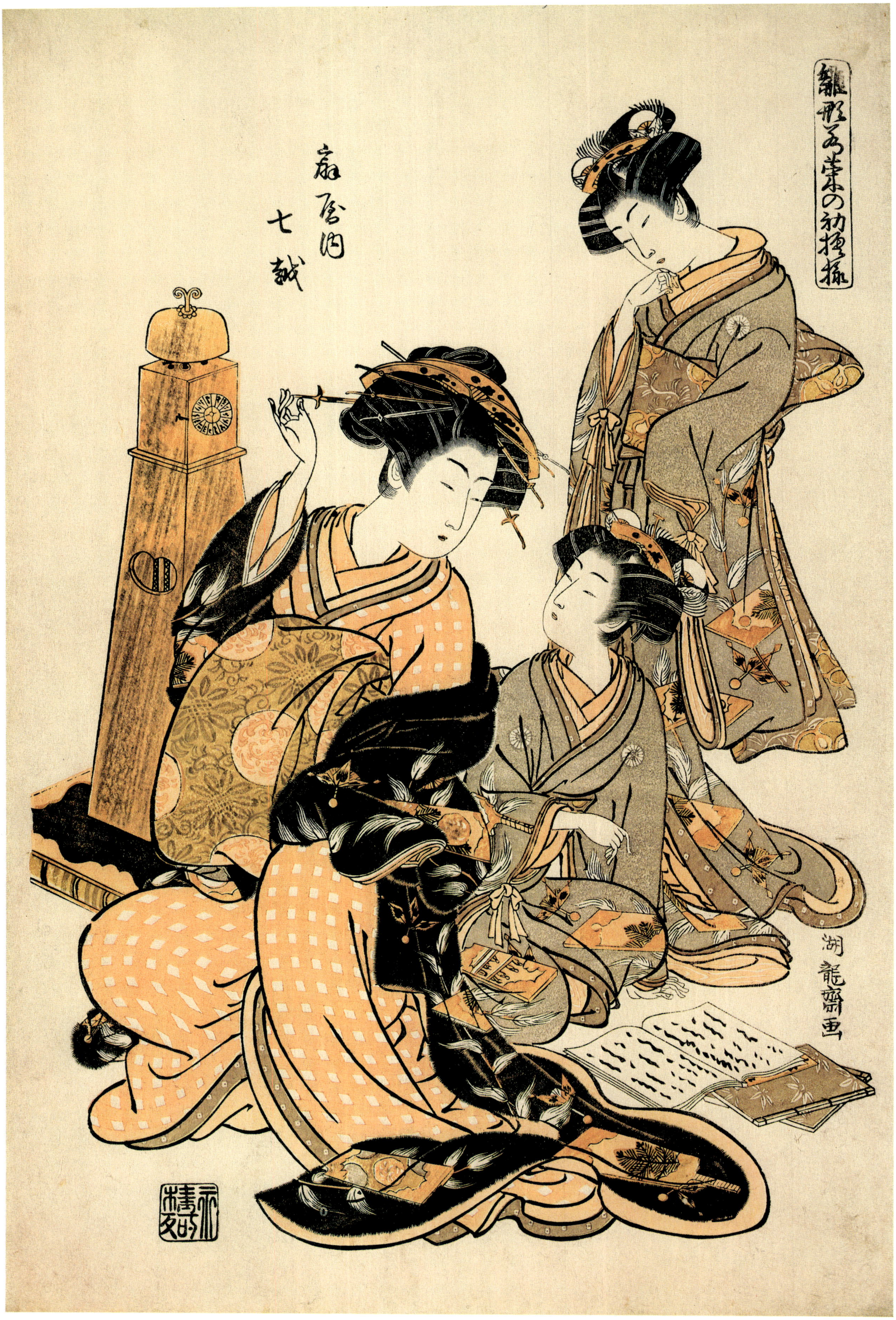
雛形若菜の初模様
扇屋内
七越
湖龍斎画

possible that these prints, like those of Shiba Kōkan, were all done after Harunobu's death, but in this case it is charitable to suppose that Harunobu himself bestowed the name *Haruhiro* on his pupil.

Koryūsai was a samurai. The Edo writer Shikitei Samba, in notes which he added between about 1818 and 1821 to the manuscript of *Ukiyo-e ruikō*, our most important, yet at times sketchy, source for the lives of *ukiyo-e* artists, says: 'His common name (*zokushō*) was Shōbei, and he was a *rōnin* [wave man, or samurai without allegiance] of the Tsuchiya house, in Ogawa-machi.' Samba further informs us that Koryūsai's clan name (*sei*) was Isoda and his ordinary name (*na*) was Masakatsu, and these two names do appear on some of his prints. One print bears, beside his signature, the inscription *Bukō Yagenbori no inshi*, 'Hermit of Yagenbori, in [the city of] Edo, Musashi [Province].' This address dates from the later part of his career, and it has been presumed that he gave up print-making in the early 1780s. Two illustrated books, one published in 1781 and the other a few years later, reveal artistic interests which reached beyond *ukiyo-e* and, as a samurai, he may have received instruction in the Kanō school of painting. Unusually for an *ukiyo-e* artist, he was awarded the honorary religious rank of *hokkyō* (Bridge of the Law), and occasionally used this title, even in his prints.

Almost all Koryūsai's considerable output of *ukiyo-e* prints belongs to the 1770s. His early work is hard to distinguish from that of Harunobu, but a turning point was reached with the series entitled *Hinagata wakana no hatsu moyō*, 'First Designs of the Young Leaves, in Pattern Form' (page 74), published jointly by Nishimura and Tsutaya Jūsaburō. This series of *ōban* prints, numbering over 140 designs, appeared during the later 1770s, probably being continued over several New Year seasons. It depicts courtesans and their attendants, from individual houses in the Yoshiwara. The names and affiliations of the girls are given, and they are portrayed as statuesque, richly dressed beauties, coiffured in the new *tōrōbin* and *shusubin* fashions, with hair combed back over crescent-shaped struts and secured with decorative pins and combs. These fashions swept through Edo around 1775, and the less complex styles of Harunobu's time and of the early 1770s completely disappeared. It is easy to guess that Koryūsai's prints helped to popularize the new styles; they also helped to establish *ōban* as the standard size for *nishiki-e*. The series was continued, in the early 1780s, with a further eleven designs by Torii Kiyonaga, and several other artists copied the idea.

Koryūsai's early work (page 72) closely resembles that of Harunobu, and in many cases is actually based on it. His erotic albums in particular are often confused with those of Harunobu. In general, his faces have sharper chins than those of Harunobu, and they are slightly longer. The curves of his drapery are crisper, and the lines of the blocks are thicker and firmer. His palette includes a mineral orange pigment, which had appeared already in Harunobu's later work, and, from the middle 1770s, bright rose and ocher colors are quite prominent. Both before and after beginning the *Hinagata* series he produced a continuous stream of the smaller *chūban* prints, often in small sets of four, six, eight or twelve designs on the same theme. Besides these, there are a number of exquisite single prints of the type called *kachōga*, (pictures of flowers and birds; page 75). Only one or two impressions of most of Koryūsai's prints survive today, so that the full extent of his output has been

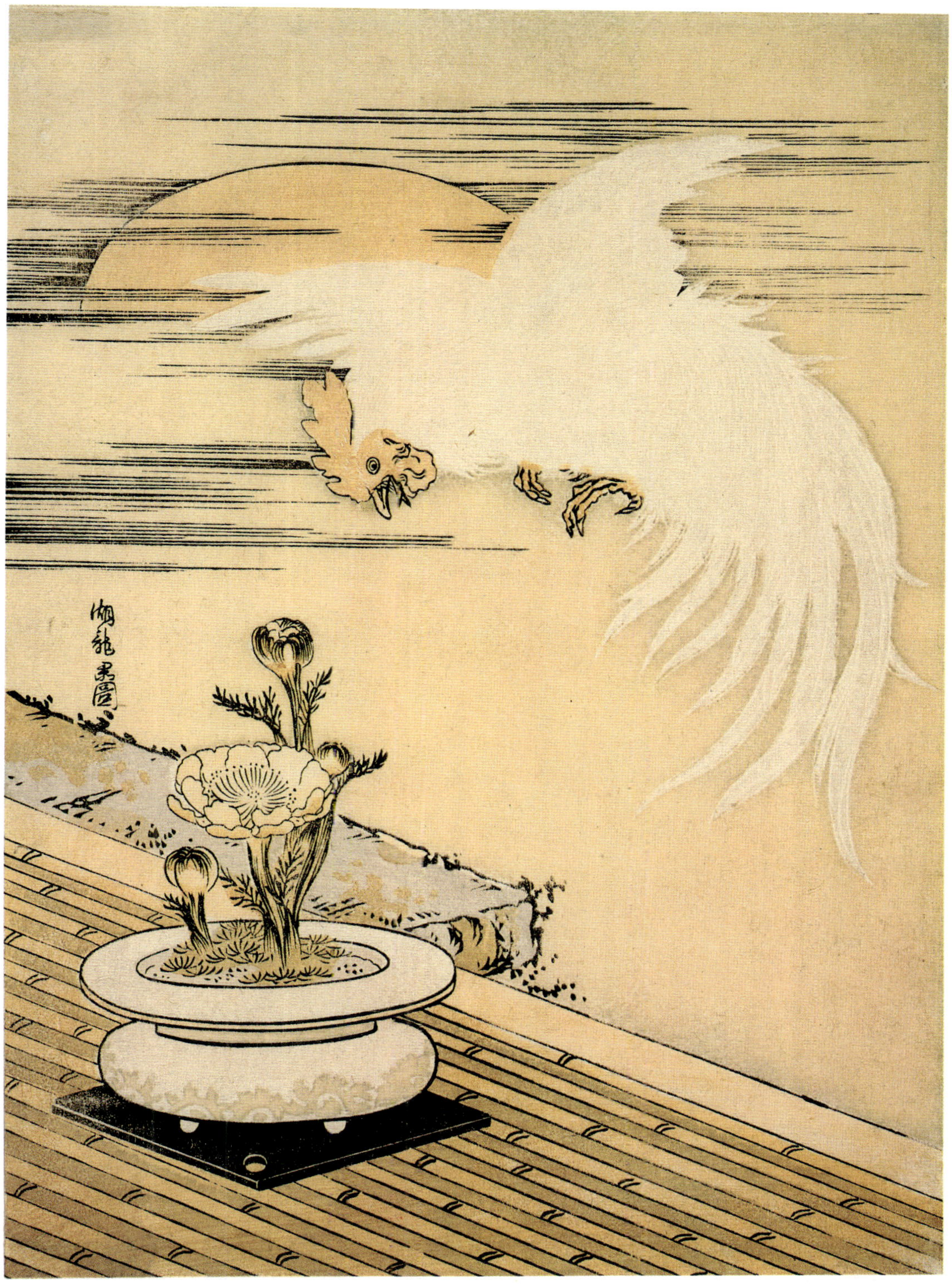

Above: Isoda Koryūsai, 'White Cockerel and Pot of Adonis,' early 1770s, *chūban*, $9\frac{13}{16}\times7\frac{1}{4}$ inches (25.1×18.4 cm). Art Institute of Chicago. A print for the New Year, with auspicious symbols. The Japanese name for the adonis, *fukujusō*, literally means 'grass of good fortune and longevity.' The white cockerel, personifying *yang*, wards off evil influences. The rising sun at once symbolizes Japan and announces a new dawn.

Left: Isoda Koryūsai: *Ōgiya-uchi Nanakoshi* (Nanakoshi, from the Ōgiya), from the series: *Hinagata wakana no hatsu moyō* (First Designs of the Young Leaves, in Pattern Form), later 1770s, *ōban*, $15\frac{5}{16}\times10\frac{3}{8}$ inches (38.9×26.4 cm). Metropolitan Museum of Art, New York. The 'Young Leaves' of the title are courtesans, who are depicted in new kimono for the year. *Hinagata*, 'Pattern Form,' refers to the pattern books for kimono, which were often illustrated by *ukiyo-e* artists. The Ōgiya, one of the best-known establishments in the Yoshiwara, was at Edo-chō, 1-*chōme*. Several other prints of the *Hinagata* series portray girls from it. The pillar clock in this print is of a type which had just been developed, under Dutch influence.

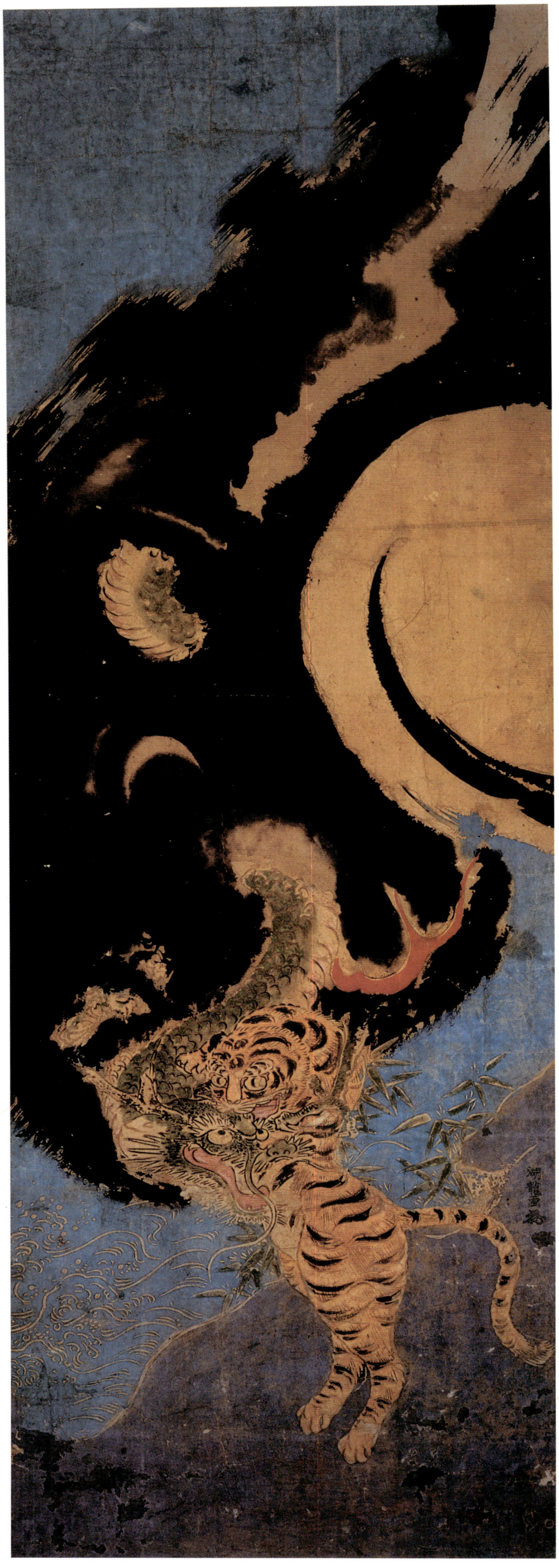

Left: Isoda Koryūsai: 'Dragon and Tiger,' later 1770s, Large *hashira-e*, $30\frac{11}{16}\times10\frac{13}{16}$ inches (77.9×27.4 cm). British Museum, London. Although paired paintings of a dragon and a tiger are common in Chinese and Japanese art, it is unusual to find them in a single work, locked in combat, or rather sexual embrace. However, *qi* (material force) in its *yang* form is represented by a dragon, and in its *yin* form by a tiger. The point where the two forces cross, or unite, is considered to be the most auspicious, charged, and balanced, in geomancy and kindred arts.

masked. A complete listing would run to well over a thousand designs, but there is still no monograph on his work, even in Japanese.

Koryūsai is best known for his pillar prints (page 72). This genre seems to have been invented by Okumura Masanobu in the early 1740s, as an adaptation of the traditional hanging scroll (*kakemono*). The term *hashira-e* denoted both the wider prints of this type, made by cutting a *hōsho* sheet vertically into two, or by joining two *ōban* pieces vertically; and the more common *hashira-kakushi*, 'pillar-hiders,' which were narrower, and were normally made by cutting a *hōsho* sheet vertically into four. Harunobu himself turned out more than 150 such long narrow designs, and Koryūsai did at least 250, including some of his most distinguished work. Among them is a small group of wide *hashira-e* in the Kanō school style, using *karazuri* and unorthodox painterly coloring effects (left). The main inspiration of these prints is Kanō painting, but in their use of dense black they remind us of Harunobu's own experiments with this effect.

The decade after Harunobu's death saw several other artists rise to prominence. One of these is Kitao Shigemasa, who enjoyed a long career in *ukiyo-e*. He illustrated his first book in 1760, and his first *nishiki-e* was a calendar for 1765. His output of single-sheet prints was surprisingly small, but includes some fine designs (page 77), and he had some outstanding pupils: Kitao Masayoshi (1764-1824), Kitao Masanobu (1761-1816) and Kubo Shunman (1757-1820). As with so many other early *nishiki-e* artists, his work has never been subjected to careful study.

Right: Kitao Shigemasa (1739-1820; attr.), 'Picking Goldfish from a Wooden Tank,' later 1770s, *ōban*, $14\frac{1}{16}\times9\frac{13}{16}$ inches (35.7×25.0 cm). Metropolitan Museum of Art, New York. The first recorded goldfish merchant in Japanese history had his business at Ueno in the Genroku period (1688-1703). By the 1720s goldfish were becoming more popular; and from the 1750s there were open-air shops selling them, especially during the summer months. In the 1770s these were superseded by wandering goldfish-sellers, one of whom is apparently depicted here selecting fish for a customer.

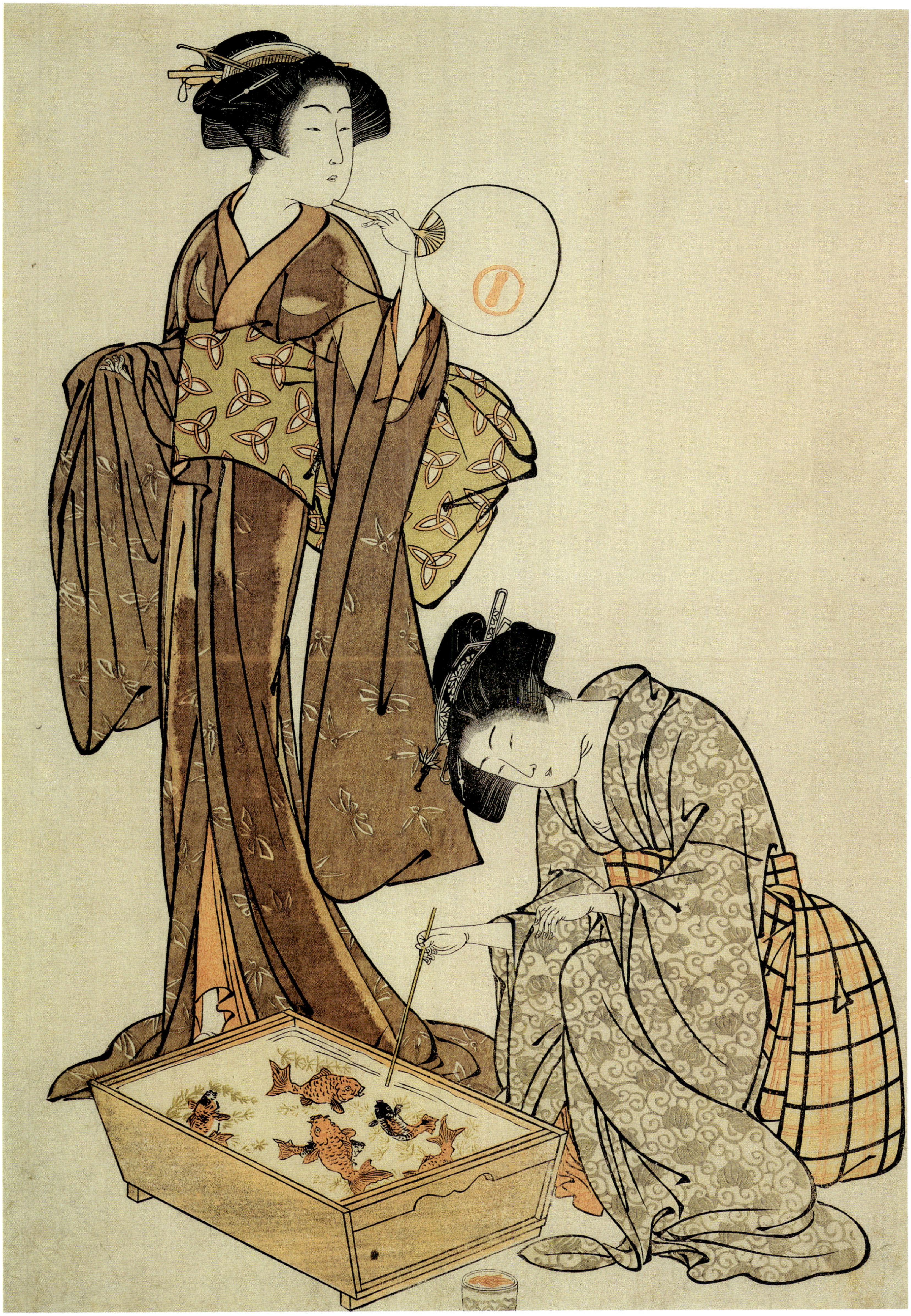

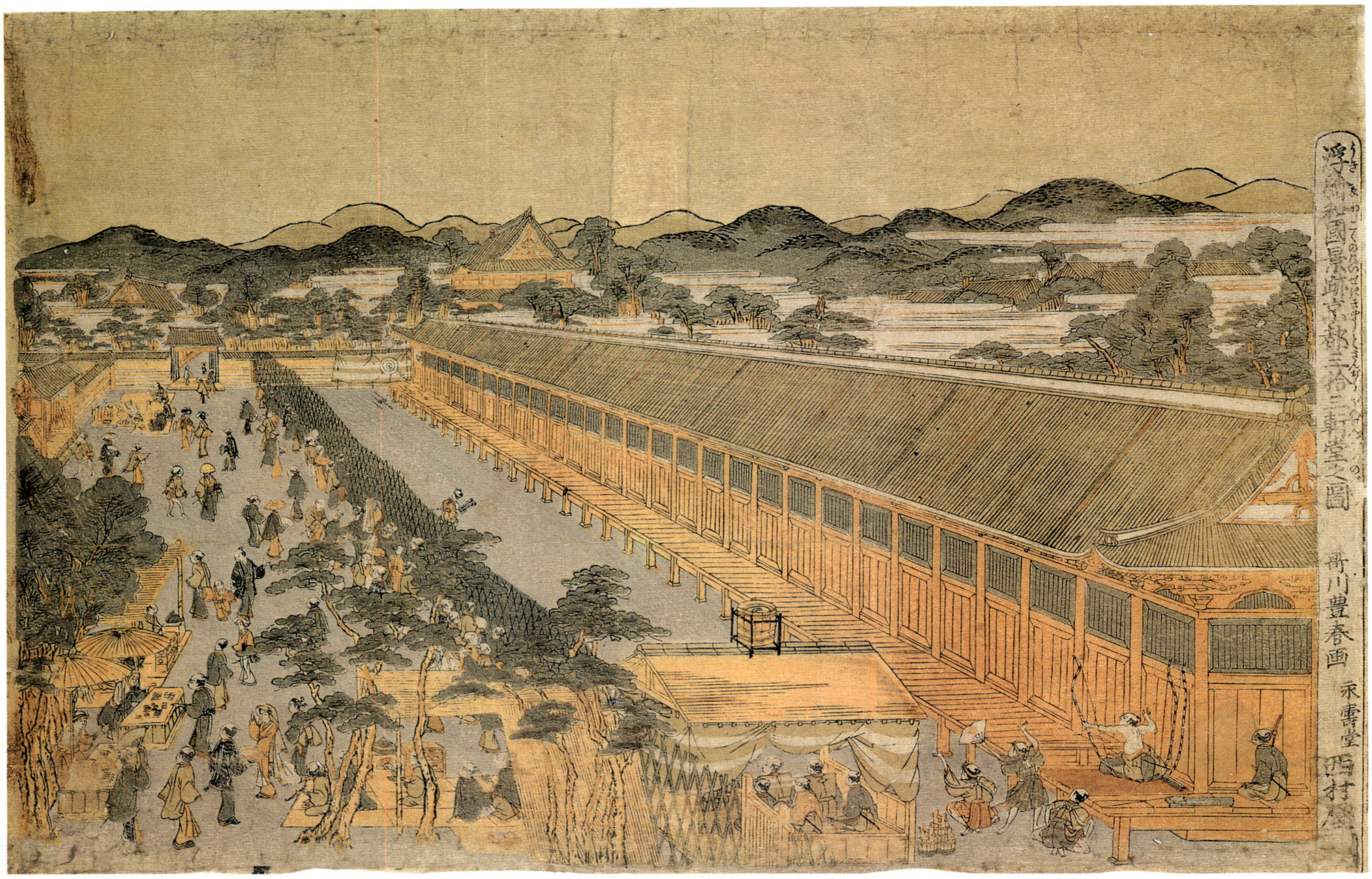

Above: Utagawa Toyoharu: *Fukagawa Sanjūsangendō tōshiya no zu* (Picture of the Piercing Arrows at the Hall of Thirty-Three Bays, Fukagawa), late 1770s, *ōban yoko-e*, 9⁹⁄₁₆×13¾ inches (23.3×35.0 cm). Portland Art Museum, Portland, Oregon. The Hall of Thirty-Three Bays, Fukagawa, modeled on the historic one in Kyoto, was first built in 1642 at Asakusa. After being destroyed by fire it was re-built in 1701 on a site near the Hachiman Shrine at Tomigaoka, Fukagawa. It was designed above all for archery practice, and survived until 1872.

Right: Katsukawa Shunshō, 'Nakamura Nakazō I and Iwai Hanshirō IV in Performance,' 1771, *hosoban*, 11¹⁵⁄₁₆×5⅜ inches (30.3×13.7 cm). Achenbach Foundation for Graphic Art, San Francisco. Nakamura Nakazō I (1736-90) and Iwai Hanshirō IV (1747-1800) were two of the most celebrated actors of the day, in male and female roles respectively. They appeared together on several occasions at the Nakamura-za in the early 1770s, the period to which on stylistic grounds this print must belong. A performance in late 1771 has been suggested, but does not quite fit what we see here. The most likely identification is a *nagauta* (long song) scene entitled *Wada sakamori eiga kagami*, from the New Year production in 1773, when Nakazō played the oil-seller Kuheiji, and Hanshirō played Temmaya Osome (a courtesan in love with him?). The piece apparently combined elements of the 'Wada's Wine-Feast' story (from the Soga Brothers cycle) and Chikamatsu's *Sonezaki shinjū*, 'Love Suicides at Sonezaki.'

Another interesting artist of the period was Utagawa Toyoharu (1735-1814), whose early studies were in Kyōto and whose main teacher in Edo seems to have been the Kanō painter and book illustrator Toriyama Sekien (1712-88). Sekien is also famous as the teacher of Utamaro. Toyoharu is best known for his *uki-e*, 'floating pictures,' prints which use extreme receding perspective and were intended to be viewed through an optical device, the *megane*. The models for these prints, and the device itself, were Dutch: the 1760s and 1770s witnessed a wave of interest in Dutch science and material culture – or rather what could be gleaned about it through the Dutch trade mission in Nagasaki. We have already seen how Shiba Kōkan tried to incorporate Dutch perspective into his *ukiyo-e*; and the prints of Harunobu, Koryūsai (page 74) and others also occasionally reflect the interest in Dutch things. Indeed, this was to become one of the main intellectual currents behind the Meiji Restoration movement of the mid-nineteenth century; and certain of the shoguns too displayed curiosity about the West, though not enough to guarantee long-term survival for their regime.

Toyoharu's earliest prints, in *uki-e* and other formats, belong to the later 1760s, and over the next twenty of thirty years he produced a long series of topographical views, mainly of scenes in and around Edo (page 78), but also from other regions of Japan. Some were on themes taken from Chinese or Japanese literature. Toyoharu deserves to be regarded as a pioneer of the landscape print in Japan, though comparable woodcut illustration (in black-and-white) can be found in a number of earlier gazetteers (the genre known as *meisho-ki* ('chronicles of famous places). In addition, as founder of the Utagawa school, Toyoharu holds a place of honor in *ukiyo-e* history. His own direct pupils included Toyohiro (1773-1828; the teacher of Hiroshige) and Toyokuni I (1769-1825; the teacher of the Utagawa artists Kunimasa, 1773-1810, Kunisada, 1786-1864, Kuniyoshi, 1797-1861, and many others). In the 1790s, thanks to his Kanō connections, Toyoharu was put in charge of a team of restorers of the Tokugawa mausoleum at Nikkō.

From time to time Toyoharu even designed prints for the theater. This was traditionally the preserve of the Torii line of artists, but in the 1770s the spotlight passed to two outsiders, Bunchō and Shunshō, who together breathed new life into the Kabuki print. Ippitsusai Bunchō worked above all in the *hosoban* 'narrow print' format which had long been conventional for actor prints, but he used *nishiki-e* technique, and his figures occupy more of the available space than in the old *benizuri-e*. Bunchō also used the *chūban* format, for domestic scenes and for small sets on literary and other themes (page 67), in the manner of Harunobu and Koryūsai. His prints are all individually composed, and their distinctive flavor makes one regret that so little is known about this artist and his work, even if he does not have the range, verve or historical significance of his more famous contemporaries.

In 1770 Bunchō together with Harunobu collaborated on a sumptuous color-printed book of actor-portraits. This three-volume publication, *Ehon butai ōgi* (The Picture Book of Stage Fans), may have been commissioned by the proprietor of the Nakamura-za, one of the main Kabuki theaters in Edo; the blocks for it were cut by Endō Matsugorō (also called Endō Goroku), who did a lot of work for Harunobu, including calendar prints and book illustrations. *Ehon butai ōgi* was a commercial success, being reprinted twice before 1772, and it did much to launch the careers of both Bunchō and the other illustrator, Katsukawa Shunshō.

Shunshō, who may have hailed from Western Japan, and like Koryūsai was of samurai origin, shared with Bunchō (and with Shigemasa) an interest in *haiku* poetry. *Ehon butai ōgi* contains a collection of *haiku* about the stage. The first syllable of Shunshō's name is written with the same character as the *Haru-* of Harunobu, but Shunshō's teacher was the minor *ukiyo-e* artist Miyagawa (later Katsukawa) Shunsui, who is known chiefly as a painter and book illustrator. Another teacher was the painter Kō Sūkoku (1730-1804), a follower of Hanabusa Itchō (1652-1724). In his early work as a single-sheet print artist Shunshō was inevitably influenced strongly by Harunobu, but, like Bunchō, and in marked contrast to Harunobu, he chose to specialize in prints of the stage, above all, *hosoban* of Kabuki actors in particular stage roles (page 79). Such prints became a staple product of Shunshō and his school, being frequently designed as diptychs or triptychs (page 80). Although the overall standard of these *pièces d'occasion* is high, their similarity can be daunting to the researcher who tries to identify and date them. As a result, there is still no complete listing of Shunshō's oeuvre, which spans some 25 years of unceasing activity until his death in 1793.

Shunshō is notable, however, for the variety as well as the quantity of his work, which includes also many prints in *chūban* and *ōban* format, and which extends well beyond the Kabuki theater, to embrace the world of the courtesan, sumo wrestling, landscape, military subjects and so on. In this diversity of subject matter he was emulated by certain of his pupils, who include several celebrated names from the end of the eighteenth century: Shunkō (1743-1812; page 81), Shun'ei (1762-1819); Shunchō (*fl* c. 1780-95); and Shunrō (later Hokusai; 1760-

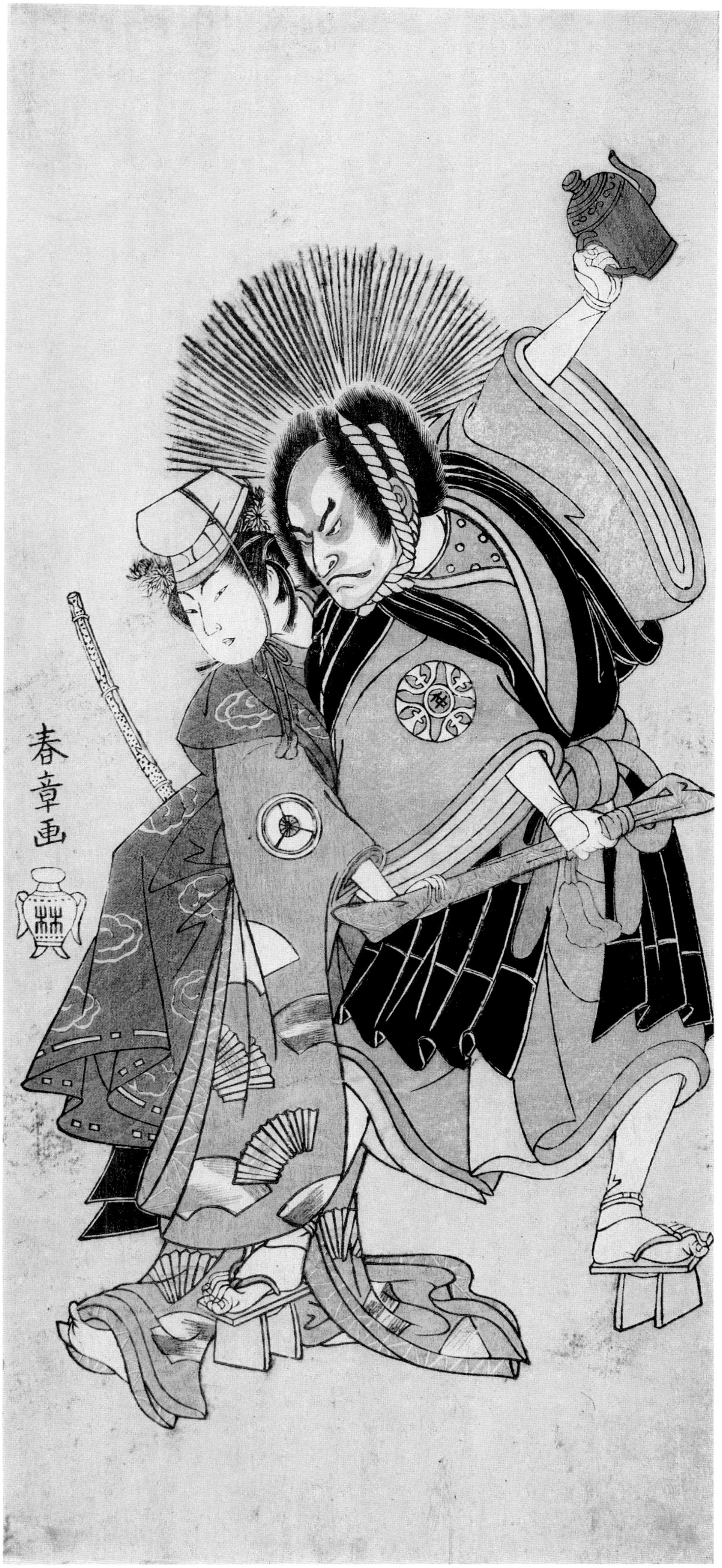

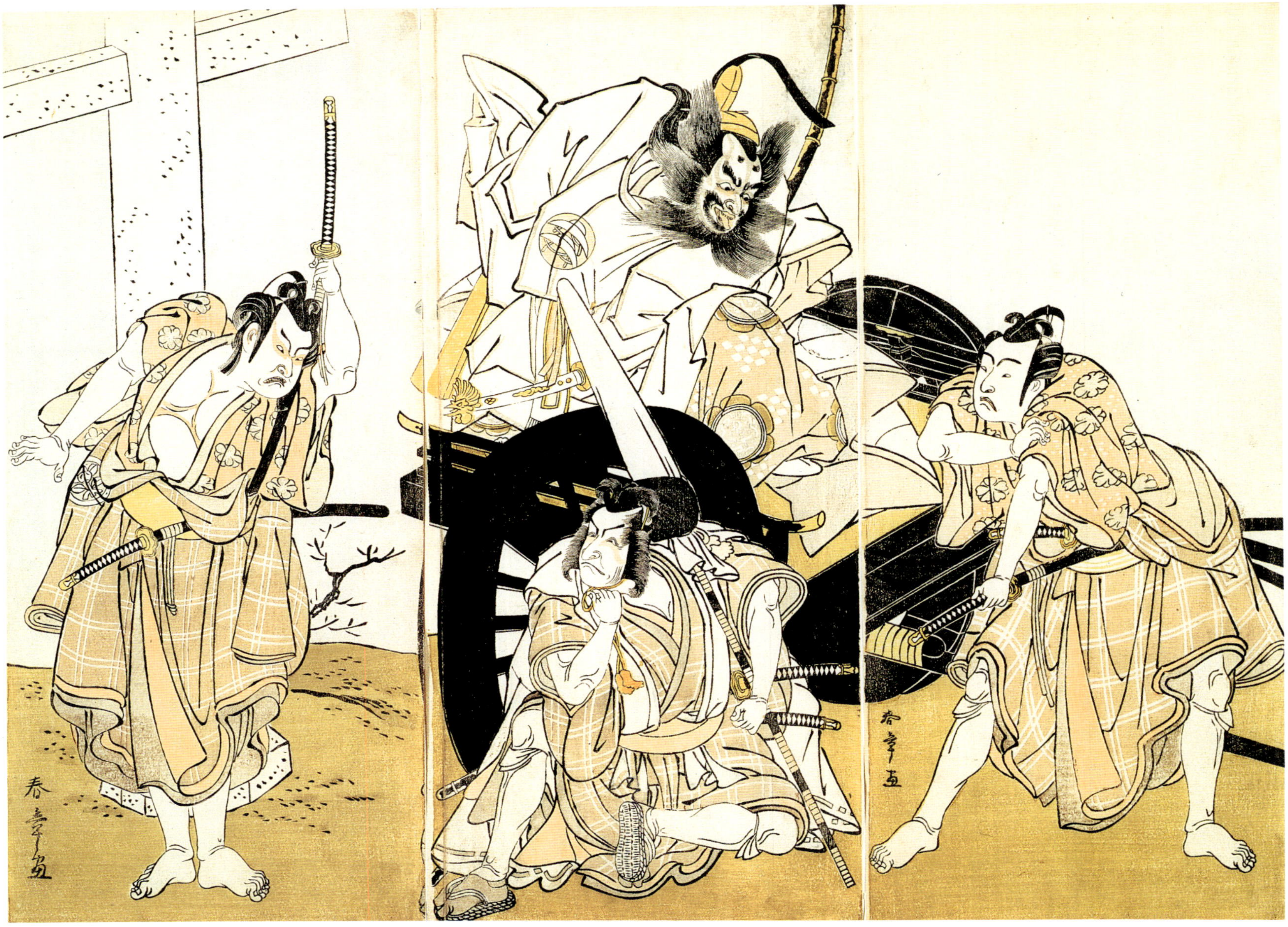

Above: Katsukawa Shunshō, 'Ichikawa Yaozō II as Sakuramaru, Nakajima Mihoemon II as Fujiwara no Shihei, Ichikawa Ebizō II as Matsuōmaru, and Ichimura Uzaemon IX as Umeōmaru,' *hosoban* triptych, $12\frac{5}{16}\times5\frac{11}{16}$ inches (31.2×14.4 cm) [R], $12\frac{5}{16}\times5\frac{13}{16}$ inches (31.2×14.7 cm) [C], $12\frac{5}{16}\times5\frac{9}{16}$ inches (31.2×14.2 cm) [L]. 1776. Art Institute of Chicago. This fine *hosoban* triptych illustrates *Kuruma-biki*, 'Pulling at the Carriage,' Act IV from the well-known play *Sugawara denju tenarai kagami*, originally written in 1746 by Takeda Izumo and others. In fact the *Kuruma-biki* scene is an addition made for the Kabuki adaptation of this puppet play. We see Sakuramaru, Matsuōmaru and Umeōmaru, three sons of the courtier and calligrapher Sugawara no Michizane (845-903), with their father's nemesis Fujiwara no Shihei in his carriage, which they have partially dismembered, at the Yoshida Shrine in Kyōto. The performance shown here was at the Ichimura-za, in the 7th month, 1776.

1849). While the founding of the Katsukawa School was technically attributed to Shunsui, Shunshō was more important by far, both as an artist and as a teacher (as in the fifteenth-sixteenth centuries Kanō Motonobu was more important than his father Kanō Masanobu). In 1776 Shunshō collaborated with Shigemasa in a memorable album about courtesans, *Seirō bijin awase sugata kagami* (A Mirror of the Forms of the Beauties of the Greenhouses Compared, see page 231 and altogether he illustrated some fifteen books, either on his own or with another artist. Shunshō also enjoys a well-deserved reputation for his paintings of female beauties and other subjects, which are polished works of art and bear witness to his early training in this medium. Of the various artists discussed in this chapter, Shunshō is the only one to have achieved real distinction as a painter as well as a print-maker.

The various natural disasters of the 1770s – drought, followed by floods, plague, and volcanic eruptions – had scarcely interrupted the even tenor of life in Edo, which was quickly re-built after the fire of 1772. Their effect may have been cumulative, however, for in 1783 a severe famine spread throughout the country. The price of rice escalated, and the population of some regions was decimated. In Edo itself there were acute shortages, and rioting. In 1784 an attempt was made on the life of the Chamberlain, Tanuma Okitsugu (1719-88), who was blamed for the catastrophes, and he was demoted in 1786. The shogun Ieharu (1737-86; r. 1760-86), who since his accession in 1760 had advanced and protected Tanuma, and who probably knew personally Kyosen and some of his friends, also died in 1786. These events, which ushered in a period of retrenchment, and greater government intervention in cultural as well as economic life, can be taken as marking the end of the second phase of *nishiki-e* and, remarkably, the beginning of its maturity as an art-form.

Right: Katsukawa Shunkō, 'Ichikawa Danjūrō V as Kazusa Gorobyōe Tadamitsu,' 1780, *aiban*, $12\frac{11}{16}\times8\frac{7}{8}$ inches (32.2×22.5 cm). Art Institute of Chicago. There are countless prints of Ichikawa Danjūrō V (1741-1806), whose prominent nose makes him easy to recognize. This particular one has been connected with a performance in the eleventh month, 1780, at the Nakamura-za, in which he appeared together with Nakamura Nakazō I (cf page 78). As Tadamitsu, Danjūrō visits the Mishima Shrine (in Shizuoka Prefecture). The idea for this fine portrait print is taken from Shunshō.

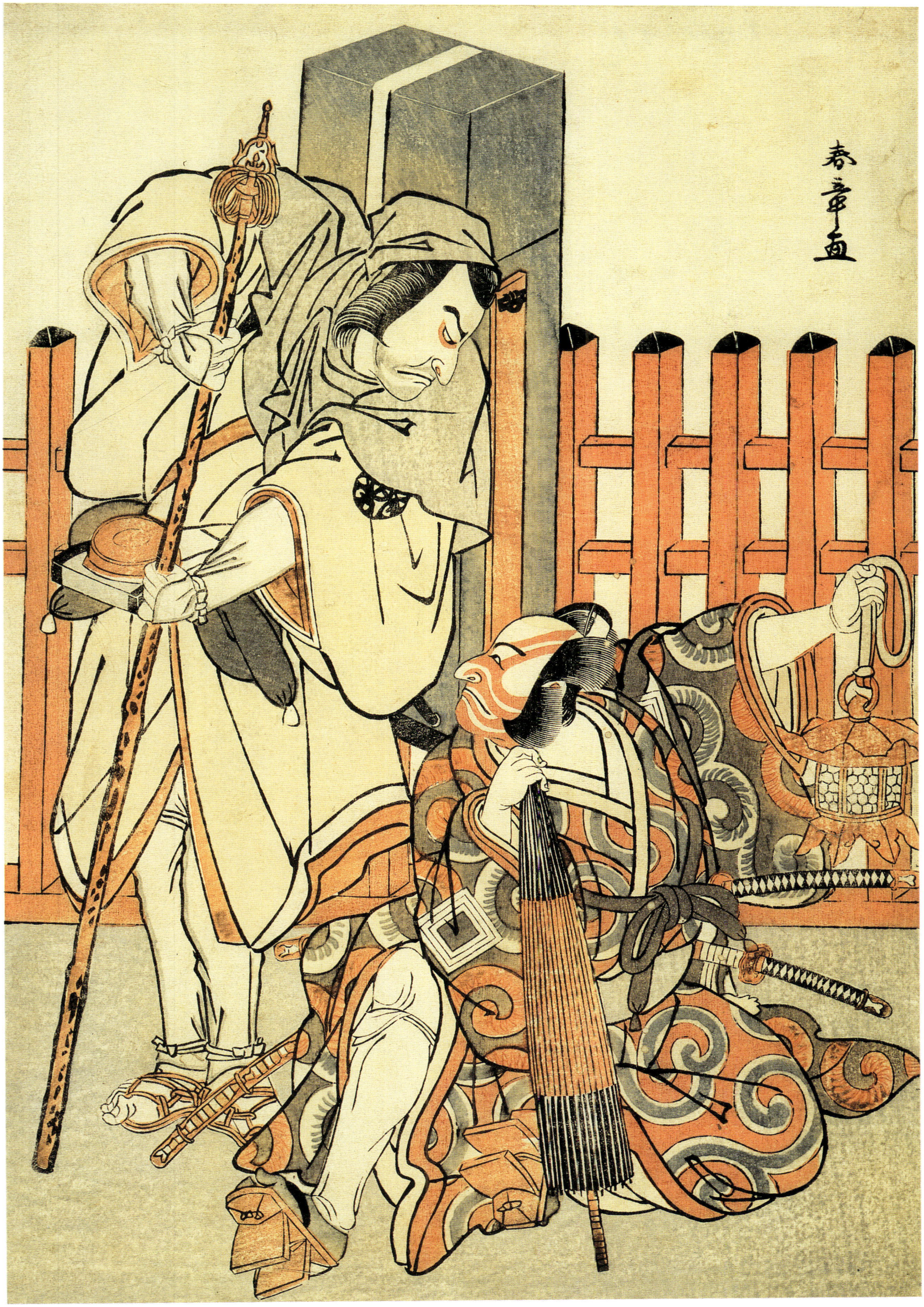
春章画

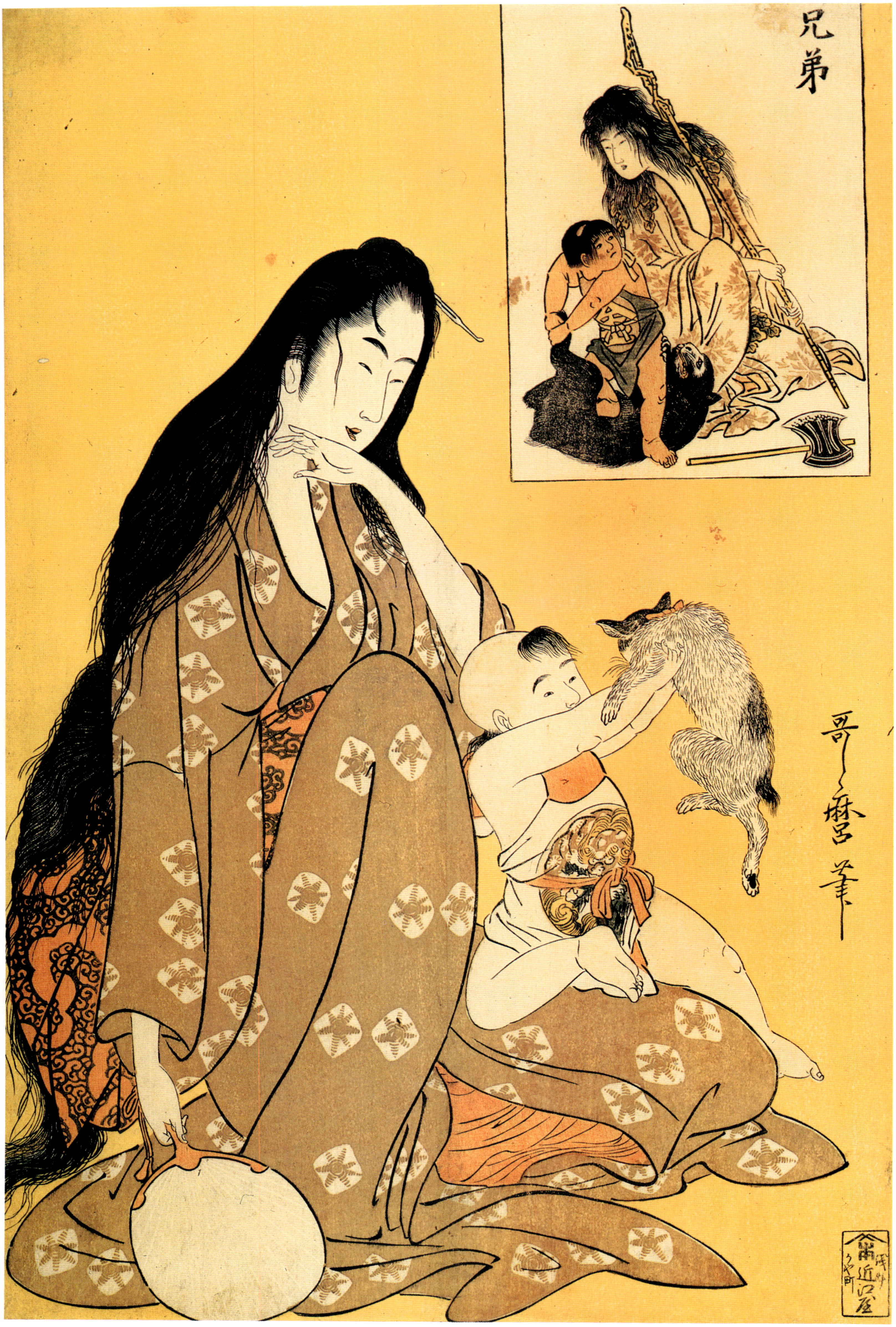
兄弟

4
The Golden Age, 1780-1810

JULIA HUTT

The period 1780-1810 is frequently referred to as the Golden Age of *ukiyo-e* and it witnessed the appearance of some of the finest prints ever produced in Japan. This was made possible by a combination of political, social and economic conditions, together with technical advances in print production, all of which coincided with the appearance of a number of highly skilled print designers.

In the period preceeding 1790, the *chōnin* (townspeople) were relatively free from government restrictions which were periodically imposed to curb overt displays of wealth. At the same time, the commercial prosperity which was enjoyed by the merchants, increasingly spread to other levels of society. This resulted not only in a growing market for the *ukiyo-e* print, but also in one that was becoming increasingly well-informed and sophisticated in its demands. Since the introduction of full-color printing (*nishiki-e*) on a wide scale significantly increased the price of a print, the emergence of an interested and prosperous market was an essential prerequisite for its continued success.

Left: Kitagawa Utamaro (1753-1806) 'Yamauba and Kintoki,' from the series 'Brother and Sister Pictures,' c.1796, 14⅕×9⅘ inches (36.1×24.7 cm). Published by Ōmiya Gonkurō. Courtesy of the Trustees of the British Museum, London.

Full-color printing opened up new and challenging possibilities for the print designer, especially in rendering emotion more realistically. Such a development was evident in print design during the 1770s and 1780s, culminating in the works of Kitagawa Utamaro (1753-1806), Tōshūsai Sharaku (*fl* 1794-95) and their many contemporaries in the 1790s. To this end, the print designer was no longer content merely to depict an outward likeness of his human subjects, but increasingly sought to capture their personalities and moods. The greater emphasis on figures as individuals led to their widespread portrayal in half-length or head-and-shoulders form. These compositions were particularly well suited to the *ōban* format (15×10¼ inches [c.38×26 cm]) which enjoyed increased popularity from the late 1780s. With their focus on facial expressions they created an emotional intensity hitherto unknown.

From the very beginning, *bijin* (beautiful women) and Kabuki actors were a main source of inspiration for *ukiyo-e* artists and the period covered by this chapter witnessed the culmination of the portrayal of the human figure in these forms. In the context of *ukiyo-e* art, the term *bijin* is used generically to refer to well-groomed women from many social levels employed in multifarious activities. *Ukiyo-e* prints in which *bijin* predominate as the main subject are extremely varied in content. On the one hand are those which depict respectable women going about their daily business, such as carrying out mundane domestic activities or taking part in outings to view cherry blossoms, to the seaside or to a temple. On the other hand, some portray courtesans, geisha and tea-house girls who ran the various establishments in the Yoshiwara. Such women were frequently shown preparing their toilet, engaged in some leisure activity or entertaining others. Some were completely innocuous in tone, while others were of a more sensual nature depicting a beauty drying herself after a bath, a young girl coyly biting her little finger or even with a few strands of hair hanging out of place on her bare neck. There were other examples that were explicit illustrations of sexual encounters. Such scenes, referred to as *shunga* (spring pictures), illustrated books or albums. A large number of print designers who were active during the late eighteenth and early nineteenth centuries also produced *shunga*.

In order to gain a fuller understanding and appreciation of *bijin* prints during this period, it is necessary to understand in more detail the women portrayed in them, as well as aspects of their lives. The majority of courtesans portrayed in prints of this period were those of the highest rank, known as *tayū* or *oiran*. They were well-educated and sophisticated women, skilled in their profession as well as being practised in literature and music. Their favor had not only to be bought but also to be won, usually through intermediaries and preliminary meetings in tea-houses, before any assignation could take place. *Tayū* were often accompanied by attendants, known as *shinzō* and *kamuro*, the latter a pair of young girls, often dressed identically and with elaborately arranged hair. The *tayū* enjoyed an extremely high status in Yoshiwara society and it was important that they should be seen to follow trends of the latest fashion, if not actually to set them.

Whatever class of woman was depicted, it became increasingly necessary for the print designer to dress her in sumptuous kimono, with meticulous attention paid to the latest hairstyle and the arrangement of hair ornaments. Indeed, these may provide important clues towards dating an otherwise undated print. It is also interesting that the leading courtesans of the day were thus often used to model the latest fashion. In this way, such prints were not only sought

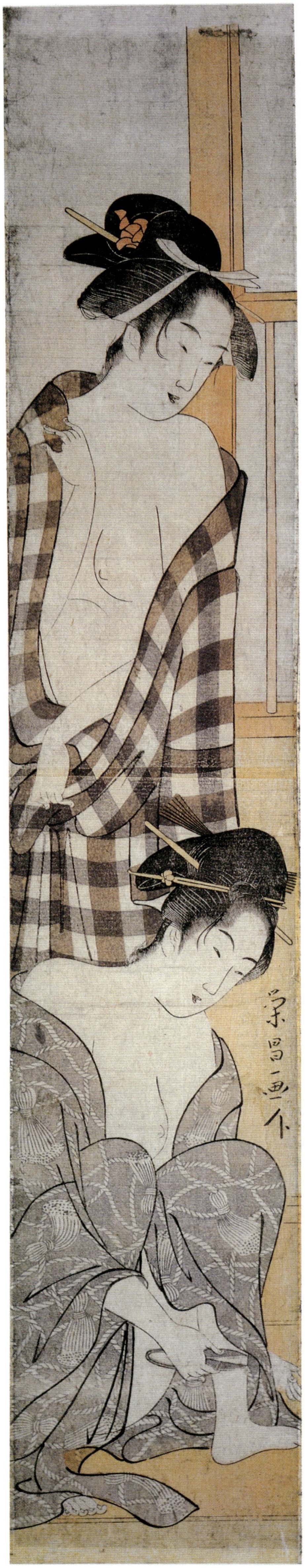

Left: Chōkōsai Eishō (*fl* 1793-99) 'After the Bath,' 1795-9, 24⅓×4⅔ inches (61.7×11.7 cm). Published by Yamaguchiya Chūsuke. Courtesy of the Trustees of the British Museum.

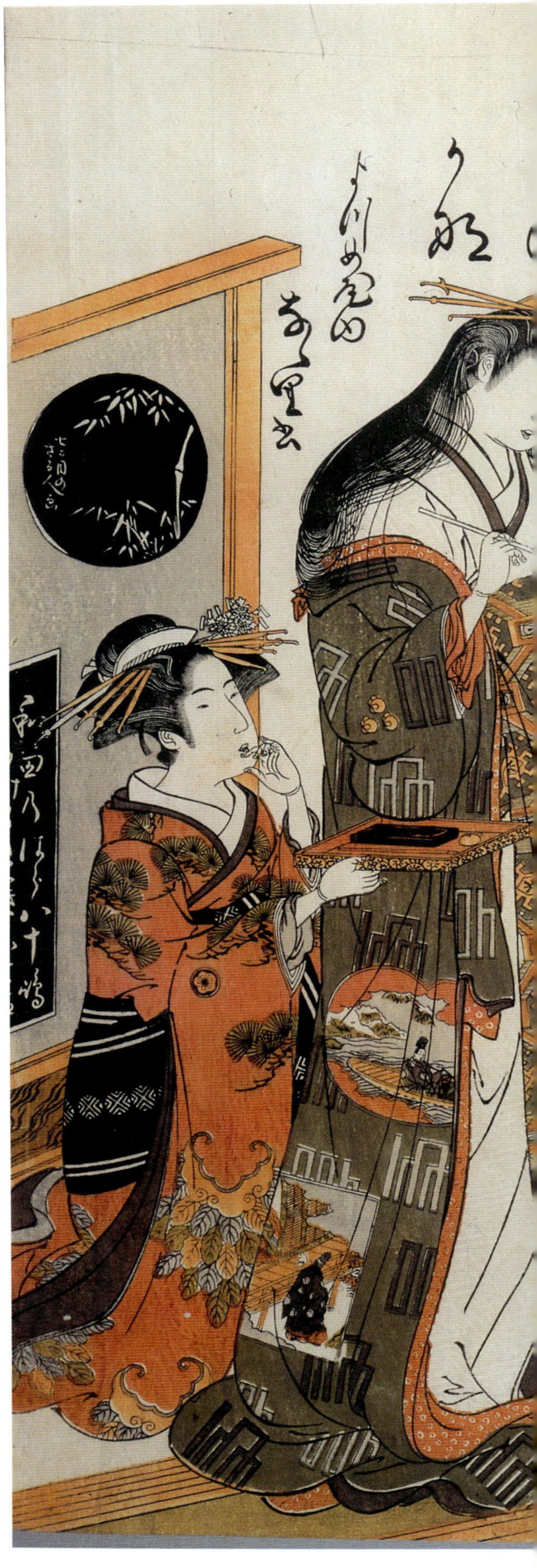

Right: Kitao Masanobu (1761-1861). 'The Courtesan Nanasato Writing Poetry (Standing) and Utagawa Reading (Seated) with Attendants,' from the series 'A Mirror Comparing the Handwriting of New and Beautiful Courtesans of the Yoshiwara' (*Yoshiwara keisei shin bijin awase jihitsu kagami*), 1784, 15×10 inches (38.1×25.4 cm). Published by Tsutaya Jūsaburō. Courtesy of the Trustees of the British Museum, London.

after by men as mementos of an amorous liaison or as a pin-up but also by women as fashion plates.

In *bijin* prints of the period, it is not uncommon to come across situations, such as viewing cherry blossoms, in which the protagonists could equally be either respectable women or courtesans from the Yoshiwara. There are, however, certain features which may serve to distinguish one from the other. By this period, for example, it had already become customary for courtesans to secure the *obi* (sash) elaborately tied at the front instead of at the back. In addition, the courtesan generally went around barefoot or, during the winter, made use of high clogs, known as *geta*, while other women wore special socks, known as *tabi*. The title or series title of a print may also have provided further information, together with the use of the *mon* (family badge) of the brothel. The names of popular courtesans were frequently recorded on prints.

The most talented and successful print designers ultimately created a 'type' of woman through their prints which per-

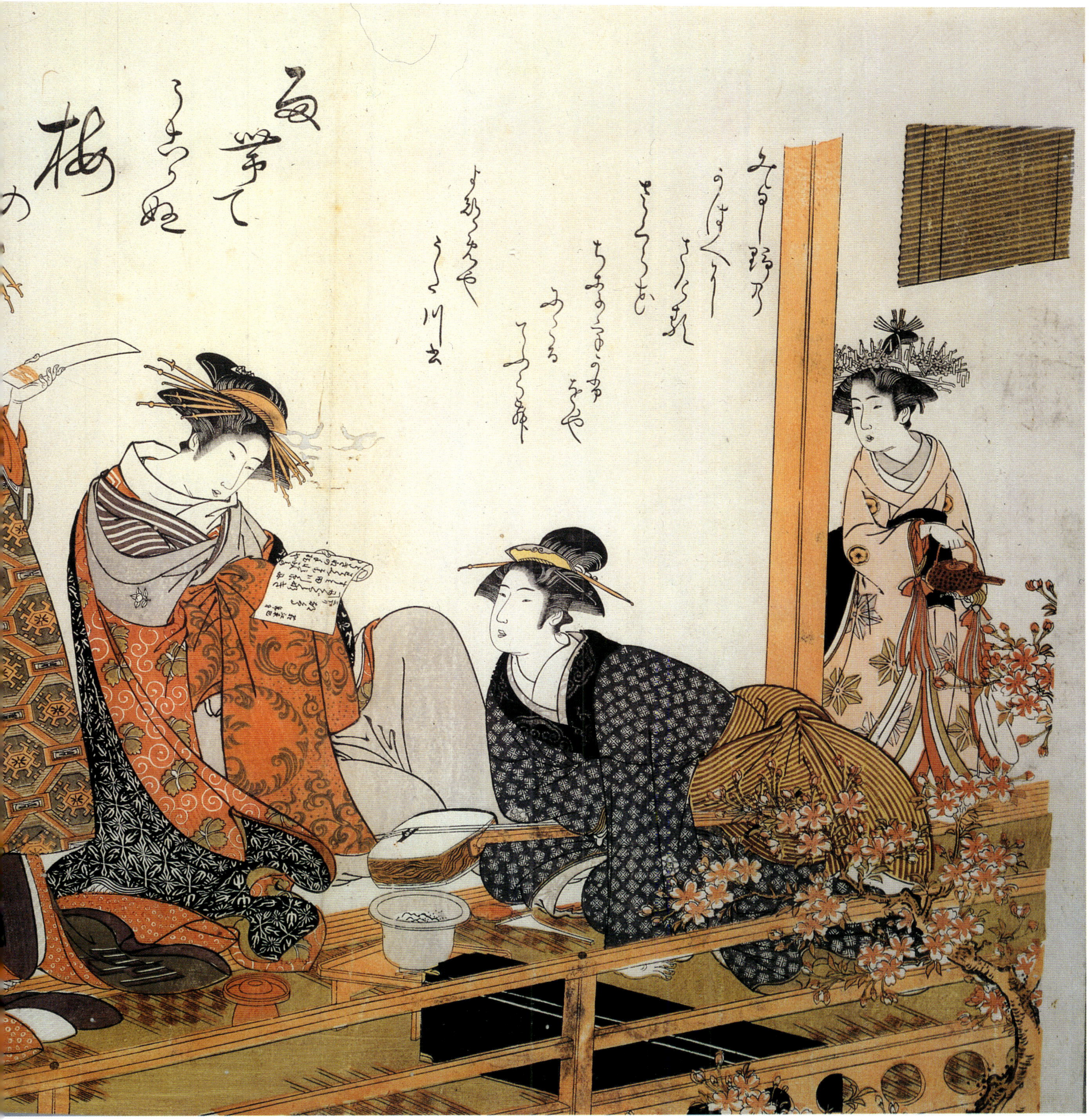

sonified their ideal of feminine beauty and which served to characterize their work. It is this which distinguishes those designers who were purely imitative from those whose creativity and insight set them apart. Suzuki Harunobu (?1725-70), for example, portrayed a type of woman who was slim, dainty and coy and who was immediately recognizeable as a product of his imagination, just as Utamaro, Eishōsai Chōki and others did too.

In the field of *bijinga* (pictures of beautiful women), the designer Kitao Masanobu (1761-1816) spanned both the 1770s and 1780s and may be seen as ushering in the Golden Age. Masanobu, who also worked under the name Santō Kyōden, was the leading pupil of Kitao Shigemasa (1739-1820). Much of his artistic activity was expended on providing illustrations for books, *kyōka* ('mad poem,' a form of light verse in 31 syllables) and, above all, for popular novels. He is best remembered, however, for an album in the *ōban* format entitled 'A Mirror Comparing the Handwriting of New and Beautiful Courtesans of the Yoshiwara' (*Yoshiwara keisei shin oijin awase jihitsu kagami*), which was published in 1784 by Tsutaya Jūsaburō, the leading print publisher of the time. The album contained seven diptychs, each of which portrayed two courtesans with their attendants, together with a poem written in the courtesan's own calligraphy (see above). This serves to illustrate that high-ranking courtesans were well educated and that this was considered an important and integral part of their professional training. Masanobu's figures, like those of Shigemasa and Isoda Koryūsai (*fl.* c.

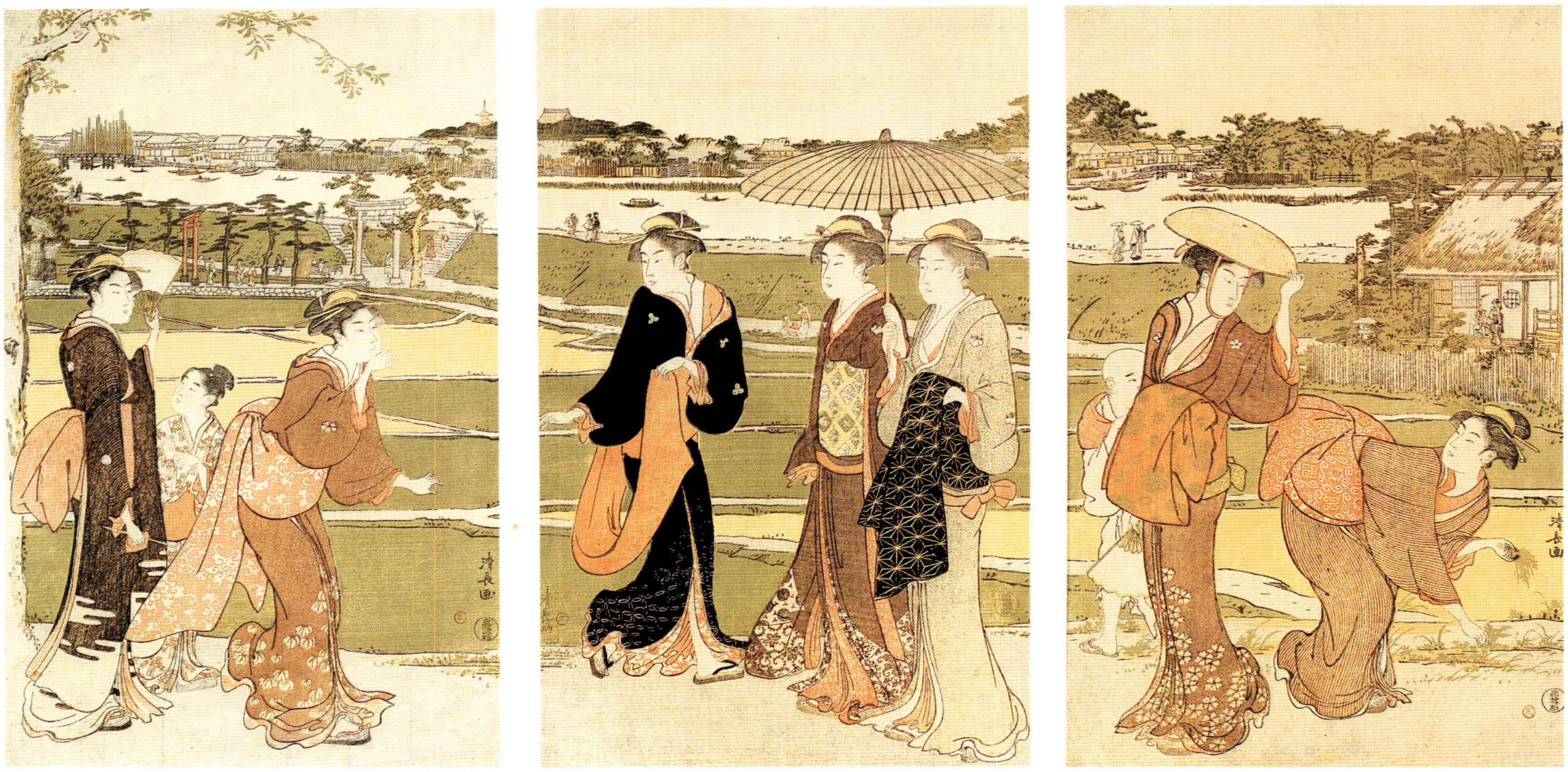

1764-88), were more solid and robust than those of Harunobu. Additionally, the women in the album are portrayed considerably taller than prevailing convention. This allowed them to display the most sumptuous kimono to full advantage, with the height of the figure balanced by the volume of material cascading to the floor. Although the influence of this album was considerable, Masanobu gave up designing prints in 1790 in order to pursue a career as a writer.

Torii Kiyonaga (1752-1815) was the son of an Edo bookseller, and the foremost pupil of Torii Kiyomitsu (c. 1735-85). As a member of the Torii family, he designed prints of Kabuki actors and theatrical billboards. However, during the early 1780s he expanded his repertoire to include *bijinga*. He eventually became the most influential designer in this field, a position which, until then, had been occupied by Koryūsai. Kiyonaga had developed a personal style by the early 1780s which was distinctive and far-reaching in its influence (above). Kiyonaga's mature style is characterized by solid, majestic figures which, like those found in Masanobu's album, are of a slightly exaggerated height. Despite this, Kiyonaga's figures, more realistically portrayed than ever before, are generally shown enjoying some leisure activity. Although the format was not new, he made frequent use of the diptych and triptych and masterfully grouped his figures across the resulting wide expanses in a unified manner (below). His figure compositions, which were arranged in such a manner that the figures were contained within the edges of the sheet were usually set outdoors against a background landscape, which served to unify the compositional whole. The fact that he used such settings enabled him to portray women from the Yoshiwara district and from other social groups mixing freely on neutral ground. Although elements of landscape had already appeared in earlier *ukiyo-e* prints, it was the detailed and consistent use of landscape that made the works of Kiyonaga so different in this respect.

The appearance of background land-

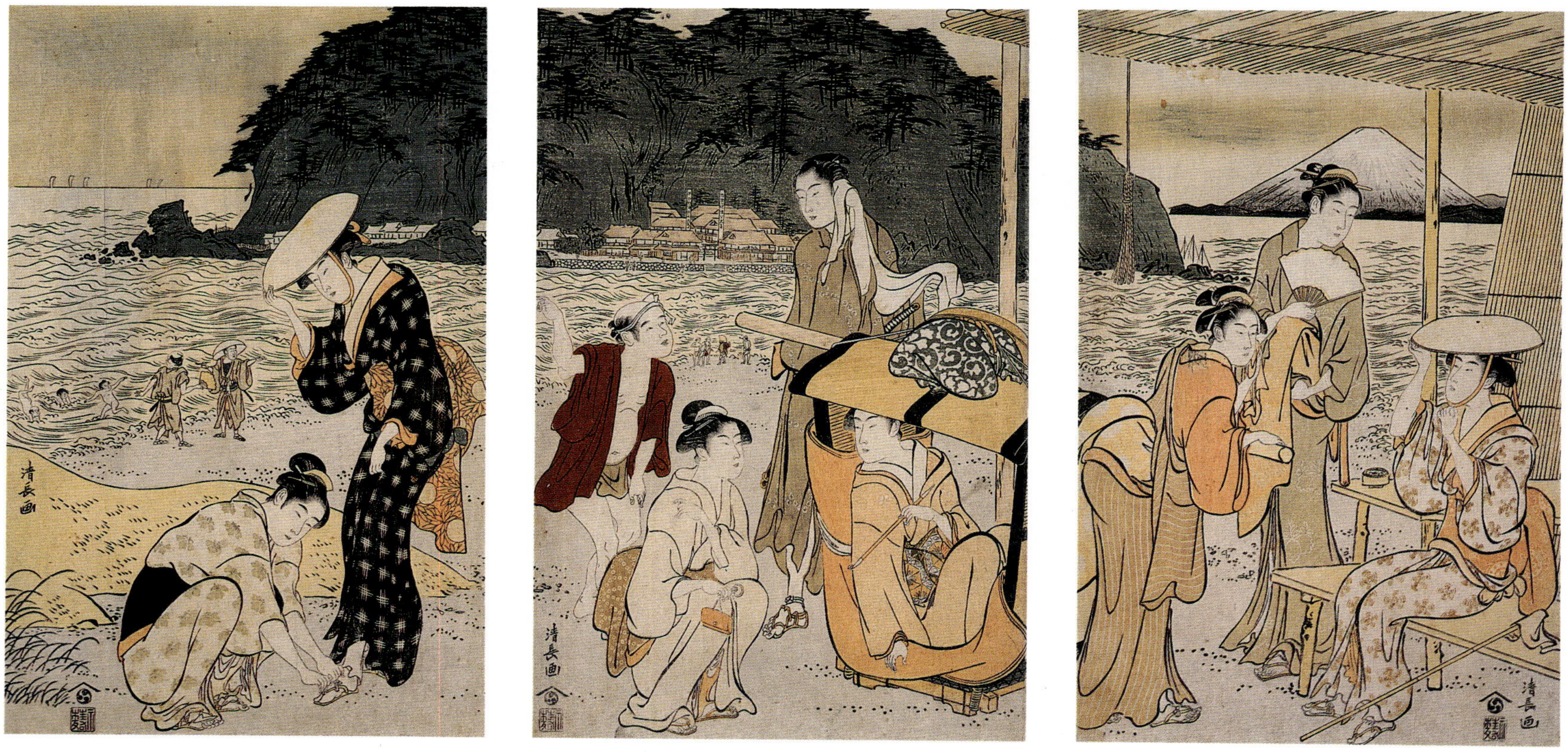

Left: Torii Kiyonaga (1752-1815) 'A Walk in the Suburbs,' 1780 triptych, 15½×30 inches each (38.7×76.2 cm). Published by Takatsuya Isuke. Courtesy of the Trustees of the British Museum, Victoria and Albert Museum, London.

Below left: Torii Kiyonaga (1752-1815) 'Women Visiting Enoshima,' c.1785-8, triptych, 14½×9⅔ inches (37.0×24.5 cm). Published by Nishimuraya Yohachi. Courtesy of the Trustees of the British Museum, London.

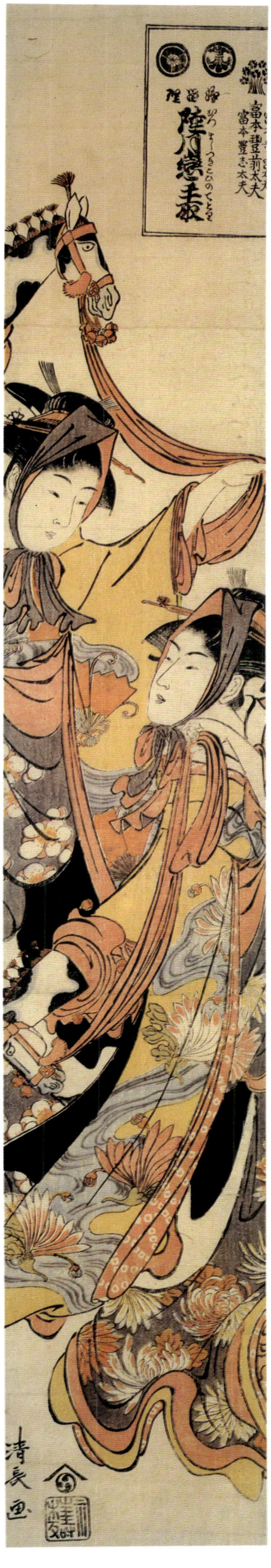

Right: Torii Kiyonaga (1752-1815) 'Actors Doing the Spring Dance,' 1782, *hashira-e*, 26⅕×4½ inches (66.7×11.6 cm). Published by Nishimuraya Yohachi. Courtesy of the Trustees of the British Museum, London.

scape as an important and integral part of Kiyonaga's compositions may, in part, be attributed to the influence of Western perspective. Traditional Japanese painting did not make use of scientific perspective but instead sought alternative means to produce the effect of recession and depth on a two-dimensional surface. These included depicting nearer objects lower down and further ones higher up, or the convention of looking down on a scene as though the roof had been removed, together with the use of diagonal lines to draw the viewer's eye back. During the 1730s, however, Japanese artists were introduced to Western perspective by means of an illustrated Chinese translation of a European treatise by A. Pozzo, entitled *Perspective Pictorum et Architectorium* (published in Rome, 1693 and 1712). Painters such as Shiba Kōkan (1747-1818) and Hiraga Gennai (1726-79), as well as print designers, including Okumura Masanobu (1686-1764) and Torii Kiyotada (*fl* 1720-50), experimented with this new concept. In the field of *ukiyo-e*, isolated examples of vanishing perspective began to appear, most notably in architectural settings, such as theater interiors. In particular, the print designer Utagawa Toyoharu (1735-1814), the founder of the Utagawa school, may be singled out for special attention. A pupil of Toriyama Sekien (1712-88), a somewhat undistinguished Kanō school painter who later turned to book illustration, specializing in the supernatural, Toyoharu spent his early working years designing prints of *bijin* and actors, before turning to historical subjects and perspective landscapes, frequently combining the two. His main contribution lay in a number of *uki-e* ('floating' or 'perspective' prints) which reveal a fusion of Western and indigenous elements to produce what is essentially a Japanese scene. In this he not only influenced Kiyonaga, but indirectly lay the foundations for the great landscape prints of Katsushika Hokusai (1760-1849) and Utagawa Hiroshige (1797-1858) some fifty years later.

Kiyonaga also excelled in prints in the tall, narrow, *hashira-e* (pillar print) format. Such a size, which had already been used to great effect by Koryūsai during the previous decade, provided a challenge to the inventive skills of the print designer. Kiyonaga frequently succeeded in fitting more than one figure into the limited confines of the print in a meaningful and interesting composition while, at the same time, using elements of the design, such as diagonal lines, to draw the viewer's eye up and down the print (left).

Around 1787 Kiyonaga became head of the Torii family and almost entirely gave up designing prints at the height of his career. He had broken much new ground in print design and established a naturalistic style which was popular and influential. There were few, if any, contemporary print designers who were not indebted to him in one way or another, particularly Shunzan, Shunman, Toyokuni and Utamaro, though his main follower was Katsukawa Shunchō. Kiyonaga also had a son and pupil, Torii Kiyomasa (*fl* 1777-95), who was active between 1793 and 1795, though there are few surviving works by him.

Katsukawa Shunchō (*fl* c. 1780-1800) was a pupil of Katsukawa Shunshō (1726-93), an innovative and talented designer of Kabuki prints. Although Shunchō produced theatrical prints, he is best known for his *bijinga*, which closely follow Kiyonaga's style (right). Shunchō revealed enormous competence rather than originality and the finest of his works are comparable to those of Kiyonaga. He, too, mastered the *hashira-e* format and also used the diptych and triptych to benefit and expand his compositions. Katsukawa Shunzan (*fl* 1782-98) was yet another pupil of Shunshō who worked in the style of Kiyonaga, though few works by him have survived.

Another print designer of note during this period was Kubo Shunman (1757-1820), who first studied under Katori Nahiko (1723-82) and subsequently became a pupil of Shigemasa. Although his prints from the mid 1780s were clearly influenced by Kiyonaga, Shunman was an original and creative artist. His prints from this early period also indicate that he was skilled at conveying the mood and atmosphere of a composition, with the result that they range from relaxed and informal to refined and elegant (overleaf).

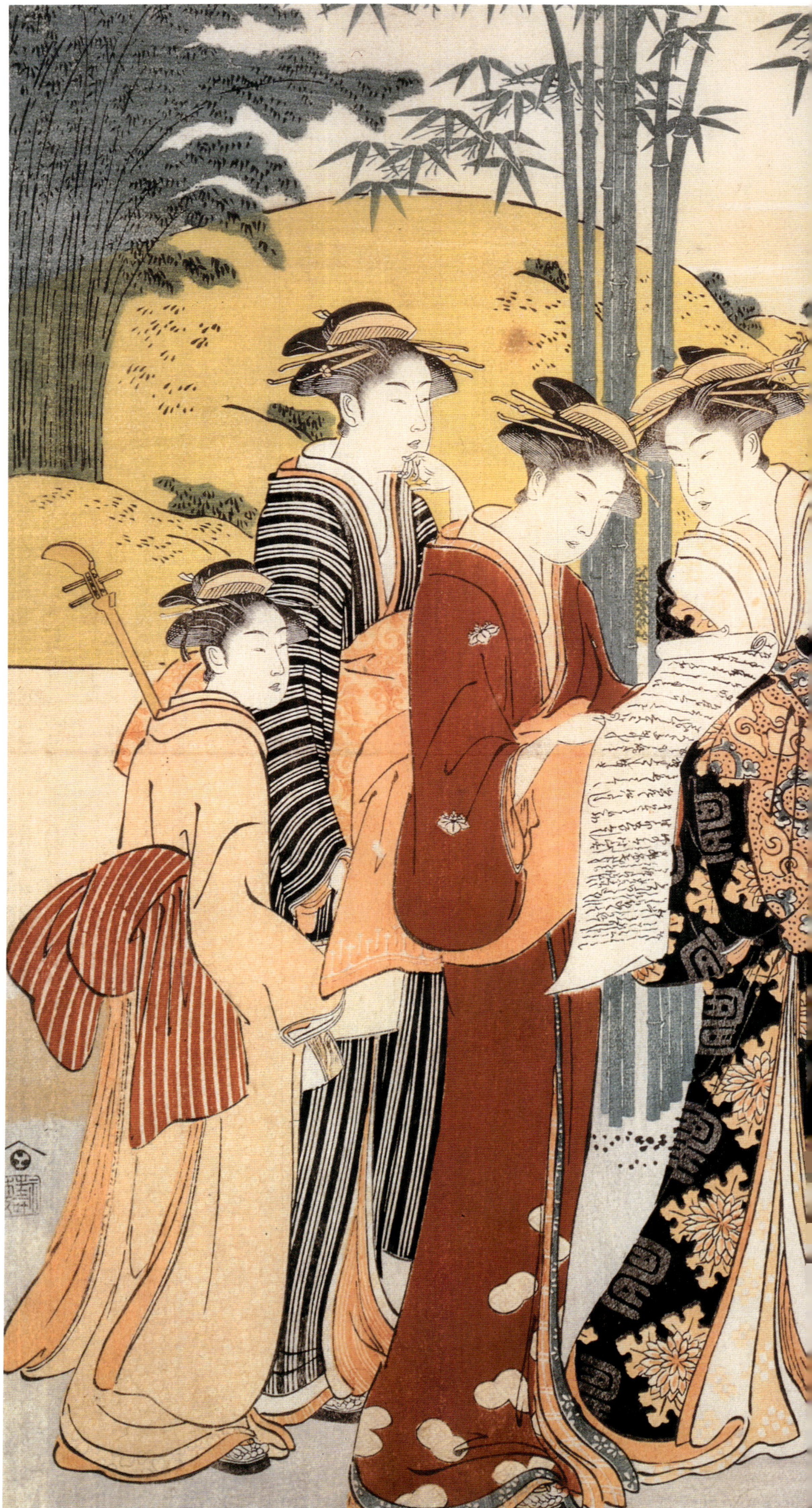

Right: Katsukawa Shunchō (*fl* c. 1780-1800) 'The Seven Sages in Modern Dress,' c.1788 diptych, 14½×9½ inches each. (36.7×24.2 cm). Published by Nishimuraya Yoohachi. Courtesy of the Trustees of the British Museum, London.

Overleaf: Kubo Shunman (1757-1820) 'The Shikian Restaurant,' c.1787-8 diptych, 14¼×9⅔ inches (36.3×25.3 cm). Published by Shūeido. Courtesy of the Trustees of the British Museum, London.

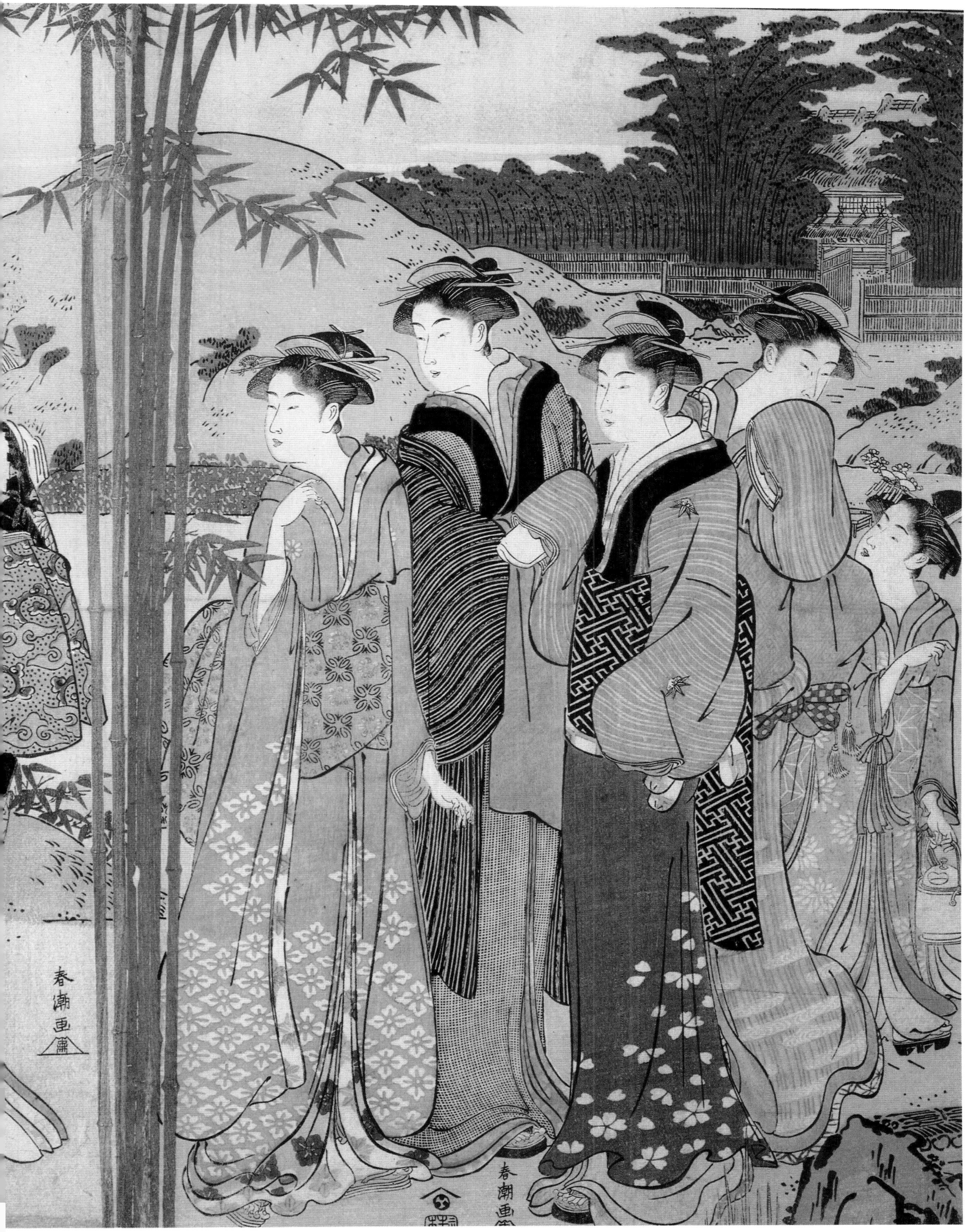
春潮画
春潮画

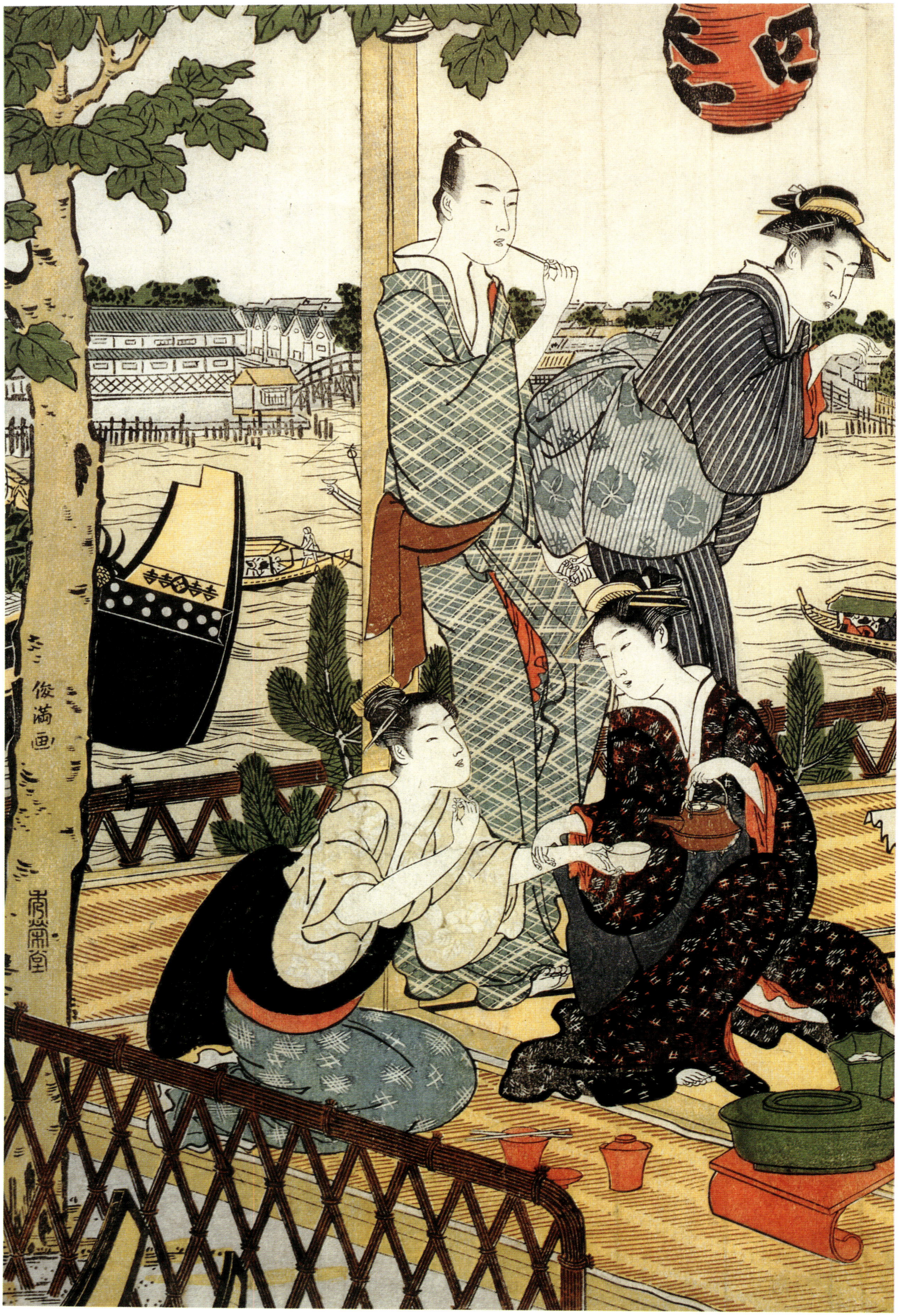
俊満画

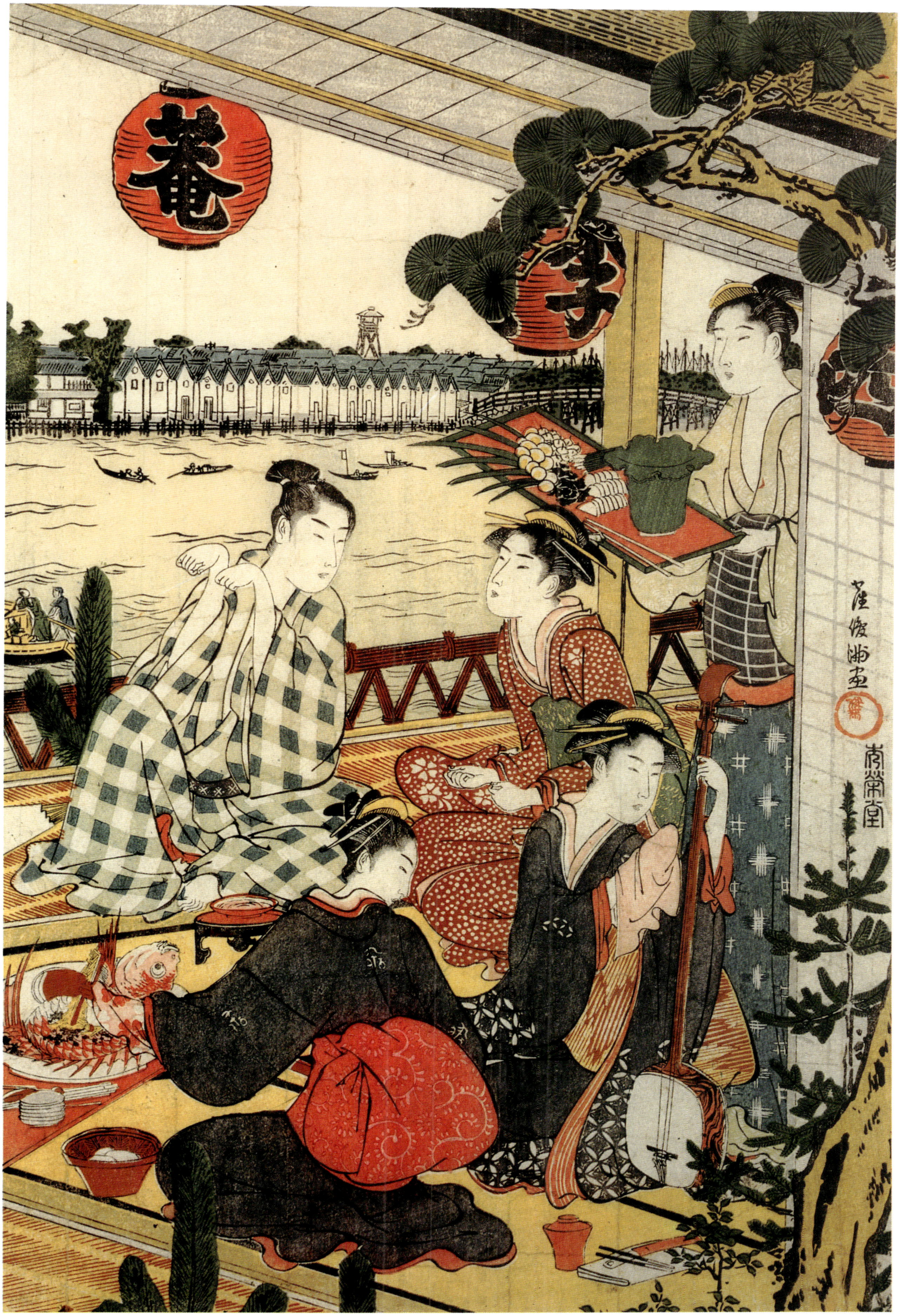

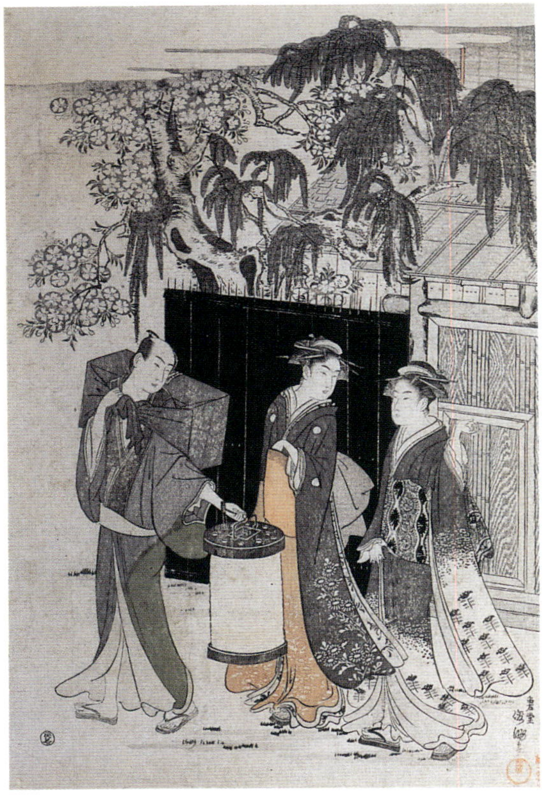

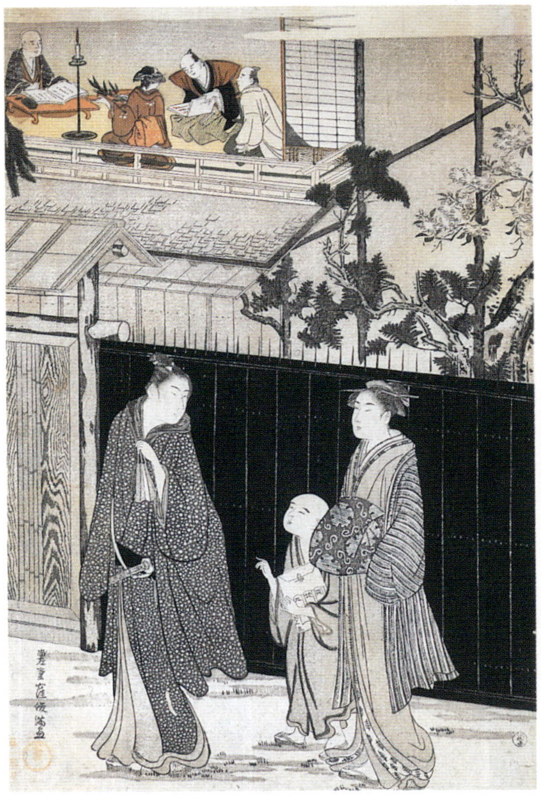

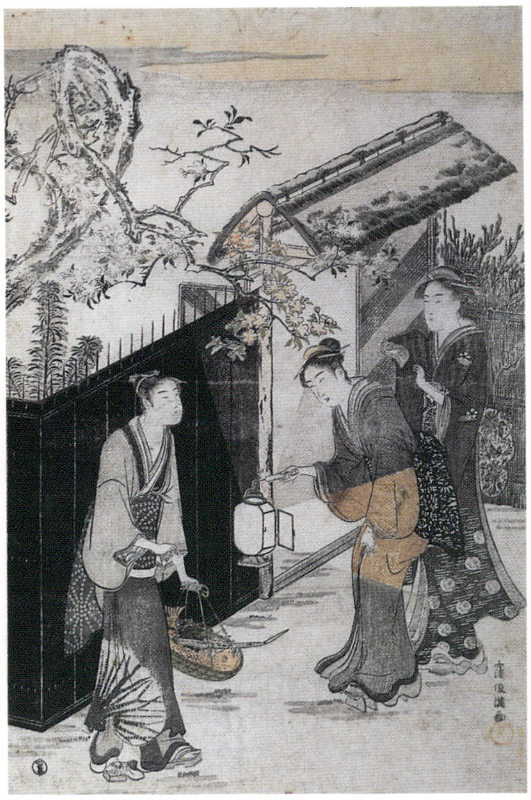

Above: Kubo Shunman (1757-1820) 'A Poetry Meeting at Night,' c.1787-8 triptych, 14⅘×10 inches each (37.5×25.5 cm). Published by Fushimiya Zenroku. Courtesy of the Trustees of the British Museum, London.

Right: Kitagawa Utamaro (1753-1806) 'Drying Clothes,' c.1785-90, two sheets of a triptych 14⅔×9½ inches (37.2×24.2 cm). Published by Iwatoya Kisaburō. Courtesy of the Trustees of the British Museum, London.

Below: Kitagawa Utamaro (1753-1806) 'A Pair of Lovers,' frontispiece from 'Poem of the Pillow (*Uta makura*), 1788, 9¾×14¾ (24.8×37.4 cm).' Courtesy of the Trustees of the Victoria and Albert Museum, London.

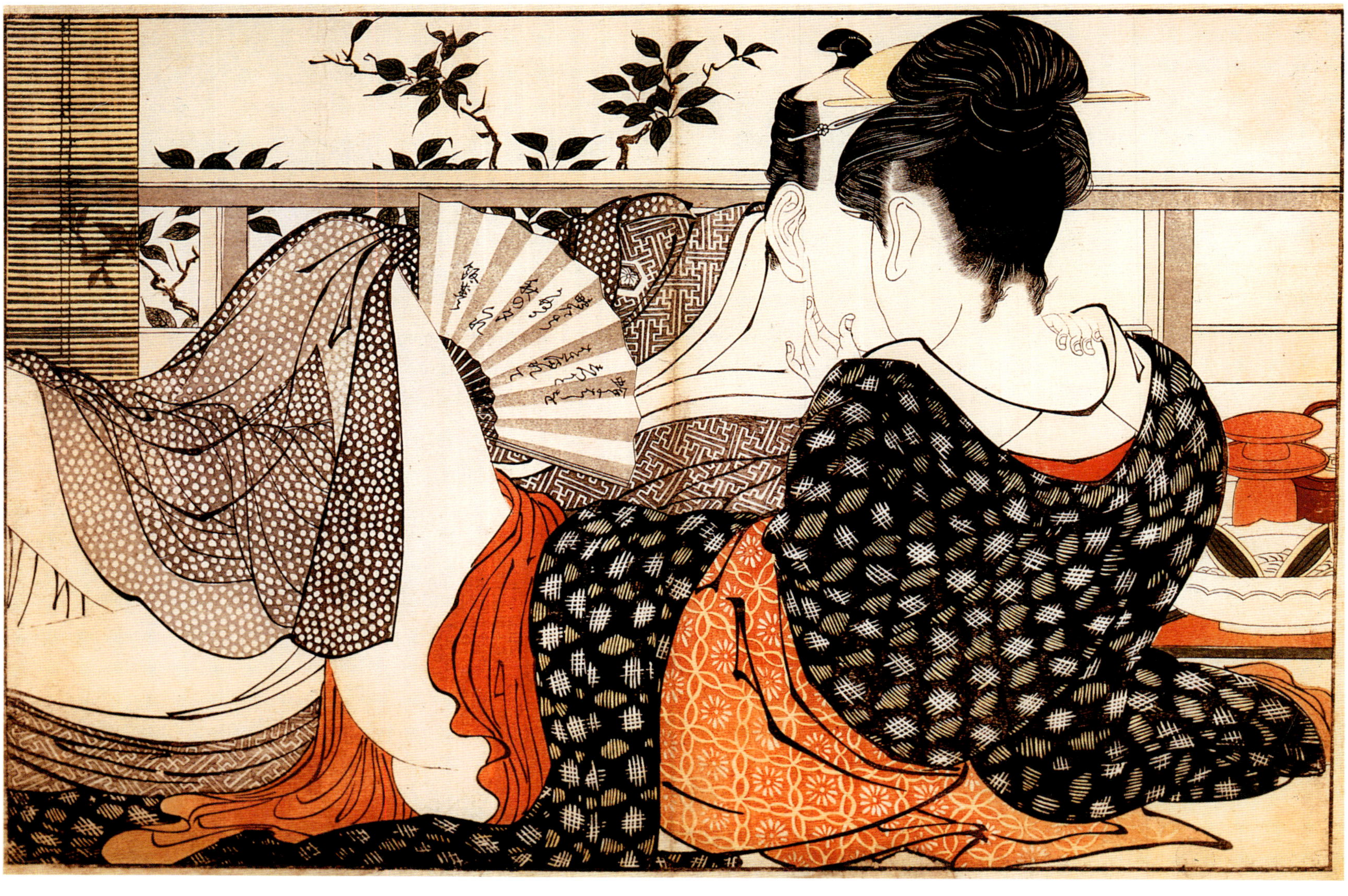

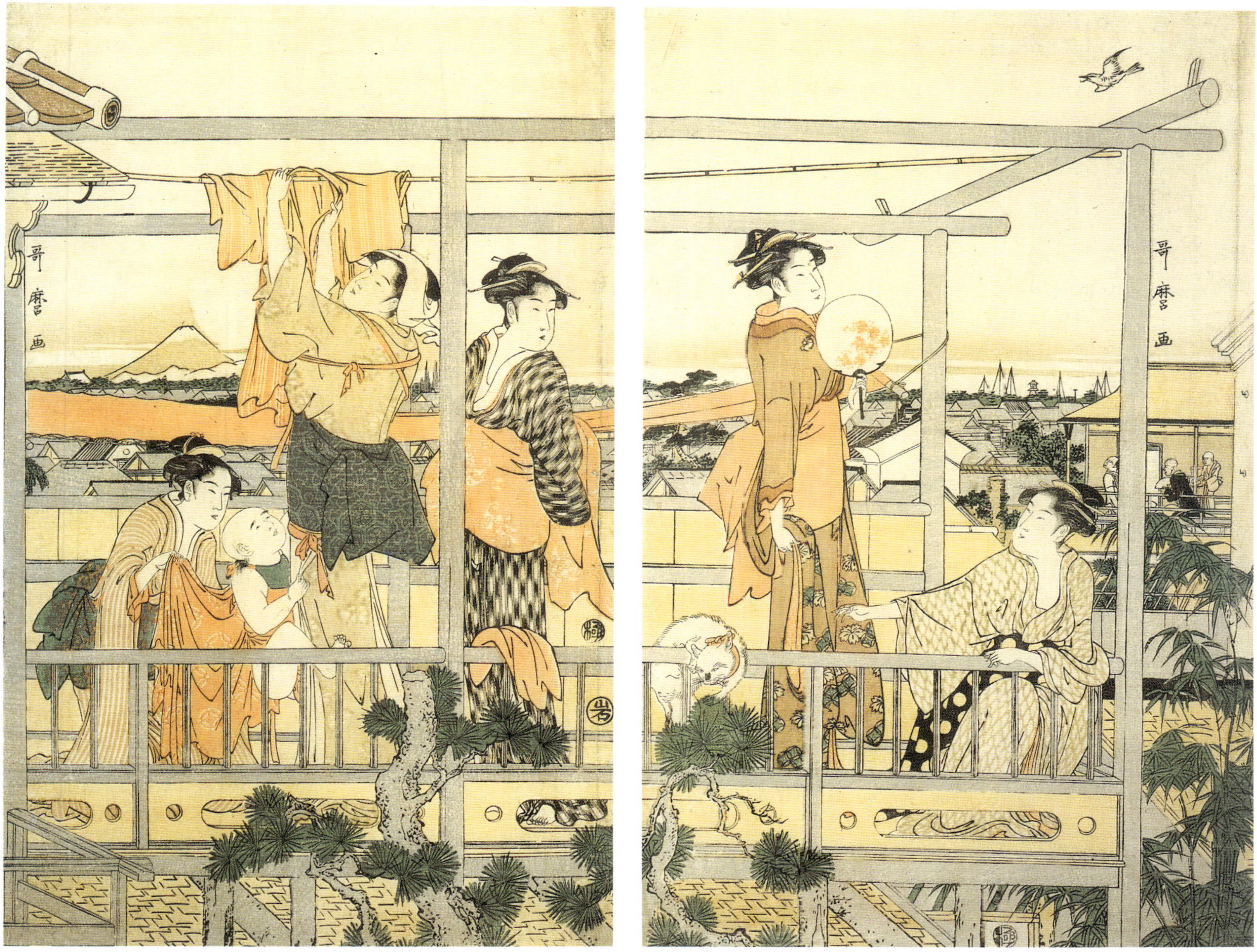

Among some of Shunman's finest works are those which make use of subdued color schemes, known as *benigirai-e* (red-hating pictures), in which shades of gray predominate, heightened by small areas of pastel colors. *Benigirai-e* may well have been adopted as a result of the Kansei Reforms of 1790 in an attempt to tone down the sumptuous color schemes found on *ukiyo-e* prints but, once established, it became popular in its own right, with Shunchō and Hosada Eishi (1756-1829) also producing examples. One of Shunman's most famous prints was a hexatych published between 1787 and 1788, entitled 'The Six Crystal Rivers' and printed in *benigirai-e*. A particularly fine and interesting example, however, is entitled 'A Poetry Meeting at Night' (page 92). In this, Shunman has cleverly attempted to depict the scene true to life by using the muted colors of night time, with contrasting areas of brighter colors shown up by the light of various lamps. Such an effect was very much in keeping with the move towards greater realism evident in *ukiyo-e* prints of the period.

Apart from designing individual sheet prints, Shunman also illustrated books and albums, and was a gifted painter and writer of *kyōka*. In connection with his poetry, Shunman undoubtedly had dealings with the various poetry groups in Edo, many of which commissioned print designers to produce *surimono* for them. Interestingly enough, Shunman gave up designing sheet prints in the 1790s and concentrated on painting and *surimono*. His *surimono*, examples of which he printed himself, are among some of the finest ever produced.

In the field of *bijin*, the decade of the 1780s undoubtedly belonged to Kiyonaga and his concept of feminine beauty. The 1790s, however, came to be dominated by Utamaro, one of the greatest *ukiyo-e* print designers and probably the best known in the West. Kitagawa Utamaro (1753-1806) was a pupil of Toriyama Sekien. His earliest extant works, dating from around 1775, were illustrations for popular literature and theatrical publications of little artistic merit. Then, in 1783, Utamaro moved to lodge with the publisher Tsutaya Jūsaburō where he stayed until Jūsaburō's death in 1797. Tsutaya Jūsaburō was an educated and cultivated man who gathered around him many of the literary and artistic personalities of the day, and who possessed an uncanny ability to bring out the best in his artistic protegés. He became the most successful publisher of the period, renowned for his high standards and with many of the leading artists of the day, including Kitao Masanobu, Shunman, Sharaku and Utamaro, working for him. Even though Utamaro was slow to reach maturity, his work began to flourish from around the time of the collaboration with this remarkable publisher. Kitao Masanobu (1761-1816), for example, who also lodged with Tsutaya Jūsaburō, was some eight years younger than Utamaro, while Torii Kiyonaga was a year older, and yet both print designers had reached their peak and influenced Utamaro before he himself rose to prominence.

During the late 1780s and early 1790s, Utamaro's most notable works included a number of illustrated books and albums, such as the 'Picture Book of Selected Insects' (*Ehon mushi erabi*), 1778 'Gifts of the Ebb-tide' (*Shioi no Tsuto*),

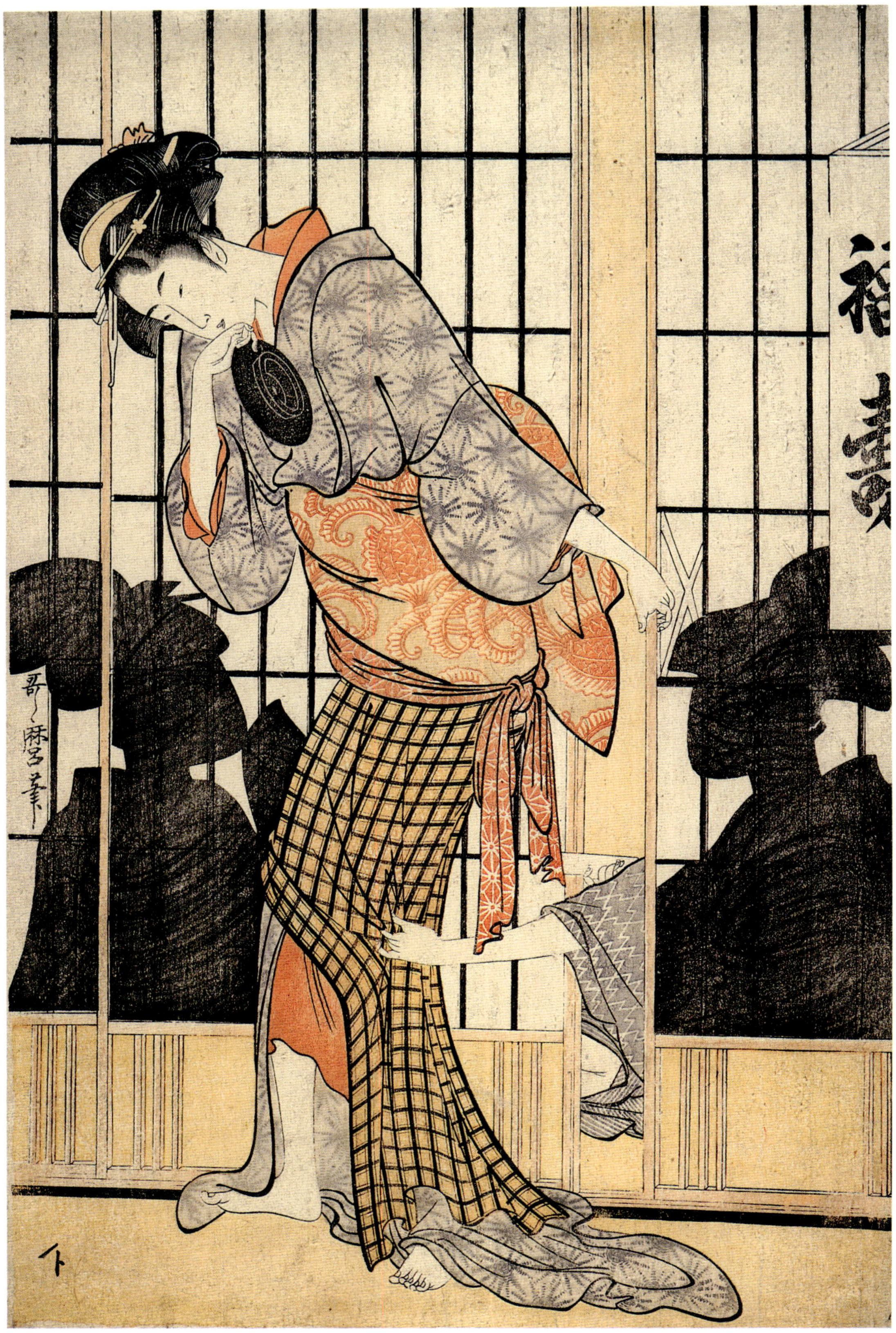

Left: Kitagawa Utamaro (1753-1806) 'Girl Leaving a Sake Party,' early 1790s, 15×10 inches (38.2×25.3 cm). Published by Yamaguchiya Chūsuke. Courtesy of the Trustees of the British Museum, London.

Right: Kitagawa Utamaro (1753-1806) 'Yearning for Her Lover,' from the series 'Six Selected Types of Love' c.1793, woodblock with tinted mica background, 15×9⅘ inches (38.3×25.1 cm). Published by Tsutaya Jūsaburō. Courtesy of the Trustees of the British Museum, London.

c.1790; see page 230) and the 'Birds Compared in Humorous Ditties' (*Moma chido kyōka awase*), c. 1791, often referred to as the 'Insect,' 'Shell' and 'Bird' books respectively. *Kyōka* accompany the illustrations in each book, which extend over a double-page spread. They are as remarkable for the choice of subject as for the superb quality of printing and use of color. In 1788 there also appeared the 'Poem of the Pillow' (*Uta makura*) probably the finest example of Utamaro's *shunga* works (page 92).

This influence of younger on older artists is paralleled in Western art in the influence of Masaccio on Masolino or Leonardo on Verrocchio.

The majority of Utamaro's *bijin* prints from the period 1785-1790 reveal the strong influence of Kiyonaga (page 93). By the early 1790s, however, Utamaro had developed a style which was unmistakably his own. Rather than portraying an idealized view of a woman, Utamaro's *bijin* are portraits of existing women, particularly the tea-house attendants Okita, Ohina and Ohisa who were all favorite models of the artist. It is hard for those unfamiliar with the conventions of Japanese art to appreciate such prints as portraits since they do not conform to the traditional Western image of a portrait as a true likeness. This is borne out by the stylized manner in which the facial features were portrayed, that is two lines for the eyebrows, almond-shaped eyes, a hook for the nose and a small mouth with slightly parted lips. The fact that such economy of brush, a simple thin line, with areas of flat color and with no attempt to suggest light and shade, could convey so much is a tribute to the skills of the *ukiyo-e* artist. Utamaro's interest in the *bijin* went far beyond her surface beauty; he was, above all, concerned with capturing the essence of her personality, character and mood.

Utamaro is perhaps best known for a number of half-length and 'large-head' (*ōkubi-e*) portraits of *bijin* which were published during the early 1790s and which were startlingly different from anything that had gone before (pages 95, 96 and 98). The prints show a woman seen from close up and depicted from just below the waist upwards, or the head and shoulders alone, against a background

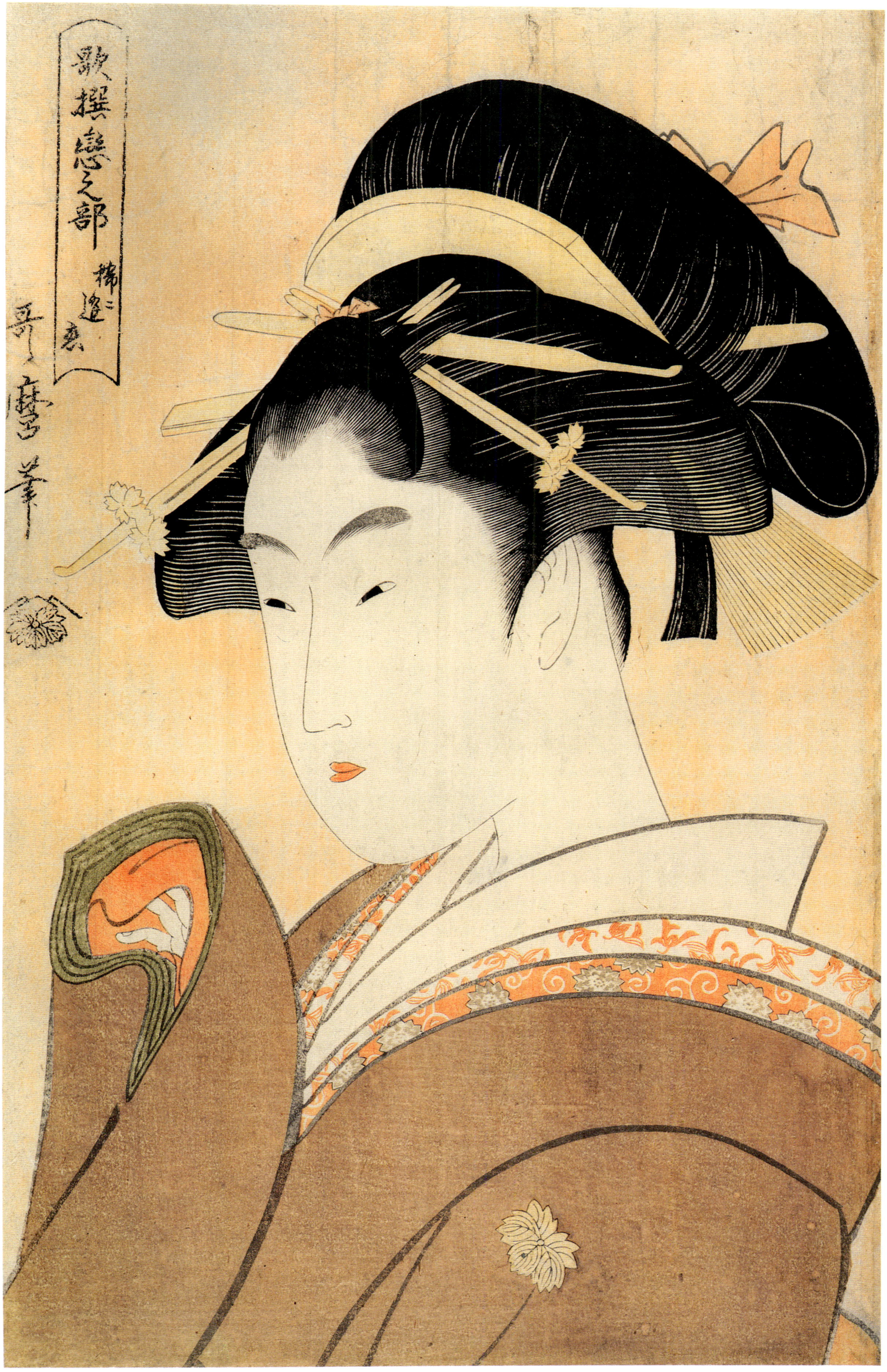
歌撰戀之部
稀ニ逢戀
歌麿筆

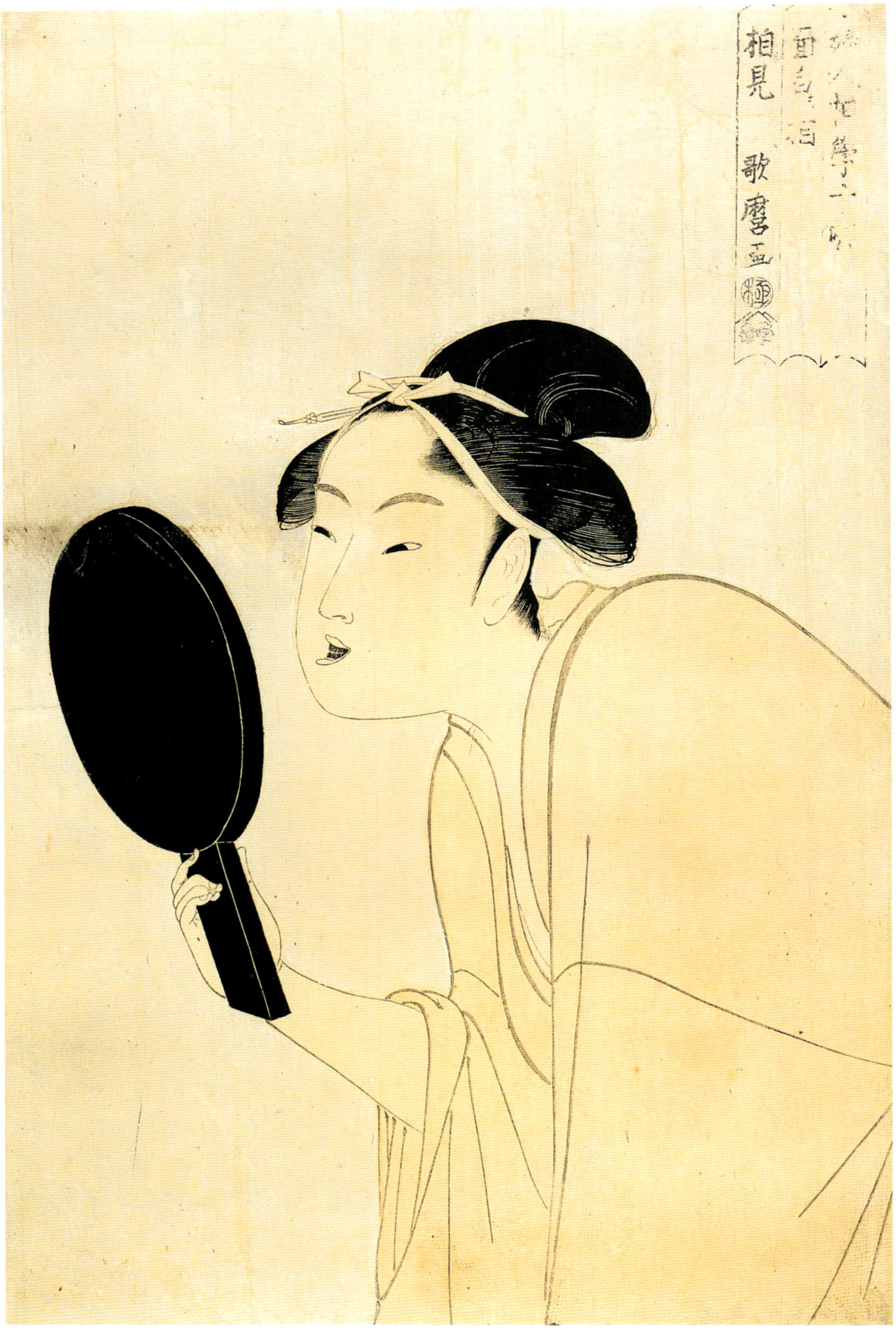

Left: Kitagawa Utamaro (1753-1806) 'Young Woman with Blackened Teeth Examining Her Features in a Mirror,' from the series 'Ten Facial Types of Women (*Fujin sōgaku jitlai*), c.1792-93, 14⅖×9⅔ inches (36.5×24.6 cm). Published by Isutajū,' Courtesy of the Trustees of the British Museum, London.

Right: Kitagawa Utamaro (1753-1806) 'The Fickle Type,' from the series 'Ten Female Faces,' c.1792-93, 13⅘×9⅔ inches (35×24.7 cm). Published by Tsutaya Jūsaburō. Woodblock with powdered mica background. Courtesy of the Trustees of the British Museum, London.

devoid of any drawing, but embellished with mica. The lack of any background imagery served to focus attention on the subject, while the mica had the effect of pushing her forward in bold relief. It should also be remembered that, when in pristine condition, the mica provided a bright metallic surface which, in the majority of cases, is now a pale shadow of its former glory. Neither the use of mica nor the half-length figure was in itself new, though Utamaro was the first to use them consistently. The new close-up view of the woman allowed the artist to concentrate on her as an individual capable of displaying emotion. This allowed a greater degree of intimacy and informality, often of a sensuous nature.

Utamaro also designed many full-length portraits of women and groups of women, as individual prints or as multiple-sheet prints. 'Women Preparing Material for Kimono' (page 98) for example, which is in the form of a triptych, reveals a group of women preparing material for making kimono. It makes use of the 'transparent' device much favored by Utamaro, with the face of a woman seen through a piece of gauze which she holds across her face.

It has already been noted how Kiyonaga's *bijin* tended towards a certain elongation of form. In a series of prints published around 1795 entitled the 'Twelve Hours of the Green Houses' (*Seirō jūniji tsuzuki*), Utamaro adopted a similar exaggerated height for his female figures, a fashion which lasted until approximately 1800 (page 99). In order to achieve this unnatural height, the women were portrayed with a backward curve of the body, formed at one end by the layers of clothing sweeping the ground and, at the other, by excessively ornate hairstyles. Prints which make up this series, moreover, are portrayed on a yellow background sprinkled with gold powder. Yellow backgrounds were popular from around 1793 and yellow grounds sprinkled with gold powder were probably used in place of mica after this was banned in 1795.

Utamaro was prolific in his output and continually sought new and interesting

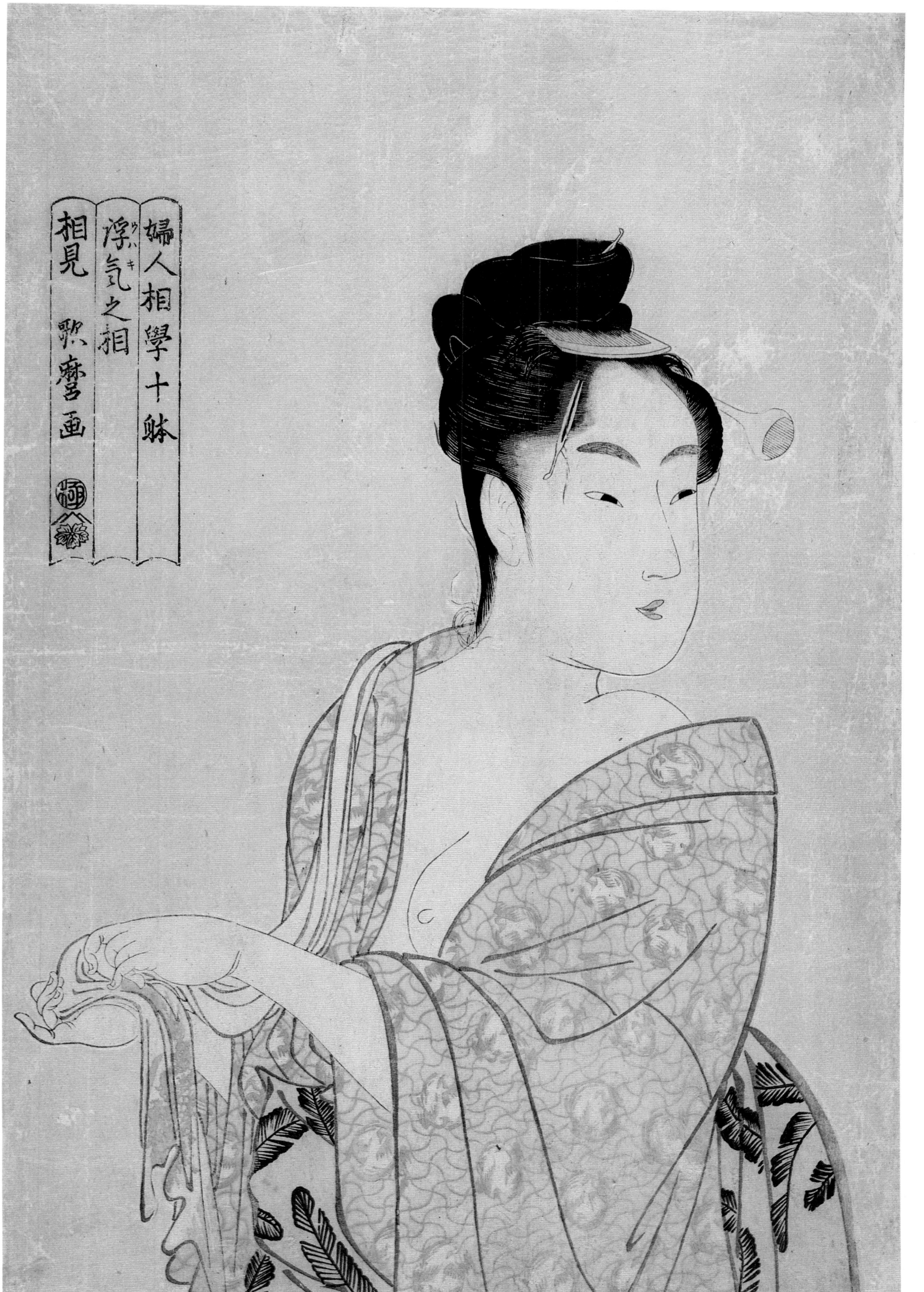
婦人相學十躰
浮氣之相
相見 歌麿画

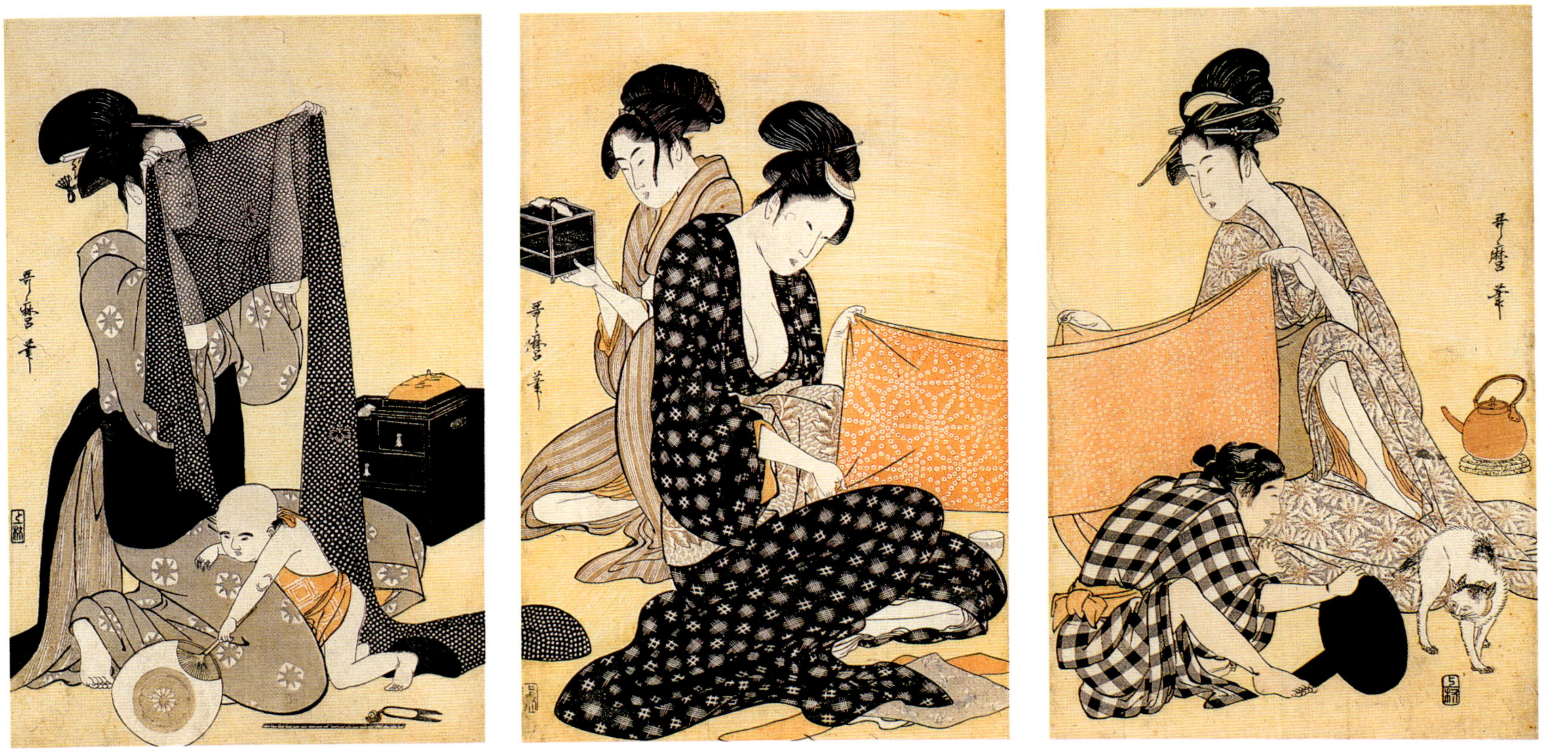

Above: Kitagawa Utamaro (1753-1806) 'Women Preparing Fabric for Kimono,' c.mid. 1790s, triptych, 15⅕×10 inches (38.6×25.4 cm) each. Published by Uemura Yohei. Courtesy of the Trustees of the British Museum, London.

Right: Kitagawa Utamaro (1753-1806) 'The Niwaka Festival,' from the series 'Geisha from the Green Houses at Niwaka' (*Seirō niwaka onna geisha no bu*), 1790s, 15⅖×10⅕ inches (39.2×26 cm). Published by Tsurukin. Courtesy of the Trustees of the British Museum, London.

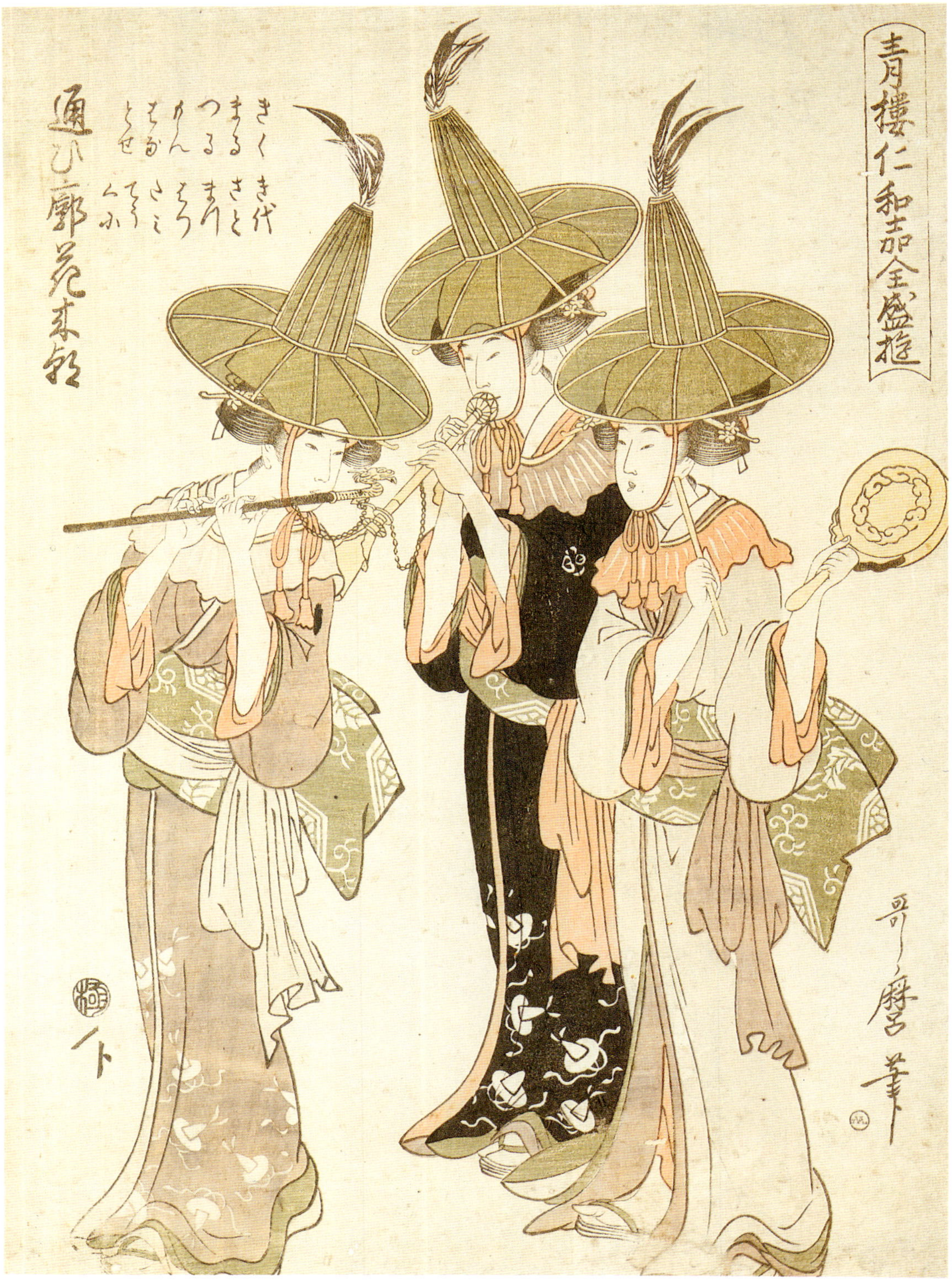

Far right: Kitagawa Utamaro (1753-1806) 'Hour of the Rat,' (*Ne no koku*), from the series 'Around the Twelve Hours of the Greenhouses' (*Seirō jūniji tsuzuki*), c.1795, 15⅕×10⅕ inches (38.6×25.9 cm). Published by Tsutajū. Courtesy of the Trustees of the British Museum, London.

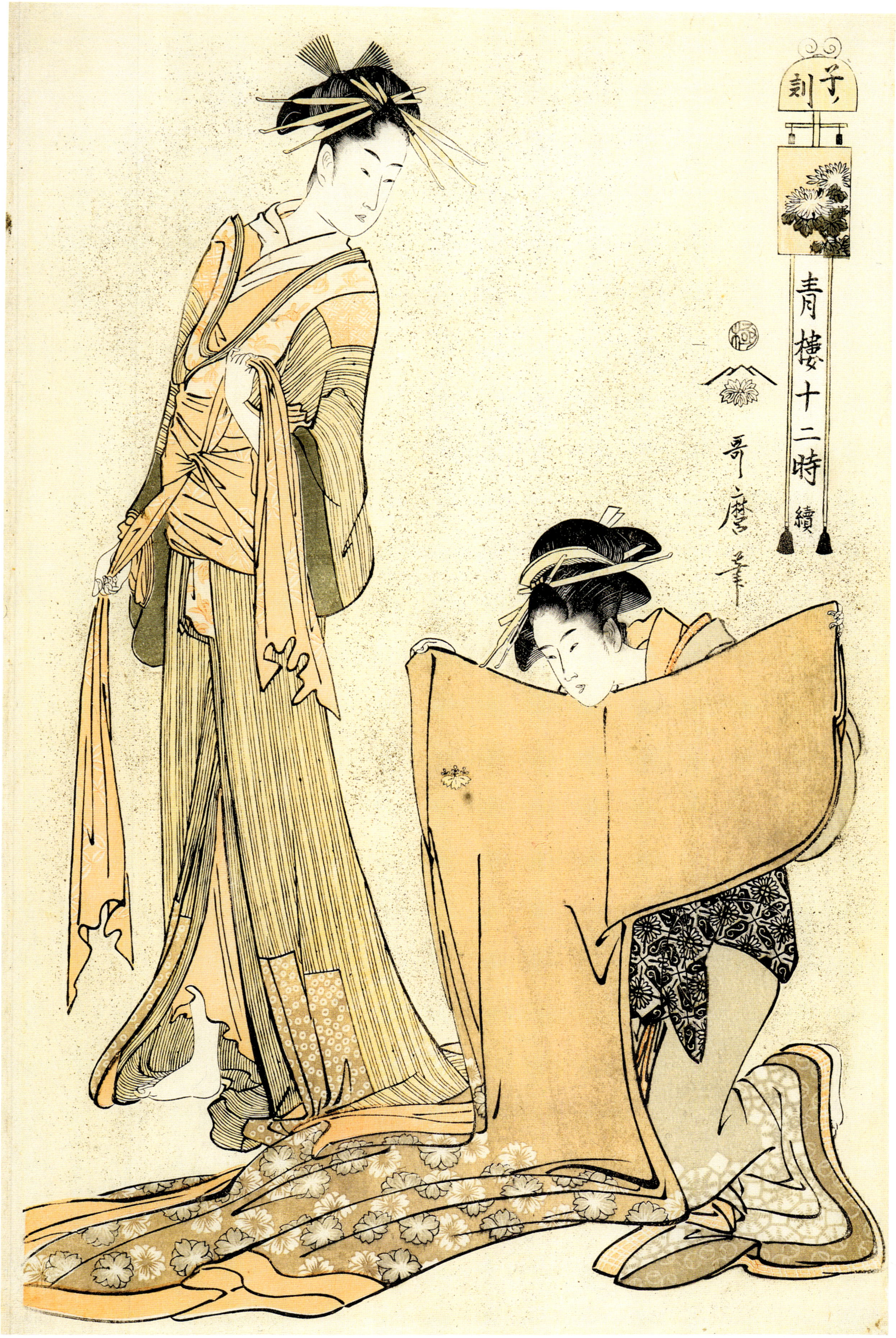
子ノ刻
青樓十二時 續
哥麿筆

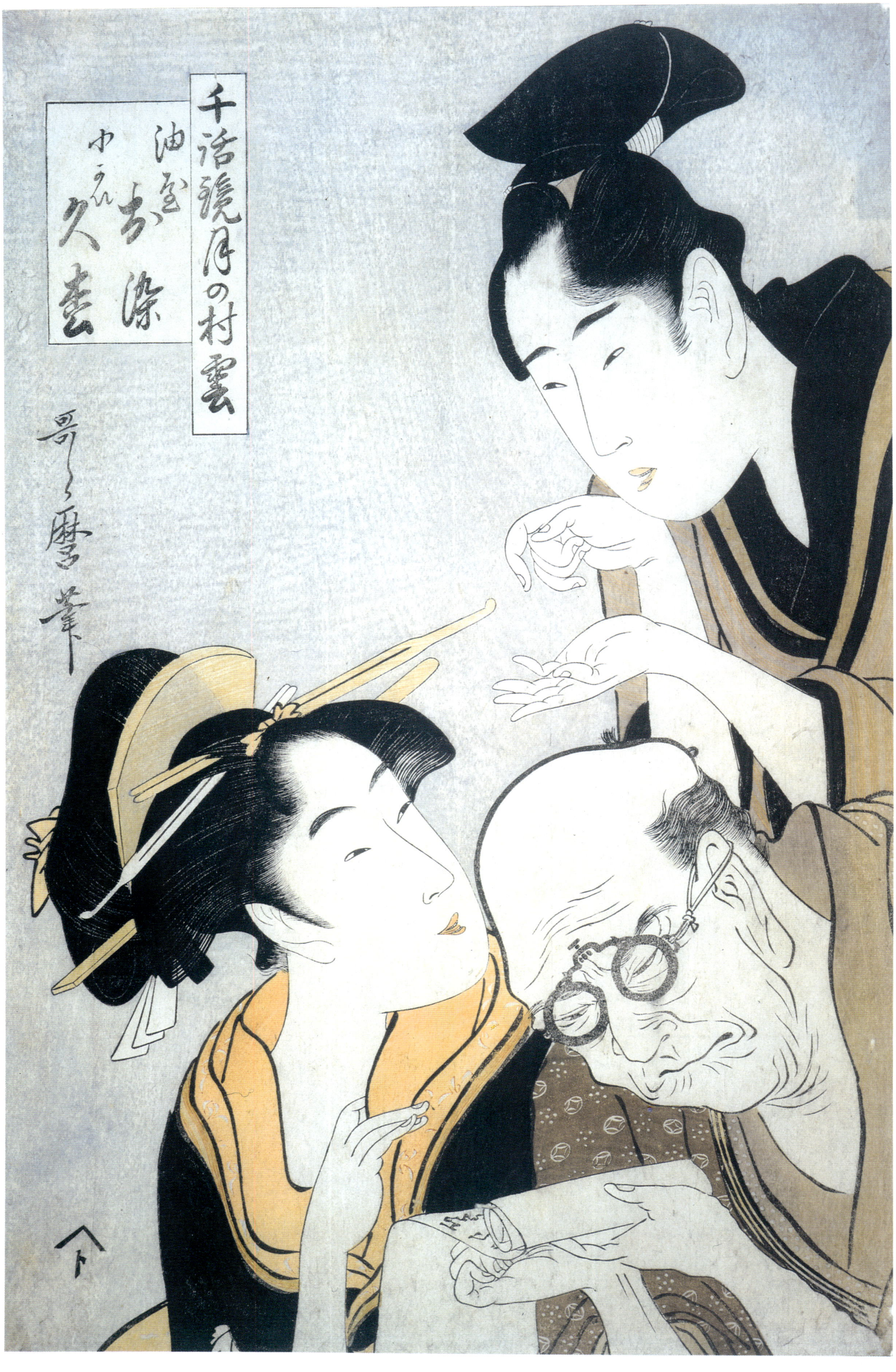
千話鏡月の村雲
油屋 お染
久松
哥麿筆

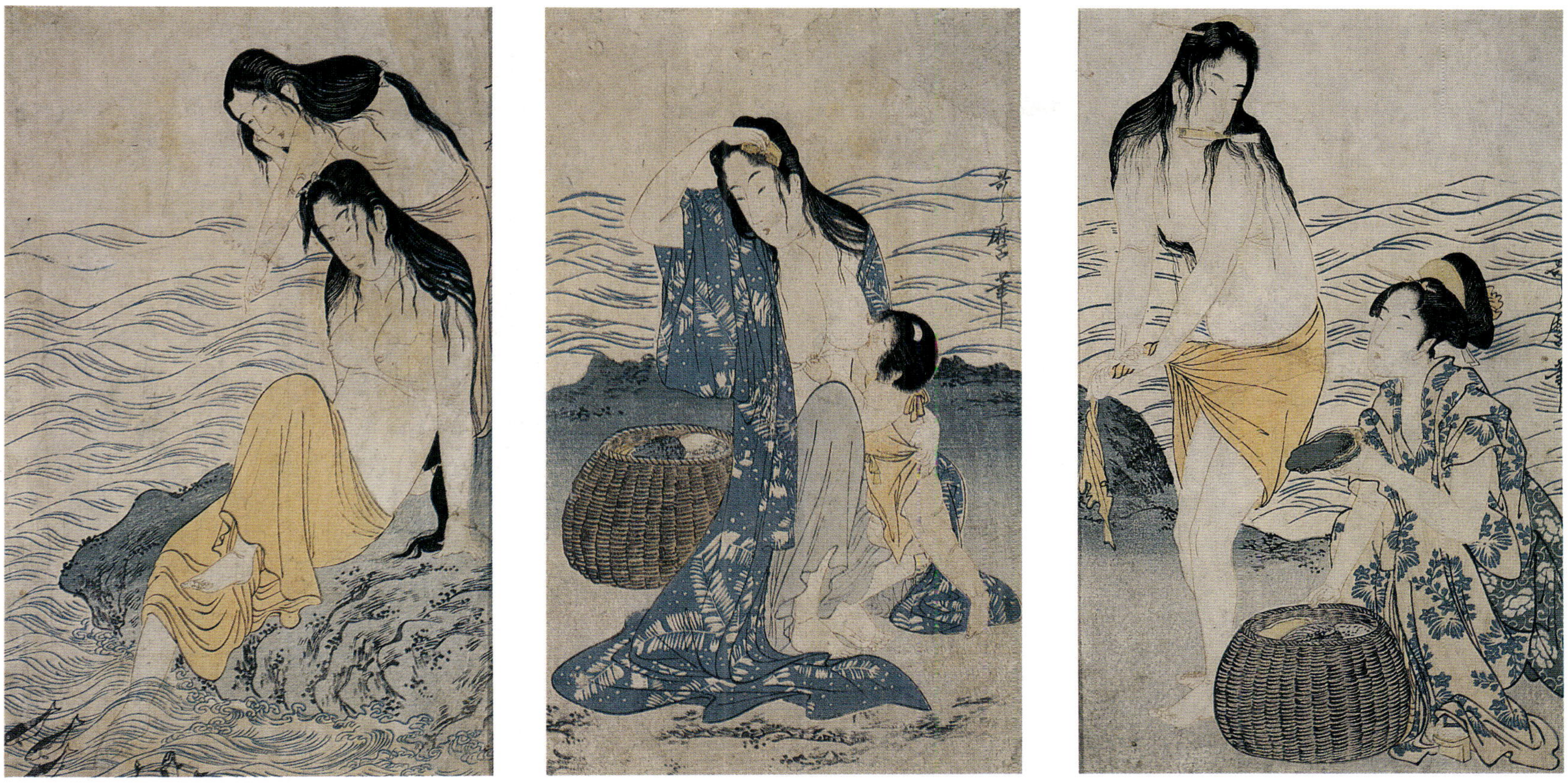

Above: Kitagawa Utamaro (1753-1806) 'Awabi Fishers,' c.1798, triptych, 14⅖×10⅕ inches (36.5×25.9 cm) each. Courtesy of the Trustees of the British Museum, London.

Left: Kitagawa Utamaro (1753-1806) 'The Lovers Osome and Hisamatsu frustrated,' from the series 'A Mirror of Flirting Lovers' 1795-1800, 15×10 inches (38.2×25.7 cm). Published by Yamaguchuya Chūsuke (*Chiwa kagami tsuki no mura-kumo*),' Courtesy of the Trustees of the British Museum, London.

settings in which to display women and to explore their emotions and states of mind. There are, for example, numerous examples of prints illustrating the Niwaka festival during which courtesans and geisha burlesqued the procession of the Korean ambassadors (page 98). Utamaro was also fascinated by the emotional aspect of pairs of lovers and this formed the basis of several sets of prints. In the series entitled a 'Mirror of Flirting Lovers' (*Chiwa kagami tsuki no mura-kumo*), published between 1795 and 1800, each print is composed of three figures, the lovers, who are immaculately turned out, and a third person who, by contrast, is old, wrinkled or in some way unsightly (page 100). Utamaro was interested in all types of women, not just the well-groomed *bijin*. This is exemplified by women diving for *awabi* shells in the sea (above), a far cry from the women of the Yoshiwara, as well as portrayals of legendary figures of Yamauba and Kintoki. The illustration of the latter not only allowed for an intriguing design, with the wild appearance of Yamauba and the dark red skin of her infant son Kintoki, but also for an interesting study of their emotions. Utamaro also increasingly sought novel technical devices, such as the use of a red outline (instead of the normal black), or even none at all (page 102).

Throughout his life, Utamaro used different signatures which may be used to help date a print. His earliest works, for example, are signed Toyoaki. He subsequently adopted the name Utamaro, adding *ga* to it before 1791-92 and *hitsu* afterwards, both meaning 'painted (by),' but with slightly different nuances.

In his last few years, Utamaro fell foul of the laws prohibiting the depiction of historical or important persons by the publication of a print which portrayed a very loosely disguised Hideyoshi. For this, he was imprisoned in 1805. At the same time, a noticeable lowering of standards is evident in his prints, yet he still produced some fine examples. In addition, some works assigned to him were undoubtedly the work of his pupil Utamaro II.

Although Utamaro dominated the field of *bijinga* from the 1790s onwards, there were several other artists who worked alongside him, such as Hosoda Eishi. Eishi was of samurai origin, the son of a government official who was in receipt of an annual stipend. He studied Kanō school painting and spent his early years working as a painter, until he turned to designing *ukiyo-e* prints at the age of 30. This was an unusual step for someone of his background, since *ukiyo-e* was essentially produced for the *chōnin* by the *chōnin*. Eishi specialized in the portrayal of *bijin*, first under the influence of Kiyonaga, and then Utamaro, with the works of these two artists forming the basis of his style. Although he was an artist of no great originality, Eishi's works reveal certain qualities which set them apart. His compositions frequently allude to classical themes, for example, and he designed sets of prints which illustrate Japanese classical literature, such as the 'Tale of Ise' and the 'Tale of Genji.' The latter consists of a set of nine triptychs which may be considered among his best works. Such prints, known as *mitate-e* (travesty prints), which parody classical themes, were given contemporary interest by setting them in the present rather than the past, with the women displaying the latest fashion.

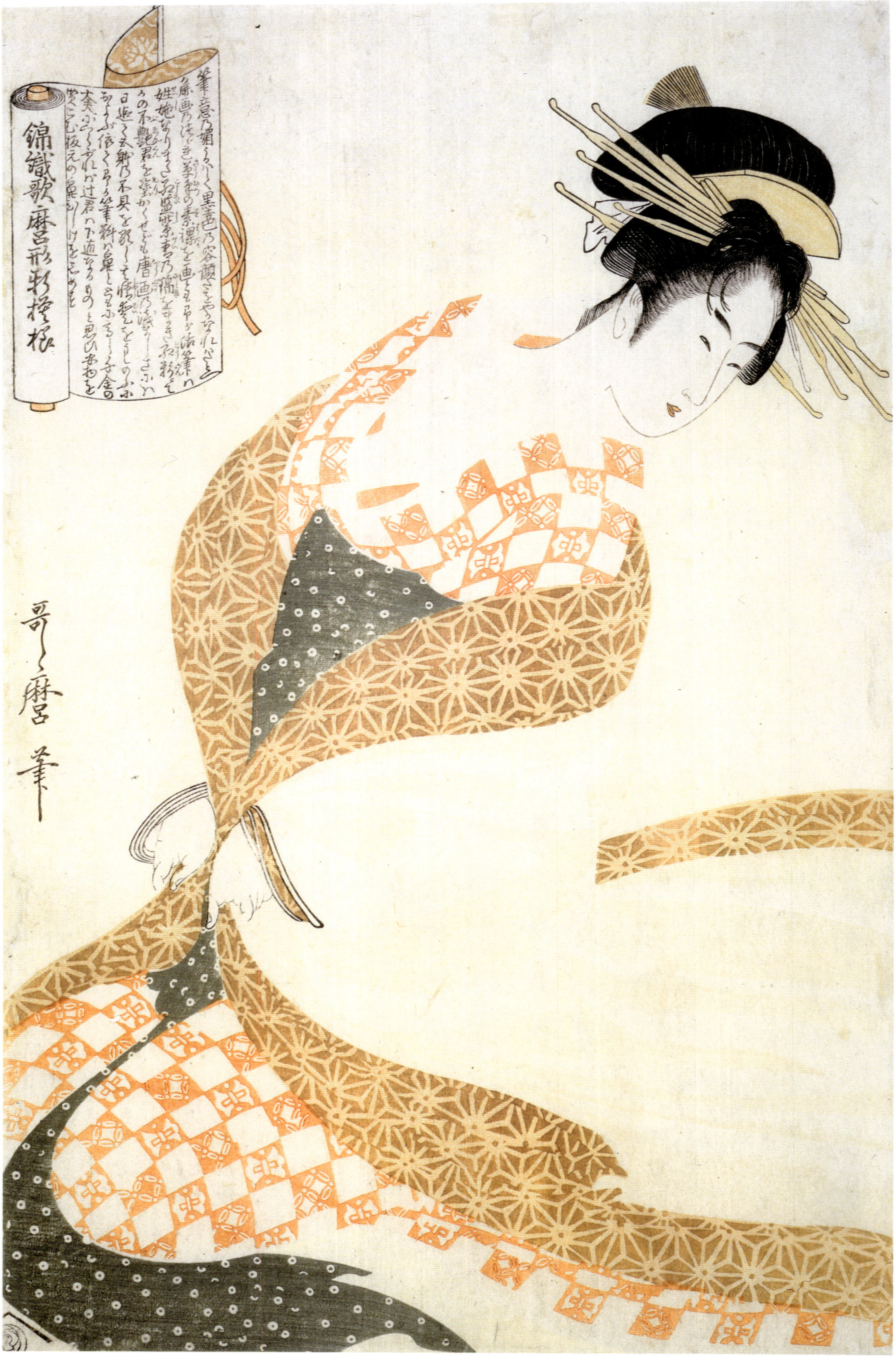
錦織歌麿形新模様
哥麿筆

Left: Kitagawa Utamaro (1753-1806) 'The Outer-robe', from the series 'New Patterns of Brocade in Utamaro's style' (*Nishiki ori Utamaro gata shui-moyō*), c.1797, 14⅗×9⅘ inches (37.3×25.0 cm). Published by Tsutuya Kiemon. Courtesy of the Trustees of the British Museum, London.

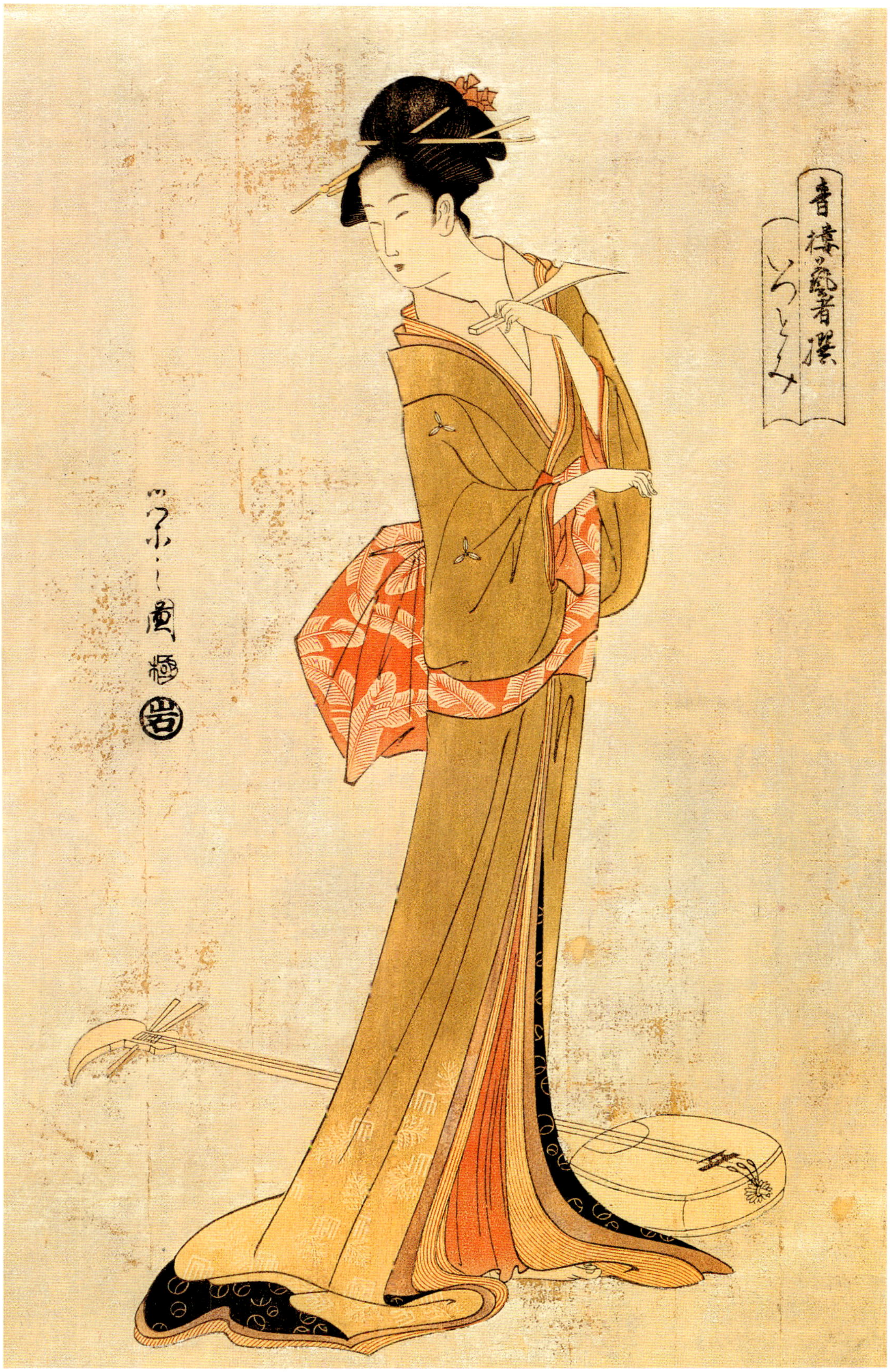

Right: Hosoda Eishi (1756-1829) 'The Courtesan Itsutomi with a Samisen,' from the series, 'A Selection of Beauties from the Green Houses' (*Seirō geisha sen*), c.1796-7, 15½×10⅕ inches (39.4×26 cm). Courtesy of the Trustees of the Victoria and Albert Museum, London.

In the case of the print seen above, moreover, additional interest was added by the use of *benigirai-e*. Between the years 1795 and 1800, Eishi also designed a number of full-length, as well as *ōkubi-e* portraits, the former exhibiting the curved and exaggerated stature characteristic of *bijin* prints of the period (page 104), set against plain, colored grounds, and often embellished with mica. In general, Eishi's prints are characterized by a refined elegance, though his figures lack the emotional insight which make Utamaro's *bijin* so powerful. Around the turn of the century, Eishi gave up designing prints and during the remainder of his life produced a great number of paintings in the *ukiyo-e* genre.

Eishi had several competent pupils and followers, namely Eishō, Ichirakutei Eisui, Chōkyōsai Eiri and Rekisentei Eiri. Chōkōsai Eishō (*fl* 1793-99), who was the most prolific among them, specialized in 'large head' portraits of *bijin* (pages 104 and 105). His ideal of feminine beauty was more robust and down to earth than that of Eishi. Rekisentei Eiri (*fl* 1790s), on the other hand, portrayed fragile and willowy women. Ichirakutei Eisui (*fl c.* 1789-1801) specialized in 'large-head' portraits of courtesans (page 106), which also display his considerable technical virtuosity.

Another print designer who specialized in *bijin* portraits and who was more or less contemporary with Utamaro, was Eishōsai Chōki. What is particularly noteworthy about this artist is the fact that among the bulk of his work, which was competent but somewhat undistinguished, are a small number of prints of exceptional beauty, published by Tsutaya Jūsaburō. These were, for the most part, half-length portraits of women, with serene expressions and set against an atmospheric ground, the two unifying perfectly to bring about a composition of poetic calm (pages 107 and 109). The resulting overall effect is powerful and yet extremely peaceful.

The period from 1780 to just after the turn of the century was dominated by the portrayal of *bijin*, culminating in the works of Utamaro. By the early 1800s,

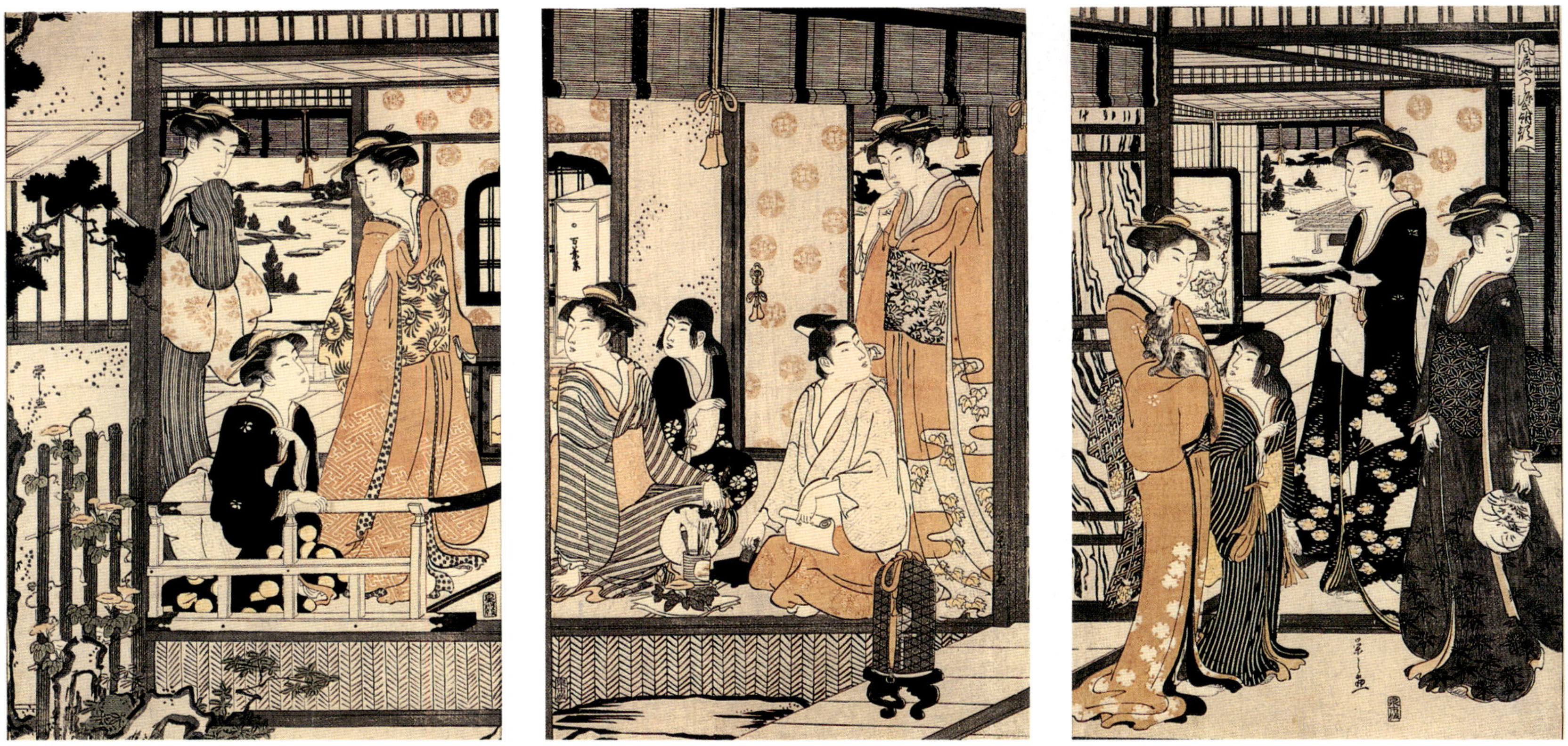

Above: Hosoda Eishi (1756-1829) 'Morning Glory' from the series 'Genji in Modern Dress,' c.1791, triptych, 14⅔×9⅘ inches (37.2×25.0 cm) each. Published by Izumiya Ichibei. Courtesy of the Trustees of the British Museum, London.

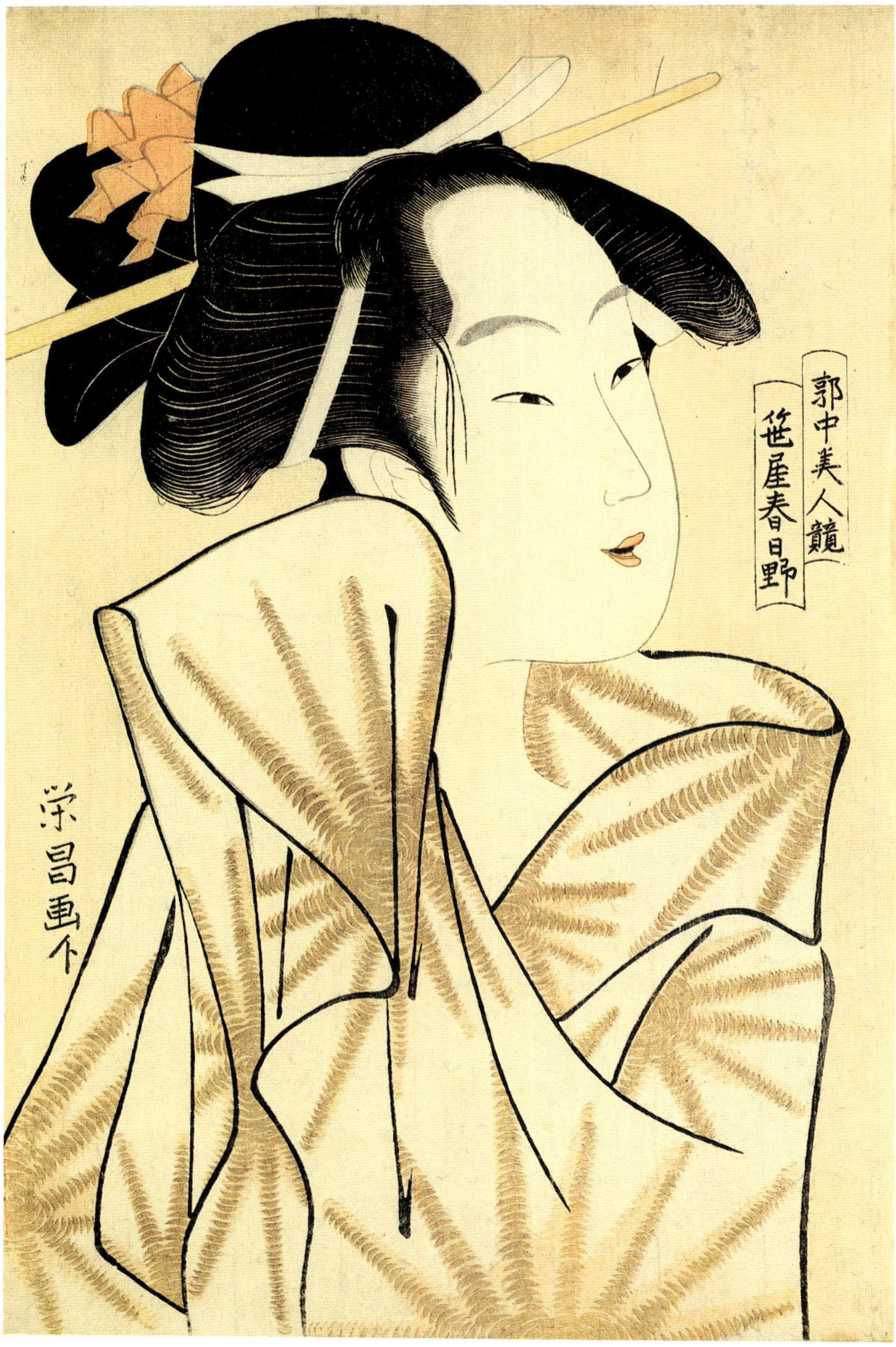

Left: Chōkōsai Eishō (*fl* 1793-99) 'The Courtesan Kasugano of the Sasaya Drying her Hair,' from the series 'A Comparison of Beauties within the Quarter,' (*Kakuchu bijin kurabe*), c.1795, 14¾×9¾ inches (37.5×24.8 cm). Published by Yamaguchi Chūsuke. Courtesy of the Trustees of the British Museum, London.

Right: Chōkōsai Eishō (*fl* 1793-99) 'The Courtesan Yosooi of the Matsabaya,' 1790s, 15×10 inches (38.4×25.4 cm). Published by Yamaguchi Chūsuke. Courtesy of the Trustees of the Victoria and Albert Museum, London.

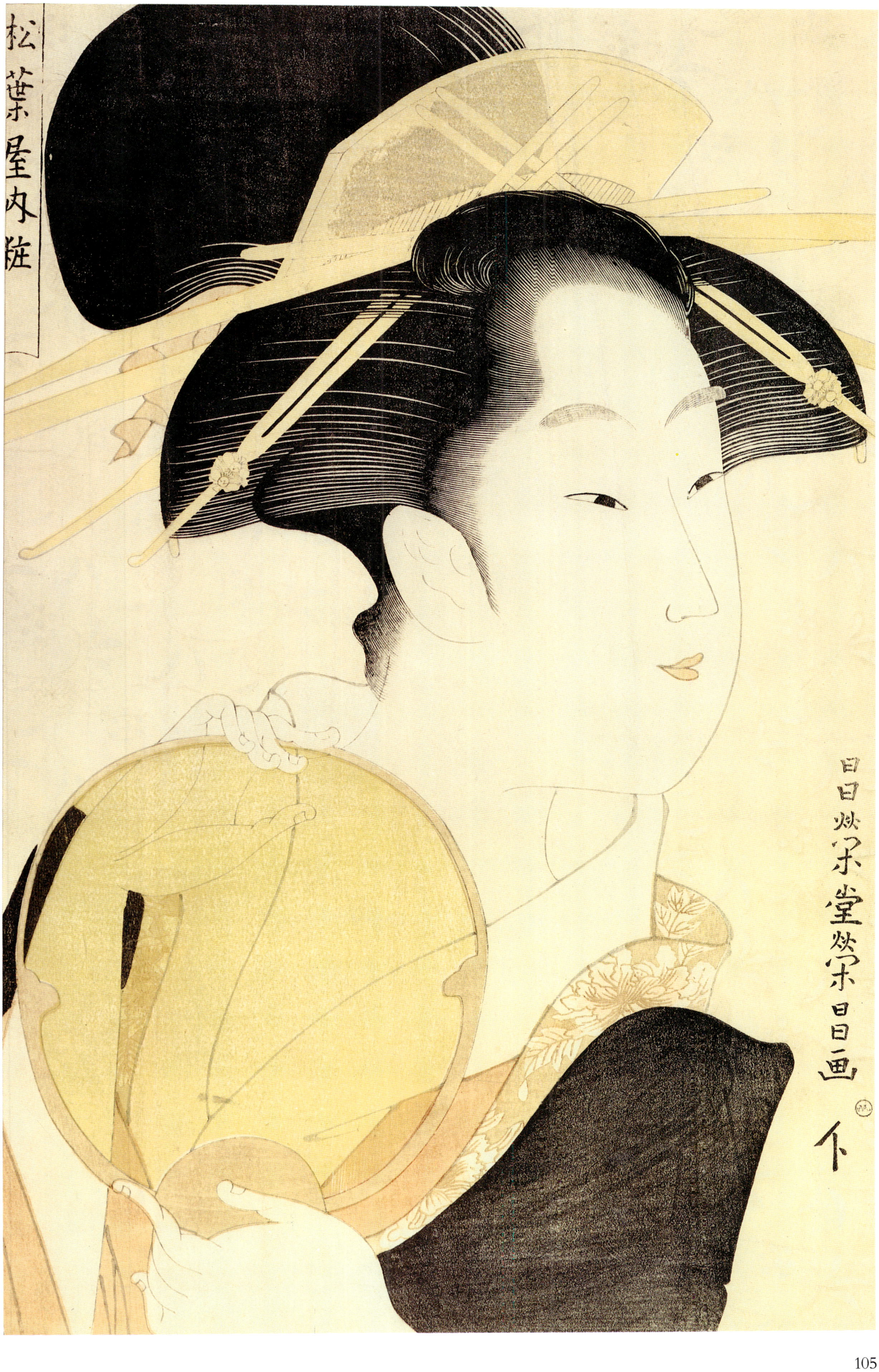
松葉屋内粧
昌栄堂栄昌画

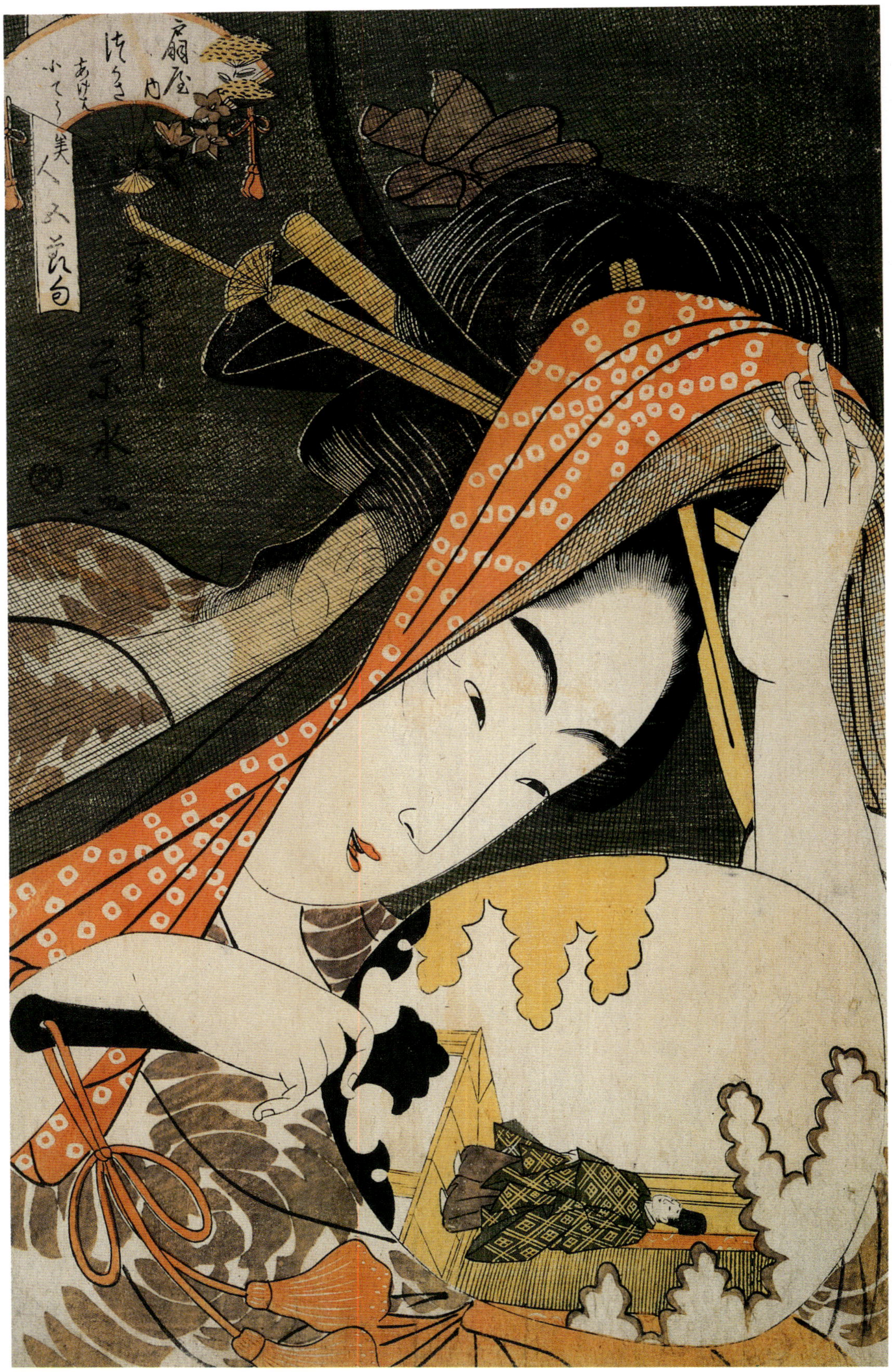

Left: Ichirakutei Eisui (*fl* 1789-1801) 'The Tanabata Festival,' from the series 'Beauties of the Five Festivals,' (*Bijin gō-sekku*), c. 1797-1800, 14½×10⅕ inches (37×25.9 cm). Published by Maruya Bun'emon Courtesy of the Trustees of the British Museum, London.

Right: Eishōsai Chōki (*fl* late 1780s-early 1800s) 'Catching Fireflies,' c.1795, 15×9⅘ inches (38.2×25.0 cm). Published by Tsutaya Jūsaburō. Courtesy of the Trustees of the British Museum, London.

however, the works of such artists who had not already given up this genre displayed an overall decline in quality and standards. In a sense, too, their very popularity may have contributed to this since over-production, together with the absence of a figure such as Tsutaya Jūsaburō and his insistence on high standards, resulted in poor quality and design. It was also as though Utamaro and his contemporaries had, for the time being, explored all possible facets of the portrayal of *bijin* and had brought it to its logical conclusion. It is true that Utamaro had many followers who continued working after his death, most notably Kikumaro (*fl* 1830; also known as Tsukimaro) and Utamaro II, but they contributed nothing new to the subject. It was not until some ten years later, that artists such as Kunisada (1786-1865), Keisai Eizan (1787-1867) and Eisen (1790-1848) produced some interesting *bijinga* prints, though it is probably true to say that the prints of Utamaro and some of his contemporaries have never been surpassed.

Between 1780 and 1810, there was a continuing interest in theatrical prints. In the same way that Utamaro had attempted to portray individual women, Bunchō and Shunshō in the 1770s also portrayed known actors, with identifiable personal characteristics, instead of stereotyped figures in specific acting roles. Whereas in the field of *bijin* print designers from the 1790s onwards were able to concentrate on the woman alone and her mood, those specializing in actor prints strove to combine the actor as an individual with the dramatic role he was playing. Print designers also produced 'large-head' actor prints which concentrated on the face of the actor as well as on his range of expressions. Another popular device was to portray the actor in a melodramatic, fixed pose (*mie*). This pose, which was the culmination of a dramatic and emotional build-up, frequently involved a peculiar stance, with crossed eyes and a fixed glare. In the hands of a skillful print designer, the portrayal of the *mie* readily lent itself to the most spectacular and vivid compositions and was used for great dramatic effect.

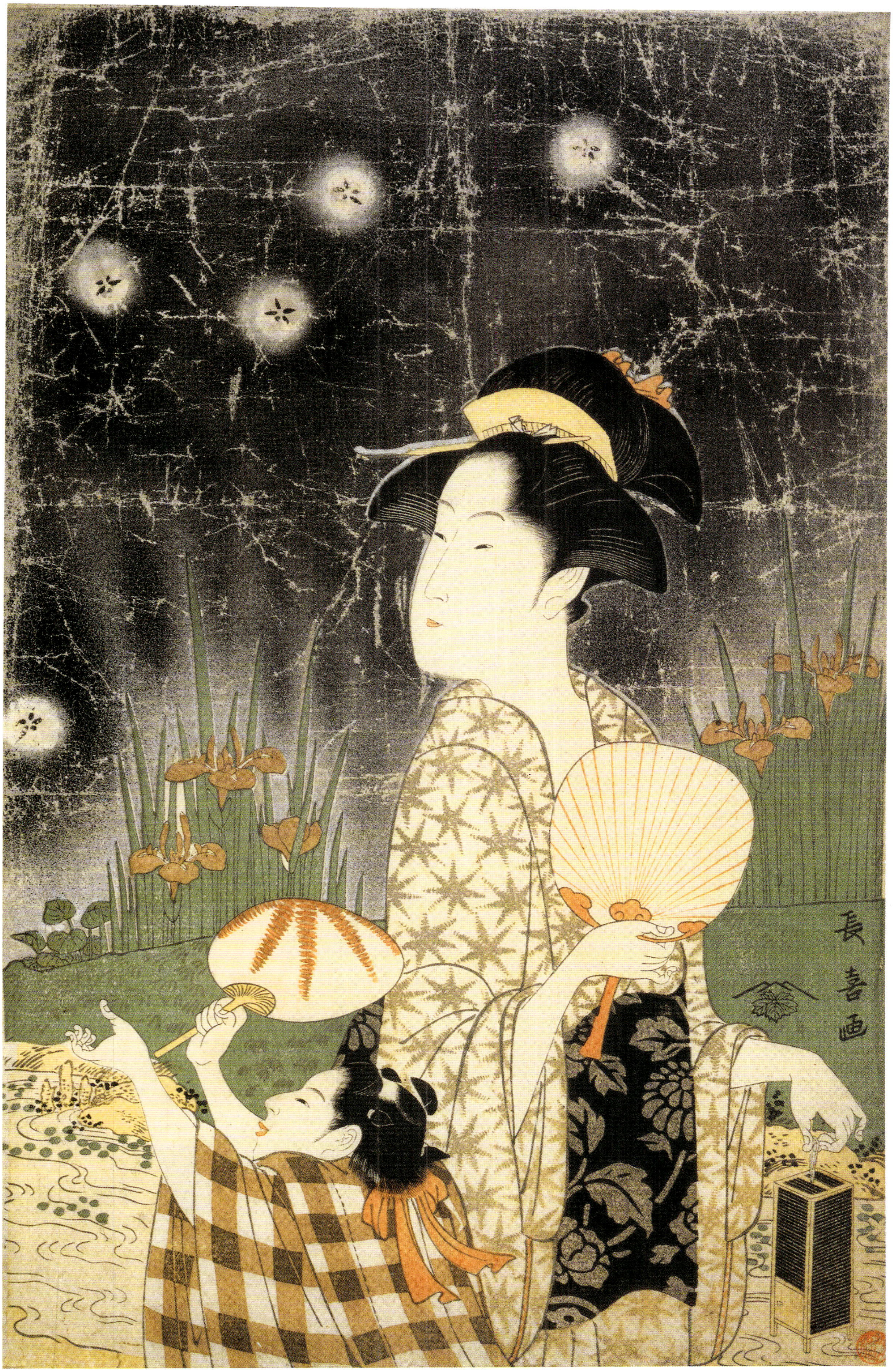
長喜画

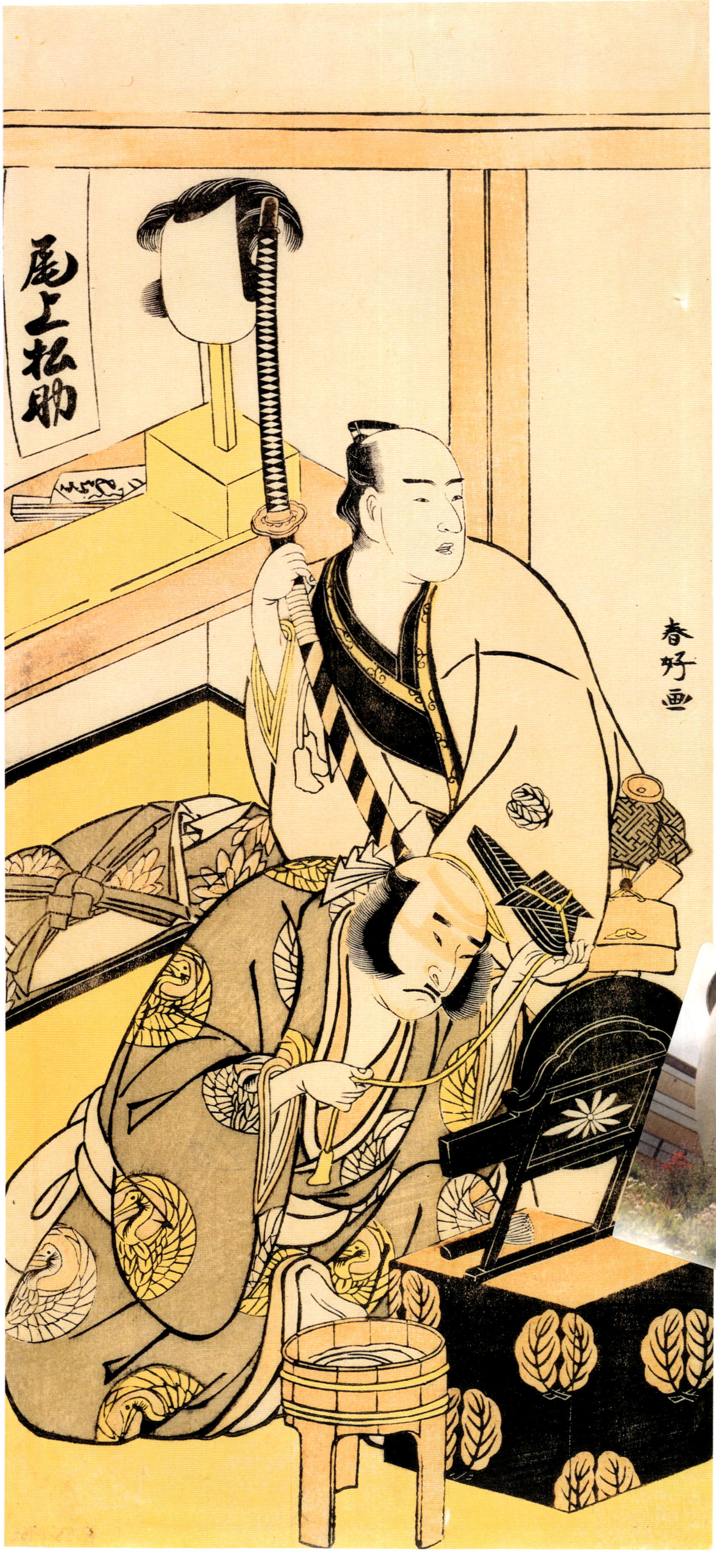

Left: Katsukawa Shunkō (1743-1812) 'The Actor Onoe Matsusuke in his Dressing Room with his Dresser,' 1785, 12×5 inches (30.5×14 cm). Courtesy of the Trustees of the Victoria and Albert Museum, London.

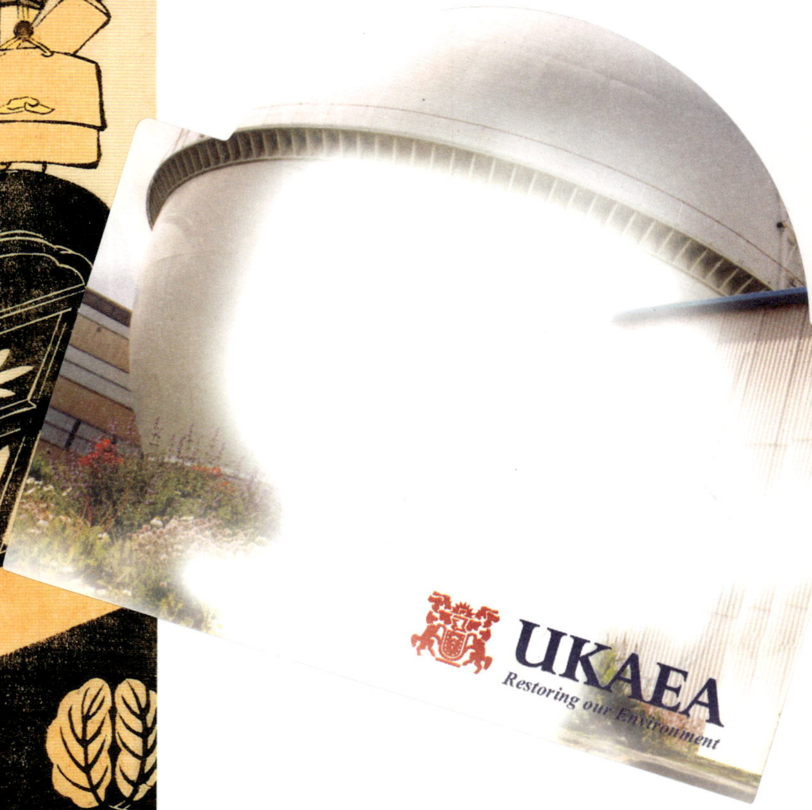

Right: Eishōsai Chōki (*fl* late 1780s-early 1800s) 'Sunrise on New Year's Day,' c.1795, 14⅕×9½ inches (36.0×24.2 cm). Published by Tsutaya Jusaburō. Courtesy of the Trustees of the British Museum, London.

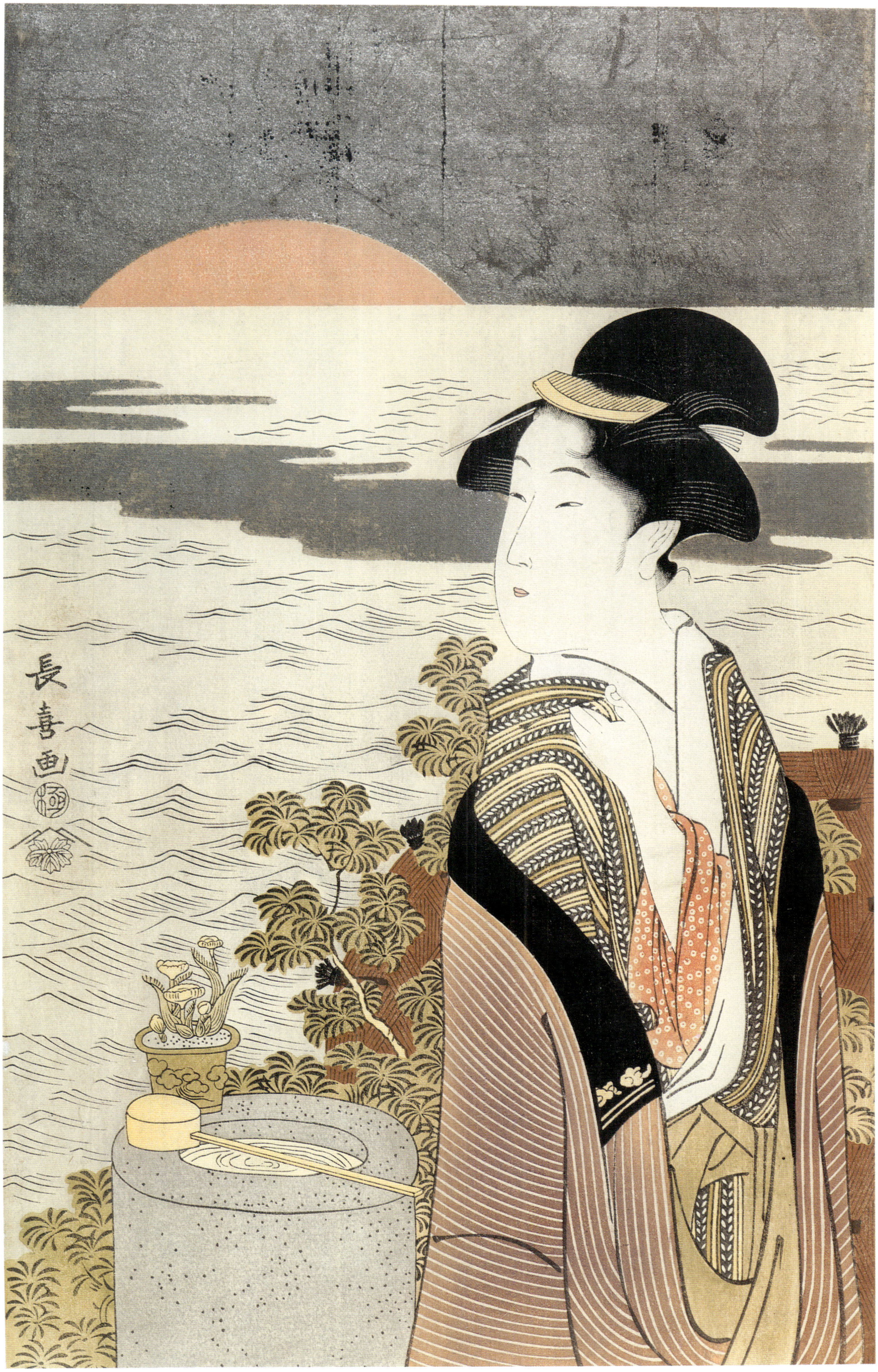
長喜画

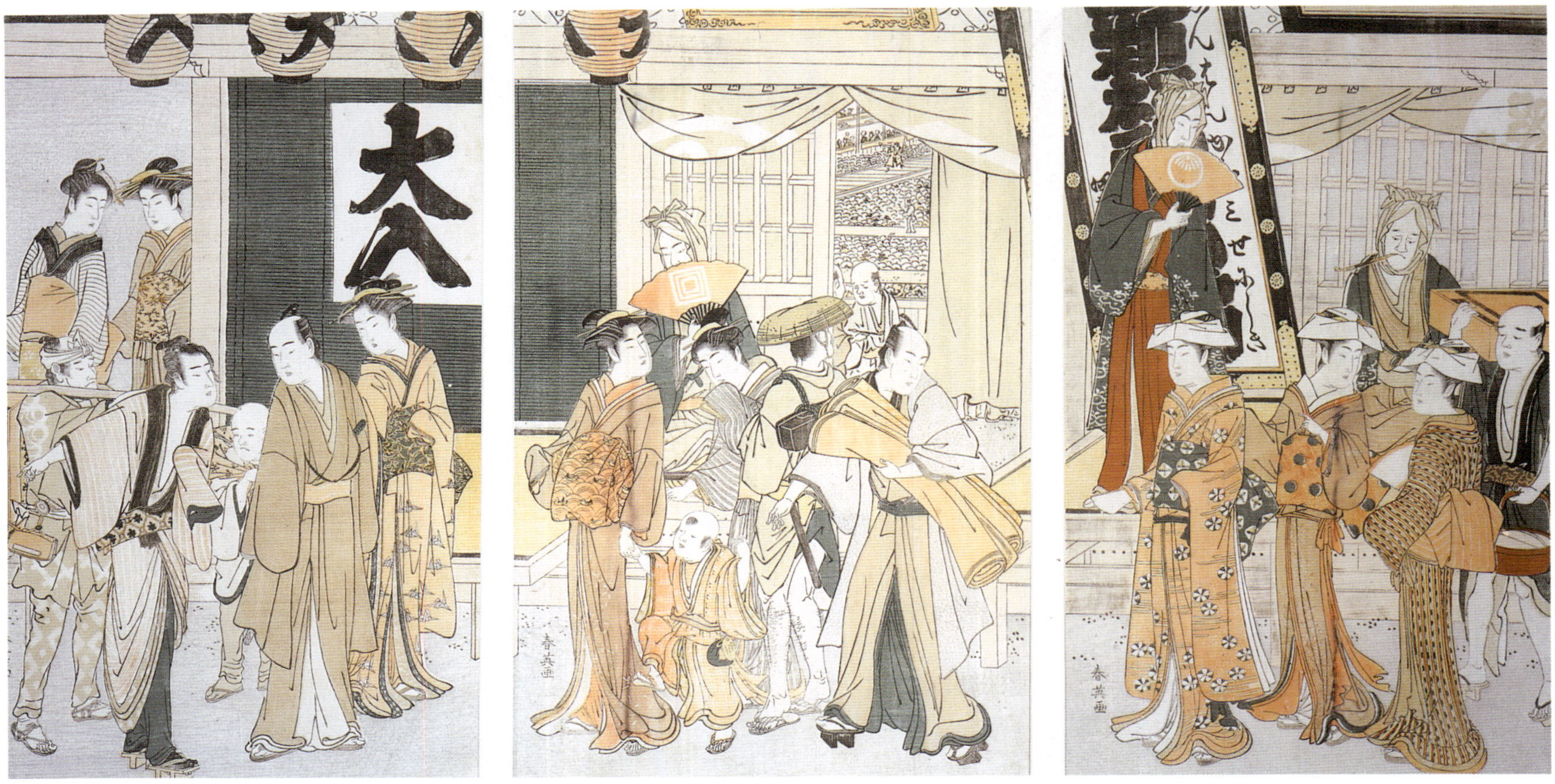

Above: Katsukawa Shun'ei (1762-1819) 'A Newly Published Brocade First Night,' c.1795, triptych, 15×9⅘ inches (38×25 cm) each. Courtesy of the Trustees of the British Museum, London.

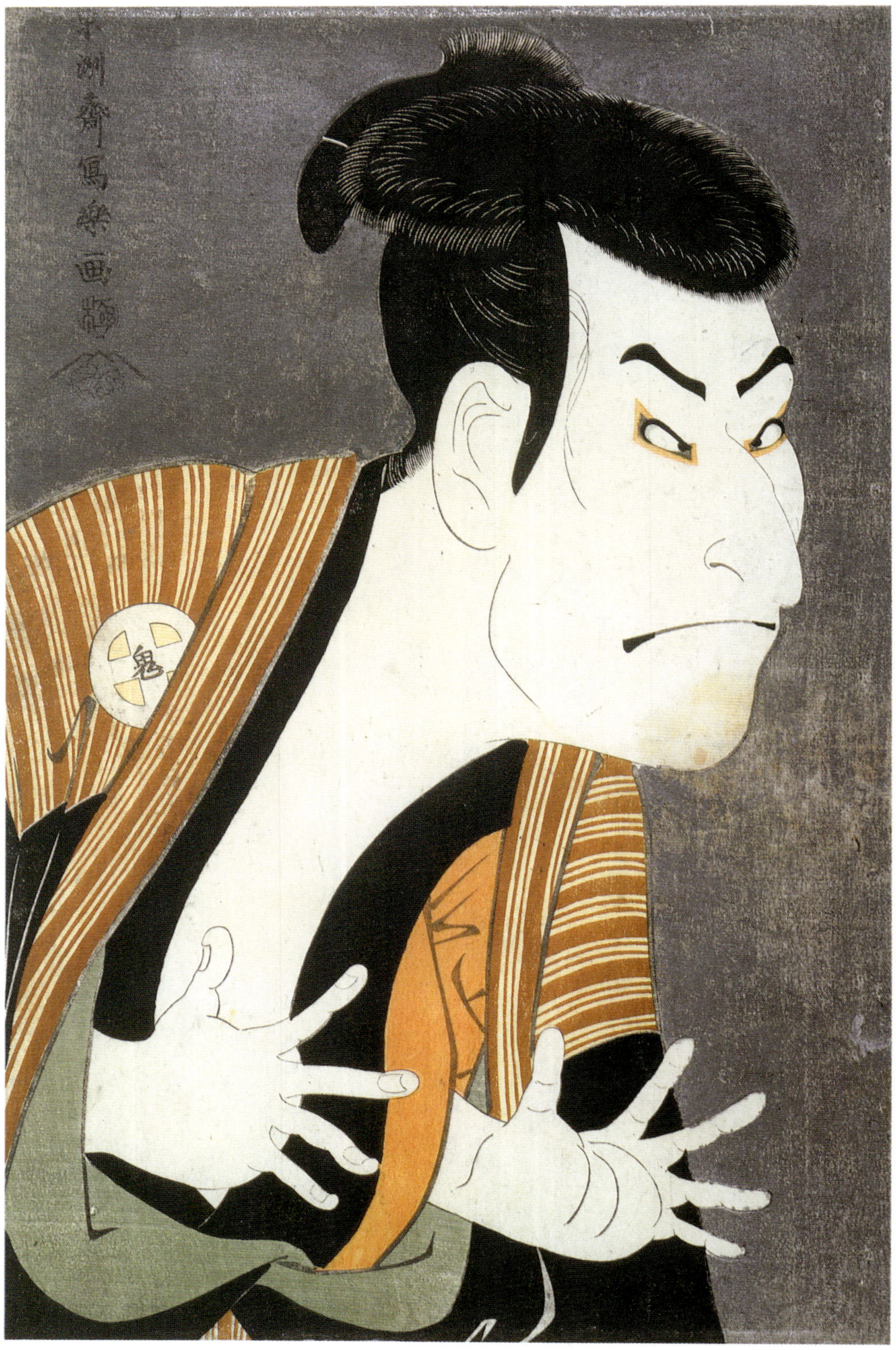

Right: Tōshūsai Sharaku (*fl* 1794-95) 'The Actor Ōtani Oniki,' 1794, triptych, woodblock with powdered mica background, 14⅕×9⅔ inches (36.2×24.4 cm). Published by Tsutaya Jūsaburō. Courtesy of the Trustees of the British Museum, London.

Far right: Tōshūsai Sharaku (*fl* 1794-95) 'The Actors Nakajima Wadaemon and Nakamara Konozo, woodblock with powdered mica background,' 13⅘×9½ inches (35.0×24.2 cm). Published by Tsutaya Jūsaburō. Courtesy of the Trustees of the British Museum, London.

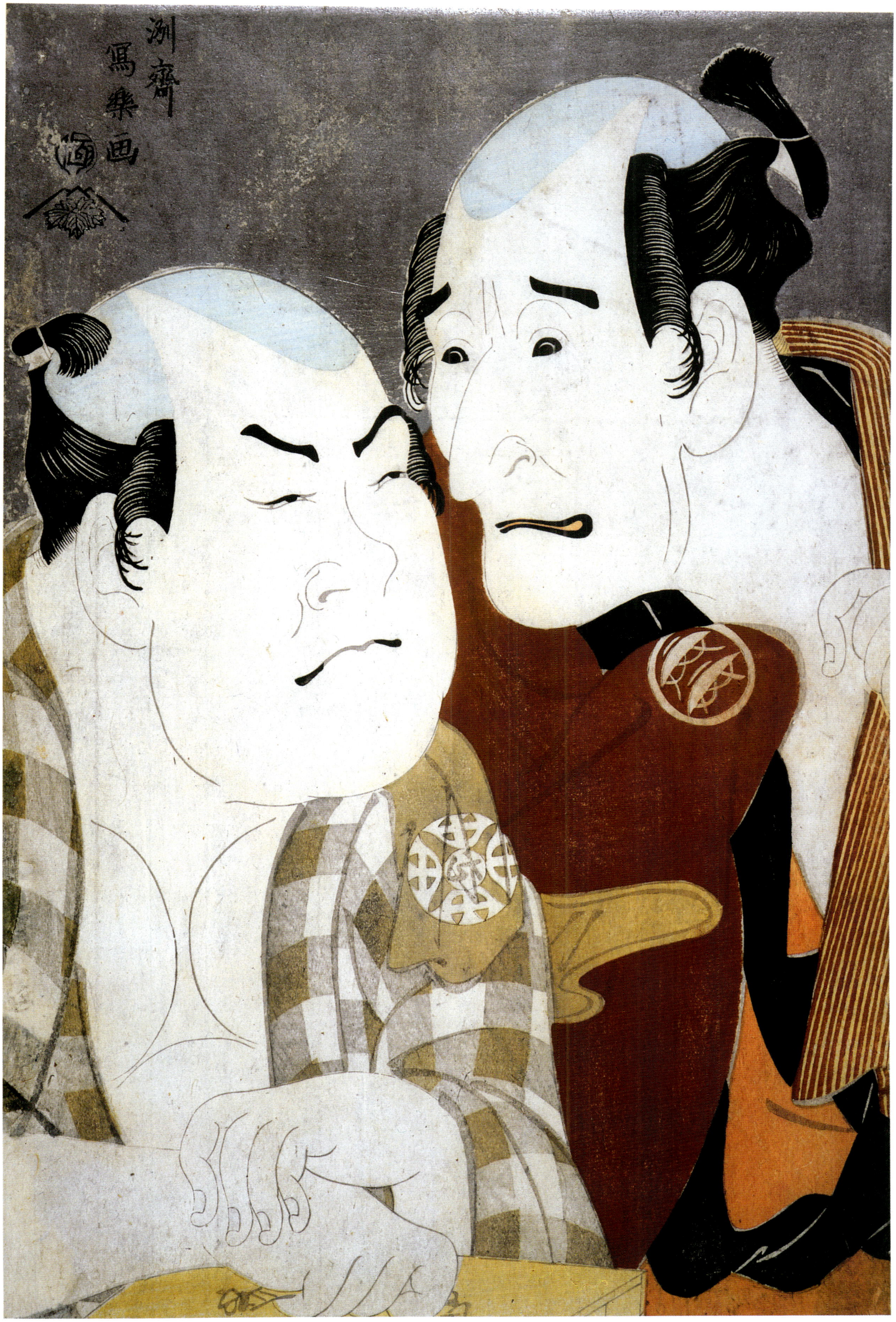
洲齋
寫樂画

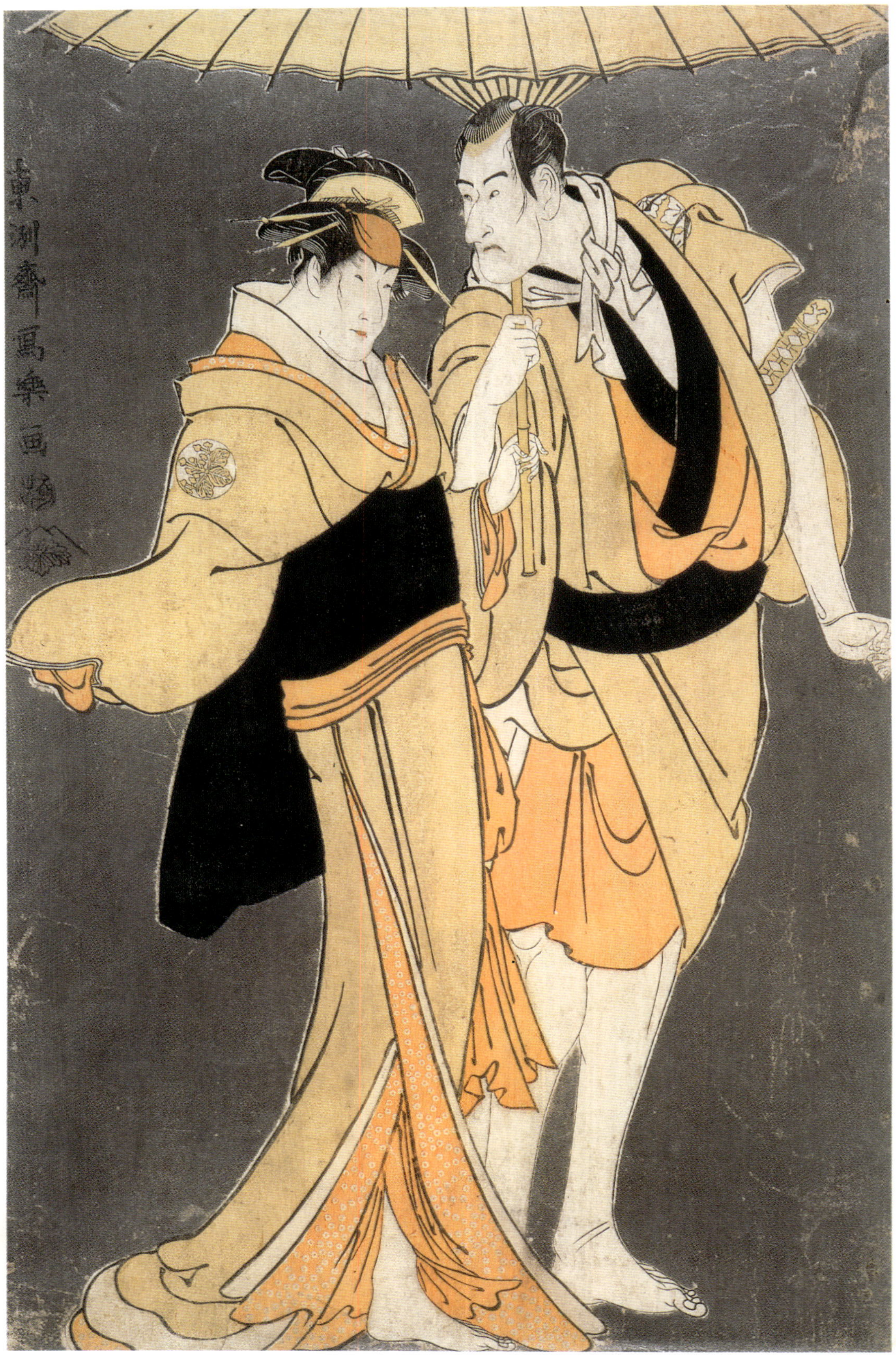

Left: Tōshūisai Sharaku (*fl* 1794-95) 'Actors as the Lovers Umegawa and Chūbei,' 1794, woodblock with powdered mica background, $14\frac{1}{5}\times9\frac{2}{5}$ inches (36.0×23.8 cm). Published by Tsutaya Jūsaburō. Courtesy of the Trustees of the British Museum, London.

Right: Utagawa Toyokuni (1769-1825) 'Snow' (*Yuki*), from the series 'The Three Beauties,' (*San bijin*), $14\frac{2}{3}\times10$ inches (37.3×25.7 cm). Courtesy of the Trustees of the British Museum, London.

Overleaf: Utagawa Toyokuni (1769-1825) 'The Actors Ichikawa Danjūrō VII and Segawa Kikunojō IV,' 1810, diptych, $15\times20\frac{1}{2}$ inches (38.1×52.1 cm) each. Published by Yamaguchiya Tōbei. Courtesy of the Trustees of the Victoria and Albert Museum, London.

Bunchō gave up designing prints in the 1770s, while Katsukawa Shunshō turned his main artistic attention to painting *bijin* in the 1780s, though he was an able teacher with a number of talented pupils including Shunchō, Shunzan, Shunkō, Shun'ei and Shunrō. Both Shunchō and Shunzan specialized in *bijin* prints and have already been discussed, while the prints of Shunrō, who is better known as Hokusai, belong to another chapter.

Among those pupils of Shunshō who specialized in theatrical prints, Katsukawa Shunkō (1743-1812) was the most prolific. In the early 1770s, he began producing actor prints in the tall, narrow *hosoban* ($12\frac{1}{4}\times5\frac{3}{4}$ inches [32×14.5 cm])format, which are often indistinguishable from those of his teacher. He also continued his initiative by portraying actors involved in offstage activites (page 108). In 1787 Shunkō suffered a stroke which paralyzed his right arm but, undaunted, he continued to work with his left arm, producing a number of 'large-head' portraits during the 1790s.

Although Katsukawa Shun'ei (1762-1819) was a fellow-pupil of Shunshō, he was considerbly younger than Shunkō. Shun'ei was particularly instrumental in pioneering actor *ōkubi-e* producing examples as early as 1790. During the 1790s, he became the leading member of the Katsukawa school, working in a lively manner, which was combined with an attempt to capture the emotion of the actor and his role (page 110). Shun'ei's most notable pupil was Katsukawa Shuntei (1770-1820), who not only designed actor prints, but also *bijin*, landscapes, including some in Western style, *surimono*, and warrior prints.

The 1790s was a highly creative and innovative period for actor prints as seen in the work of Tōshūsai Sharaku. Despite his position of importance in the history of *ukiyo-e*, however, Sharaku remains one of its greatest enigmas. His fame lies in the appearance of 150 prints and drawings, the prints of which were published by Tsutaya Jūsaburō, together with a few drawings, over a ten-months period between the fifth month of 1794 and the first month of 1795. He appeared apparently out of the blue, working in a fully developed style, and disappeared back into obscurity after a short period of highly

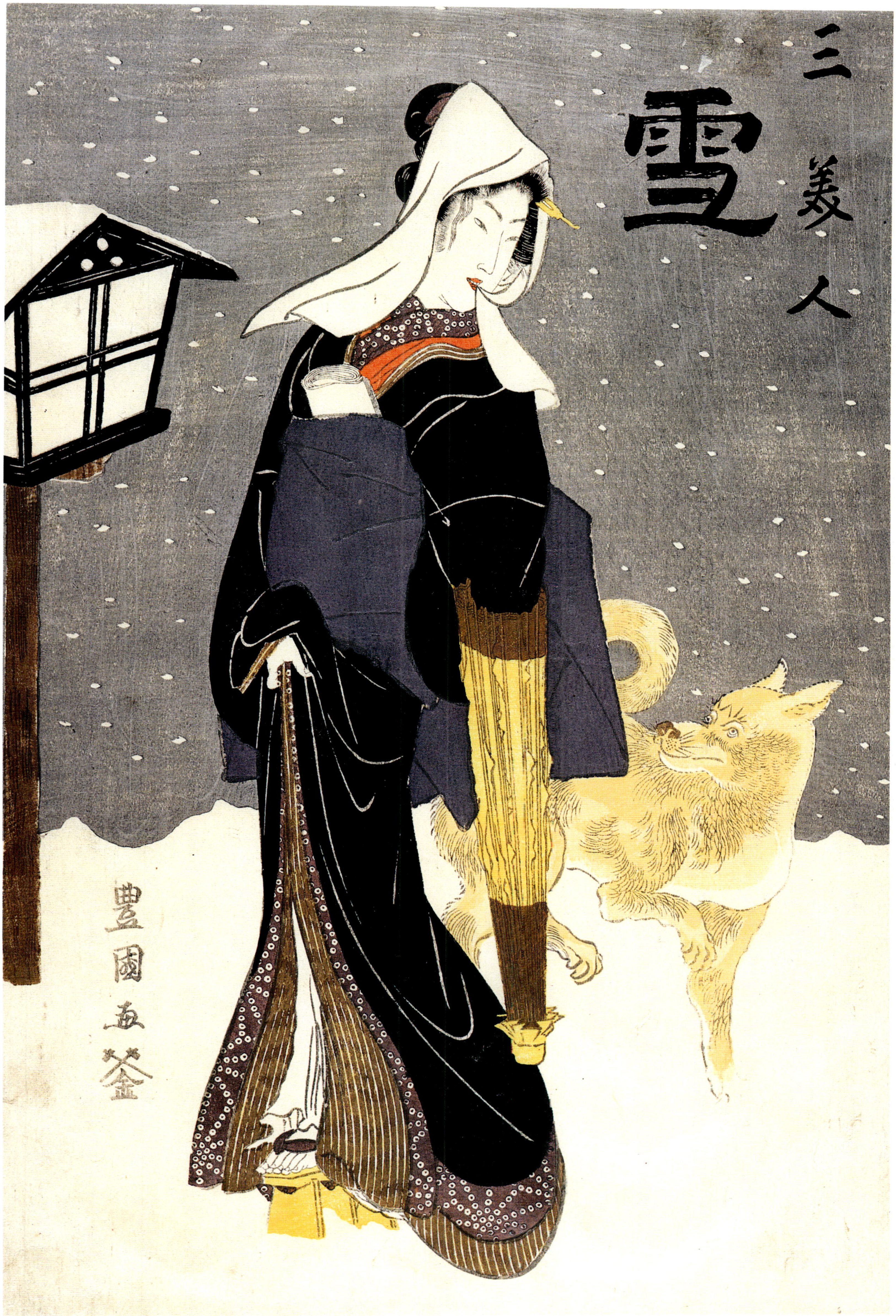
雪
三美人
豊國画

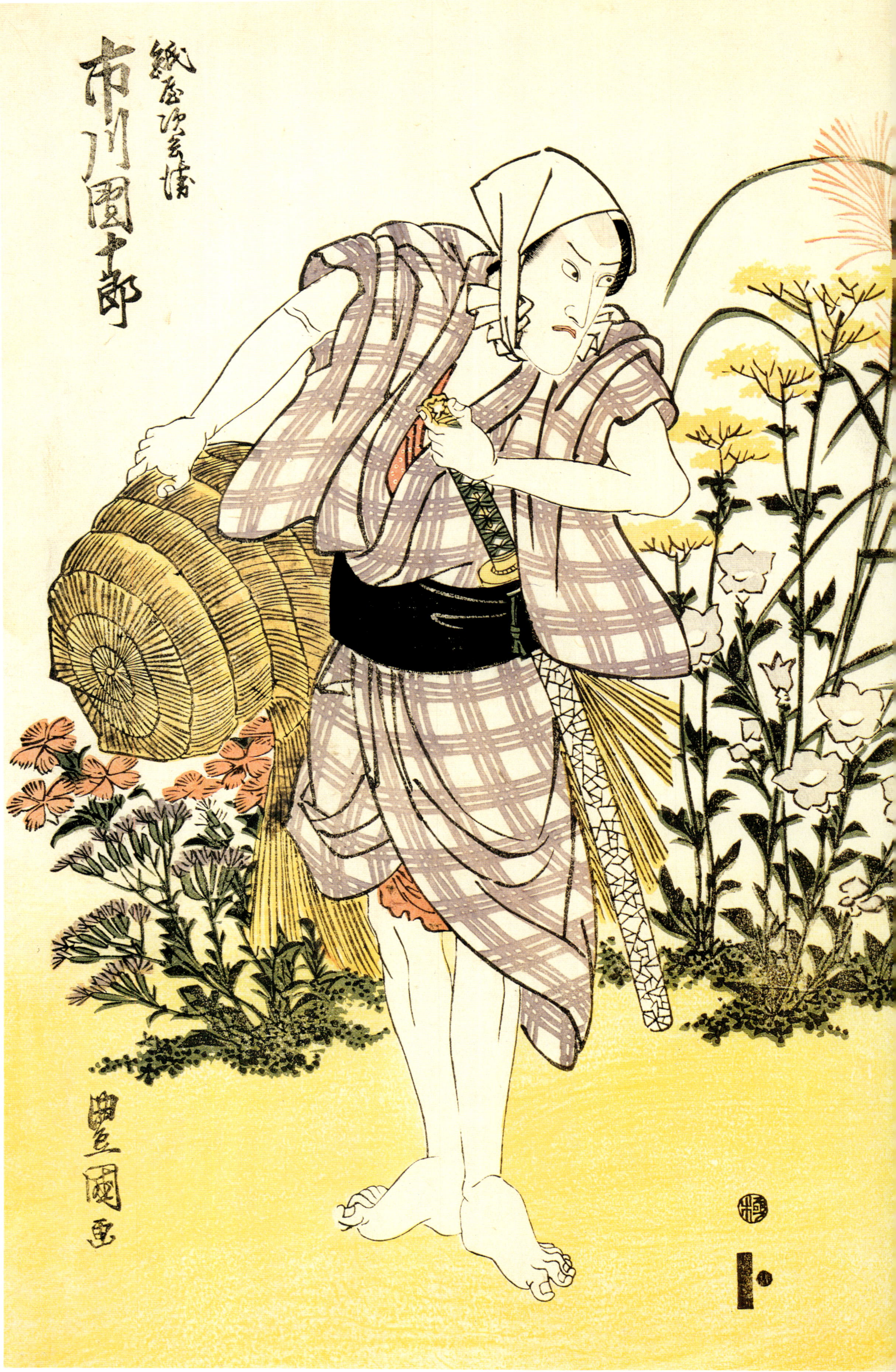
市川團十郎
豊國画

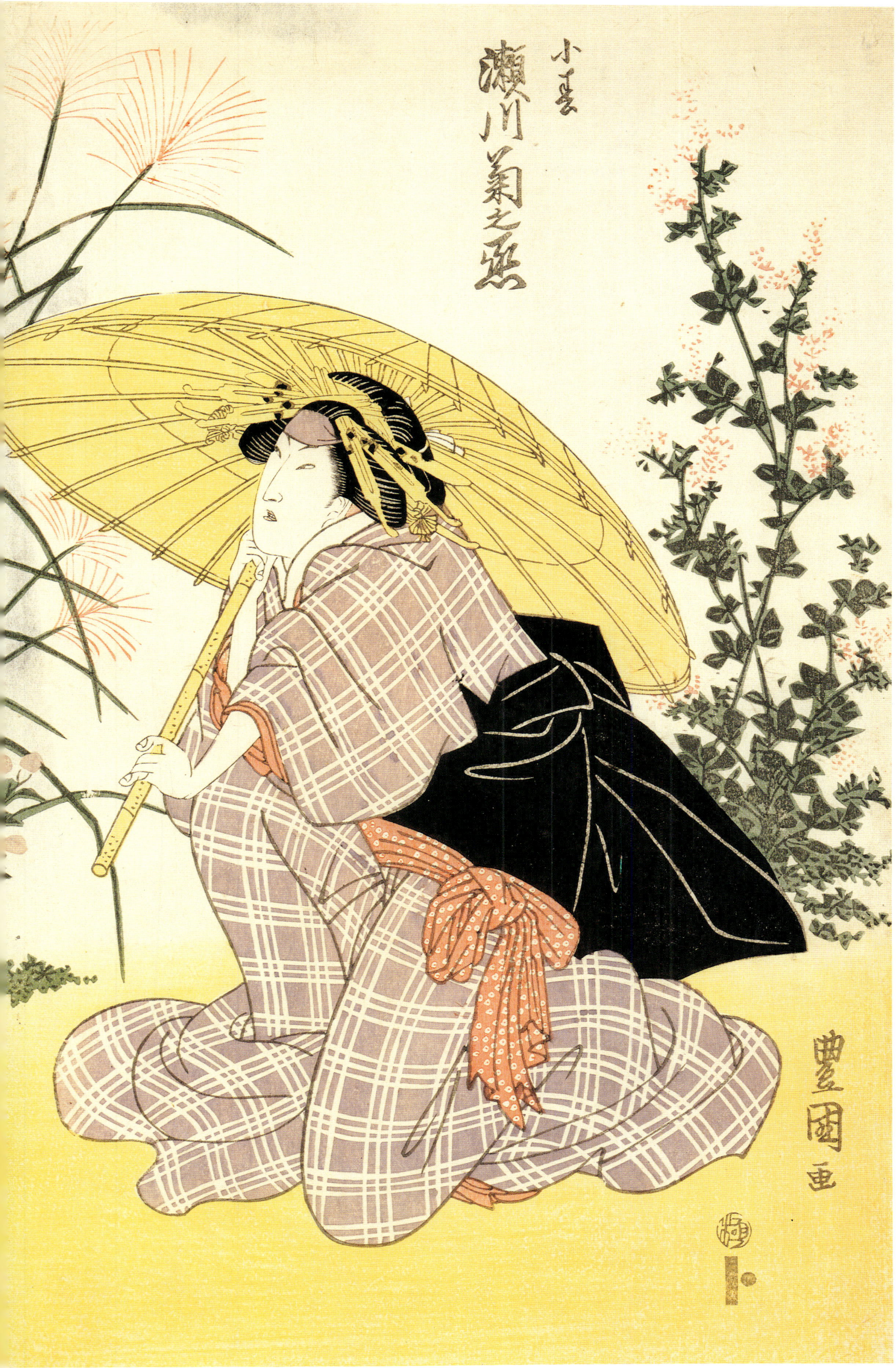
瀬川菊之丞
豊國画

creative and productive artistic activity.

According to one theory, Sharaku was a Nō theater dancer in the service of one of the daimyō, while others suggest that he must have had a close connection with the Kabuki theater to have depicted its actors in such detail and with so much insight. And yet, although there is no biographical or stylistic evidence for this, it is hard to imagine that Sharaku was an untrained amateur. Despite such a short and prolific period of activity, it is possible to identify the plays and actors which Sharaku depicted and hence divide his prints chronologically into four stylistic groups. The first group, which dates to the fifth and sixth months of 1794, consists of 28 prints in the *ōban* format which are among his most famous. They are all in the form of 'large-head' portraits of actors, mostly depicted on their own, though sometimes in pairs, against a mica ground of dark purple or gray (page 110 and 111).

Sharaku's manner of depiction is unmistakable. He sought to portray the personality of the actor combined with the dramatic force of his role. To this end, he was influenced by the figure compositions and characterization of Bunchō and Shunshō, and also by the 'large-head' portraits of Shunkō and Shun'ei. Perhaps the strongest influence, however, were the prints of Utamaro and his psychological probing into the character and mood of the women he portrayed. Sharaku similarly attempted the same but went beyond the bounds of realism into the realms of caricature. In addition, Sharaku's depiction of actors was frequently uncomplimentary, drawing attention to the haughty manner and vanity of many actors of the period. Such shortcomings in their personalities were then exaggerated for expressive effect.

Sharaku's second period dates from the seventh and eighth months of 1794 and includes 38 designs of actors (page 112) of which thirty are individual portraits on a yellow ground in the small, narrow and vertical *hosoban* size, while the remaining eight depict pairs of actors against a white or dark mica ground in the *ōban* format. Sharaku's third and fourth groups in-

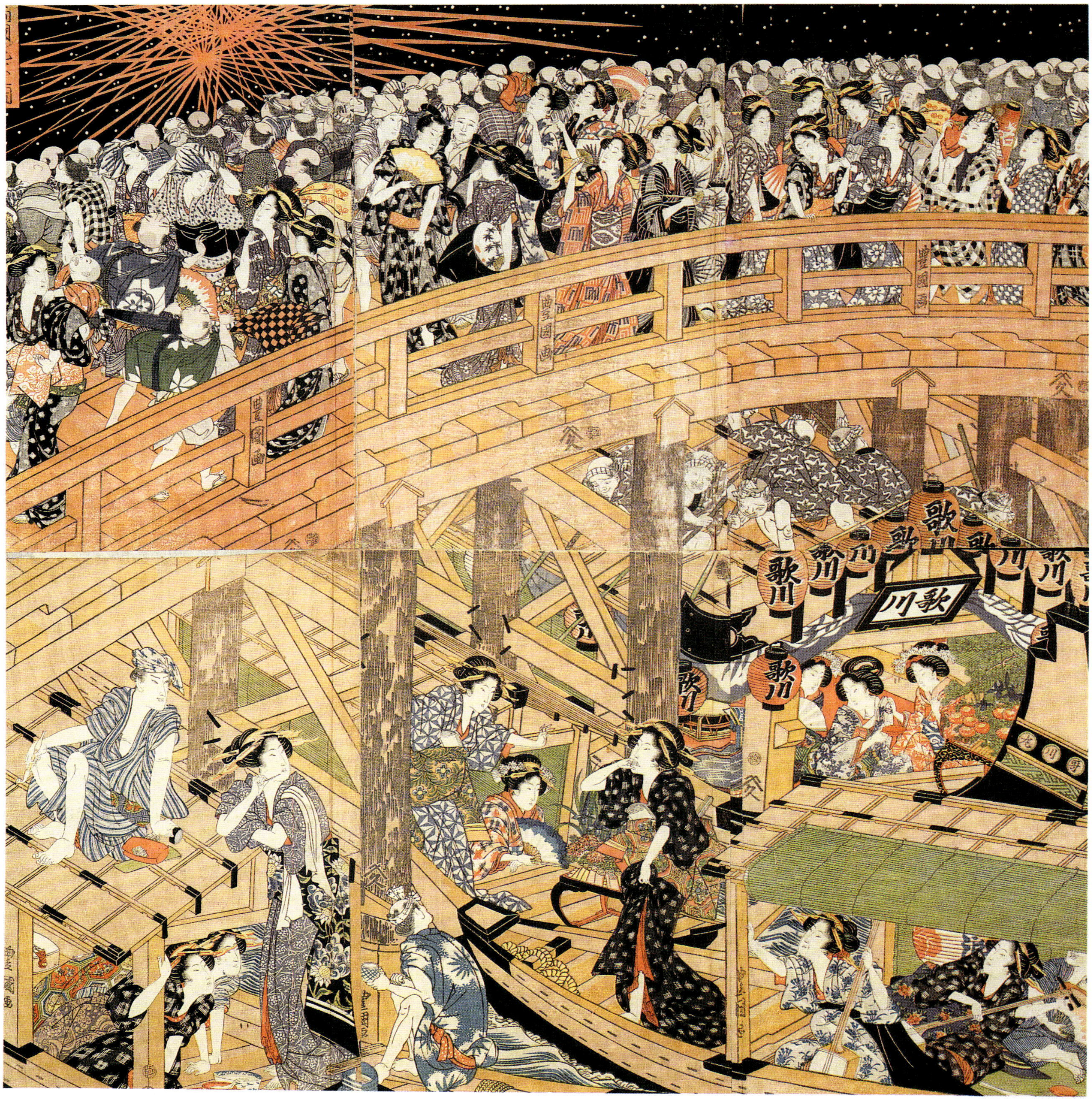

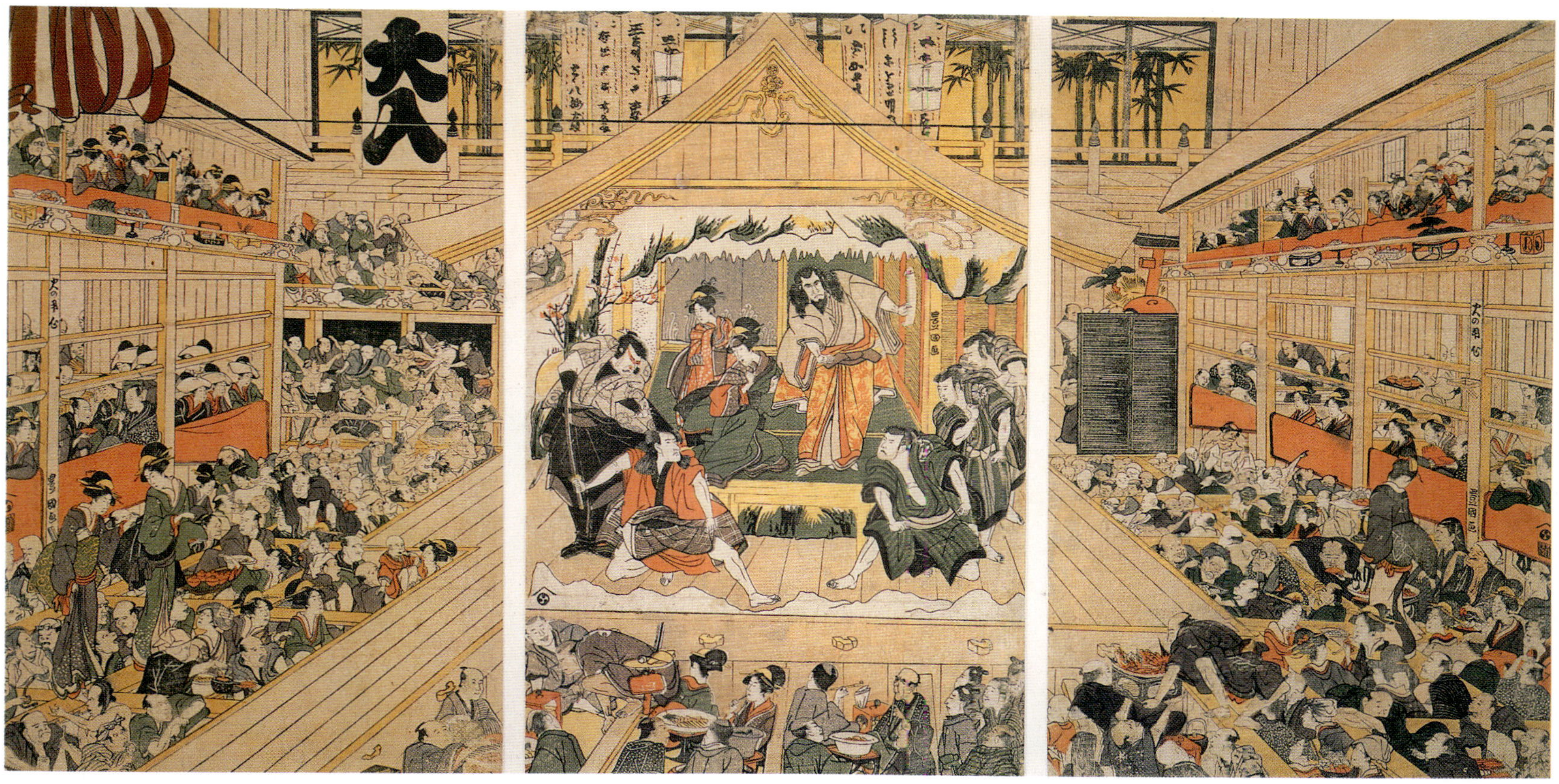

Left: Utagawa Toyokuni (1769-1825) 'Fireworks near Ryōgoku Bridge,' hexaptych. Courtesy of the Trustees of the Victoria and Albert Museum, London.

Above: Utagawa Toyokuni (1769-1825) 'Inside a Kabuki Theater,' triptych, 14⅘×9⅘ inches (37.7×24.9 cm) each. Published by Nishimuraya. Courtesy of the Trustees of the British Museum, London.

clude the bulk of his prints. These include a variety of compositional forms, ranging from the half- to the full-length portrait, as well as group compositions, in individual sheets, triptychs and even some pentaptychs, in the *hosoban* and *aiban* sizes. The first month of 1795 constitutes Sharaku's final period and is marked by 15 prints with signatures different from the other groups. Although some are extremely fine works, there is an evident overall decline in creativity and quality.

There has been much speculation as to why Sharaku abruptly ceased designing prints as suddenly as he had started. In the past, some art historians have put this down to his unpopularity as a print designer. It was argued that the majority of his prints portrayed the actors in such an unflattering way so as to offend not only the actors, but also their fans, the theatergoing public and, hence, many of the people who bought the prints. This, however, does not appear to have been the case. In the short space of ten months, Sharaku was extremely prolific. There are more surviving 'large-head' portraits by Sharaku than by any other contemporary artist, which suggests that they were considered worth preserving, both at the time and subsequently. In addition, some of Sharaku's prints went into second editions. All in all, the above factors suggest that Sharaku was far from unpopular in his own time and, indeed, he seems to have had a considerable and far-reaching effect on contemporary print designers in all fields. Despite various theories, the reasons for his abrupt disappearance from the print scene have not been satisfactorily explained.

During Sharaku's brief period of artistic activity, the only challenge to his supremacy in the field of actor prints lay in the person of Utagawa Toyokuni (1769-1825). Toyokuni entered the workshop of Toyoharu at an early age and began his career by designing book illustrations. He subsequently became one of the most productive print designers of the day, having studied in succession the styles of his contemporaries such as Kiyonaga, Shunchō, Shunman, Utamaro, Chōki and Eishi, together with Shunshō, Shun'ei and Sharaku for theatrical prints. Toyokuni was an eclectic artist who was quite at ease working in a wide variety of styles. He borrowed quite unashamedly from one designer after another, depending on whichever was currently in vogue, rather than working in the manner of one teacher. At his best, he frequently equalled and sometimes surpassed the works of his masters. His prints are rarely imitative copies, since he possessed a creative and intuitive feel for his compositions. He had the ability to assess what was popular at any one time and to recreate his own version of it.

Toyokuni worked in a bright and lively manner, with colorful compositions. The actors portrayed in his later prints best characterize his style, with long, lean faces, a pointed nose, a thrusting jaw and a thin sinewy line for the lips. He is often criticized for a lack of sensitivity and a coarseness in his prints, especially when compared to artists such as Utamaro and Eishi. However, Toyokuni was a true *ukiyo-e* artist who was enormously popular and produced prints of a direct and immediate appeal, although he

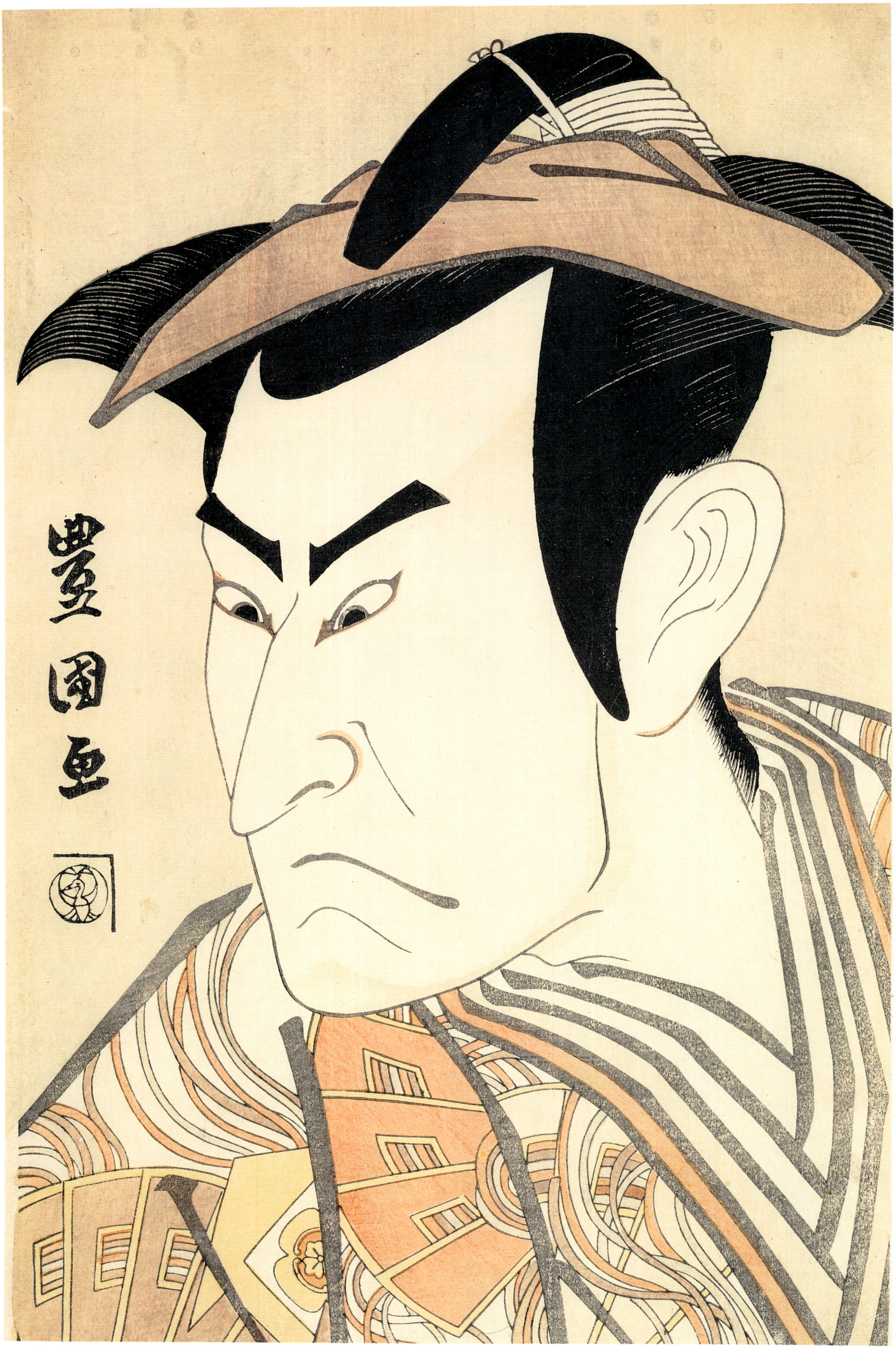
豊國画

Left: Utagawa Toyokuni (1769-1825) 'Portrait of the Actor Onoe Matsusuke as the Villain Kudō Suketsune,' 1800, 14⅝×9⅝ inches (37.2×24.6 cm). Courtesy of the Trustees of the Victoria and Albert Museum, London.

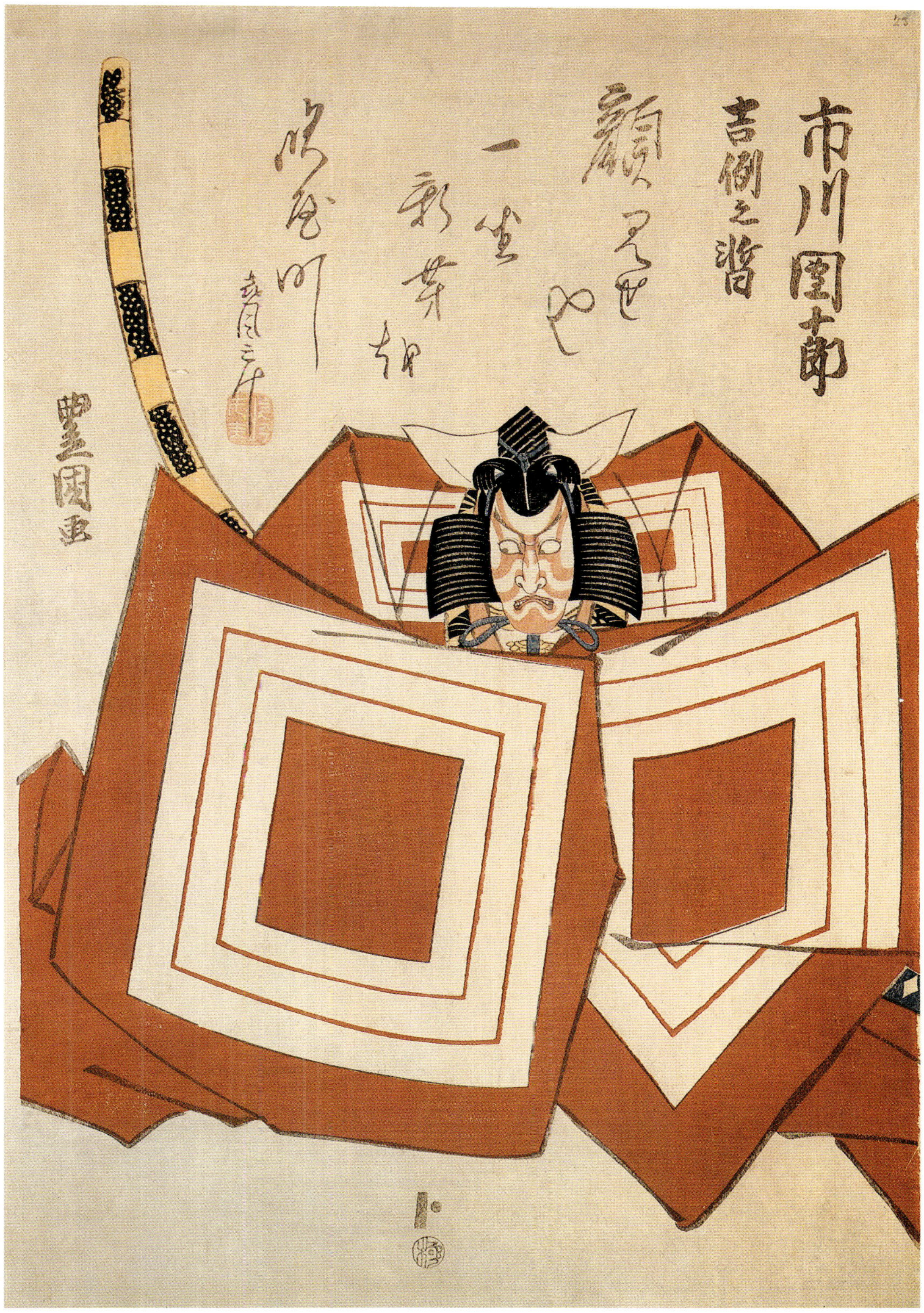

Right: Utagawa Toyokuni (1769-1825) 'Portrait of the Actor Ichikawa Danjūrō VII in the *Shibaraku* Role,' 1807, 15¼×10¾ inches (38.7×40 cm). Courtesy of the Trustees of the Victoria and Albert Museum, London.

will probably always remain an artist that many 'love to hate.'

Although Toyokuni designed some fine examples of *bijin* prints (page 112), particularly those in the style of Kiyonaga and Utamaro, it is for his theatrical prints that he is best remembered. The period of 1794-95 during which Sharaku's prints appeared, roughly coincided with the publication of a series of prints by Toyokuni entitled 'Portraits of Actors on Stage' (*Yakusha butai no sugata-e*; 1794-96), which established his reputation as a print designer. Indeed, during this period, Sharaku and Toyokuni, working for the rival publishers, Jūsaburō and Nishimuraya Yohachi, competed to design prints for the current plays. The disappearance of Sharaku, however, left the field open to Toyokuni who became the unrivaled master of the theatrical print. Among his actor prints, Toyokuni produced almost every conceivable type and combination of compositions, full-length, half-length and 'large heads,' individually, in pairs (page 114) and triples or in groups, in individual and multiple-sheet formats (pages 116 and 117). Of particular note are his 'large-head' actor portraits on gray grounds of the late 1790s, some of which almost entirely fill the sheet (page 118). In his later years he made particular use of the diptych and triptych format which he used to great dramatic effect, together with a more detailed background instead of plain colored grounds.

The period covered by this chapter also witnessed the emergence of numerous talented actors, such as Ichikawa Danjūrō VII. Since Ichikawa Danjūrō I had created the *Shibaraku* (wait a moment!) role in 1697, this had proved a great specialty of successive Danjūrō actors. The striking red costume with the family crest of concentric squares, together with the long sword and striped red and white face make-up, made the role extremely popular with print designers for the design opportunities it offered them. Toyokuni produced several versions of the *Shibaraku* role which resulted from his close association with and admiration of the actor Danjūrō VI.

Toyokuni dominated the field of actor prints for almost three decades until his death in 1825. Like so many other print designers, however, his later works suffered from over-production and as a result declined in quality. Nevertheless, Toyokuni presided over a flourishing workshop and trained a large number of pupils including Toyohiro, Kunimasa, Kunisada and Kuniyoshi. Utagawa Kunimasa (1773-1810) was the most senior of his pupils, producing the finest

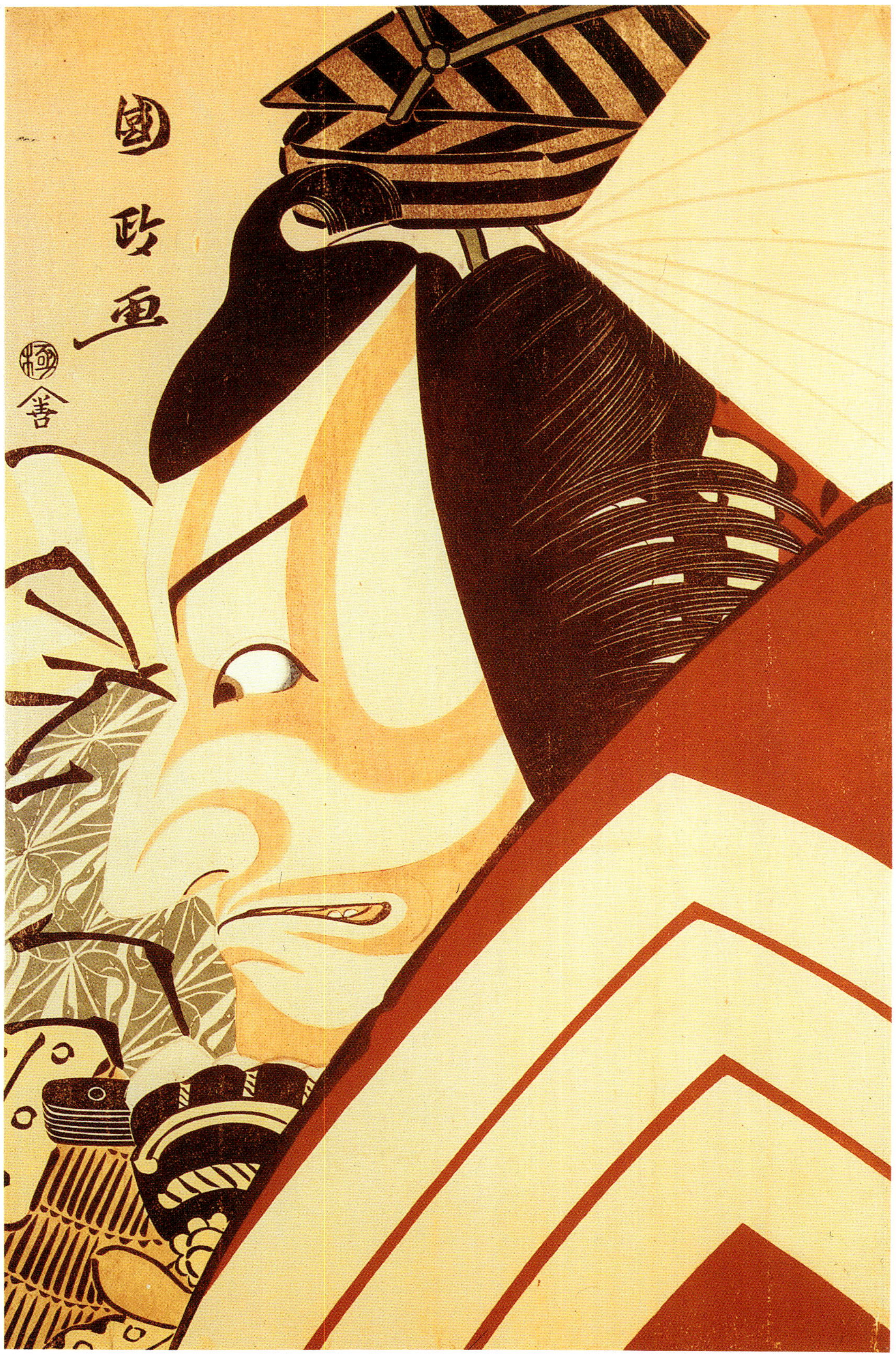

Left: Utagawa Kunimasa (1773-1810) 'The Actor Ichikawa Danjūrō V in a *Shibaraku* Role,' Courtesy of the Trustees of the British Museum, London.

Right: Utagawa Kunimasa (1773-1810) 'The Actors Sawamura Sōjurō III and Segawa Kikusaburō,' 1798, 14¾×9¼ (37.5×23.4 cm). Published by Tsutaya Kinsuke.

of his works between 1795 and 1804. His most notable works were a number of 'large-head' actor portraits produced in 1795 and 1796, of bold and striking composition (page 119). Kunimasa also went on to design half- and full-length portraits (page 121). Utagawa Toyohiro (1773-1829), on the other hand, was a fellow pupil of Toyoharu along with Toyokuni and was a versatile artist, designing *surimono* and prints of *bijin* and landscapes. He was also the teacher of Hiroshige, who became one of the greatest exponents of the landscape print.

The year 1790 saw a new wave of government austerity designed to curb overt displays of luxury which, among others, introduced censorship of prints. Despite such measures, the 1790s was one of the most highly creative periods in the history of *ukiyo-e*, with many leading print designers. By the early nineteenth century, however, a marked decline in the quality and standards of *ukiyo-e* prints had become evident. As prosperity spread among the *chōnin*, prints came within the purchasing power of larger sections of the population than ever before who were less discerning and sophisticated in their tastes. Since the print run often had to be increased accordingly, standards of printing frequently deteriorated. Furthermore, the majority of artists who had played such a vital role during the 1790s were either dead, in old age or had ceased designing prints altogether. This decline in standards and lack of creative impetus, however, was only shortlived, for some of the major developments in *ukiyo-e* prints were yet to come, as we shall see in Chapter 5 of this book.

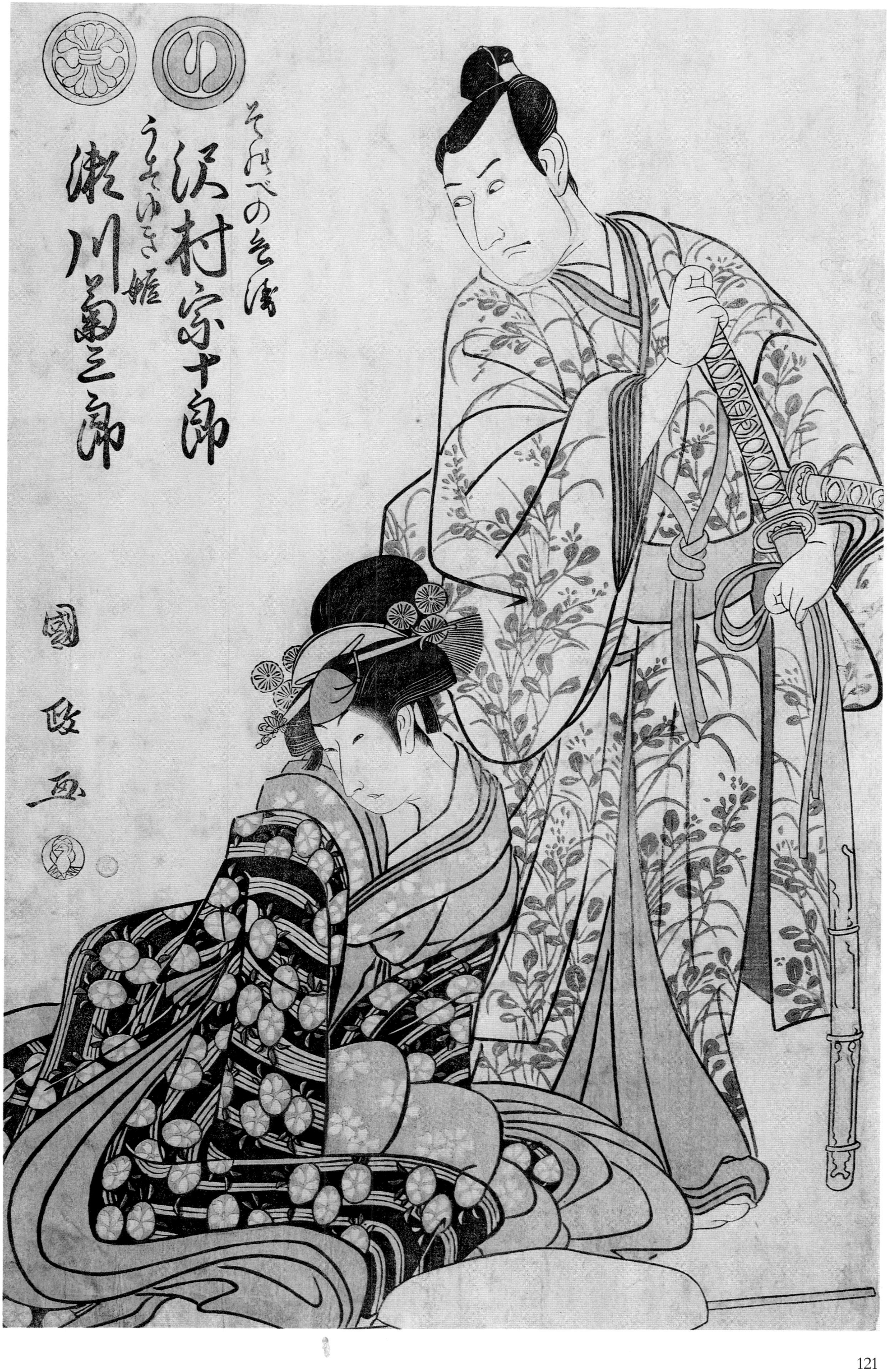
沢村宗十郎
瀬川菊三郎
國政画

Sumo Wrestling Prints LAWRENCE BICKFORD

The roots of modern-day sumo may date as far back as the Yayoi period (300BC-AD300) when it was performed as an agrarian wrestling ceremony (*sumai*) to beseech the *kami* (deity) to provide a fruitful harvest. However, by the Edo period (1600-1868), sumo had evolved away from a religiously imbued ceremony to become a sport popular among townspeople and as a result sumo wrestlers and tournaments became suitable subjects for the *ukiyo-e* artist. Before the Temmei era (1781-89), *ukiyo-e* broadsheets illustrating sumo were relatively rare. The absence in early *ukiyo-e* of sumo imagery is not surprising as *Kanjin sumō* did not establish itself as a major Edo entertainment until the 1750s, building up its popular following only slowly. From the short period between 1782 and 1795, however, sumo's popularity had grown such that it matched even that of the flamboyant Kabuki theater.

Katsukawa Shunshō (1726-92), the principal innovator of the sumo print, appears to have been attracted by the sensational matches between the two sumo champions Tanikaze and Onogawa. The exciting competition between these two goliaths fueled what is sometimes considered the first golden age of sumo and this period paralleled the golden age of the *ukiyo-e* print. Following the lead of Shunshō, many Katsukawa artists began producing sumo prints and, with the assistance of Shunshō's senior pupil, Katsukawa Shunkō (1743-1812), they implemented the ideas he had formulated. The Katsukawa sumo prints were in high demand, and sold without significant competition from other artists.

As the Katsukawa school was the foremost in the depiction of Kabuki actors, it is not surprising that their repertoire of sumo prints bore some resemblance to them. This might not have been viewed as unusual since sumo and Kabuki co-existed as forms of entertainment for the Edo-period townsman (*chōnin*), and as a result a camaraderie sprang up between the actors and wrestlers that was to last throughout the Edo period. Prints exist which depict these two groups relaxing together and their close contact resulted in an exchange of various elements. For example, in the *uki-e* (perspective print) by Katsukawa Shunshō (below left), a line of wrestlers are depicted approaching the ring from the right with Tanikaze bringing up the rear while another line leaves to the left; Onogawa is seen resting his hand on a post. Both lines follow special pathways through the audience. These walkways had been strewn with flowers, hence the name *hanamichi* (flower path), and this element was borrowed by the Kabuki theater. Conversely, the custom of a functionary onstage striking together wooden clappers (*hyoshige*) to catch the audience's attention and the advertising drum tower visible in the background to the left of the ring in the same print were conventions taken by sumo from Kabuki. While Kabuki staged its performances in permanent theaters, sumo bi-annual tournaments occurred in temporary arenas erected within temple grounds east of the Sumida River and not far from the famous Ryōgoku Bridge. The *dohyōiri* (ring-entering, below) was a colorful tournament event in which the senior wrestlers strutted in gorgeous brocaded aprons (*keshomawashi*) that would have been presented to them by their sponsors. Many posed for their portraits in these splendid costumes.

The essence of professional sumo was the brief matches which were equivalent to Kabuki's stage action. Unlike Kabuki prints which depicted the flamboyant attire and make up of the Kabuki actor, sumo prints offered little variety. The wrestlers did not fight in their colorful *keshomawashi*; instead, they wore only scant loincloths as seen in the 1784 print by Shunshō of Edogamine and Kimenzan (above). For a number of artistic reasons, sumo was a difficult subject to portray in prints. No publisher would produce a print unless it had a chance of being profitable and this meant that a wrestling bout should appeal equally to the supporters of both contestants. Neutrality became a pragmatic imperative, even though it did not inspire great action art. Moreover, since the contestants had to be illustrated on a equal stance, the action appeared more like ballroom dancing than wrestling. To this complication was added the lack of anatomical correctness. The faces of both participants had likewise to be given equal visibility. Shunshō's oversized print represents one of the artist's more successful efforts to create a realistic depiction of his subject despite commercial constraints.

In addition to the illustration of sumo wrestlers in the ring, another popular format was the recording of the life of the wrestlers outside the ring. Wrestlers were shown walking Edo's streets near Ryōgoku Bridge or re-

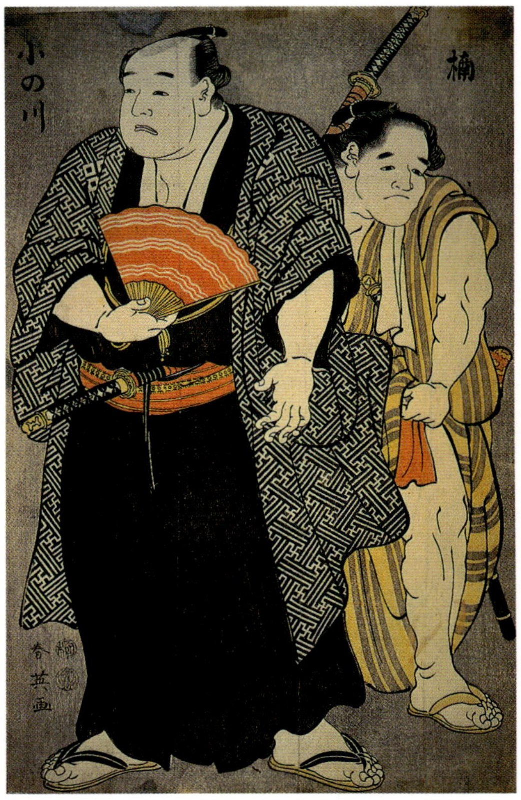

Above: Katsukawa Shunshō (1726-92) 'Sumō Match between Edogamine Genji (left) and Kimenzan Tanigorō (right) with the *gyōjj* (referee) Shikimore Tadanosuke,' 1784, *bai ōban*; 14⅞×20 inches (37.8×50.8cm). The names of the wrestlers appear on the left and right, respectively with name of the *gyōji* in upper left followed by the artist's signature. Bickford collection.

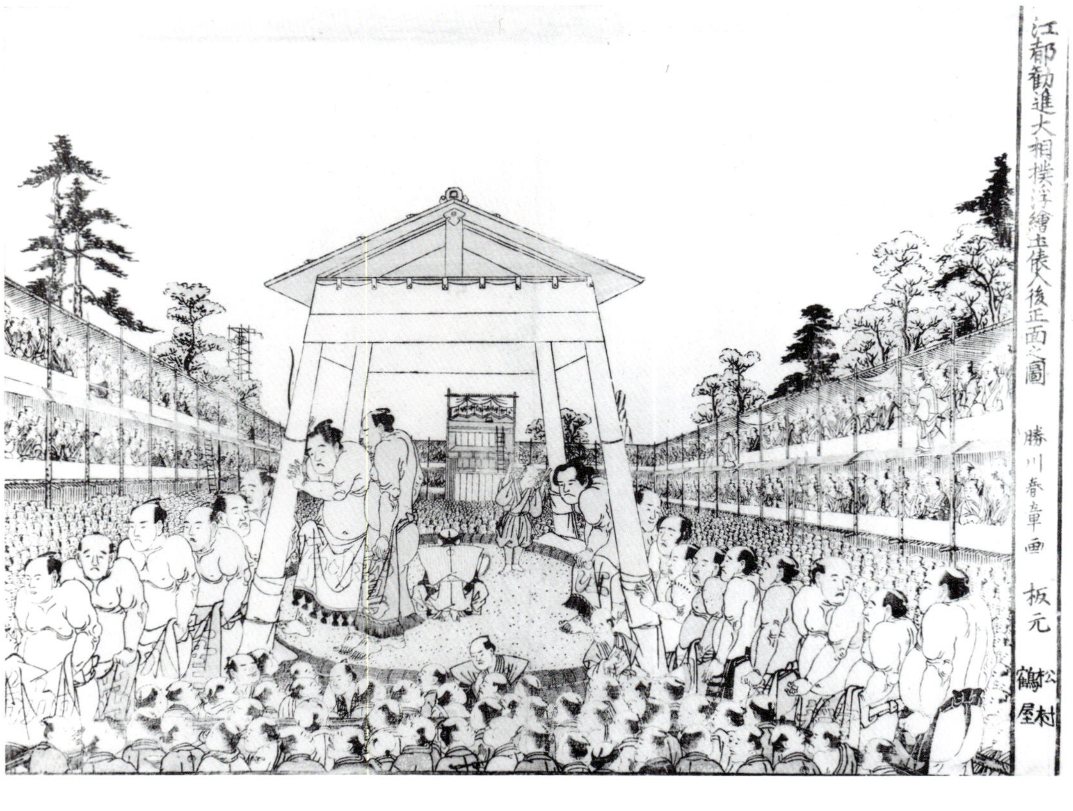

Below left: Katsukawa Shunshō (1726-92) 'Perspective Print Illustrating the Ring-Entering Ceremony,' (*Edo kanjin ōzumō ukie dohyōiri ato shōmen no zu*), c. 1784. Large *ōban-ukie*. Publisher: Matsumura/Tsuruya. Title, artist's and publisher's names in right margin. Bickford collection.

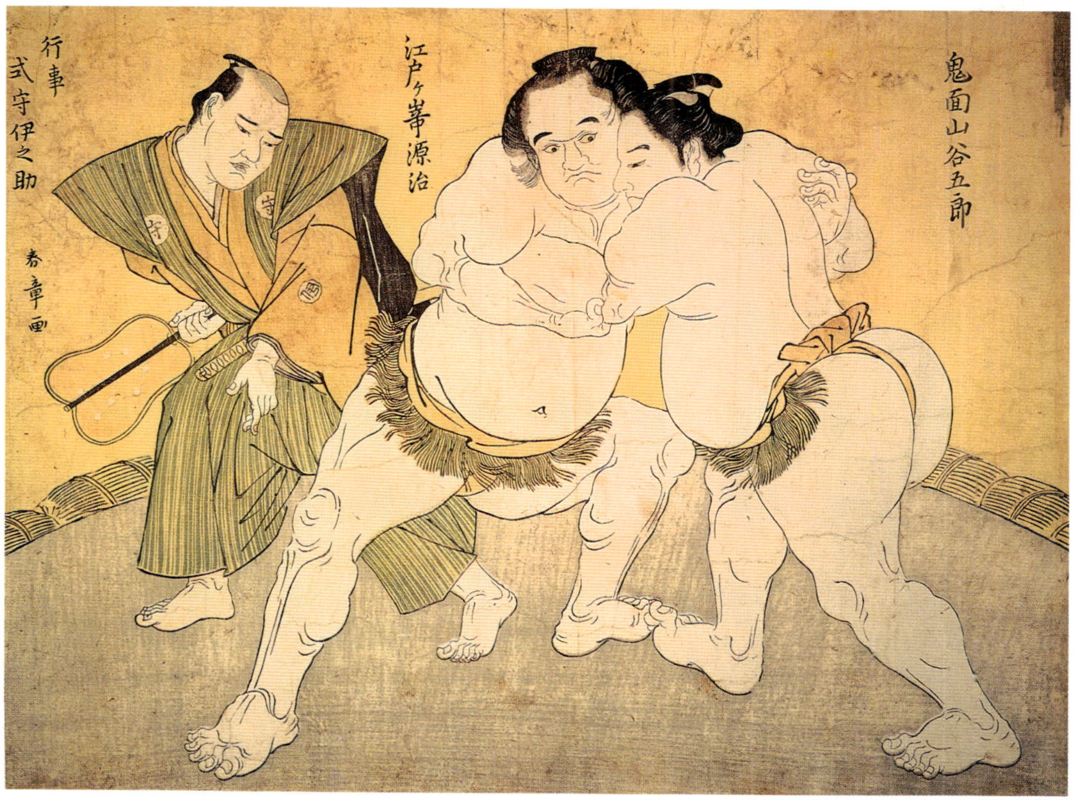

laxing in teahouses and other public places. The pictorial contrast between *bijin* (beautiful women) and wrestlers became a popular theme, as can be seen in the example by Shunchō illustrated here (below).

Only four Edo-period print designers can be considered as masters of the *sumo* print judging from their sustained contributions to the field: Katsukawa Shunshō, Shunkō and Shun'ei (1762-1819) and Toyokuni Kunisada (1786-1865). They shared a personal interest in the sport and are known for their innovative approach to this demanding genre. Other print designers like Katsushika Hokusai (1760-1849) and Toyokuni Kuniyoshi (1797-1861) also produced sumo prints but they were relatively unimpressive when compared to the above artists. Hokusai left the field after 1794, and the only promising sumo prints by Kuniyoshi were influenced by Kunisada. The four sumo masters, however, were deeply committed: Shun'ei, for example, continued designing sumo prints until his death, although he had abandoned a promising career in actor portraiture 20 years earlier.

Above: Katsukawa Shun'ei (1762-1819) 'Grand Champion Onogawa promenading with Sword-bearing Attendant,' c. 1793, *ōban*; 16⅛×10⅜ inches (42.1×26.3cm). Published by Tsuruya Kiemon. Bickford collection.

Right: Katsukawa Shunchō (flc. 1780-95) 'Grand Champion Onogawa with the Takashimaya Waitress Ohisa,' c. 1793, *ōban*; double *okubi-e*. 16¾×9⅜ inches (42.5×23.9cm). Published by Tsuruya Kiemon. Names appear to the left of the figures. Bickford collection.

Below: Katsukawa Shunshō (1726-92) 'Tokeshima Urauemon and Yatsugamine Suemon of the Tōhō (East Side),' c. 1783, *ōban*; 14⅞×10 inches (37.7×25.3cm). Published by Matsumura Tatsuemon. Signed in lower left. Bickford collection.

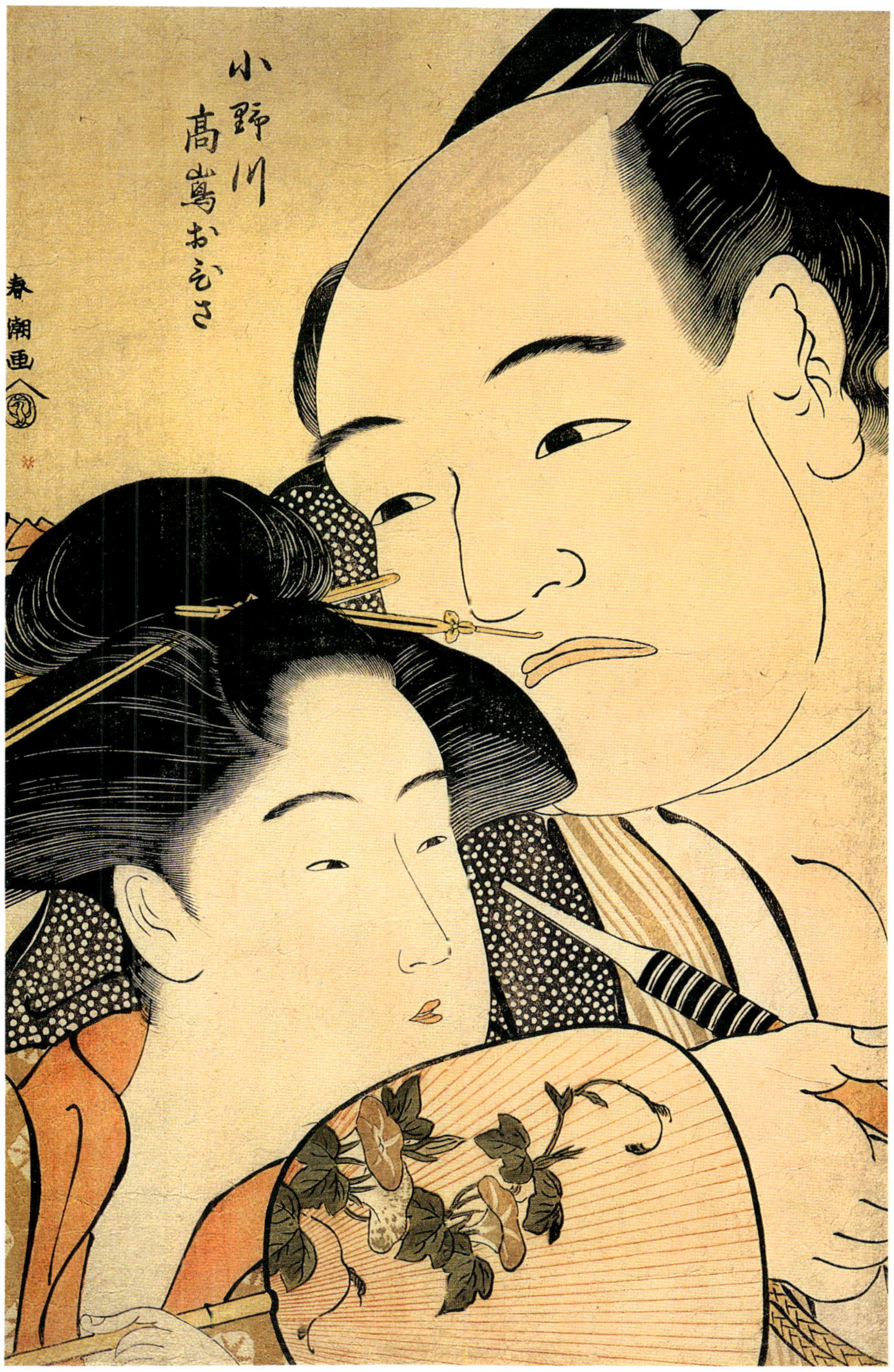

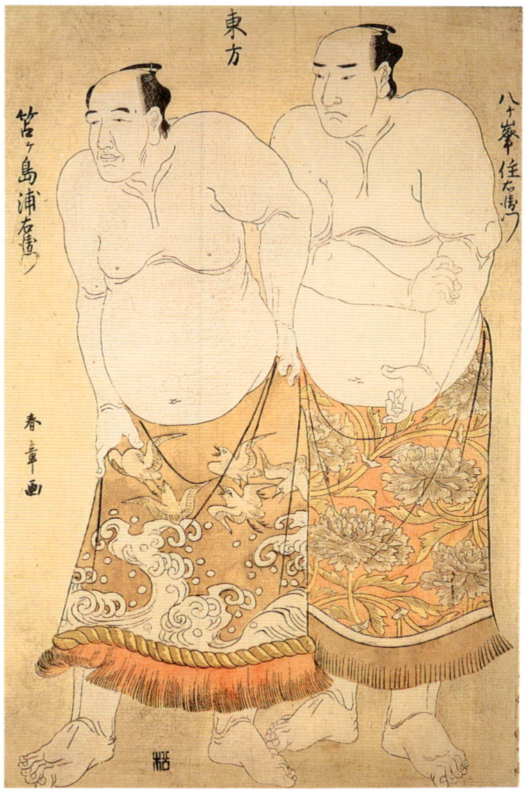

5
The Nineteenth Century until the Meiji Restoration

JONATHAN BENNETT

By the last quarter of the eighteenth century, the structure of Edo-period society was firmly established; the city of Edo, for example, was a bustling economic and cultural center and boasted a population of approximately one million. The merchant class, who played an instrumental role in the emergence of the *ukiyo-e* broadsheet, had achieved a relative level of financial success by acting as creditors of many daimyo, feudal domains and even the *bakufu*. However, in 1783 the country was beset by a difficult period marked by a series of epidemics, famines and natural disasters. The widespread shortages and chaos that ensued prompted nationwide peasant uprisings (*hyakushō ikki*) and to add to the misery the city of Kyoto was swept by fire in 1788. It was quite clear that measures were now drastically needed to alleviate the conditions that now assailed the country. In an attempt to deal with worsening conditions, Tokugawa Ienari (1786-1837), who was only fifteen when appointed shogun in 1786, engaged his regent Matsudaira Sadanobu (1758-1829) to formulate a series of sumptuary edicts that would encourage frugality and would, it was hoped, guide the country through this unfortunate period.

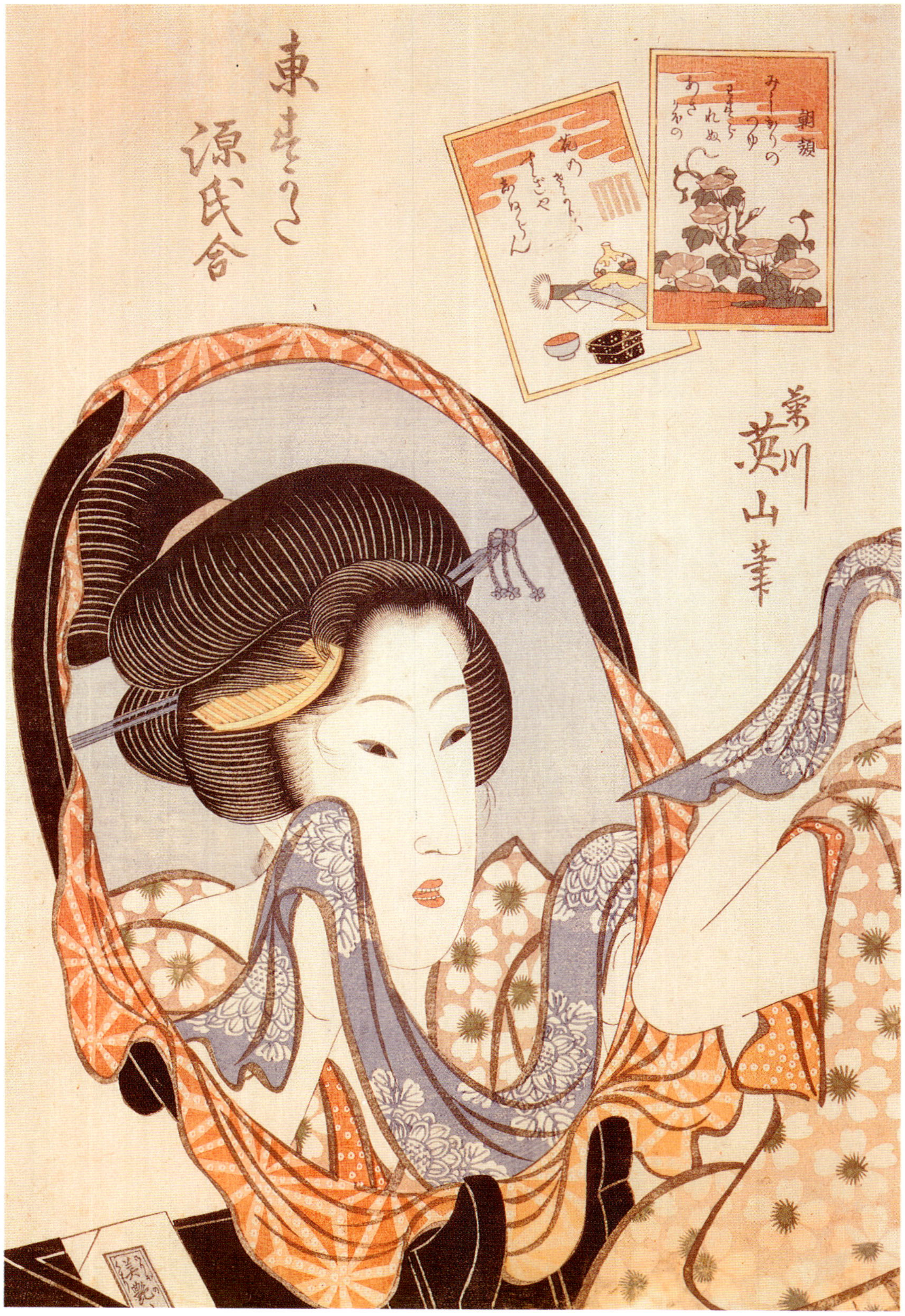

Right: Kikukawa Eizan (*fl* 1804-29) 'Woman at her Mirror,' from the series' Genji Comparisons, Edo-style,' c. 1830, 15¼×10½inches (38.8×26.7 cm), Courtesy of the Trustees of the Victoria and Albert Museum, London.

Far right: Kikukawa Eizan (*fl* 1804-29) 'A Courtesan Fetching Water,' from the series 'Fashionable Beauties; Eight Views of Tomiga,' c. 1815, 15×10¼ inches (38×26 cm), The Whitworth Art Gallery, University of Manchester.

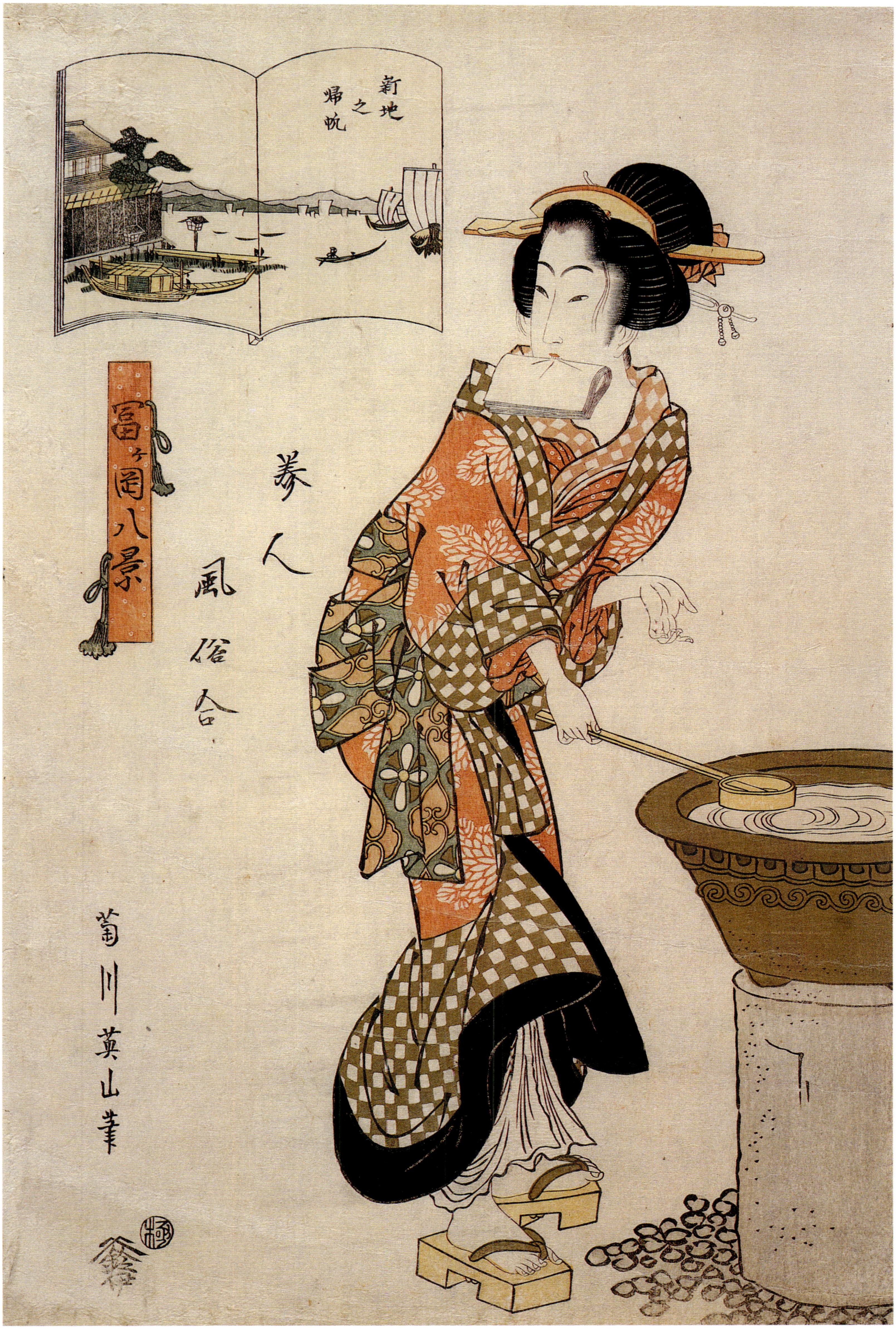
新地之帰帆
冨ヶ岡八景
美人風俗合
菊川英山筆
極

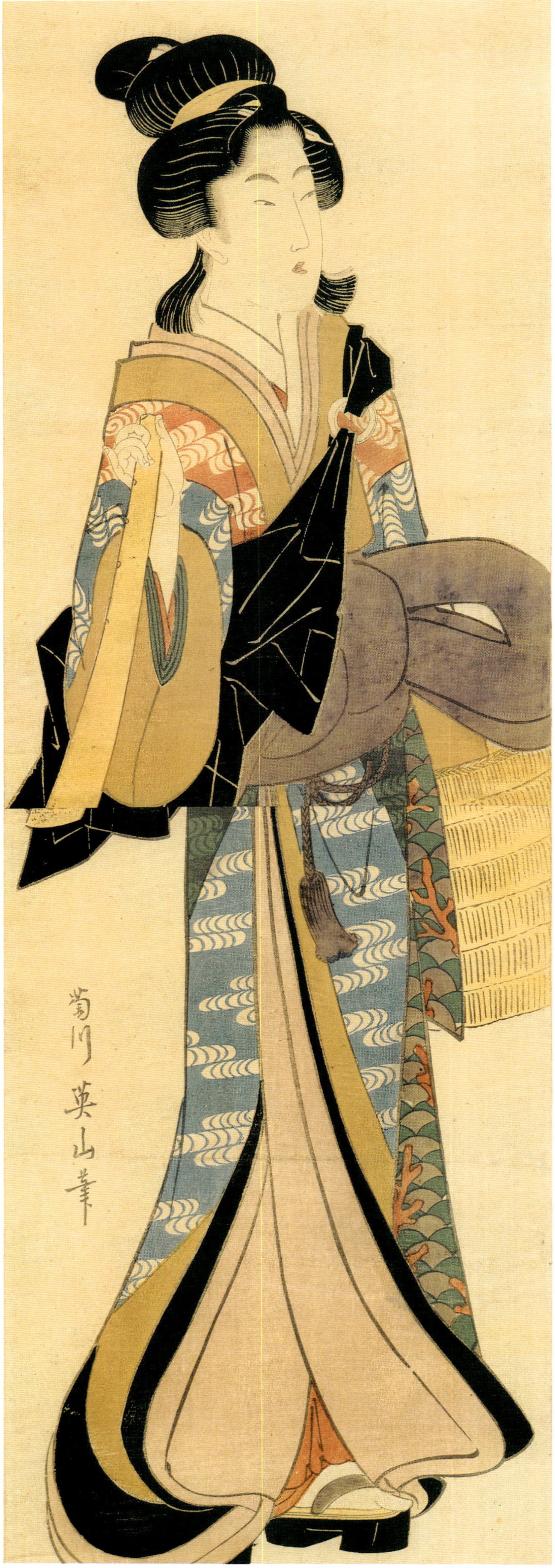

Left: Kikukawa Eizan (1787-1867) 'Courtesan Dressed as a Komusō,' c. 1815, *kakemono-e*, 28×9¾ inches (71.1×24.8 cm), Courtesy of the Trustees of the Victoria and Albert Museum, London.

At the beginning of the nineteenth century these edicts were still in effect; however, it was to become increasingly apparent that Matsudaira's formula for economic and social stability was not particularly successful. Luxurious display and uninhibited spending typified the years between around 1810 and 1830; (the merchant class continued to cement their position as creditors which caused members of the samurai class to fall deeper into debt.) Further crop failure plagued the country in 1833-7: by the 1830s the power of the shogunate was on the decline with a debased currency and official expenditure exceeding income. In a last attempt to regain economic stability, the government once again attempted to cut extravagance by issuing a series of edicts in the 1840s known as the Tempō Reforms. The reforms were led by Mizuno Tadakuni (1793-1851). The increasingly weakened position of the Tokugawa shogunate was soon to set the stage for a tide of revolt which eventually sought to overthrow the shogunate, to return to imperial power and most importantly to open the doors of the country to the West.

The fluctuating economic and social climate in Japan at the end of the eighteenth and in the early years of the nineteenth century no doubt had a profound impact on the course of *ukiyo-e*. In many ways, as discussed by Richard Kruml in Chapter 1, the restrictions placed on prints often resulted in innovations in styles and techniques. The 1810s to the 1830s, for example, represented an apogee in the history of *surimono* production. As privately commissioned prints, *surimono* were exempt from government censorship and therefore could showcase a range of elaborate and refined printing techniques; it marked a period when *surimono* production evolved as a profession in its own right. In the early years of the nineteenth century, the single-sheet print, however, entered into a phase that continued until the end of the century that was marked by an almost baroque interpretation of established themes such as *bijinga* and actor's portraits. It was only with the introduction of other genres, such as landscape and history, by contrast, that nineteenth-century printmakers were provided with outlets for innovation and artistic expression.

Right: Keisei Eisen (1790-1848) 'Oiran on Parade,' c. 1830, *kakemono-e*, 29×9¾ inches (73.7×24.8 cm). Published by Sanoya. Courtesy of the Trustees of the Victoria and Albert Museum, London.

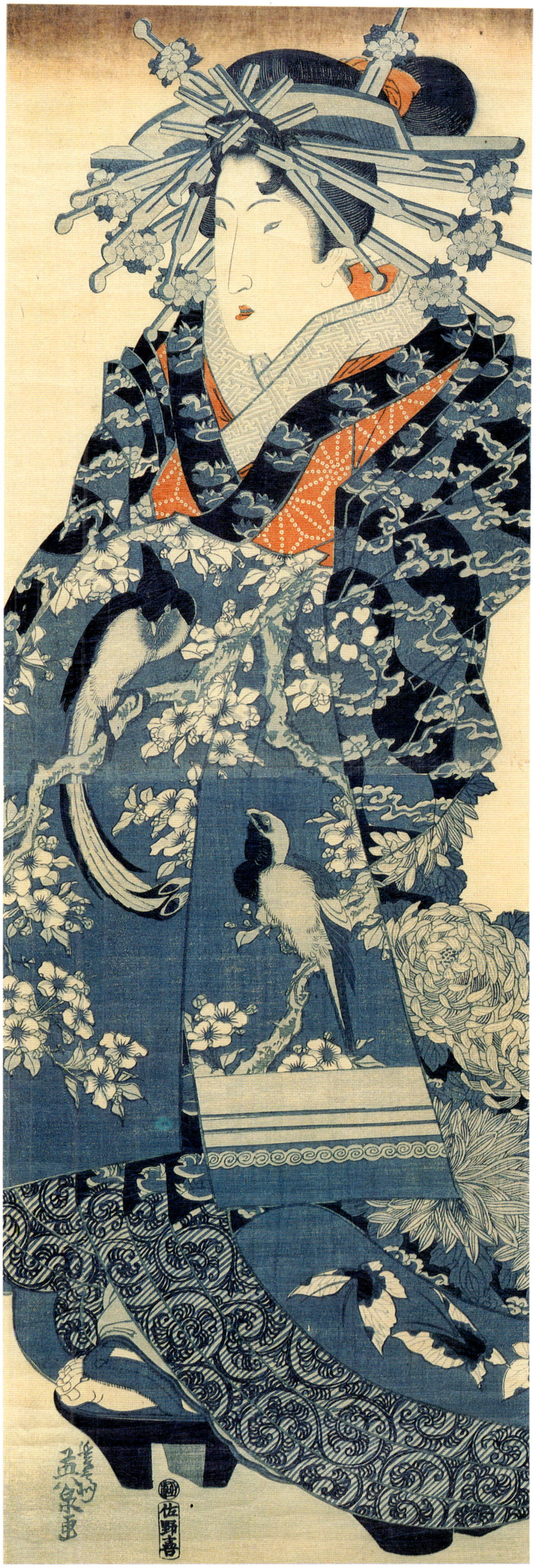

THE HEIRS TO THE BIJIN TRADITION

Following the death of Utamaro, the production of *bijinga* was carried on by the pupils of the great master. Utamaro II (d.1831?), Tsukimaro or Kikumaro (c.1808-30) and Hidemaro (*fl* 1810s-20s) continued to produce prints of beauties, competent but lacking their teacher's sense of composition and style. The designs tend to be rather cluttered up and none of Utamaro's pupils can be credited with any creative innovation in the genre.

Outside of the Kitagawa school only a few others were active in the field, the most interesting being perhaps Torii Kiyomine (1787-1868). He was a pupil of Kiyonaga and contrary to the artists mentioned above, his prints have a distinct style and feeling. Katsukawa Shunsen (1760-c.1830), one of the last pupils of the Katsukawa school, produced prints in a manner closely related to Shunchō and Shunzan. In his later years his small output became very similar to that of Eizan, who dominated the genre of *bijin* after Utamaro's death.

Kikukawa Eizan (1787-1867) was the principal designer of prints of women from the death of Utamaro in 1806 until 1820, when the more voluptuous figures of his pupil Keisei Eisen began to supplant his more refined style. The decadent flavor to his representations of women appeals to the modern Japanese collector. He was the son of a Kanō-style painter and fan-maker. His teachers were quite diverse: he worked under Suzuki Nanrei and Totoya Hokkei and he was strongly influenced by his artistic predecursor, Utamaro.

The print by the artist illustrated on page 125 brings in a classical comparison. The elegant, if slightly dishevelled, courtesan biting on a wad of paper napkins (a traditional gesture of passion) looks back as if alarmed as she bends to dip some water from the water butt. The print comes from the series 'Fashionable Beauties, Eight Views of Tomiga,' a classical theme originally derived from the Chinese 'Eight Views on the Xiao and Xiang Rivers.' Her form echoes the distant sails returning to harbor shown in the book-shaped cartouche above her

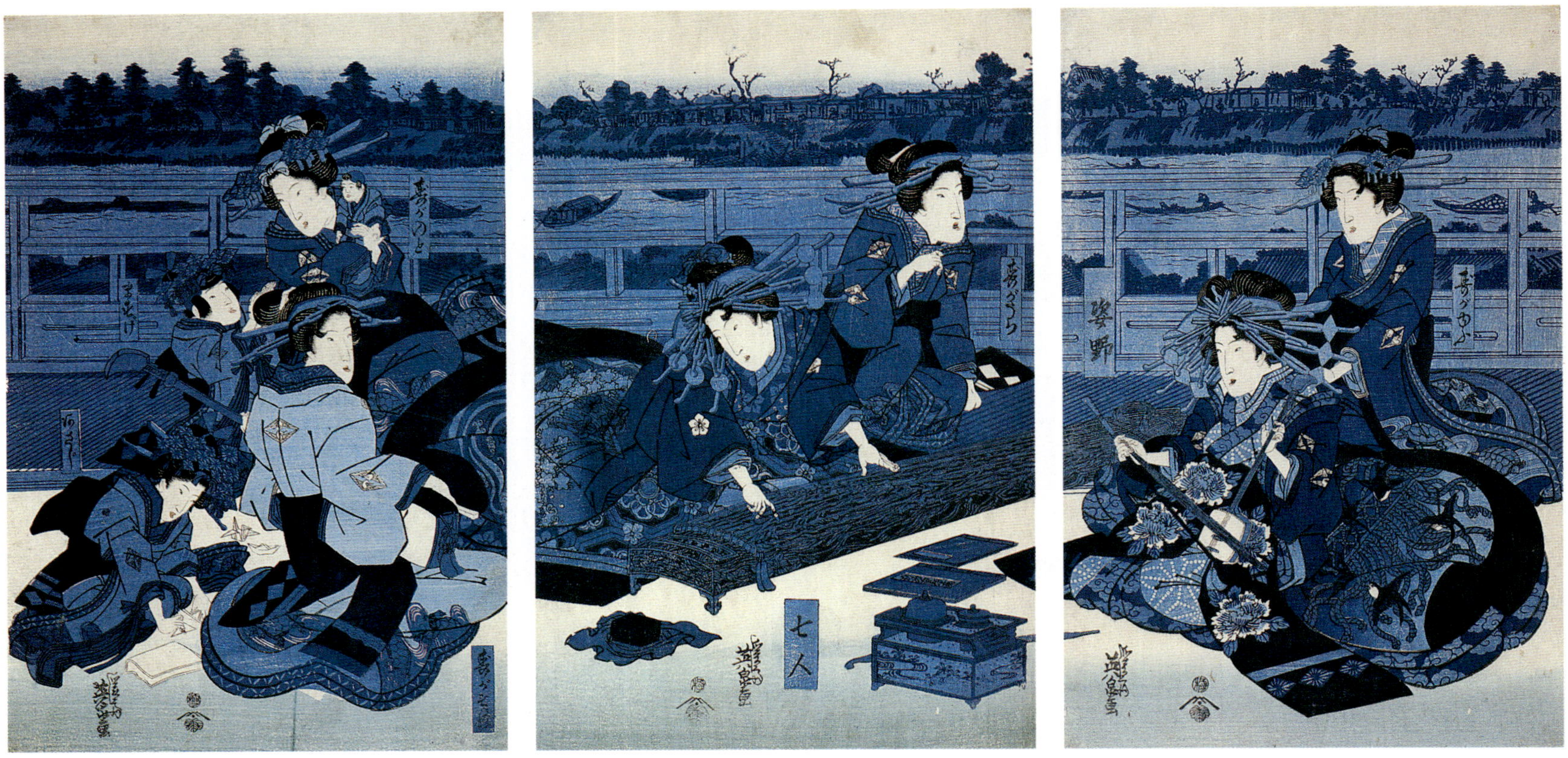

Above: Keisai Eisen (1790-1848) 'The Grand Courtesans Sugatano and Nanabito with Attendants,' c. 1830, *aizuri-e* triptych, 14⅜×35½ inches (36.5×90 cm). Published by Tsutaya Kichizō. The Whitworth Art Gallery, University of Manchester.

shoulder. Presumably the wad of paper in her mouth suggests the sail, a rather louche basis for the comparison.

Eizan seems to have been one of the prime movers of the *kakemono-e*, a format used to provide a cheaper printed equivalent to the hanging scroll painting and made up of two upright *ōban* sheets arranged vertically to provide a single image, usually of a *bijin* but sometimes of nature subjects (e.g. carp, hawk), legendary scenes (especially Shōki, the demon-queller), or landscapes. A very fresh and simple image from about 1815 depicts a courtesan dressed as a *komusō*, or wandering monk (page 126). She carries the concealing basket hat in one hand and the *shakuhachi* flute in the other, reminding one that this anonymous garb was often used by samurai when they visited the Yoshiwara (the brothel district), which was officially off-limits to them. In general Eizan's designs are characterized by elegant elongated beauties with rather dream-like features.

By 1820 Keisai Eisen (1790-1848) gradually took over from his master as the main artist in the field of *bijinga*. This style has a much earthier flavor, as can be seen from a *kakemono-e* (page 127). The *aizuri-e*, 'blue-colored print' of an *oiran*, a senior courtesan, on parade, dates from around 1830. Eisen was the first, in 1829, to make use of *berorin*, the newly imported Prussian blue, a pigment already used in Osaka four years earlier. He started a fashion for *bijin* prints executed only in this new color. His women tend to be less elongated than Eizan's almost hunch-backed, with facial expressions which are not in the least serene or dreamlike. One notices that the curving lines of Eizan have been replaced by shorter, straighter lines. The splendid pictorial sash-ends flatten and broaden the figure and the mass of combs obscures the coiffure. Much of this reflects the gorgeous formality of a senior courtesan parading through the Yoshiwara. However, one must acknowledge

Right: Keisai Eisen (1790-1848) 'Seven O'Clock in the Morning, Rising Time,' from the series 'A Mirror of the Beauties of the Present Day,' c. 1825, 15⅜×10¼ inches (39×26 cm). The Whitworth Art Gallery, University of Manchester.

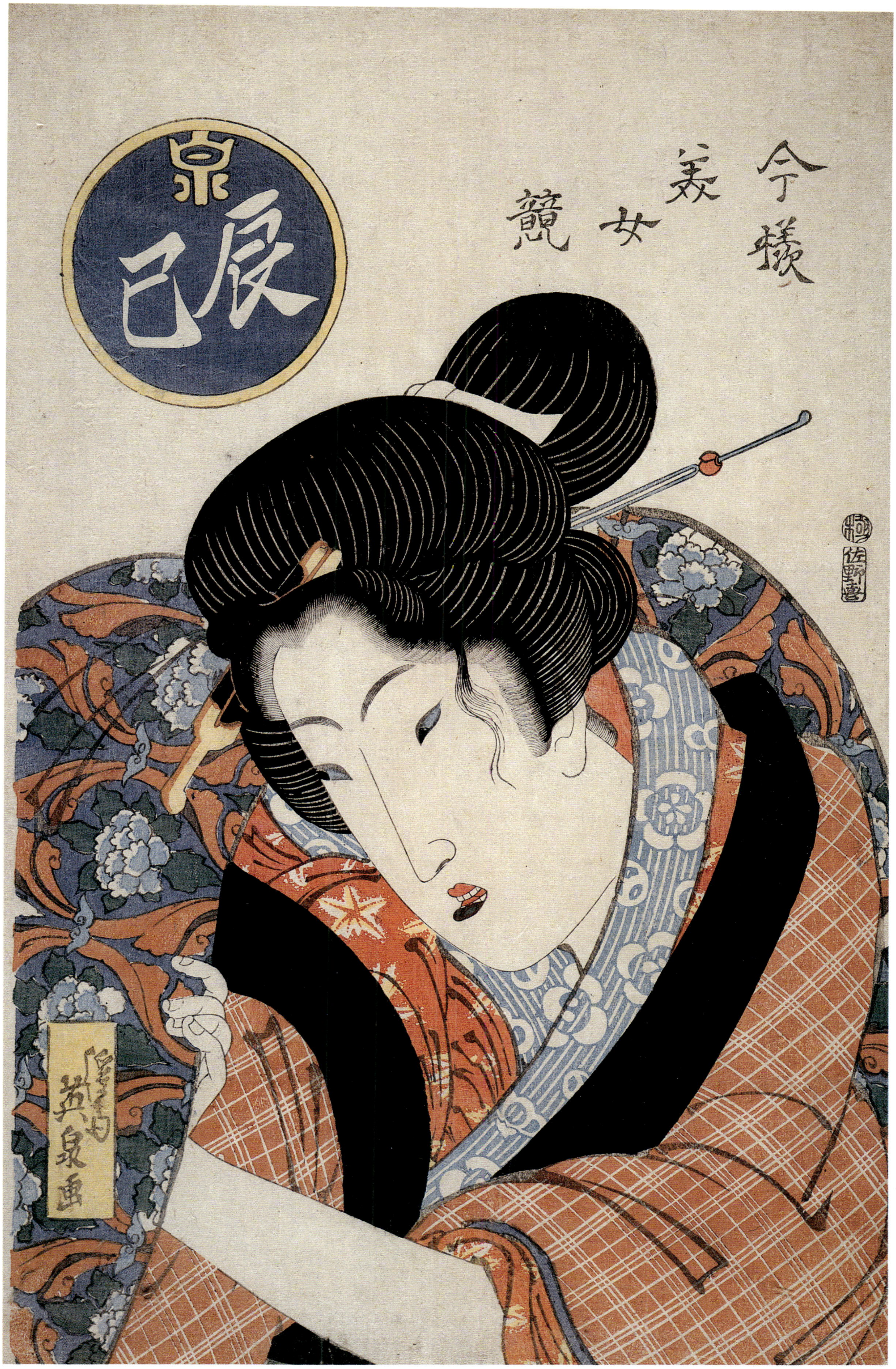
今様
美女
競
英泉画

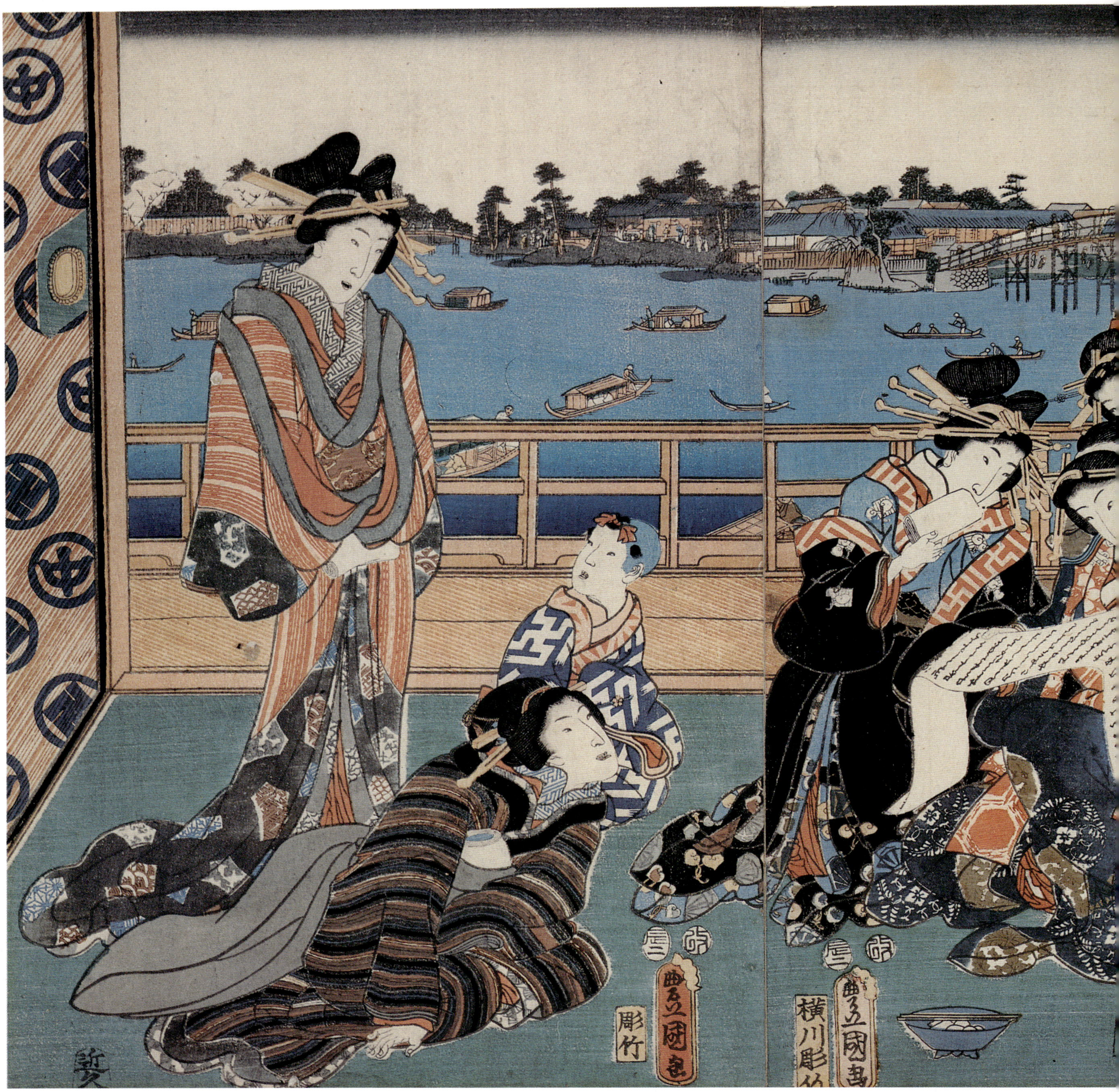

Above: Utagawa Kunisada (1786-1865) 'Three Courtesans Exclaiming over a Love Letter,' 1856, 13¾×35½ inches (35×90 cm). Published by Ibaya Sensaburō. The Whitworth Art Gallery, University of Manchester.

that fashions in kimono and hair decoration were particularly grandiose around the start of the 1830s, reflecting the ephemeral prosperity of the period. '7 O'clock in the Morning: Rising Time,' (page 129) from the series 'A Mirror of the Beauties of the Present Day,' is by contrast intimate in the extreme, showing the waking girl's face at pillow level engulfed by rich fabrics as she pushes back the coverlet.

The final example of Eisen's work in the context of *bijinga* is another *aizuri-e* print, a triptych scene of 'The Courtesans Sugatano and Nanabito,' which brings together the depictor of women and the landscape artist, in a scene of courtesans making music on an upper floor overlooking the Sumida River, presumably at dusk. The grand courtesans, notable again for the great profusion of their combs, play the *koto*, a harp played on the floor, and the *kokyū*, the Japanese violin, accompanied by another courtesan on the *samisen*. There is charming detail in the little apprentice courtesans, one folding paper shapes and the other asking for a doll.

Eisen was, in retrospect, one of the most interesting of the *ukiyo-e* artists of the late Edo period. He was something of an anarchist, lived a rough, rather antisocial life, and was a talented writer who contributed to the *Mumei-o zuihitsu*, or

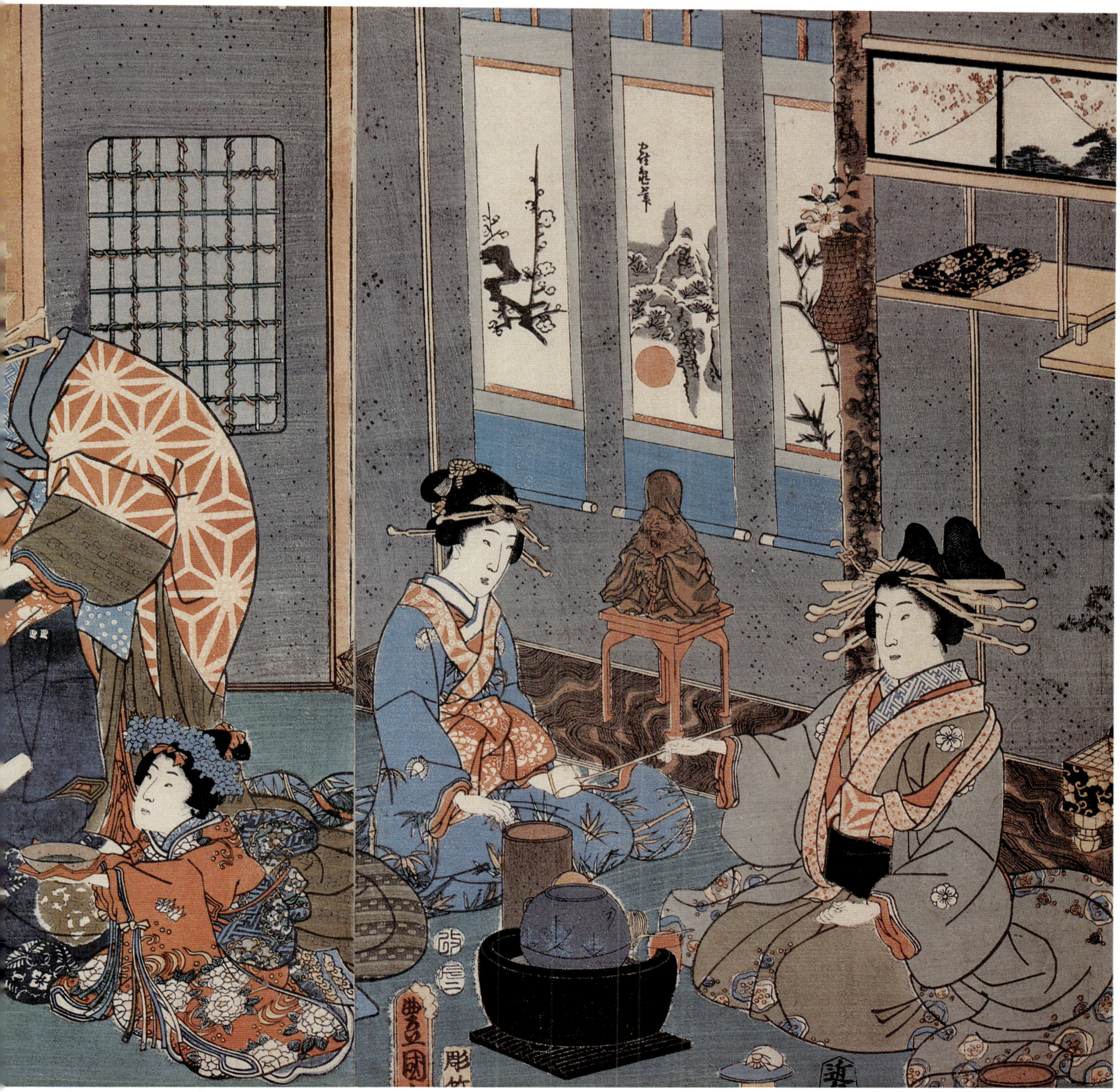

Zoku ukiyo-e ruikō, probably the most important contemporary source on the floating world of the period.

Another, this time full color, triptych depicts 'Three Courtesans Exclaiming over a Love Letter' in an upper room also overlooking the Sumida River, attended by lesser courtesans and their apprentices including one boy. It was designed a quarter of a century later by Utagawa Kunisada (1786-1865) in 1856 for the publisher Ibaya Sensaburō and evokes the cultured milieu of the prestigious courtesan. The woman holding the bamboo dipper in the right-hand panel is preparing tea at the brazier before her; a page offers a cup to the recipient of the letter, but she is too engrossed to notice. With Kunisada we come to the first great exponent of the Utagawa school style, derived from Toyokuni and his master Toyoharu. He was the most prolific *ukiyo-e* artist, carrying out an estimated 40,000 images in his sixty-year career. He is certainly the artist most frequently encountered by the collector in dealers' shops and at auction, often in poor quality late impressions of popular images which exemplify the decline in the role of the publisher from arbiter of taste to virtual sweat-shop owner by the mid-century, churning out images using garish pigments until the blocks wore flat. Such images caricature the artist at his best. Early impressions of his prints, even late in his career, have a consistent high standard of design and feeling for color and detail.

The charming fan-print, 'Touch and Textile' (page 132), from a set of three 'Comparison Between the Three Pairs' of senses and the objects of those senses, published by Ibaya Sensaburō in 1855, evokes the rich texture of the material: the woman stares unseeing to one side as she assesses the quality by feel. The print bears the signature *Toyokuni ga*, the name of his master which Kunisada took in 1844, ignoring the claims of Toyoshige (who had received the title Toyokuni II on the master's death), and calling him-

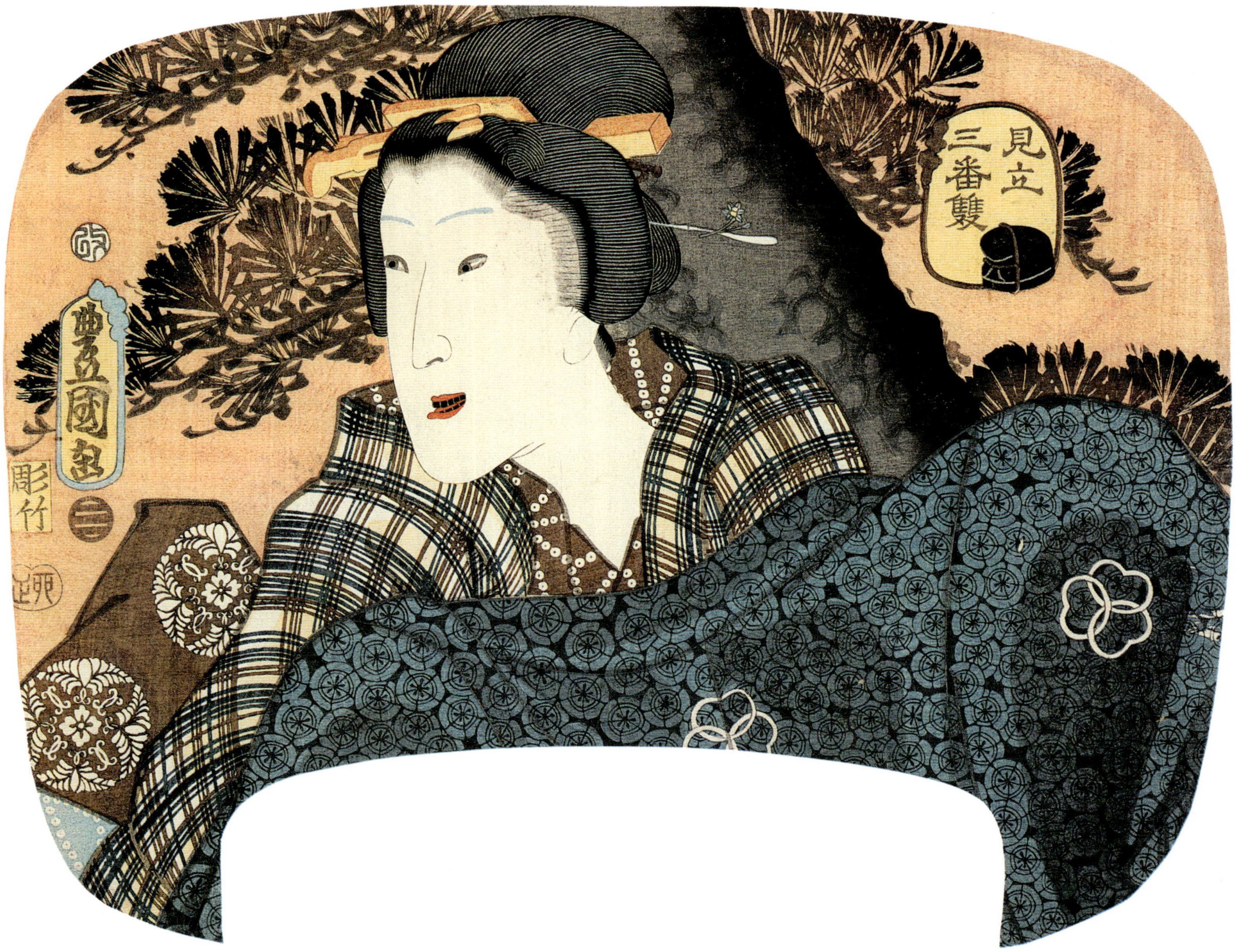

Above: Utagawa Kunisada (1786-1865) 'Touch and Textile,' 1855, from the series 'Comparisons between the Three Pairs,' 1855, 8½×11½ inches (21.6×29.2 cm). Published by Dansendō. Courtesy of the Trustees of the Victoria and Albert Museum, London.

Right: Utagawa Kuniyoshi (1798-1861) 'Woman with Wine Cup,' from the series 'Excellencies of Mountain and Sea Illustrated' (*Sankai medetai zue*), 1853, 13¾×9½ inches (35×24 cm). Courtesy, the Whitworth Art Gallery, University of Manchester.

self 'second-generation Toyokuni.' Modern usage refers, confusingly, to Kunisada as Toyokuni III.

Utagawa Kuniyoshi (1798-1861) became a pupil in the studio of Toyokuni at the age of 13, in 1811. This first known works are illustrations for a book called *Gobuji Chūshingura*. His early years were largely devoted to book illustration and actor-prints in the tradition of the Utagawa school. One of the senior pupils of Toyokuni, Utagawa Kuninao (1793-1854), exerted a considerable influence on him. This is evident in the several series of beauties which he designed, largely during the 1840s and 1850s. The series 'Instructive Reference-Index of all Sorts of Proverbs' (*Tatoe-gusa ashie hayabike*), published by Aritaya Kiyoemon around 1843, is full of life and grace, enlivened by the imaginative detail of the octupuses crawling around the coral outcrop on which she sits. The encyclopedic title for this set of prints reflects that the Tempō Reforms of July 1842 were in their full force at the time, banning frivolous subjects, especially courtesans, and insisting that each print published should be approved by a named censor and bear his seal. Artists were careful to avoid the penalties, either by turning to landscape or heroic subjects, or by inventing rather bogus themes as the occasion for their depictions of fashionable beauty.

The final print in this group (page 133) dates from 1853, late in the artist's career, and is particularly interesting as a collaboration between Kuniyoshi and his elder daughter Acho, a talented pupil who continued to work with her father even after her marriage to a Nihonbashi fishmonger. It comes from a set of 70 or more under the general title 'Excellencies of Mountain and Sea Illustrated' (*Sankai medetai zue*), following the general scheme of a woman shown in half length before a cartouche illustrating a provincial industry, carried out by the daughter and bearing her signature *Yoshitori-jo*. The half-dressed courtesan holding a winecup in one hand as she examines the nails of the other seems to bear little relationship to the inset scene of peasants boiling silkworm cocoons to separate the thread, and shows the extent to which the Tempō rules had become a dead letter by this time.

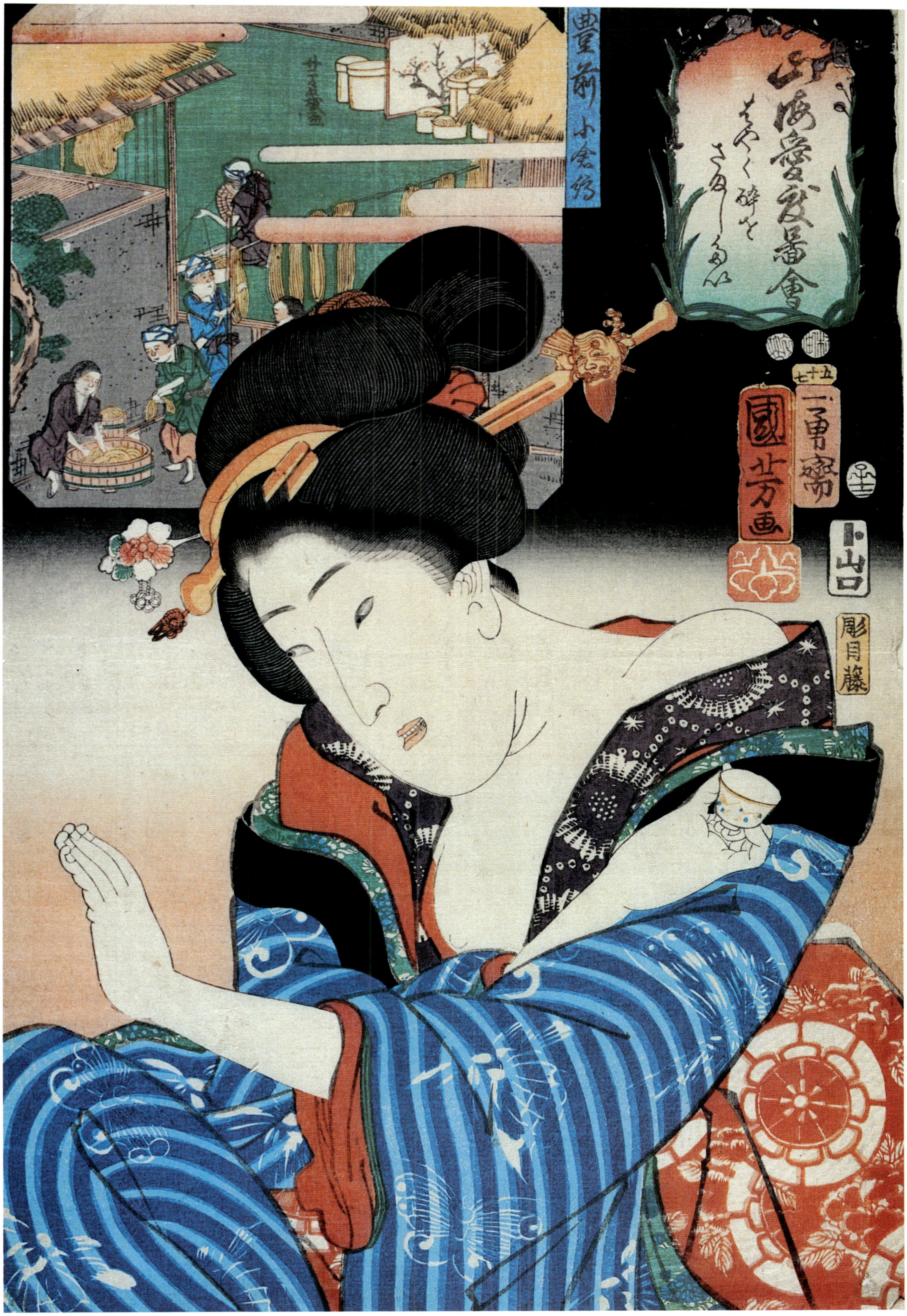
豐前 小倉
山海愛度圖會
一勇齋
國芳画

TOYOKUNI'S PUPILS: NINETEENTH-CENTURY ACTOR PRINTS

The Kabuki theater remained one of the greatest themes for prints throughout the early and mid-nineteenth century, with the significant exception of the reforms of Tempō in 1842. This edict brought official persecution of the popular theater to a head, and for a while Kabuki itself was in danger of total suppression. The theaters were eventually relocated in *Saruwakachō* (Young Monkey Street), far from the Shogun's palace. At the same time, theatrical subjects were banned in prints, and although ways were found to circumvent this, actors' names do not re-appear on prints until around 1862, leading to considerable problems of identification.

Prints of the drama in the early to mid-nineteenth century were overwhelmingly the province of the Utagawa school. Kunisada was the most notable exponent of the Kabuki-tradition within the Utagawa school. He firmly took control after the death of Toyokuni in 1825. Stylistically the development in the Kabuki field runs parallel to that in the genre of *bijinga*: during the 1820s and early 1830s, backgrounds tended to be simple. They were left blank, printed in a single light color or decorated by a minimal unifying motive. Gradually the backgrounds were filled in and given dramatic coloring. Technically the prints improved to standards not achieved before: ample use of blindprinting, burnishing and shading was made as well as of the highest paper quality. A fan portrait (page 135) by Kunisada shows 'The Actor Iwai Kumesaburō as Oritsu,' the wife of the robber Ishikawa in the production of *Masaga no shiranami* at the Nakamura-za in May 1831. The great Iwai family specialized in *onnagata*, women's roles, and had been active since the beginning of the eighteenth century. This vivid record of the actor's performance would have been on sale within a month of the start of the production. Fan prints on Kabuki subjects were popular, providing the performer's admirers with an emblem of their hero which could be flaunted publicly; they are now rare as a result of this kind of use.

Below: Keisai Eisen (1790-1848) 'Sadakurō Robbing Yoichibei in Act V of *Chūshingura*,' c. 1830, 9¼×14⅜ inches (23.5×35.6 cm). Published by Sōshūya. Courtesy of the Trustees of the Victoria and Albert Museum, London.

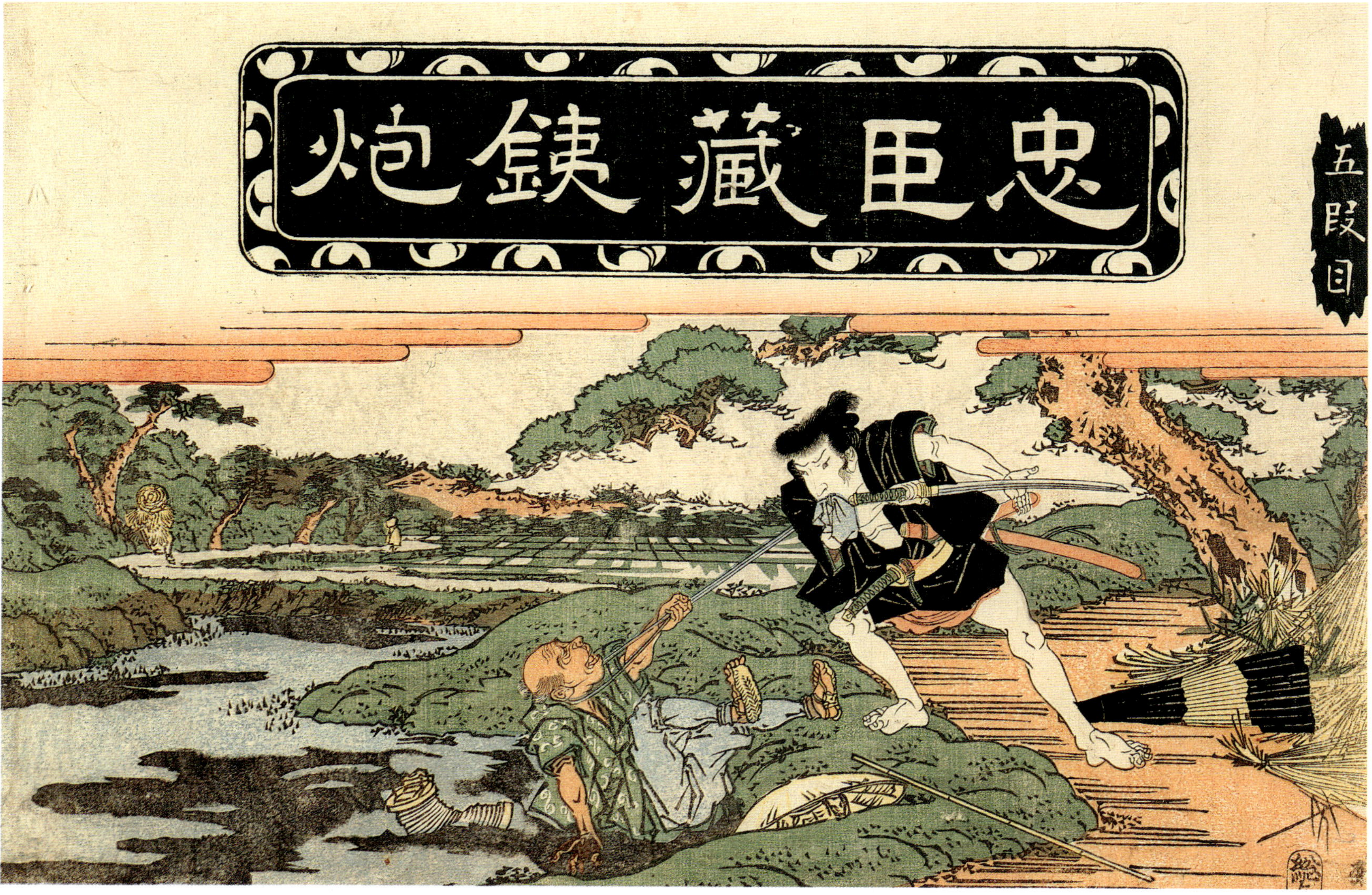

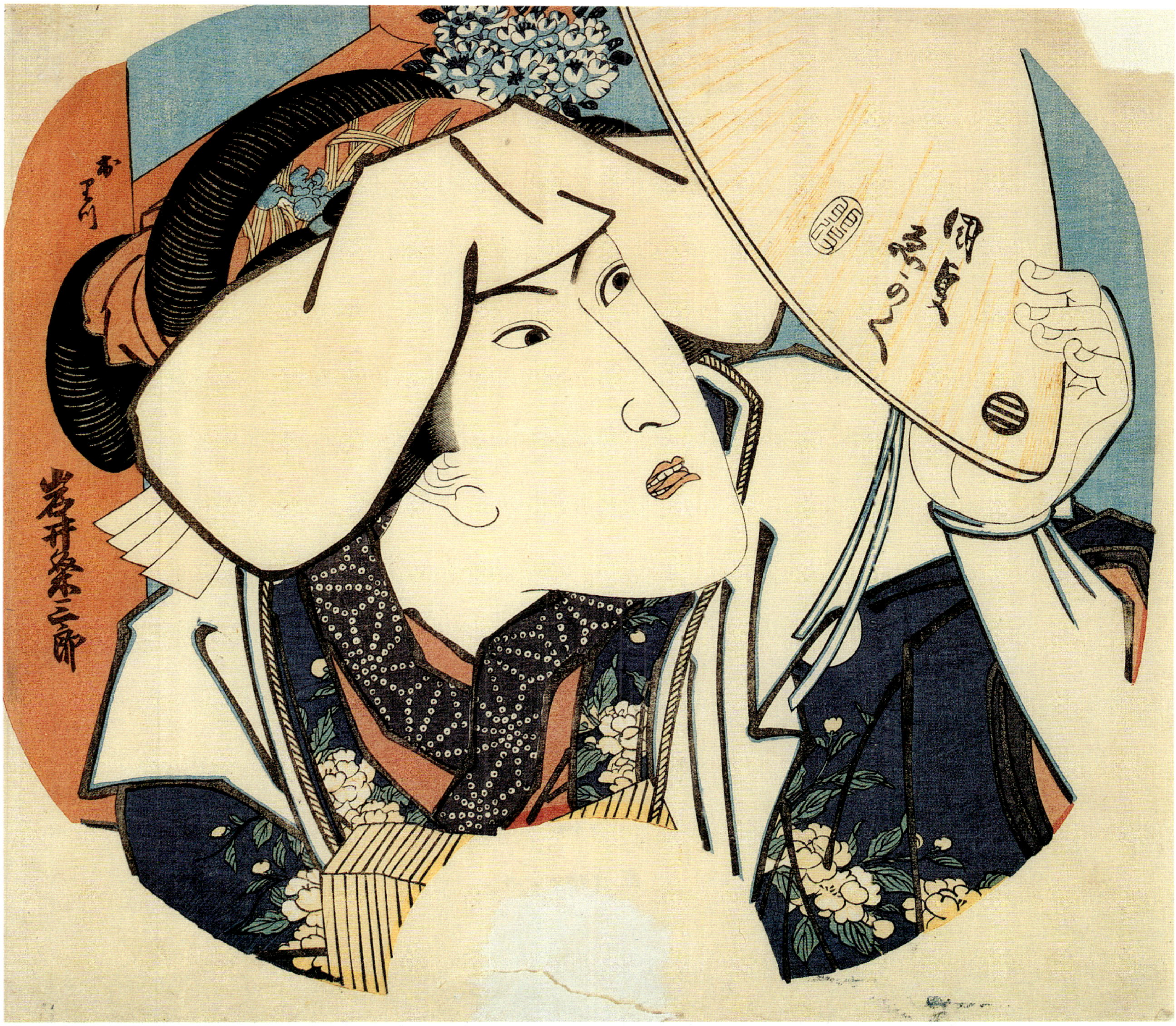

Above: Utagawa Kunisada (1786-1865) 'The Actor Iwai Kumesaburō as Oritsu,' fan print, 9×10⅝ inches (22.9×27 cm). Published by Dansendō. Courtesy of the Trustees of the Victoria and Albert Museum, London.

Right: Utagawa Kunisada (1786-1865) 'An Actor Playing Otsuji the Wet-nurse Doing Penance under a Waterfall,' 1835, 14×20 inches (35.6×20 cm). Published by Ebisuya. Courtesy of the Trustees of the Victoria and Albert Museum, London.

In a *surimono* triptych (page 136) by the same artist from around 1835 of 'A Scene from *Sukeroku*,' we see the same actor as on the fan, now promoted to the new title Iwai Hanshirō VI, as the courtesan Agemaki, standing to the right of her lover, the plebian hero Sukeroku. He is frequently shown in this defiant attitude, with parasol raised and sword and flute stuck in his sash, an emblem of the city-dweller's dislike of repressive feudal authority. The role was a specialty of the Ichikawa family, and is played here by Ichikawa Danjūrō VII, the greatest actor of the age, who himself exemplified many of these qualities. Danjūrō was to be exiled from Edo in 1842 on various sumptuary charges including infringing samurai privilege by 'wearing real armor on stage, made of leather and metal' and 'insolently and outrageously refusing to know his place,' in the words of the official indictment.

The third example by Kunisada dates from 1855 and shows the problems of identification commonly presented by the Tempō ban. It is a diptych of 'Otsuji the Wet-Nurse doing Penance under a Waterfall,' with a child-actor as Taniya Hōtarō, seeing the apparition of the spirit of Zōzu-san. The absence of any indication of names, and the landscape setting, dissociate the image from the stage, at least as far as the censors were concerned. The foremost *onnagata* actor of the time, Bandō Shuka, died in the same month the print was produced, and it has been suggested that the spirit is a memorial portrait of the man.

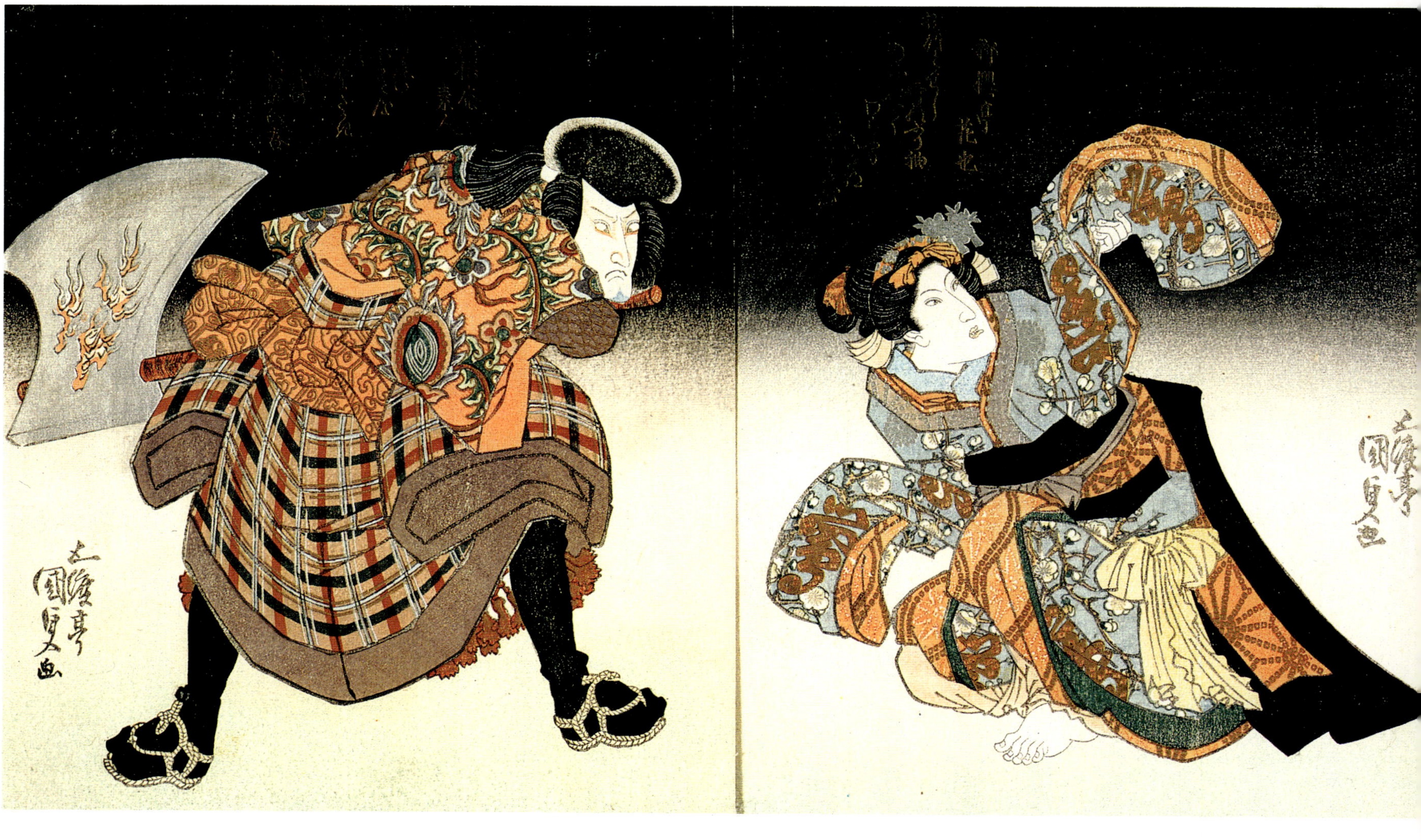

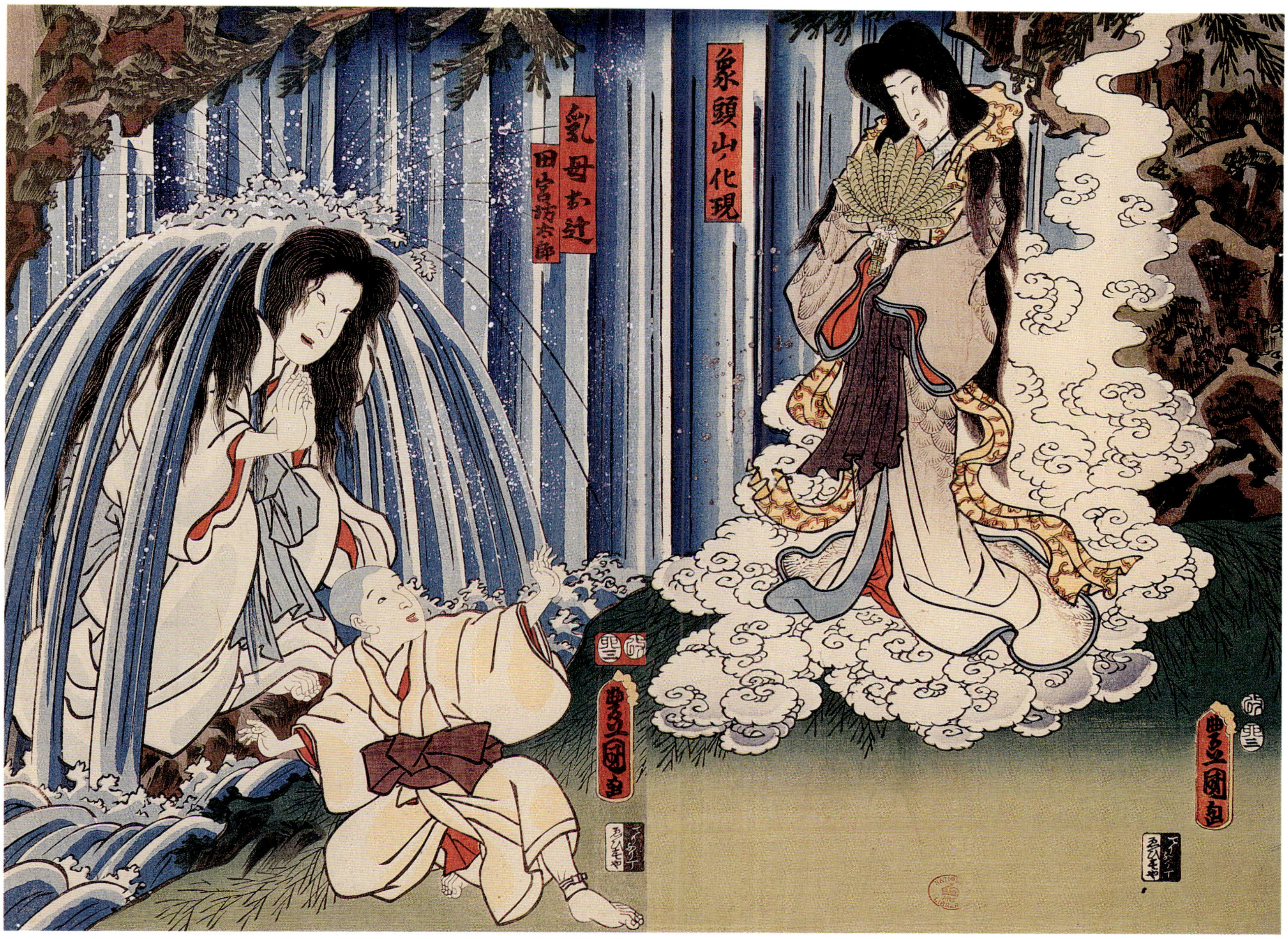

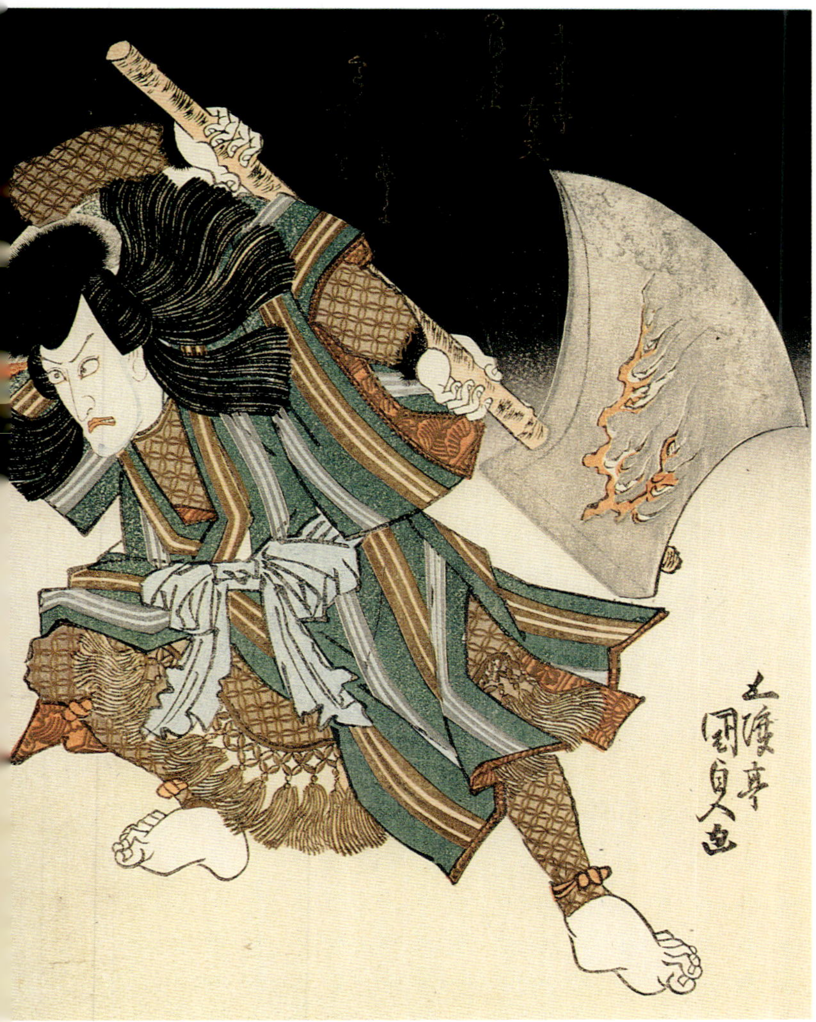

Left: Utagawa Kunisada (1786-1865) 'Scene from *Sukeroku*,' c. 1835, *surimono* triptych, 8½×22½ inches (21.6×57.2 cm). Courtesy of the Trustees of the Victoria and Albert Museum, London.

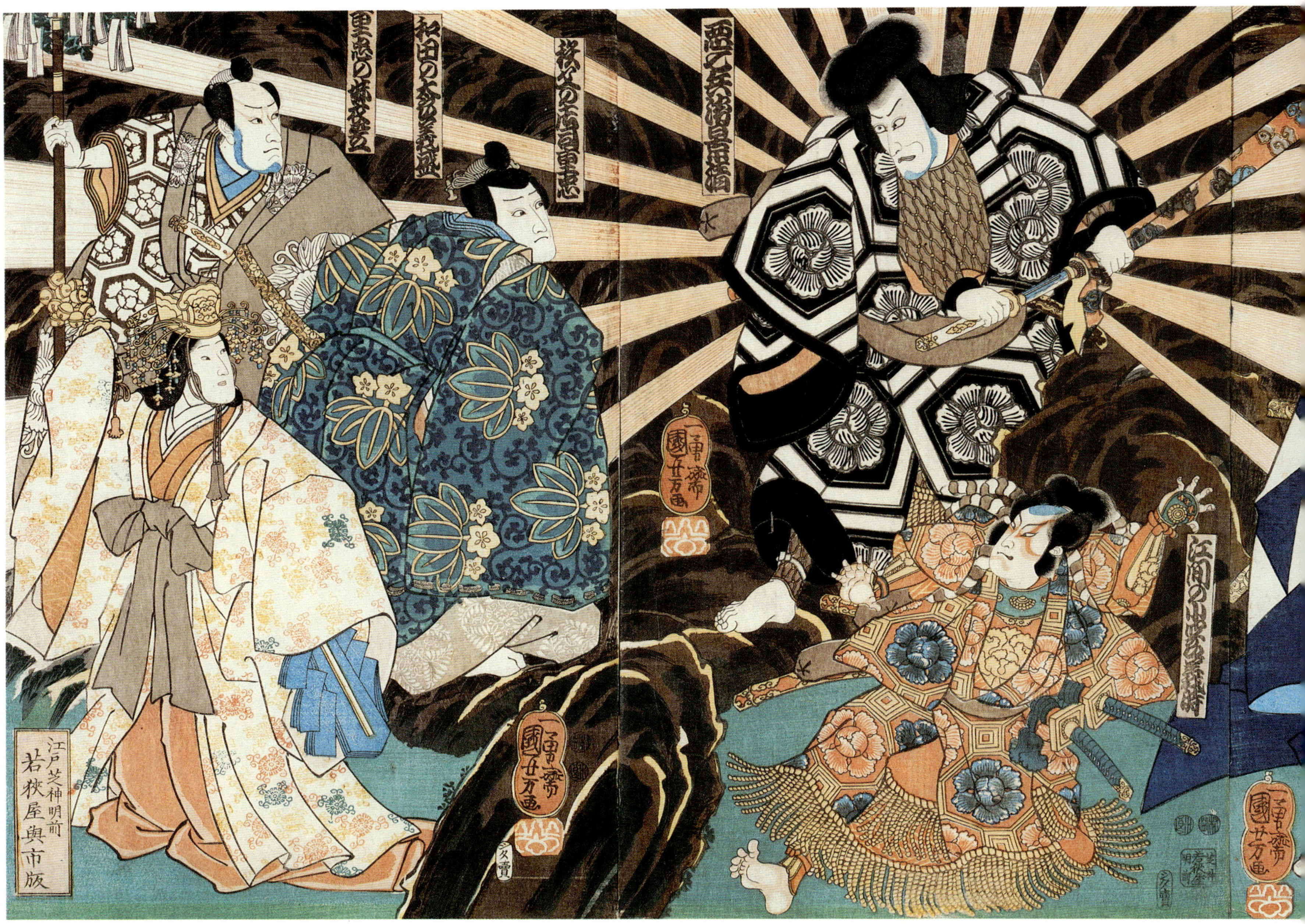

Above: Utagawa Kuniyoshi (1798-1861) 'Scene from *Oedo Kagekiyo,*' 1850 triptych, 14³⁄₁₆×28⅝ inches (36×72.7 cm). Published by Wakasaya Yoichi. Courtesy of the Trustees of the Victoria and Albert Museum, London.

Kuniyoshi produced dramatic subjects in considerable numbers. An interesting triptych from 1850 shows 'A Scene from *Oedo Kagekiyo*,' (page 138) produced at the Kawarazaki theater. The Taira warrior Kagekiyo bursts from a cave drawing his sword upon a disconcerted gathering of his Minamoto enemies. This might appear to be simply a heroic print. Kagekiyo, however, has the distinctive features of Ichikawa Danjūrō VII, who we last saw in the role of Sukeroku. The great actor had just been allowed back from exile in Ōsaka and this print thus commemorates one of his earliest performances back in his home town.

An illustration designed by Eisen of around 1830 (page 134), testifies to the enormous popularity of the *Chūshingura* drama, which is still performed every year. The labyrinthine plot, divided into 12 acts, tells how the evil Moronao angers his aide Enya-hangan into drawing his sword in the palace, a capital offence for which he must commit *harakiri.* The 47 *rōnin*, the dead man's redundant samurai retainers, eventually succeed in capturing and beheading Moronao, after which they anticipate the law by committing mass *harakiri*. The play is based on actual events in 1701-3. Enormous numbers of prints exist on this subject, not only ones depicting actors in character. Hokusai and Hiroshige both produced series of illustrations of similar type to the example by Eisen reproduced here, 'Sadakurō Robbing Yoichibei in Act V of *Chūshingura*,' published by Sōshūya Yohei. Yoichibei, the father-in-law of one of the *rōnin*, Kampei, is robbed and murdered while returning home from selling Kampei's wife to a brothel to fund the vendetta. However, Kampei, who is hunting nearby, mistakes the robber in the twilight for a wild boar and shoots him, so the money is saved. It is impressive how Eisen combines a dramatic subject and violent action, in which he was by no means a specialist, with landscape, a genre for which he is much better known.

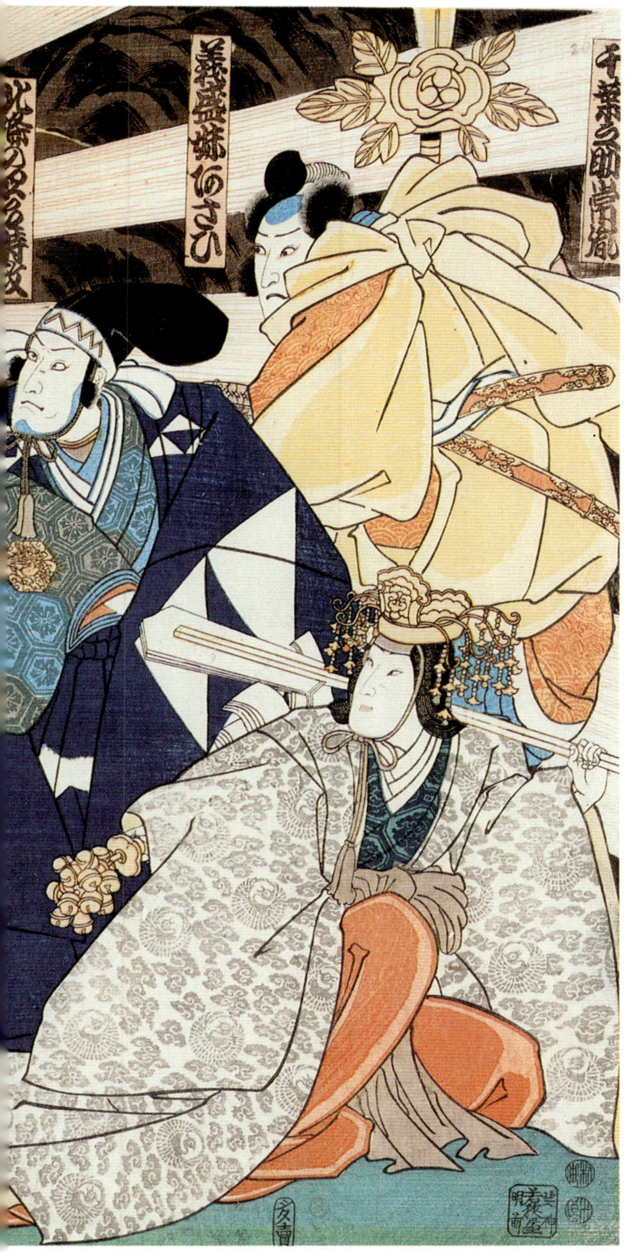

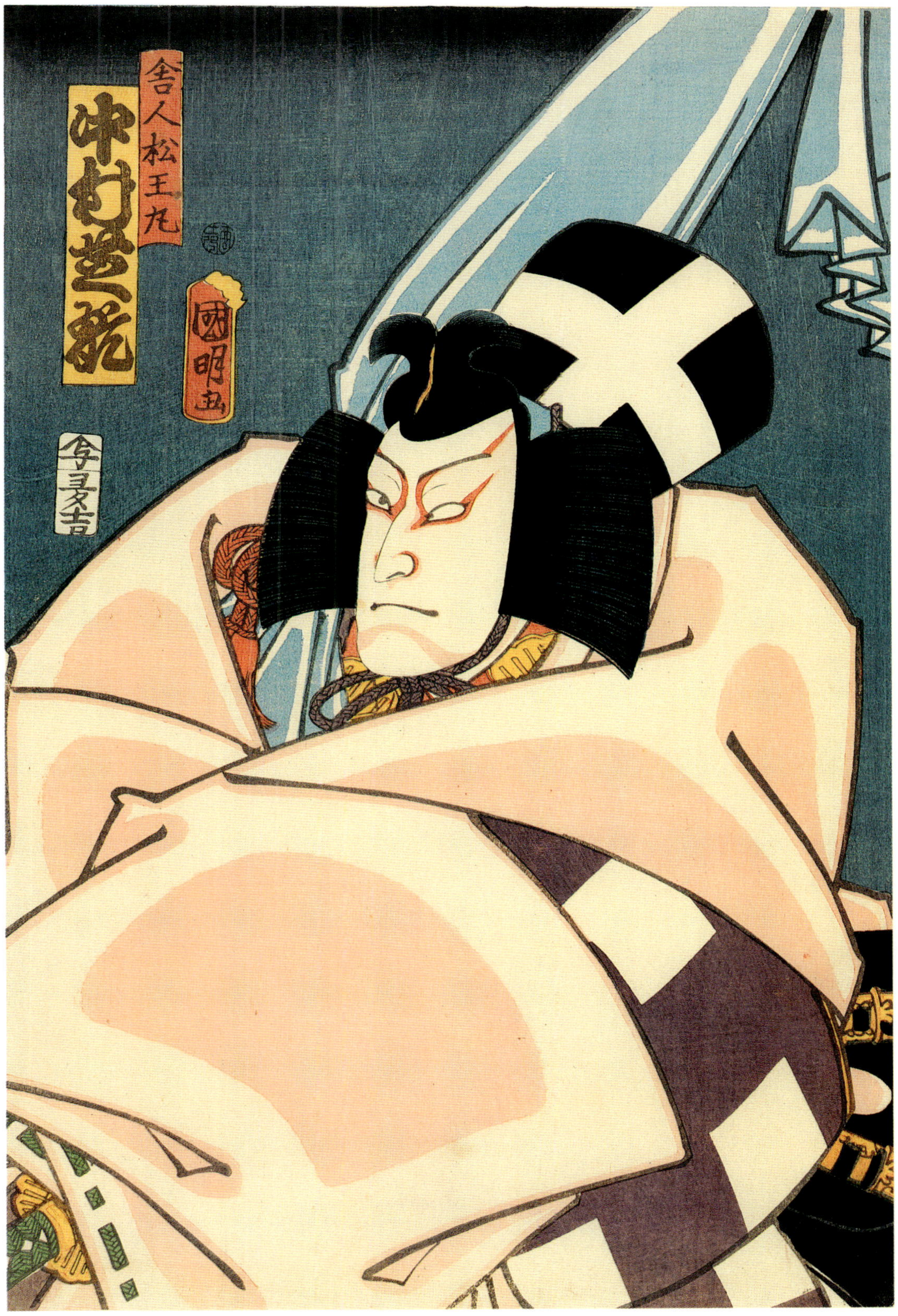

Right: Hachisuka Kuniaki II (1835-68) 'The Actor Nakamura Shikan as Toneri Matsuōmaru in *Sugawara*,' 1861, 14½×10 inches (36.8×25.4 cm). Published by Hori Takichi. Courtesy of the Trustees of the Victoria and Albert Museum, London.

Below: Toyohara Kunichika (1835-1905) 'Tengushi Okatarō Attacks Amma no Chuichi with a Kitchen Knife,' 1868, triptych, 14½×28¼ inches (36.2×71.8 cm). Published by Yorozuya Zen. Courtesy of the Trustees of the Victoria and Albert Museum, London.

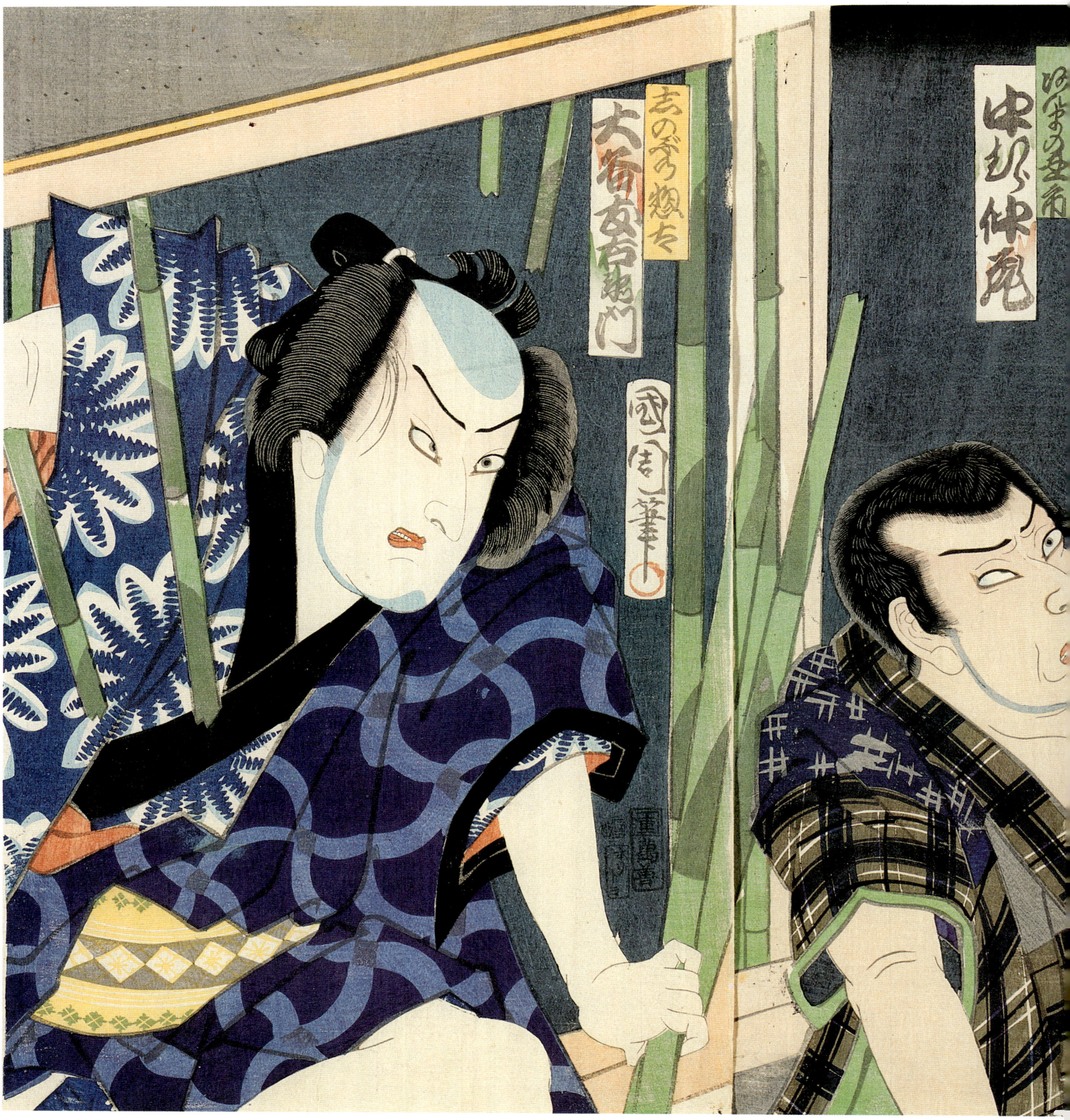

Other Utagawa artists continued the style well into the 1870s. Kuniaki (1835-68), a pupil of Kunisada, produced this powerful half-length portrait of 'The Actor Nakamura Shikan as Toneri Matsuōmaru in the play *Sugawara* in 1861. The actor is shown in the *hippari no mie* pose, with eyes crossed and glaring, connoting one of those moments of extreme emotional tension in Kabuki which are announced to the audience by the beating of a clapper on a board; all movement gradually freezes into a still tableau which is held for a considerable while. Matsuōmaru, a follower of the villain of the piece, is forced to sacrifice his son's life to save Sugawara's son.

In a triptych of 1868 (page 140) we move from the hieratic pageantry of the *jidaimono* plays on classical historical subjects, to an example of the *kizewamono*, plays dealing with the underworld and the poor which were a late development of the *sewamono* genre, the plays of common folk. Kunichika (1835-1905), another pupil of Kunisada, presents us with a characteristically vital image of mayhem in 'Tengushi Okatarō Attacks Amma no Chūichi with a Kitchen Knife,' the characters played by Ichimura Kakitsu and Nakamura Nakazō respectively, while Otani Tomoemon bursts through a bamboo partition to intervene. Kunichika resembles his master in that his reputation has been the victim of his enormous output, but his best work is bold and exciting. His *ōkubi-e* (large-head portraits) and his innovative use of the triptych format, showing one actor dramatically spread out over three sheets, make him the last great exponent of the Utagawa actor-print tradition.

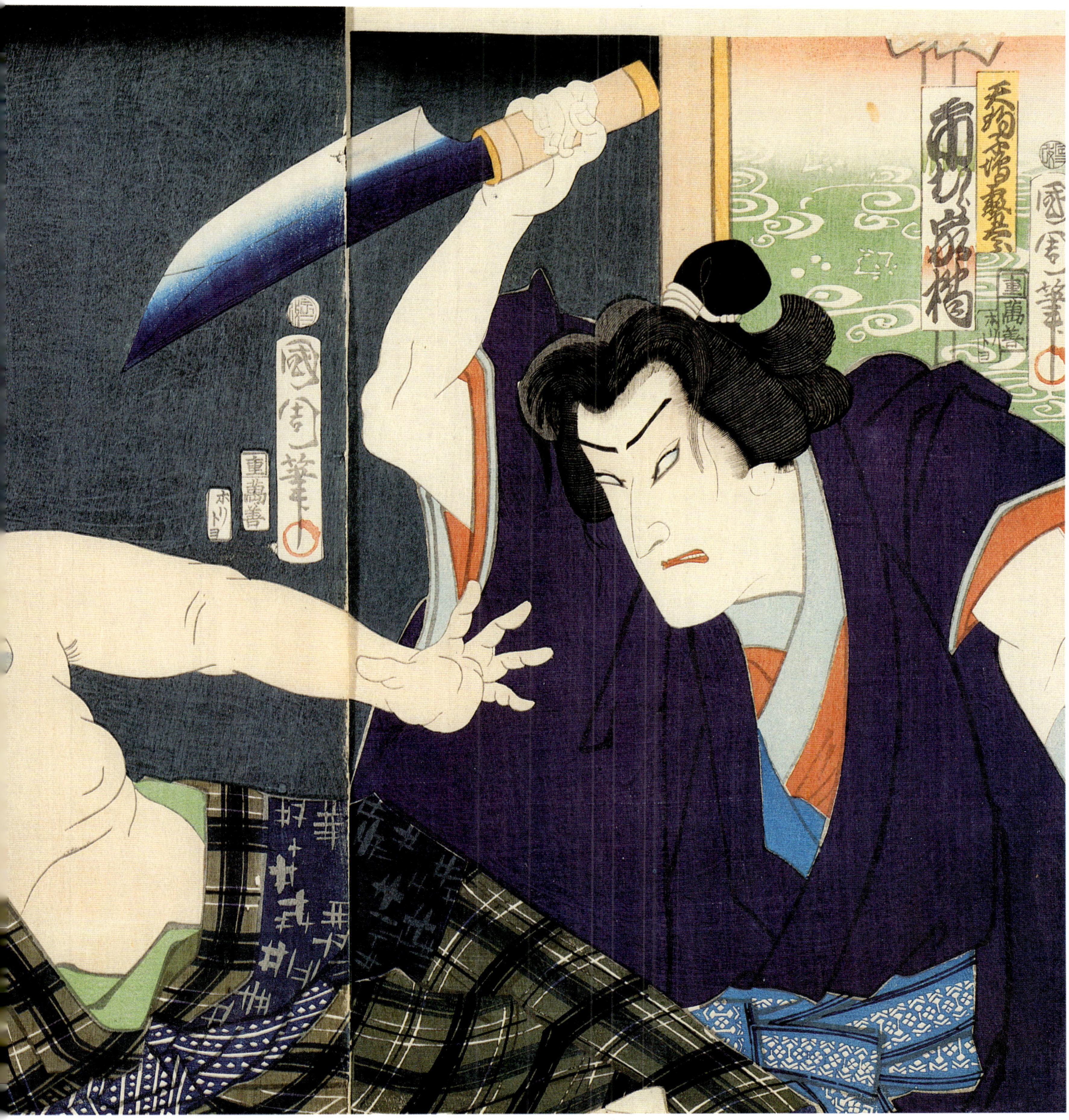

KUNIYOSHI WARRIORS

Kuniyoshi's heroic prints are occasionally hard to distinguish from the prints of the Kabuki theater and share much the same subject matter. However, there is a great difference in intention between a depiction of a performance by a named actor, produced for the actor's fans, and a depiction of the remote historical or mythological event which is the subject of the performance. For some critics in the past, this divergence from genre was an aberration which greatly devalued these prints. Despite Sir Lawrence Binyon's notable enthusiasm for the artist in *Painting in the Far East* (1908), it was half a century before Kuniyoshi's immense dramatic gusto and versatility were widely accepted among academics and collectors. The re-evaluation of Kuniyoshi's previously slighted prints on heroic subjects is mostly due to B W Robinson, whose monographs of 1961 and 1976 should be turned to by anyone interested in this striking artist.

We are probably better equipped to appreciate the samurai themes depicted in so many of Kuniyoshi's heroic prints than were our predecessors. The postwar Japanese cinema created a new image of traditional Japan for us in films such as *The Seven Samurai*; an image quite as powerful as that created a hundred years ago by the *ukiyo-e* print, and quite as incomplete, substituting the stylized violence of Tōshirō Mifune for the somewhat depraved elegance of Utamaro which had so delighted fin-de-siècle Paris. This is not the place to discuss the influence of the nineteenth-century print on the twentieth-century cinema, but it is worth mentioning, if only because it is difficult to look at the heroes of the '108 Heroes of the Suikoden' or to examine a triptych like 'The Soga Brothers Fight in the Rain' without particular images from Kurosawa's films coming to mind.

Kuniyoshi was born in 1798 the son of a silk-dyer Yanaga Kichiemon who was a personal friend of the artist Toyokuni. This friendship is an illustration of how little perceived gap there was between the plebian print-artist and any other successful artisan in Japan's stratified society. It probably helped the artist to join Toyokuni's atelier as an apprentice in 1811. Even before then he had received some artistic training from Katsukawa Shuntei (1770-1820) who can be credited with the production of the first heroic prints in the *ōban* format, and Utagawa Kuninao (1793-1854). The work at Toyokuni's studio would have given him a full training in the standard Utagawa subjects, actor-portraiture and women, while Kuninao is known to have been trained also in Kanō school ink painting and may have passed these methods on to the boy.

Around 1814 Kuniyoshi left the studio, taking on the art-name by which he is known, and became a professional artist. Robinson recounts how in the lean years that followed, he was for a time reduced to scavenging discarded *tatami* mats, which he repaired and sold. Gradually he became known and commissions began to come his way, but it was not until the publication by Kagaya Kichiemon in 1827 of the first five plates of the '108 Popular Heroes of the Suikoden' (*Tsūzoku Suikoden gōketsu hyaku-hachinin no hitori*) that he made his name.

In number 69 from the set (page 143) we see an underwater battle between the wrestler Tammeijirō Genshōgo and an armored foe. The headlong plunge of the antagonists, scattering startled fish to either side, does not conceal the richly worked Chinese armour or the hero's intricate tattoo. Tattoos in this series were used as patterns by fashionable tattooists. Kuniyoshi himself was tattooed.

Right: Utagawa Kuniyoshi (1798-1861) 'Tammeijirō Genshōgo Fighting an Armoured Man Underwater,' from the series '108 Chinese Heroes of the *Suikoden*' (*Tsūzoku Suikoden gōketsu hyakuhachinin no hitori*), 1827, 15×10⅜ inches (38.1×26.4 cm). Published by Kagaya Kichiemon. Courtesy of the Trustees of the Victoria and Albert Museum, London.

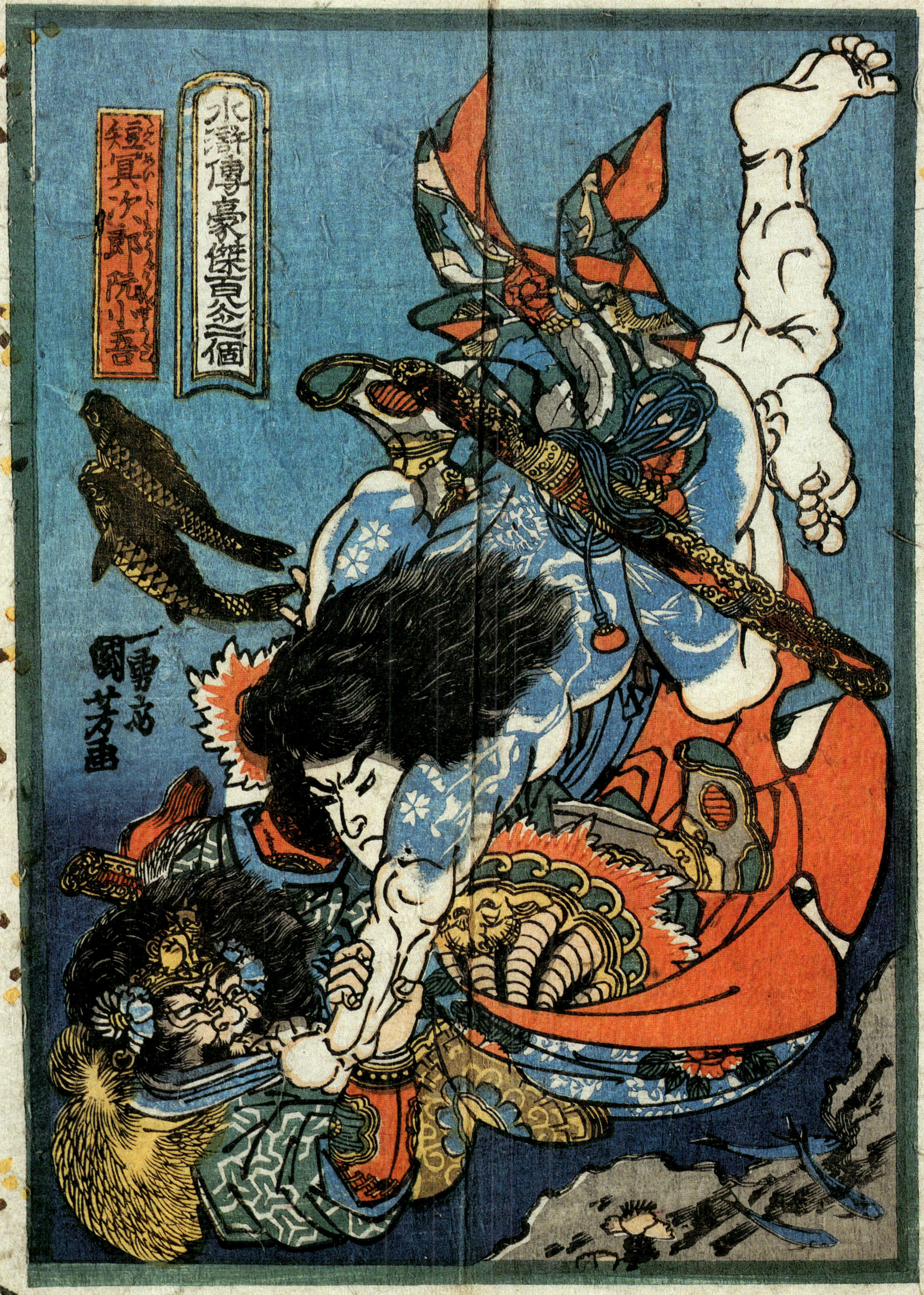
水滸傳豪傑百八人之一個
短冥次郎阮小吾
一勇斎國芳画

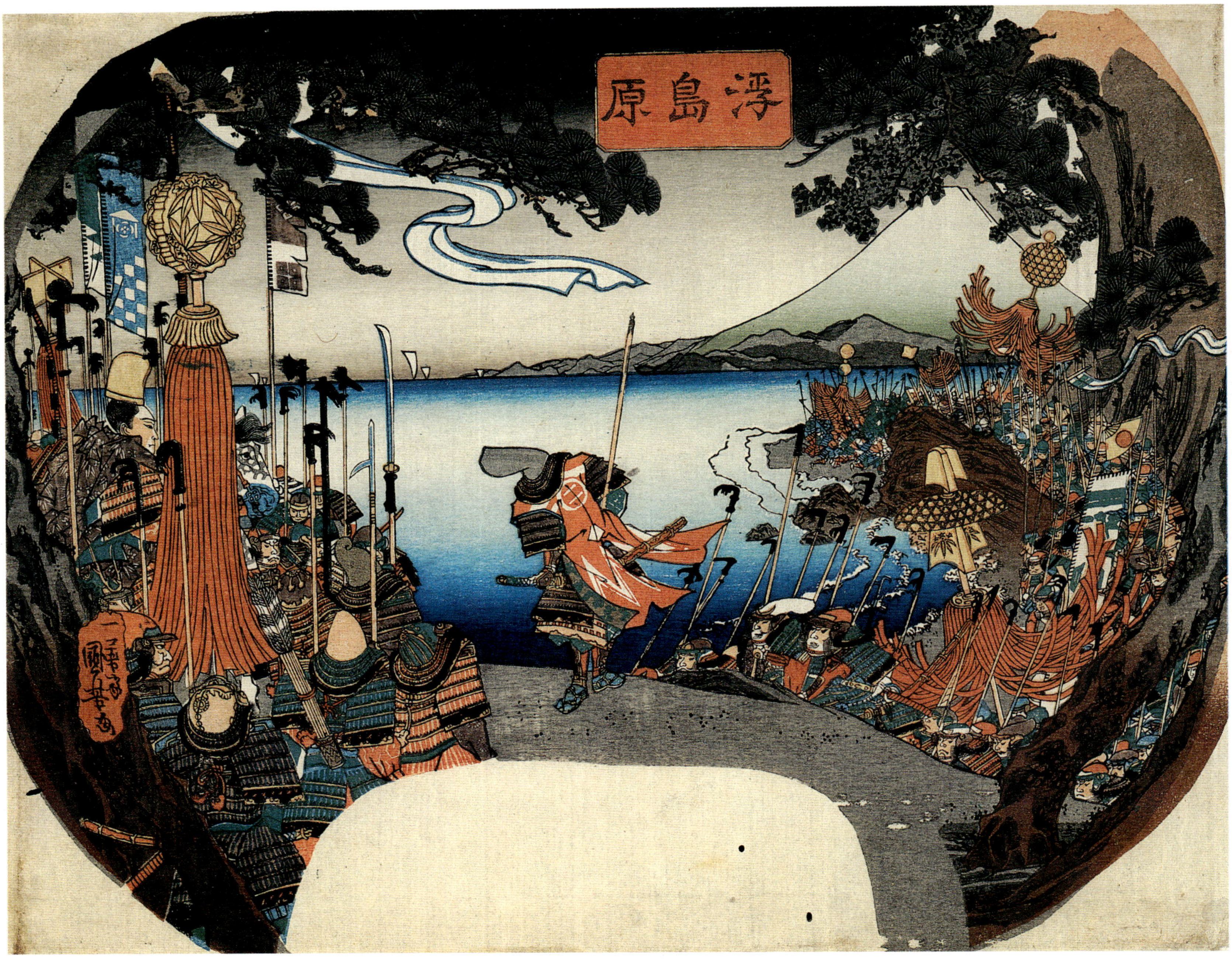

Above: Utagawa Kuniyoshi (1798-1861) 'The Plain of Ukishima,' c. 1840, fan print, 8½×11⅛ inches (21.6×28.3 cm). Courtesy of the Trustees of the Victoria and Albert Museum, London.

The *Suikoden* was a loose translation, by the popular novelist Bakin, of the semi-historical Chinese romance *Shuihe-quan*, recounting the exploits of a twelfth-century outlaw gang. It had been published serially, starting in 1805 (with illustrations by Hokusai), and had been very well received. Kuniyoshi's illustrations of the subject were so popular that he not only completed the full set of 108 but also created several parallel series.

A series of prints from around 1840 contrast with the almost claustrophobic action of *Suikoden*, pulling back to show the figures as part of the landscape. They are scenes from the life of Minamoto Yoshitsune who commanded the armies that destroyed the Taira power in the twelfth century. His half-brother Yoritomo was set up as shogun, only to be hounded to death by Yoritomo who was jealous of his popularity. A fan print (page 144) shows an episode in the hero's story when the revolt against the Taira is under way. Yoshitsune's troops join with those of Yoritomo on the plain of Ukishima. The hero's bowing figure is silhouetted against the bay, with the giant profile of Fuji on the horizon and the mass of Yoritomo's followers to his right, so that he looks isolated and already threatened; this impression is confirmed when one examines the cold stares of Yoritomo and his henchmen. The tall headpiece worn by the bowing figure is a general's helmet shaped as a courtier's cap.

While it cannot be said that the ban on actor-prints promulgated in the Tempō Reforms forced Kuniyoshi to produce heroic triptychs, as he had already designed a considerble number, he certainly benefited by their greater popularity now that the competition was suppressed, bringing them out more frequently than before.

A spectacular triptych of 'Mitsukuni Defying the Skeleton Specter' (page 145), from around 1844/5, provides an interesting example of a subject related to the drama produced under the Tempō ban. The story comes from the tenth century, and recounts how the witch Takiyasha, the daughter of the rebel Taira no Masakado, and her brother Yoshikado, joined the robber gang of Iga no Jutarō. This was produced as a play *Sōma dairi* (The Palace of Sōma), at the end of 1844. In this scene the witch calls up the giant apparition to frighten the hero Mitsukuni, possibly the most memorable image produced by the artist.

Another triptych (page 145) on a supernatural subject, 'Raiko Tormented by the Earth Spider' (1843), got Kuniyoshi in trouble with the authorities for political satire. It depicts the hero Raiko (*Minamoto no Yorimitsu*, 944-1021), who had been commissioned by the Emperor to

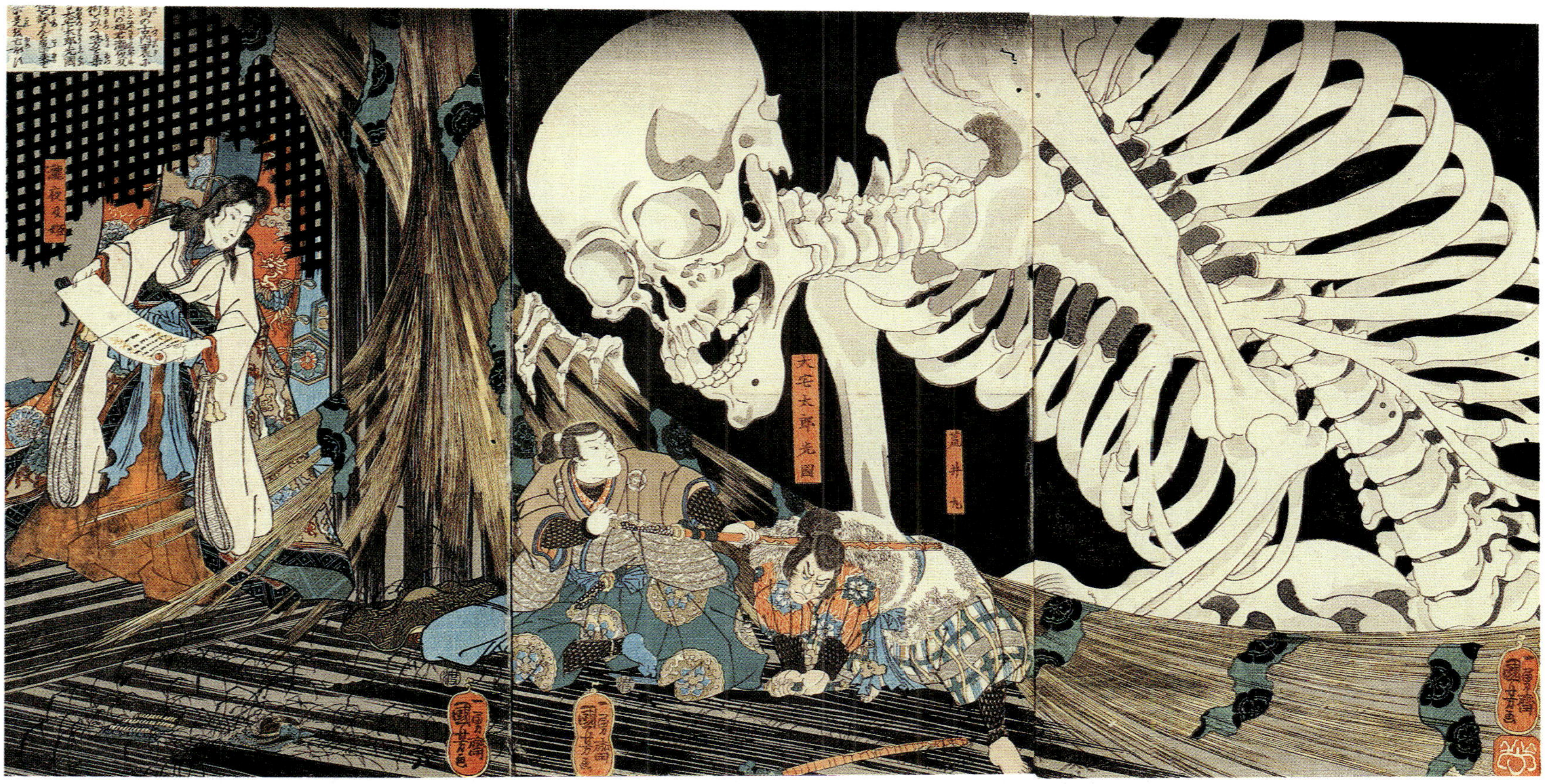

Above: Utagawa Kuniyoshi (1798-1861) 'Mitsukuni Defying the Skeleton Specter,' c. 1845. triptych, 13¾×27¾ inches (34.9×70.5 cm). Courtesy of the Trustees of the Victoria and Albert Museum, London.

clear the country of bandits. He is shown in feverish sleep in the right-hand panel while his four faithful retainers play *gō*, unaware that he is being haunted by the spider and his goblin retinue. (When the four retainers tracked the bandit to his lair and killed him, Raiko's health was immediately restored.) Kuniyoshi was reprimanded for the print and the blocks were destroyed, as the Shogun Ieyoshi and his chief minister Mizuno were said to be caricatured among the spider's grotesque retainers. The example of the print reproduced here may well be from a pirate edition brought out because of the notoriety of the original, especially as it bears no censor's seal which was obligatory after 1842.

Below: Utagawa Kuniyoshi (1798-1861) 'Raiko Tormented by the Earth Spider,' c. 1843, triptych 14½×30 inches (36.8×76 cm). Published by Dansendō. Courtesy of the Trustees of the Victoria and Albert Museum, London.

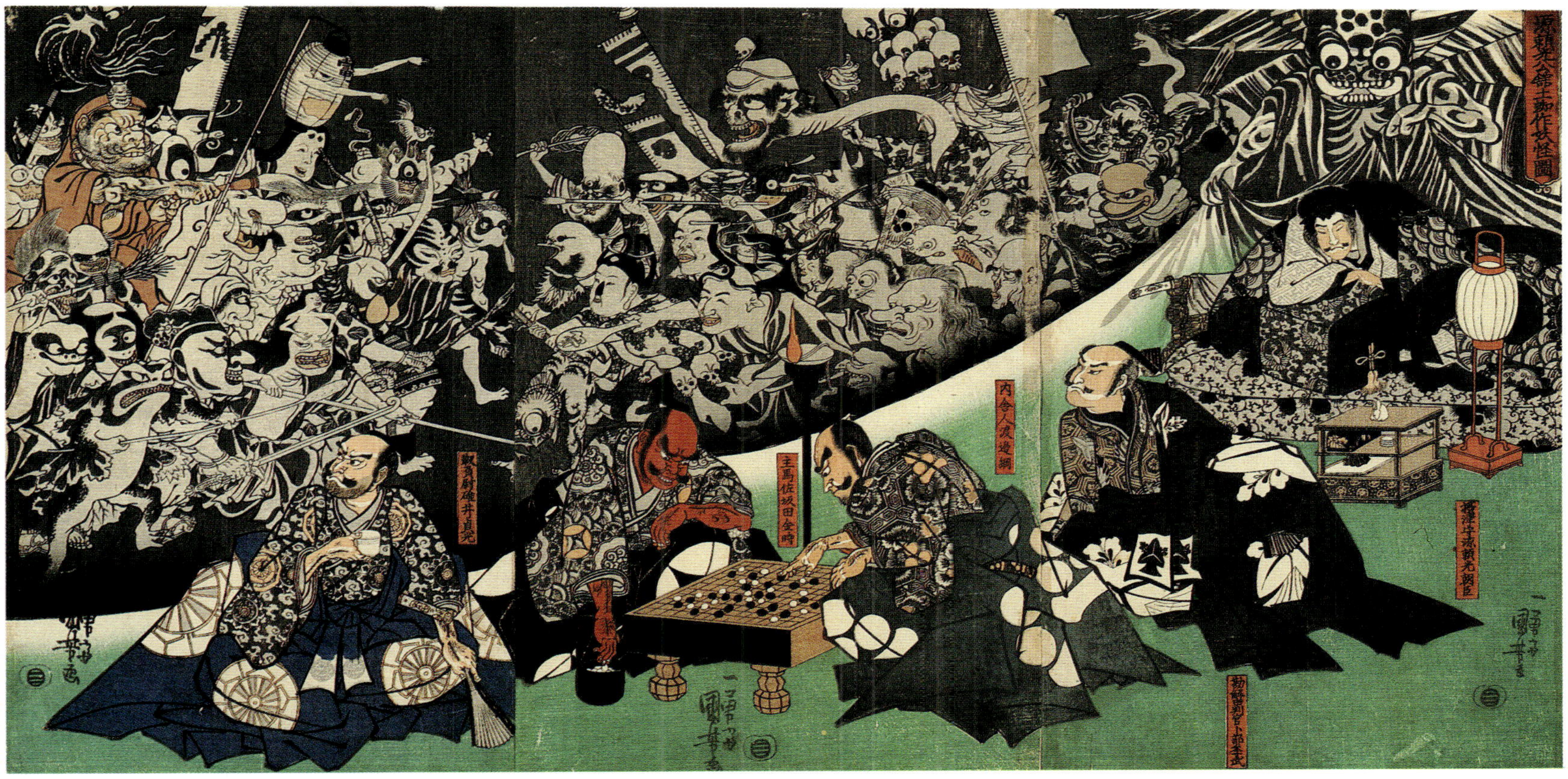

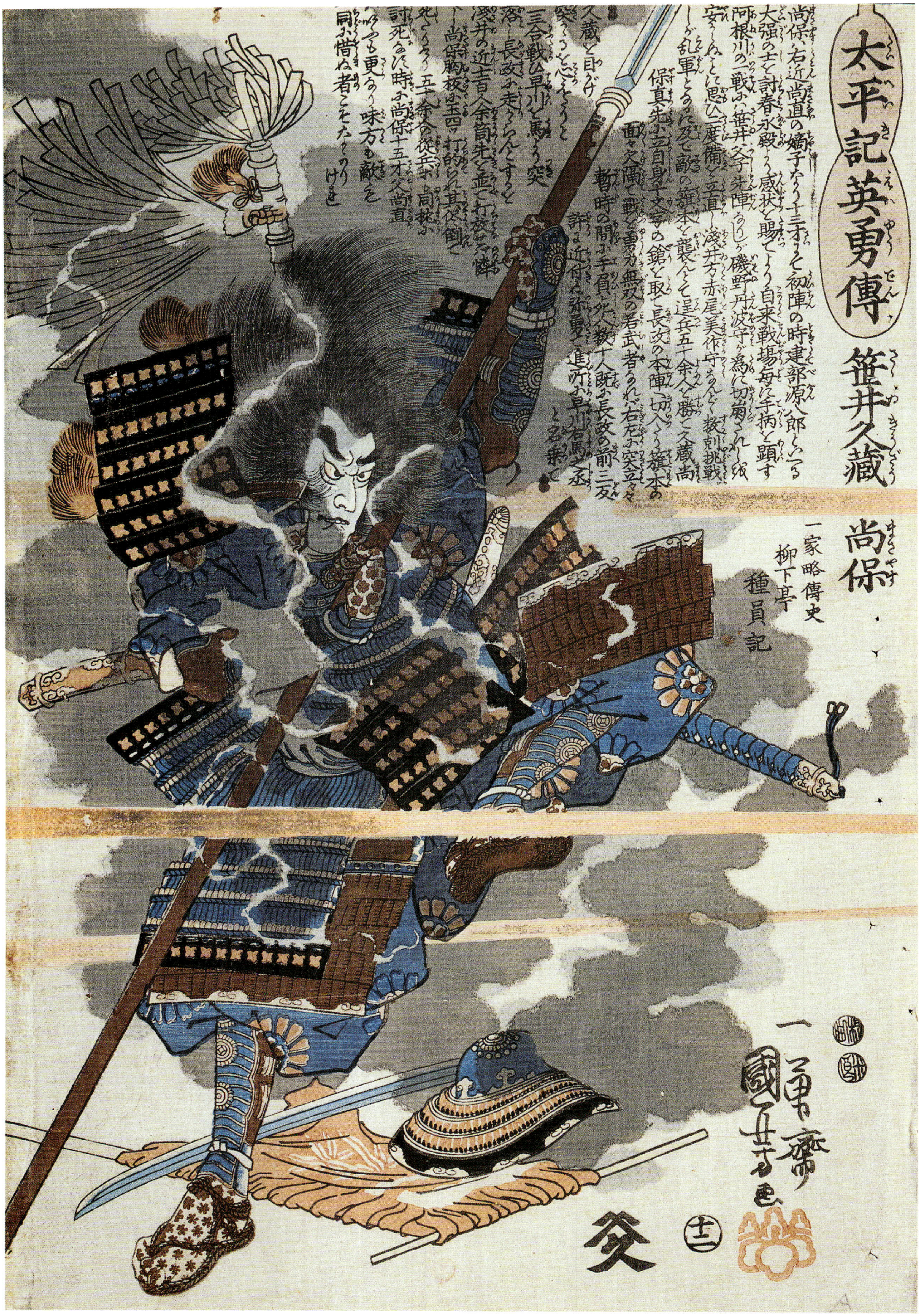
太平記英勇傳
笹井久藏
尚保
一家略傳史
柳下亭
種員記
一勇齋國芳画

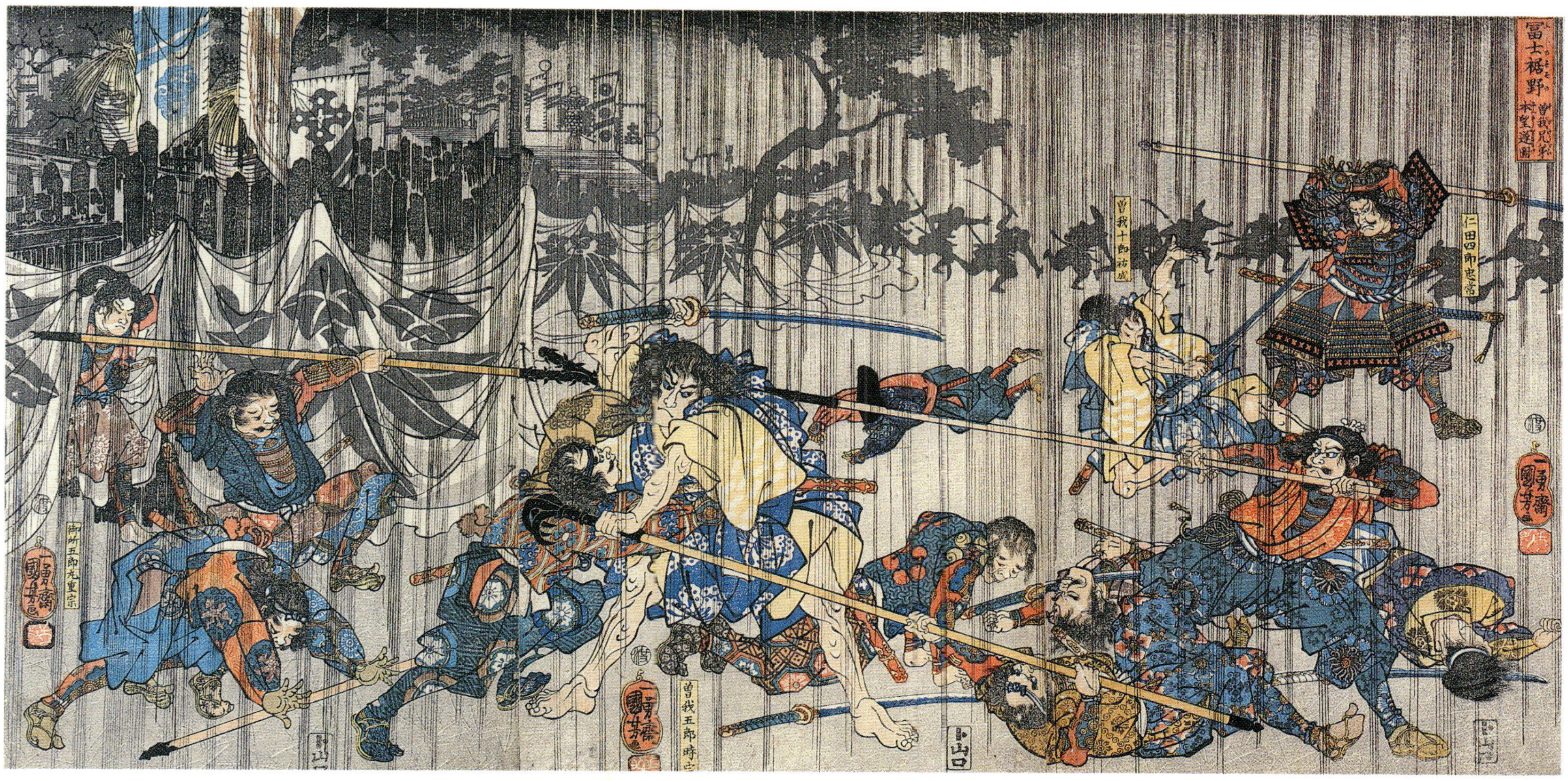

Above: Utagawa Kuniyoshi (1798-1861) 'The Soga Brothers' Last Fight in the Rain on Suso Moor,' c. 1845, triptych, 14⅜×28⅝ inches (36.5×73.6 cm). Published by Yamaguchiya Tōbei. British Museum, London.

Another triptych (page 147) is again a subject from early history produced in the mid-1840s, 'The Soga Brothers' Last Fight in the Rain on Suso Moor.' In 1193, shortly after the final defeat of the Taira, the Shogun Yoritomo held a grand hunting party on Suso moor at the foot of Mount Fuji. The young samurai brothers Jūrō Sukenari and Gorō Tokimune, determined to revenge the murder of their father fifteen years before by the courtier Kudō Suketsune, found their way into his tent on a rainy night and killed him. They are the heroes of many Nō and Kabuki dramas, appearing frequently in prints. The brothers were apprehended as they made their escape. In the right-hand panel we see the death of Jūrō, while in the center Gorō, struggling towards the Shogun's tent, is about to be tripped and captured by the bodyguard Gorō Maru who is emerging from the tent enclosure at the left. The inexorable downpour seems to be an image of the brothers' fate. Yoritomo sentenced the captured Gōro to be beheaded with a blunt sword, but also in a gesture of singular even-handedness, erected a shrine commemorating the brother's filial loyalty.

Kuniyoshi produced series of single-sheet prints on heroic themes throughout his career, either depicting figures full- or half-length beneath a rectangular title panel, or, as in the example shown (page 146), integrating text and image. The 'Death of Sasai Masayasu' printed around 1848/9 is from the series 'Biographies of Heroes of the Taiheki' (*Taiheki eiyū den*), and shows the warrior attempting to break into the camp of Asai Nagamasu at the battle of the Aregawa in 1570. It is a gruesome tour de force of great spirit, showing a man literally coming to pieces in a volley of musketry.

Left: Utagawa Kuniyoshi (1798-1861) 'The Death of Sasai Masayasu,' from the series 'Biographies of Heroes of the Taiheki' (*Taiheiki eiyū den*), c. 1849, 14⅛×9½ inches (35.9×24.1 cm). Published by Yamamotoya Heikichi. Courtesy of the Trustees of the Victoria and Albert Museum, London.

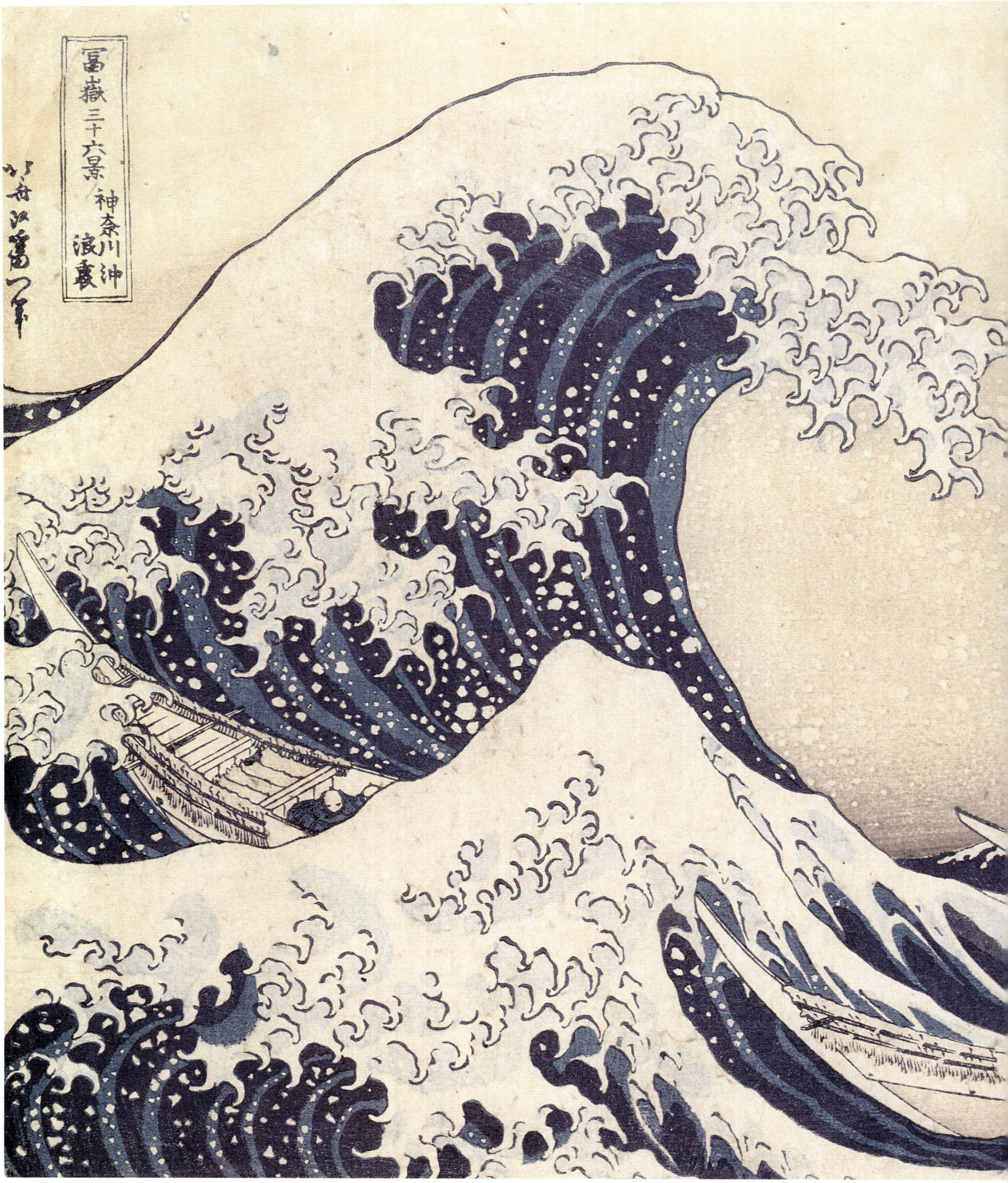

Katsushika Hokusai (1760–1849) 'The Great Wave of Kanagawa,' from the series '36 Views of Mt. Fuji' (*Fugaku sanjūrokkei*), 1831, 9⅞×14⅝ inches (25×37.1 cm). Published by Nishimura Eijudō. Courtesy of the Trustees of the Victoria and Albert Museum, London.

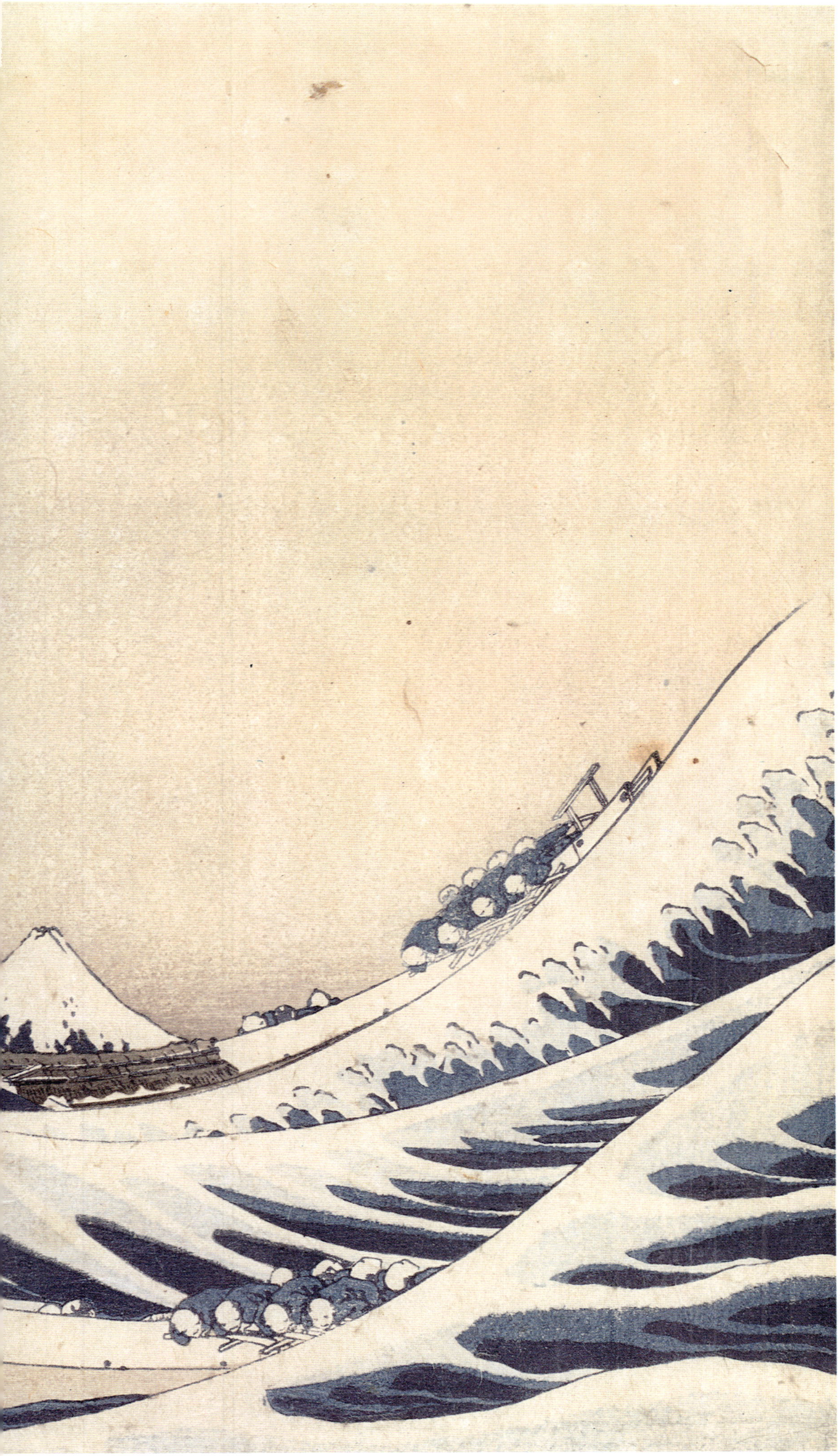

THE LANDSCAPE PRINT: HOKUSAI, HIROSHIGE AND THEIR FOLLOWERS

Katsushika Hokusai (1760-1849) is the most protean Japanese artist, eccentric, diverse, vigorous and immensely productive. It is astonishing to consider that the flood of landscape and bird and flower subjects produced in the 1830s came from a man in his seventies. The *surimono* and illustrated books from the last decade of the eighteenth century onward constitute in themselves a tremendous achievement, while his scroll paintings are equally respected in his native country. Richard Lane's summary catalogue lists 118 print series (including *surimono*) and about 220 illustrated books up to the early 1830s where I pick up the story, and some 40 more books from then until his death. However, although we are only dealing with a fraction of the artist's total oeuvre, it includes some of the most marvelous images in Japanese art, and many of the most famous.

In 1831 the Edo publisher Nishimura Eijudō announced the publication of 'the "36 views of Mount Fuji' [*Fugaku sanjū-rokkei*], by Hokusai, decorated with Prussian blue. We have already discussed the impact of this newly imported pigment on the *bijin* prints of Eisen, who from around 1829 designed a succession of *aizuri-e*, pictures printed almost entirely in shades of blue. It seems likely that the new pigment was also a major spur for Hokusai in the design of this new series. Indeed, the first editions of the 36 prints were printed with blue rather than black outlines, though the supplementary set of 10 *Ura Fuji* (Fuji from the Other Side), and later editions of the whole set revert to black outline.

'The Great Wave at Kanagawa' (page 148) is quite possibly the most famous image in Japanese art, ever since it aroused the astonished admiration of the impressionists at the end of the nineteenth century, and inspired Debussy's composition *La Mer*. It exemplifies the rich potential of the new pigment in a single decorative statement, bringing a new naturalism to the depiction of the waves, a favorite subject in the Edo period which was used extensively in the painted decoration of doors and screens. Mankind is represented by the unfortunate mariners in their coasting boats, hanging on desperately as the vessels are flung around like matches. The sacred mountain appears in the distance like a minor wave among greater, the use of the low eye-level demonstrating assured grasp of western perspective in a work which some might see as entirely exotic and Japanese.

Below: Katsushika Hokusai (1760-1849) 'Fuji above the Lightning,' from the series '36 Views of Mt. Fuji' (*Fugaku sanjūrokkei*), 1831, $9\frac{7}{8} \times 14\frac{5}{8}$ inches (25×37.1 cm). Published by Nishimura Eijudō. Courtesy of the Trustees of the Victoria and Albert Museum, London.

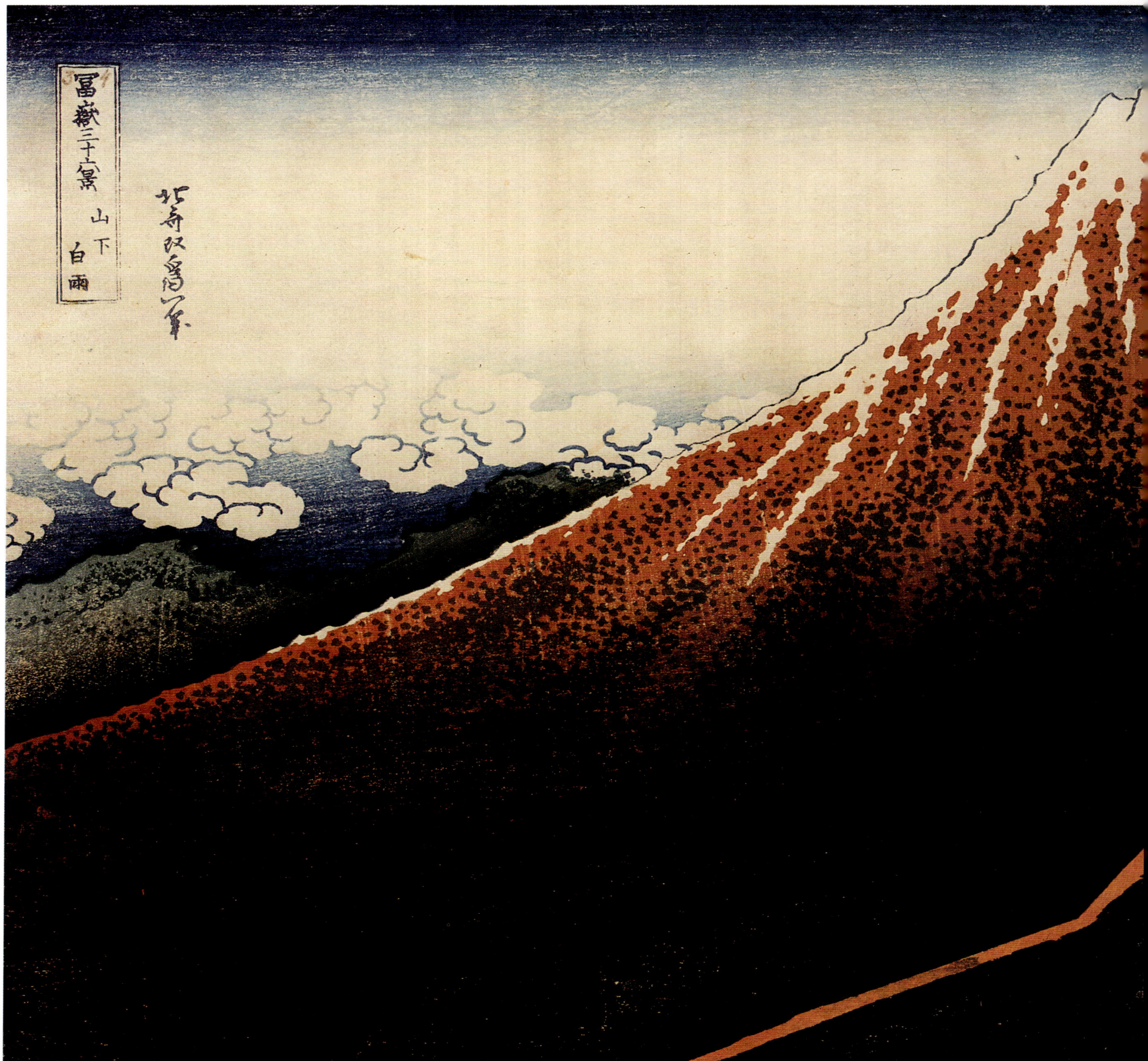

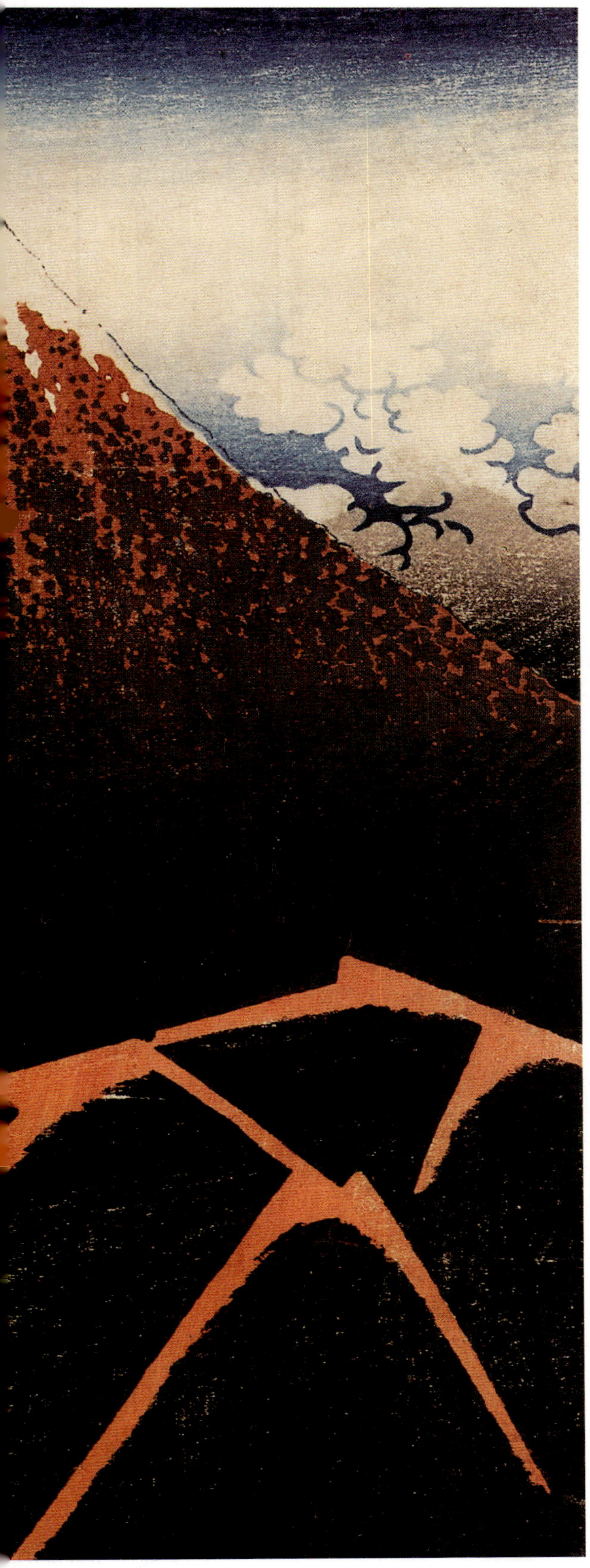

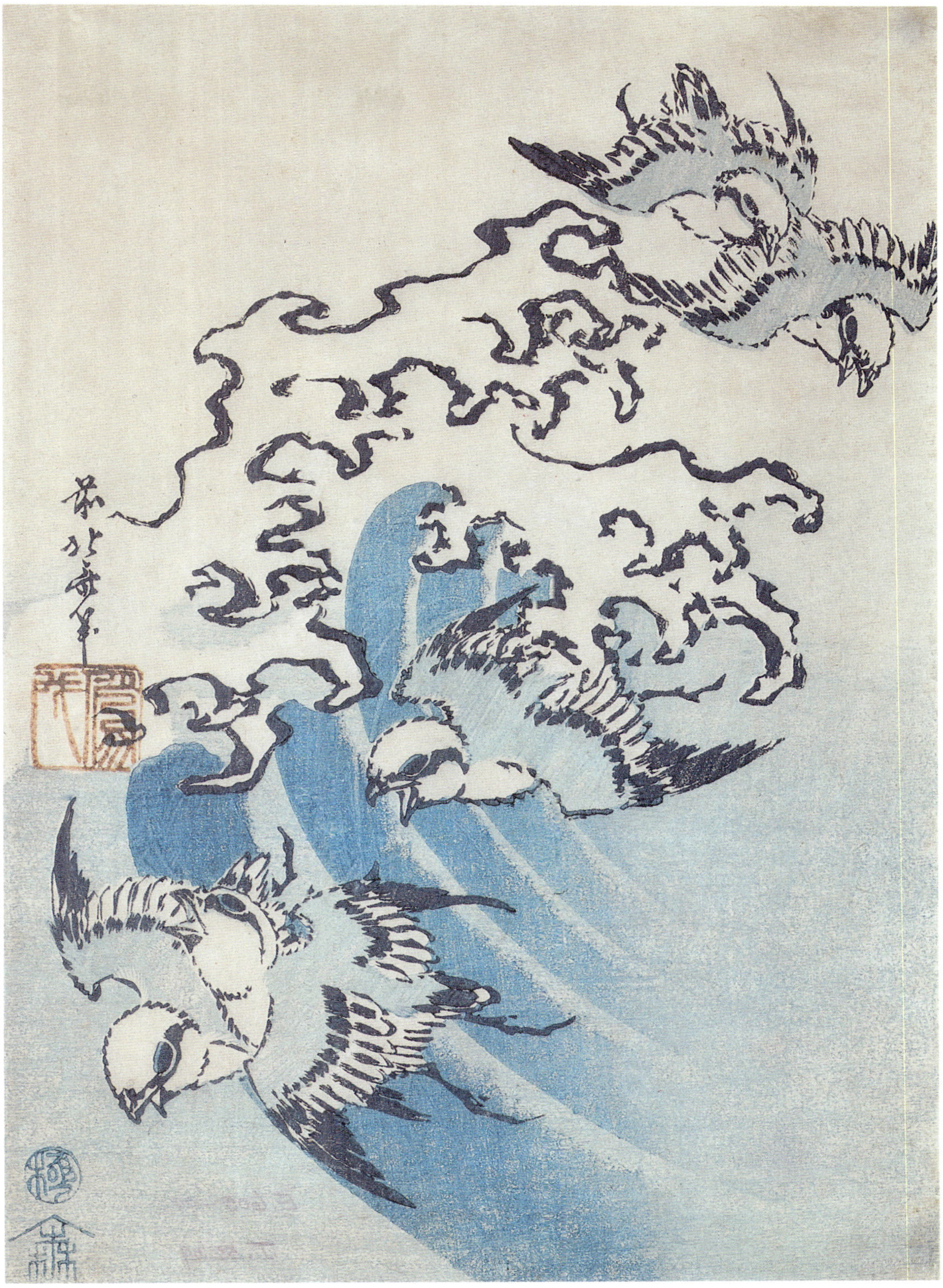

Above: Katsushika Hokusai (1760-1849) '*Chidori* Plovers Flying across a Breaking Wave,' c. 1831, 10×7⅛ inches (25.2×18.1 cm). Published by Moriya Jihei. Courtesy of the Trustees of the Victoria and Albert Museum, London.

It is interesting to illustrate (page 151) a small *aizuri-e* print from around the same time, on the related theme of '*Chidori* Plovers Flying Across a Breaking Wave,' birds which are referred to poetically as metamorphosed droplets of sea-spray. This shows a lyrical exploration of the potential of the new pigment in a closely related context.

Fuji is the highest peak in Japan and the symbol of the beauty of the country. It is a Shinto shrine, regarded as a god since early times. Indeed, at the time the series was issued there was an upsurge in religious veneration of the mountain among the Edo populace. 'Fuji above the Lightning' (page 150) presents a majestic close view of the mountain rearing from the darkness of a thunderstorm around its base to catch the last rays of the evening sun on its summit. This print, and its counterpart the 'Red Fuji,' present a primeval vision of the great peak, showing not a trace of the presence of man. In this respect, while they are among Hokusai's masterpieces, they are atypical of his work, where busy humanity is usually to the fore.

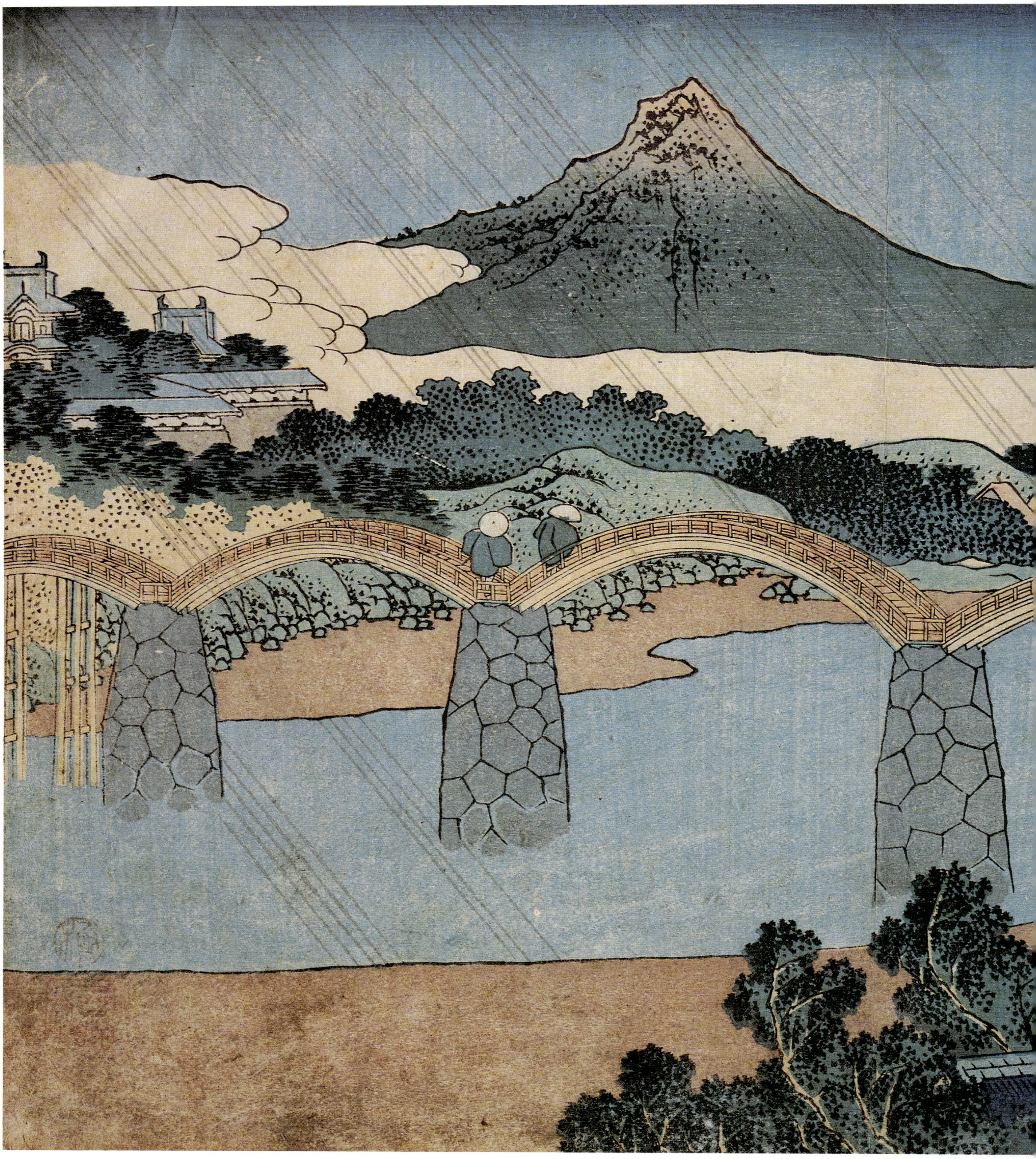

Katsushika Hokusai (1760-1849) 'Kintai Bridge, Suō Province (*Suō no kuni, Kintai-bashi*),' from the series 'Wondrous Views of Famous Bridges in all the Provinces' (*Shokoku meikyō kiran*), 1831-32, 10⁵⁄₁₆×16inches (26.2×40.9 cm). Published by Nishimura Eijudō. The Whitworth Art Gallery, University of Manchester.

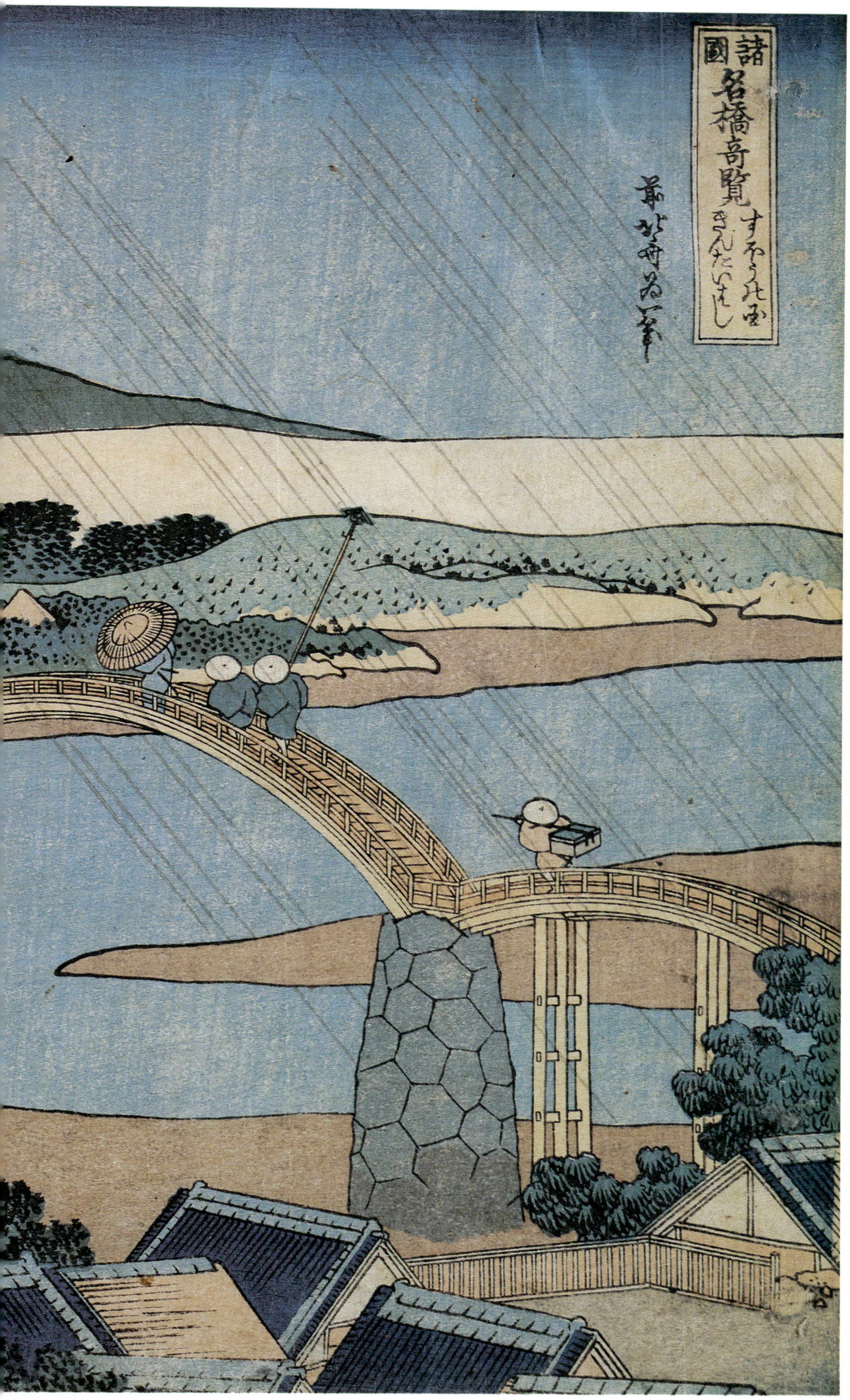

The early 1830s were a time of immense creativity for the ageing artist. The set of 11 prints of bridges 'A Journey along the Bridges in All the Provinces' (*Shokoku meikyō kiran*) appeared in 1831-32. Hokusai was fascinated by bridges and 'The Kintai Bridge in Suō Province' (page 152), is a detailed portrait of a specific bridge, a slender five-arched wood structure on massive piers of stone. Hokusai takes an architect's interest in these apparently frail constructions slung across a void to confront the elements. A group of travelers are overtaken by a squally shower of rain as they cross the bridge toward a daimyo castle among the trees on the far side. Hokusai uses traditional conventions for depicting clouds in several of these prints, as is witnessed by the unnaturalistic band dividing the distant mountain, from the middle ground.

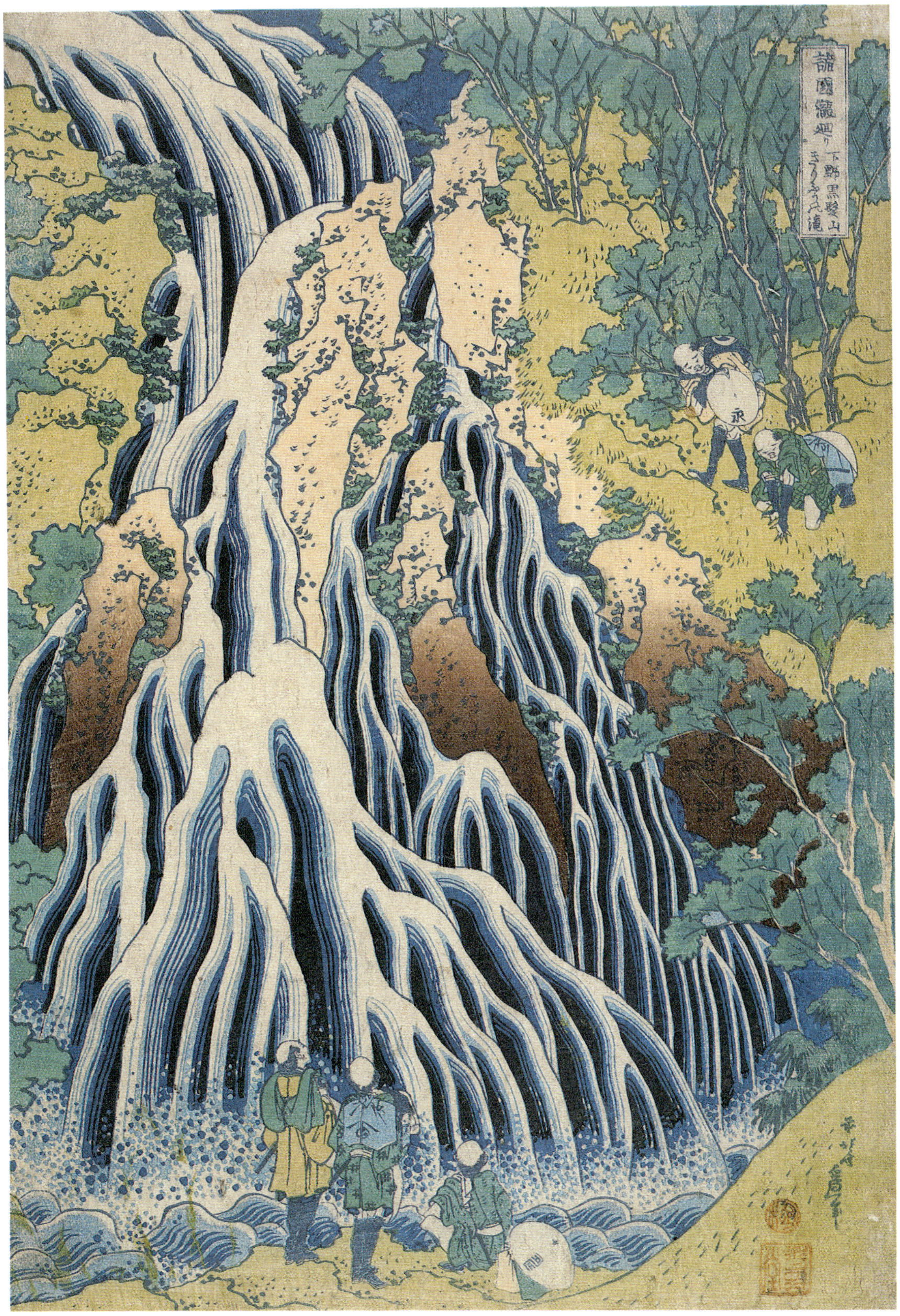

Left: Katsushika Hokusai (1760-1849) 'Kirifura Fall in Kurokawa Mountain,' from the series 'A Journey to the Waterfalls of All the Provinces' (*Shokoku taki meguri*), c. 1832, 15×10 inches (38.1ax25.4 cm). Published by Nishimura Eijudō. Courtesy of the Trustees of the British Museum, London.

The same years saw the production of 'A Journey to the Waterfalls of All the Provinces' (*Shokoku taki meguri*), of which eight are known, majestic depictions of falling water which explore the dark and light dynamics of the *berorin* dye to the full, creating compositions of almost abstract force in which the artist uses a vertical format to encompass the downward rush of the water. 'Kirifuri Fall in Kurokami Mountain' (page 154) shows a group of Edo tourists dwarfed and deafened by the spectacle.

Hokusai also produced his most distinguished *kachōga* ('bird-and-flower') compositions around the early 1830s. A small *chūban* size picture depicting iris, pinks and a kingfisher (page 155) comes from a set of ten which was published by Eijudō around 1832. It is a strongly composed group, enlivened by the rather tough-looking kingfisher, twisting in flight to dart between the leaves of the *shaga* iris. The 'one-corner' composition, firmly depicted line and brilliant coloration have a decorative immediacy which places the print firmly in a tradition deriving from Chinese painting from the Ming and earlier periods, as has always been acknowledged by Japanese critics.

Right: Katsushika Hokusai (1760-1849) 'Kingfisher and Shaga Iris,' *chūban*, 9×6½ inches (22.9×16.5 cm). Published by Nishimura Eijudō. Courtesy of the Trustees of the British Museum, London.

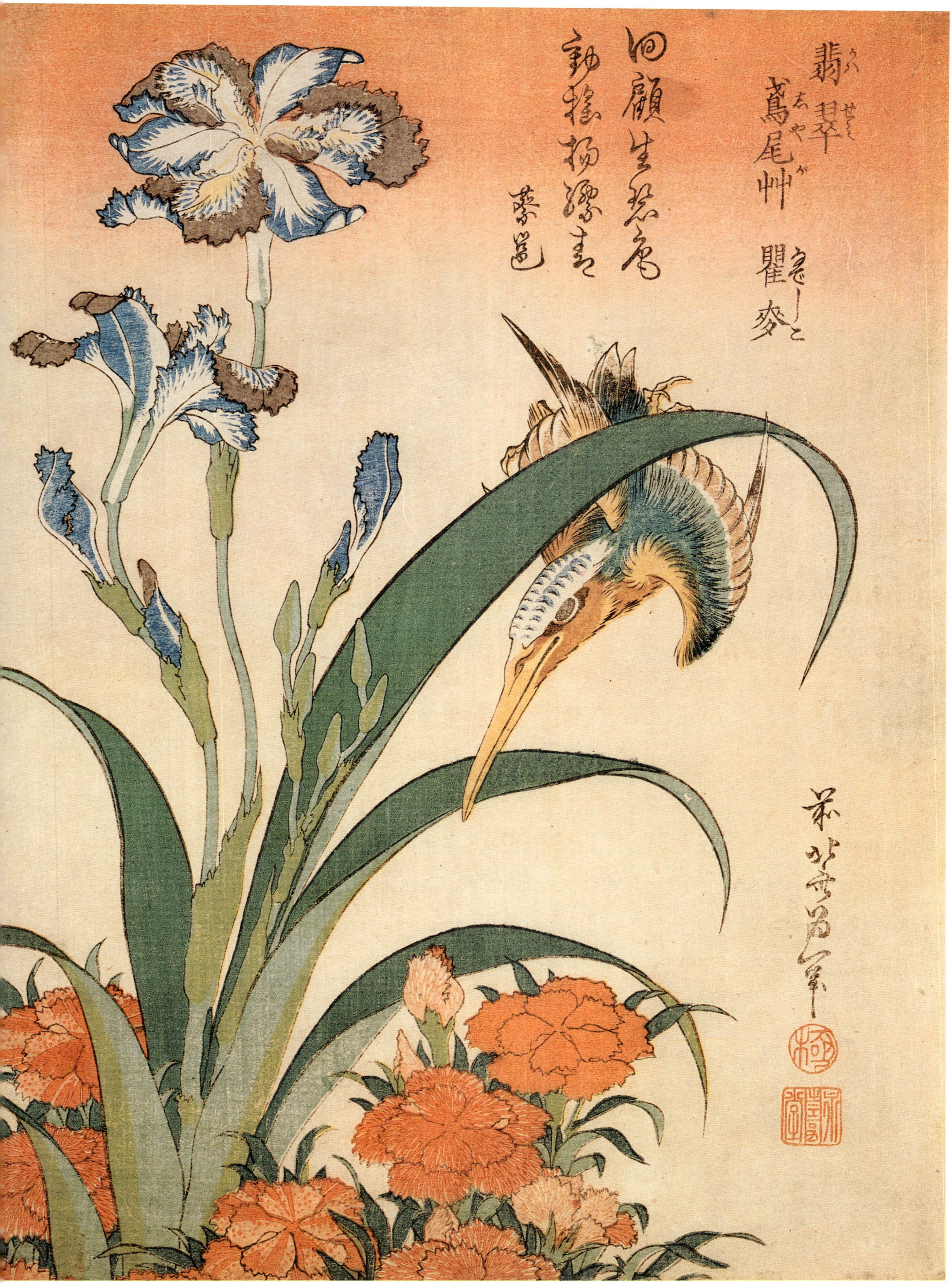
翡翠
鳶尾艸
瞿麥

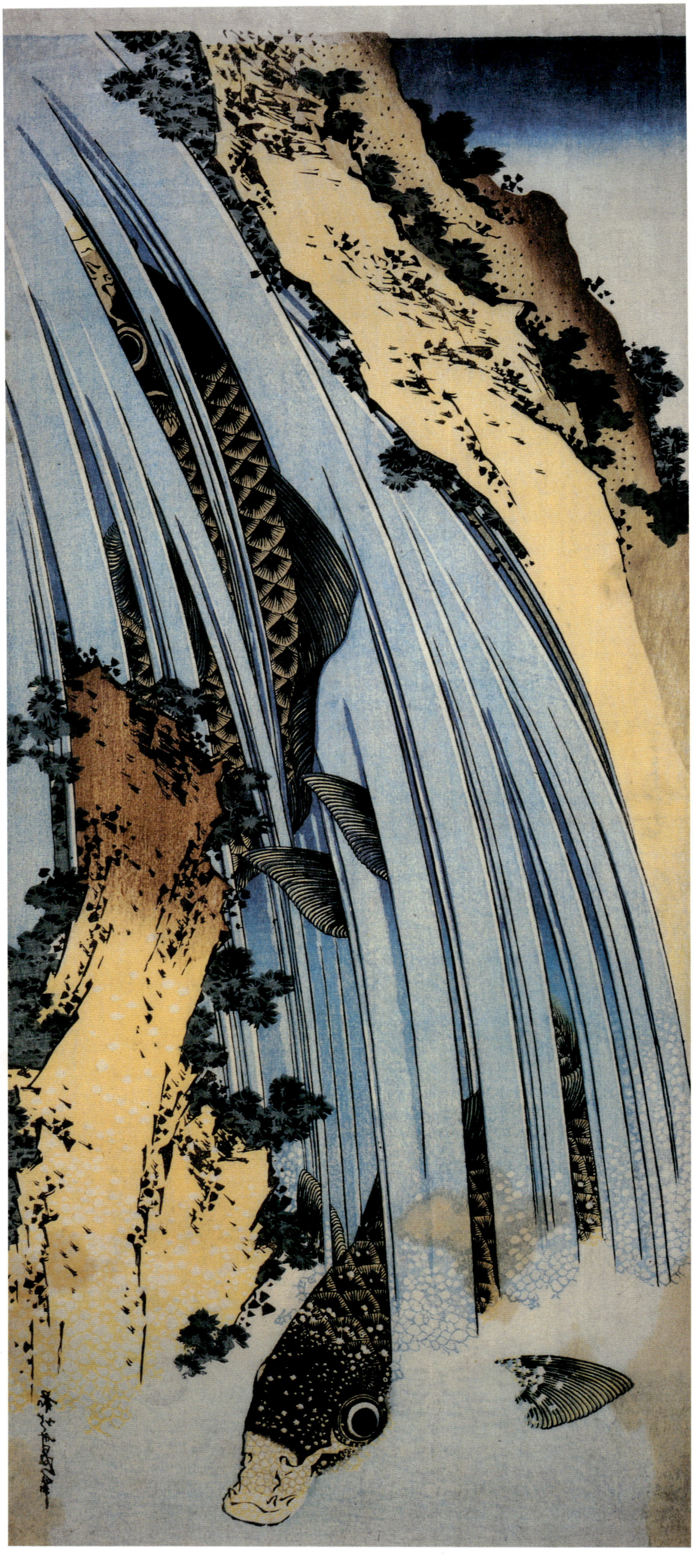

Left: Katsushika Hokusai (1760–1849) 'The Carp and the Waterfall,' 1832–35, *kakemono-e*, 20½×9 inches (52×23 cm). Published by Moriya Jihei. Courtesy of the Trustees of the British Museum, London.

Right: Katsushika Hokusai (1760-1849) 'Cranes on a Snowy Pine,'1832-33, , 20×9 inches (52×23 cm). Published by Moriya Jihei. Courtesy of the Trustees of the British Museum, London.

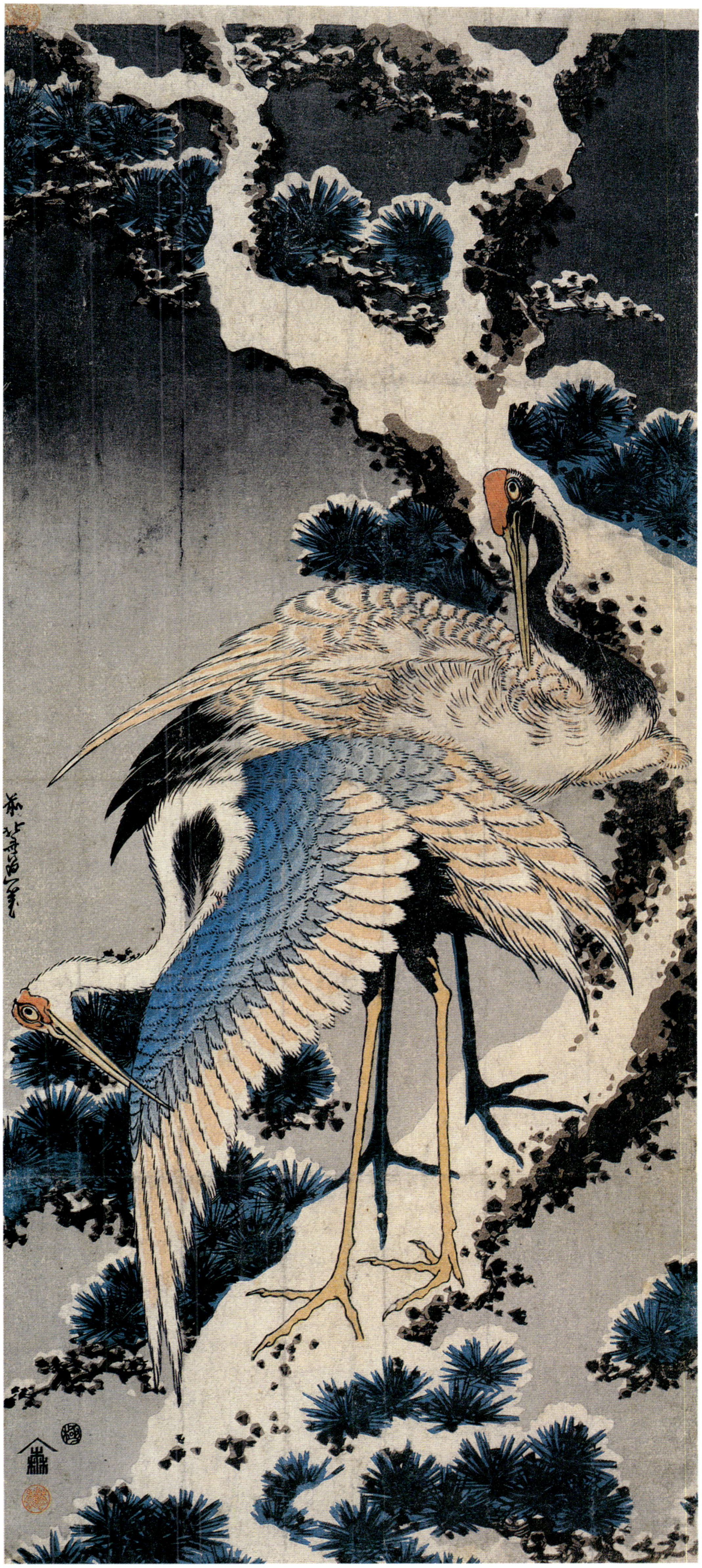

The 'Carp in a Waterfall' (page 156) of 1832-33 is another exercise in the Chinese manner, depicting a popular traditional subject. Carp which ascended the waterfalls at Longmen were reputed to become dragons, an emblem which in China was taken to symbolize the successful scholar passing the Imperial exams to join the government. In Japan it became an emblem of courage associated with the boys' festival on May 5. It is in the long *naga-ban* format, from a rare set of five which includes the supremely elegant 'Cranes on a Snowy Pine' (page 157) which I also illustrate. The famous declaration made by Hokusai around this time is worth recording here, as it refers specifically to *kachōga*:

From the age of five I have had a mania for sketching the forms of things. From about the age of fifty I produced a number of designs, yet of all I drew prior to the age of seventy there is truly nothing of any great note. At the age of seventy-two I finally apprehended something of the true quality of birds, animals, insects, fish and of the vital nature of grasses and trees. Therefore, at eighty I shall have made some progress, at ninety I shall have penetrated even further the deeper meaning of things, at one hundred I shall have become truly marvelous, and at one hundred and ten, each dot, each line shall surely possess a life of its own.

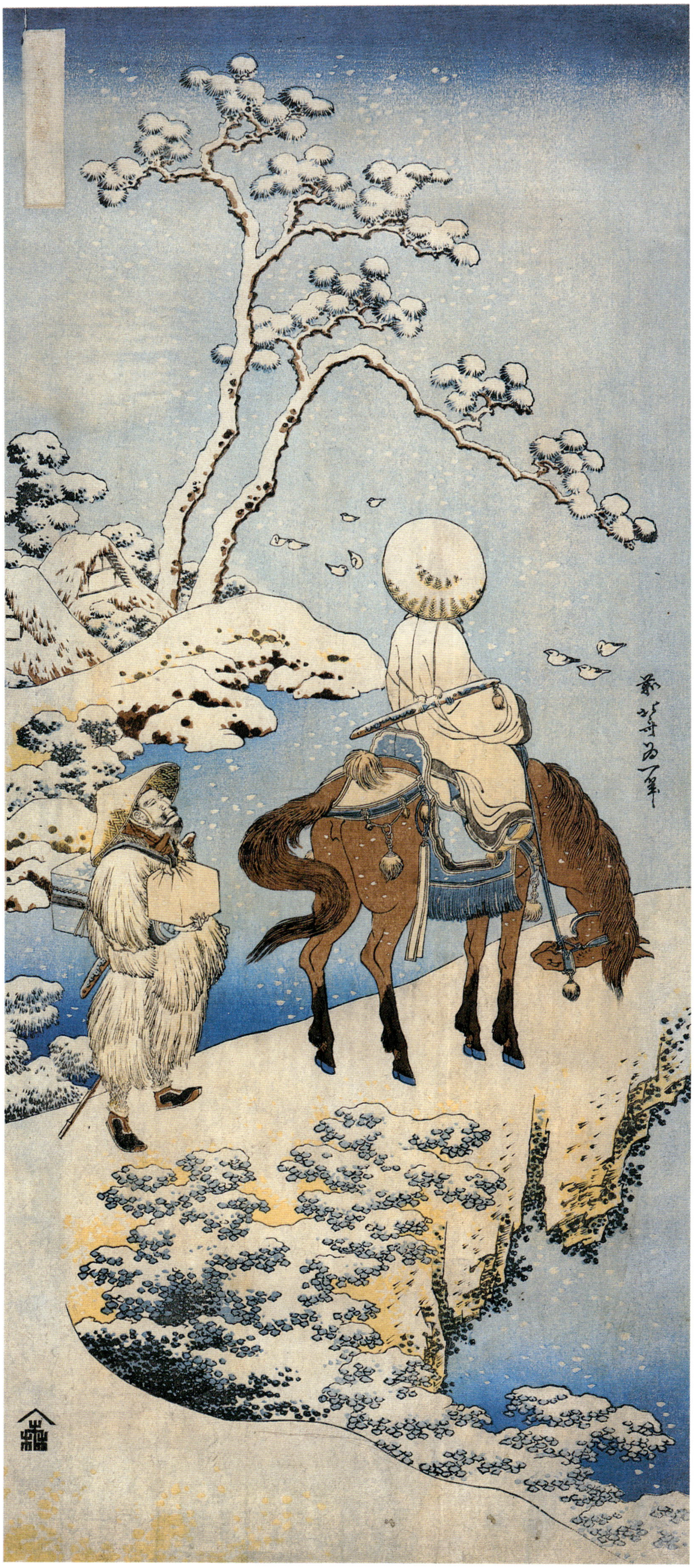

Left: Katsushika Hokusai (1760-1849) 'Tōba Exiled,' from the series 'A True Mirror of Chinese and Japanese Poems' (*Shika shashinkyō*), c. 1840, *kakemono-e*, 19⅝×8¾ (49.8×22.1 cm). Published by Moriya Jihei. Courtesy of the Trustees of the British Museum, London.

Hokusai works within the traditions of Japan, unlike the '36 Fuji' set with their Western perspective of local topography. The set 'A True Mirror of Chinese and Japanese Poems' (*Shika shashinkyō*) of 1832-33 is in the same hanging scroll format and also shuns Western convention. This poignant image (page 158) is traditionally identified as the Chinese exiled poet and calligrapher Tōba (Su Dongbo), pausing on his journey into exile through the snow to stare across a lake. Hokusai opens out the landscape vertically, interpreting motifs almost musically rather than with any interest in topographical description, the pines on the promontory echoing the theme of the figures on the spur. Sky and water are not differentiated. A Westerner might find this hard to interpret without the waterbirds seated on the blue surface. Several other prints in the series use the same palette of a predominant blue with details picked out in the red vegetable dye *beni*.

Right: Katsushika Hokusai (1760-1849) 'The Horsetail Gatherer' (*Tokusa-kari*), from the series 'A True Mirror of Chinese and Japanese Poems' (*Shika shashinkyō*), c.1840, *kakemono-e*, 19$\frac{11}{16}$×9 inches (50×23 cm). Published by Moriya Jihei. Courtesy of the Trustees of the British Museum, London.

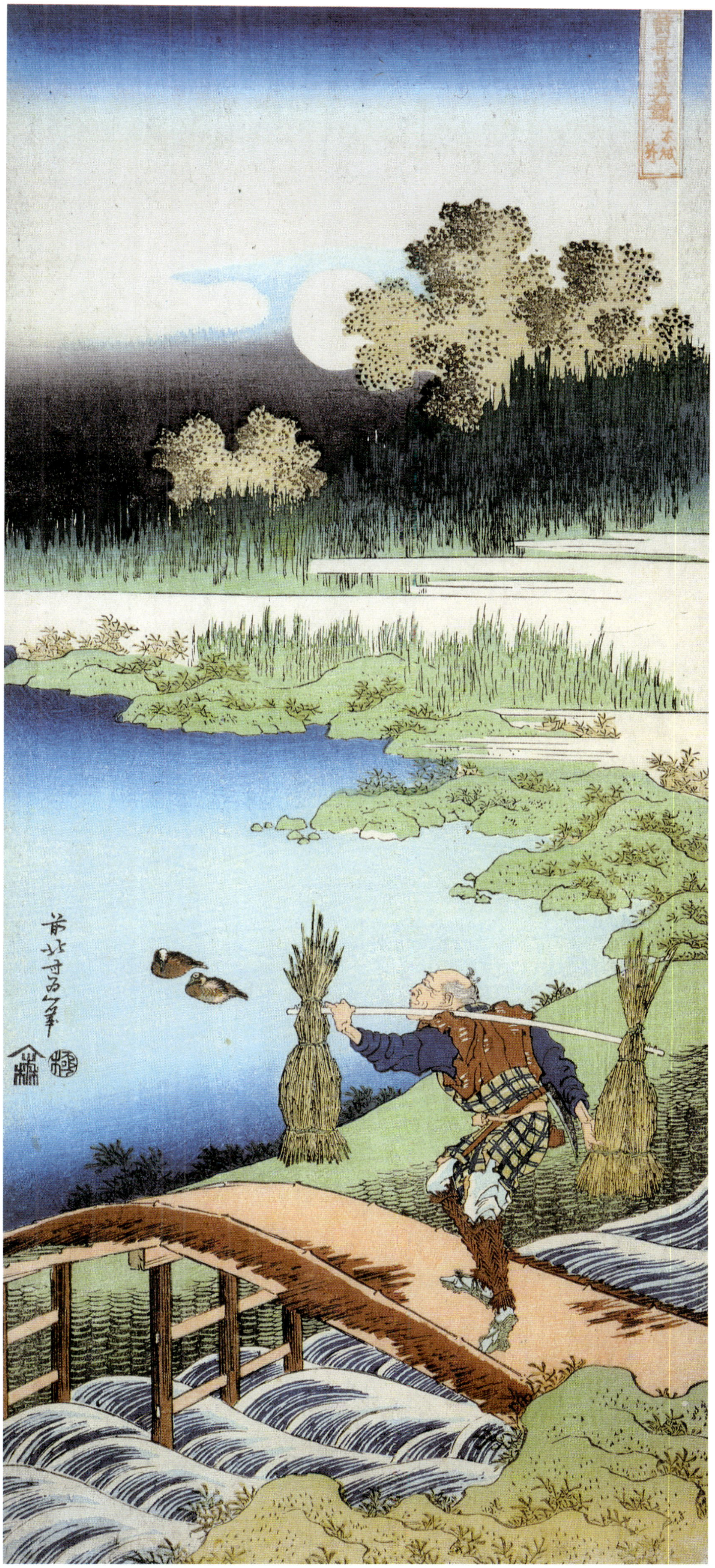

An evocative moonlit landscape (page 159) from the same series as by contrast on a Japanese literary theme, a famous section from the Nō drama *Tokusa-kari*, referring to the full moon emerging from the trees as the old reed gatherer searches for his lost child among the mountains. Indeed, both the green and blue coloration and the use of horizontal bands of mist recall the Tosa court style.

Another poetic project from around 1840 resulted in some of the most beautifully printed and expressive images in Hokusai's work, but was never completed. Though drawings exist for almost all the others, only 27 prints were actually carried out in the series '100 Poems Explained by the Nurse' (*Hyakunin isshu uba ga etoki*). It is based on a classical thirteenth-century anthology familiar to all literate Japanese, but evidently without the pulling power of Hiroshige's Edo and Kisokaido series which were then appearing.

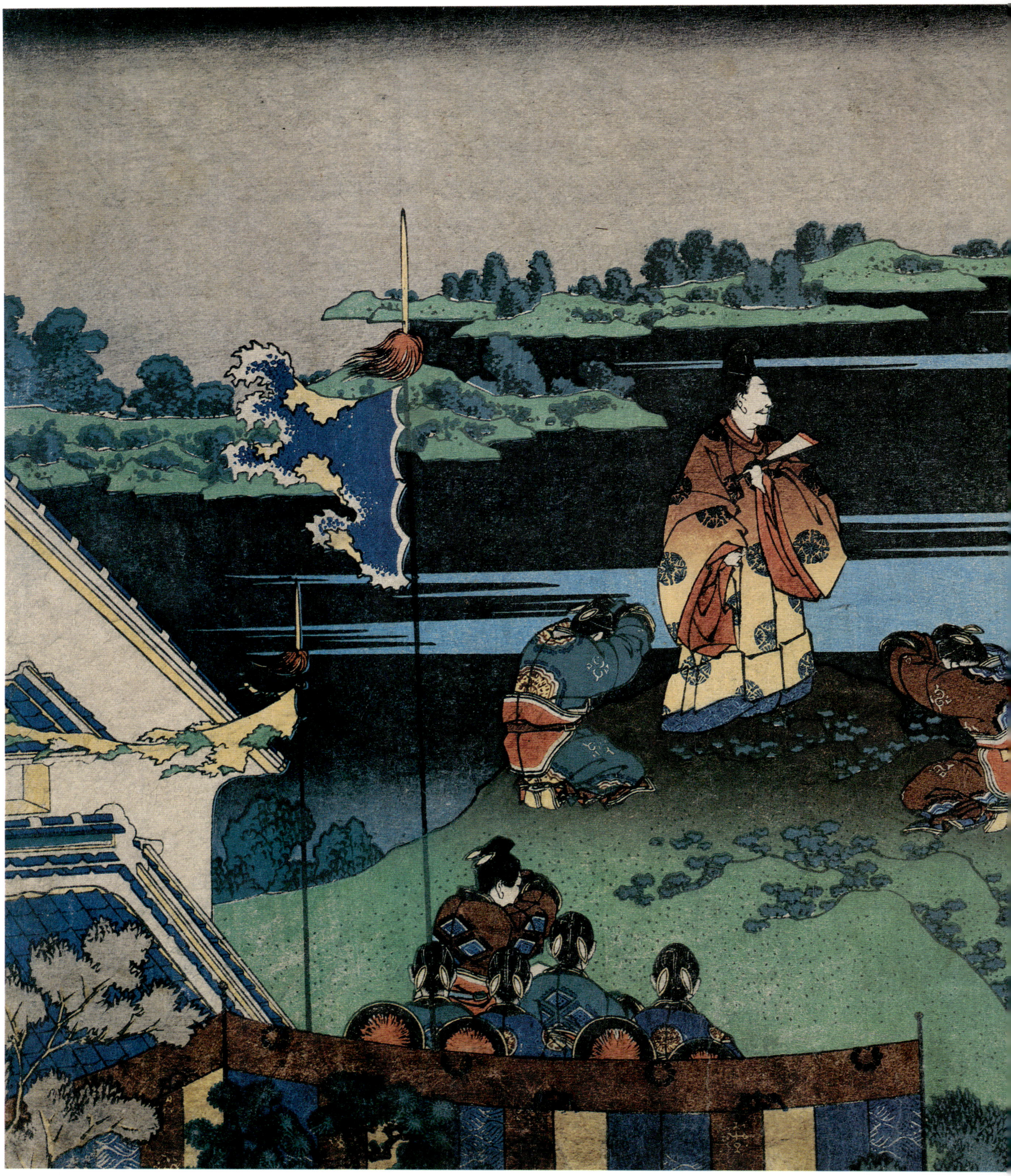

Katsushika Hokusai (1760–1849) 'The Exiled Poet Nakamarō' (*Abe no Nakamarō*), from the series '100 Poems Explained by the Nurse' (*Hyakunin isshu uba ga etoki*), c.1838. Courtesy of the Trustees of the British Museum, London.

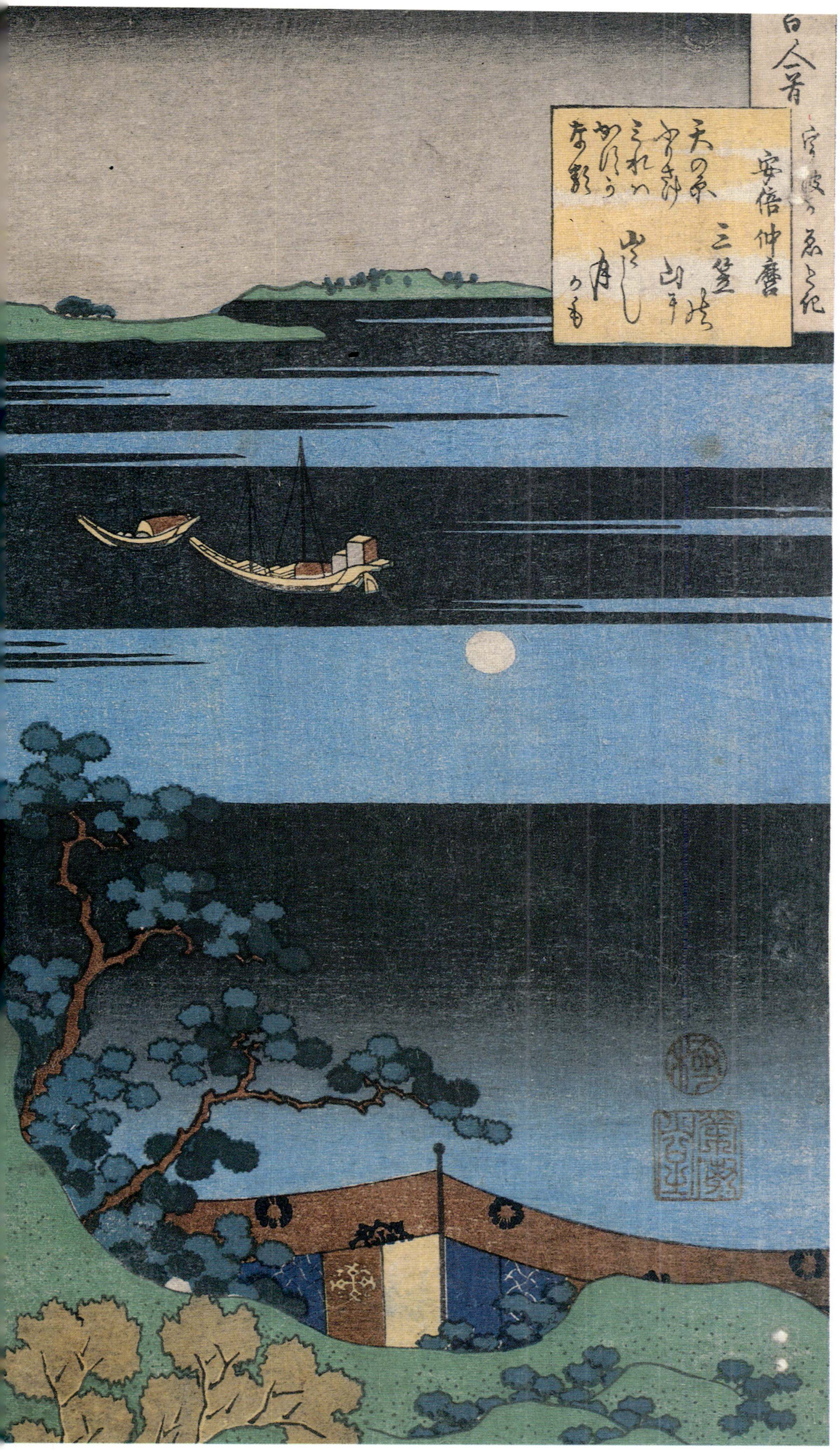

'The Exiled Poet Nakamaro' shows the eighth-century poet, an imprisoned ambassador to China, gazing at the reflected moon in the sea, illustrating the famous lines 'O can it be that the moon I see wandering out into the wilderness of the sky is the same moon that rises over Mikaos Hill in my own Kasuga?' The extraordinarily fine printing with its rich palette and clearly defined detail, and the courtly subject and references to Tosa styles point this to be an expensive print produced for a luxury market at a time when many publishers were printing cheap editions of poorly defined prints for an undiscriminating clientele.

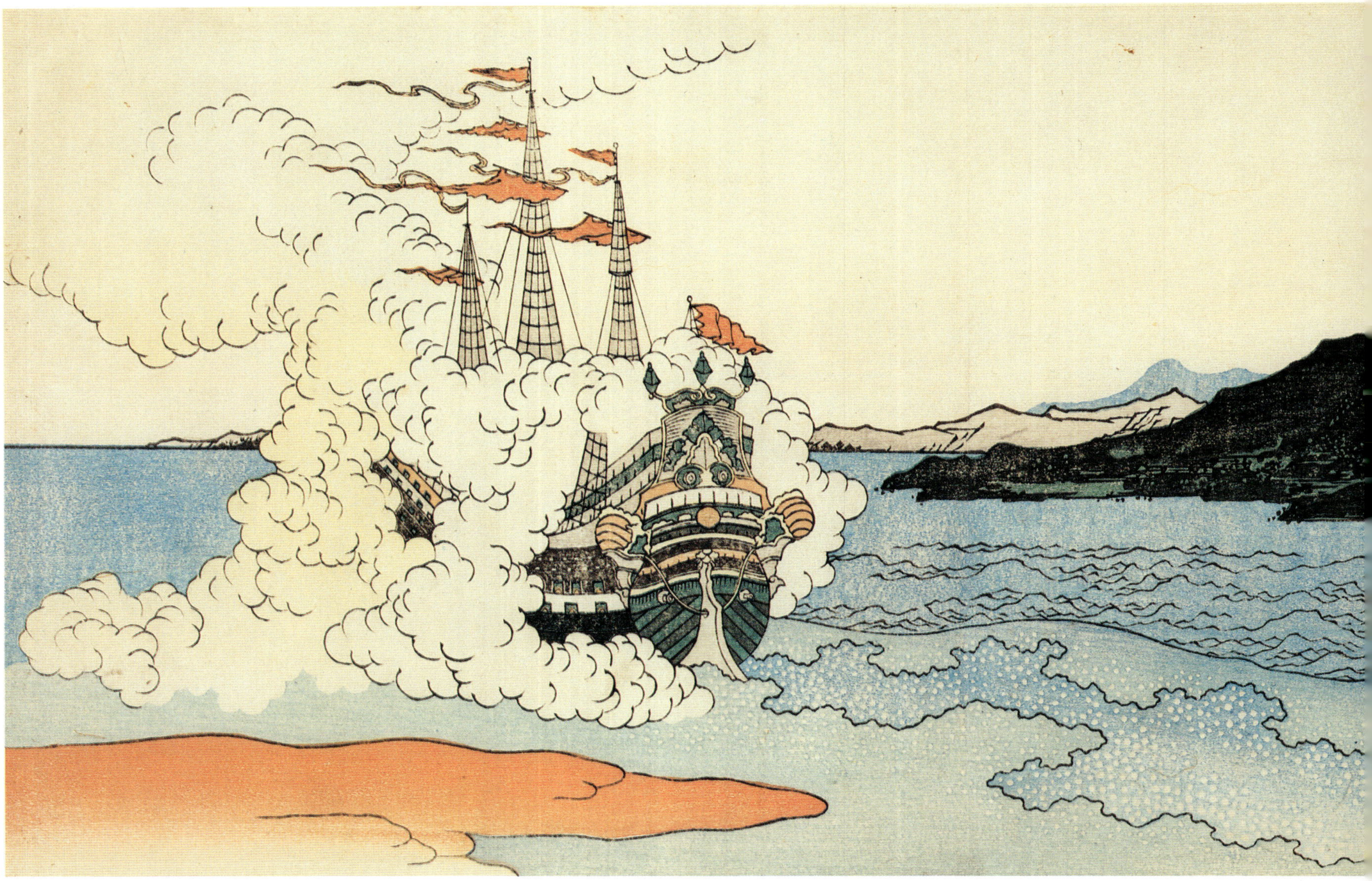

Above: Totoya Hokkei (1780-1850) 'Mount Tateyama in Hizen Province,' from the series 'Famous Places of all the Provinces' (*Shokoku meisho*), 1835-40, *tanzaku*, 5⅛×15 inches (13×38 cm). Published by Nishimura Eijudō and Nakamuraya Katsugorō. Courtesy of the Trustees of the Victoria and Albert Museum, London.

Right: Yashima Gakutei (c. 1786-1868) 'Fleet Returning to Harbor at Mount Tempō,' from the album 'Fine Views of Mount Tempō' (*Tempōzan shōkei ichiran*), 1838, 10×14½ inches (25.4×36.8 cm). Published by Takaki. Courtesy of the Trustees of the Victoria and Albert Museum, London.

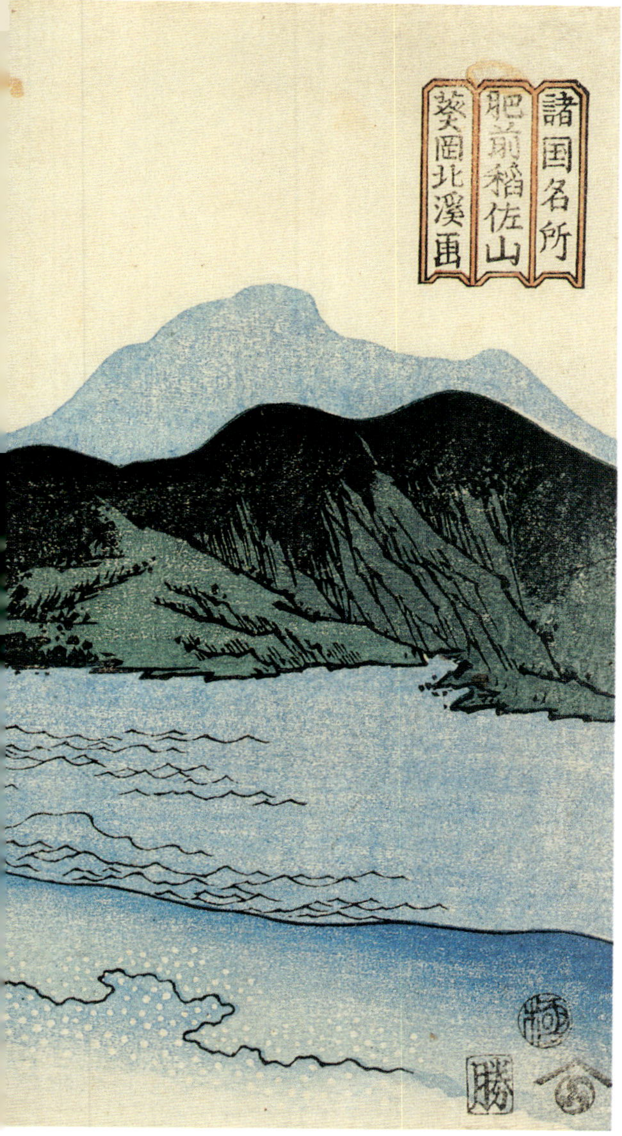

Hokusai changed the path of the Japanese print by his introduction of landscape as a major subject and had a considerable number of followers in both Edo and Osaka, including Shōtei Hokuju (*fl* 1789–1818), Shinsai Ryūryūkyo (1764?–1820), and the artist's daughters Nakajima Oi (*fl* 1820s–40s) and Katsushika Otatsu. Totoya Hokkei (1780–1850), a senior pupil of Hokusai and a former fishmonger is notable among these. He was a specialist in *surimono* who also created a famous landscape series 'Famous Views in the Provinces' (*Shokoku meisho*), a set of 13 prints in large *tanzaku* format, published in the late 1830s. 'Mt Inasa in Hizen Province' (page 162), shows a European galleon of archaic type clearly derived from a sixteenth-century *Namban* screen, standing off the port of Nagasaki and firing a salute. It will be remembered that until 1853 when Admiral Perry made his forceful intervention, Nagasaki was the only port of Japan open to Europeans. The slight formal stiffness of the execution is well suited to the almost fairy-tale strangeness of this visitor from another place and time.

Yashima Gakutei (c. 1786–1868), a pupil of Hokkei, was a *surimono* artist and illustrator of books who produced a superb album of six *ōban* views of Osaka in 1838, 'Fine Views of Mount Tempō' (*Tempōzan shōkei ichiran*). 'The Stone Bridge at Shinzan, Aji River, Osaka' hovers between *surimono* and *ukiyo-e* in its immaculately detailed printing, positive use of strong color and sure design, echoing Hokusai's fascination with bridges and with people. The slightly doll-like figures are differentiated with some care, boating or taking a walk to enjoy the breeze off the sea. The striking vision of a 'Fleet Returning to Harbor at Mount Tempō' from the same series, provides an almost Wagnerian image.

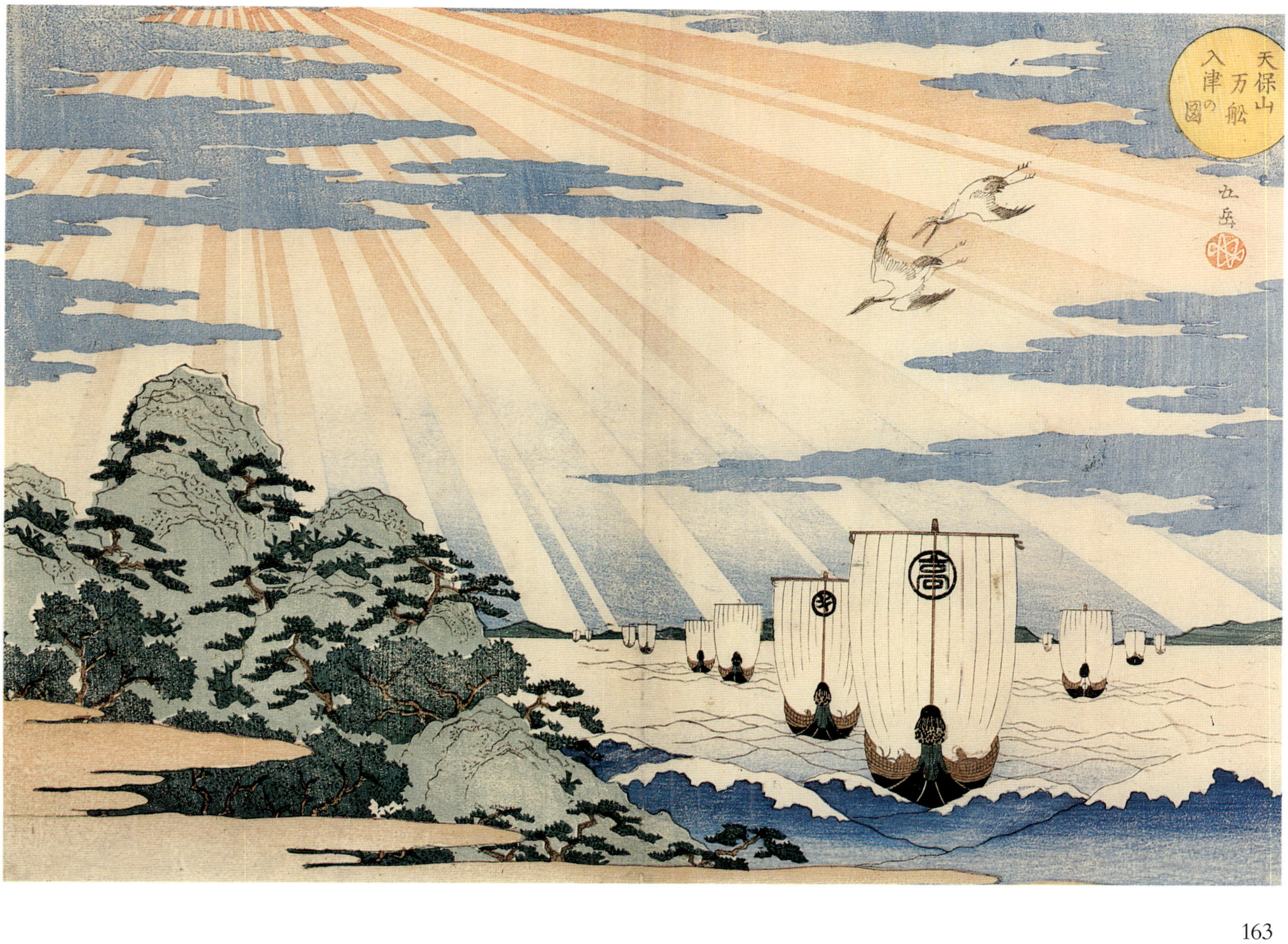

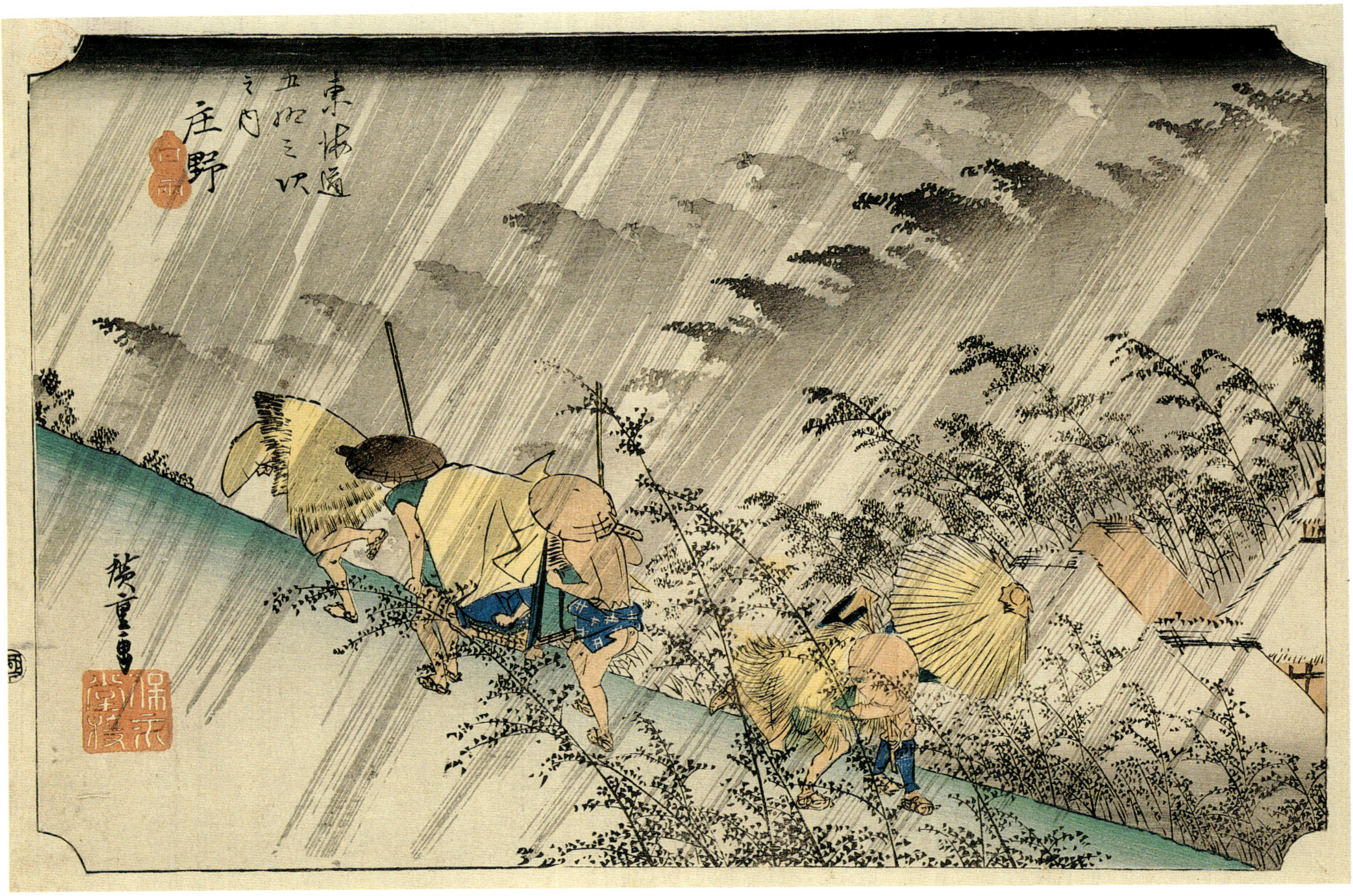

Above: Utagawa Hiroshige (1797-1858) 'Sudden Rainstorm at Shōno' (*Shōno haku-u*), from the series '53 Stations of the Tokaido' (*Tōkaidō gojūsan tsugi no uchi*), 1833, 9½×14⅓ inches (24ax36.4 cm). Published by Hōeidō. Courtesy of the Trustees of the Victoria and Albert Museum, London.

The only other artist to rival Hokusai in the nineteenth century was Utagawa Hiroshige (1797-1858). He was the son of an Edo fire warden, and succeeded him in the hereditary post when he died in 1809. Two years later, at the age of fourteen, he became a pupil of Utagawa Toyohiro. He graduated with the right to use the surname Utagawa and was given the new personal name of Hiroshige after only one year's study. His position as firewarden, which he retained until he was 27, protected him from the desperate poverty which bedeviled the young Kuniyoshi, and returned to torment Hokusai throughout his life. He produced many capable figure prints up to 1830, but it was the example of Hokusai's '36 Views of Mount Fuji' which made him a landscape artist. 'Famous Places of Edo' (*Tōto meisho*), a set of ten prints issued around 1831, showed a tremendous advance over his earlier work, displaying the almost affectionate feeling for nature and man which characterizes so many of his best landscapes.

The '53 Stations on the Tokaido' (*Tōkaido gojūsantsugi no uchi*), published in 1833, made Hiroshige's reputation unassailable. The Tokaido highway runs along the coast for much of its length between the Shogun's capital at Edo and the Imperial capital at Kyoto. Hiroshige made the sketches for his great series while attending on a slow ceremonial procession bearing gifts from the Shogun to the Emperor during 1832. The new idea of travel for pleasure had become fashionable among the inhabitants of the larger towns, and collecting prints of sights along the way was a popular part of the phenomenon.

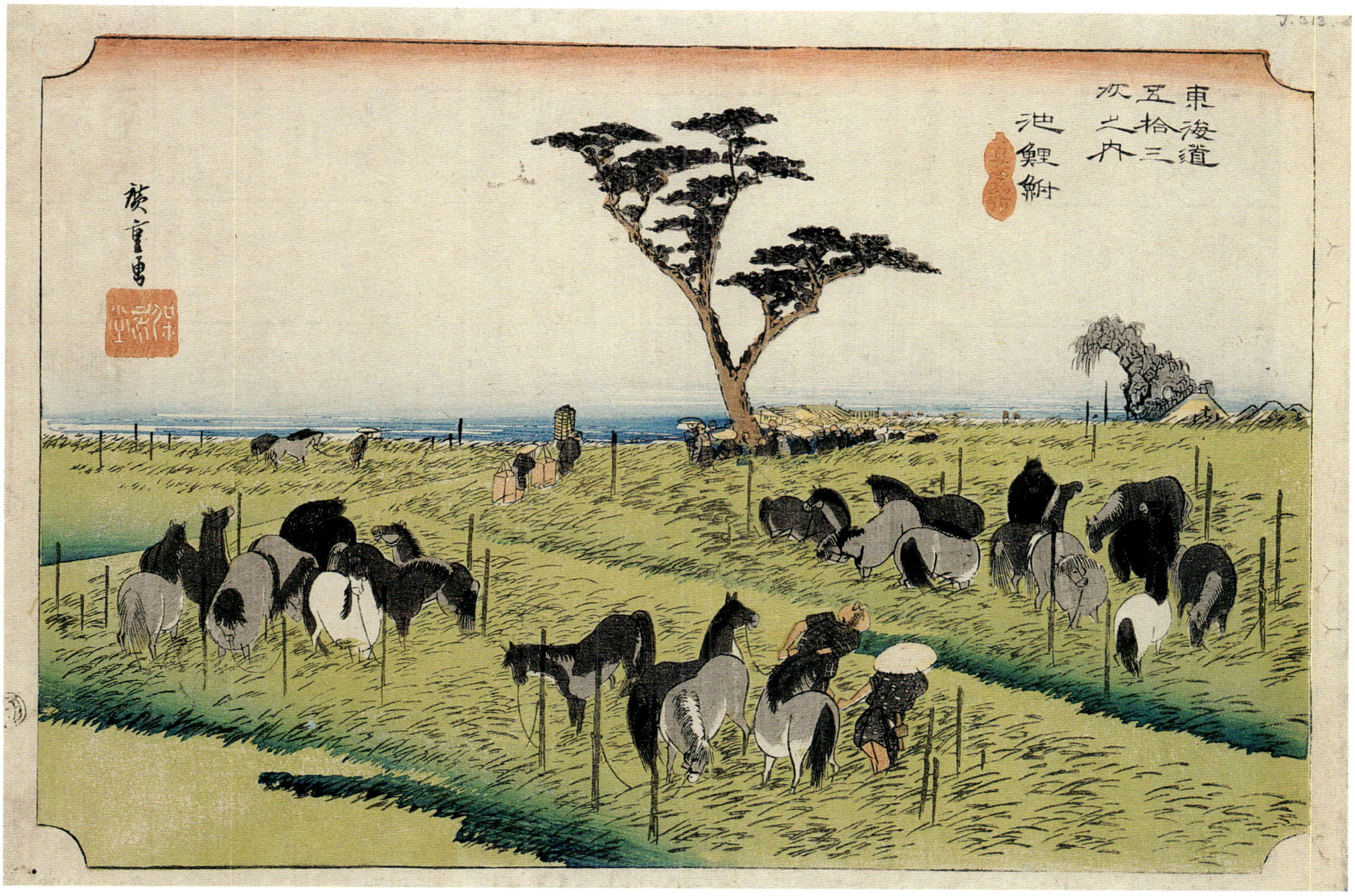

Above: Utagawa Hiroshige (1797-1858) 'Chiryū, the Summer Horse Fair' (*Chiryū shuka uma ichi*), from the series '53 Stations of the Tokaido' (*Tōkaidō gojūsan tsugi no uchi*), 1833, 9½×14⅓ inches (24ax36.4 cm). Published by Hōeidō. Courtesy of the Trustees of the Victoria and Albert Museum, London.

'Sudden Rainstorm at Shōno' (page 164) may well be the most famous of all Hiroshige's prints, with unencumbered travelers running for cover in a sudden summer storm while the palanquin bearers must plod stolidly on. Behind the figures, which are picked out in bright yellows and browns, rank after rank of windblown bamboo are printed in successively paler shades of ink monochrome as they recede in the downpour, making an atmospheric contrast with the frantic group in the foreground. The extensive use of uncolored ink line and wash effects recalls Hiroshige's early training in Kanō school methods by the fireman Okajima Rinsai. While the dynamic composition, with its bold triangular divisions, and the active group in the foreground may recall Hokusai, the figures are far more part of the landscape than one finds in the works of the older master whose figures tend to contrast with the world of nature. This may be because Hiroshige's figures are overprinted with the slanting rain; but also, since we can hardly see a single face, they remain anonymous.

'The Summer Horse Fair', from the same series, with its flat marshy fields, engaging tethered horses and cluster of potential buyers gathered under a pine, does not pretend to the intensity of the former image but has its own tranquil lyricism, and seems more recognizably close to nature than so many of Hokusai's tautly constructed images in '36 Views of Fuji.' The popularity of the first Tokaido set led Hiroshige, at the behest of his publishers, to bring out some twenty more series on the same subject in the course of his career.

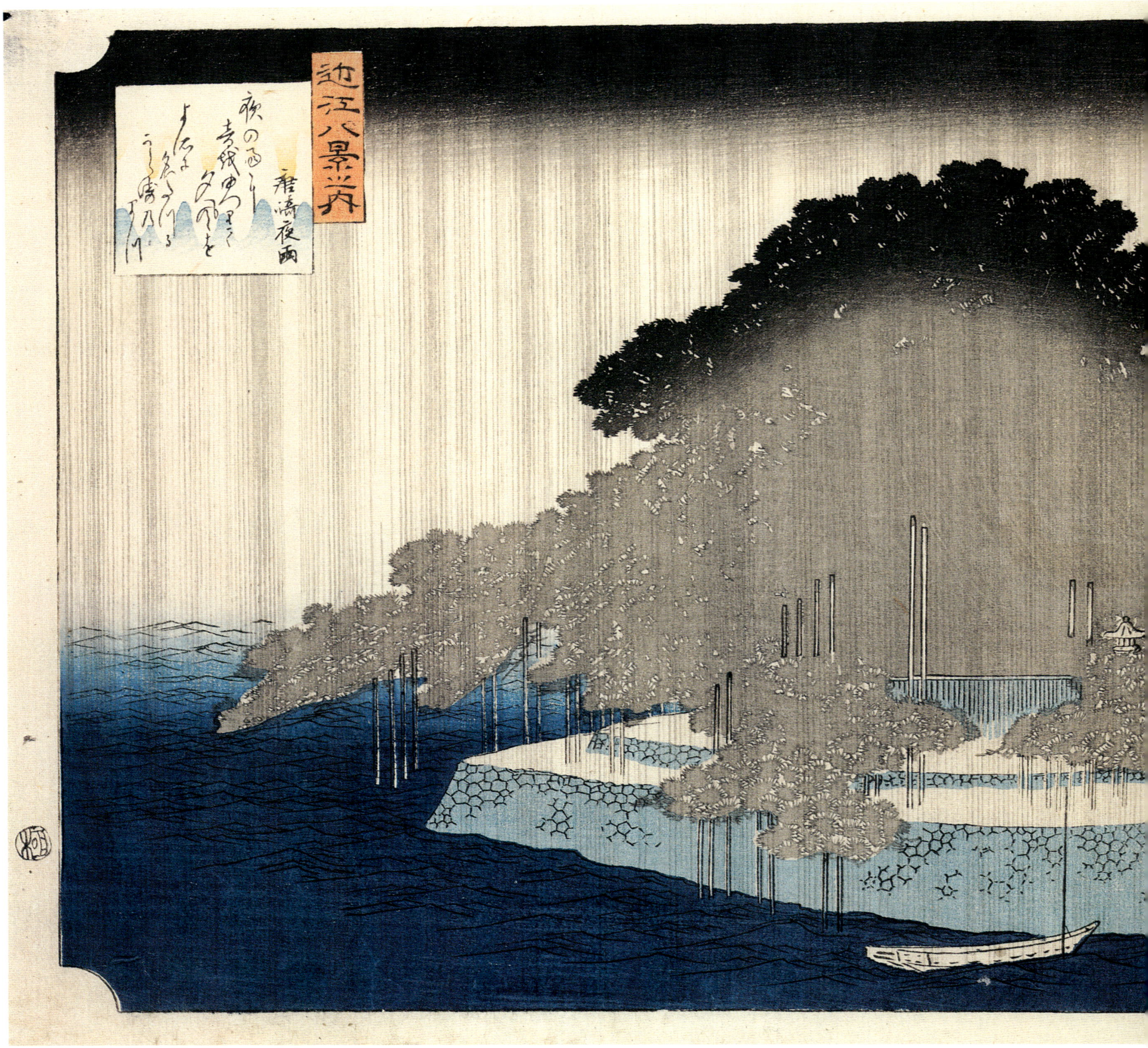

Above: Utagawa Hiroshige (1797-1858) 'Night Rain at Karasaki' (*Karasaki no yau*) from the series 'Eight Views of Lake Biwa' (*Ōmi hakkei no uchi*), c. 1834, 9×13 inches (2.9×33 cm). Published by Hōeidō and Eikyūdō. Courtesy of the Trustees of the Victoria and Albert Museum, London.

The 'Eight Views of Lake Biwa' (*Ōmi hakkei*) were also worked up from sketches made on his 1832 Tokaido tour, and published around 1835. They were based on the early Chinese 'Eight Views of Xiao and Xiang Rivers,' naturalized in a Japanese setting. 'Night Rain at Karasaki' (page 166) shows the pine tree at Karasaki shrine, which was so large that its great limbs had to be supported on stakes. Its brooding ancient shape looms out of the cold downpour, with the distant cone of Mount Fuji appearing as a faint echo to one side. The artist was to produce at least 24 more *Ōmi hakkei* sets in the course of his career.

Hiroshige also had success in the early 1830s with bird and flower subjects which display a leaning towards the impressionistic style of the Kyōto-based Shijō school, creating poetic images which occasionally verge on the sentimental. In this *ō-tanzaku* print of a pair of *oshidori*, mandarin ducks, swimming beneath overhanging flowers (page 167), published about 1832, we see the traditional emblem of marital felicity beneath the inscription in *kyōka* verse:

I have seen the parting of the inseparable *oshidori*
It portends a storm in the morning;

a wordly sentiment, alluding to marital discord which seems to bear little relation to the quiet and almost pensive pair depicted by the artist. Another *ō-tanzaku*

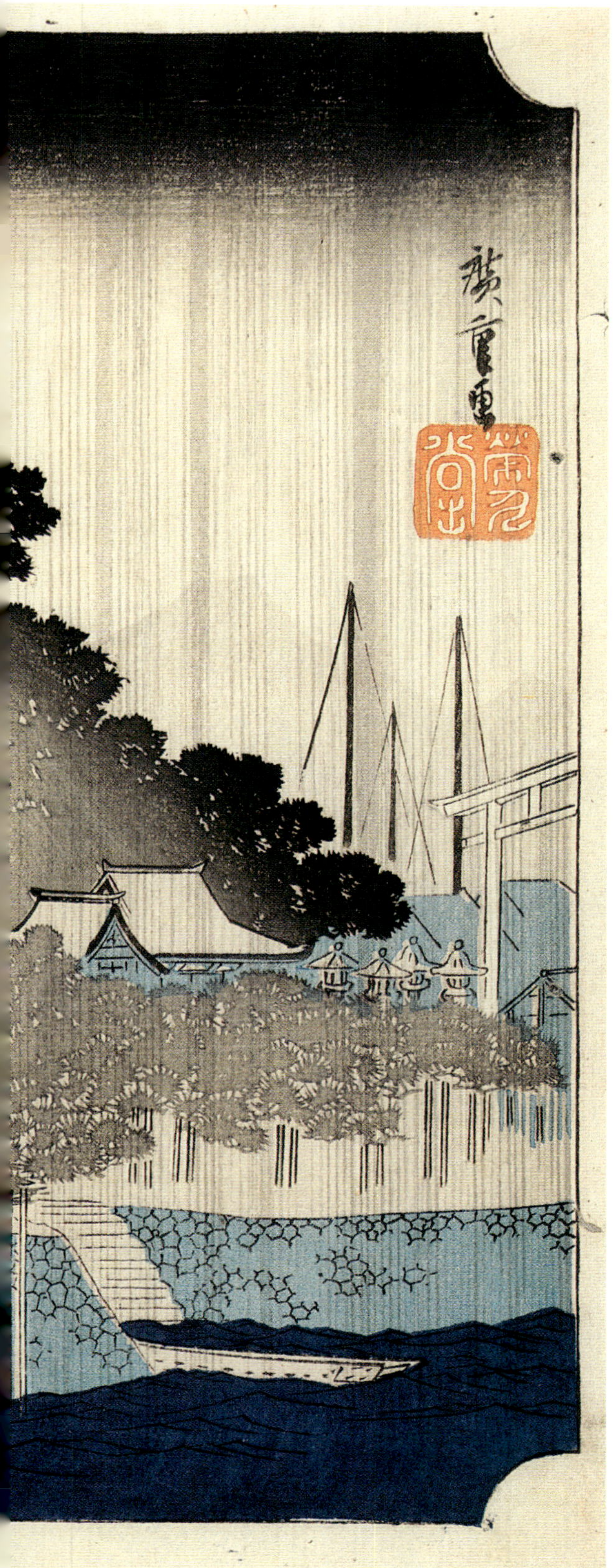

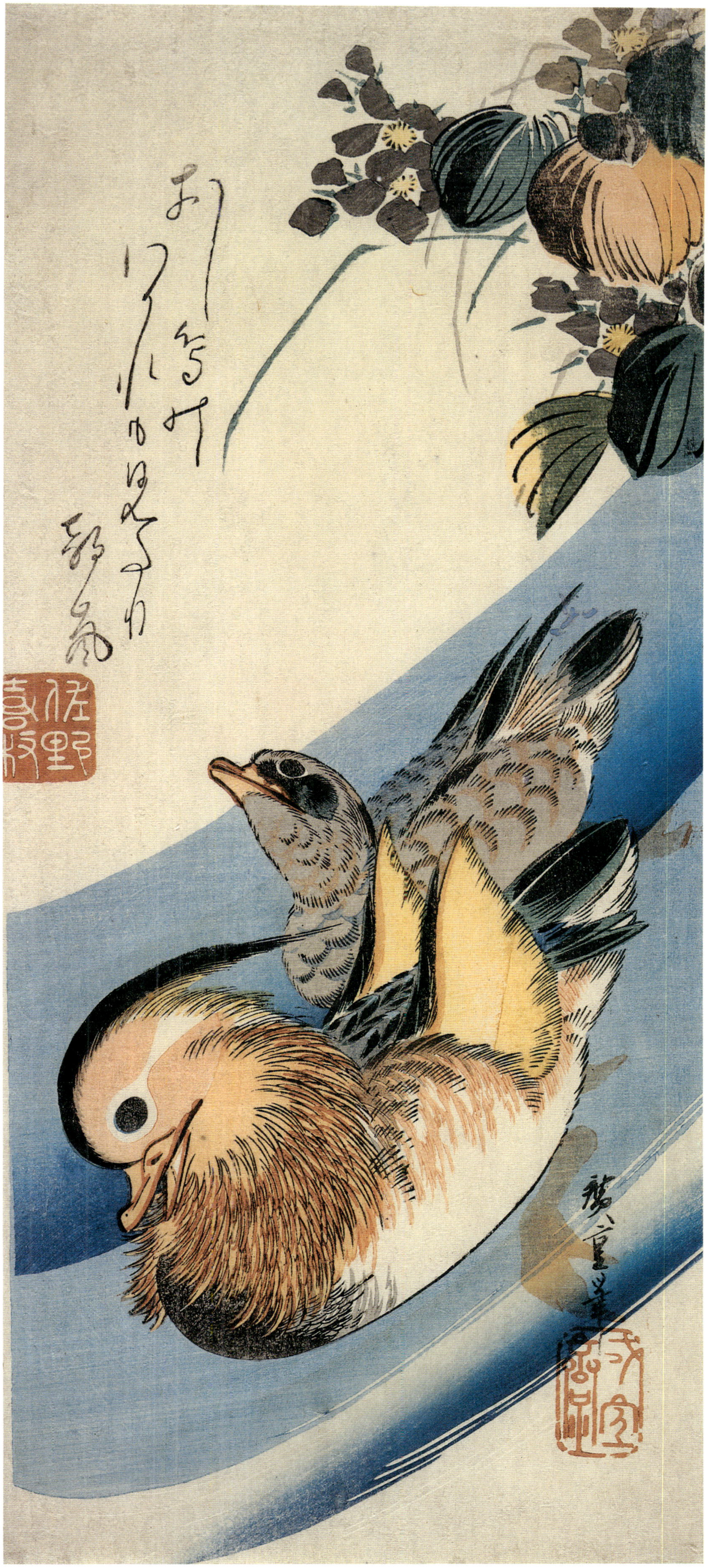

Right: Utagawa Hiroshige (1797-1858) 'A Pair of Mandarin Ducks,' c. 1832, *ō-tanzaku*, 14⅜×6⅝ inches (36.5×17 cm). Published by Eirindō. The Whitworth Art Gallery, University of Manchester.

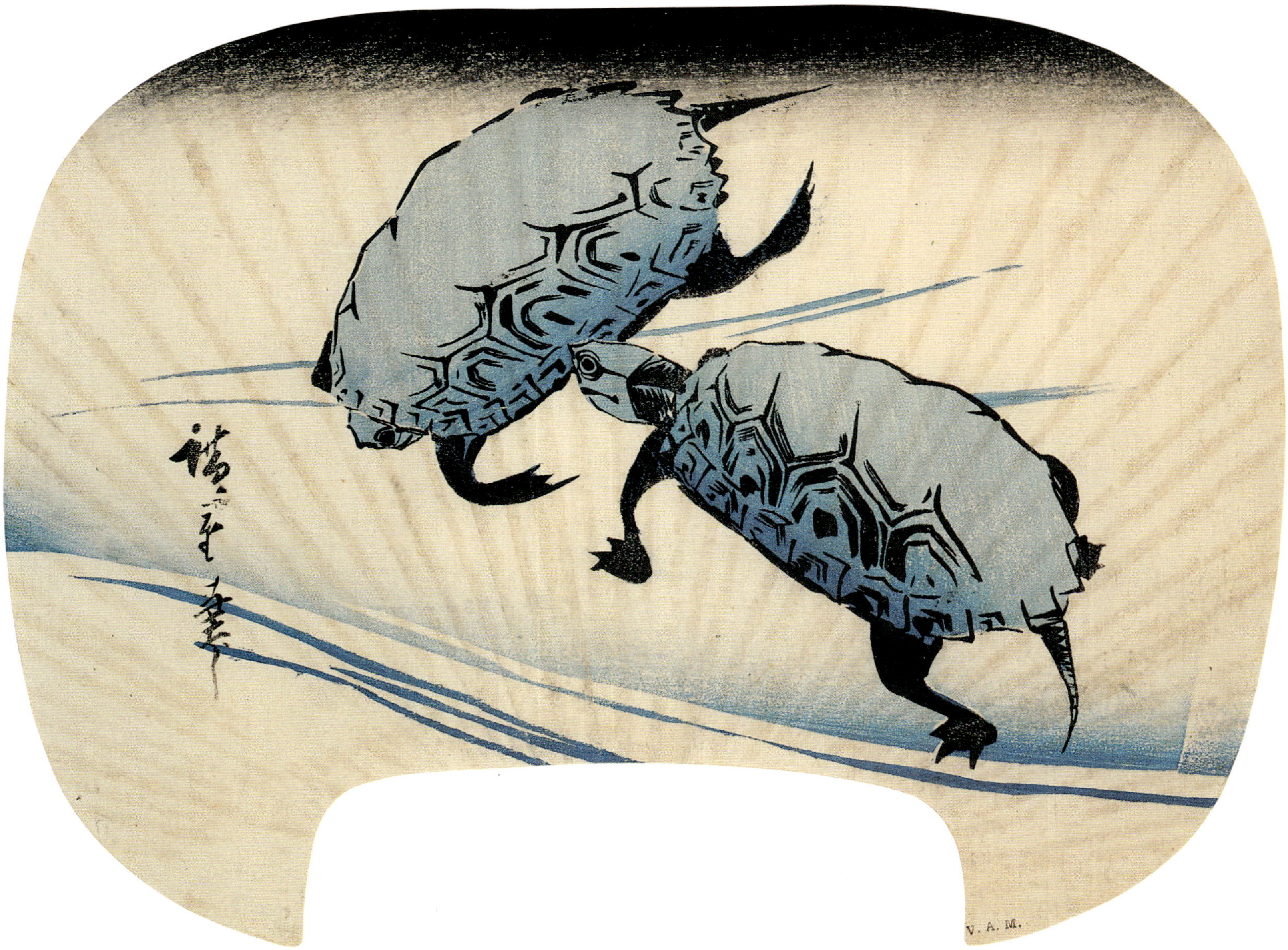

Above: Utagawa Hiroshige (1797-1858) 'Two Terrapin Swimming Underwater,' c. 1830, fan print, $8\frac{3}{8} \times 11\frac{1}{4}$ inches (21.3×28.6 cm). Courtesy of the Trustees of the Victoria and Albert Museum, London.

Right: Utagawa Hiroshige (1797-1858) 'A White Heron Landing Behind a Clump of Sweet Flags,' c. 1832, *tanzaku*, $14\frac{7}{8} \times 6\frac{5}{8}$ inches (37.8×17 cm). Published by Shorindō. Courtesy of the Trustees of the Victoria and Albert Museum, London.

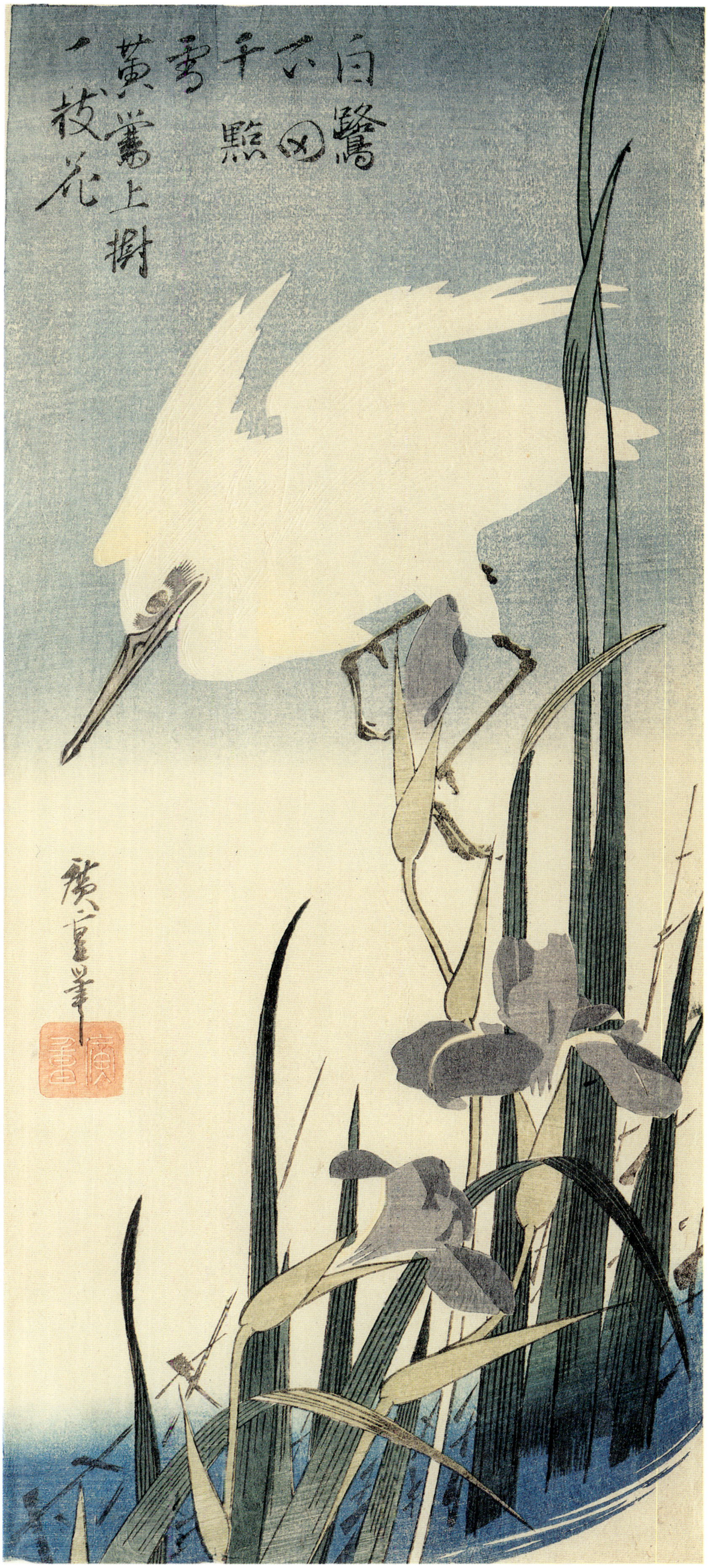

print depicting 'A White Heron Landing Behind a Clump of Sweet Flags' presents us with an image of quiet and mysterious beauty that at the same time conveys a sense of movement, not only in the bird but also in the leaves and flower heads, pushed back by the breeze.

A rare fan print of 'Terrapins Swimming Underwater' (page 168) further demonstrates the artist's ability to convey life and movement with a minimum of means using their relative position to emphasize how one beast merely hangs in the water while the other swims downwards energetically.

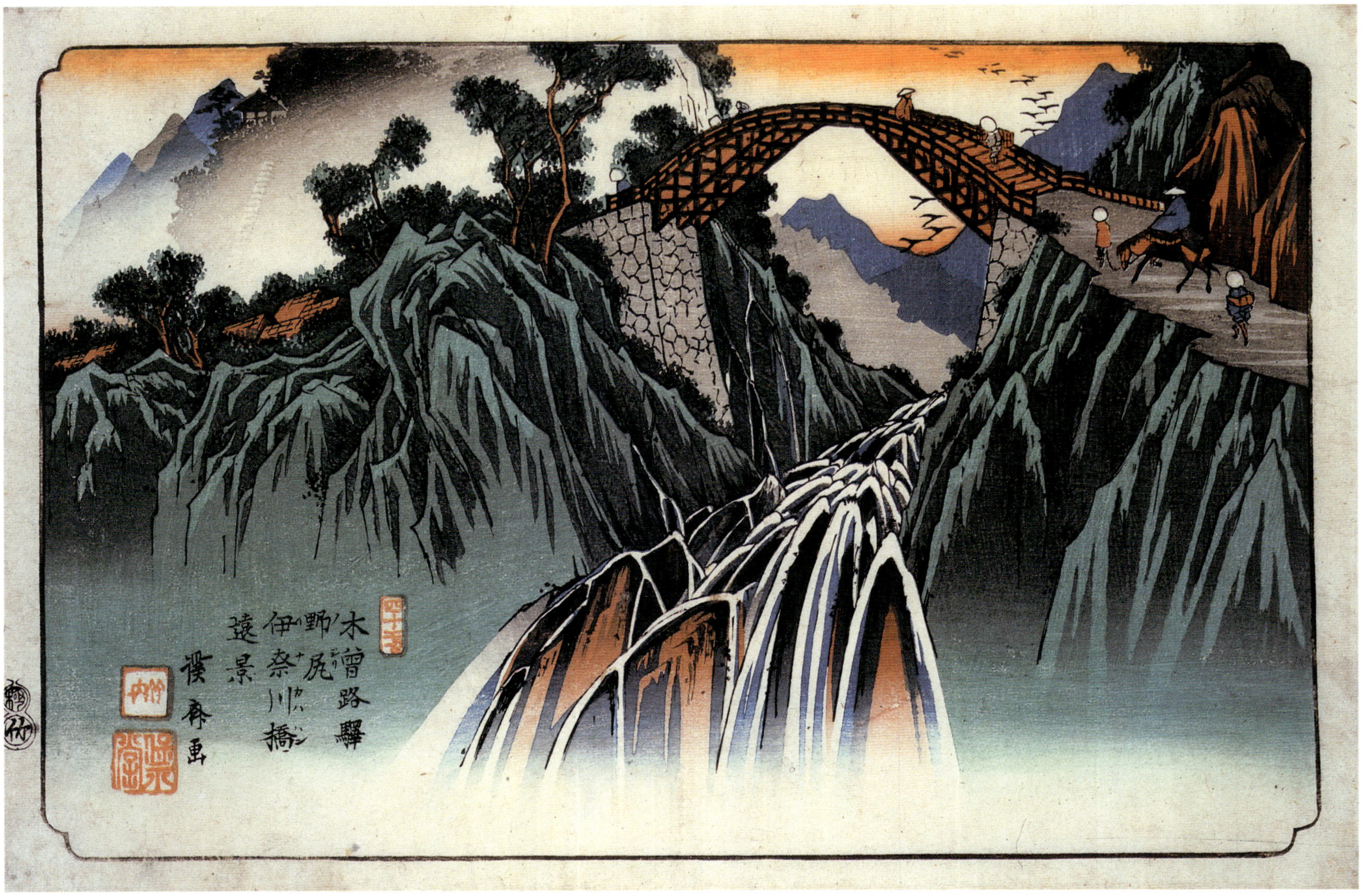

Above: Keisai Eisen (1790-1848) 'Inagawa Bridge at Nojiri,' from the series 'From the 69 Stations of the Kisokaido' (*Kisokaidō rokujūkyū tsugi no uchi*), late 1830s, 10¼×14½ inches (26×36.8 cm). Published by Hōeidō and Kinjudō. Courtesy of the Trustees of the British Museum, London.

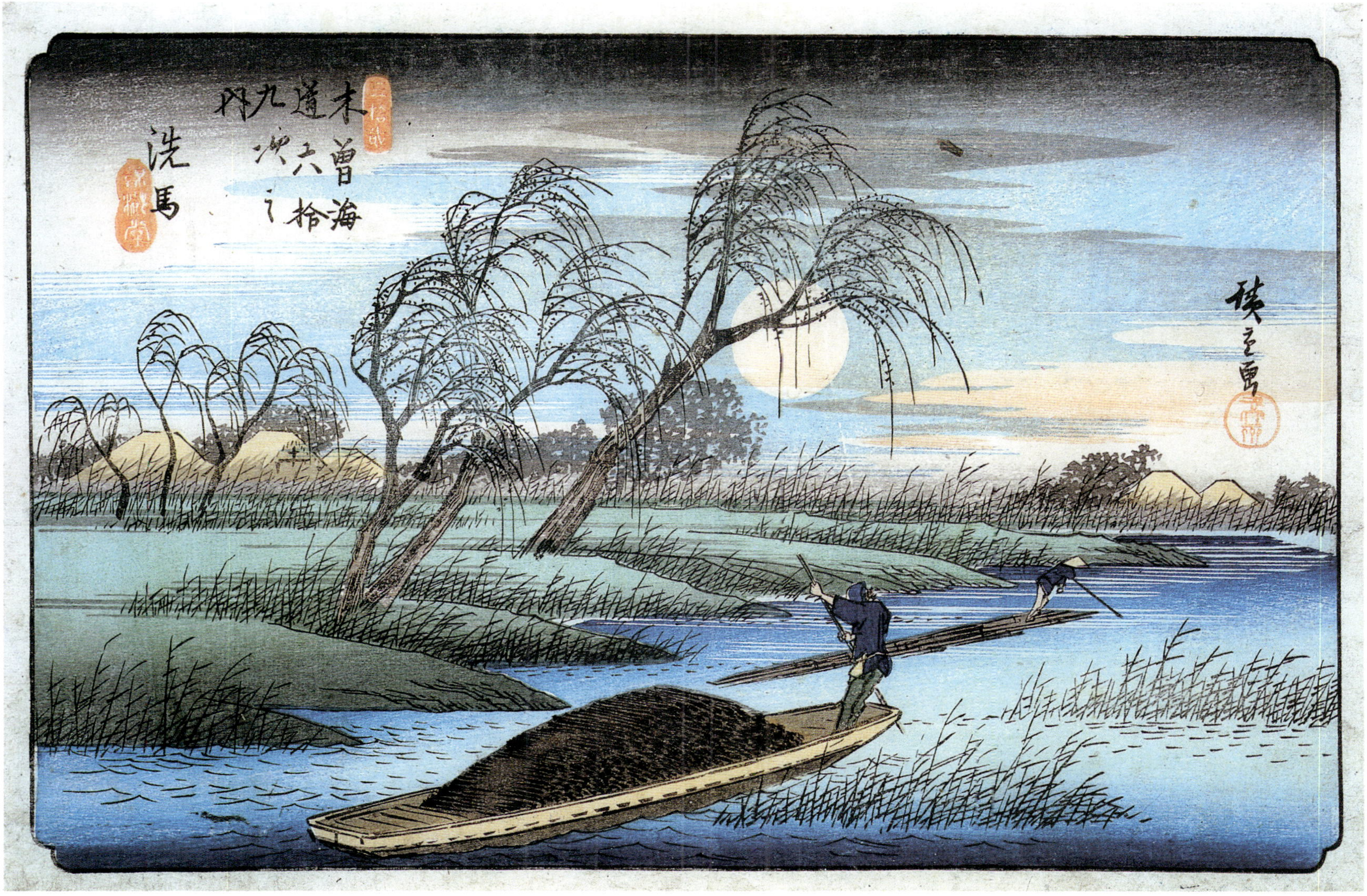

Above: Utagawa Hiroshige (1797-1858) 'Full Moon at Seba,' from the series 'From the 69 Stations of the Kisokaido' (*Kisokaidō rokujūkyū tsugi no uchi*), late 1830s, 10¼×14½ inches (26×36.8 cm). Published by Hōeidō and Kinjudō. Courtesy of the Trustees of the British Museum, London.

The next major project Hiroshige undertook was the 'From the 69 Stations of the Kisokaido' (*Kisokaidō Rokujūkyū-tsugi no uchi*) of the late 1830s, depicting scenes on the inland highway from Edo to Kyoto, which led through the mountains. It was started by the publishers Hōeidō, with Eisen designing the images, became a collaboration between Eisen and Hiroshige and the two publishers Hōeidō and Kinjudō, and ended with Hiroshige and Kinjudō alone. Eisen's 'Inagawa Bridge at Nojiri' (page 170), probably the most famous of the 23 images contributed by him, demonstrates the influence of both Hokusai and Hiroshige. The vibrantly graphic torrent recalls the Hokusai 'Waterfalls' set, and contrasts with the more evocative 'Hiroshige' background, with its weary travelers and flight of wild geese. The bridge is famous for the outline of its underside which recalls Mount Fuji. Later editions were simplified in design to reduce costs, removing the geese, and also removing Eisen's signature in the hope that it would pass as a Hiroshige.

'Full Moon at Seba' (page 171) shows Hiroshige at his best, and depends as much on the manner of the Kanō school and literati painting as on *ukiyo-e*. The willows leaning over the stream draw the eye to the straining figures of the watermen, poling their craft under the rising moon. The rich colors of this early edition of the print are one of the acknowledged beauties of Hiroshige. This aspect of the artist's work most suffers in large later editions. Fewer, cheaper and more raucous dyes were used, and printed from worn blocks at the behest of publishers determined to profit from selling cheaply in volume. Richard Lane remarks that the Japanese divide impressions of Hiroshige prints into nine grades according to quality, and even medium-grade impressions are becoming hard to find in good condition.

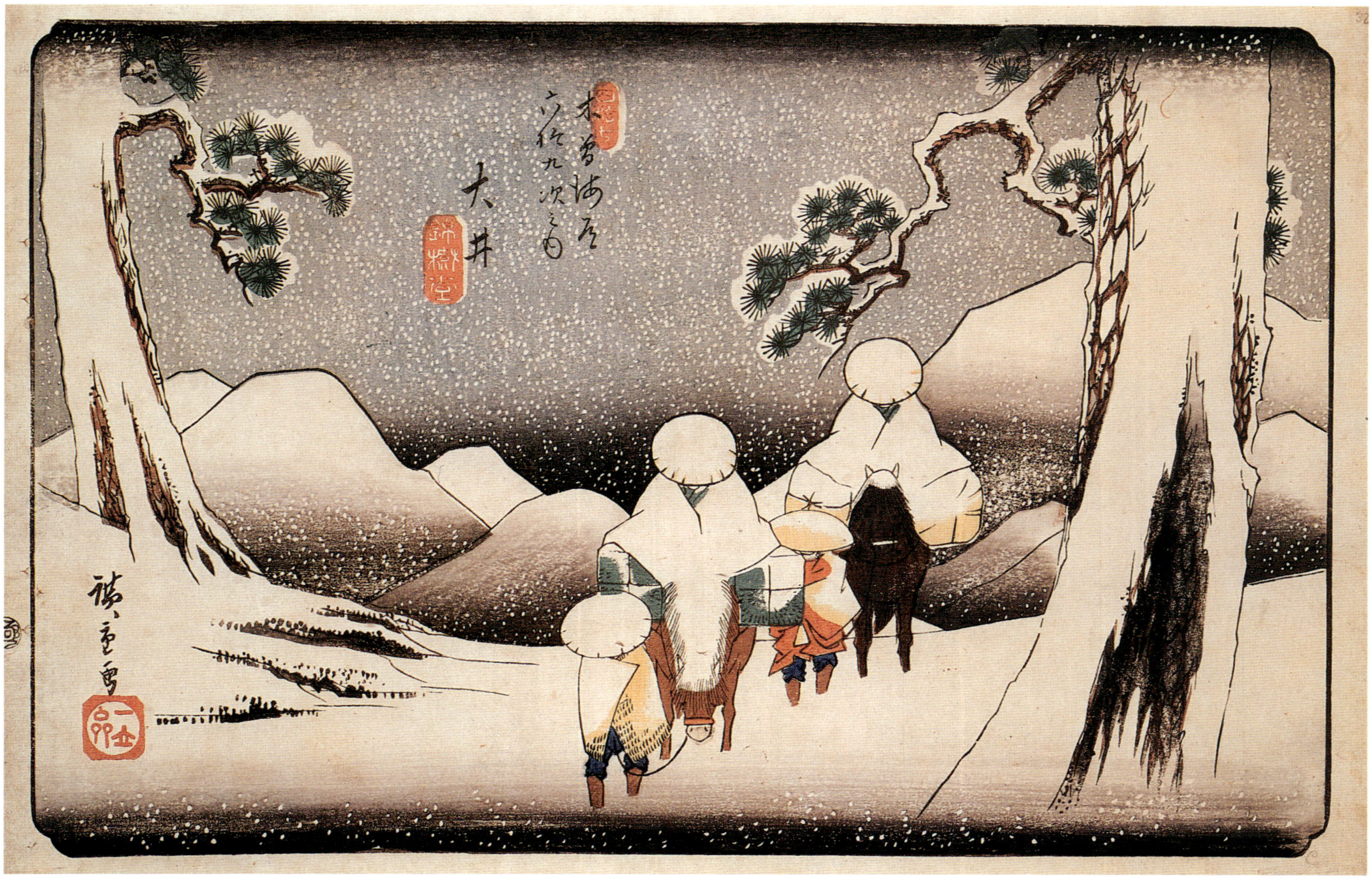

Above: Utagawa Hiroshige (1797-1858) 'Travelers in the Snow at Ōi,' from the series 'From the 69 Stations of the Kisokaido' (*Kisokaidō rokujūkyū tsugi no uchi*), late 1830s, 10¼×14½ inches (26×36.8 cm). Published by Hōeidō and Kinjudō. Courtesy of the Trustees of the British Museum, London.

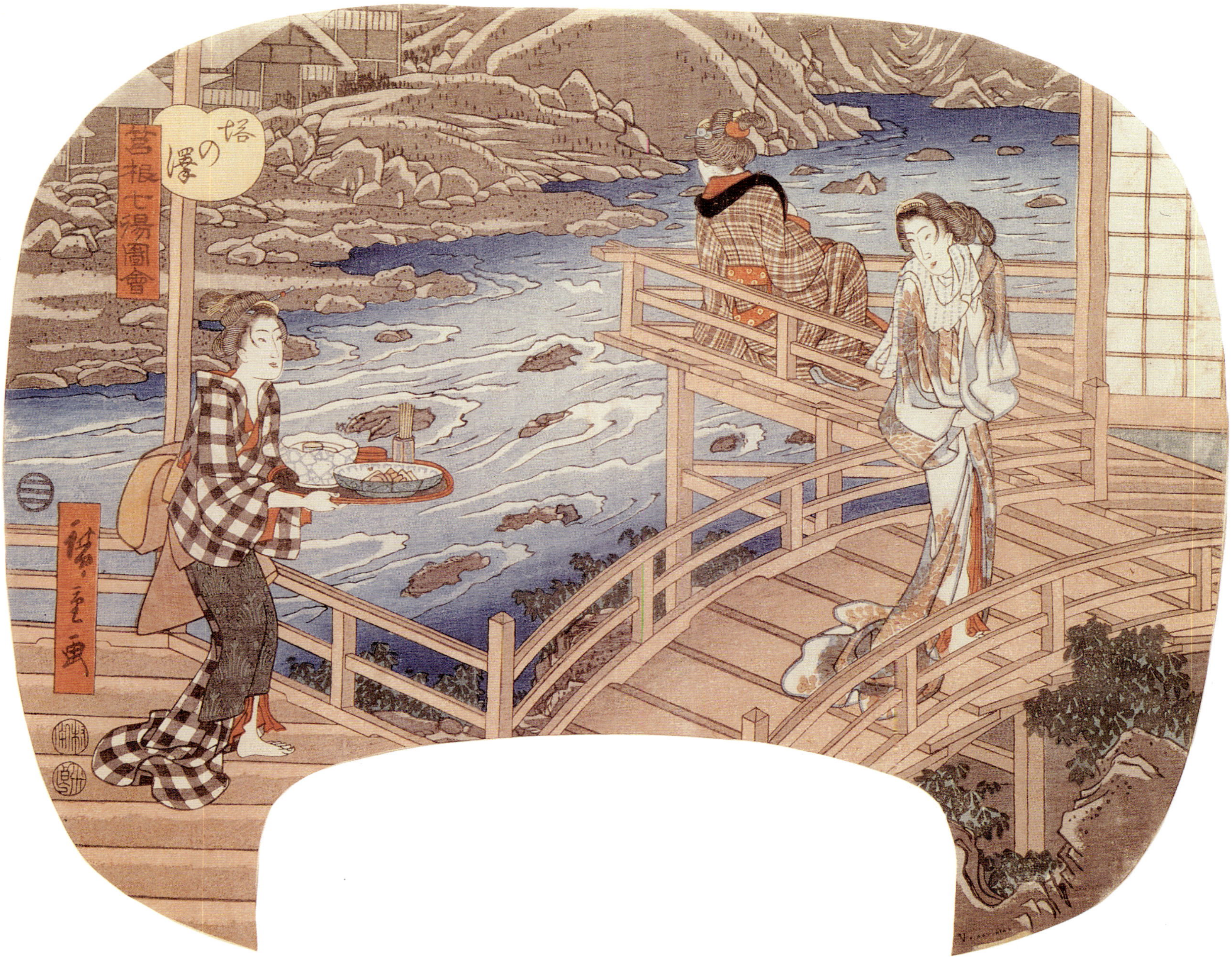

Above: Utagawa Hiroshige (1797-1858) 'Water' from the series 'The Pride of Edo Compared with the Five Elements,' 1846, fan print, 8⅝×11½ inches (21.9×29.2 cm). Courtesy of the Trustees of the Victoria and Albert Museum, London.

The print of 'Travelers in the Snow at Ōi' is another image from the same series, with its hapless travelers sympathetically described as they struggle forward through the blizzard, heads bowed. Their round hats and the regularly shaped mountains in the background, which echo the shapes of the rider's shoulders, introduce an oddly geometric element to the composition, as forms are simplified by the enshrouding snow.

The demands of publishers for quantities of new images resulted in large numbers of new series in the 1840s and early 1850s, some of which are mediocre in quality. However, many fine compositions were also produced. The unusual fan-print 'Water' (page 173), from an 1846 set of five, 'The Pride of Edo Compared with the Five Elements,' depicts the *Ocha no mizu*, the canal which supplied water for the Shogun's tea. The gorgeously dressed woman standing on the foredeck of the pleasureboat reflects the lingering effects of the Tempō Edicts of 1841-43 which it will be remembered forebade prints of courtesans or frivolous subjects. Here, and in others of the same series, fashionable women are prominent in what purport to be landscape subjects. While the lady on the boat has the shaven eyebrows of a married woman, a night scene from the same series shows a woman walking alone at night carrying a lantern, with bare feet rather than the socks worn by virtuous women.

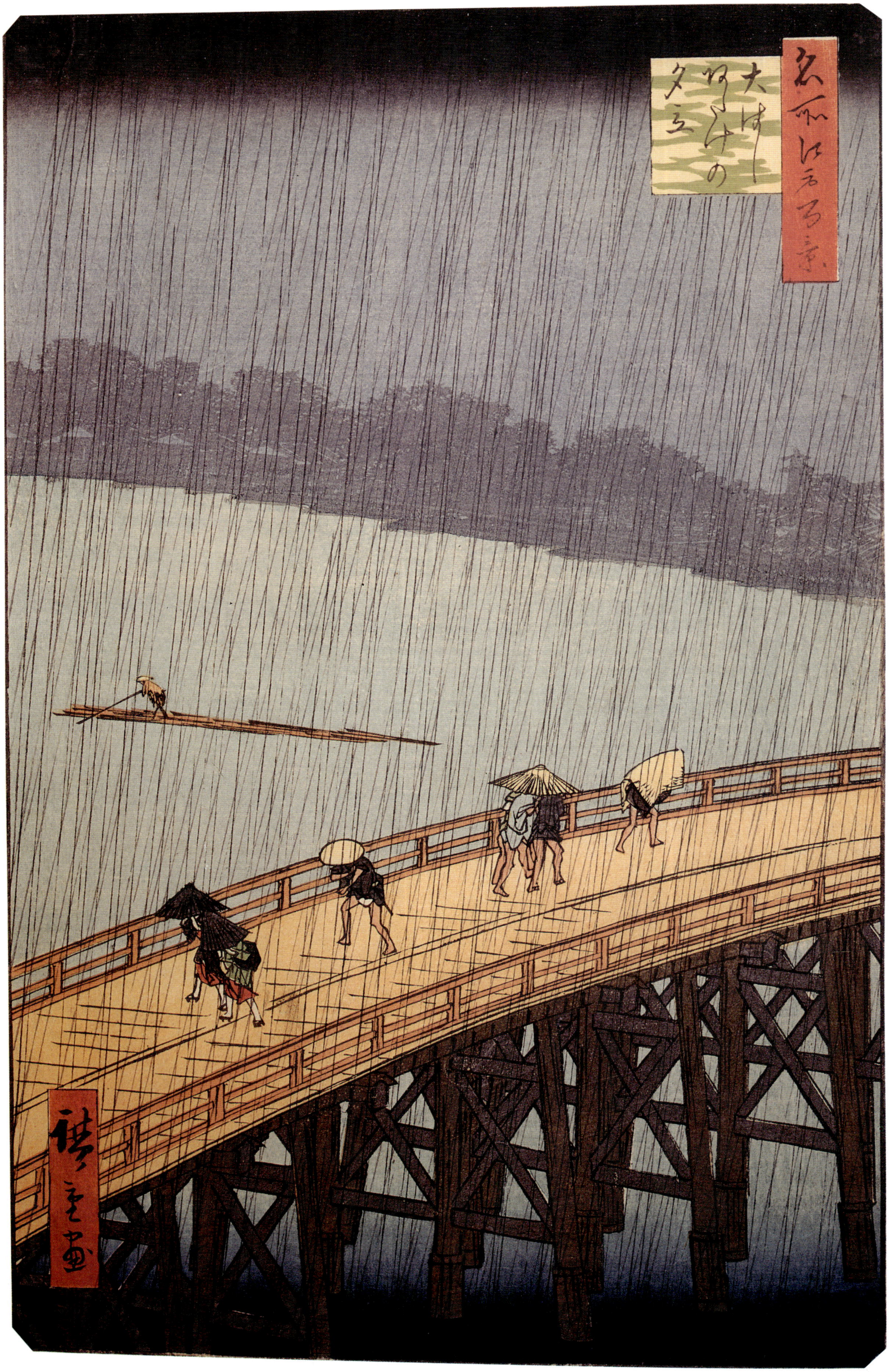

Left: Utagawa Hiroshige (1797-1858) 'Sudden Shower at Ōhashi Bridge at Ataka' (*Ōhashi, atake no yūdachi*), from the series '100 Views of Edo' (*Meisho Edo hyakkei*), 1857, 14⅛×9¾ inches (35.9×24.8 cm). Published by Uoya Eikichi. The Whitworth Art Gallery, University of Manchester.

The '100 Views of Edo' (*Meisho Edo hyakkei*), a set of 119 prints in upright format published between 1856 and 1859 (so that it was partly a posthumous publication for the artist, who died of cholera in the fall of 1858), was the artist's last great series and contains some dozen masterpieces. The 'Sudden Shower at Ōhashi Bridge at Atake' (page 174) was one of the earliest Japanese images to be well known in the West. Indeed, Vincent van Gogh made a copy of it in oils in 1888. The print must have seemed challengingly strange and yet sympathetic to the impressionists and their successors with its succinctness, mastery of the transient atmospheric effect, and tilted horizon. The high viewpoint opens up a vast sweep of the Sumida river which makes the anonymous figure poling his raft of logs almost a necessary accent and indicator of recession.

Saruwaka-chō, a fascinating view in the theater street from the same series, by contrast uses a strong single vanishing point that recalls the *uki-e* perspective pictures of the previous century. The depiction of shadows to convey the strength of the moonlight is rare in the Japanese print, which normally adheres to Far Eastern convention and eschews chiaroscuro. The theaters are on the left, with intent figures outside touting for custom from the crowds in the street, and we gain a vivid sense of Edo as a metropolis, a sense which is rare in this series.

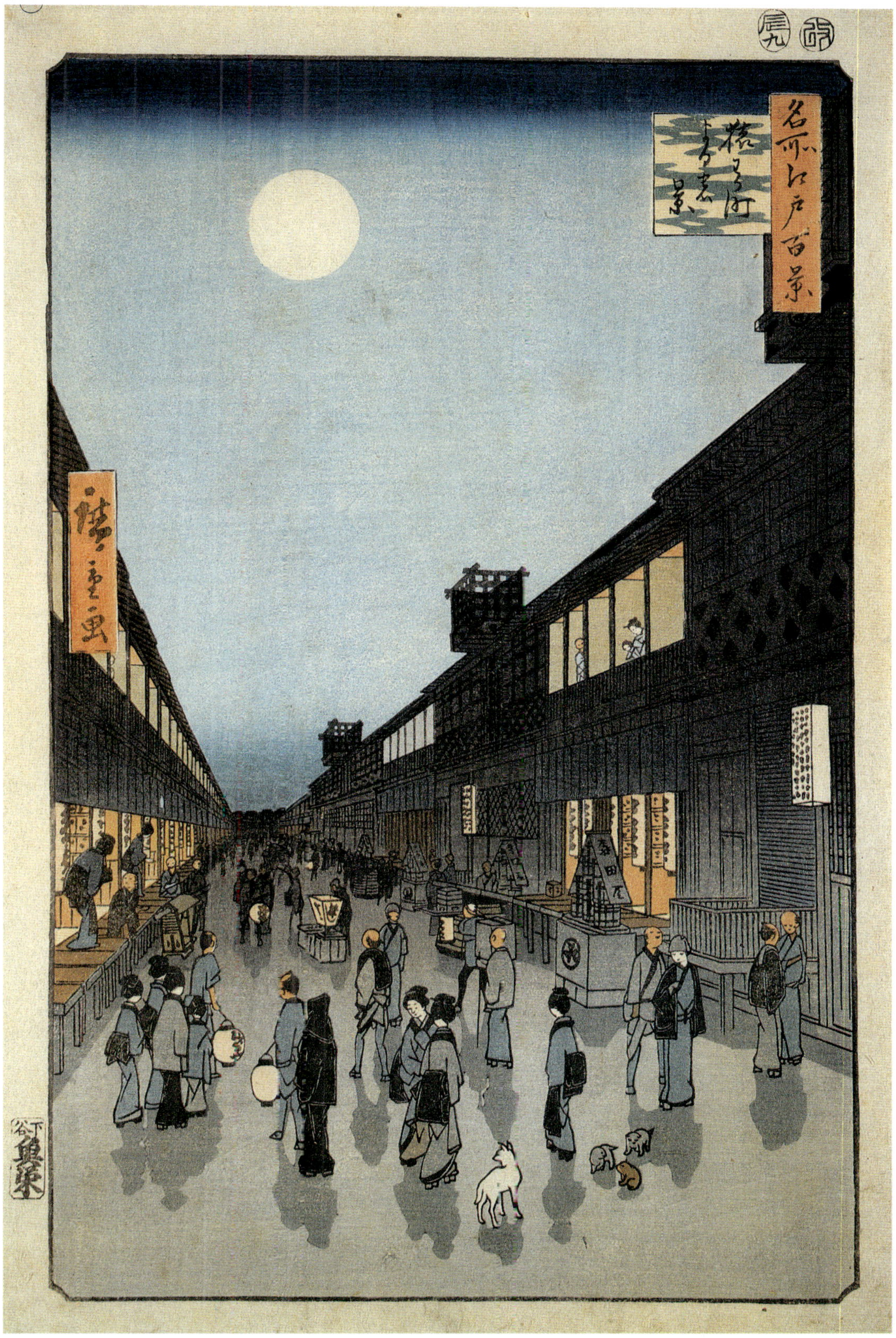

Right: Utagawa Hiroshige (1797-1858) 'Saruwaka-chō Theater,' 1856, from the series '100 Views of Edo' (*Meisho Edo hyakkei*), 1857, 14⅛×9¾ inches (35.9×24.8 cm). Published by Uoya Eikichi. The Whitworth Art Gallery, University of Manchester.

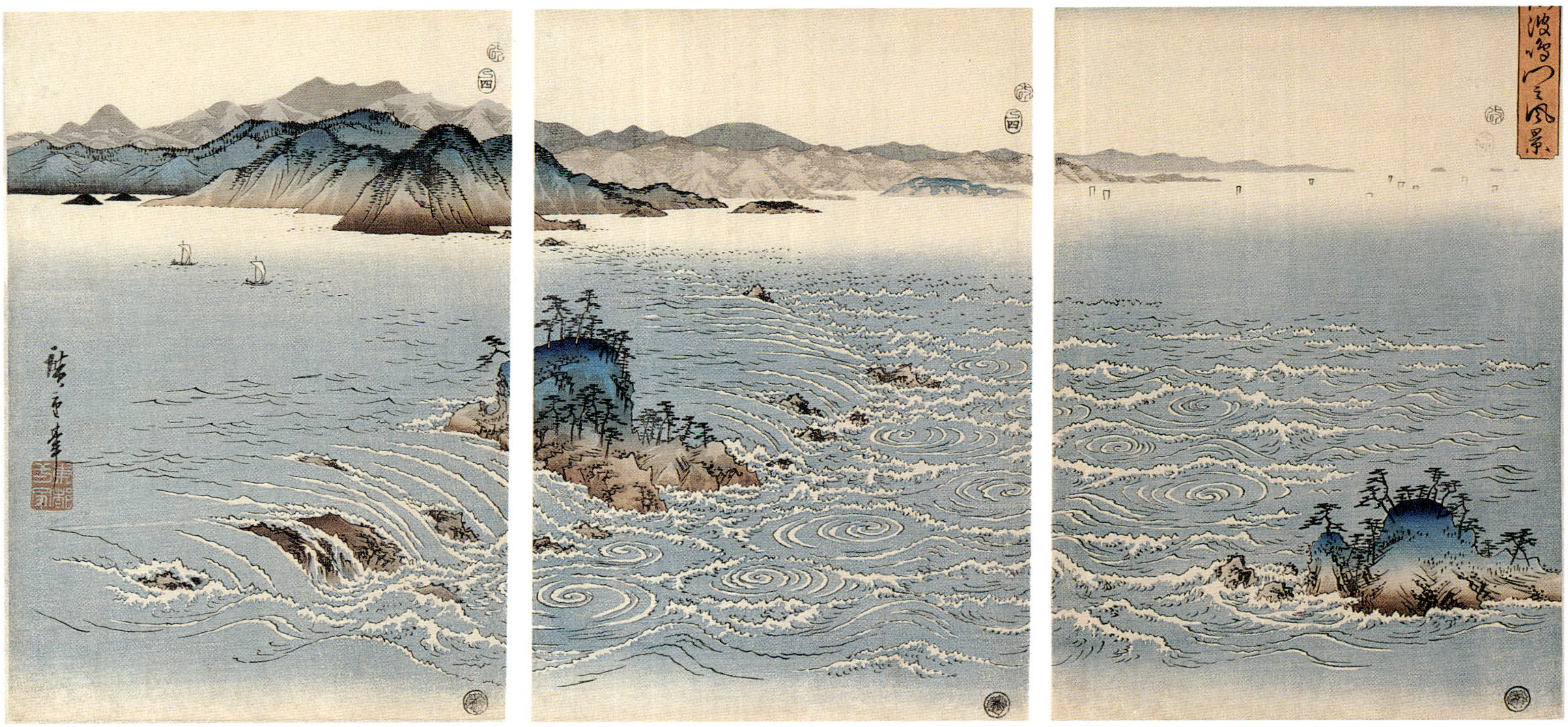

Above: Utagawa Hiroshige (1797-1858) 'The Whirlpools at Naruto in the Province of Awa,' 1857, 14½×29½ inches (37×75 cm). Courtesy of the Trustees of the Victoria and Albert Museum, London.

In 1857 Hiroshige designed a set of three landscape triptychs, on the traditional theme of 'snow, moon and flowers,' which have a breathtaking grandeur leading one to regret he did not survive to do more landscapes in this format. 'The Whirlpools of Naruto in the Province of Awa' (page 176), between the islands of Awaji and Shikoku, represents the 'flowers' of the set, as the whirlpools are poetically described as *nami no hana*, flowers of the waves.

The memorial portrait of Hiroshige which Kunisada designed in 1858 carries the artist's farewell verse:

Leaving my brush behind
In Edo
I set forth on a new journey
Let me sightsee all the famous views
In Paradise!

Indeed, he had probably run out of famous views to depict in Japan.

Hiroshige was succeeded by his adopted son who took the name of Hiroshige II upon his death, and retained it up to 1865 when he divorced the artist's daughter and moved to Yokohama. Then another pupil became Hiroshige III, retaining the title until his death in 1894. Both produced numbers of prints in the style of the master, often including comic incidents to enliven a formula which was becoming stale.

Hiroshige's Utagawa school contemporaries, notably Kunisada and Kuniyoshi, were also caught up in the fashion for landscape in the early 1830s. They made prints of quality and produced many memorable images on which they display an eclectic range of influences. Kunisada lifts details from an 1824 book by Kawamura Bunpō (1779-1821), *Bunpō sansui gafu*, while certain Kuniyoshi prints, such as 'Sosan Returning to his Mother,' from 'Twenty-four Paragons of Filial Piety' (*Nijūshi kō dōji kagami*) of around 1840, are virtual transcriptions of European engravings.

Kuniyoshi's 'Seaweed Gatherers at Ōmari' (page 177), from the series 'Famous Views of the Eastern Capital' (*Tōto Meisho*), published around 1833, shows a sympathetic interest in the humble labour of the figures on the boat in the foreground which reflects the example of Hiroshige, while the clouds have a European model, demonstrating the artist's fascination with the fusion of European styles into Japanese tradition.

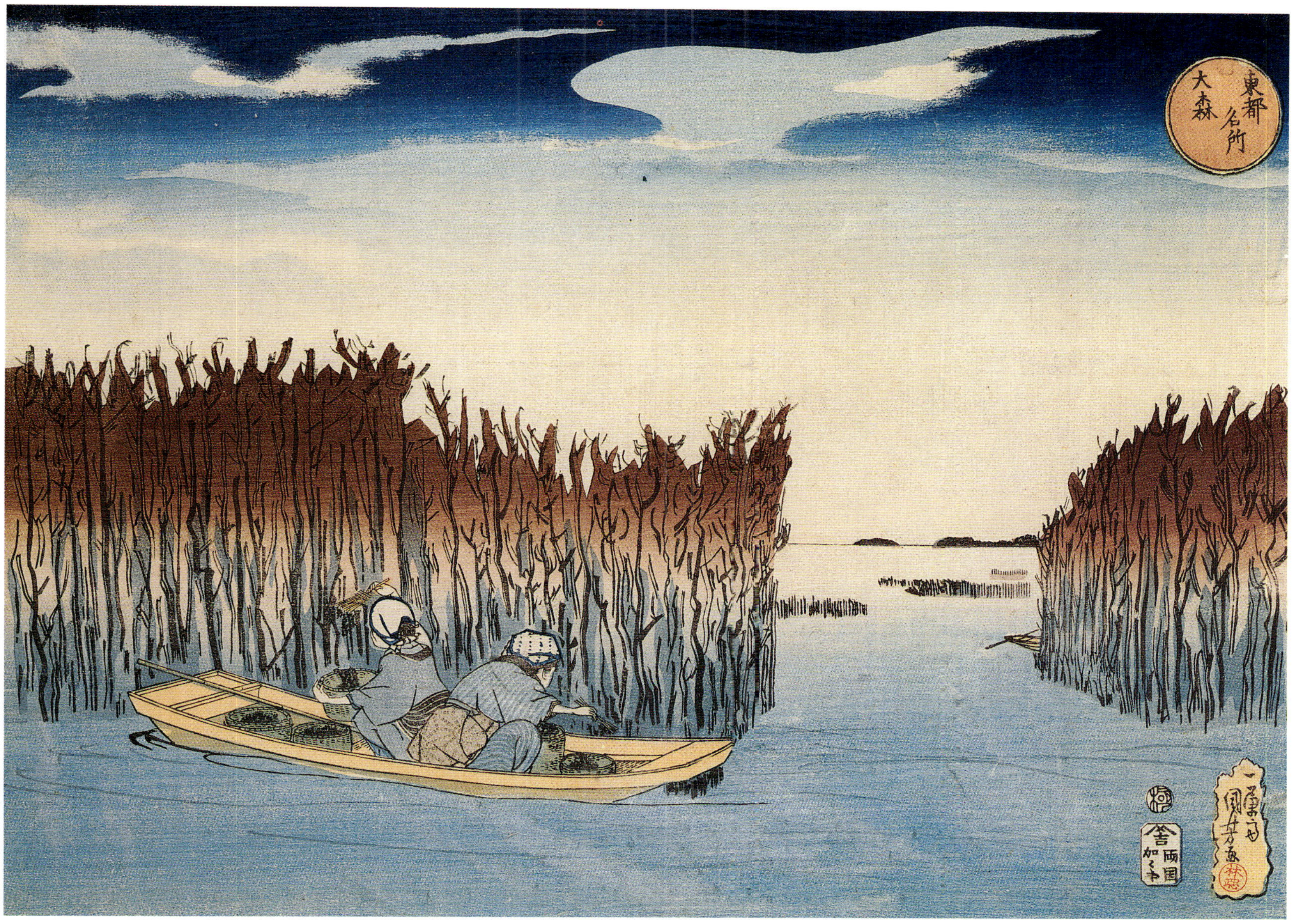

Above: Utagawa Kuniyoshi (1798-1861) 'Seaweed Gatherers at Ōmari,' from the series 'Famous Views of the Eastern Capital' (*Tōto meisho*) c. 1833, 9ax13⅜ inches (23×34 cm). Published by Kagaya Kichibei. Courtesy of the Trustees of the Victoria and Albert Museum, London.

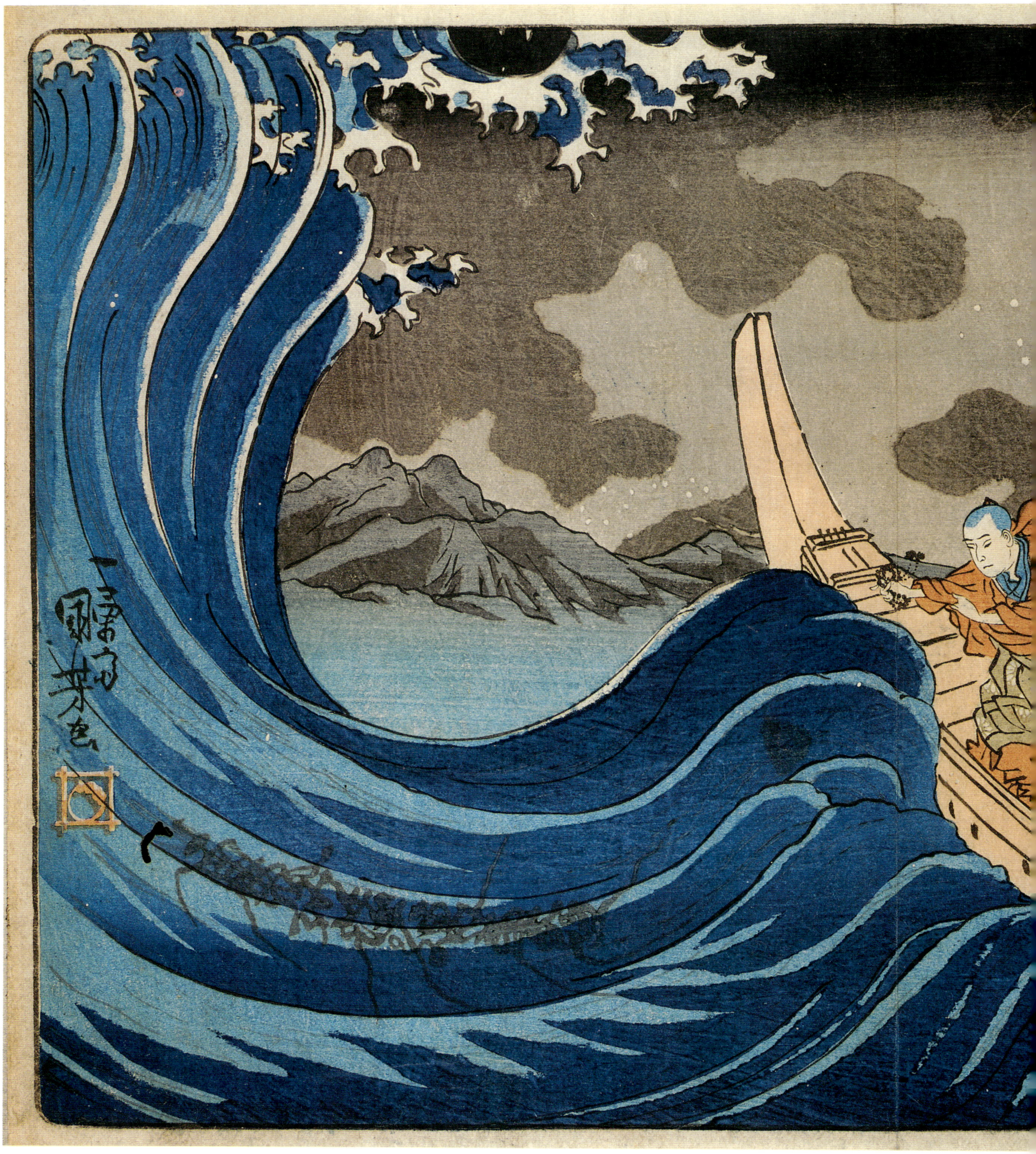

Utagawa Kuniyoshi (1798-1861) ‘Nichiren Calming the Storm,’ c. 1835, from the series ‘The Abridged Biography of the Buddhist Priest, Nichiren, Illustrated’ (*Kōsō go-ichidai ryaku zu*), 8¾×3³⁄16 inches (22.2×36 cm). Published by Ebiya Rinnosuke. Courtesy of the Trustees of the Victoria and Albert Museum, London.

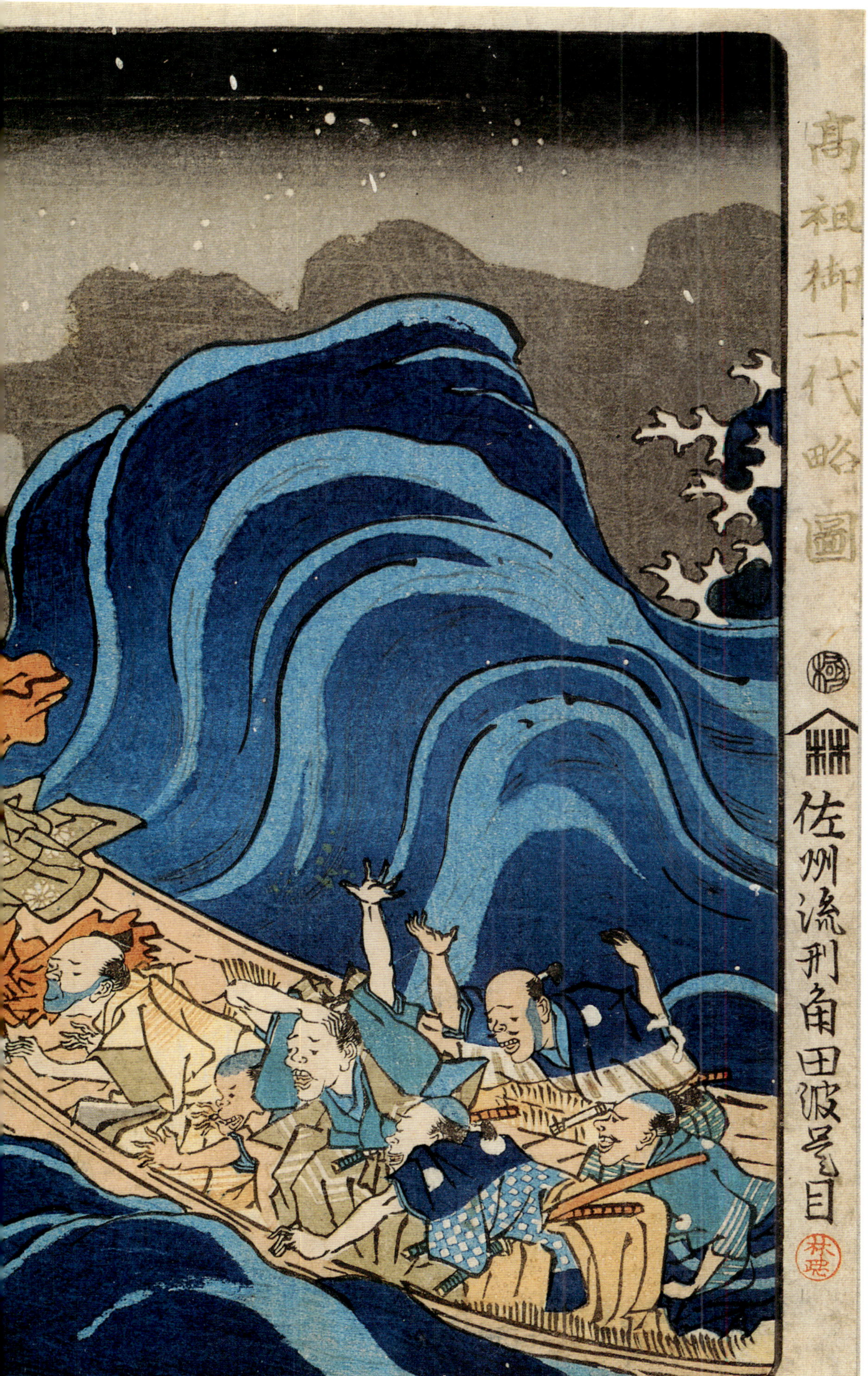

The print of 'Nichiren Calming the Storm' (page 178), from the series 'The Abridged Biography of the Buddhist Priest Nichiren, Illustrated' (*Kōsō go-ichi-dai ryaku zu*), which was published around 1835, by contrast shows a manifest debt to Hokusai's 'Great Wave at Kanagawa'. The theme of the sea in storm recurs with exciting bravura variations throughout Kuniyoshi's career, exploiting the rich potentialities of the Prussian blue dye to the full. The ten prints of the Nichiren set have from the first been praised among European collectors for their evocative landscape content. Here the thirteenth-century saint traveling into exile calms the sea by the recitation of a sacred mantra, which appears in magical script on the face of the waves. A much more soothing marine image is 'Fuji on a Clear Day' (page 180), from the series '36 Views of Fuji Seen from the Capital' (*Tōto Fuji-mi sanjūrokkei*), published around 1843. This presents us with an appealing and breezy view of the sacred mountain.

Kuniyoshi produced a series of the '100 Poets' (*Hyakunin isshū no uchi*), published around 1840, about the time Hokusai brought out his series on the same subject, and obviously in competition. The evocative image of the poet Ariwara no Narihira (825-880) watching maple leaves floating down the Tatsuta River in fall is steeped in the aristocratic gravitas and rich decorative values of the Tosa school.

Below: Utagawa Kuniyoshi (1798-1861) 'Fuji on a Clear Day,' c. 1843, from the series '36 Views of Fuji seen from the Capital' (*Tōto Fuji-mi sanjūrokkei*) 9×13¼ inches (22.9×33.7 cm). Published by Murata. Courtesy of the Trustees of the Victoria and Albert Museum, London.

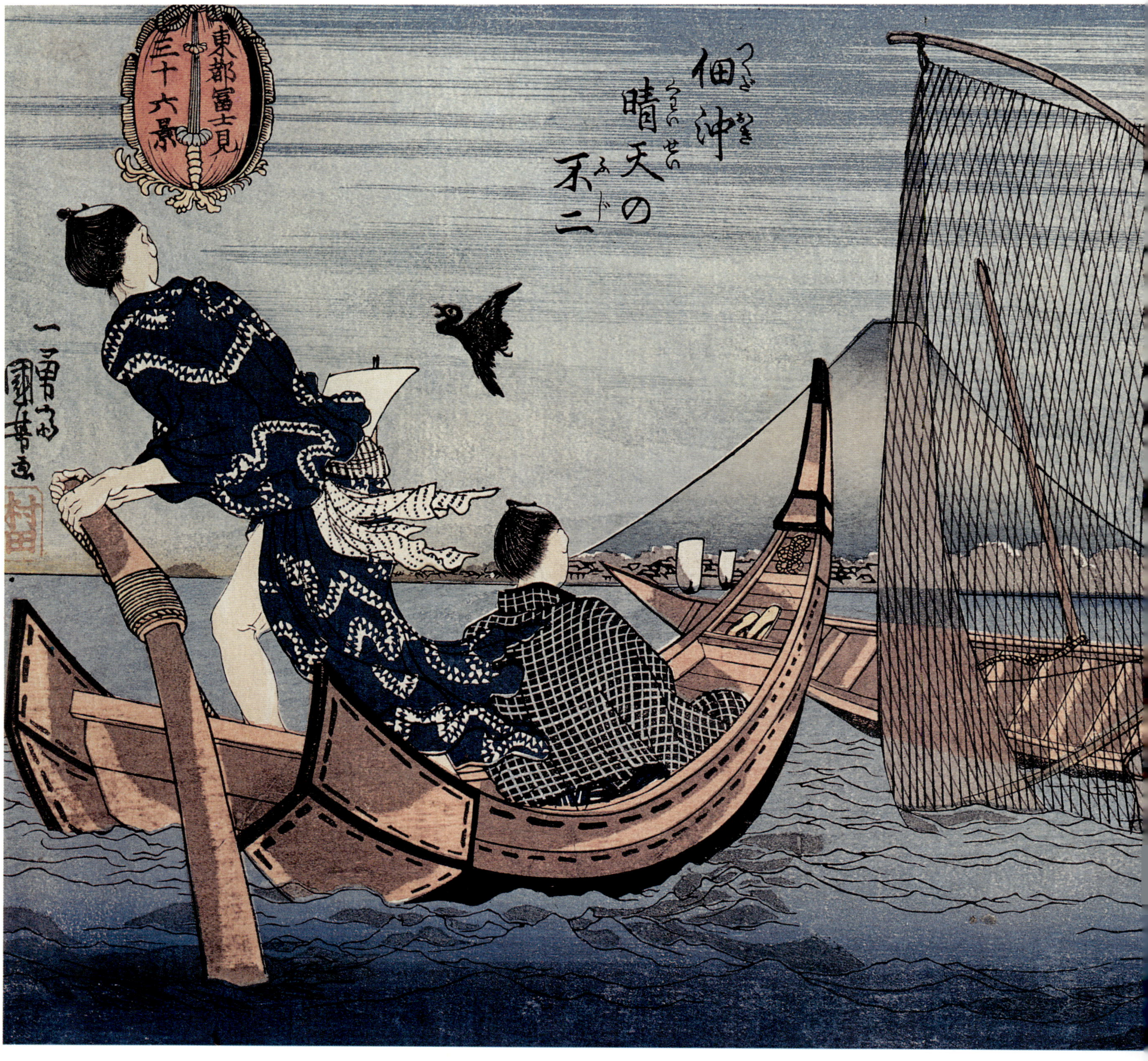

Right: Utagawa Kuniyoshi (1798-1861) 'Ariwara Narihira by the Tatsuta River,' c. 1840, from the series '100 Poets' (*Hyakunin isshū no uchi*), 14⅛×9½ inches (35.9×24.1 cm). Courtesy of the Trustees of the Victoria and Albert Museum, London.

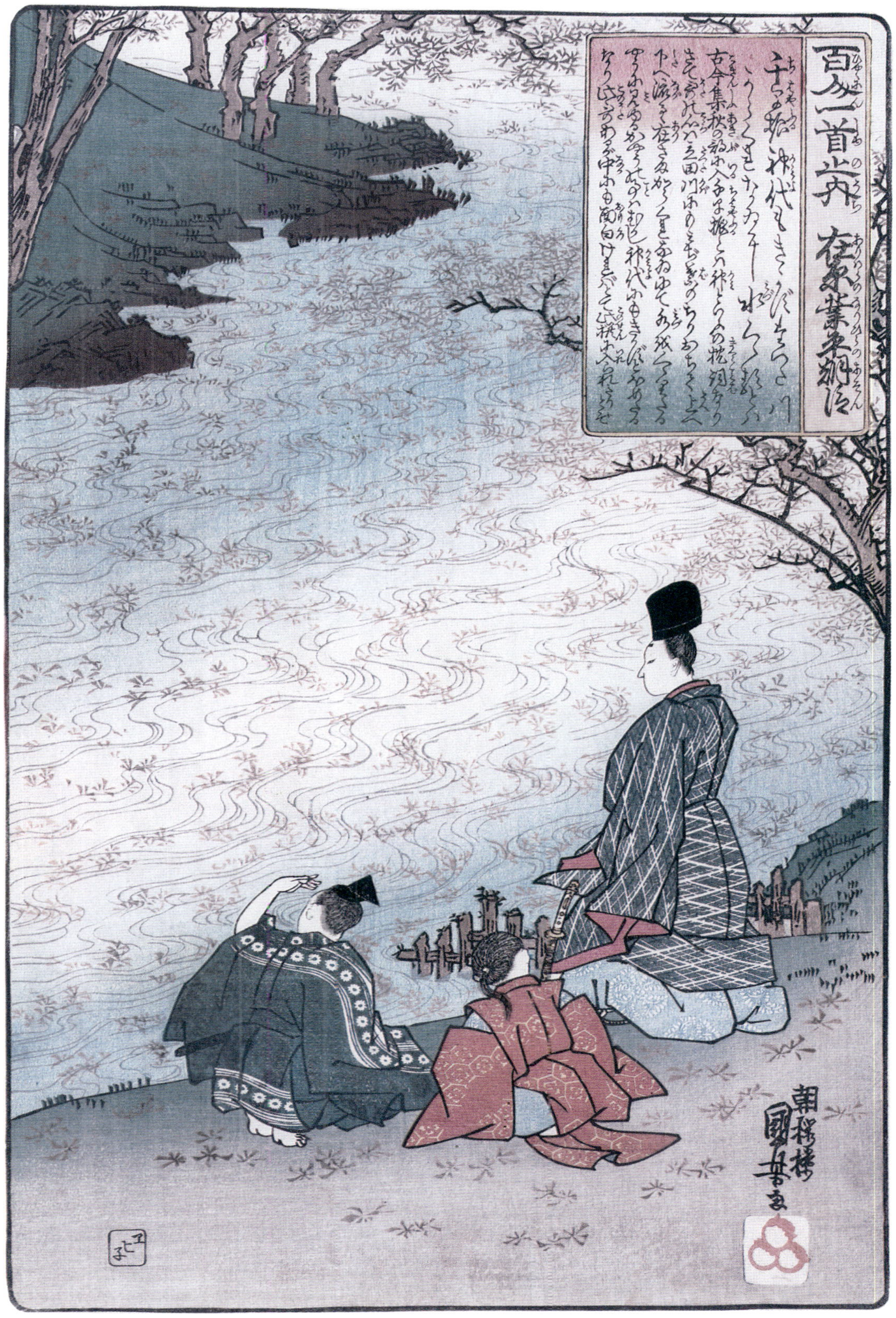

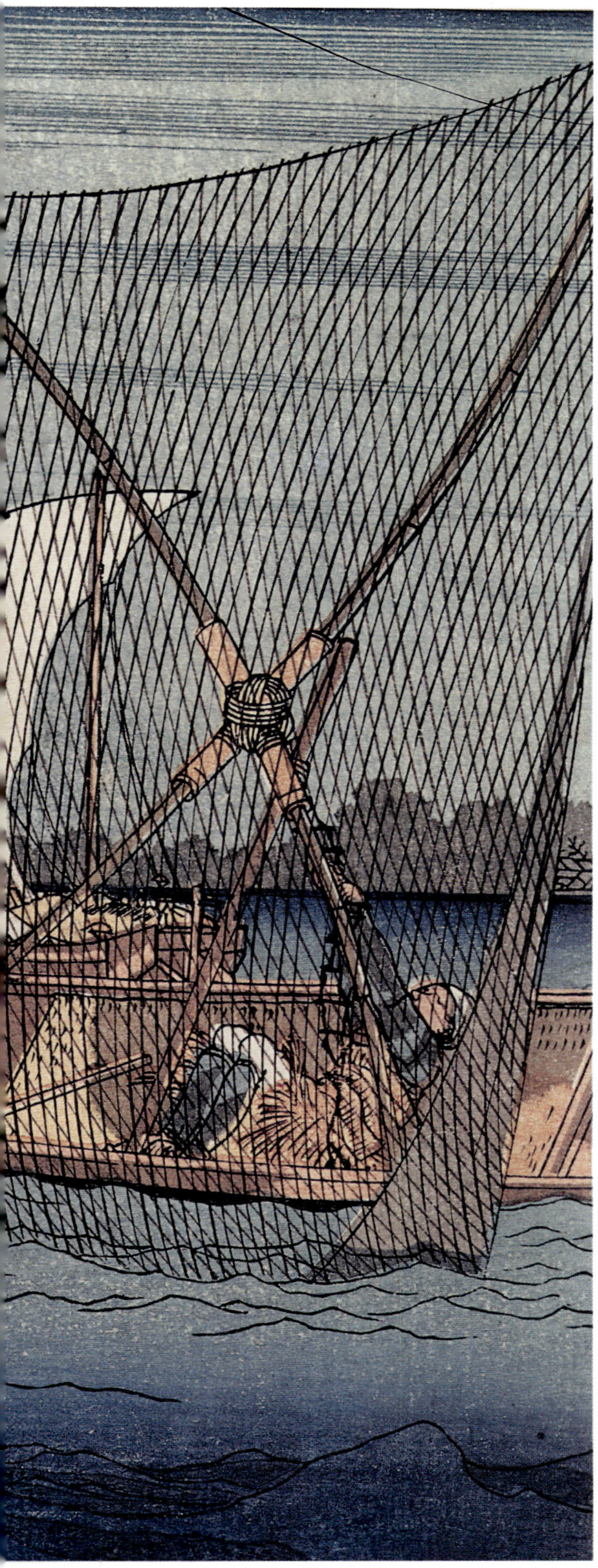

Our survey of the developments of the last decades of the Edo period has highlighted the growth to maturity of the landscape prints. Following the death of Hiroshige this genre was virtually to disappear in the last decade before the Meiji Restoration, only to be revived by Kiyochika in the 1880s. (See pp 184-201). The heroic tradition was firmly entrenched through the prolific efforts of Kuniyoshi. His pupils would expand the genre in the Meiji period: in the hands of Yoshiiku, Yoshitoshi and, to a lesser extent, Kyosai, historic and heroic prints came to dominate the 1870s and 1880s. Graphics printed in large series by extremely prolific artists characterize the late Edo period. Editions were huge: it is estimated that editions of 20,000 prints pulled from a single set of blocks may well have been possible. (See pp 28-43). Printing techniques became increasingly refined and from 1829 onwards foreign pigments were added to the palette of the artists and publishers. First Prussian blue and later, in the 1850s, aniline and ecoline dyes provided the possibilities for new striking color-combinations.

All in all, the achievements of the six decades of the nineteenth century are quite considerable and it seems proper to reconsider such derogatory concepts as 'the period of decadence and decline.' These judgments based on taste have hampered the study of people like Eizan, Eisen and, above all, Kunisada.

The Osaka Printmakers JONATHAN BENNETT

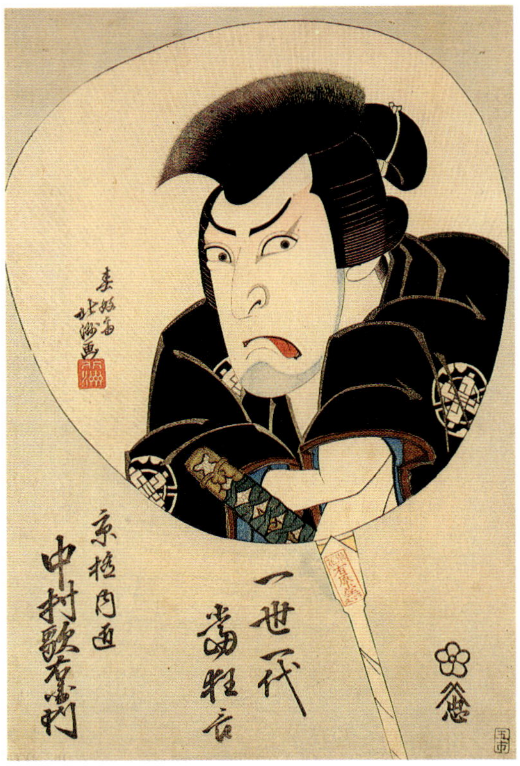

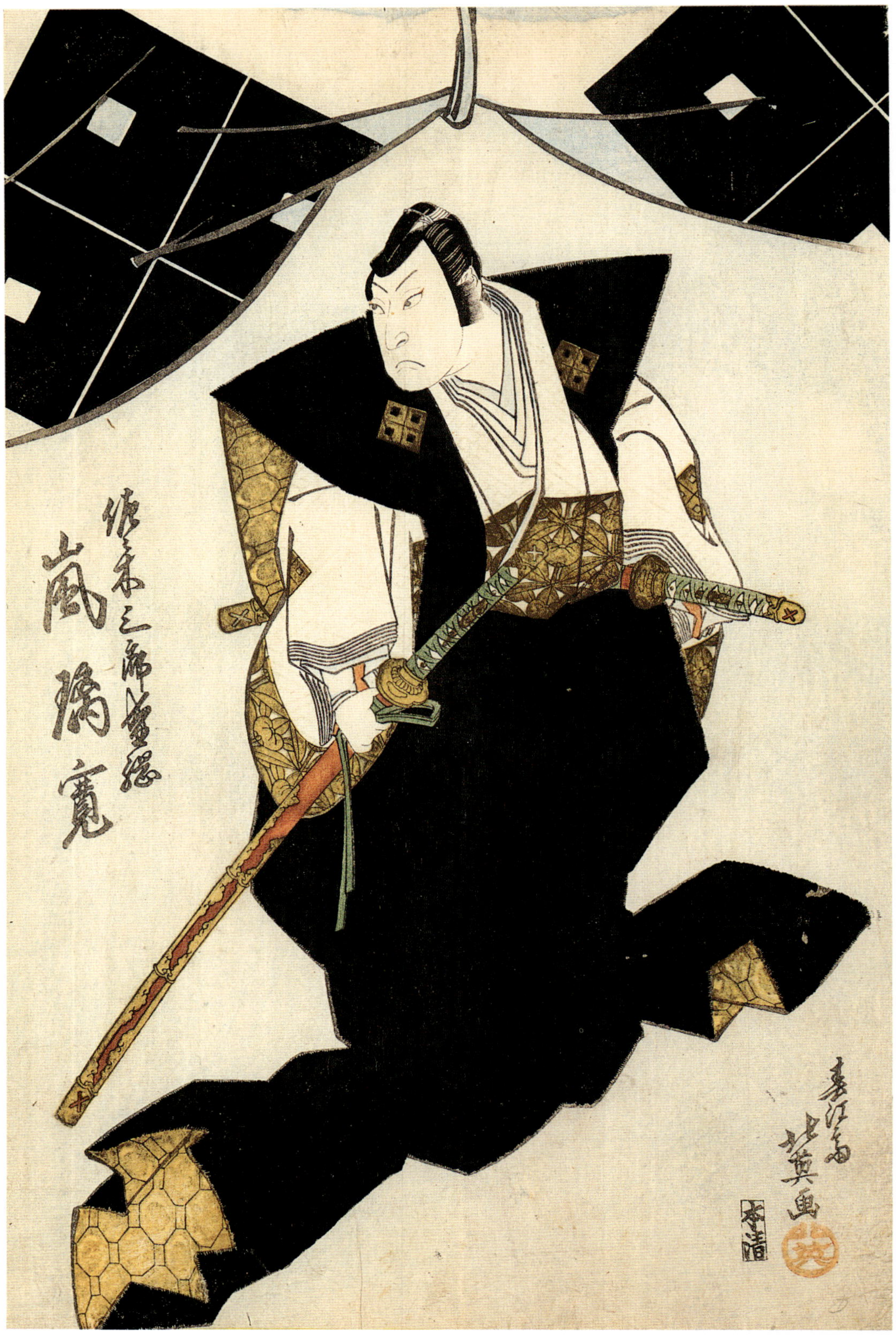

The city of Osaka, the commercial neighbor of the imperial capital Kyōto, was dominated by great merchant and banking dynasties. While Edo, the center of government, was the stronghold of the independent artisan and shopkeeper, Osaka was a city of clerks, dependent upon paternalistic employers and unable to indulge themselves in the libertine and luxurious like their Edo counterparts. It is partly for this reason that the Osaka *ukiyo-e* concentrates entirely on Kabuki subjects; partly also because Edo prints were widely available in the city. There remained a clear commercial niche for depictions of local dramatic heroes in recent productions, but the number of prints produced was always miniscule compared to that of Edo artists. Many designers in Osaka were part-time or amateur, and private patronage seems to have been as important as public sale in supporting the genre. This rather compromising scenario produced exceptional images by such artists as Shunkōsai Hokushū (*fl* 1810-32), Shunkōsai Hokuei (*fl* 1824-37), Utagawa Kunimasu (*fl* 1834-52), Gosōtei Hirosada (d. 1863), Nagahide and Nakamura (*fl* 1805).

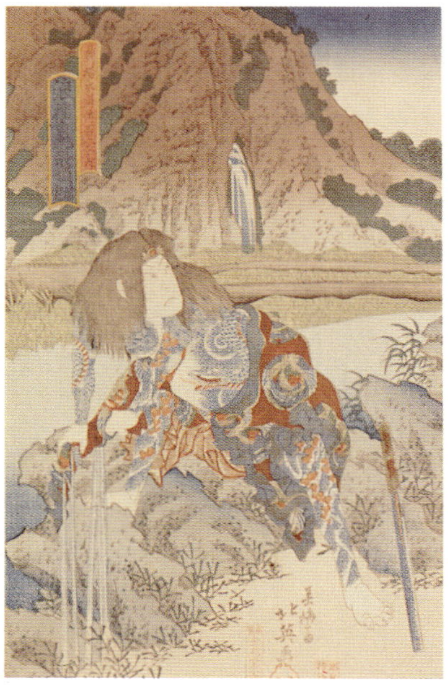

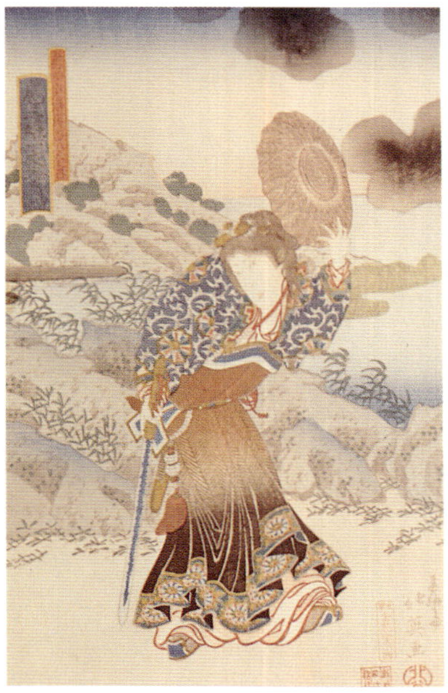

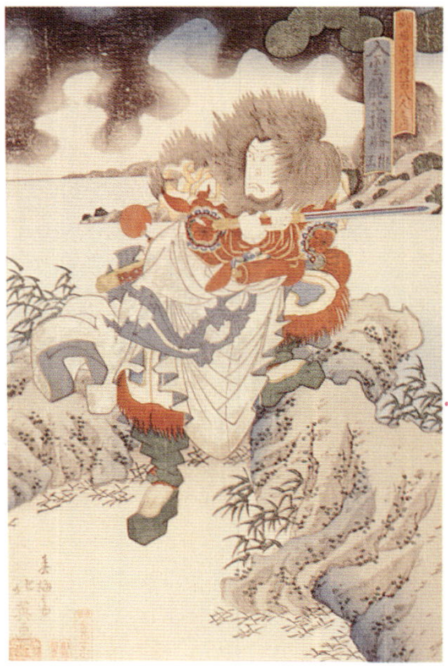

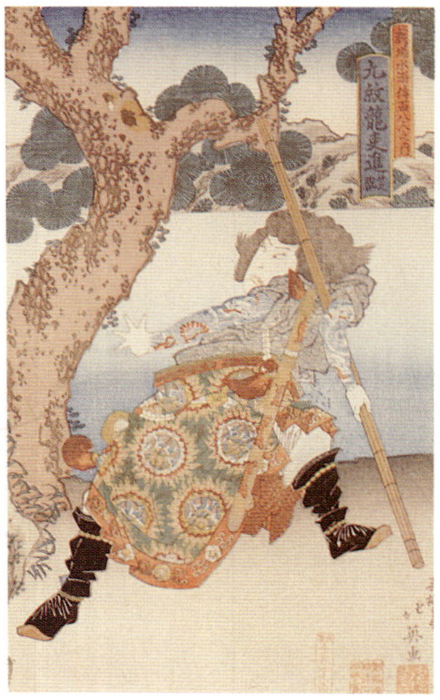

Hokushū's 'Nakamura Utaemon III as Kyōgoku no Takumi in Hikosan Gongen Chikai no Sukedachi,' was published in March 1825. The Elvis-like shock of hair denotes a villain as decent people shaved the top of the head. This print records a 'retirement' performance by Utaemon III which was so well received that he continued to act until his death in 1838. Hokushū was the leading actor portraitist in Osaka for two decades, in collaboration with the brilliant block-cutter Kasuke, and was noted for his skill in conveying the emotional charge signaled by the *mie* grimace.

The short-lived Hokuei, a pupil of Hokushū, was an important and prolific figure, whose depiction of faces is indistinguishable in style from either his master or several other Osaka masters. The characteristic prominent bulging eyes and large oval jaw combine his 'Arashi Rikan II as Sasaki Saburō Moritsuna,' with the thin downturned mouth of the popular actor Arashi Rikan II to convey a misleadingly doleful effect. Hokuei was a pioneer in the application of *surimono* metallic pigments and embossing techniques to the actor print, along with the block-cutter Kasuke with whom he collaborated after 1832.

A polyptych by Hokuei, 'Three Heroes of *Suikoden* capture Kosanjō Ichijōsei, the Female Chief of a Rival Band,' published by Tenki around 1835. This masterpiece of Osaka printmaking has an unusually well developed landscape setting for an actor print, displaying the influence of Hokusai's illustrations to the translation of *Suikoden*, the last episode of which appeared in 1828, as well as Kuniyoshi's print series. We recognize the features of Arashi Rikan II, as the wonderfully tattooed Rorihakuto Chōjun on the left and of Nakamura Utaemon III as Ju-unryū Kosonsho at second from right. The hero on the right, Kumonryū Shishin, is probably played by Nakamura Shikan; the captured chief is unknown. The odd electrified stasis of the figures conveys the *Kabuki* convention whereby action is frozen into a still tableau at moments of extreme tension, a feature that made the drama extraordinarily suitable for reproduction in prints.

Kunimasu, a pupil of Kunisada, used the name Sadamasu until spurred by the example of his master, who changed his name to Toyokuni in 1844. He was a wealthy man who spent his fortune on establishing his own school of print design, and had many pupils. In his print 'The Fight on Gojo Bridge,' c.1835, the splendidly overequipped Oger Benkei V represents yet another appearance by Nakamura Utaemon III, while Nakamura Shikan (later Utaemon IV) plays the apparently effete Yoshitsune who is to defeat him. The dots over the latter's eyes denote noble birth (not illustrated).

The Tempō ban brought all printmaking in Osaka to a halt for five years until 1847 when Kunimasu's pupil Hirosada courageously designed a set of small portraits of unnamed actors, with titles suggesting they were likenesses of legendary heroes. These were passed by the censor and a new *chūban* size portrait genre was born using the brilliant mineral dyes now available and printed with meticulous precision. While Hirosada became the leading designer in this new wave, his master Kunimasu produced prints closely comparable in quality and style. In 'Actor as the Priest Saigyō Hōshi before Mount Fuji,' the anonymous actor is portraying the twelfth-century nobleman-turned-monk Saigyō Hōshi who eulogized Fuji in his poems and is distinguished by his pilgrim's hat and staff.

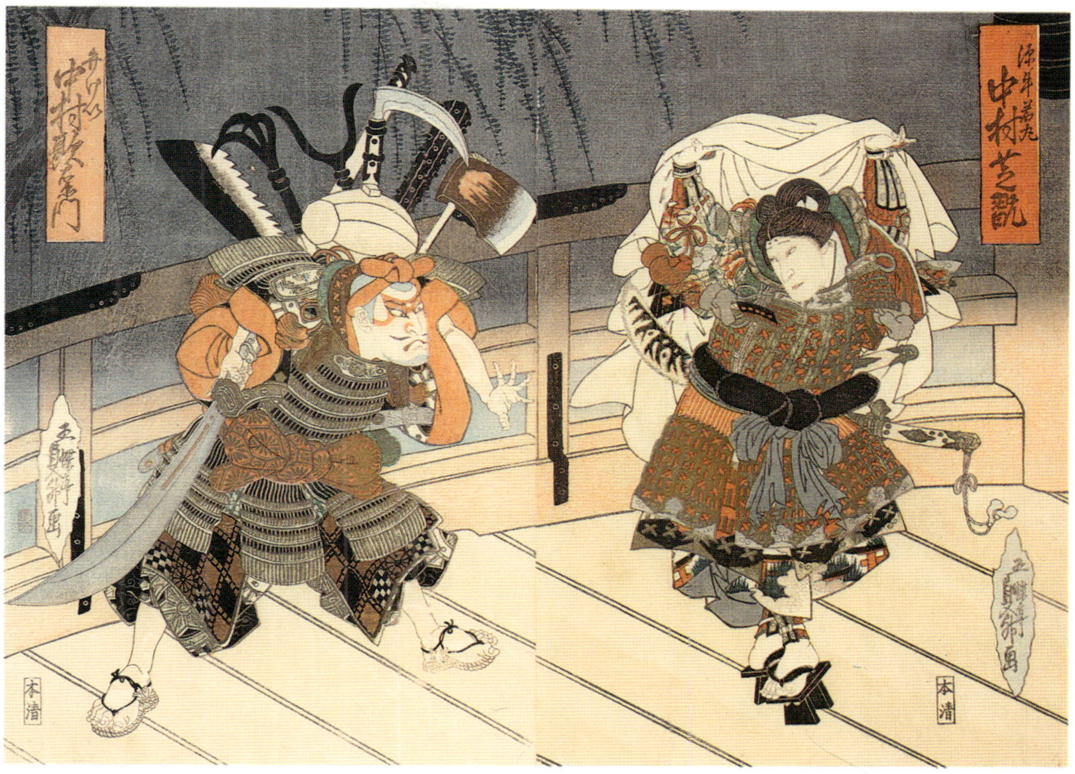

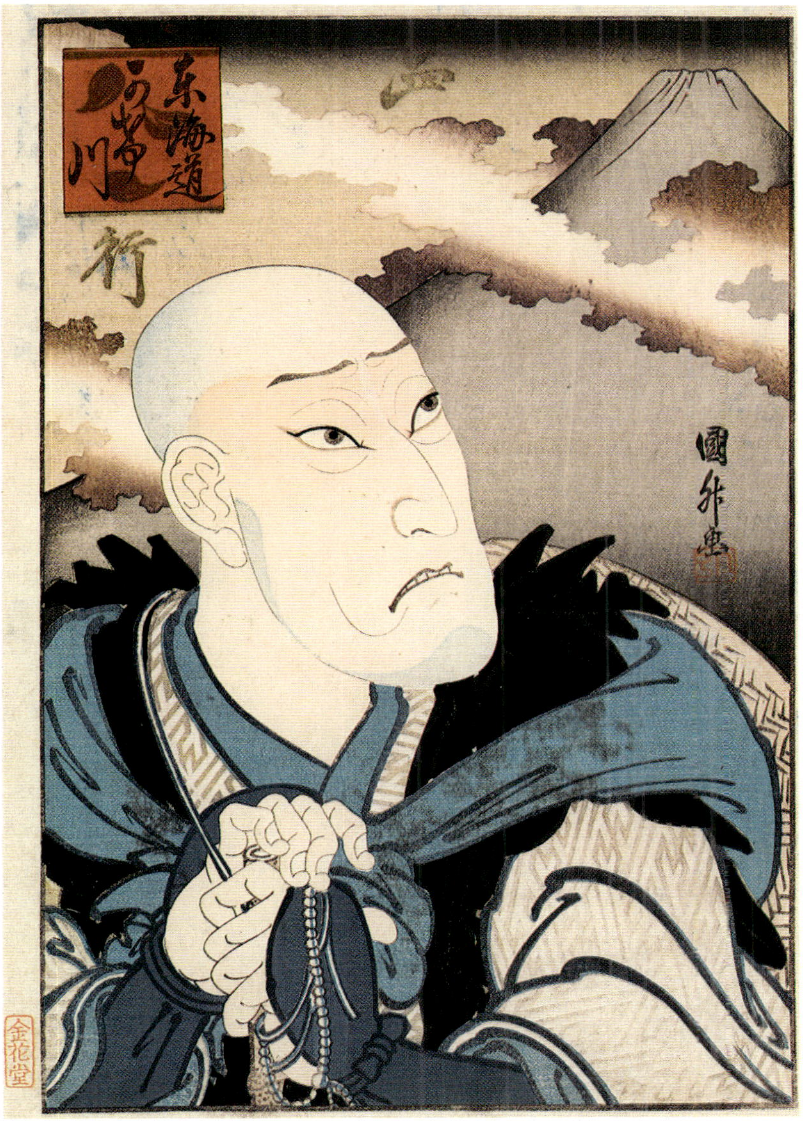

Above left: Shunkōsai Hokushū (*fl.* 1810-32) 'Nakamura Utaemon III as Kyōgoku no Takumi,' 1825, 14½×10 inches (36.8×25.4 cm). Published by Ariharadō.

Left: Shunkōsai Hokuei (*fl.* 1824-37) 'Arashi Rikan II as Sasaki Saburō Moritsuna,' c. 1830. Published by Honsei.

Below left: Shunkōsai Hokuei 'Three Heroes of *Suikoden* Capture Kosanjo Ichijōsei,' c. 1835, teraptych, 14⅝×40½ inches (37.2×109.2 cm). Published by Kinkadō Konishi.

Above right: Gosōtei Hirosada 'Act I of Sugawara,' 1851, *chūban* diptych, 10×14¾ inches (25.4×37.4 cm). Published by Daijin.

Right: Kunimasu 'Actor as the Priest Saigyō Hoshi,' c.1848, *chūban*, 9⅞×7⅛ inches (25.1×18.1 cm). Published by Tenkei.

All the above prints are reproduced courtesy of the Trustees of the Victoria and Albert Museum, London.

6
Woodblock Prints of the Meiji Period

CHARLOTTE VAN RAPPARD-BOON

The Meiji period (1868-1912) was a time of tremendous upheaval in Japanese art and in many apsects constituted an abrupt break with the traditions of the preceding Edo period (1600-1868). Scholars in the past have often argued that the Meiji period signifies the unfortunate downfall of the indigenous arts, with the influence of Western arts delivering a decisive blow to their development. As a result, many books on Japanesea art, including those on woodblock prints, end with the Meiji Restoration of 1868. However recently this situation has been redressed through several exhibitions on Meiji art and artists and today we are able to sympathize much more with the arts of the period which is unique in its fostering of a number of hybrid art forms. This appreciation also extends to the woodblock print.

The deteriorating infrastructure of the Tokugawa shogunate coupled with the mounting pressure of the Western powers to gain entrance to Japan contributed, in 1858, to the end of over 200 years of Japanese seclusion. It was already apparent to members of the Japanese intelligentsia before the country's opening in the 1850s that, if Japan were to compete with the modern industrialised nations and not be colonized like other Asian regions, it was necessary to open the borders and adopt Western science and technology. With the subsequent change that was brought about with the Meiji Restoration in 1868, involving the dissolution of the shogunate and the reinstatement of the emperor, Japan entered a new period which was marked by rapid modernization and industrialization.

As part of this modernization, the government entered into a phase of what they labelled *bummei kaika* (civilization and enlightenment) and the first two decades of the Meiji period witnessed an almost blind assimilation of Western technology and culture. Everything Western was seen as better, more advanced and preferable as Japanese elements. The government, as part of this process, established institutions like the *Kōbu bijutsu gakkō* (Technical Art School) in 1876 which was set up on the campus of the Imperial College of Technology in Tokyo. Foreigners like Antonio Fontanesi were employed to teach painting, sculpture or architecture at the school. Talented men like Fontanesi were engaged at the school not so much for their potential artistic contribution, but for their role as disseminators of Western technology and civilization.

However, the wholesale borrowing of Western culture that came to typify the early decades of the Meiji period was met with resistance in the 1880s particularly by advocates of traditional arts. Ironically, one of the most active spokesmen against the indiscriminate assimilation of Western-style arts was the American Ernest Fenollosa (1853-1908). Fenollosa arrived in Tokyo in 1878 to teach philosophy and economics at Tokyo University. Subsequently he became interested in the traditional arts and, alarmed at the disregard towards them, he established such societies as the *Ryūchikai* in 1879 and the *Kangakai* (Painting Appreciation Society) in 1884. Together, with his follower Okakura Tenshin (1862-1913), Fenollosa encouraged the establishment of the Tokyo Art School in 1887 which promoted traditional as well as neo-traditional (viz, *Nihonga*) arts. The Technical Art School suffered in the wake of this emerging trend and many Western-style artists underwent a difficult period: bitter fighting occurred between these rival factions, with a struggle surfacing between those artists who adhered to the artistic tenets of the past and those who wanted to incorporate 'modern' Western elements in their work. The parallel between this struggle and the social and political upheavals of the period have not always been made sufficiently clear.

While this split is probably the most clearly delineated in Meiji painting, this was not always the case with Meiji-period printmaking. Woodblock printing, for example, which during the Edo period was regularly assimilating and refining new techniques and styles, appears in the nascent years of the Meiji period to cling to past conventions.

For example, one of the most interesting early Meiji prints is a depiction made by Yamamoto Hosui in 1877 of the battle at Kagoshima during the Satsuma rebellion. This print, which is obviously very much influenced by Goya's depcition of the terrors of war, was made on the lithographic stone. If we remember that very little actual fighting between troops had

Right: Toyohara Chikanobu (1838-1912) 'Beauty behind a Folding Screen' from the series 'New Beauties' (*Shin bijin*), 1897. Published by Akiyama Buemon. R O Müller Collection. Meiji prints like this of *bijinga* (pictures of beautiful women) are nostalgic reminders of *ukiyo-e* works by such Edo-period artists as Kitagawa Utamaro (1753-1806).

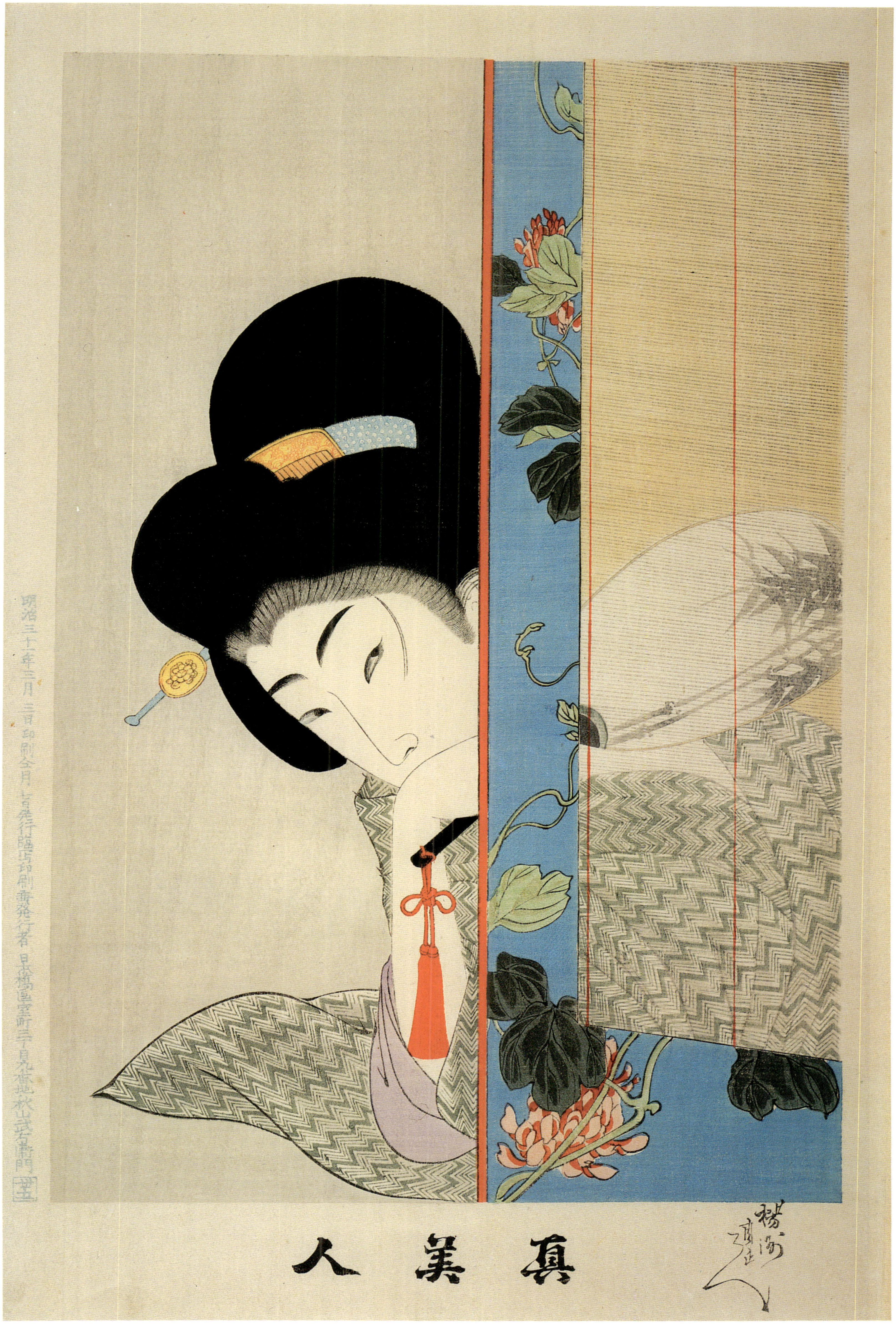
真美人

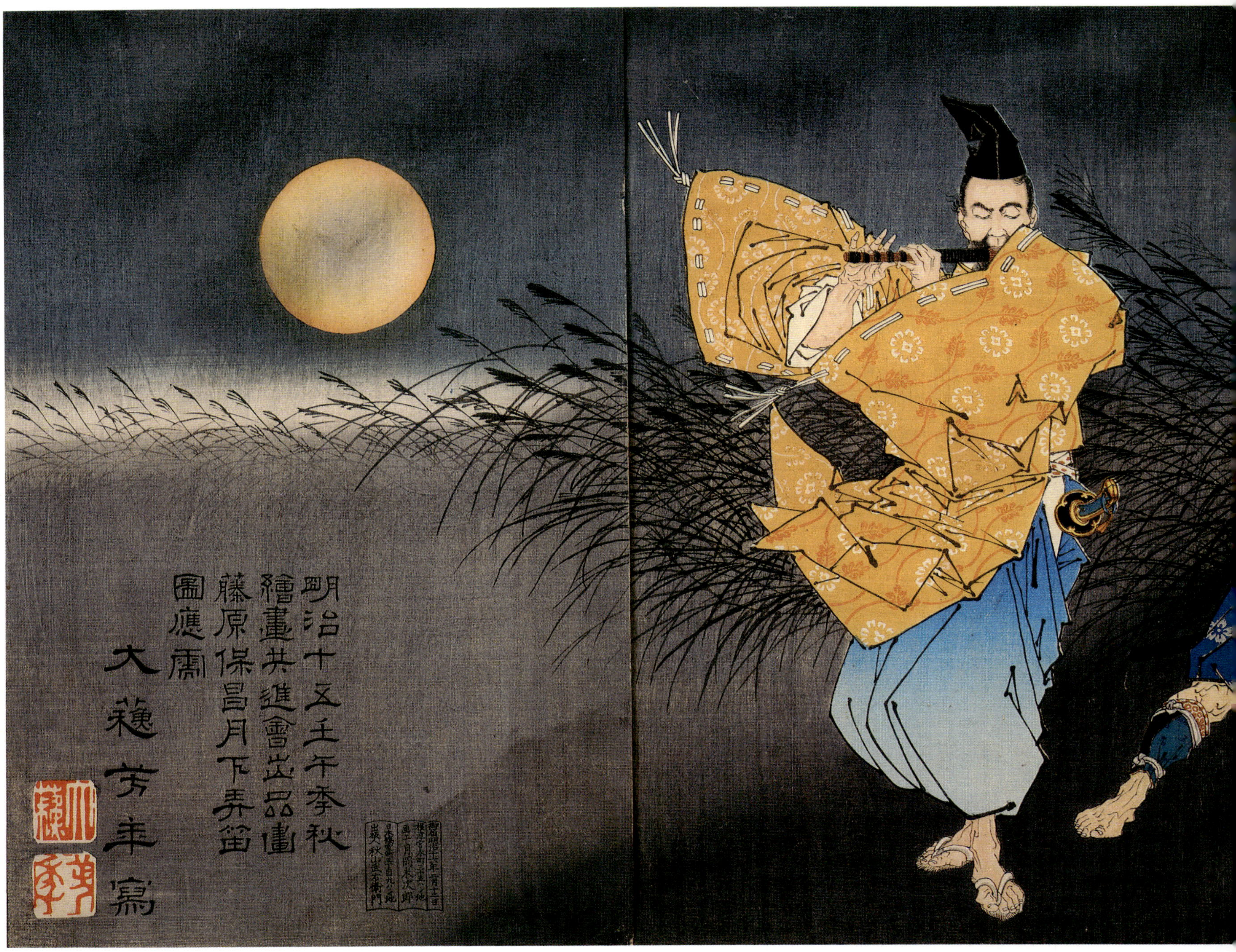

taken place in Japan during the last centuries, this extraordinary print seems to convey more of what actually happened than the prints by Yoshitoshi and his followers of the same event which show the fighters mostly in heroic Kabuki-like stances.

New developments, however, were taking place in engraving and photography. Even when depicting the many interesting new things introduced by Westerners, the Meiji woodblock artist did so in a thoroughly traditional manner. On the other hand, much information about the Meiji period and the many facets of the rapid Westernization of Japan can be gained from these prints. Interest in western life and western objects had already been brought to fruition during the early 1860s, in Yokohama prints, in which the lifestyle of Westerners who sojourned in the treaty ports, was observed in sharp, humorous detail. Paradoxically, artists such as Utagawa Sadahide in his pre-Meiji book *Record of Things Seen and Heard at the Open Port of Yokohama (Yokohama kaikō kembun shi,* 1862-65) strikes a much more modern note than his contemporaries who continued to depict 'Japanese' subjects such as courtesans and beautiful women in commonplace poses. It is not certain that this conservatism in the woodcut print was due to the artists alone. Sadahide was one of the first print artists whose work was exhibited officially outside Japan. Ten of his prints with views of Edo were shown at the International Exposition in Paris in 1867, which demonstrates that he had gained official recognition by this time. He is also one of the first artists in whose work Western stylistic elements are incorporated in a completely convincing manner. His deft use of Western perspective is combined with such typical *ukiyo-e* elements as the abrupt cutting off of the representation by the border of the picture plane, and shading to indicate modelling of the figures is juxtaposed with flat planes. Sadahide's work certainly influenced the later artists of the Utagawa school, who specialized in prints report ing actual events of the Meiji period, but most of these artists lacked his power of expression and depicted the much-changed Meiji world in the manner of their Tokugawa forebears.

In the unstable economic conditions of the Meiji period when many craftsmen were forced to turn to other means of livelihood as they lost their sources of patronage, it might as well have been the publishers who clung to the well-known subjects which had sold well. The demise of many of the well-known artists who could have initiated new fashions and styles to the public must have played a role too. When it eventually became clear that there was still a market for *ukiyo-e* prints, not only the quick, cheap and often rather shoddy broadsheet but also for the more expensive luxury edition, publishers again took up large ambitious series. As a result, artists like Yoshitoshi and Kiyochika were able to develop new styles. Many of the major artists who are included in a discussion of Edo period *ukiyo-e* died not long before the advent of the Meiji period: Utagawa Hiroshige in 1858, Kuniyoshi in 1861 and Kunisada in 1864. They each had a great number of

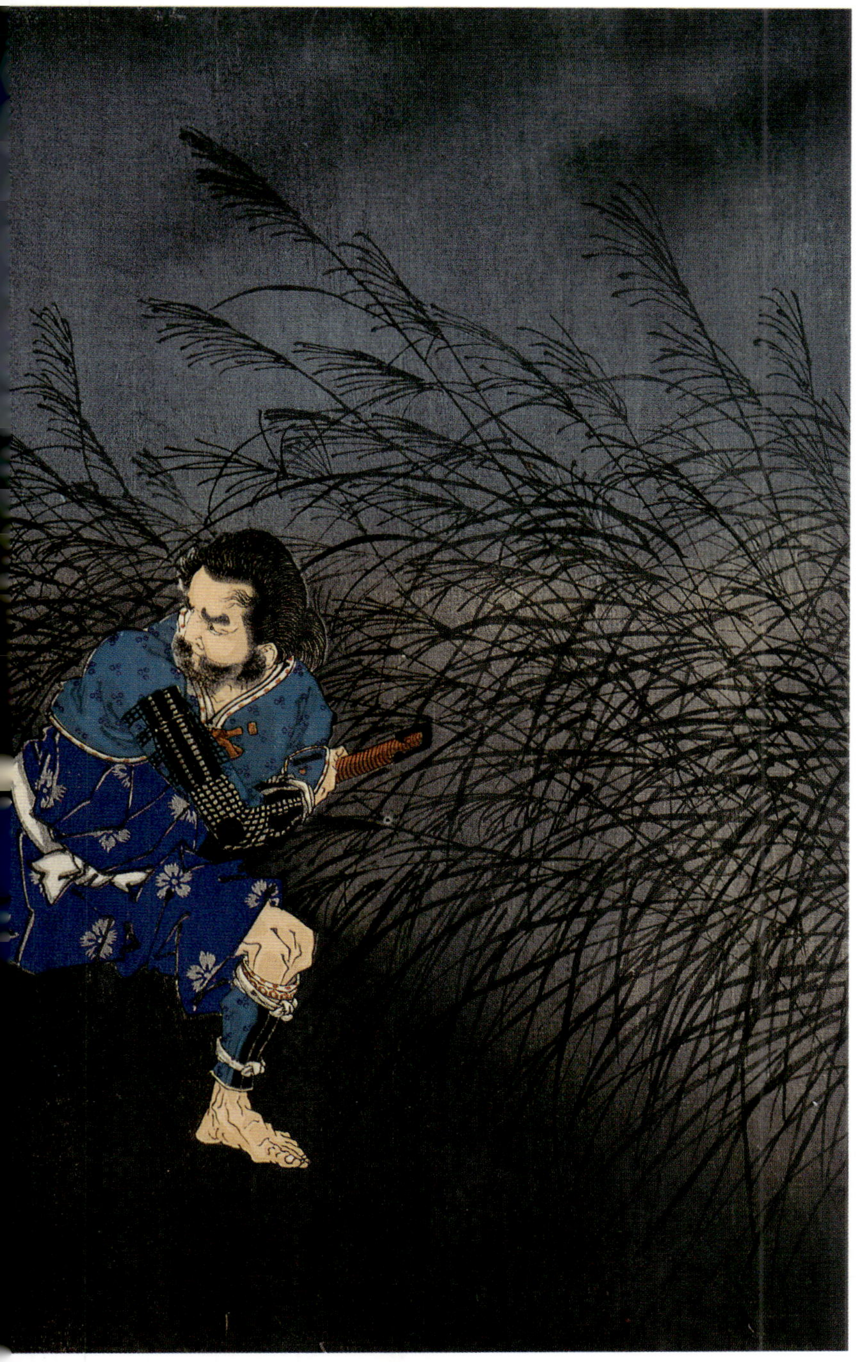

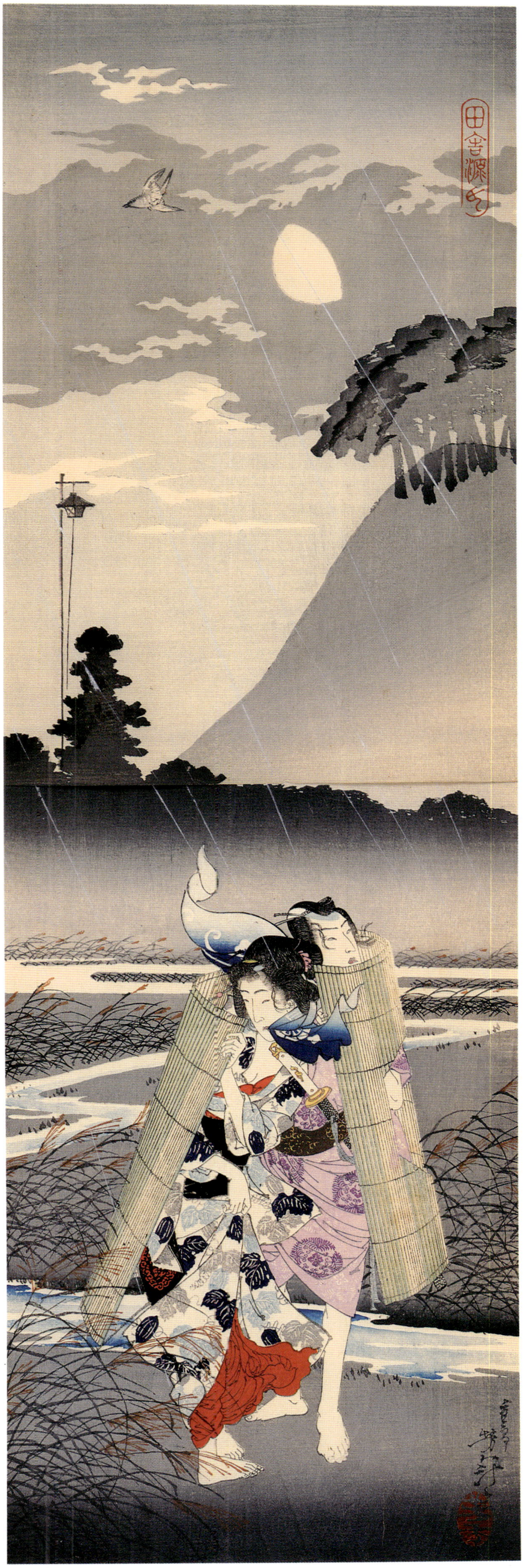

Above: Tsukioka Yoshitoshi (1839-92) 'Yasumasa Playing the Flute by Moonlight' (*Fujiwara no Yasumasa gekka roteki zu*), 1863, *ōban* triptych. Published by Akiyama Buemon. R O Müller Collection.

Right: Tsukioka Yoshitoshi (1839-92) 'Genji in the Countryside' (*Inaka Genji*), 1885. Published by Matsui. R O Müller Collection.

pupils, but only a few followed in a style derived from their masters. Indeed, the only artist who would have a lasting influence in the early Meiji was Kuniyoshi whose pupils Taiso Yoshitoshi (1839-92) and Kawanabe Kyōsai (1831-89) continued his legacy.

TAISO YOSHITOSHI

The most important artists in the early years of the Meiji period was Taiso [Tsukioka] Yoshitoshi. Yoshitoshi, though coming from a samurai background, had a classical *ukiyo-e* grounding. He was educated in the workshop of Utagawa Kuniyoshi, where the main repertoire of the Utagawa school, actor prints and beautiful women had been enlarged to include the portrayal of scenes from the history of Japan and from the life of the classical heroes. This was caused probably as much by contemporary interest in history and legends which would continue well into the Meiji period, as by the more severe censorship laws during the 1850s and 1860s. This iconographical development was not only to exert a profound influence on Kuniyoshi's own pupils, such as Yoshitoshi and Kyōsai, but also on Meiji print artists in general. The great interest in Meiji times in the history of Japan and in the early chronicles such as the *Kojiki* (*Record of Ancient Matters*, c.712) and the *Nihon shoki* (*Chronicles of Japan*, c.720) was frequently reflected in the subject matter of the woodcut print.

Yoshitoshi started with designing series of prints with heroes very much in a style similar to his master. However a penchant for the spectral, the macabre and the downright bloody soon became very evident in his work. Many authors have seen a parallel between Yoshitoshi's subject matter and his own personality in which a strongly depressive and even sadistic side can be discerned. Yet generally, at the end of the nineteenth century there was a fascination with horror stories and the depiction of repulsively detailed murders and slayings. These themes were treated by many more artists than Yoshitoshi. The same 'romantic agony' can be found in the work of many writers of the time, for example in the diaries of Masaoka Shiki or somewhat later, in a famous story such as *Rashōmon* by Akutagawa Ryuūnosuke (1915).

At the same time that Yoshitoshi designed gruesome but intriguing series like '100 Ghost Stories from China and Japan' (*Waka hyaku monogatari*, 1865) and the collaborative work with Utagawa Yoshiiku (1833-1904) 'Twenty-eight Famous Murders with Poems' (*Eimei nijūhasshūku*, 1866), he also designed prints reporting comtemporary events, such as the arrival of the admiral Perry's 'Black Ships' (British Museum, London) and prints depicting the Satsuma rebellion and the suicide of the Satsuma leader, Saigō Kiyomori. In these prints influence of Western art is much more obvious than in Yoshitoshi's better-known later series. Of these early series certainly one of the most interesting depicts the officers of the shōgunal forces in the fighting of 1868. In order to escape the censorship laws the subjects are disguised with the names of well-known heroes of the *Taiheiki* and the *Taikōki*, but depicted in modern dress. This disguise, apparently to avoid the still severe censorship laws, is so elaborate that one must wonder whether contemporaries were able to penetrate it. Nevertheless it is one of the few instances when we see Yoshitoshi greatly influenced by Western art and the incorporation of this together with a convincing realism in the portrayal both of the faces and the anatomy, makes this an unusual endeavor. On the whole Yoshitoshi's artistic outlook is fairly conservative and the renewal he brought about in the art of *ukiyo-e* has more to do with a fresh way of looking at well-known subjects and in the original choice of subjects than with style.

In the late 1860s his production declined and he seems to have entered a period of profound depression. This corresponded to a period during which the demand for woodblock prints waned. With the 1870s, however, the production of woodblock prints was revived not so much due to the re-emergance of traditional publishers, but to a more modern invention, newspapers. Important Tokyo newspapers, such as the *Postal News* (*Yūbin hōchi shimbun*) or the *Tokyo Daily News* (*Tōkyō nichinichi shimbun*) started to publish color supplements. These were printed in the woodcut technique and designed by the most important artists of the day. Yoshitoshi was commissioned to design prints for newspapers. He exceled in these and this, together with his regained health, enabled him to undertake again the effort of larger series. At this time he took the artist name Taiso (Great Resurrection) to indicate his newly found equilibrium. Most of his important work dates to this period with the series like the '100 Views of the Moon' (*Tsuki no hyakushi*, 1885-92), 'New Forms of 36 Ghosts' (*Shinkei sanjūrokkaisen*, 1889-92), 'A New Selection of Brocade Prints from the East' (*Shinsen Azuma nishiki-e*, 1885-9). '100 Views of the Moon' (see introduction) is considered by most scholars to be Yoshitoshi's masterpiece. The range of subject matter is drawn from legend, Kabuki and Nō plays, scenes from daily life and illustrations of classical poetry. It exhibits a diversity of styles with inspiration from 'classical' *ukiyo-e*, Shijō and Nanga and the variety of subject matter is very unusual in the history of the Japanese woodcut. Before Yoshitoshi, only an artist ike Katsushika Hokusai (1760-1849) had been able to muster such a wide variety in style and composition. One well-known print from the 'Moon' series (Rijksmuseum, Amsterdam) is a highly unusual depiction of one of the most touching love stories from *The Tale of Genji* when the protagonist Prince Genji becomes enamored with a beautiful commoner (Yūgao, literally 'Evening glory') after having seen her handwriting on a fan. This is the moment of the story which is illustrated by most *ukiyo-e* artists, but Yoshitoshi has not shown the handsome prince gazing at the fan, but rather, he shows the ghost of the girl who – neglected by Genji after his love has disappeared – has slowly pined away in a distant house. The evening glory, the flower offered on the fan, which had been the cause of the Prince's love, surrounds her and her form is so transparent that even the tendrils of the plant are visible through her robes. This atmosphere of resigned melancholy can often be found in Yoshitoshi's later work and is especially obvious in the Moon series. Even in a well-known story, like that of the Soga brothers, the artist does not show the scene of a heroic attack, that would have created one of the action-filled prints much enjoyed by the Meiji public. Instead, he shows Soga no Tokimune after the brother's revenge, when his brother has already been killed and Tokimune, looking up at a cuckoo flying in front of the moon – a symbol of the transcience of life – realizes that he too, will shortly have to forfeit his own life.

The same unusual method of slightly altering well-known stores is shown in the aforementioned series, 'A New Selection of Brocade Prints from the East,' with horizontal diptychs and in a set of vertical diptychs. The set of vertical diptychs which was begun in the 1880s uses a format which had been rarely used in *ukiyo-e* prints before, though Japanese artists seem always to have enjoyed the challenge of an unusual format. This is apparent in the pillar prints designed in earlier times. A print from this set, 'Genji in the Countryside,' (page 187) (1885), is again based on the Genji story. However, this time the figures – a prostitute and Genji – are disguised in modern dress and illustrated running through a desolate landscape, their only protection being a rough, straw sleeping mat. The other horizontal *ōban* diptych series shows a close connection with the illustrations Yoshitoshi had designed for newspapers some years earlier. Their subject matter of scenes of violence and gruesome murder, is also comparable:

only in this diptych series they do not represent contemporary events but stories from the recent past which had been made into Kabuki plays. A print of a fight between sumo wrestlers and the fire brigade (Rijksmuseum, Amsterdam) is striking for the contrast between the dark background and the sparsely colored subjects. The action is organized along a diagonal with elements like the ladder and the fireman's hook extending outside the border of the print – a device often used by modern cartoonists.

Also in other series such as the '36 Ghosts' there is often a splendid depiction of violent action that often seems to transcend even the borders of the prints themselves. Yoshitoshi took over one of Kuniyoshi's most effective stylistic inventions, such as the portrayal of action from the front as it moves towards the onlooker. This is something completely new in *ukiyo-e* which makes a much more dramatic impact of the print possible. Yoshitoshi stepson, Kōgyo (1869-1927) was to use the same device in depicting Nō plays (right), another new subject in woodblock prints, and another of Yoshitoshi's pupils, Gessan, would use it to great effect in triptychs depicting the Russo-Japanese war.

Other pupils of Kuniyoshi, such as Yoshifuji (1827-87) or Yoshiiku mostly designed work comparable to that of Yoshitoshi, often imitating their successful rival, but one of them expanded this subject range to include animals and flower and bird prints.

KAWANABE KYŌSAI

Kawanabe Kyōsai (1831-89) was slightly older than Yoshitoshi. By the time Yoshitoshi entered Kuniyoshi's workshop in 1850 Kyōsai had long since left and was already associated with the official Kanō painting school. In 1852 he was repudiated on account of his dissolute life in which apparently the love for sake played an important part, as one of his artist's names was Shōjō, after the mythical small red-haired goblins who are known for their drunkenness. Kyōsai did not design many single-sheet prints, but he was a very original and humorous book illustrator. He also developed an interest in the history of art and his book *Kyōsai gadan* (Discussions of Painting by Kyōsai, 1887), not only contains an interesting autobiography but also examples of all the main schools of Japanese painting and illustrations to Western methods of drawing. In book illustration Kyōsai's work seems mostly influenced by the Shijō style, but in his other work the full range of Japanese painting styles can be found. His early series depicting the 48 loyal retainers from the story of *Chūshingura* (1886; Rijksmuseum, Amsterdam) is clearly influenced by the many series Kuniyoshi designed of the same subject. He used a similar style of portraying action which is seen from the front as described above, coupled with, on occasion, extreme fore-shortening. This last element was also introduced by Kuniyoshi who probably took it from Western examples. On the other hand, a print showing two crows on the trunk of a flowering plum tree reminds us of Kyōsai's training in the Kanō school (c. 1870; Rijksmuseum, Amsterdam). The print imitates a *sumi-e kakemono* done in broad brushstrokes and with a single color accent in the red seals of the artist. The seals refer to the birds and read: 'flying over every country'; and to the artist, read 'like a void.' These prints of birds were for a long time the only prints from

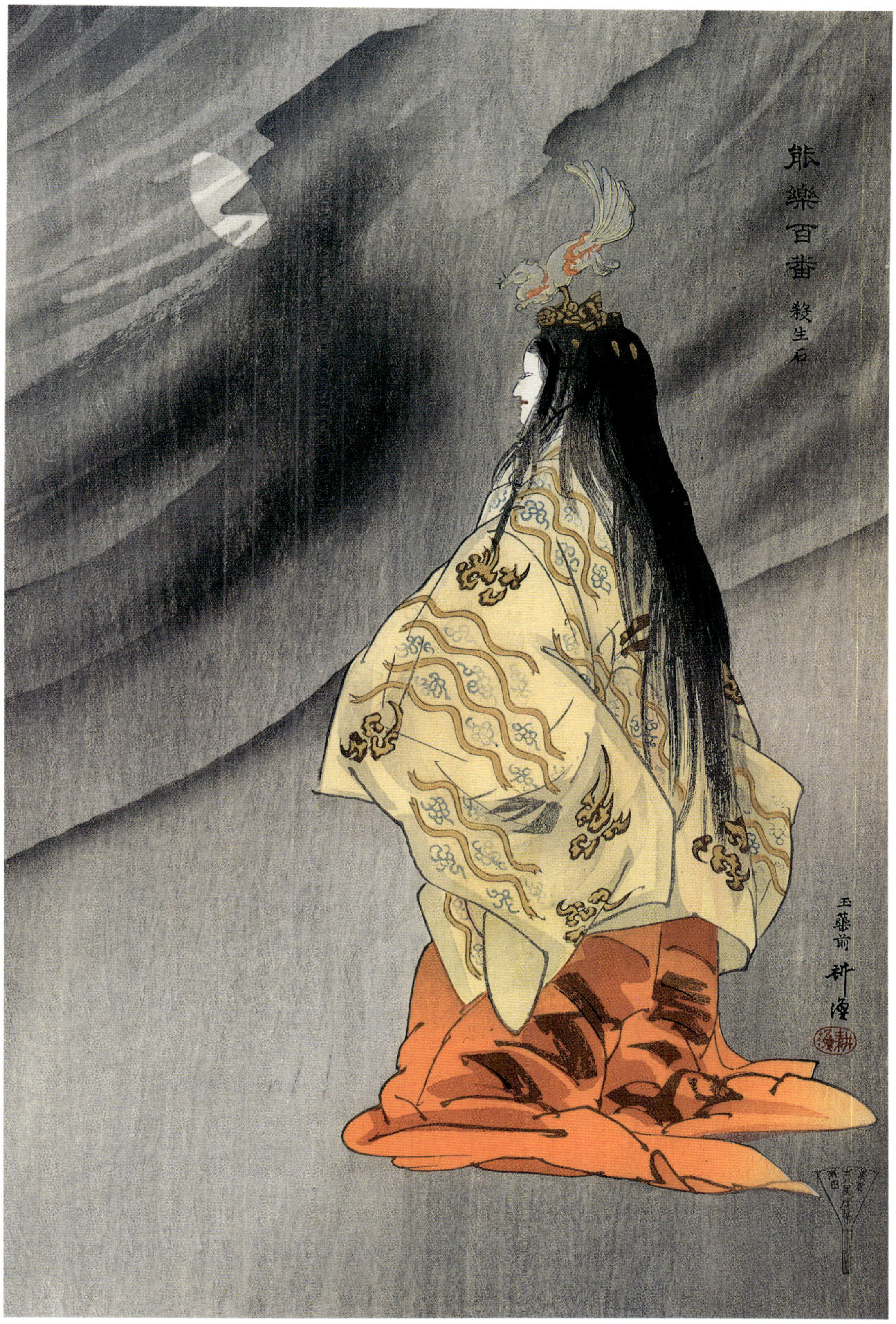

Above: Tsukioka Kōgyo (1869-1927) 'An Actor in the Nō Play Death Rock (*Sesshōseki*)' from the series 100 Nō Plays' (*Nōgaku hyakuban*), c. 1900. Published by Daikikuya, R O Müller Collection.

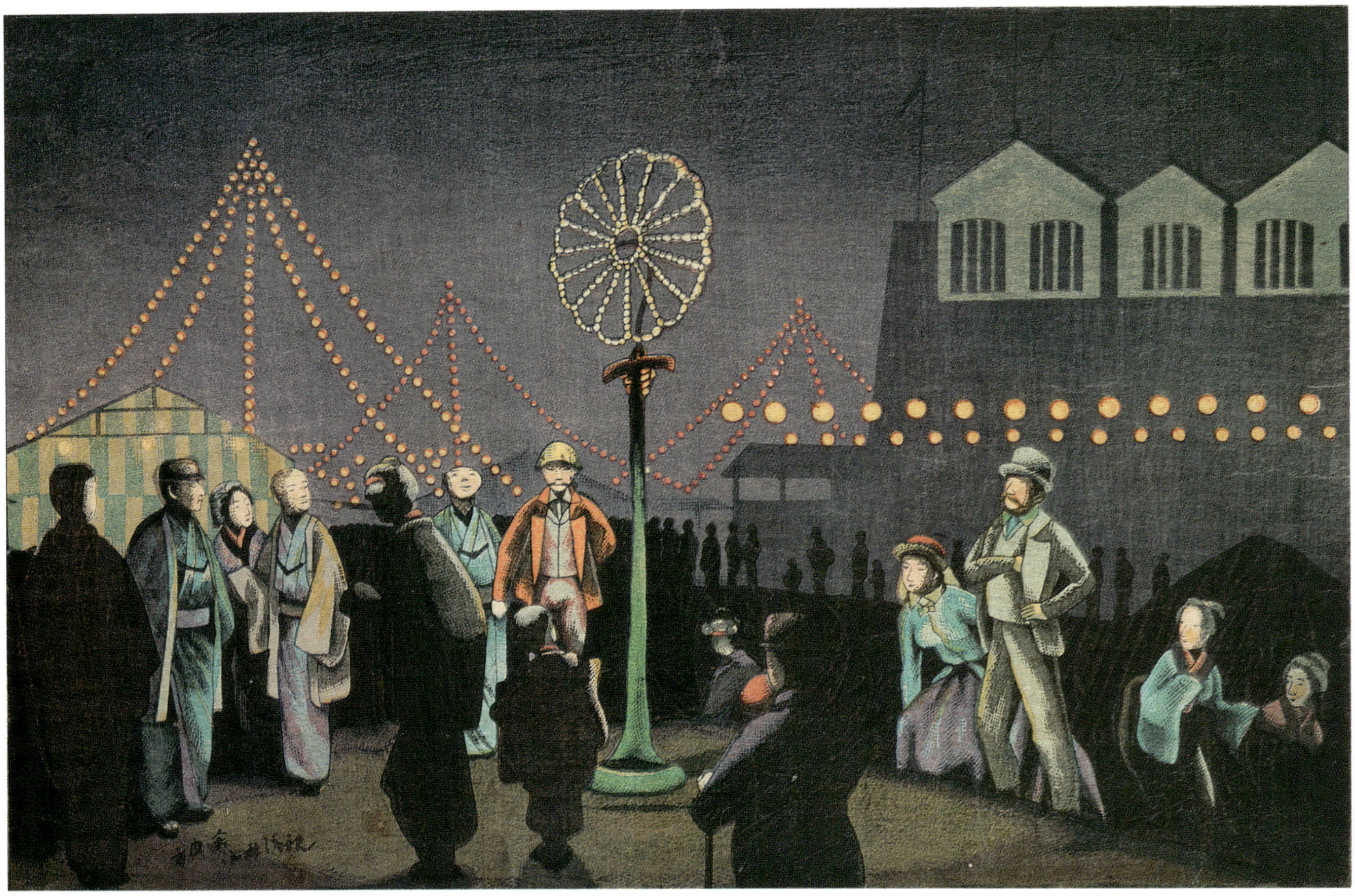

Above: Kobayashi Kiyochika (1847-1915) 'Gaslight Illumination at the First Domestic Industrial Exhibition,' 1877. Published by Heikichi Matsuki. Courtesy Abe Publishing Co Ltd, Gallery Kabutoya, Pallas Inc.

the Meiji times that were acceptable to most writers on *ukiyo-e* and we find them thus at the end of many books on the subject, as, for example, in the famous series by Vignier and Inada.

ACTOR AND OTHER TRIPTYCHS

If both Yoshitoshi and Kyōsai followed in part of the example of their teacher Kuniyoshi in depicting heroical subjects, the original tradition of the Utagawa school, i.e., the actor print, was not lost in the Meiji time either. After some initial difficulties the Kabuki theater saw a great revival during the Meiji period, both in the classic drama and in more modern plays. One of the instigators of this revival was the great actor Ichikawa Danjūrō IX (1839-1903) and it is therefore not surprising that more than three-quarters of Meiji actor prints depict this popular actor. An artist like Toyohara Kunichika (1835-1900) had been trained under Utagawa Kunisada and thus directly continued the tradition of Toyokuni. We see this clearly in his many series in the *ōban* format with 'large-head' actor portraits, though Kunichika's prediliction for the more intense colors of aniline dyes recently made available from the West, makes his prints something of an acquired taste. His flamboyant compositions however, become even more pronounced in what must be considered to be one of the most important inventions in Meiji printmaking: the Triptychs with a half-length figure of an actor in close-up. There is something inherently contradictory in such triptychs which becomes readily apparent when we compare two Kunichika triptychs. In one of geisha viewing the fireworks at Ryōhoku Bridge on a summer night (Rijksmuseum, Amsterdam), though the composition is certainly made to be enjoyed on all three sheets, we might still take out one sheet and have a most satisfying picture. As this had been the case with all triptychs from Kiyonaga onwards, quite often when looking at a single sheet we do not realize that it once formed part of a greater whole. With a triptych like the one depicting the actor Ichikawa Danjūrō as Sandanji I as Akiyama Kiimori Amid Flames' from the series 'New Plays from the Meiji Theater' (*Meijiz Shinkyōgen*, 1894), this would not have been possible. In this case, a separate sheet of the triptych makes no sense at all, as we have to see all three sheets together. Ichikawa Danjūrō was also the subject of three famous triptychs by Yoshitoshi in which the actor is portrayed in the same manner in half-length figure. One of these show Danjūrō as the depraved monk Seigen, who in defiance of his monastic vows falls in love with a princess and, stricken by madness, pines away. Like the

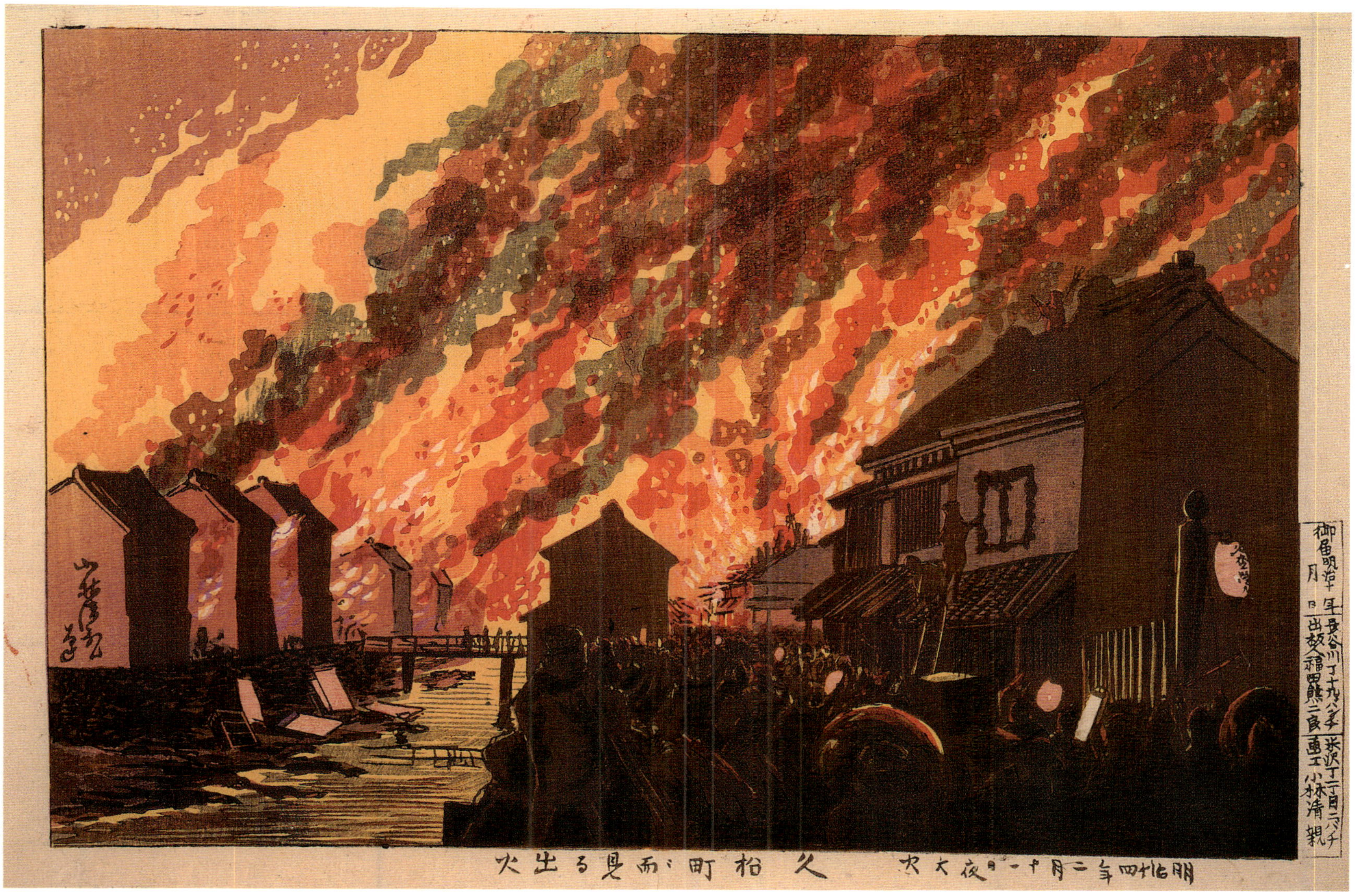

Above: Kobayashi Kiyochika (1847-1915) 'The Outbreak of the Fire as Seen from the Hisamatsu Quarter,' (*Hisamatsushō yori miu shukka*), 1881, Published by Fukuda Kumajirō. R O Müller Collection.

Kunichika triptych the figure spreads over the three sheets in a kind of horrifying close-up.

One could easily describe the history of Meiji prints by showing only triptychs. All Meiji artists designed them and some of their best and most original work is found in them. Publishers in general seem to have lavished great care on their production and it is astonishing how they were able in the case of actor or war triptychs to produce these prints which often needed more than ten color blocks for printing, within a few days of an actual event or performance. The heyday of the triptych was during the Sino-Japanese War 1894-5 when more than 300 triptychs were designed by all the major artists of that period. Both the writers Lafcadio Hearn (1850-1904) and Tanizaki Jun'ichirō (1886-1965) have described the excitement of the public whenever new war triptychs were published and we cannot doubt that during the Sino-Japanese war, these prints had the same actuality that actor prints had possessed during the Edo period.

Interest in these prints stems from a fairly recent date and it is mainly due to two excellent essays by Donald Keene and a book by N Chaikin on the subject that we have begun to appreciate these triptychs as works of art. This was the last great flowering of the *nishiki-e* as popular prints. Contemporary writers noted that shortly after the Sino-Japanese war production fell off sharply. The fickle Tokyo public finally transferred its preference to more modern media, like photography or lithography. Publishers who tried to survive turned to another public at first mainly consisting of connoisseurs at home, later of the foreign market.

KOBAYASHI KIYOCHIKA

As had been said above, the role of the publisher in the revival of Meiji printmaking was of great importance. It is clear that they often tried to imitate series which had popular success. Thus one of Yoshitoshi's last series '32 Aspects of Women' (*Fūzoko Sanjūnisō*, 1888), inspired by Utamaro's series on the same subject, was followed shortly by comparable series by other artists.

In one case it was probably the publisher who was the primordial cause of an artist, in this case Kiyochika, the artist who nowadays seems to epitomize Meiji printmaking, to design prints at all. In Kiyochika we encounter for the first time an artist who was not educated in an *ukiyo-e* workshop. Kobayashi Kiyochika was born into a samurai family in Tokyo who had been minor shogunal retainers. His early interest in art was later overshadowed by the need to provide for his family during the vicissitudes of the Meiji

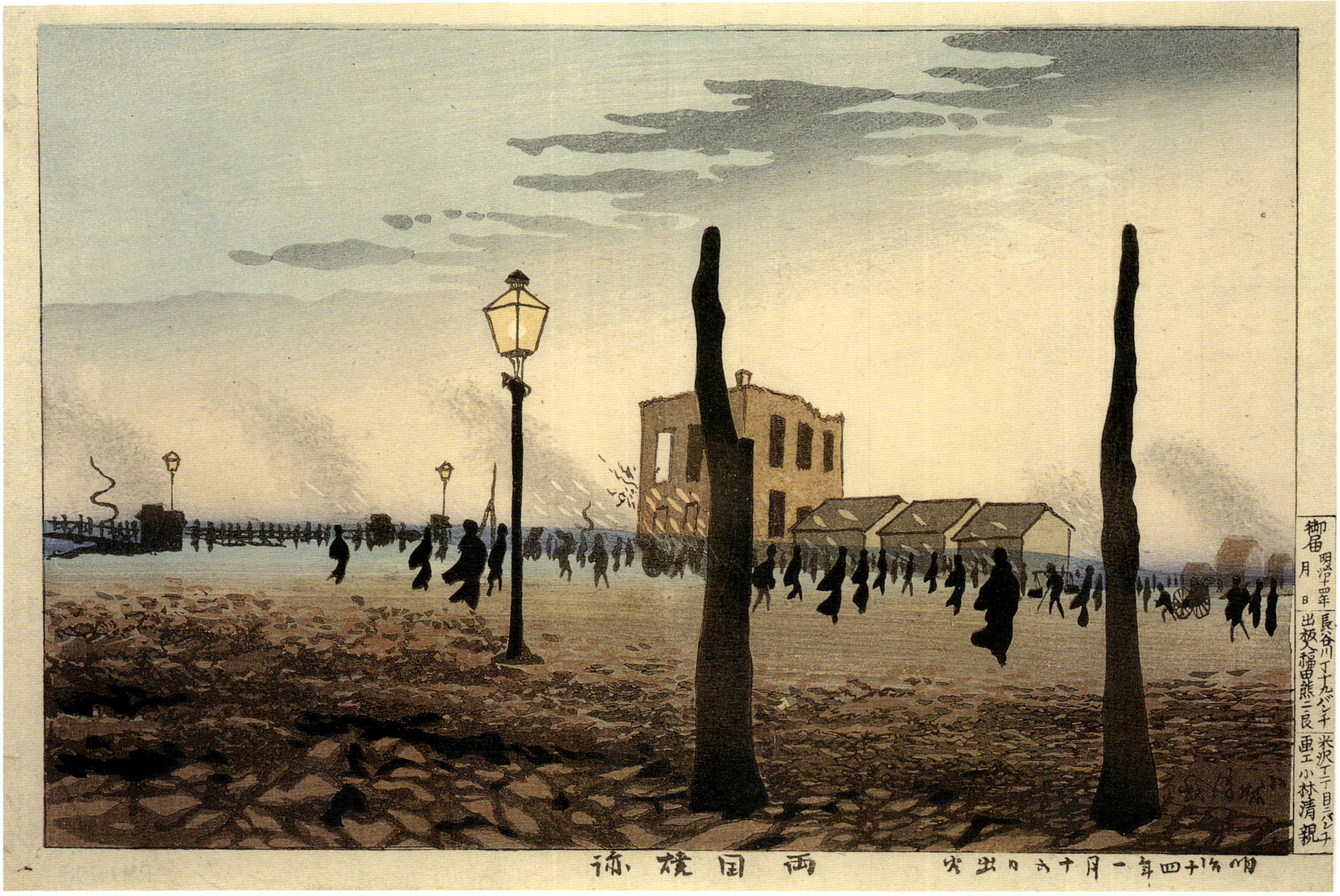

Above: Kobayashi Kiyochika (1847-1915) 'Ryōgoku After the Fire' (*Ryōgoku no yakekato*), 1881, Published by Fukuda Kumajirō. R O Müller Collection.

Restoration. The family fled to the far provinces with the last shogun. Kiyochika seems to have led a wandering, uncertain life, even showing off his swordsmanship with a group of itinerant performers. He only took up art again after he returned to Tokyo in 1874. Although some scholars have attempted to associate Kiyochika with various teachers, he is now considered to have been mostly self-taught. His humorously drawn autobiography illustrates a scene from his early years with him walking away from his first drawing teacher because the latter's drawing of plum blossom was not naturalistic enough.

We do not know why in 1876 the publisher Matsuki Heikichi issued prints by what must then have been a completely unknown artist. Moreover, these woodcuts, which look sometimes more like engravings, lithographs or photographs, did not belong to one of the current fashionable genres. Even so they must have pleased the fickle Tokyo public who were able to see examples like the 'Cat and Lantern' in the first Domestic Industrial Exposition, in 1877 (page 190). During the following years Kiyochika continued to publish with Matsuki and then later, in 1879, with Fukuda Kumajirō, a series of nearly a hundred prints with views in and around Tokyo. This set is one of the highlights of Meiji printmaking. It took up a theme perfected by Hiroshige in which well-known scenes around the capital were shown during different times of the day and different seasons. Kiyochika clearly had a prediliction for night scenes and snow scenes and it is in these that his novel technique is manifest. Whereas Yoshitoshi still adhered to the existing tenets of the *ukiyo-e* print, such as black outline and often unmodulated color planes, Kiyochika used a technique which seems to reflect the watercolor sketches which formed the basis for his prints. The woodcut imitates thin overlapping washes and sometimes even the scribblings and hatchings of a pencil. Even a certain gaucheness in the depiction of the figures seems to contribute towards the atmospheric mood of the prints. 'Ryōgoku after the Fire' (above) shows a desolate scene after a big conflagration which broke out in Kanda in 1881. The sketch from which it was made has survived and if we compare the two, we can see how Kiyochika changed the rather tranquil sketch into a print where the figures, whipped by the wind, wander through the desolate quarter.

The modern feeling of this set does not prepare us for Kiyochika's next landscape series: '100 Views of Musashi' (*Musashi hyakkei no uchi*) of 1884. Here Kiyochika emulates not only Hiroshige's subject

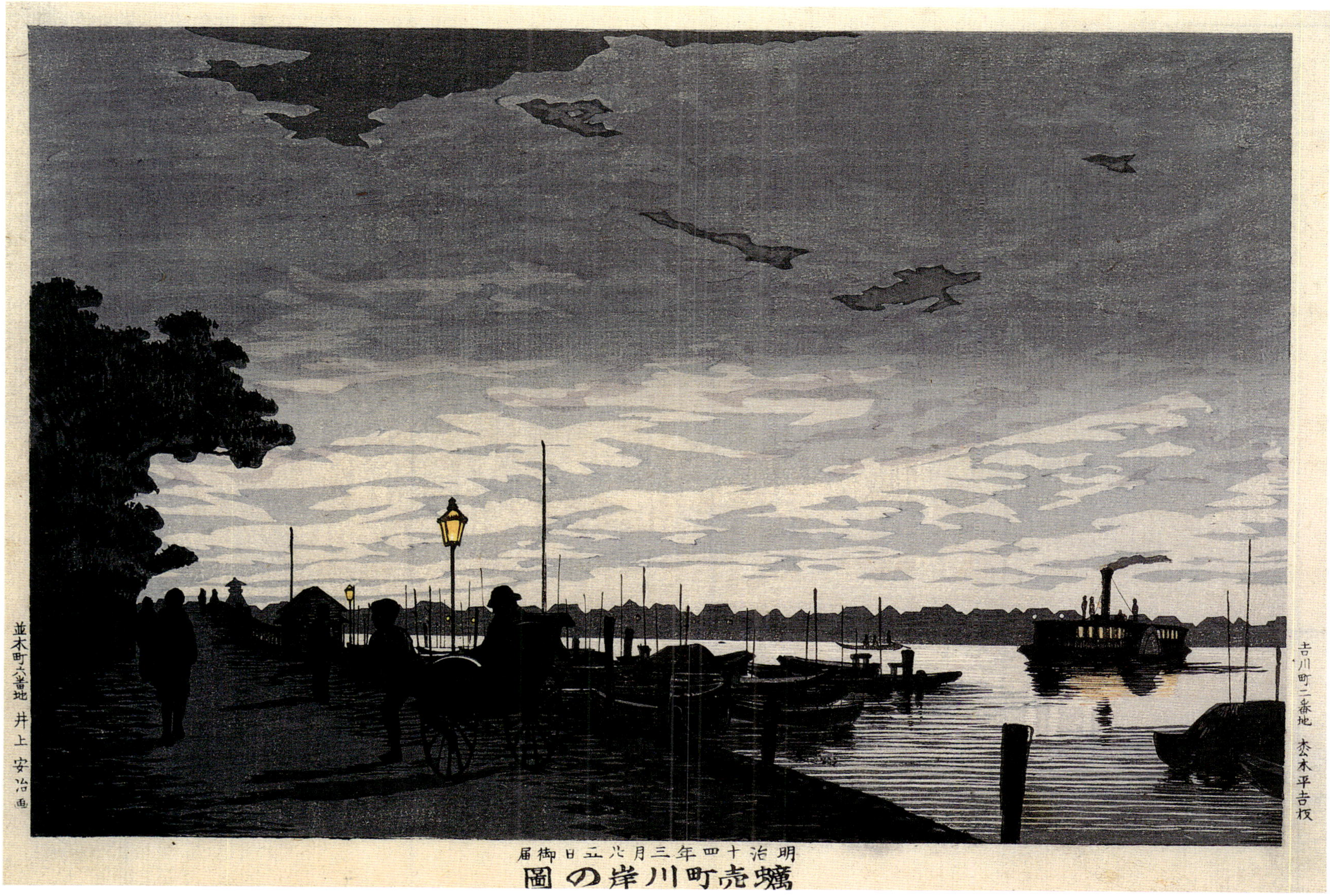

Above: Inoue Yasuji (1864-89) 'View of a Riverbank at the Kakigara Quarter' (*Kakigatachō kawakishi no zu*), 1881. Published by Matsuki Heikichi. R O Müller Collection.

matter, but also his style, by returning to a black outline and adopting such typical Hiroshige stylistic devices as the close-up figure used as a repoussoir, cut off by the picture border. Again I think that this change in Kiyochika's style reflects not only a change in his own artistic outlook, but also in popular taste too. The general return to the past in the works of a conservative artist like Yoshitoshi is less obvious than in those of an innovative one like Kiyochika. Over the years Kiyochika would return more and more to a classical style and would often depict scenes from the glorious past. The poet Taira no Tadanori (1144-84) writing his last poem on the eve of the battle at Dan-no-ura, in which he is to be killed, is one such subject (Rijksmuseum, Amsterdam). The print reflects the loneliness of the warrior who has lost his companions and has to spend a solitary night:

When twilight comes
under the shade of this tree
I take up my dwelling
this night, only a flower
will be my host.

This print belongs to a very rare series depicting some of the great classical poets. The rarity indicates that it was either meant as a small luxury edition or had no great public success. It is not influenced by Utagawa Hiroshige, as is most of Kiyochika's later work, but by the work of Hokusai, when he, like Kiyochika, late in his life turned away from landscapes and designed illustrations to classical poetry in his series 'A Mirror of Japanese and Chinese Poetry' (*Shika sashinkyō*, 1832-3) and '100 Poems Explained by the Nurse' (*Hyakunin uba ga etoki*, c. 1838).

When Kiyochika designed this print in the fifth month of 1884 the glorious wars were not all in the past. There was an actual war with China going on in Korea. The fighting there caused a great outpouring of nationalistic fervor at home which was reflected in literature and in thousands of prints. Each heroic feat, immediately after it was reported in Japan, was portrayed by the artists and published within a few days. In these prints, there is a strain not only of extreme jingoism, but also of more or less overt racism. For many years they had been nearly completely forgotten due to Japanese and foreign aversion against the martial side of the Japanese character. Recently they have been the subject of various publications and we are thus able to see that some represent excellent works of art.

Kiyochika especially excelled in triptychs which depicted not only the heroic side of war, but also, as in the triptych

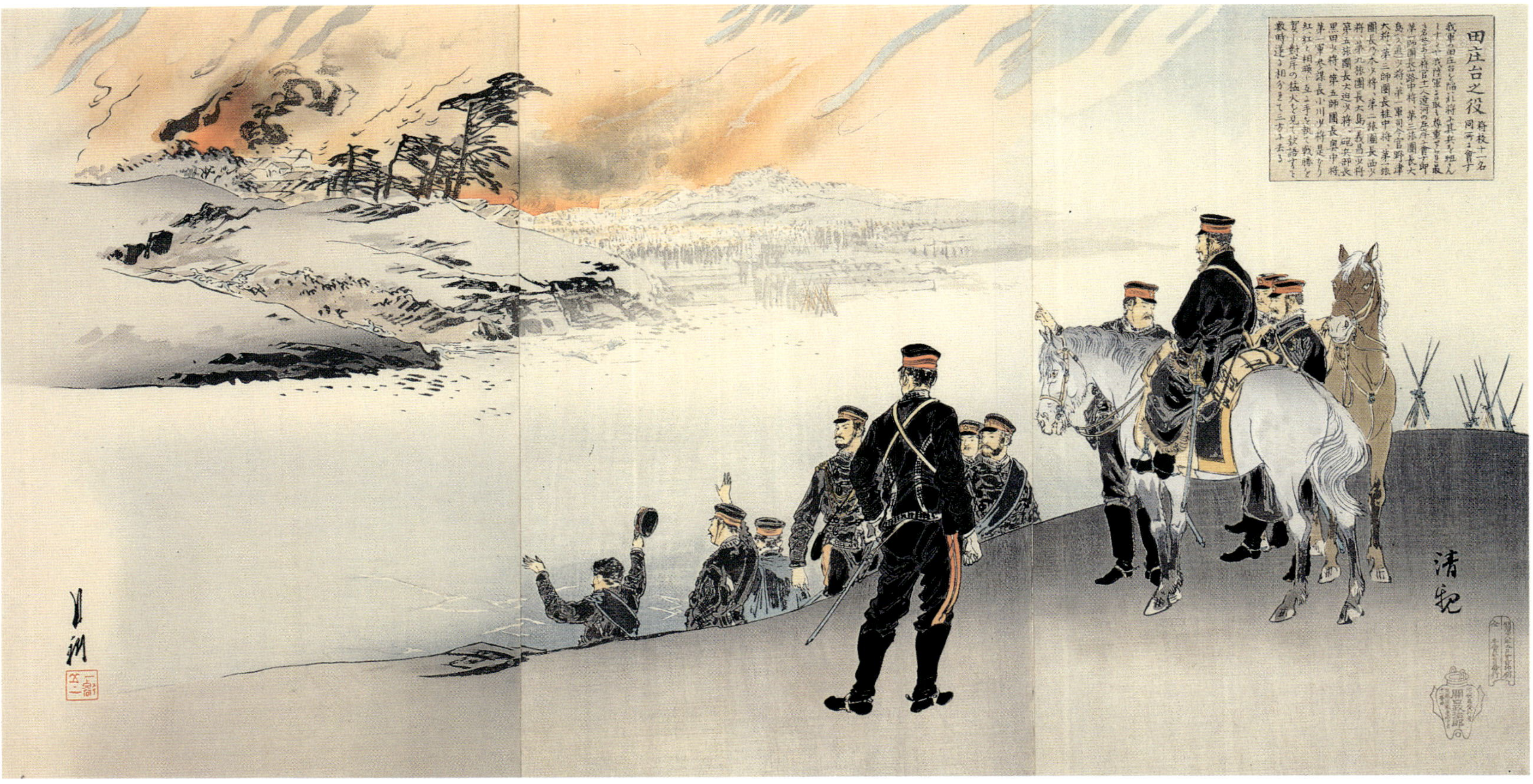
田庄台之役
清親

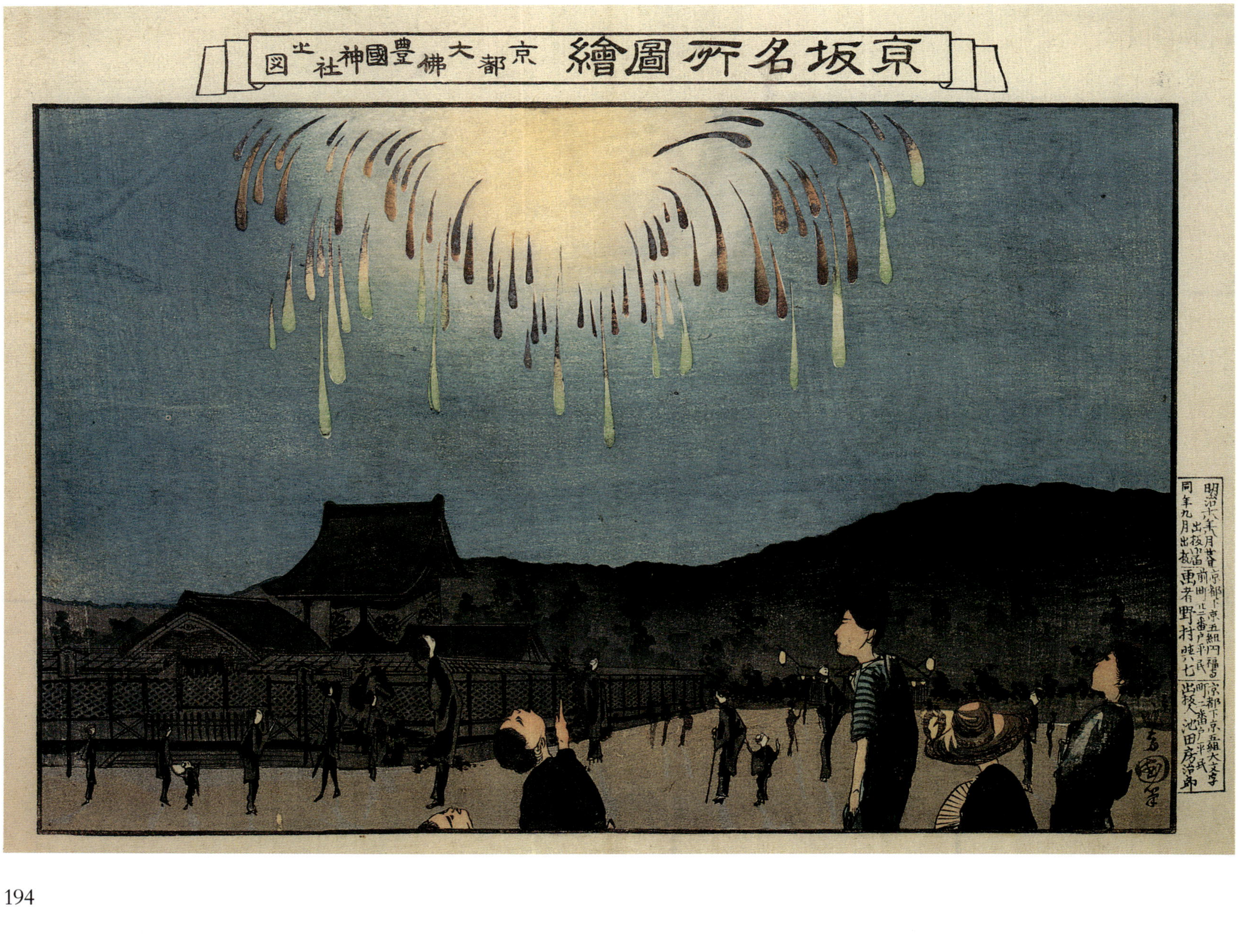
京坂名所圖繪
京都大佛豊國神社之図

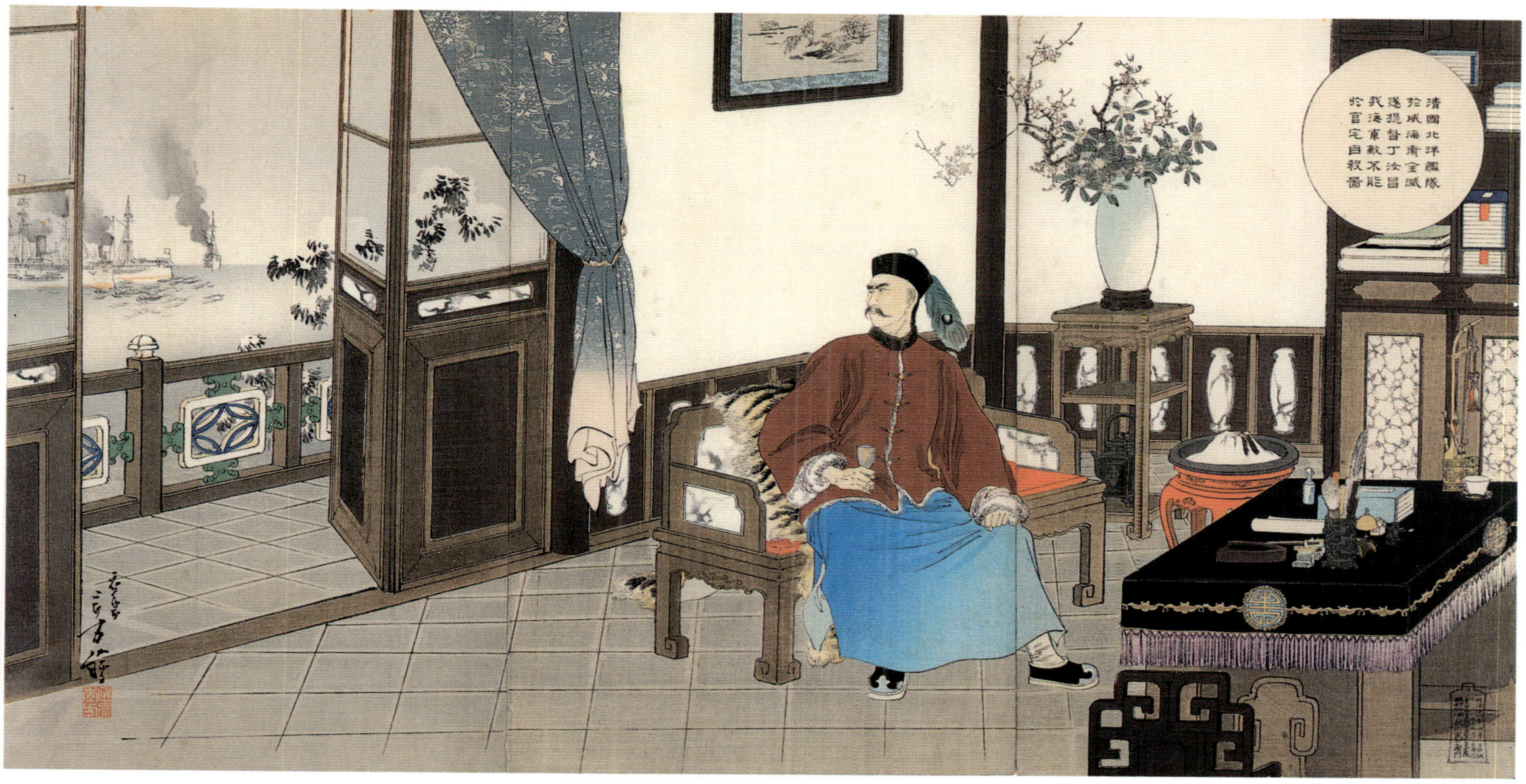

Above left: Ogata Gekkō (1859-1920) and Kobayashi Kiyochika (1847-1915) 'Battle at Denshodai,' triptych. R O Müller Collection.

Above: Mizuno Toshikata (1866-1908) 'Ting Ju-ch'ang Commits Suicide after the Defeat of his Peiyang Fleet,' triptych, 14½×12½ inches (36.8×31.8 cm). Philadelphia Museum of Art, Given by Mr Peter Benoliel (Funds Contributed).

Left: Inoue Yasuji (1864-89) 'Fireworks.' R O Müller Collection.

described above, in the loneliness of standing at watch at night in a foreign country, in the coldness of lying in a trench in the winter and in the horror of a death by drowning at sea.

A rare war triptych by Kiyochika shows the Battle at Denshodai (above). In this he collaborated with the artist Ogata Gekkō whose work is discussed below.

Kiyochika had few pupils and his style had little influence until long after his death, when in the 1920s artists such as Kawase Hasui (1883-1957) would take up his early lyrical manner of depicting the Japanese landscape. His most gifted pupil, Inoue Yasuji (1864-89; see left), who died very young, is best known for the copies he made after his master's work, especially the series with views in and around Tokyo. A print with the ferryboat in Kakigarachō was made after a Kiyochika print published in 1881. Prints such as 'Fireworks' (left) reveal that as an independent artist he showed great promise.

Another print from the Sino-Japanese War depicted here is also unusual in this genre, because it depicts the enemy with sympathy. By the artist Mizuno Toshikata (1866-1908), it portrays the admiral Ting Ju-ch'ang who committed suicide at the end of the war when his navy had lost a dicisive naval battle with the Japanese on 20 February 1895 (above). The Japanese who often wrote derisively about the cowardice of the Chinese soldier admired Tin Ju-ch'ang especially because of his suicide, and this is revealed in the dignified composition by Toshikata. Toshikata had been a pupil of Yoshitoshi and had succeeded his teacher as illustrator to one of the Tokyo newspapers, the *Yamato shimbun*. His prints, however, cover a much greater range than those of his master as he also created prints of beautiful women and actors' portraits. Toshikata's women are much sweeter than those of Yoshitoshi, who often seem to have a rather shrewish character. The influence of Western art was especially flattering in prints with beautiful women as the use of shading and modeling and the interest in correct anatomy, revived a genre which had become extremely repetitious during the nineteenth century. These 'modern' women seem much more lively and more interesting persons than the courtesans depicted by earlier masters. Some typical Meiji subjects, like the reportage prints or the historical prints were to die out almost completely at the turn of the century and certainly would not survive into the Taishō era (1912-26). But the prints with beautiful women would experience a great revival in the twentieth century, both with the artists working in *shin hanga* (new prints).

Between 1900 and 1910 Toshikata's most gifted pupil Kaburagi Kiyokata (1878-1972) designed the most beautiful work in this genre, both as illustrations to contemporary novels and to the literary journal *Bungei kurabu* (The Literary Club). Though Kiyokata's women are most often still clothed in traditional Japanese dress, there is no mistaking them for anything other than twentieth-century women (page 196). Their expressions whether sentimental, wistful or serious, such as the violin player from the *Bungei kurabu* (page 196) show a greater range than had been usual in *ukiyo-e*

Right: Kaburagi Kiyokata (1878-1972) 'Girl Looking at an Insect on a Lamp,' 1900s. R O Müller Collection.

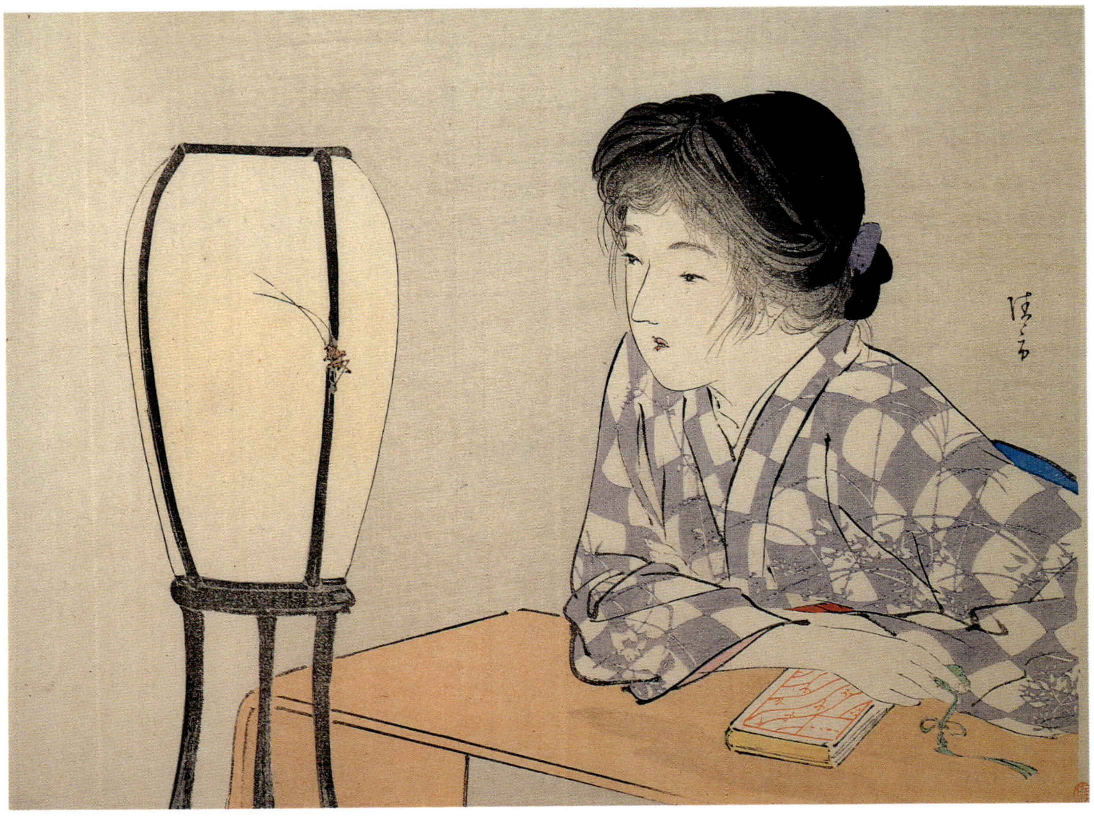

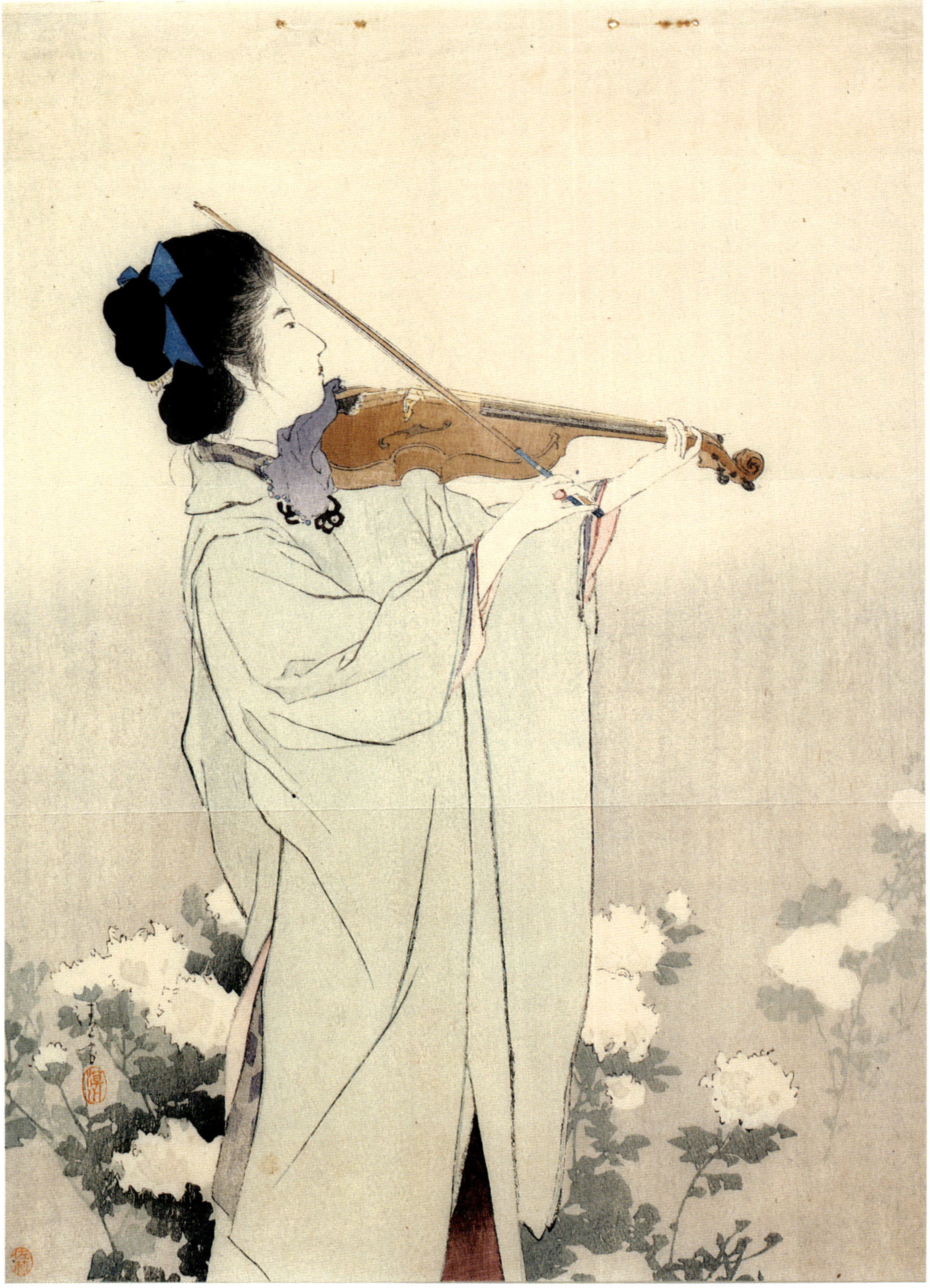

Left: Kaburagi Kiyokata (1878-1972) 'Morning Dew' from *Bungei karabu* (The Literary Club), 1903. $12\frac{1}{16} \times 8\frac{3}{4}$ inches (30.3×22.2 cm). The Metropolitan Museum of Art, New York, Gift of Lincoln Kirstein, 1959.

Right: Kaburagi Kiyokata (1878-1972) 'The Third Month,' 1900s. R O Müller Collection.

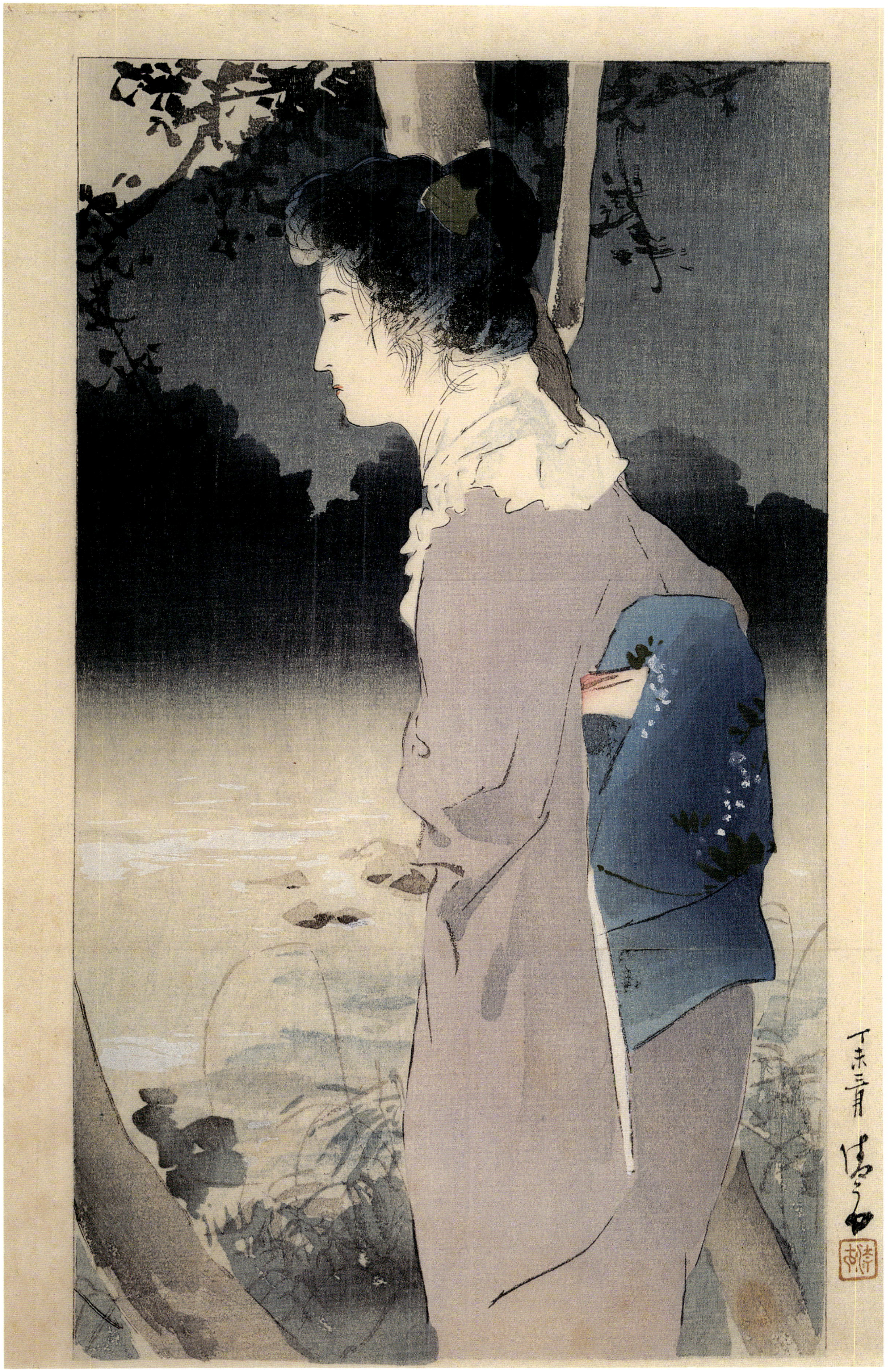

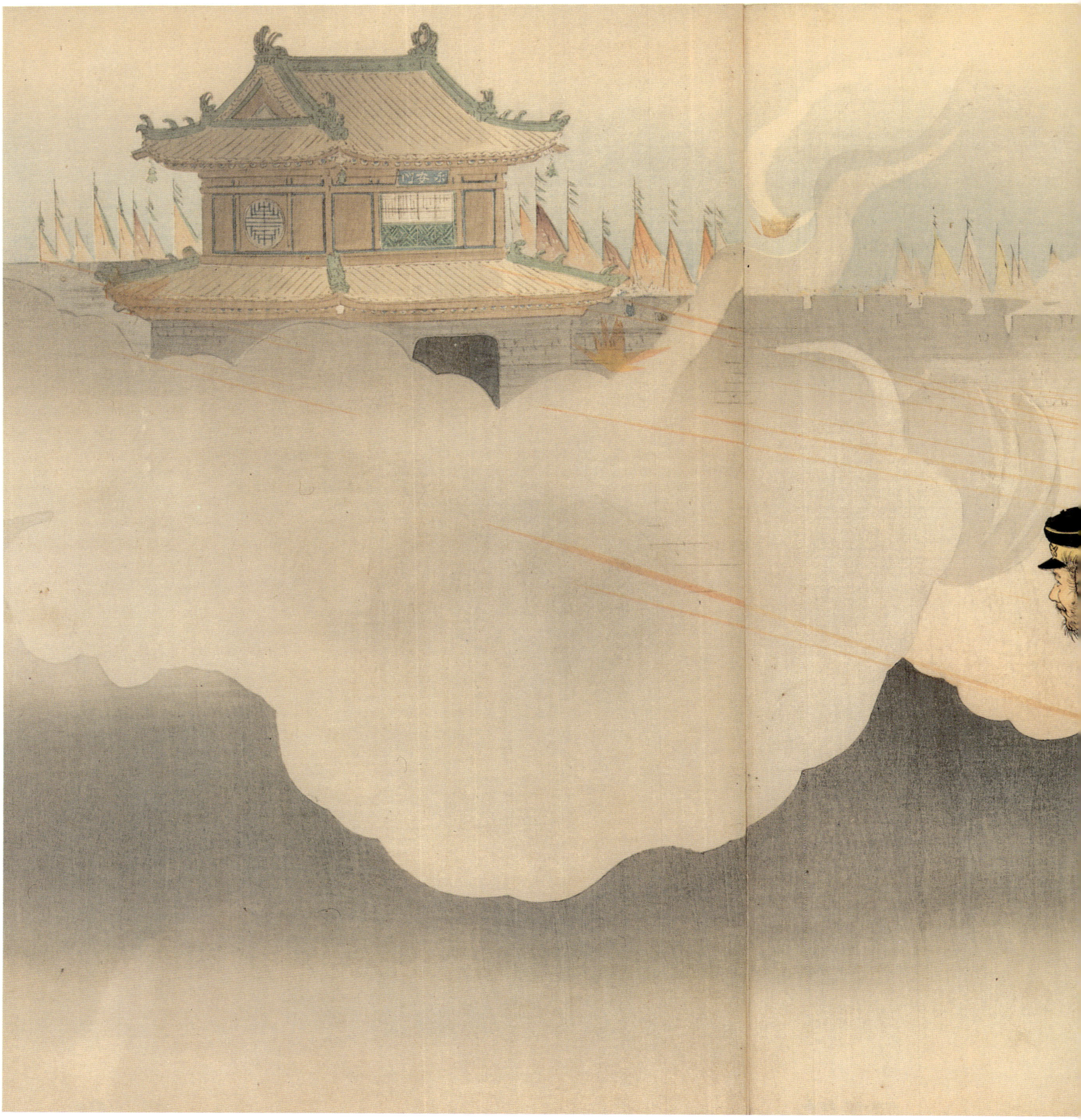

Above left: Ogata Gekkō (1859-1920) 'During the Attack on Chinchou, Onoguchi Tokuji Blasts the Gate of the Enemy Fort,' (*Dai nigun kinshūjō kōgeki kōhei jōhōtei sotso Onoguchi Tokuji shi banshi o kashite bakuyaku o sōchi shi jōmon o Hakai suru zu*), 1894, 14½×12½ inches (36.8×1.7 cm). Published by Matsuki Heikichi. Philadelphia Museum of Art; Given by Mr Peter Benoliel (Funds Contributed).

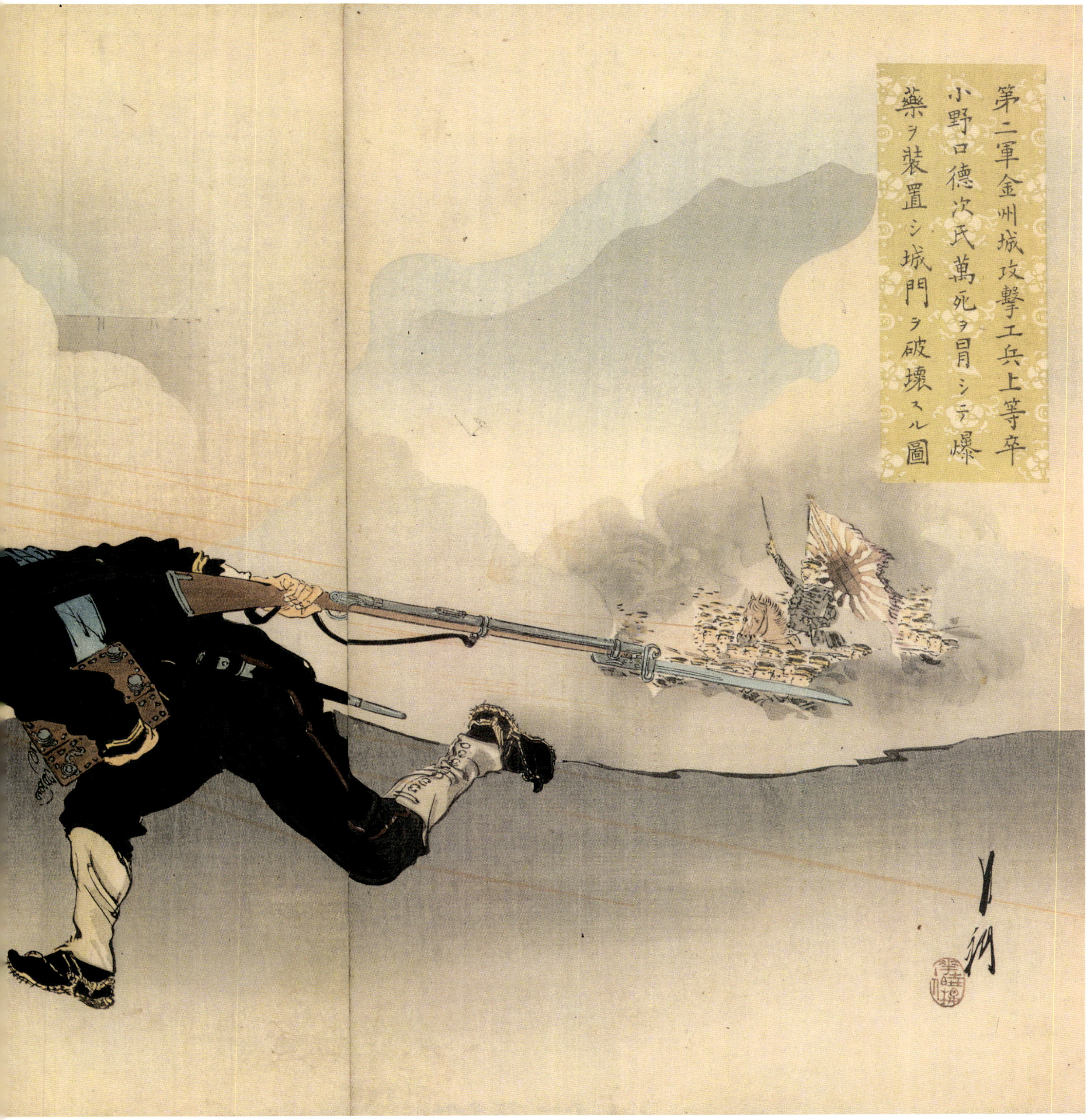

prints, enhanced by a subtle use of colors mainly in pale pastel shades (page 197).

OGATA GEKKŌ

The range of subjects that characterize Toshikata's work was also seen in the work of Ogata Gekkō (1859-1920). Gekkō also designed many triptychs of the Sino-Japanese war, some of them showing the Chinese in rather ugly racist caricatures. The triptych illustrating the private engineer Onoguchi bombing the enemy fort (above) has none of these elements, however, as it concentrates on a single heroic action by a simple soldier. In this triptych the extent of Western influence on Japanese prints is clear. As had been the case with Kiyochika's prints there is the use of soft watercolor-like washes. Depth, modeling and a full use of shadows contribute towards a picture that could as well have been designed in the West. Artists who designed war triptych, like Gekkō, were strongly influenced by Western illustrators working for magazines such as the *Illustrated London News*. In turn these magazines, when writing about the war, often illustrated the articles with copies after the Japanese triptychs! A triptych Gekkō designed together with Kiyochika is reproduced on page 194.

Although Gekkō did work for newspapers, perhaps his most enchanting work is in woodcut prints of simple subjects in a style close to that of the Maruyama/Shijō school, such as the vines tossing in a fall wind, depicted here (page 200). As true *ukiyo-e* subject matter became increasingly unpopular, the woodcut as a broadsheet reflecting current events entered a swift decline after the Sino-Japanese War. Consequently, a new genre of woodcuts appeared, typified by these Maruyama/Shijō style prints by Gekkō. These woodcuts, principally of still-lifes – flowers, birds, and landscapes – were printed in a careful, extremely luxurious technique. They are technically comparable to earlier *surimono*. Whereas the war triptychs or series such as the Yoshitoshi 'Moon' series had been printed in large editions and in Yoshitoshi's case often in many re-editions, this kind of de-luxe print was issued in limited numbers. Similar prints had been published early in the Meiji period of Shibata Zeshin's (1807-91) work and here we already see that these prints were frequently close reproductions of an artist's painted oeuvre.

Zeshin's humor is seen in one of his more irreverent works shows the Death of the Buddha as a radish lying on a chopping board, surrounded by mourning vegetables. Zeshin's prints not only exist in various versions, but also the same subjects can be found in his paintings. An artist such as Zeshin, who in his own day was best known for his painting and his lacquerwork, falls somewhat outside the scope of this chapter which concentrates on the continuation of the *ukiyo-e* tradition.

However, works in this tradition were to be of major influence in the twentieth century, when the print as a popular broadsheet ceased to be produced and was replaced either by illustrative prints, like the female portraits of Kiyokata; or prints produced mostly for an export market, such as the landscapes by Hasui and the Yoshida family; bird prints by Ohara Shōson (Koson, right); or prints made for the small clientele of knowledgeable Japanese conoisseurs. These prints were often not in the *ukiyo-e* tradition but in a decorative style. In concluding we can see that the Meiji period is not a period of downfall in Japanese printmaking. Its many often conflicting tendencies and its inventions of new modes of expression were to lead to the revival of printmaking in the twentieth century. Once this period is placed into the proper historical perspective, we can start to enjoy Meiji prints as the products of one of the most interesting periods in Japanese history.

Below: Ogata Gekkō (1859-1920) 'Hawk on a Pine Tree in front of Mount Fuji,' from the series '100 Views of Mount Fuji,' c. 1890. Published by Matsuki Heikichi. R O Müller Collection.

Right: Ohara Koson (1877-1945) 'Bats in Front of the Full Moon,' c. 1910. R O Müller Collection.

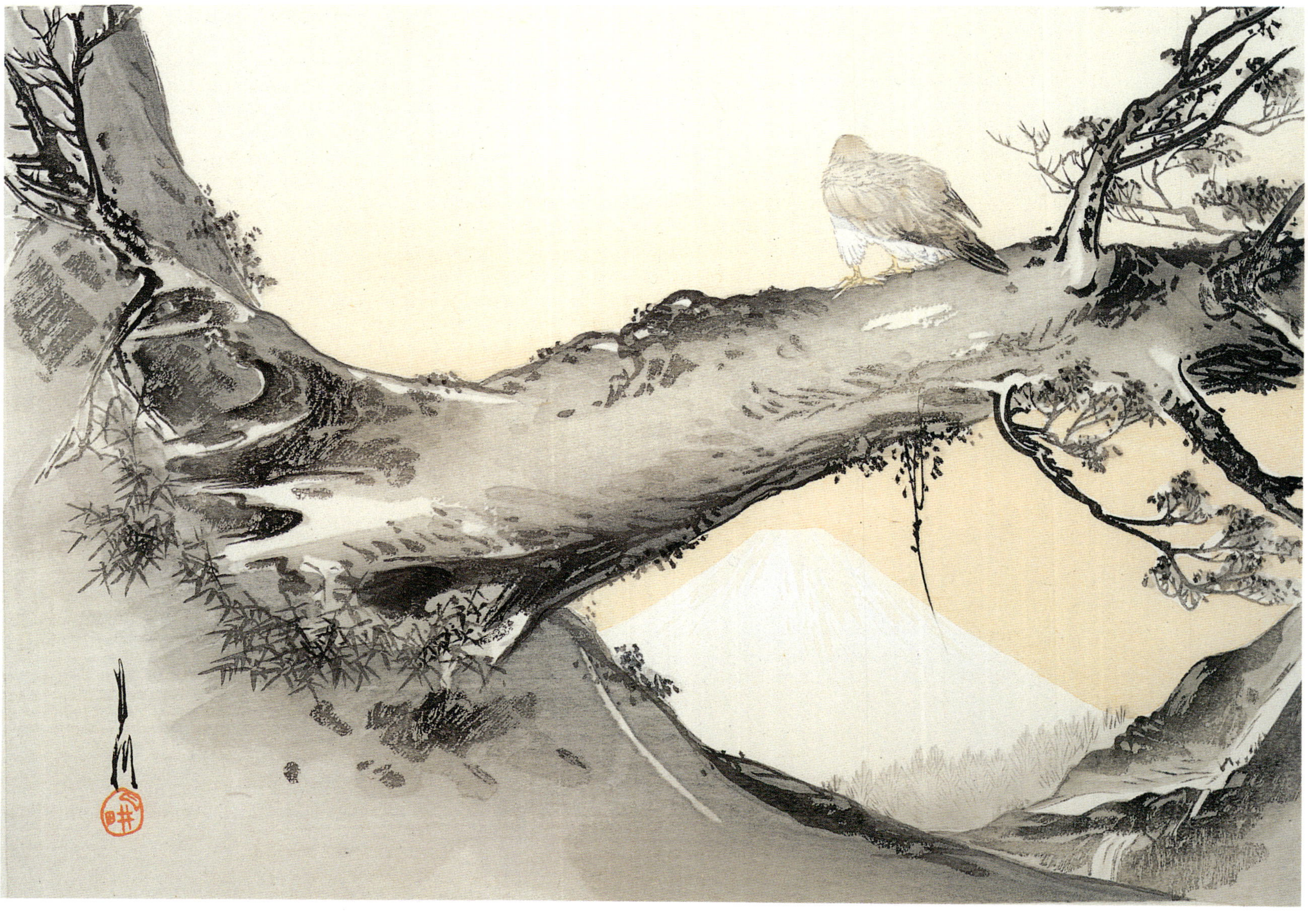

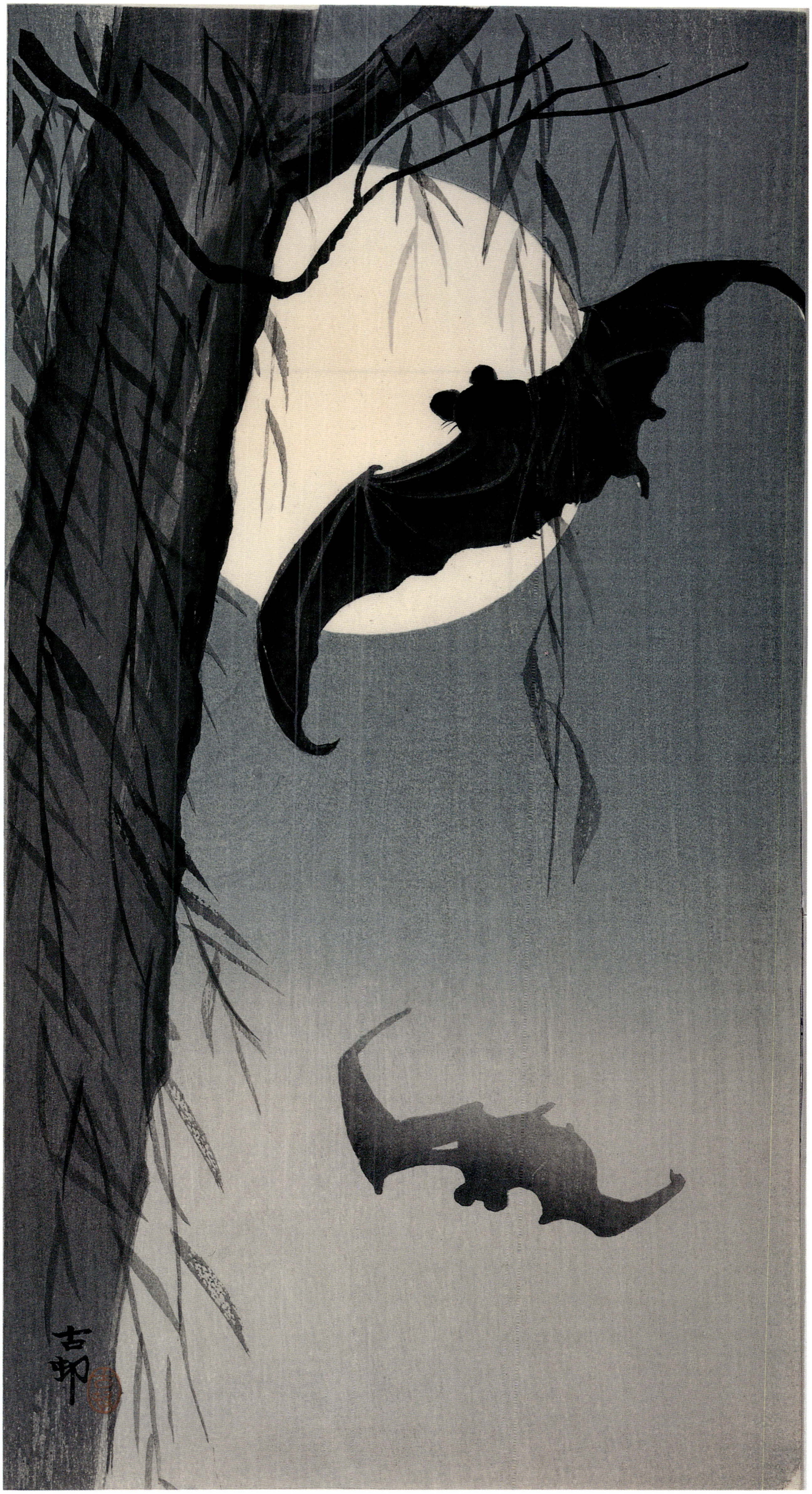
古邨

7
The Advent of Sōsaku hanga

AMY NEWLAND

While the Meiji period marked the final phase of *ukiyo-e,* it was also a watershed in the development of Western-style painting and printmaking. In the 1870s Western-style painting (*yōga*) was taught at the *Kōbu bijutsu gakkō* (Technical Art School) which was established in 1876 by the Ministry of Industry as part of the Imperial College of Technology. Despite the mounting opposition against *yōga* at this time (the Technical Art School was closed in 1882) by advocates of traditional painting (*Nihonga*) such as Ernest Fenollosa (1853-1908) and Okakura Tenshin (1862-1913), a number of societies were nonetheless formed which provided the *yōga* artist with opportunities to meet others of like mind. For example, the *Meiji bijutsukai* (Meiji Art Society), the first *yōga* group, was set up by the painter Asai Chū (1856-1907) and others in 1889, and the *Hakubakai* (White Horse Society) by the painters Seiki Kuroda (1866-1924), Fujishima Takeji (1867-1943) and others in 1896. The future of *yōga* was guaranteed when, in the same year as the founding of the *Hakubakai,* Seiki Kuroda organized a department of Western-style painting at the *Tōkyō bijutsu gakkō* (Tokyo Art School; later the Tokyo University of Fine Arts and Music) which was established in 1887 with the assistance of Fenollosa and Okakura as an institution for instruction in *Nihonga.* The inclusion of *yōga* as part of the school's curriculae was a decisive win for *yōga* supporters and in the early twentieth century, the Tokyo Art School became the fountainhead of the *sōsaku hanga* (creative print) movement.

By 1900 Japanese artists were travelling to Europe, particularly to France, and were consequently well versed in contemporary developments in European art. Those artists who were unable to travel abroad were kept abreast of European trends either through contact with the artists who had themselves visited the West such as Kuroda, Aoki Shigeru (1882-1911) and Fujishima Takeji or through foreign art journals and select exhibitions in Japan. To Japanese *yōga* artists Western art did not only have a impact stylistically but also ideologically since the adoption of Western painting styles was accompanied by the adoption of the ideology of Western artists. Underlying this was the concept which held that the artist was an integral part of the creative process and that as such it demanded that he play a significant role in it. This Western-based ideology had a profound effect on Meiji artists, shaping the course of Japanese painting and printmaking history. It was especially evident in the print movement, the seeds of which were planted in the first decade of the twentieth century, called *sōsaku hanga.*

As the name *sōsaku hanga* (creative prints) implies, the fundamental precept was that the artist should play an important role in all stages of the creative process, from the initial stages of design to the final stages of carving and printing. As a result, *sōsaku hanga* is often viewed in contradistinction to *shin hanga* (new prints, a style in which the artist assumed a lesser role in the creative process, see Chapter 8), viz, the 'modern and Western' versus the 'traditional and Japanese.' However, when viewing *sōsaku hanga* artists and their work, it is sometimes difficult to draw neat divisions between the two styles. For example, Yoshida Hiroshi (1876-1950), who, although a Western-style painter, is generally associated with the *shin hanga,* not *sōsaku hanga,* movement. Or, as with the work of *sōsaku hanga* pioneers like Ishii Hakutei (1882-1958) and Fujishima Takeji who did not carve their own work, but rather entrusted their designs to the skilled craftsman Igami Bonkotsu (1875-1935). Perhaps the most important elements that characterize a *sōsaku hanga* artist are his training in Western-style art and at, least in theory, the acknowledgment of the idea that the artist should be at the core of the creative process. Therefore it is the ideological differences, perhaps more than any technical considerations, that defined the division between *sōsaku hanga* and *shin hanga.*

Yamamoto Kanae (1882-1946) is generally accepted as the inventor of *sōsaku hanga.* At the age of ten Kanae was apprenticed to Sakurai Gyoun, a craftsman in Western-style wood engraving, with whom he learned *koguchi mokuhan* (literally, cross-grain woodcuts; it is this carving across the grain that distinguished a wood engraving from a woodcut which is carved along the grain). He later enrolled in the department of Western art at the Tokyo Art School. In 1904, while still a student, Kanae produced a small woodcut executed only in black and yellow ochre called 'Gyōfu' (Fisherman). The print was published in the July issue of *Myōjō* ('Bright Star,' also translated 'Venus'), a magazine of Western-style poetry, Japanese classical 31-syllable poetry (*tanka*) and graphic arts which was begun in 1900 by Yosano Tekkan (1873-1935). In 'Gyōfu,' Kanae's training in *koguchi mokuhan* is clearly evident in the use of the knife to create expressive line

Right: Yamamoto Kanae (1882-1946) 'Bathing,' 1918, 12⅘×9½ inches (32.5×24 cm). Courtesy Abe Publishing Co Ltd, Gallery Kabutoya, Pallas Inc.

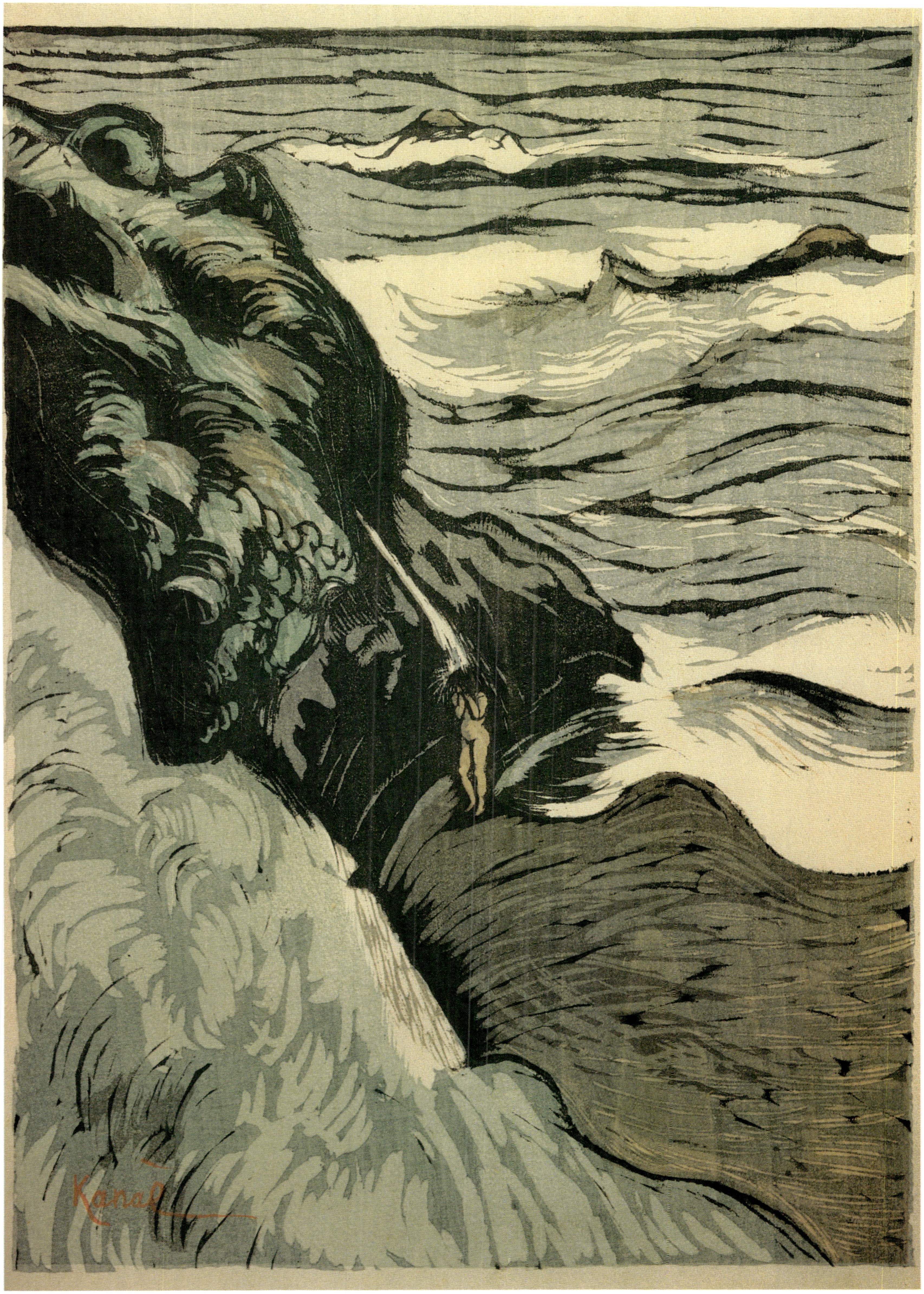
Kanae

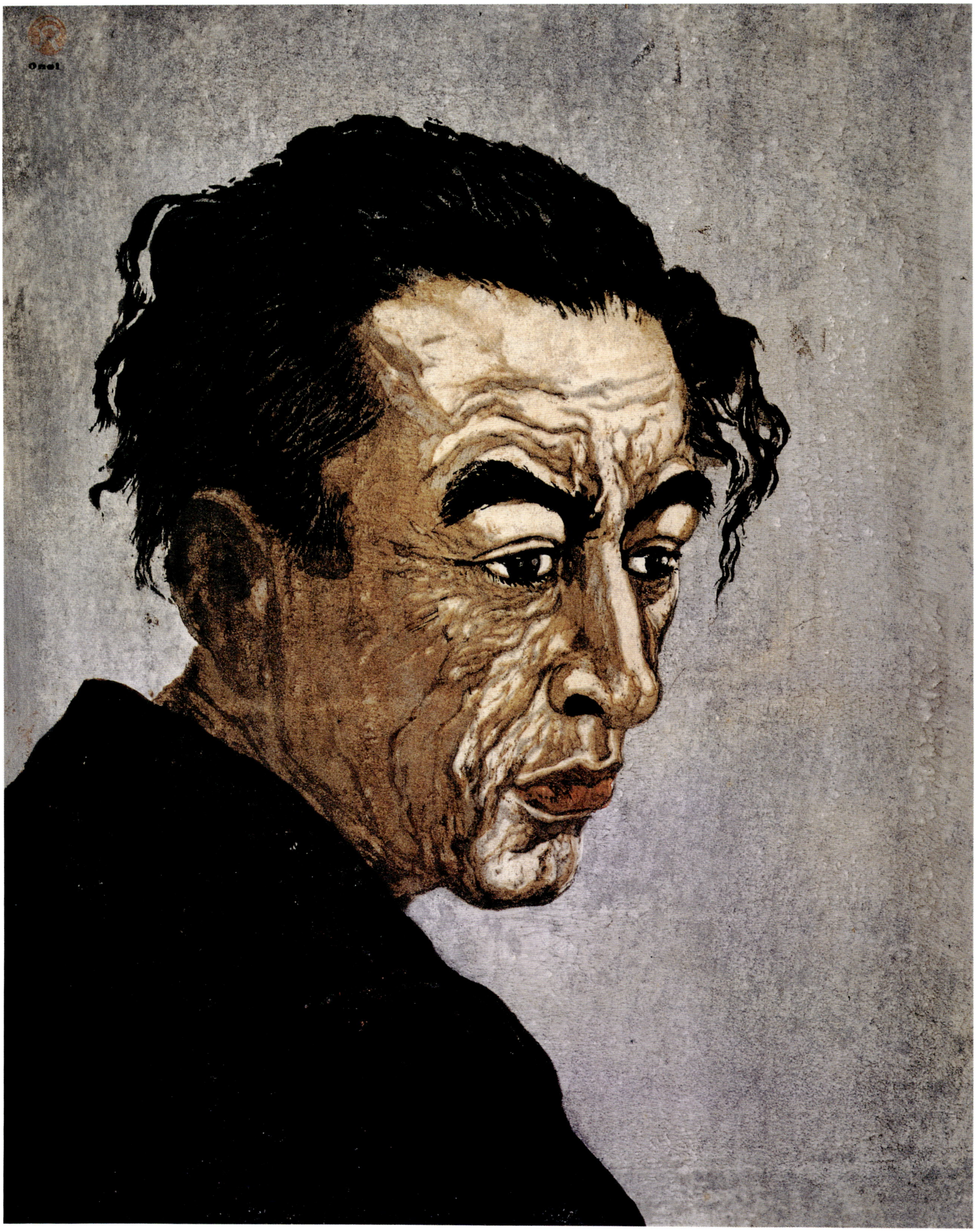

Above: Onchi Kōshirō (1891-1955) 'Portrait of Poet Sakutarō Hagiwara,' 1943, 20⅗×16½ inches (52.5×42 cm). Courtesy Abe Publishing Co Ltd, Gallery Kabutoya, Pallas Inc.

effects, so much so that Kanae referred to this print as a *tōga* (knife picture). In the same issue of *Myōjō* the painter, printmaker and close friend of Kanae's, Ishii Hakutei, describes 'Gyōfu' as a painterly woodcut in which the artist's knife has become the brush.[1] In fact, 'Gyōfu' was so distinct technically from anything known at the time that many scholars view it as marking the beginning of the *sōsaku hanga* movement. As seen in his much later print 'Bathing' (1918; page 203), Kanae's work has a decidedly Western flavor in which the emphasis has moved away from line to color.

Students at the Tokyo Art School like Kanae had access to a number of European art journals such as the German *Der Sturm, Simplicissimus* and *Jugend*. Inspired by these publications, Kanae, in the spring of 1907, collaborated with fellow students at the School, Ishii Hakutei and Morita Tsunetomo (1881-1933), to publish the first issue of *Hōsun* (literally, 'One's Mind'). *Hōsun* is considered the first arts magazine to showcase works by artists who were later recognized as *sōsaku hanga* pioneers. Significantly, in the fall of 1907, the *Bunten* was initiated by the Ministry of Education, partially modelled after the Salon d'Automne in Paris. It was an important outlet for *yōga* artists to exhibit their work. The publication of *Hōsun* and the founding of the *Bunten* marks a prosperous period in the development of contemporary Japanese art. Over the course of *Hōsun*'s five-year existence, many *sōsaku hanga* artists like Sakamoto Hanjirō (1882-1969), Oda Kazuma (1882-1956) and Hirafuku Hyakusui (1877-1933) as well as leading writers and critics such as Kinoshita Mokutarō (1885-1945) contributed to the publication. The paramount role that *Hōsun* played in the history of printmaking and *sōsaku hanga* is undeniable: it represented one of the early artistic outlets for the *sōsaku hanga* artist, who, unlike his *shin hanga* counterpart, did not have the same publisher/artist association and therefore had few opportunities, at least initially, to publish their work.

Kanae left to study in France in 1912, returning in 1917. A year later he, with Sakamoto and others, formed the *Nippon [Nihon] sōsaku hanga kyōkai* (The Japanese Creative Print Society) which became the *Nihon hanga kyōkai* (The Japanese Print Society) in 1931. The formation of this society consolidated and made official the *sōsaku hanga* movement. It was at this time that the term 'sōsaku hanga' came into currency. In 1919 the society successfully mounted its first exhibition, comprising 189 works by 25 artists, at the Tokyo department store Mitsukoshi. The exhibit contained mostly woodblock prints but also included etchings, lithographs and mono types and it marked the first exhibition of prints to be held in Japan. That year the arts magazine, *Mizu-e*, devoted a special issue to *sōsaka hanga*. In the same year Kanae left Tokyo and organized a research center of arts for farmers in a remote mountain village in Nagano prefecture, and thereafter his involvement in printmaking substantially decreased.

Unlike Yamamoto Kanae, who was actually trained as a printmaker, many *sōsaku* artists were initially students of oil painting and in a few instances worked for only a relatively short period as printmakers. One such artist was Ishii Hakutei. Considered one of the *sōsaku hanga* 'pioneers,' Hakutei was the eldest son of a *Nihonga* painter. He began his artistic career as an apprentice in the printing department of the Finance Ministry (Ōkurashō) and later became a pupil of the Western-style painter Asai Chū. He was active in the formation of artistic and literary groups in the formative years of *yōga* and contemporary literature. As mentioned above he was one of the three artists involved in publication of the seminal magazine *Hōsun* as well as taking part in the establishment of such artistic and literary groups as the *Pan no kai* (Bread Group). The group was set up in 1908 by artists and writers who met on a regular basis, to drink and to discuss pertinent contemporary issues.

Perhaps Hakutei's most notable works as a *sōsaku* printmaker are the series *Tōkyō jūni kei* (Twelve Views of Tokyo and the *Nihon fūkei hanga* (Prints of Japanese Scenery). The first, 'Twelve Views of Tokyo,' was started in 1910, the year Hakutei left for two years of study in Europe, and finished in 1916. Two prints were completed before his departure, seven after his return and three were never executed. Each picture in the series illustrates a geisha busying herself with a specific activity and behind her, enclosed in a cartouche, a scene which has some association with her. This compositional device is clearly drawn from the nineteenth-century *ukiyo-e* printmakers Keisai Eisen (1790-1848) and Utagawa Kunisada (1786-1865). In the scene entitled 'Asakusa' (British Museum, 37.8×26.0 cm, see Smith [1983], cat. 5), for example, the background cartouche portrays the temple of Kinryūzan. In the treatment in this scene and others in the series of the figure and the background scene Hakutei adroitly combines *ukiyo-e* conventions with Western elements: the realistic rendering of the seated woman in 'Asakusa,' who is tying a *kotsutsumi* (small hand drum), recalls his training as a Western painter, softened by the delicate treatment of line and the rhythm of the drapery. Hakutei left the carving of the Twelve Views to the master carver Igami Bonkotsu who was trained in a studio of a late Edo-period craftsman.

Hakutei was also one of six contributors to the ambituous *sōsaku hanga* project *Nihon fūkei hanga*. Issued from 1916-20 under the supervision of the publisher Nakashima Jūtarō, the *Nihon fūkei hanga* consisted of ten sections composed of five prints each by the artists Sakamoto, Morita, Ishii Tsuruzō, Kosugi Misei, and Hirafuku Hyakusui. Hakutei himself produced three of the sections. After this project, Hakutei ceased making prints and returned to painting, the medium for which he is best-known.

Sakamoto Hanjirō was encouraged to study *yōga* in Tokyo by Aoki Shigeru who hailed from Kurume, the same town in Kyushu, as Sakamoto. While Sakamoto's reputation is primarily as a painter heavily influenced by late Impressionism (he studied in France from 1921 to 1924), he was nevertheless active in early *sōsaku* history. He played a role in the establishment of the *Nippon sōsaku hanga kyōkai* and participated in *Hōsun* as well as collaborating in joint works (*rensaku*) such as the above-mentioned *Nihon fūkei hanga*. The idea of collaboration was an important part of the *sōsaku hanga* scene and over the years these artists joined forces numerous times to publish print portfolios or contribute to print journals. Sakamoto also designed the series *Tosa sanjū ezu* (36 Views of Tosa, c. 1925 (British Museum, 25.8×37.5 cm, see Smith [1983], cat. 11). The name Tosa is the former name for the region around the city of Kōchi on the island of Shikoku. The series illustrates the urban scenes and landscapes in and around the city. The textured surfaces of Sakamoto's prints closely resembles the impressionistic feel of his paintings which were based on an acute observation of his surroundings. As states Yamamoto Kanae after seeing Sakamoto's work at the 1924 *Nikakai* (Second Division Society) exhibition: 'seeing is of immense significance, and therein lies a reality that has been depicted by Mr Sakamoto for the first time.'[2] Sakamoto was never comfortable in the urban environment of Tokyo and after his return from France, he went back to his native Kyushu where he remained for the rest of his life.

Sakamoto's work contrasts sharply that of his contemporary Oda Kazuma. Kazuma is accredited with the introduction of the *sōsaku sekihanga* (creative lithograph) to the movement.[3]. Born in Tokyo he learned lithography from the minor printmaker Kaneko Seijirō. While he was working as an artist in the Koshiba printing studio in Tokyo in his early 20s, he encountered the work of Europeans such as Emil Orlik (1870-1932, see Chapter 1), a Prague-born artist who was in Japan during the later Meiji period.

Oda later worked in Osaka with Morita Tsunetomo as an artist on the Imperial Newspaper. Oda was active in the *yōga* circles of the period and in addition to being a member of such groups (as were many *yōga* artists) as the *Pan no kai* and *Nippon sōsaku hanga kyokai*, he was responsible for the formation of the *Yōfū hangakai* (Western-style Print Society) in 1929 and wrote several scholarly studies on *ukiyo-e* like the *Ukiyo-e to sashi-e geijutsu* (Ukiyo-e and the Art of Illustration). Oda's naturalistic style is seen in prints such as 'View of Mihonoseki, Izumo' (British Museum 36.5×24.3 cm, see Smith [1983], cat. 71). In works such as this Oda's debt to the *ukiyo-e* landscape tradition, especially as developed by Utagawa Hiroshige (1797-1858), is apparent in the utilization of climatic elements like rain and clouds to create a particular mood. The slanted pattern of rain that moves from the top right to left of the composition juxtaposes the boats in the foreground and the seated guests in the inn to the left appear oblivious to the torrential rainstorm outside.

The Kyushu-born artist Fujishima Takeji was initially trained as a painter in the naturalistic Shijō school under Kawabata Gyokushō (1842-1913) and later was a student of Western-style painting at the Tokyo Art School. Fujishima was well-known as an oil painter of Western-style figures (viz, *The Black Fan,* 1908-9, Bridgestone Museum of Art, Tokyo) and landscapes in which 'the use of brush and of light and shade is not aimed at recreating the subject but is directed exclusively by compositional necessity . . . he is clearly attempting to use brushstrokes and coloring for direct expressive effect.'[4] This effect, influenced by Paul Cézanne, who Fujishima said 'resembles the stillness of the East,'[5] is also visible in his prints. In 'The Stand at the Races' (British Museum, 26.7×19.8 cm, see Smith [1983], cat. 8) which illustrates a number of spectators in the stands, Fujishima has used only one color – a pale shade of purple – and the diagonal compositional elements are conceived of as contrasting areas of color, decorative shading and white. Although this print dates from around 1905 it is still unclear if it was done before or after Fujishima's European studies in 1905-10 with the artists Charles Carolus-Duran and Fernand Corman at the Académie Colarossi in Paris. However, the flat compositional quality and use of color might suggest a later date.

The pioneering generation of artists like Kanae and Hakutei was followed in the 1910s to 1930s led by figures like Onchi Kōshirō (1891-1955). Born in Tokyo, the son of a tutor of the Imperial family, Onchi received a formal artistocratic education. Rebelling against the wishes of his family, he entered in 1910, the Tokyo Art School where he studied *yōga* and sculpture. There he met Fujimori Shizuo (1891-1943) and Tanaka Kyōkichi (1892-1915) and in 1914 they formed the magazine *Tsukuhae* (Moonglow) which featured poetry and woodblock prints. The publication of *Tsukuhae* ceased after Tanaka's death in 1915. The *Tsukuhae* artists – unlike those of the earlier *Hōsun* – cut their own blocks and executed their own carvings. Compared to the earlier *Hōsun*, the prints featured in *Tsukuhae* were more progressive and it featured the first abstract woodblock print which was by Onchi. Onchi, whose influence as an artist would be felt by a number of creative print artists, was an innovative artist who constantly sought to expand the vocabulary of prewar Japanese printmaking; he worked in both abstract and figurative themes. His name has since became a shibboleth of the *sōsaku hanga* movement.

Onchi was also an accomplished poet and associated with the literary cycles of the period. In 1916 he collaborated with the free-verse poet Hagiwara Sakutarō (1886-1942) in the poetry magazine *Kanjō* (Feeling) and in the same year he illustrated Hagiwara's well-known book of poems *Tsuki ni hoeru* (Howling at the Moon, 1916). Hagiwara was an instrumental figure in promoting Japanese colloquial verse and the often suggestive quality in his poetry was on several occasions seen by the Imperial Censor's board as having a corrupting influence:

Hard as I hug your breasts, your body
Hard-presses mine that we
May squeeze from the abandoned place
Overshaking ecstacy;
And, as I love you piercingly
I'll stain your stainless skin
With ooze from blue bruised grasses
Such juiciness was in.(from *Ai ren* from *Tsuki ni hoeru*)[6]

Onchi made a portrait of the poet called *Hyōtō no chosha,* (The Author of Ice Island) as a memorial a year after the poet's death. The psychologically penetrating pose as depicted by Onchi captured the ethos of a poet who felt that 'poetry was a lonesome consolation for his wounded soul.' The original print was executed as a memorial to the poet a year after his death in a small edition of only seven impressions (Onchi was interested little in running large editions). It was reprinted in 1949 by the artist's student Sekino Jun'ichirō (b. 1914) (page 204).

Another artist of this 'prewar' generation was Munakata Shikō (1903-75). While he was not directly associated with the *sōsaku* movement, he shared with the *sōsaku hanga* artist the desire to design and carve his own work 'fulfilling its ideal

Right: Munakata Shikō (1903-1975) 'Shells' from the series 'A Homage to Shōkei,' (*Shōkei hanga saku*) dated 1956, 22×15 inches (55×39 cm). Courtesy Abe Publishing Co Ltd, Gallery Kabutoya, Pallas Inc.

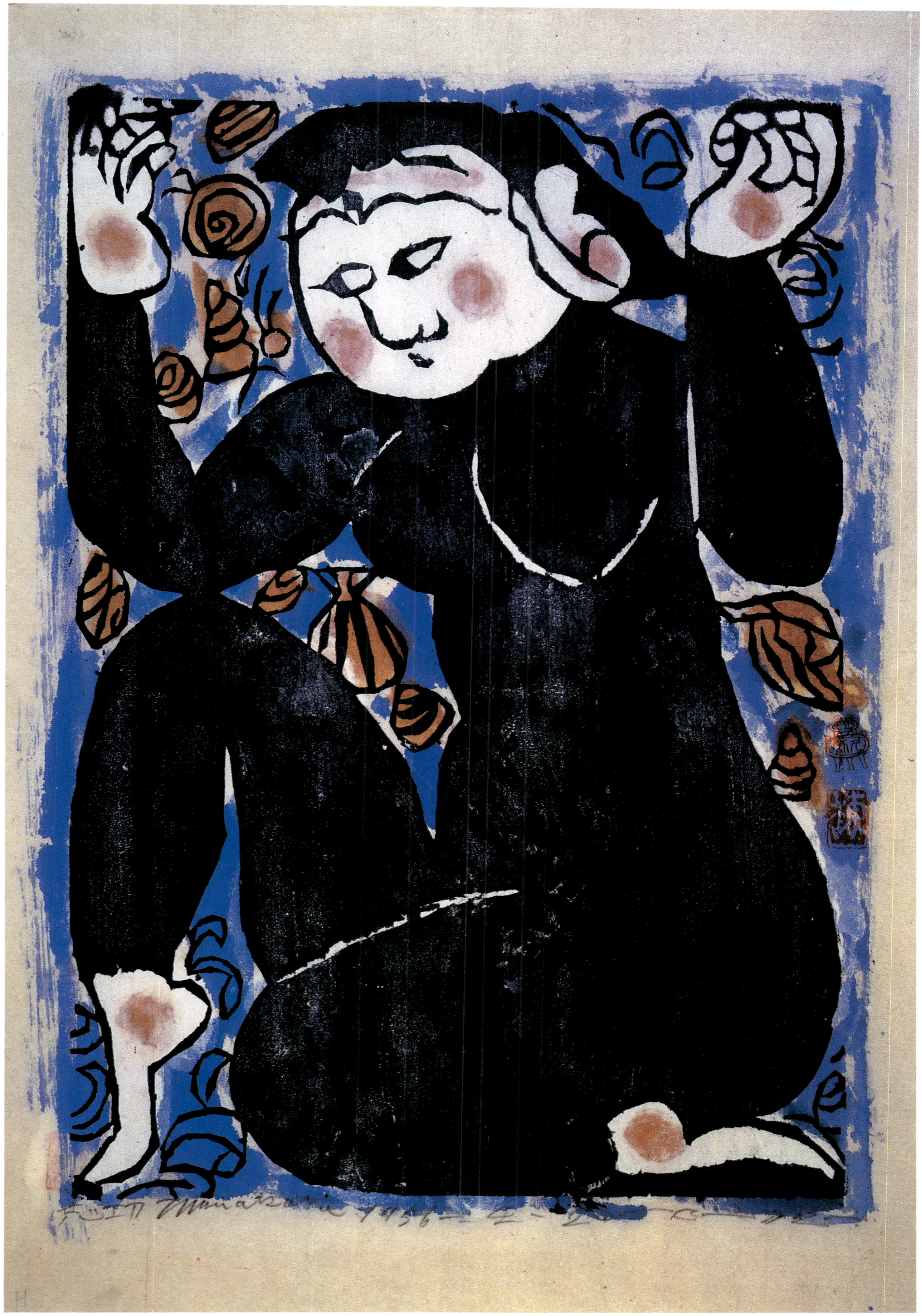

[*sōsaku hanga*'s] of raising the print to the level of high art.'[7] Shikō differed fundamentally from the creative print artists, however, in his refusal to be influenced by foreign traditions stating that 'we have to go back to the ancient Buddhist prints for the real art of woodblock.' The individual, energetic style that he developed was characterised by a sharpness and strength of line and a spontaneity in execution.

Munakata was one of 15 children of a blacksmith from Aomori prefecture. He first studied oil painting and after meeting the woodblock artists Hiratsuka Un'ichi (b. 1895) and Shimokawa Kihachirō he became interested in woodblock prints. The direction that Munakata's work and ideology would take from the 1930s onwards – his critics sometimes labelled him a *kamigakari* (obsessed with God) – was less in accordance with contemporaries like Onchi than with the artists, philosophers and writers affiliated with the Folk Art (*mingei*) movement led by the philosopher and aesthe Yanagi Sōetsu (1889-1961). Religious themes would eventually dominate his work such as the series A Hommage to Shōkei (*Shōkei hanga saku*) which dedicated to the *mingei* potter Kawai Kanjirō (1890-1966). Kawai's kiln was named Shōkei-yō (page 207).

The *sōsaku hanga* movement weathered the devastation of World War II. The years of the American dominated Allied Occupation (1945-52) were marked by tremendous social and economic changes that altered many patterns of Japan's prewar culture: the Emperor Hirohito (1901-89) renounced his claims to Shinto divinity; wholesale land reforms were instituted converting tenant farmers into land owners and *zaibatsu* (industrial conglomerates) were decentralized and organized.

In the face of the changes imposed on Japan, *sōsaku hanga* artists still remained active and in 1946 the Japanese Print Society produced three companion series that were nostalgic reminders of prewar Japan and no doubt made for Western audiences in mind. These were the *Tōkyō kaikō zue* (Nostalgic Views of Tokyo); *Nihon jozokusen* (Customs of Japanese Women) and *Nihon minzoku zufu* (Native Customs of Japan). The *Tōkyō kaikō zue,* a portfolio of 15 prints issued by Fūgaku Publishers, was based on an earlier, larger edition begun in 1928 and completed in 1932 called *Shin Tōkyō hyakkei* (One Hundred Views of New Tokyo). The original series was executed five years after the Great Kantō Earthquake which shook the Tokyo plain and caused widespread destruction. The 1946 version not only involved artists from the first series but also newer contributors and together they included Onchi, Maekawa Sempan (1888-1960), Saitō Kiyoshi (b. 1907), Hiratsuka Un'ichi, Kawakami Sumio (1895-1972), Yamaguchi Gen (1896-1976), Maeda Masao (b. 1904), Sekino Jun'ichirō and Azechi Umetarō (b. 1902). The block for Onchi's 'Tokyo Station' (British Museum, 24.5×18.4 cm) a building which still stands today, was the only selection from the original set which did not require recarving.

Yamaguchi Gen was a pupil of Onchi at the Tokyo Art School and through him he met other *sōsaku* printmakers like Sekino Jun'ichirō. He eventually exhibited with the *Nippon sōsaku hanga kyōkai* and the *Kokugakai* (National Painting Society), a group formed in 1918 by *Nihonga* painters, which after 1928 was represented only by Western-style painting. While Yamaguchi's abstract style is considered to be closely modelled on his teacher, his contribution to the *Tōkyō kaikō zue*, 'Meiji Shrine' (British Museum, 19.7×28.1 cm) reveals his competency in representational subjects and the underlying softness that become characteristic of his post-war style.

Yokohama born Kawakami Sumio became acquainted with printmaking about the time he graduated from junior high school. Later, during his studies at the Aoyama Academy, he was educated in Western-style art by a junior instructor. From the age of 17 to 18 he travelled to the United States and spent time in Washington and Alaska where he worked at odd jobs. A few years after his return to Japan, Kawakami assumed a post as English teacher at a junior high school in Utsunomiya in Tochigi prefecture and produced prints in his free time. Although he exhibited with the *Kokugakai* and *Nippon sōsaku hanga kyōkai,* he led a relatively isolated existence and had little contact with *sōsaku* artists. Kawakami's works reveal his fascination with the strange interpretation of the customs of the first foreigners (Dutch and Portuguese) in Japan in the late sixteenth century and the events surrounding their arrival. This interest was no doubt fueled by the numerous scholarly works concerning the first foreigners in Japan that were being published during the early Showa period. His work was also influenced by the influx in Western culture after the Meiji Restoration in 1868. His colorful depiction of a street scene in the *Tōkyō kaikō zue,* 'Night in Ginza' (British Museum, 18.3×24.2 cm, see Smith [1983], cat. 87), a similar image from the *Shin Tōkyō hyakkei,* provides a glimpse at the Japan of the 1920s when Western dress and culture was all the rage, when young women, as seen in the foreground of the print, had bobbed hair just like the flappers in the West. These *moden garu* (modern girl) strolled down the avenues of the fashionable districts like the Ginza. In this print, these women contrast the

Right: Jun'ichirō Sekino 'Portrait of Munakata Shikō,' 1968, 26⅕×21 inches (66.8×53.3 cm). Courtesy The Portland Art Museum, Oregon Art Institute, The Vivian and Gordon Gilkey Graphic Arts Collection.

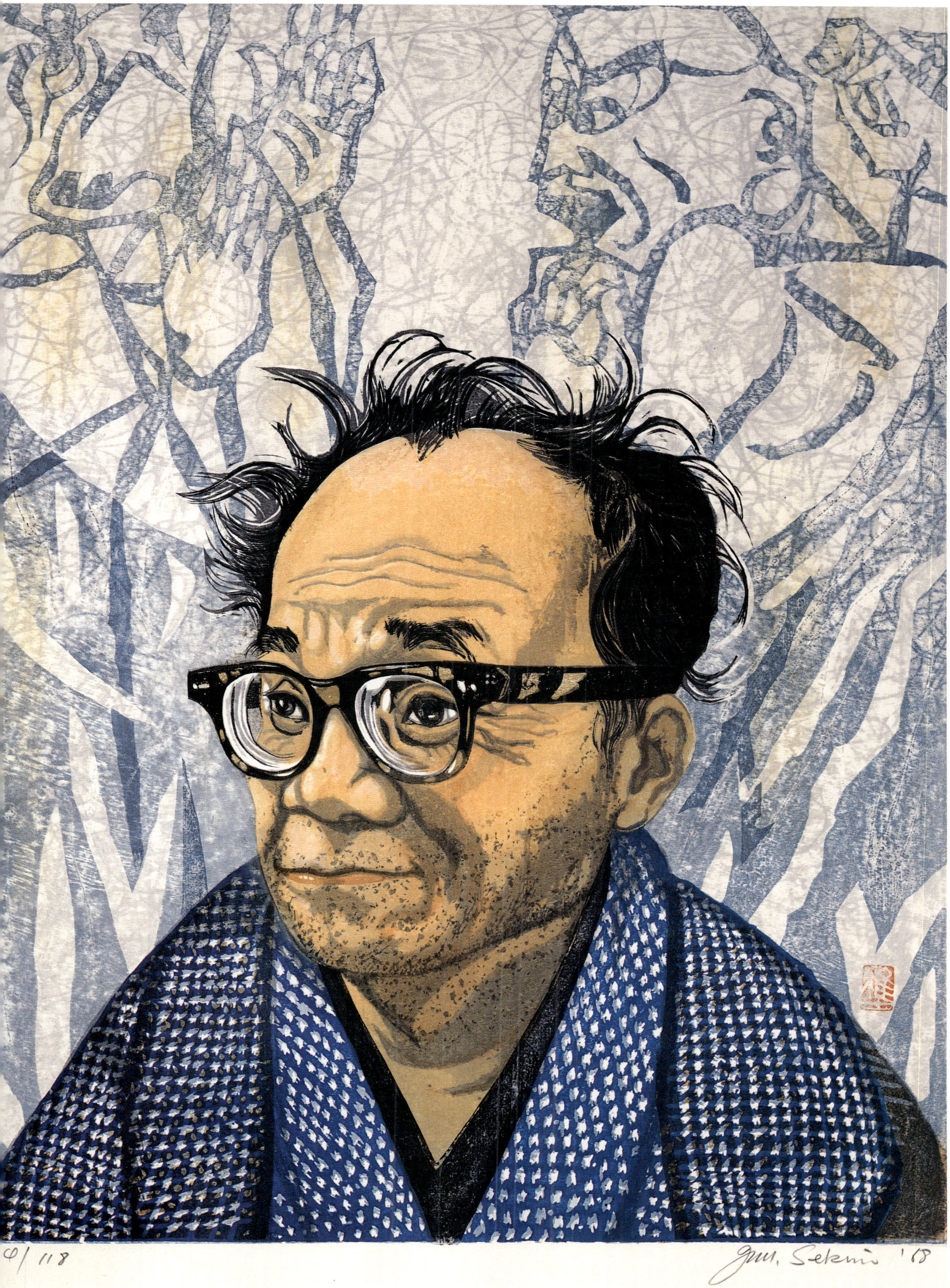

kimono-clad woman who oddly enough stands with her back turned towards them.

Hiratsuka Un'ichi was introduced to Western-style painting in 1913 when Ishii Hakutei visited and taught a watercolor class in Hiratsuka's home town of Matsue. Two years later he went to Tokyo to study Western-style painting. At this time, he rekindled his acquaintance with Ishii who encouraged Hiratsuka to pursue his interest in printmaking. Ishii introduced him to the master carver Igami Bonkotsu who was instrumental in executing the blocks for Ishii's *Tōkyō jūni kei*. Hiratsuka subsequently learned to carve in the traditional manner of *ukiyo-e* and his skill in traditional carving techniques was an anomaly among *sōsaku* practitioners. His first exhibited woodcuts were two pieces submitted to the 1916 *Nikakai*. The *Nikakai* was instituted by a group of Western-style painters in 1914 in reaction against the *Bunten* which by this time had become a bastion of conservative painting. He later was recognized as one of the most active and influential *sōsaku hanga* pioneers, not only as an artist but also as a respected craftsman, teacher and writer. He, for example, formed the magazine *Han* (Printing) in 1928 with Munakata and Azechi; in 1927 he published an important book on printmaking techniques; in 1931 he set up the printing division within the *Kokugakai*; and in 1950 set up the Hiratsuka Print Institute in Tokyo. Hiratsuka's works, which are principally landscapes and urban scenes, are delineated by a clarity of line and a stillness in feeling as is evinced by the print 'Akasaka Detached Imperial Palace' (British Museum, 18.1×24.3 cm). The Akasaka Detached Imperial Palace, constructed between 1909-19, was the residence of the crown prince. Modelled on the buildings of Versailles and the Louvre, it was designed by Katayama Otōkuma (1854-1917) and today stands as a representative example of late Meiji-period architecture. In his print, Hiratsuka places the building into a deeply receding background, a compositional device already evident in his early series, *Tōkyō shinsaiseki fūkei* (Scenes of Tokyo After the Earthquake, 1924). Like many *sōsaku* artists, Hiratsuka's distinctive line is created by the use of a flat knife and V-shaped chisel (*aisuki*).

Among the artists in the *Tōkyō kaikō zue*, one about whom little has been written but whose contribution to the project was nonetheless noteworthy was Maeda Masao (b. 1904). He was a student of *yōga* at the Kawabata Art School and of woodblock printing under one of the leading *yōga* painters of the early twentieth century, Umehara Ryūzaburō (1888-1986). Early in his career he became acquainted with the *sōsaku* artist Hiratsuka Un'ichi, after which time he produced inspiring scenes of Tokyo and of ancient castle towns. A number of his prints are also chilling reminders of the devastation of War. In the *Tōkyō kaikō zue,* however, he offers an impressionistic view of the grand gate, the 'Akamon', at the Imperial University (*Teikoku daigaku*) (British Museum, 20.1×27 cm).

Maekawa Sempan, Sekino Jun'ichirō and Saitō Kiyoshi contributed prints to all three of the 1946 portfolios. The artists of the *Nihon josokusen* additionally included Kawanishi Hide (1894-1965) and Onchi. The series contained both English and Japanese text and illustrated images of Japanese women from different regions. As Smith states, the text 'lays great emphasis on the simple beauty of the Japanese female dress, and one may speculate on the direction in which the American occupiers were gently being led.'[8] The *Nihon minzoku zufu*, included the work of the artists like Maekawa, Saitō, Sekino, Yamaguchi and Kawanishi and of the three series is possibly the most quaint evocation of Japan's traditional life. Like *Tōkyō Kaikō zue*, these two series also reveals the variety of styles of the *sōsaku hanga* artist. Born into a Kyoto merchant family, Sempan studied *yōga* under Asai Chū and later Kanokogi Takeshirō at the *Kansai bijutsuin* (Kansai Art Institute) while assisting with the family business. He first went to Tokyo in 1911 where he worked as a cartoonist and illustrator in newspapers and magazines like the *Kokumin shimbun* (The People's Newspaper) and *Yomiuri shimbun* (Yomiuri Newspaper). It was at this time that he encountered and was deeply impressed by the work of Minami Kunzō at his landmark one-man exhibition prints in 1911. Kunzo's style profoundly influenced Sempan's nascent style. Maekawa participated in the *sōsaku hanga* movement from its inception and displayed his work in its first exhibition in 1919. His experience as a cartoonist is bore out by his simple treatment of compositional motifs and in his ability to effectively create a disquieting atmosphere as seen in 'Night in Shinjuku' (British Museum, 18×24 cm) in the Tokyo series. In 'Night in Shinjuku' the lonely figure and the cropped automobile in which are seated two silhouetted, anonymous figures presents an eery view of Shinjuku, today a bustling area of downtown Tokyo. By contrast, Sempan's *maiko* of Kyoto in the series *Nihon josokusen* (British Museum, 27×21 cm), mirroring perhaps Sempan's interest in Japanese folk prints, borders on a sweet, almost 'folksy' image. It relays an aesthetic different from the realistic beauty of Hakutei or even the idealized *bijin* of *ukiyo-e* artists like Kitagawa Utamaro.

Sekino Jun'ichirō's interest in printmaking was already surfacing during his years at junior high school when he and several of his schoolmates formed a printing collective. Later he studied etching, design and oil painting and first exhibited his work (a copperplate etching) in the 1936 *Teiten*. The *Teiten* (Imperial Art Academy Exhibition) was the latter day version of the *Bunten*; the change occurred in 1919. He moved to Tokyo at about the same time where he made the acquaintance of Onchi. Onchi introduced him to members of the *sōsaku* circles and the older artist's style would have a tremendous impact on Sekino. Sekino's works are especially striking in the use of line as in, 'The Benkei Bridge, Akasaka' (British Museum, 17.9×24 cm) in *Tōkyō kaikō zue* and relaying a sculptural quality as seen in the face of the old man leading the 'Oiran's Street Procession' (British Museum, 24.2×18.3 cm, See Smith [1983], cat. 89) from the *Nihon minzoku zufu*. Here, an *oiran,* a high-class courtesan, dressed in a sumptuous kimono, high wooden geta and bedeckled with lavish hairpins, is illustrated parading through the street in an effect to show off her beauty and perhaps entice future patrons. Sekino's figurative studies often appear to capture the sitter in a moment of thought as seen in the 'Maid of Northern Japan' (British Museum, 24.1×18.2 cm) from the *Nihon josokusen* and is continued in later works such as the 1968 'Portrait of Munakata' (page 209). The unidealized treatment of Munakata as the unkempt artist, who is in this print depicted before one of his prints from the series *The Ten Great Disciples of Buddha* (1939), conveys in a poignant manner the personality of the subject in a fashion similar to Onchi's 'Portrait of Hagiwara.'

Sōsaku artists of the older generation such as Hiratsuka were particularly important in encouraging younger artists, such as Azechi Umetarō. In 1920 Azechi was in Tokyo working as a printer in the *Naikaku insatsukyoku* (Interior Ministry of Printing) and pursuing his painting studies, when Hiratsuka noticed his work. Hiratsuka advised him to consider a career as a printmaker and in 1927 he submitted prints to the Seventh annual exhibition of the *Nippon sōsaku hanga kyōkai*. Azechi's initially produced urban scenes and landscapes in a painterly fashion but after the War his interest in mountaineering (he actually wrote a book about it) influenced his choice of subjects which focused on the illustration of the scenes and the inhabitants of Japan's mountainous regions (see 'Snowman'). 'Fighting Bulls in Iyo' (British Museum, 20.9×27 cm) from *Nihon minzoku zufu* represents something of a departure in Azechi's work, but nonetheless retains his typical painterly style.

Saitō Kiyoshi, a native of the mountainous area of Aizu, went to Tokyo at the age of 25 (1931) where he studied design at the *Jiyū kenkyūjo* (Free Research Studio). It was not long before he began to make prints and in 1936 he entered his prints for the first time in the 5th exhibition of the *Nippon sōsaku hanga kyōkai*. He also showed works in the exhibitions of the *Kokugakai*; and of the *Zōkei hanga kyōkai* (Formative Print Association), founded in 1937 by the printmaker Ono Tadashige (b. 1909). Saitō was a completely self-taught printmaker, unfamiliar with the traditional of printing with multi-blocks. As a result, he devised a system whereby he used a single block to print his works. Commenting about his early years in Tokyo and his view of printmaking: 'During this period I was painting in oils and because I felt resistence towards works that were "print-like", I created pieces as I chose. Even today, I enjoy the prints of that period.'[10]

Saitō's print style was bold, simple and painterly; he often depicted snowy landscape views of Aizu as seen in his contribution to the *Nihon minzoku zufu*. The figure in 'Winter in Aizu' (British Museum, 22.2×27.8 cm) in the series with his turned back and wearing a traditional snow cape, became a leitmotif in Saito's landscape works. Saitō's compositions appealed greatly to audiences outside of Japan, particularly in America, and consequently he has become internationally recognized.

Unlike many *sōsaku hanga* artists, who lived in Tokyo, Kawanishi worked from the port city of Kobe which was culturally isolated compared to metropolis like Tokyo. Kawanishi comments about the lack of appreciation of *yōga* in Kobe during his youth when he mounted an exhibition after his graduation from a school of trade, 'For the city of Kobe, this was the first exhibition of *yōga*. I arranged 31 works – primarily oils, but also pastels and rough sketches – that pleased me. At this point I was not yet making prints.'[9]

Kawanishi was, like Saitō, a self-taught printmaker, and was initially impressed by the works of Yamamoto Kanae. Kawanishi might be best remembered for his series of Kobe scenes such as *Kobe jūnikagetsu fūkei* (Scenes of Kobe in the Twelve Months, 1931) and *Kobe hyakkei* (100 Views of Kobe, 1962, no doubt the name a reference to Edo-period *ukiyo-e* series like the 100 Views of Edo. However, his piece in the *Nihon josokusen*, 'Kobe Bar Girl' (British Museum, 24.0×17.9 cm), demonstrates the striking style he evolved based on vibrant contrasts of primary colors and strong, flat shapes. The almost masculine depiction of the young girl's arms which are folded in front of her, hands and face perhaps represents the Kawanishi's image of the 'modern' working class Japanese woman.

The majority of the prewar generation members of the movement continued to work after the War such as Onchi as did second generation artists like Watanabe Sadao (b. 1913). In 1962 both Azechi and Watanabe together with other members of the *sōsaku hanga* movement participated in the publication by James A. Michener called *The Modern Japanese Print: An Appreciation.* While some scholars suggest that *The Japanese Print* represented the peak of old-style *sōsaku hanga* it did, in fact, contain works by a younger generation of *sōsaku hanga* artists as well. The ten works in the book were chosen by a competition held by the publisher Charles E Tuttle were meant to represent the richness and power of the modern Japanese print movement.'[11]. Watanabe's contribution to the book is entitled 'Listening' and depicts in a very mannered style, a bearded figure. His use of stencils in this piece reflects his training under Serizawa Keisuke, a stencil artist working in the *mingei* vein. Like many of his works, 'Listening' is executed on crumpled paper (*momi-gami*). The subject matter of this and many of Watanabe's prints are distinguished by their religious overtones. As the artist writes the book, 'I have always aspired to portray stories and episodes from the Bible. In this disturbed world, I would like to be able to heed the voice of Heaven. The person shown in this print is no one in particular but was created in this spirit.[12]

Concurrent with the activities of the old *sōsaku hanga* guard, a new generation of artists were coming to the forefront following the War. These individuals were also among those in *The Modern Japanese print* such as the woman artist Iwami Reika (b. 1927). Iwami first worked as a creative doll-maker and later, influenced by the work of Onchi, went on to produce prints that are a powerful contrast of light, dark and textures as in the print in Michener's book called 'Winter Composition No.' As evinced by projects like Michener's and earlier publications such as Oliver Statler's ground breaking book *Modern Japanese Prints: An Art Reborn* (1959), for the first time in its history, creative prints were seen and appreciated by Western audiences. The postwar period truly represents the 'coming of age' of the *sōsaku hanga* print.[13] This period also witnessed an influx of new cultural influences: the term *sōsaku hanga* (and the ideology underlying it), so instrumental in forging a path for Japanese printmaking in the early twentieth century, could no longer encapsulate the diversity that would come to characterise postwar Japanese printmaking.

NOTES:

1 Oda, Tadashige *Kindai nihon no hanga* (Contemporary Prints of Japan) (Tokyo, 1975), p. 10

2 Takashina, J, Shūji and Thomas Rimer with Gerald D. Boas, *Paris in Japan: The Japanese Encounter with European Painting* (Washington University in St Louis, 1987), p. 226. Reprinted from *Atelier* (October, 1925)

3 Onchi, Kōshirō *'The Modern Japanese Print: An Internal History of the Sōsaku hanga* Movement,' *Ukiyo-e Art*, no. 1 (1965), p. 15

4 *Paris in Japan, op.cit.*, p.132

5 *ibid*, p. 99

6 Wilson, Graeme, trans. *Face at the Bottom of the World* and *Other Poems by Hagiwara Sakutarō* (Charles E. Tuttle Co, 1969), p. 39

7 Smith, Lawrence, *The Japanese Print Since 1900* (British Museum Publications, 1983)

8 *ibid*, p. 110

9 *Kindai nihon no hanga, op. cit.*, p. 91

10 *ibid.*, p. 98

11 Michener, James A *The Modern Japanese Print: An Appreciation* (Tutland, VI and Tokyo 1962), p. 7

12 *ibid.*, p. 30.

13 Jenkins, Donald *Images of a Changing World: Japanese Prints of the Twentieth Century* (Portland Art Museum, 1983), p. 21

8
The Artistic Legacy of Shin Hanga

HARUO MATSUOKA

The history of *shin hanga* (new prints) is rooted in two artistic traditions: it was intended as a 'revival,' albeit short-lived, of the older *ukiyo-e* style and it paralleled the contemporary *sōsaku hanga* (creative prints) begun by Yamamoto Kanae (1882-1946; page 203).

After the middle of the Meiji period (1868-1912) the number of talented *ukiyo-e* artists was rapidly diminishing and woodblock printmaking skills were increasingly used to produce *ukiyo-e* reproductions for export. Westernization created a new outlook for Japanese artists and writers and inevitably it involved a threat to traditional art forms. The result of this was a sense of confusion in which the individual felt the paradox of choosing between remaining loyal to what would have appeared to be a vanishing past or to model himself on Western ideals. Print designers would have been no exception; the creative originality of *ukiyo-e* was questioned by many artists and a dissatisfaction with traditional printmaking methods led them to look eventually towards other forms such as *sōsaku hanga*. This confusion is alluded to by Nishimura Kumakichi, one printer of the work of the latter-day *ukiyo-e* artist Kobayashi Kiyochika (1847-1915):

> Since Kiyochika had studied Western painting, his lines were very different from those in traditional prints and extremely difficult to print. Kiyochika had seen many Western paintings, but his craftsmen had seen none. He wanted his designs printed so that they could be seen clearly even from a distance, but we printed them using traditional graded color shading. Kiyochika used to complain to us frequently.

Affected by the influx of Western printing processes such as engraving and lithography, the demand for work by woodblock artists, skilled carvers and

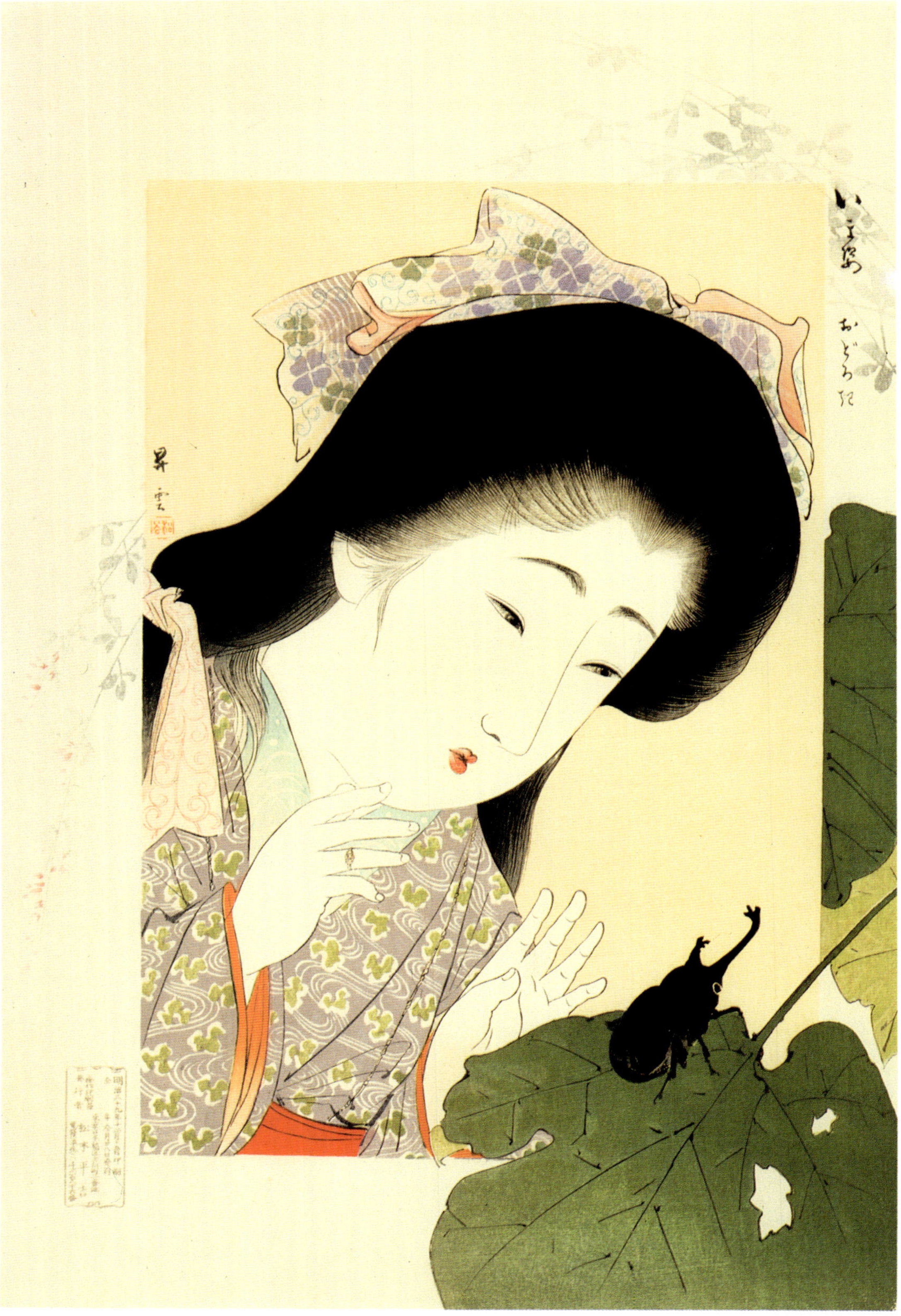

printers of *ukiyo-e* declined in the Meiji. The situation is described in the newspaper *Tokyo Asahi Shimbun* on February 25, 1908:

When the '100 Views of the Moon' (*Tsuki hyakushi*) series by the late Tsukioka Yoshitoshi (1839-92) was published, there were still many skillful carvers and printers. Since 1896 [after the Sino-Japanese War], however, the market for *ukiyo-e* has succumbed to the growing popularity of lithography, photography, and cheap chrome prints. Even if an excellent print in the *ukiyo-e* style is published, it is too highly priced because of exorbitant production costs. The only people who show interest in such prints are foreigners; thus, wholesale dealers are reluctant to continue dealing in *ukiyo-e*. As a result, woodblock carvers now have to do some drawings to make a living, and many printers have quit printing to seek other means of survival.

This excerpt clearly depicts the difficult situation that contributed to the reduction in the publication and sale of woodblock prints during Meiji-period Japan. Ironically, however, the emergence of 'Japonisme' in the mid-nineteenth century, principally among artists and collectors in France, Great Britain and America, played a major role in the growing appreciation of Japanese arts in the West – including woodblock prints and books – and by the late Meiji *ukiyo-e* was acknowledged abroad as one important part of Japan's artistic heritage.

While the history of *ukiyo-e* has been traditionally interpreted as ending with the prints of beautiful women (*bijin*) by Toyohara Chikanobu (1838-1912) and Mizuno Toshikata (1866-1908), Yamamoto Shōun (1870-1965) continued to produce prints in the *ukiyo-e* vein. Matsuki Heikichi (Taihei; 1835-91), the fifth generation Daikokuya publisher, had published the light-and-shade color prints of Kiyochika. He asked Shōun – who had received awards for his Japanese-style paintings (*Nihonga*) of beauties entered in the *Nihon bijutsuin* (Japan Art Institute), *Bunten* (Ministry of Education Art Exhibition), and *Teiten* (Imperial Art Academy Exhibition) – to design a series named *Imasugata* (Phases of Women Today, above right). Consisting of 15 close-up portraits and 13 bust portraits, the prints, published between 1906 and 1909 – an eight-year hiatus since Toshikata's last print (1899) – are a modern reflection of *ukiyo-e* beauties. 'Phases of Women Today' did not sell well, partly due to the declining popularity of woodblock prints in the face of offset printing which diminished Matsuki's power as a publisher and the devastating Great Kantō Earthquake of 1923 which destroyed all the woodblocks owned by Daikokuya. Matsuki was forced to close his publishing business and subsequently the few remaining *ukiyo-e* publishers disappeared. None the less 'Phases of Women Today' is recognized as the bridge between *ukiyo-e* of the late Meiji period and the later *shin hanga* of the Taisho period (1912-26).

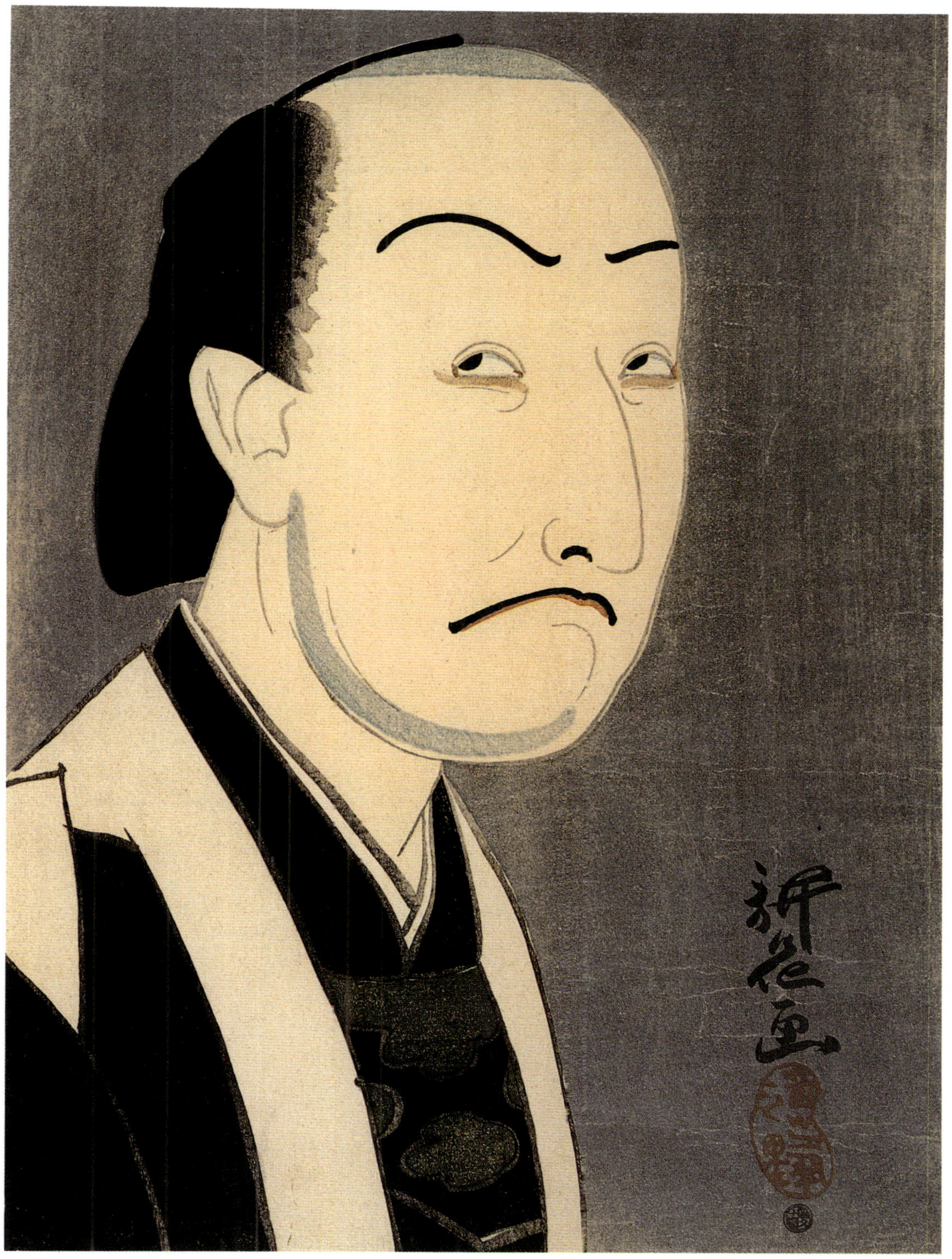

Above: Yamamura Kōka (1885-1942) Print of a Kabuki Actor. Courtesy of the R O Müller Collection.

WATANABE SHŌZABURŌ AND THE CREATION OF SHIN HANGA

Despite the disappearance of *ukiyo-e* by the first decade of the twentieth century, there were attempts to revive the *ukiyo-e* tradition and the man behind this movement was Watanabe Shōzaburō (1885-1962). In 1896 Watanabe, then 11 years old, went to Tokyo seeking work and was hired by the Yokohama branch of an antique store owned by Kobayashi Bunshichi (1868-1923). Kobayashi was very active in promoting *ukiyo-e* through organizing exhibitions, dealing and publishing. At Kobayashi's shop, Wata-

Left: Yamamoto Shōun (1870-1965) 'Surprise' (*Odoroita*) from the series 'Phases of Women Today' (*Imasugata*), 1906, 14½×10 inches (36.8×25.4 cm). Published by Matsuki Heikichi. Title in upper right. Date and publisher's name in lower left. Courtesy Abe Publishing Co Ltd, Gallery Kabutoya, Pallas Inc.

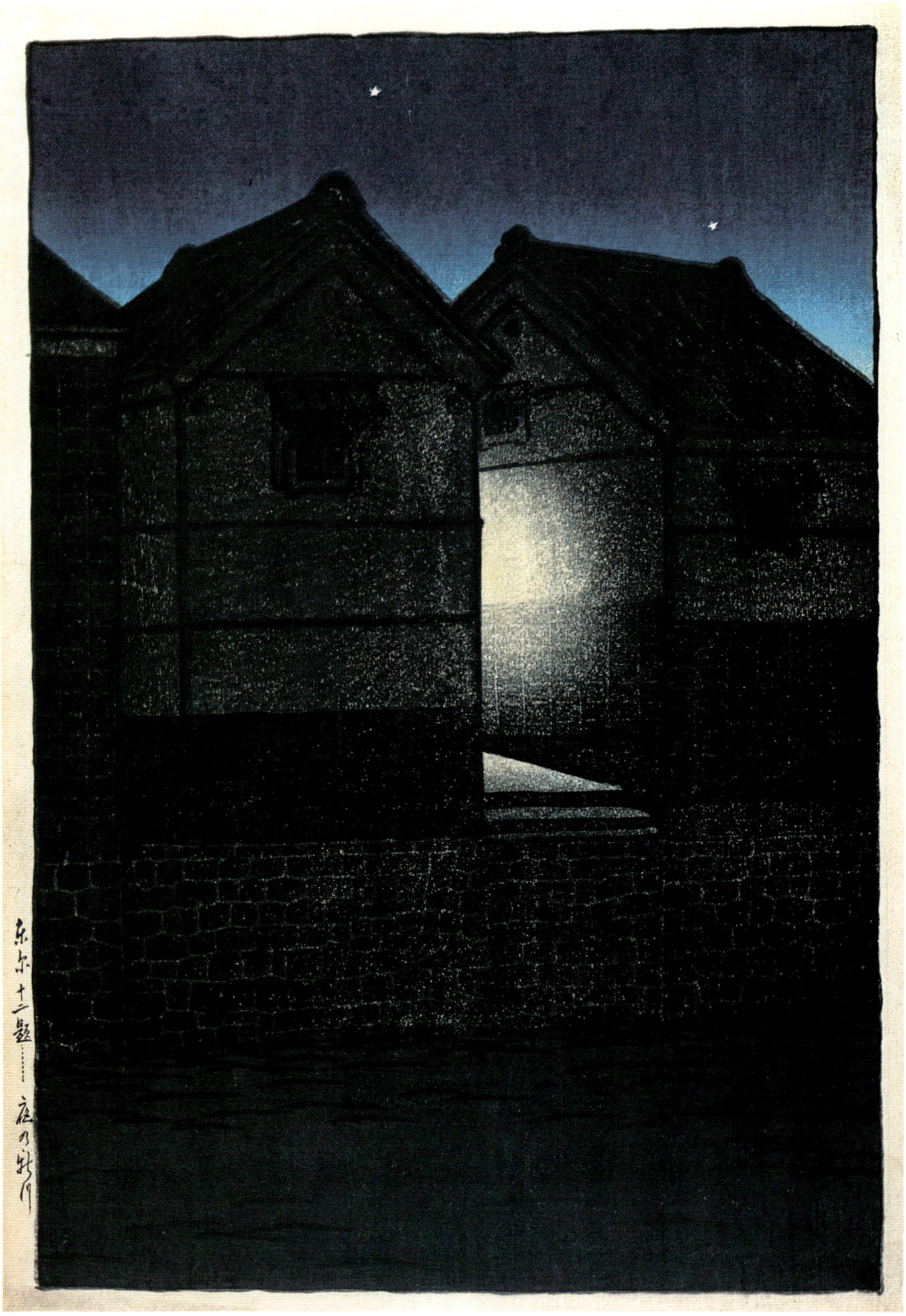

Above: Kawase Hasui (1883-1957) 'Shinkawa at Night,' (*Yoru no Shinkawa*), from the series 'Twelve Views of Tokyo' (*Tōkyō jūnidai*), 1919, 14¼×9½ inches (36.2×24.2 cm). Date and signature in lower right. Circular publisher's seal and artist's seal. Title in left margin. Published by Watanabe Shōzaburō. Courtesy Abe Publishing Co Ltd, Gallery Kabutoya, Pallas Inc.

Right: Itō Shinsui (1898-1972) 'Woman Wearing a *Datemaki* (undersash)' (*Datemaki no me*), 1921, 16×9½ inches (40.5×24 cm). Published by Watanabe Shōzaburō. Date and signature in upper right. Title in lower right. Edition number in left margin (no. 70 of 200). Courtesy Abe Publishing Co Ltd, Gallery Kabutoya, Pallas Inc.

nabe's association with *ukiyo-e* became the first step to his life-long devotion to woodblock prints and their production. On March 25, 1910 he opened his own woodblock print store at Kyōbashi Gorōbei-chō, Tokyo, just one year after his marriage to the daughter of Chikamatsu Otoju, an artisan carver of *ukiyo-e*.

Due to the vast numbers of *ukiyo-e* which had been exported to the West by 1900, the prices for those remaining in Japan soared. Watanabe expressed his grief regarding this situation, saying:

> Most of the excellent works are owned by foreigners now, and only a few are kept in Japan by those who have had foresight. Even the dealers have very few masterpieces, and those available are too expensive. It is too heavy a burden for a young scholar to purchase these prints for research.

The Tokyo *ukiyo-e* dealer Yoshida Kinbei started publishing reproductions of traditional *ukiyo-e* because of the shortage of originals and their escalating prices. By the end of the Meiji period Watanabe too began publishing *ukiyo-e* reproductions. He came to appreciate their high artistic value and the sophisticated skills necessary for carving and printing them. As a consequence of his contact with true *ukiyo-e*, Watanabe sought to revitalize the tradition in a new form, thus his creation of the term *shin hanga* (new prints). His reasons for doing so were numerous. First, as mentioned above, many examples of *ukiyo-e* were already overseas in the hands of Westerners who recognized their true value. Watanabe felt that the aim of *shin hanga* would be didactic, i.e. to educate the Japanese by deepening their understanding and love for the traditional art of *ukiyo-e*. Second, by producing *shin hanga*, Watanabe himself came to recognize and hoped others also would recognize the superb artistic craftsmanship of *ukiyo-e*. Third, the *shin hanga* he published would have the same high quality as 'original' *ukiyo-e*, enabling people to appreciate and collect them easily. Fourth, the publication of high-quality prints would become important for future research, not just for the pursuit of profit. Fifth, the creation of *shin hanga* as a contemporary form of *ukiyo-e* would become one way of encouraging artists to capture the natural beauty of the country and the lives of the people in their prints. Finally, the reproduction of traditional prints and the publication of *shin hanga* would augment the nation's artistic heritage.

Watanabe embossed the prints published with a special seal. Explaining the meaning of this seal in his shop catalogue of March 1, 1936, he states:

> Because I am the designer and the supervisor over the artist, engraver and printer, I had the idea to place my seal on an ideal art woodcut print when it is made. The characters reading *kō* (work) and *kō* (thought) were printed upon the prints in the period of reform in the 2nd year of Meiwa (1765). Most of the color-prints issued by my shop up to today are chiefly intended for abroad. Yet the high-class color-prints lately published as the successors of old ones are aimed to be appreciated by those who are interested in them at home and abroad. In signifying the incessant advancement, day and night, of woodcut color prints throughout the world, the characters 'Watanabe' in alphabet are printed on high-grade prints inside the white and black viz, day and night.

This explanation is testimony to Watanabe's extraordinary passion for publishing *shin hanga*. Once when Watanabe was asked which he held in greater esteem, *shin hanga* or *sōsaku hanga*, he

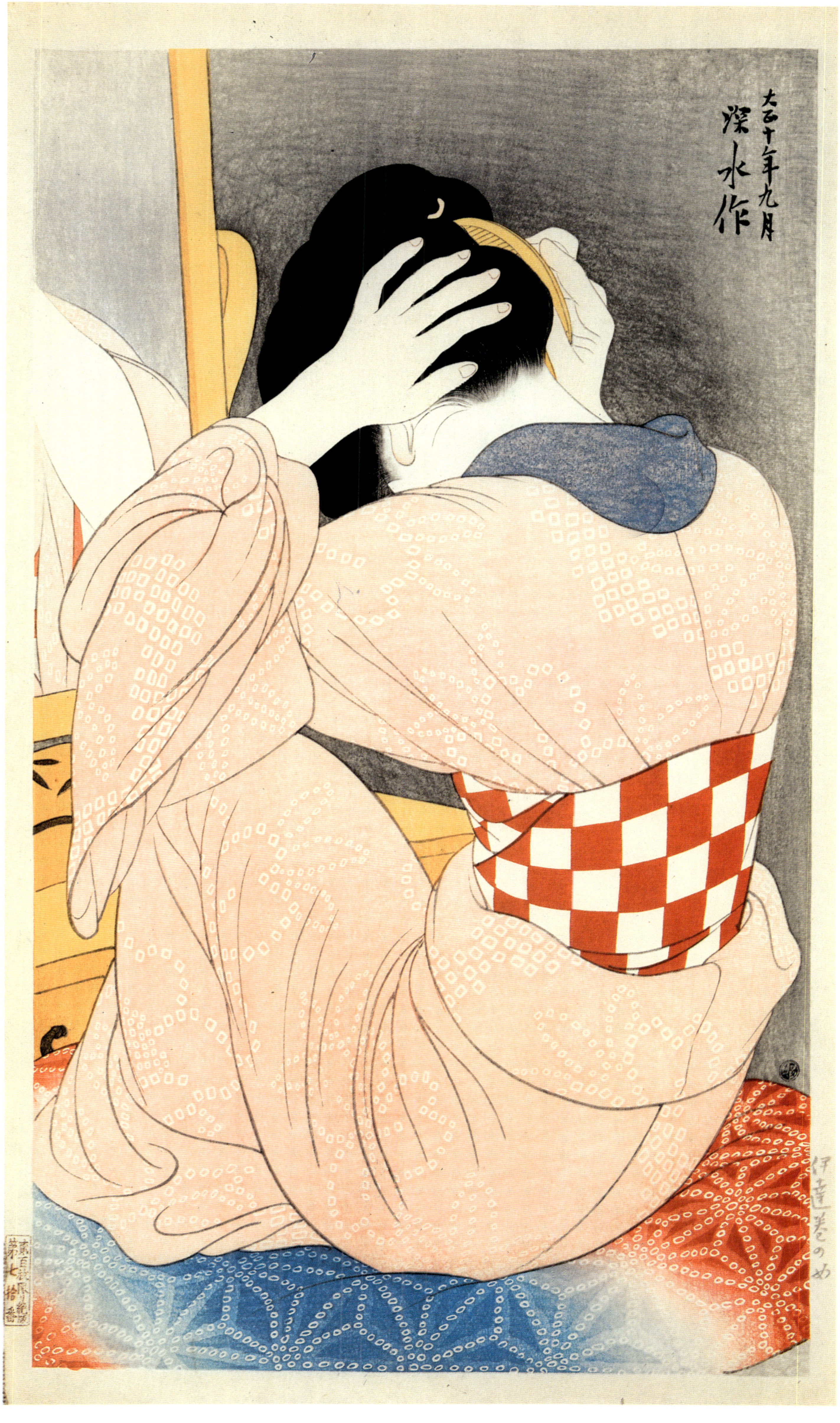

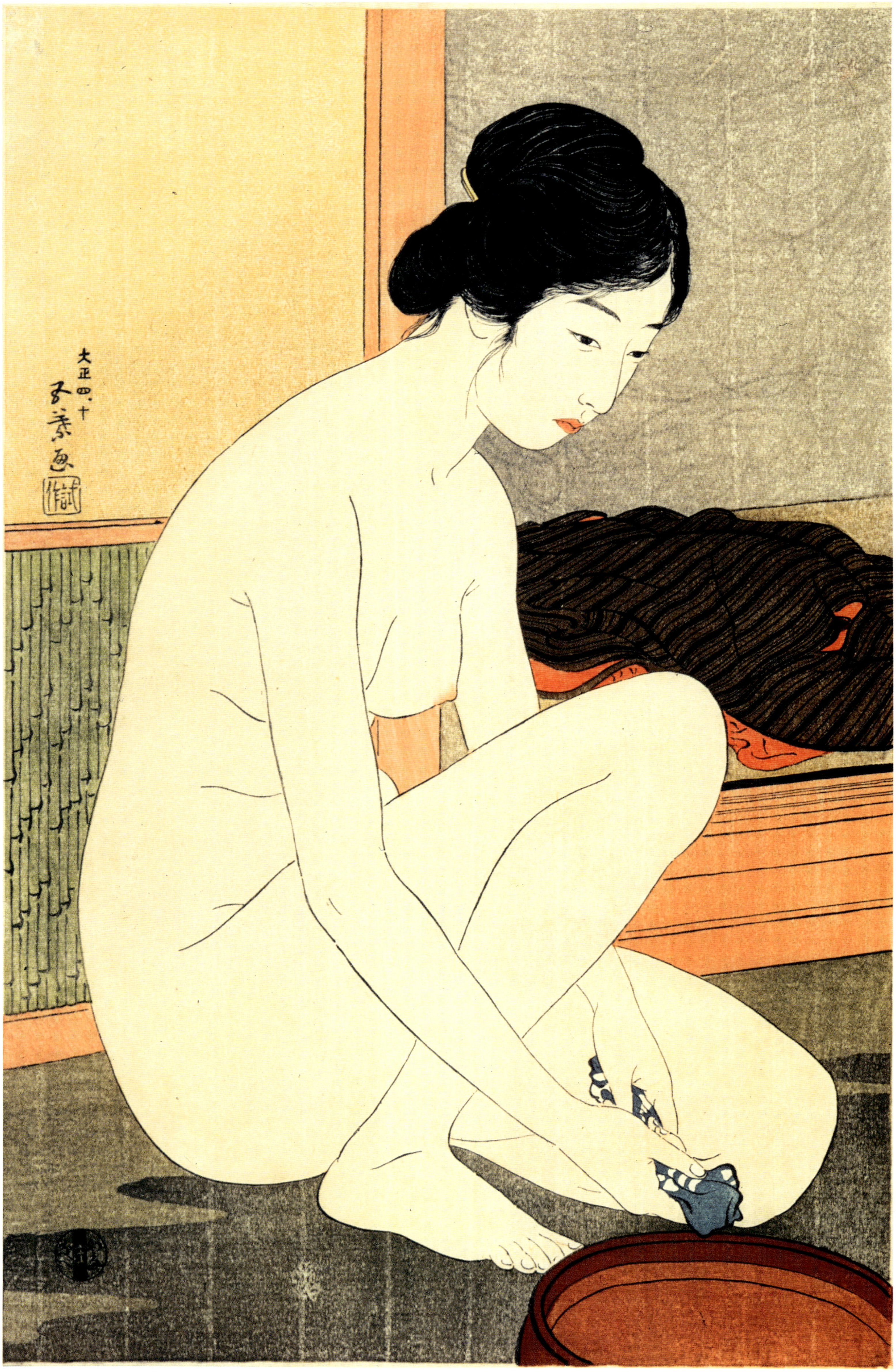
大正四、十

gave the following answer:

It is difficult to decide. The best works of *sōsaku hanga* are the ones created with great vigor by artists who have the talent to capture nature in their drawings, high skills in carving the blocks and printing, and deep understanding of the characteristics of woodblock prints. This, however, is easy to say but difficult to accomplish. It requires highly specialized carving and printing skills and great effort to create an excellent *sōsaku hanga*. Knowledge of the process and close study of other *sōsaku hanga* are not enough. If the artist is not well trained in all the areas that concern printmaking, he cannot create an excellent work, regardless of this drawing, carving, and printing skills.

I first ask of the artist to understand the characteristics of woodblock printmaking. The carver and printer work closely with the artist and make corrections until the work satisfies the artist. When the artist cannot have the carver and printer work as he wishes, I sometimes offer my advice. What is most important is for the artist to express what he wants to be in the print. Thus, it is probably best to say that the carvers and printer are the artist's assistants rather than co-workers in the creation of a print.

Watanabe believed that it was his place to supervise the creation of a new art form, and as such he played an important role in developing and encouraging artists to work in the *shin hanga* style. The first *shin hanga* print, which Watanabe published in 1915, was 'Woman at the Bath' by Hashiguchi Goyō (1880-1921) (see left), and this was followed in 1916 by a number of works by other artists that heralded the beginning of *shin hanga*. Among these were 'Before the Mirror' (page 218) by Itō Shinsui (1898-1972); 'Nakamura Ganjūrō I as Oboshi Yuranosuke' by Yamamura Kōka (1885-1942); and 'Nakamura Ganjūrō I as Kamiya Jihei' by Natori Shunsen (1886-1960). These prints and those to follow in the next few decades were evidence of Watanabe's devotion to the promotion of *shin hanga*, the 'modern' *ukiyo-e*.

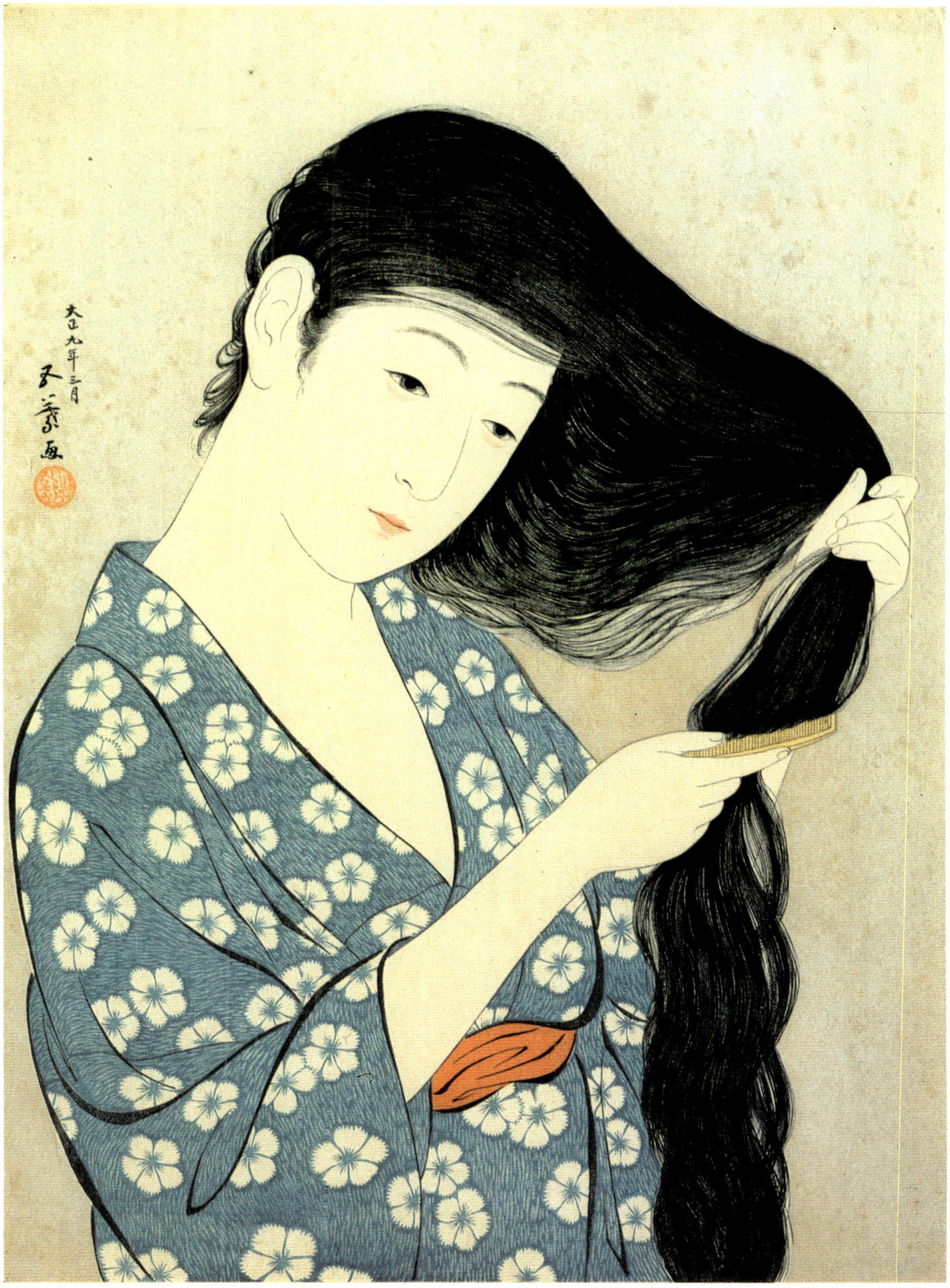

Above: Hashiguchi Goyō (1880-1921). 'A Woman Combing her Hair,' 1920, 17½×13 inches (44.5×32.8 cm). Published by the artist. Date and signature in upper left. Edition number in left margin. Courtesy Abe Publishing Co Ltd, Gallery Kabutoya, Pallas Inc.

THE ART OF SHIN HANGA

The *shin hanga* artist did not participate in every stage of the printmaking process and his involvement was generally limited to the design and coloring. In this respect the relationship between the *shin hanga* artist and his publisher was analogous to that of the *ukiyo-e* artist and publisher. This situation prompted criticism of *shin hanga* at its inception as representing a style which did not permit complete artistic expression in the same way as *sōsaku hanga*. *Shin hanga* artists and publishers were nonetheless seeking a more creative means of artistic expression. *Shin hanga* artists often worked with a repertory of imagery already familiar from *ukiyo-e*, such as pictures of beautiful women (*bijinga*), Kabuki actors, and landscapes, and at their best produced works which infused new life into the subject matter. At their worst they produced prints which were skillful, yet bordering on the 'sweet' and 'touristy.'

The artist credited with the first *shin hanga* print, Hashiguchi Goyō, first studied traditional Kanō school painting style and then *yōga* (Western-style painting). He graduated from the Tokyo Art School at the top of his class in *yōga* and after completion of his formal artistic education, he began studying *ukiyo-e*. Eventually, he became particularly knowledgeable about the lives and works of Suzuki Harunobu (?1725-70), Kitagawa Utamaro (1753-1806), and Utagawa Hiroshige (1797-1858). He published some reproductions of old prints and thoroughly researched the colors of *ukiyo-e* and printing techniques

Left: Hashiguchi Goyō (1880-1921). 'Woman at the Bath,' 1915, 19⅞×13¾ inches (50.5×35 cm). Published by Watanabe Shōzaburō. Date and signature in upper left. Circular seal of publisher in lower left. Courtesy Abe Publishing Co Ltd, Gallery Kabutoya, Pallas Inc.

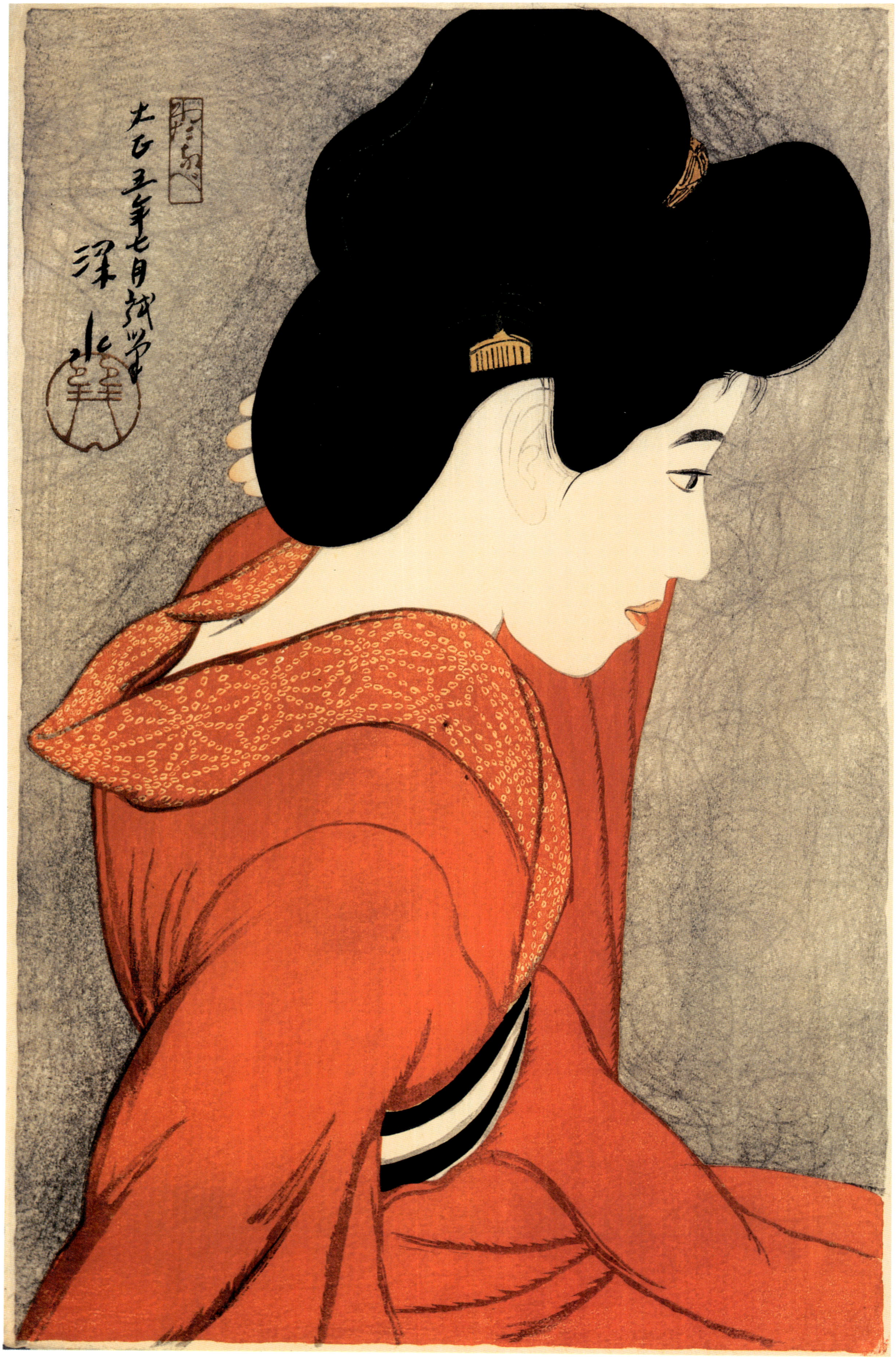
大正五年七月試摺
深水

using mica overlay. Through his research, he became acquainted with Watanabe Shōzaburō, who published his 'Woman at the Bath' in 1915. After 'Ibukiyama in the Snow' was published by Watanabe in 1919, however, Goyō issued his own prints. One reason for this decision was Goyō's dissatisfaction with the new technique of *goma-zuri* developed by Watanabe, in which the circular traces of the *baren* edge created a special swirling effect. Although he produced only a few prints, Goyō captured the beauty of Taisho-period femininity in a style inspired by the colors and printing techniques of traditional *ukiyo-e* and the flowing line of Western painting that drew inspiration from Western painting's attention to flowing lines and traditional colors and printing techniques of *ukiyo-e*.

'A Woman Combing Her Hair' (1920; page 217) is one of Goyō's masterpieces and attests to his thorough knowledge of *ukiyo-e*. The elegant and sensuous treatment of the figure is reminiscent of the work of Utamaro, who was emulated by many *shin hanga* artists. The addition of mica creates a stunning effect on the fine lines carved for the woman's glossy black hair; its thick application ensures that it does not flake off when in contact with other prints. More woodblocks than usually required are used to achieve the impression of the hair as a shining cascade, flowing gracefully from the head, down the neck, and around the shoulders, tracing the sensuous curves of the woman's body. The pattern of white flowers on the woman's *yukata* (lightweight kimono) appears to float upon her body, further accentuating her elegant and relaxed posture. The folds of the *yukata* are deepened with shading; similar shading is used on the red sash to provide depth. Goyō's red and blue colors in this print recall the colors used by Harunobu and Utamaro.

Itō Shinsui's (1898-1972) talent was discovered by Watanabe at an exhibition of students of the *Nihonga* painter Kaburagi Kiyokata (1878-1973). Watanabe's keen artistic sense told him that Shinsui would later become one of the leading Taisho print artists of Japanese beauties. In 1916 Watanabe published Shinsui's 'Before the Mirror' (left). The sharp contrast of red, black, and white in the print demonstrate the energy and talent of the young artist. Shinsui's strong, thick lines are unlike the thin, delicate lines of *ukiyo-e* and traces of his brushwork can be seen in the print. He also used uneven shading to create a three-dimensional effect. In the background of the print he avoided the traditional solid gray of *isubushi-zuri* which produces a solid untextured coloring and tends to make the print look too flat. Shinsui instead took Watanabe's advice and adopted *goma-zuri* for use in the background. The intensity of color of the woman's red kimono was obtained from a plant extract that was originally pale red which, when repeatedly applied, became a rich vermillion. This color is now impossible to reproduce. As noted on the print, 'Before the Mirror' was meant to be a work for study and reference. However, as both Watanabe and Shinsui were satisfied with the result, it was released for sale. The edition sold out quickly.

Torii Kotondo (1900-76) was adopted into the Torii family of *ukiyo-e* printmakers at the age of 15. Since the seventeenth century, the Torii School had excelled at capturing the traditional theatrical drama of Kabuki in woodblock prints and billboards. As a child,

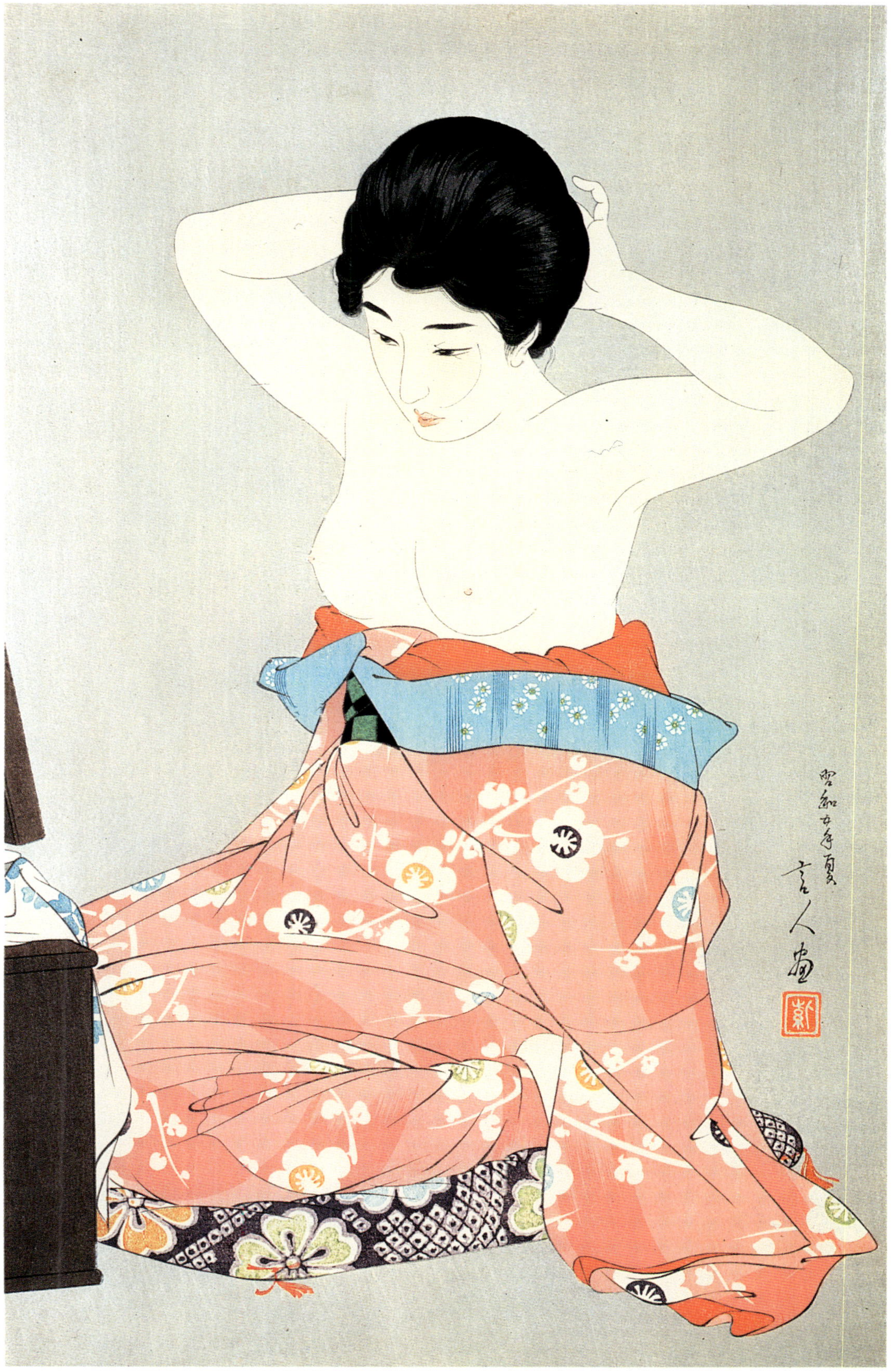

Above: Torii Kotondo (1900-76) 'Toilet,' 1930, 15⅗×10⅕ inches (39.7×26 cm). Published by Sakai Kawaguchi. Date and signature in lower right. Courtesy Abe Publishing Co Ltd, Gallery Kabutoya, Pallas Inc.

Left: Itō Shinsui (1898-1972) 'Before the Mirror,' 1916. Published by Watanabe Shōzaburō. Courtesy Abe Publishing Co Ltd, Gallery Kabutoya, Pallas Inc.

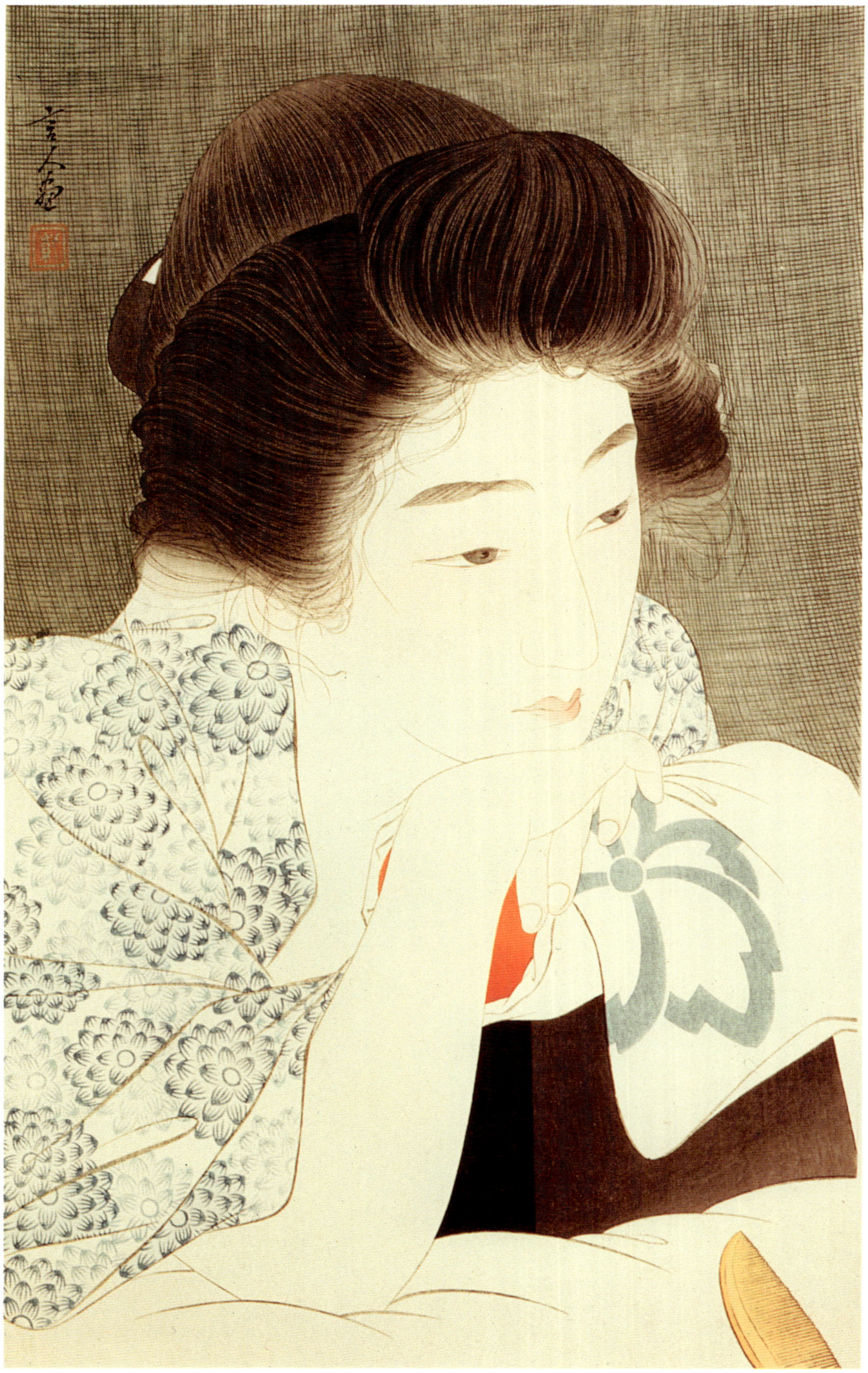

Kotondo helped his father, Torii Kiyotada IV, and learned the techniques of mixing paints and the preliminary painting of Kabuki billboard designs. At the age of 18, he became a student of Kaburagi Kiyokata and developed his talent in *bijinga*.

Kotondo became the eighth heir to the Torii school in 1929 and changed his name to Kiyotada V in 1958. While Kotondo became well-known for his *bijinga* after he began exhibiting in the *Nitten* (Japanese Art Exhibition, the successor to the *Bunten*) in the mid-1920s, he created only 21 prints of beauties under the name of Kotondo. These prints, when viewed overall, lack the wild passion of a youthful artist. Instead, they have a sophistication and dignity characteristic of the beauties of Torii Kiyonaga (1752-1815), the Torii school's fourth master, whom Kotondo held in awe and respect, and of his teacher Kiyokata. Kotondo's sensitive and graceful lines depict slender, refined Japanese beauties. Though his prints of beauties are few, their composition and their evocative illustration of the essence of Japanese femininity distinguish them as excellent examples of the *shin hanga* tradition.

The first edition of the print 'Morning Hair before Combing' (above) was the first Ikeda publication in 1930. The attention to detail is seen in the masterful technical treatment of the various com positional elements: two blocks, for example, are used for the closely woven mosquito netting in the background and three color blocks for the woman's hair. The print is exceedingly rare; the comb shown on the woman's futon was considered immoral by government censors as it suggested the languorous, sensual response of a woman who has just arisen to bid her lover farewell. The first edition printing was stopped after only 70 prints had been completed. The woodblocks and unsold prints were subsequently confiscated.

Kobayakawa Kiyoshi (1897-1948) began studying Japanese-style painting under Kiyokata at the age of 17. He also began to buy and study *ukiyo-e*, yet his interest in *ukiyo-e* and his attitude as an artist were diametrically opposed. He explained his thoughts about artistic creation in the magazine *Ukiyo-e geijutsu* (Ukiyo-e Arts) in its March 8, 1938 issue:

> I copied *ukiyo-e* and studied them, but I have found nothing to learn from them as an artist. Since only people who lived in Edo could depict the atmosphere of Edo, there is no use in copying their style. In the Showa period [1926-89], we have the art of Showa. Even if I try to draw a scene reminiscent of the time of Harunobu, my drawing would inevitably express the healthful beauties of today. I do not just draw customs and manners but try to capture the essence of the time in which we live.

Kiyoshi's first print was 'Tipsy' (right), published as part of the series 'Women's Manners of Today' in 1930. Rather than draw upon earlier themes of women of leisure, Kiyoshi drew inspiration from the ways Japanese women were reacting to the tumultuous changes affecting them. The theme reflects his interest in the illustration of the numerous faces of Japanese women in the first half of the twentieth century.

Ichikawa Toraji (1875-1964) presents us with a clear example of French influence on twentieth-century, *ukiyo-e* inspired printmaking. Toraji, who studied in Paris in the 1910s, is best known for a series of 10 large *dai-ōban* (37×49 cm) prints of nudes in strong colors, probably self-published in 1934 (right).

If, within the *shin hanga* tradition, Goyō, Shinsui, Kotondo, and others were the rightful heirs of the *bijinga* print, Natori Shunsen and Yamamura Kōka can be considered the artistic successors to the tradition of prints depicting Kabuki actors. Like many of his contemporaries, Shunsen began his career as a Japanese-style painter and worked in a rather dull, derivative style. In the 1910s he illustrated magazines and books. Watanabe approached him in 1916 and soon Shunsen was producing prints with him; by 1920 Shunsen had turned exclu-

Left: Torii Kotondo (1900-76). 'Morning Hair Before Combing,' 1930, 16⅛×10 inches (41×25.5 cm). Published by Ikeda. Signed and sealed in upper left. Printed by Ito. Engraved by Komatsu. Courtesy Abe Publishing Co Ltd, Gallery Kabutoya, Pallas Inc.

Right: Kobayakawa Kiyoshi (1897-1948) 'Tipsy' (*Horoyoi*) from the series 'Women's Manners of Today' (*Kindai jisei sho no nai*), 1930, 17⅛×10⅞ inches (43.6×27.7 cm). Published by the Artist. Date and signature in upper right. Title in lower margin. Courtesy Abe Publishing Co Ltd, Gallery Kabutoya, Pallas Inc.

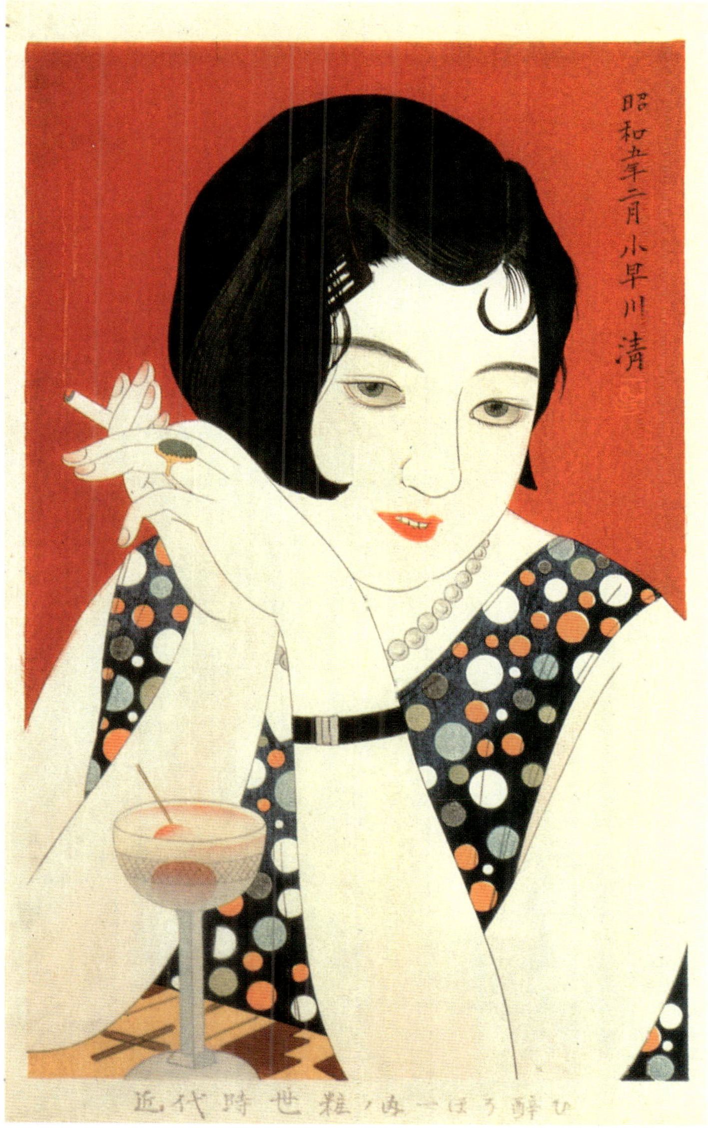

Below: Ishikawa Toraji (1875-1964) 'Dance' (*Odori*), 1934, 13×11⅘ inches (33×30 cm). Published by the Artist. Carved by Yamagishi Kazue. Signed and sealed in lower right. Courtesy Abe Publishing Co Ltd, Gallery Kabutoya, Pallas Inc.

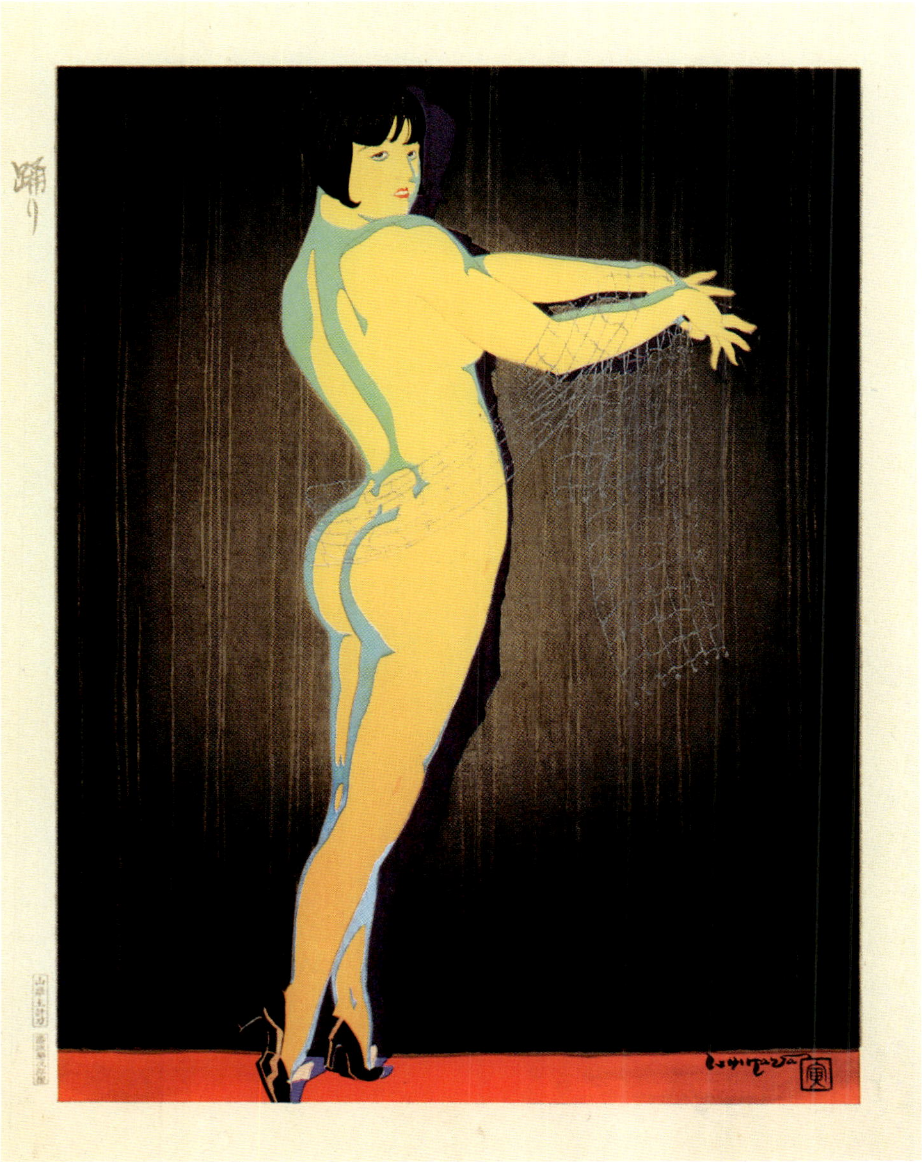

sively to printmaking. His name as a printmaker was made with a series of portraits (*ōkubi-e*) and full-length designs of actors from 1925 to 1931. These prints were initially published on a monthly basis. 'Ichikawa Chūsha VII as the actor Takechi Mitsuhide' (page 222) displays strength of line and color composition. Shunsen used paper of the highest quality and applied mica to the background to enhance the dramatic effect. After the war, Shunsen produced actor prints but was unable to achieve the same level of quality as those issued in the 1920s and early 1930s.

Yamamura Kōka (also known as Toyonari), a graduate of the Tokyo Art School, was a pupil of the prolific painter and print-designer Ogata Gekkō (1859-1920). He was persuaded by Watanabe to design prints and from about 1917 until the late 1920s, he worked periodically with Watanabe. The actor prints that he designed exhibit little influence of his teacher, Gekkō. Rather the compositonal approach and the treatment of the subject's psychological stance was inspired by the eighteenth-century print designer Tōshūsai Sharaku (*fl.* 1794-5). His strong actor prints make him the foremost representative of twentieth-century male portraiture (page 223, above right).

Kawase Hasui (1883-1957), another student of Kiyokata, was deeply moved

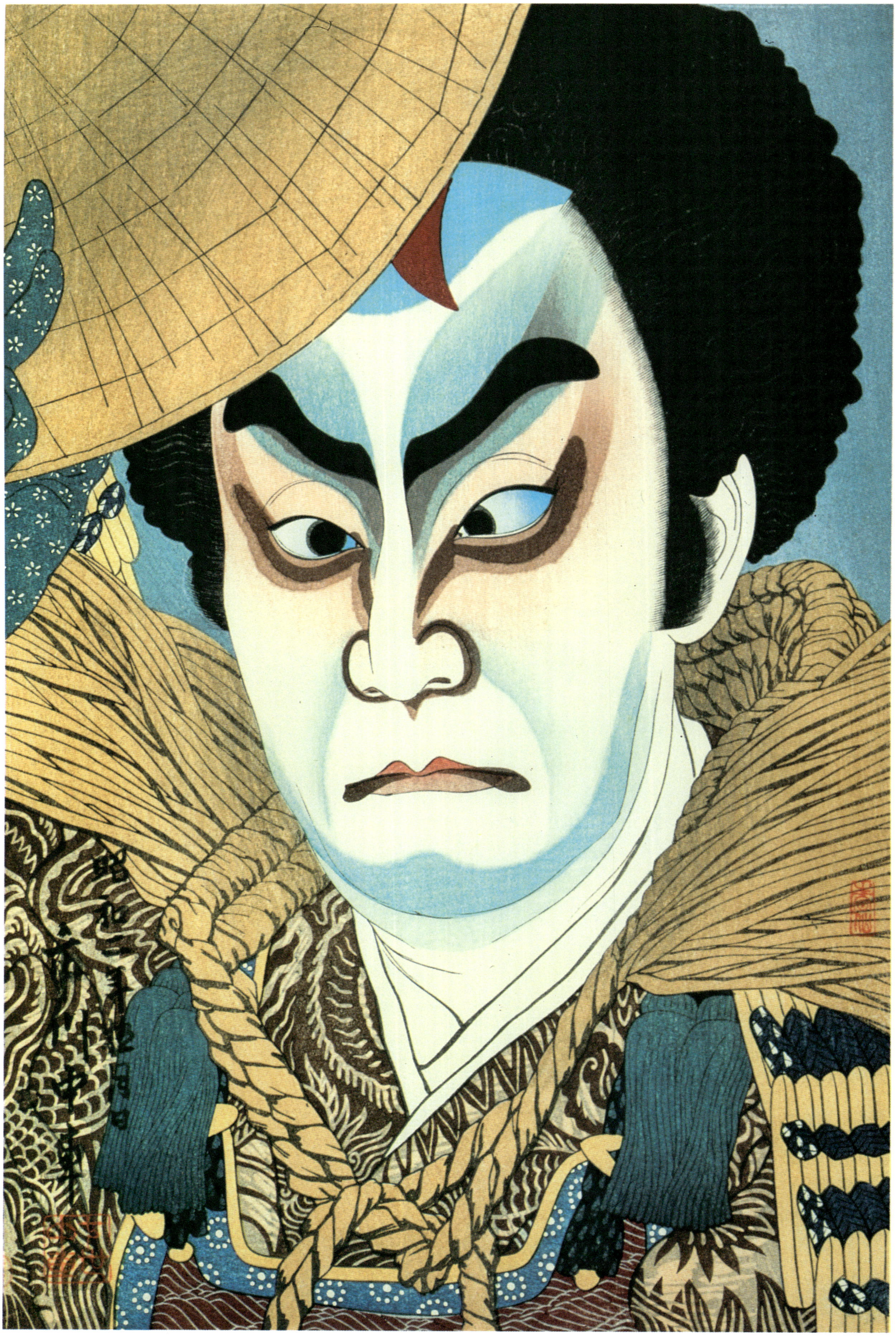

Right: Yamamura Kōka (1885-1942). 'Ichikawa Danjūrō I as Tesshinsai,' 1919, 15⅘×10⅘ inches. (40×27.5 cm). Published by Watanabe Shōzaburō. Signed and sealed in lower left. Courtesy Abe Publishing Co Ltd, Gallery Kabutoya, Pallas Inc.

Left: Natori Shunsen (1886-1960) 'Ichikawa Chūsha VII as Takechi Mitsushide,' 1927, 14⅘×10 inches (37.6×25.6 cm). Published by Watanabe Shōzaburō. Courtesy Abe Publishing Co Ltd, Gallery Kabutoya, Pallas Inc.

Below: Yamamura Kōka (1885-1942) 'The View at New Carton in Shanghai,' 1924, 15⅗×10⅗ inches. (39.8×27.1 cm). Published by Yamamura Kōka Print Publishing Association. Dated and sealed in upper left. Artist's seal in left margin. Courtesy Abe Publishing Co Ltd, Gallery Kabutoya, Pallas Inc.

by Shinsui's 'Eight Views of Lake Ōmi' (Ōmi hakkei no uchi). In 1918, his first prints published by Watanabe were 'Okane Path in Shiobara' and 'Shiogama in Shiobara' (*Shiobara Okane-michi*). He eventually became the leading *shin hanga* landscape artist, owing much to the style of the nineteenth-century landscapist Utagawa Hiroshige. His series 'The Twelve Months of Tokyo' (*Tōkyō jūni-dai*) began publicaton in 1920 but was never completed. Among the five out of twelve prints issued 'Snow at Sanjūkken-bori' (page 224) is an outstanding land-scape scene. What distinguished this print from other snow scenes was once noted by Hasui:

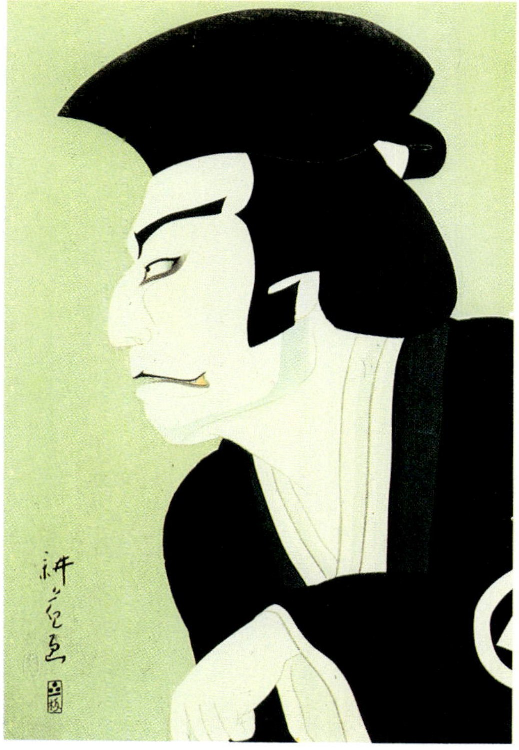

People have always been attracted by prints of snow scenes. Yet the snow in every print I have seen is a pattern of dots. I wanted to add a more realistic feeling to the image of falling snow. Whenever there was a big snow storm, I would study the swirling snow carefully. I chose Sanjūkkenbori because it had just the right atmosphere I wanted to capture.

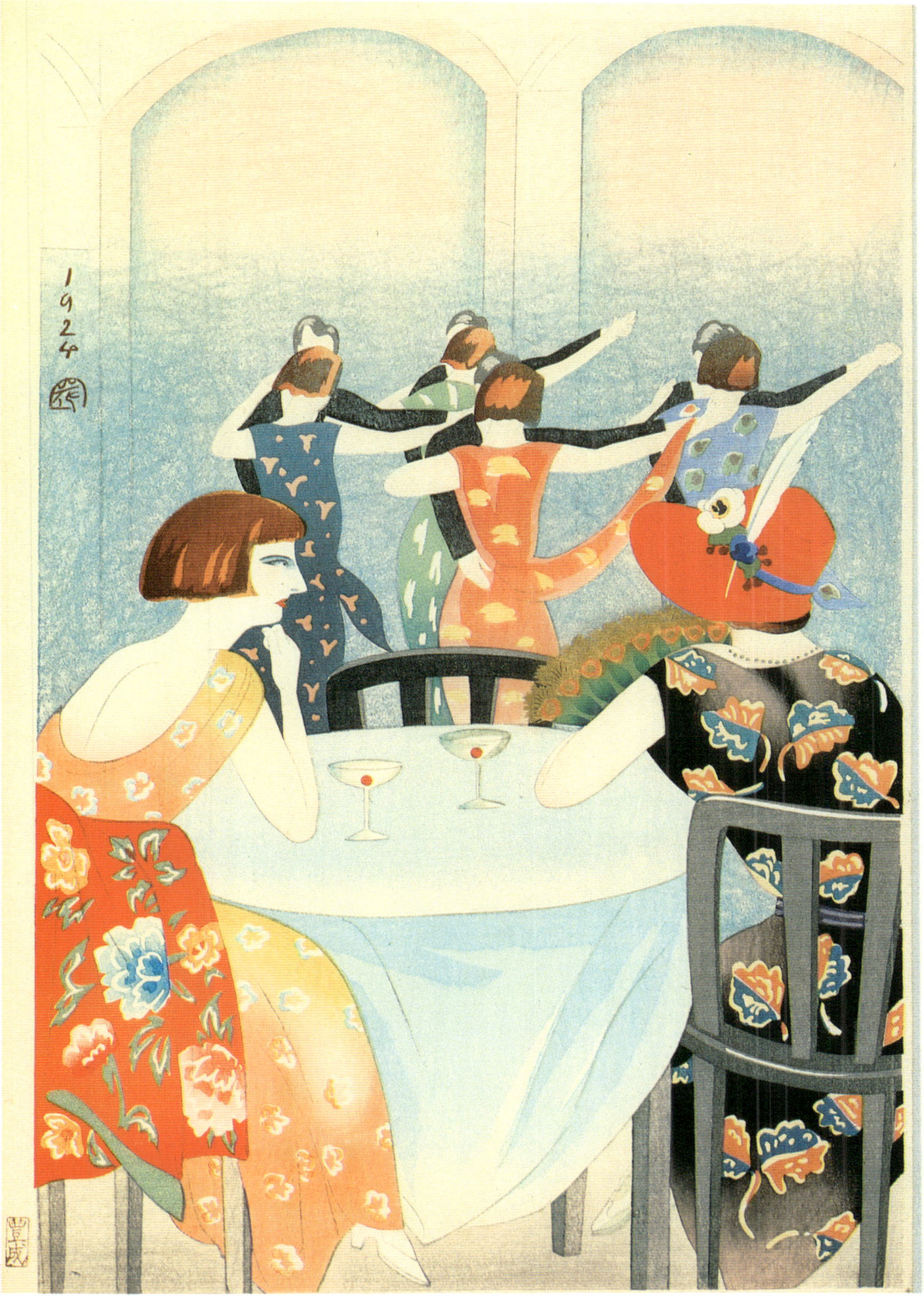

To add to the feeling of being in a snow-storm, Watanabe advised Hasui to experiment with a new technique of scratching the surface of the completed woodblock with a whetstone or scrub brush. 'Snow at Sanjūkkenbori' is so skillfully executed that it evokes a sense of being amid howling wind and swirling snowflakes.

Ishiwata Kōitsu (b. 1897) was one of the most talented of Hasui's pupils. He dealt with scenes taken from daily life, often set at dusk or night, and the intimate nature of his prints reveal an interest in depiction of the individual in his surroundings rather than nature alone. In the example illustrated (page 224) the light of lanterns provides the setting for human activity. Most of Kōitsu's work dates from the 1930s.

Yoshida Hiroshi (1876-1950) already had a secure reputation and steady income as a Western-style painter in 1920, when he became acquainted with Watanabe through the *ukiyo-e* dealer and distant relative Matsuki Kihachirō. He was persuaded by Watanabe to make the 'Sacred Garden in Meiji Shrine' which was commissioned by the Meiji Shrine Support Association and published by Watanabe. Subsequently Yoshida decided to devote his artistic talents to printmaking and of *shin hanga* artist he became one of the best-known abroad, especially in America. Between 1921 and 1932 Watanabe published seven other prints by Yoshida which included 'A Hunter's Story' (page 225). At an ex-

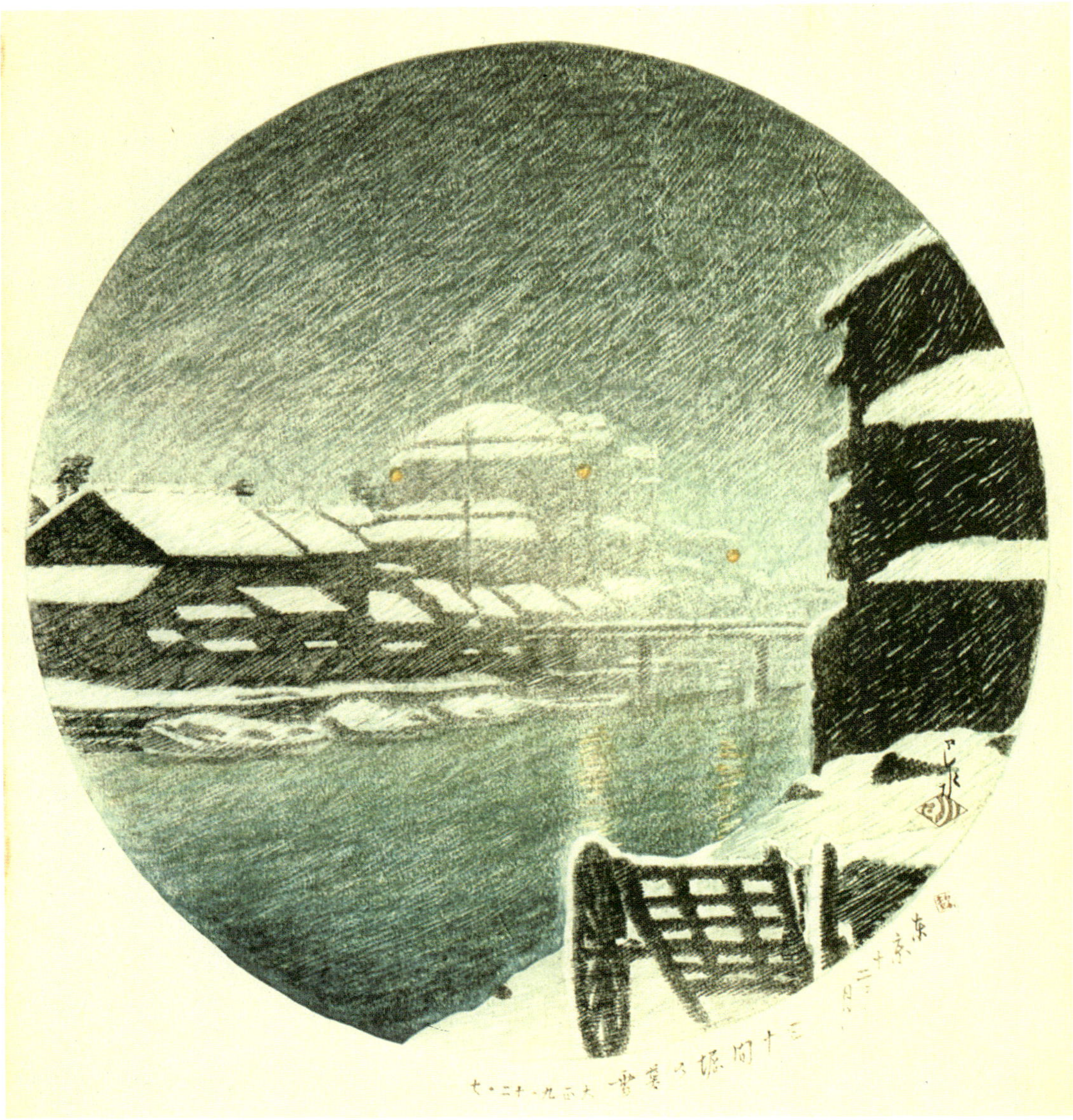

Left: Hasui Kawase (1883-1957) 'Snow at Sanjūkkenbori' (*Sanjūkkenbori no bosetsu*) from the series 'The Twelve Months of Tokyo' (*Tōkyō jūnidai*), 1920, image 10⅕ inches (26 cm). Published by Watanabe Shōzaburō. Title and date in lower right. Courtesy Abe Publishing Co Ltd, Gallery Kabutoya, Pallas Inc.

Right: Yoshida Hiroshi (1876-1950) 'A Hunter's Story,' 1922, 17⅘×13 inches (45.4×33 cm). Published by the artist. Courtesy Abe Publishing Co Ltd, Gallery Kabutoya, Pallas Inc.

Below: Ishiwata Kōitsu (b.1897) 'A Night Stall in Yokohama' (*Yokohama yomise*). 1931, 9⅖×14⅖ inches (23.8×36.4 cm). Published by Watanabe Shōzaburō. Title and date in left margin. Artist's and publisher's seals in lower left. Courtesy Abe Publishing Co Ltd, Gallery Kabutoya, Pallas Inc.

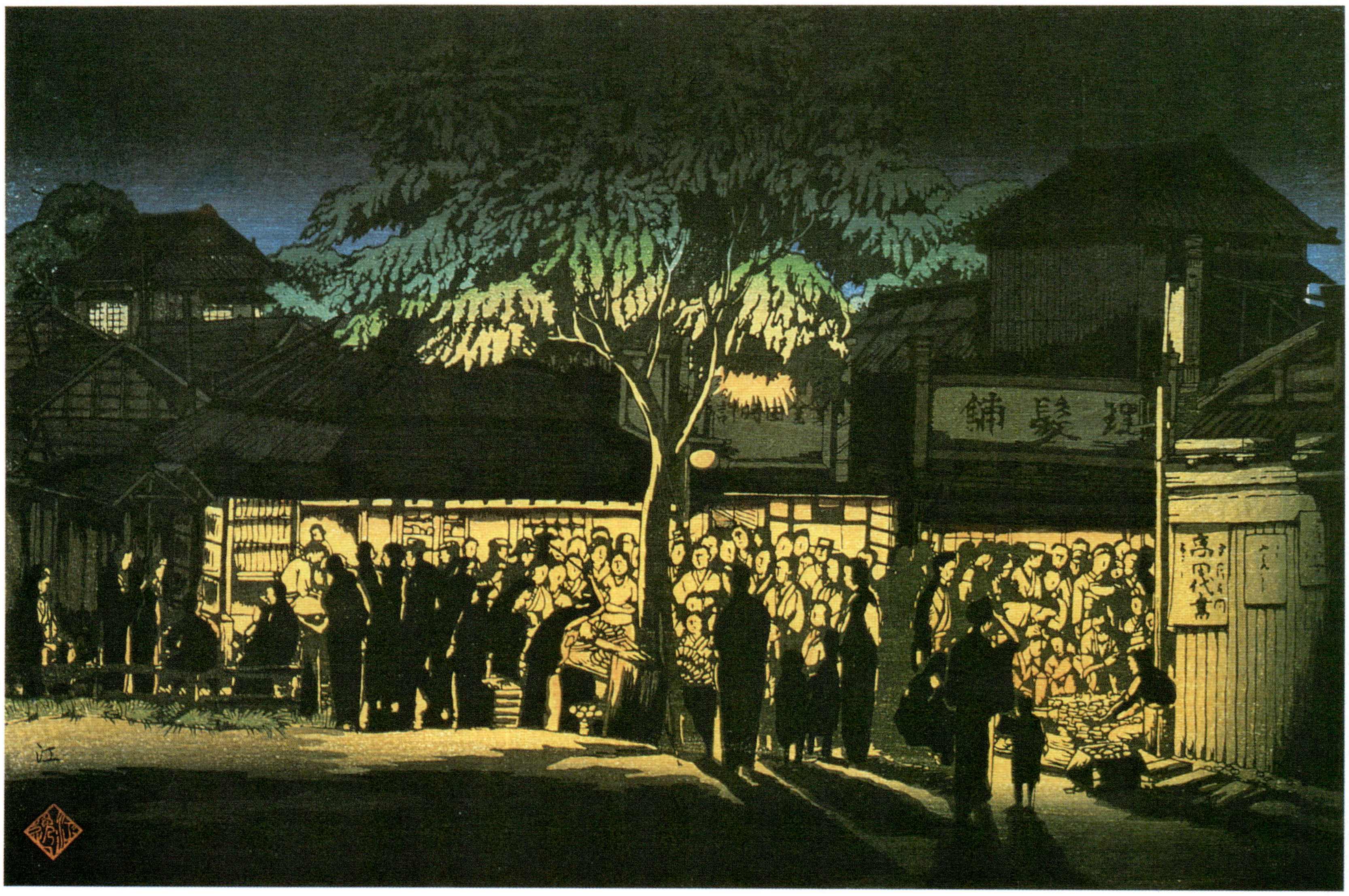

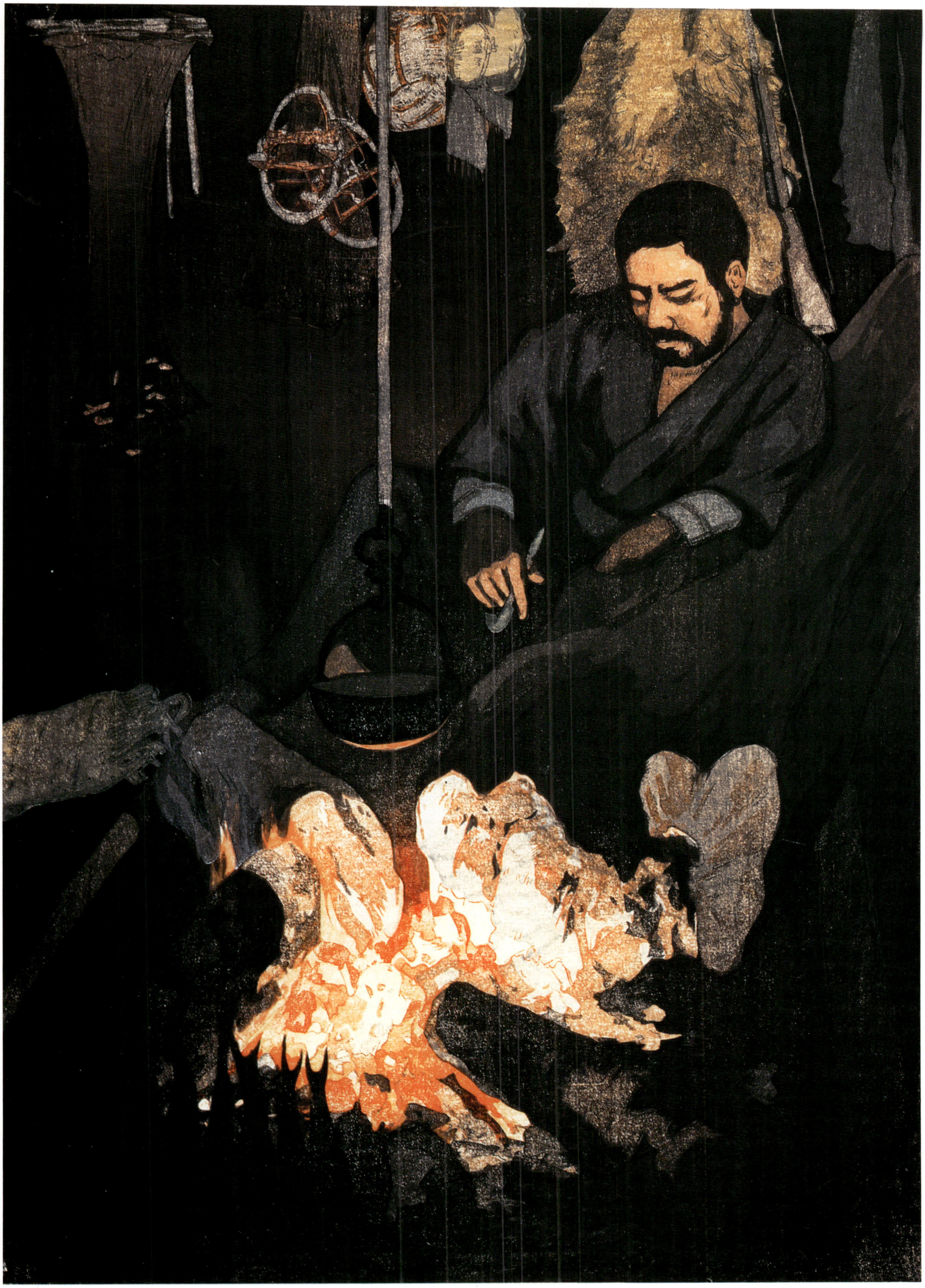

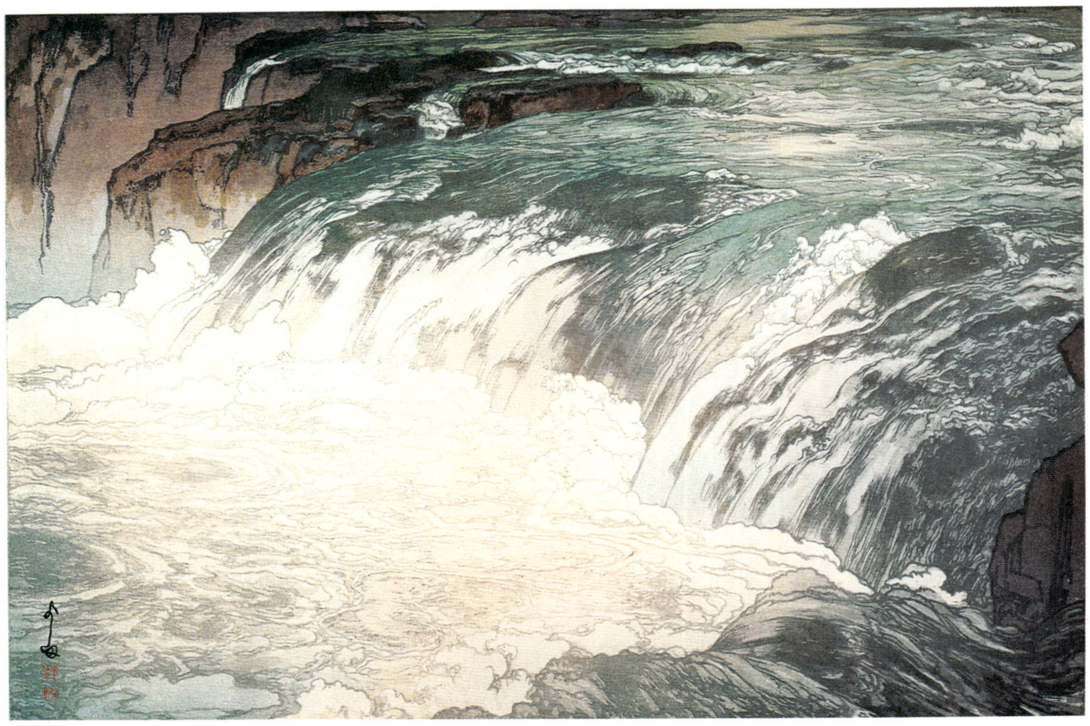

Left: Yoshida Hiroshi (1876-1950) 'Rapids' 1928, 21½×32½ inches (54.5×82.8 cm). Published by the artist. Title and date in left margin. Signature and seal in lower left. Courtesy Abe Publishing Co Ltd, Gallery Kabutoya, Pallas Inc.

hibition in 1936 at the Toledo Museum of Art, Ohio, the subtle gradations of light and shadow in 'A Hunter's Story' were compared with those of Rembrandt. The prints of Yoshida published by Watanabe reflect the artist's characteristically close attention to color gradations. In order to perfect this aspect of his work, Yoshida left Watanabe in 1925 and, hiring carvers and printers, published his own prints.

Yoshida was a seasoned traveler, having been to Europe, Africa and the United States as a young man. He had learnt in the United States that watercolors and prints were held in high esteem. His interest in traveling is reflected in the subject matter of his prints such as those in the 'Inland Sea Series' (*Seto naikai shū*) of 1926. He created six different variations of the same scene – 'Morning,' 'Forenoon,' 'Afternoon,' 'Mist,' 'Evening,' and 'Night.' The sunlight in 'Morning' (right) was cut with a tempered scalpel by Yoshida himself. The four impressions of this series entered in the Eighth *Teiten* of 1927 were highly praised and drew the public's attention.

The artist Takahashi Shōtei (1871-1944) began studying painting with his uncle Matsumoto Fūko (1840-1923) at the age of nine. Later he submitted works to exhibitions while working as an illustrator for scientific textbooks and newspapers. In 1907, with the encouragement of Watanabe, he started producing woodblock prints and by 1923 had published 500 prints. His works, varying in size from *mitsugiri* (one-third of regular *ōban* 20⅞×14½ inches [53×37 cm]) to postcard size, were mainly exported to the West, where they were avidly sought by European and American collectors. Shōtei changed his name to Hiroaki in 1921 and had eighteen *ōban* landscape prints pubished by Watanabe.

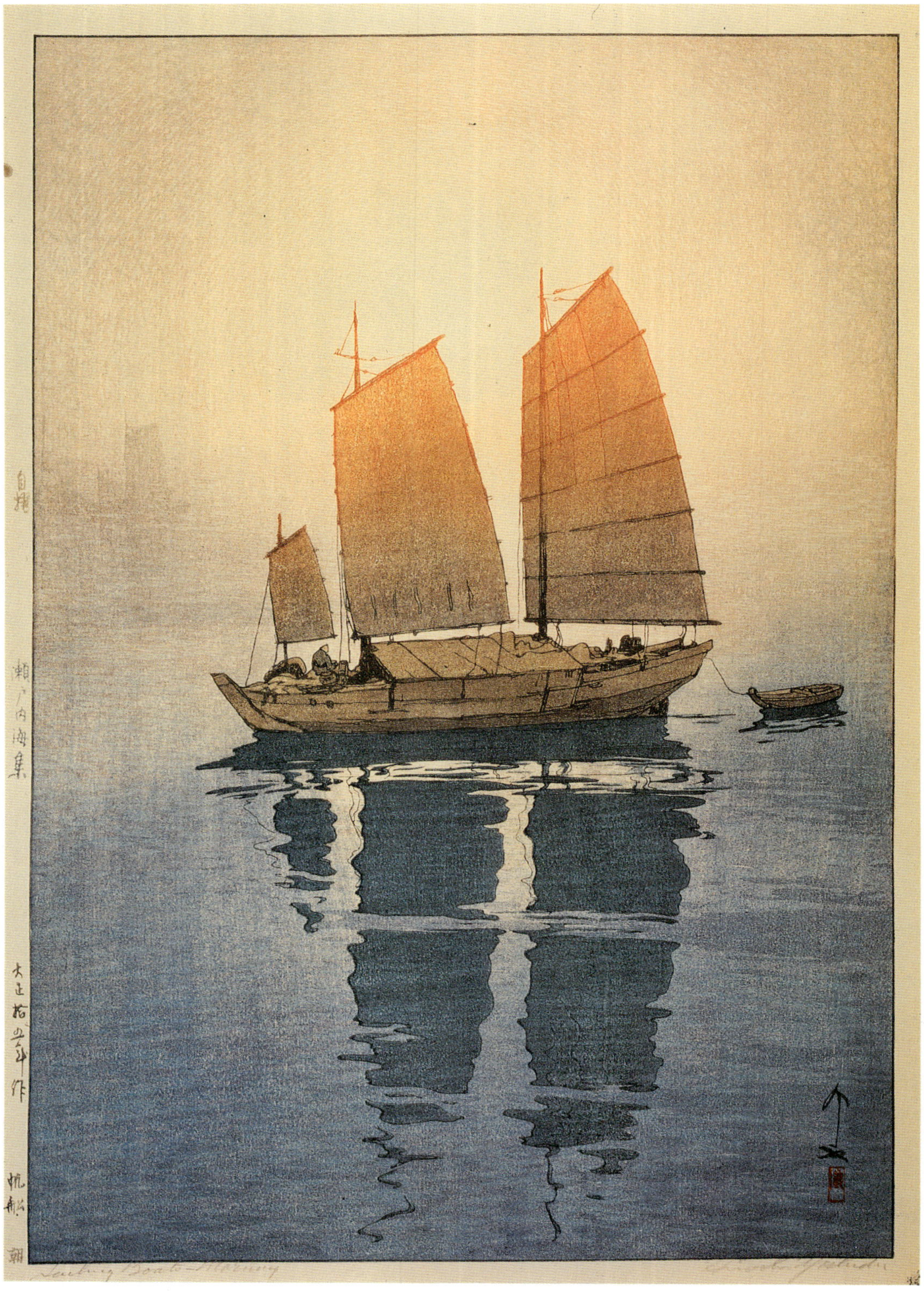

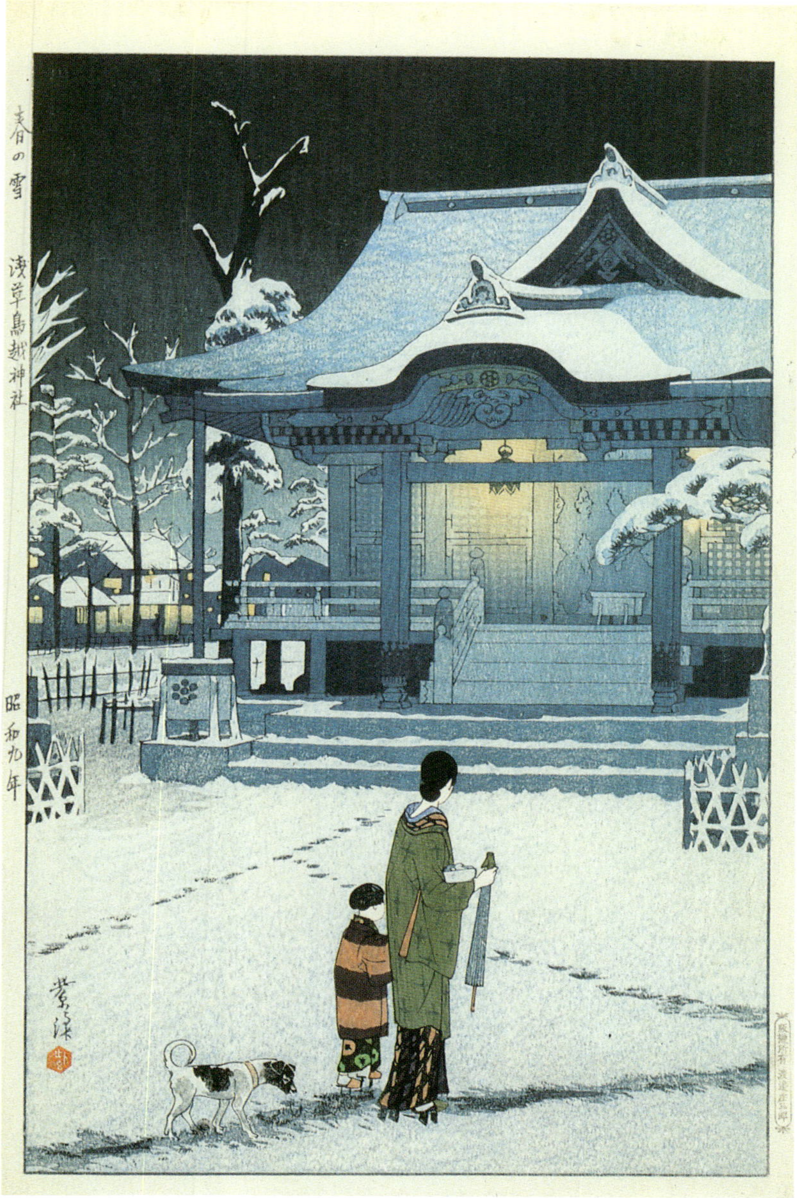

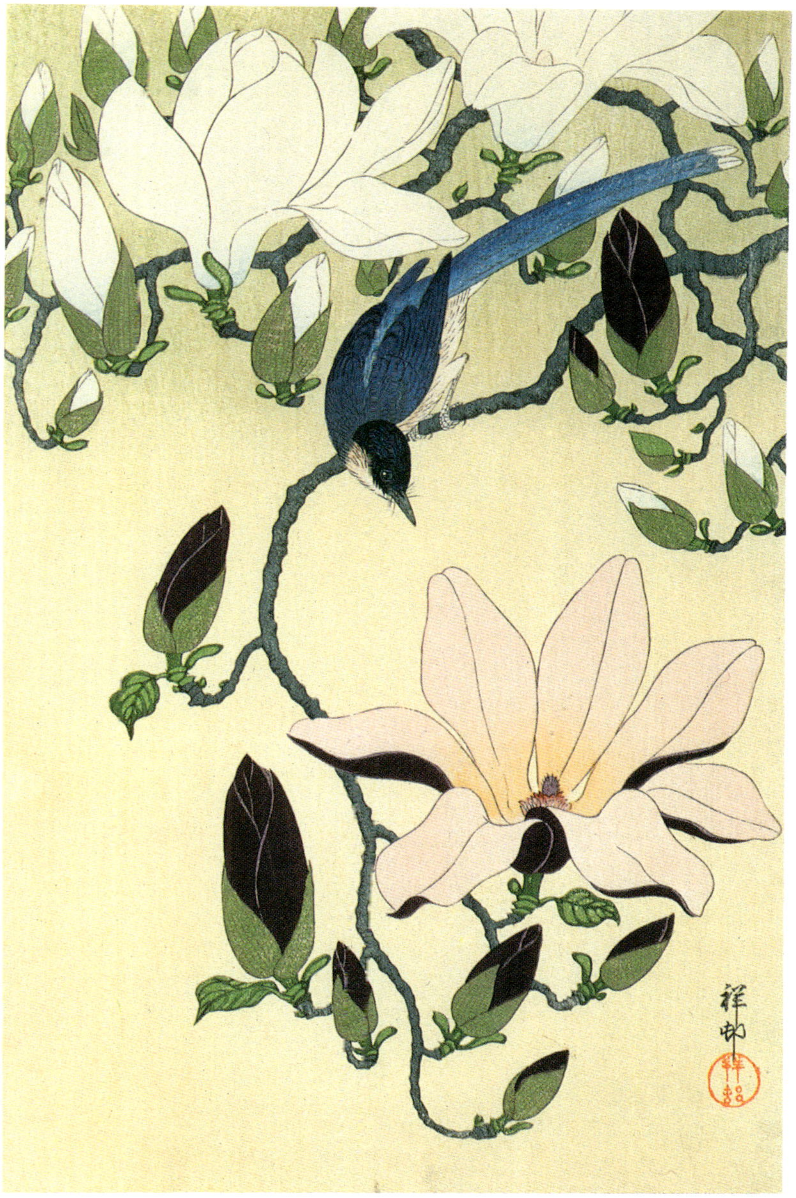

Above: Kasamatsu Shirō (b. 1898). 'Spring Snow at Torikoe Shrine, Asakusa' 1934. inches. (36×24 cm). Publisher Watanabe Shōzaburō. Title in left margin. Signed and sealed in lower left and in lower right. Courtesy Abe Publishing Co Ltd, Gallery Kabutoya, Pallas Inc.

Above right: Ohara Shōson (1877-1945). 'Magnolia and Eastern Blue Magpie,' c. 1930, 14⅖×9½ inches (36.5×24 cm). Published by Watanabe Shōzaburō. Signed and sealed in lower right. Courtesy Abe Publishing Co Ltd, Gallery Kabutoya, Pallas Inc.

Left: Yoshida Hiroshi (1876-1950) 'Sailing Boats, Morning,' (*Hansen asa*) from the series *Seto naikai shū*, 1926, 20×14⅕ inches (50.8×35.9 cm). Published by the artist. Title and date in left margin. Signed and sealed in lower right; signature in right margin. Courtesy Abe Publishing Co Ltd, Gallery Kabutoya, Pallas Inc.

A student of Kaburagi Kiyokata, Kasamatsu Shirō (b. 1898) frequently entered his paintings in the *Tatsumi kai* (Tatsumi Society) exhibition as well as the *Bunten* and *Teiten*. Watanabe published Kasamatsu's first woodblock prints in 1919. Kasamatsu specialized in landscape prints, particularly in scenes in and around Tokyo, as in the print of the Torikoe shrine in Akasaka. The frequent use of deep purple – Kasamatsu's favorite color – and the portrayal of scenes of Japanese customs and manners are two distinct characteristics of Kasamatsu's landscape prints. Watanabe had high hopes for the artist's success as a *shin hanga* designer but in 1945 Shirō left Watanabe and began to experiment with methods of printmaking (he also carved and printed his own blocks) that would later be associated with the *sōsaku hanga* movement.

Apart from the *bijinga*, actor portraits, and landscape, there were other *shin hanga* artists who made prints of nature studies, like Ohara Koson (1877-1945). Koson was trained in the naturalistic style of the Maruyama/Shijō school by the painter Suzuki Kason (1860-1919). He taught at the Tokyo Art School and was drawn to printmaking by the influential American art historian Ernest Fenollosa (1853-1908). He initially produced studies of nature (mainly birds) in the *tanzaku* format (14×7½ inches) [36×19 cm] which he signed and sealed Koson. After a hiatus from 1911 to 1926 Koson began producing works with Watanabe in the *ōban* format. He returned to design prints of birds and signed his prints with the name Shōson. Unfortunately, crudely printed versions of the artist's work were issued in endless editions before and after the war. While the prints produced during the last decade of Koson's life became garish (Koson then worked under the *gō* [artist's name] Hoson), the technical quality remained of the highest standard.

If Hashiguchi Goyō's 'Woman at the Bath' marks the beginning of the *shin hanga* movement, and the death of Watanabe Shōzaburō in 1962 the end, the period can be said to have lasted about 50 years. Despite its brief flowering in the history of Japanese woodblock prints, however, a closer look at *shin hanga* artists and their works, and at publishers like Watanabe reveals their devotion to creating prints indicative of a new age. *Shin hanga*, born of a romantic love of the past, grew into a graceful art that deserves its important place in Japanese print history.

Overleaf: Kitao Shigemasa (1739-1820) and Katsukawa Shunshō (1726-92) 'Women of the Maruya,' from 'A Mirror of Beautiful Women of the Greenhouses' Compared (*Seirō bijin awase sugata kagami*), 1776, volume 2. Courtesy of the Trustees of the British Museum, London.

9
Illustrated Books and Albums

A PICTORIAL SURVEY

The following survey begins with two examples of *ukiyo-e* in book form which are relevant to the discussion of Katsukawa Shunshō in Chapter 3 and of Kitagawa Utamaro in Chapter 4. Selections have also been added in an effort to introduce an area not covered in the text but which, nonetheless, comprise a significant part in the history of Japanese woodblock printed works: the illustrated books and albums of the 'impressionistic' Maruyama/Shijō school.

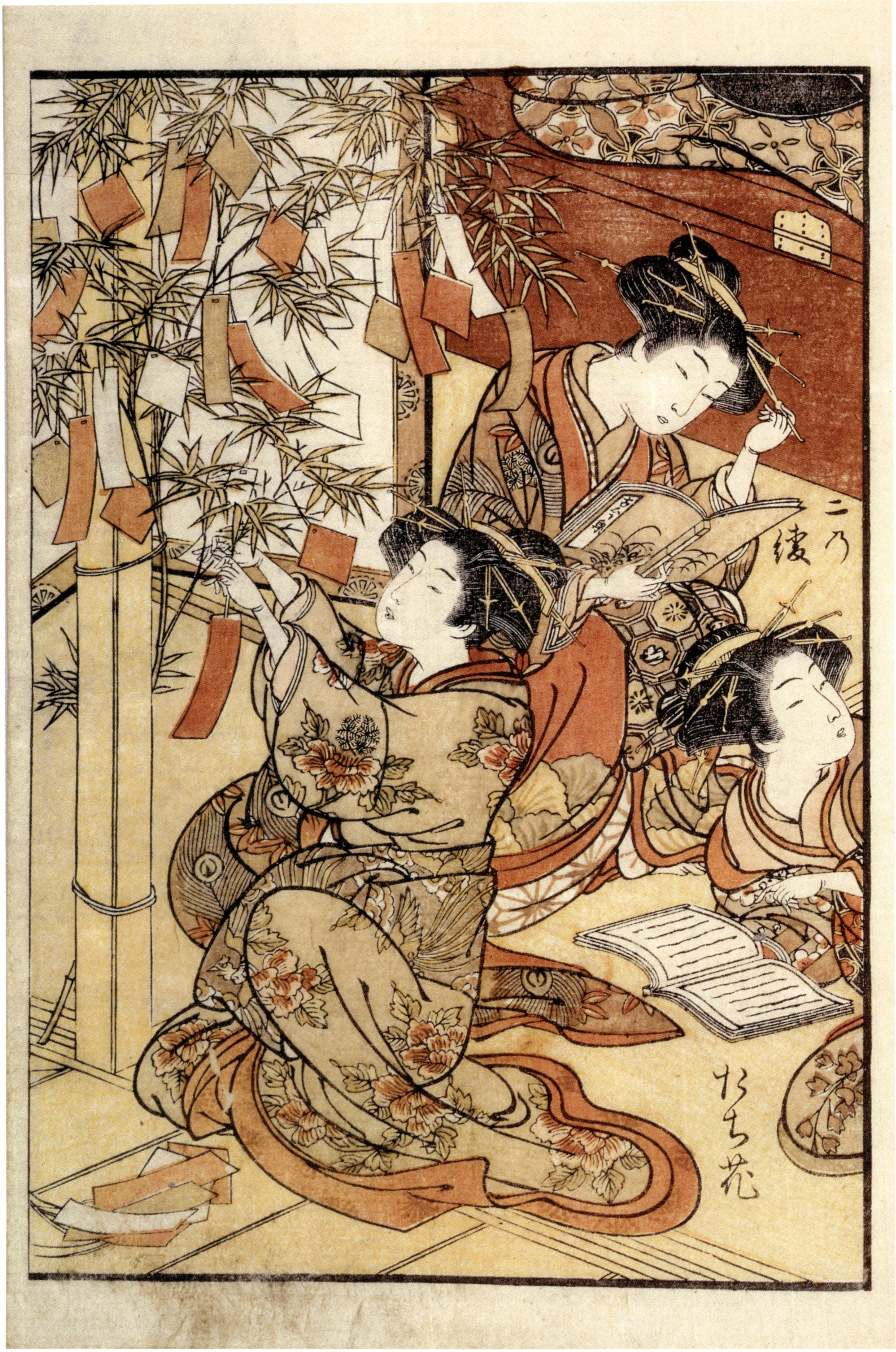

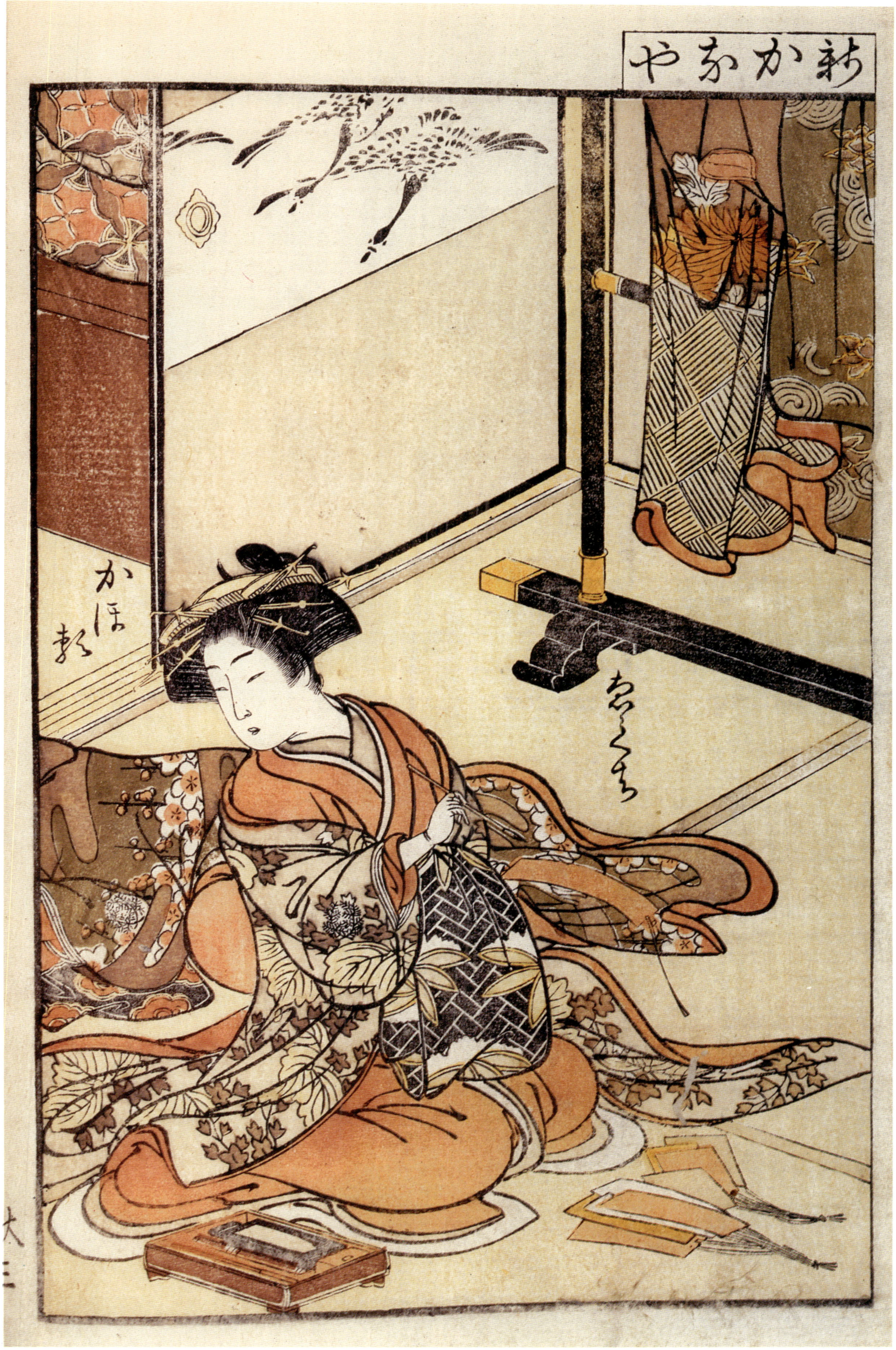

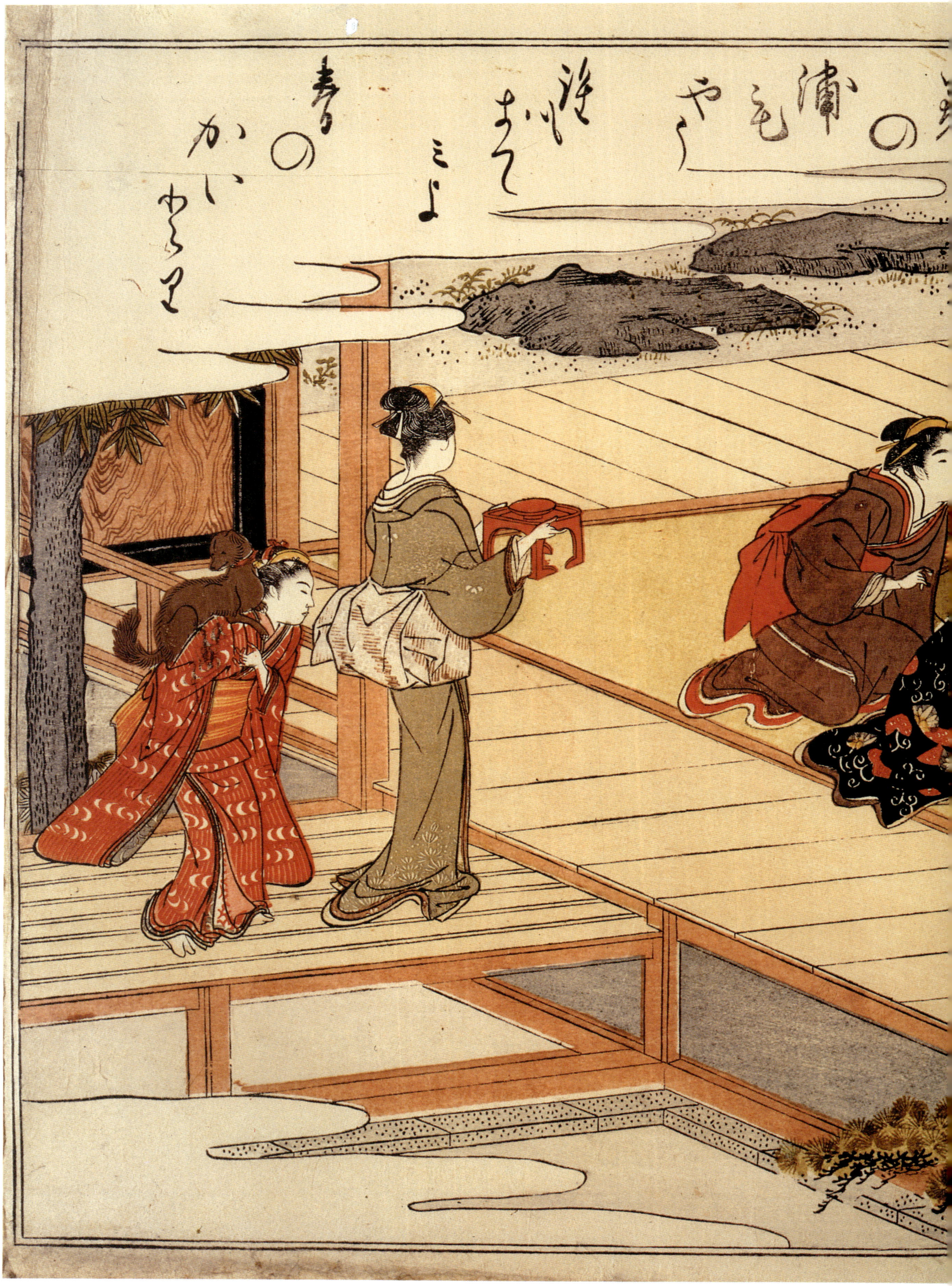

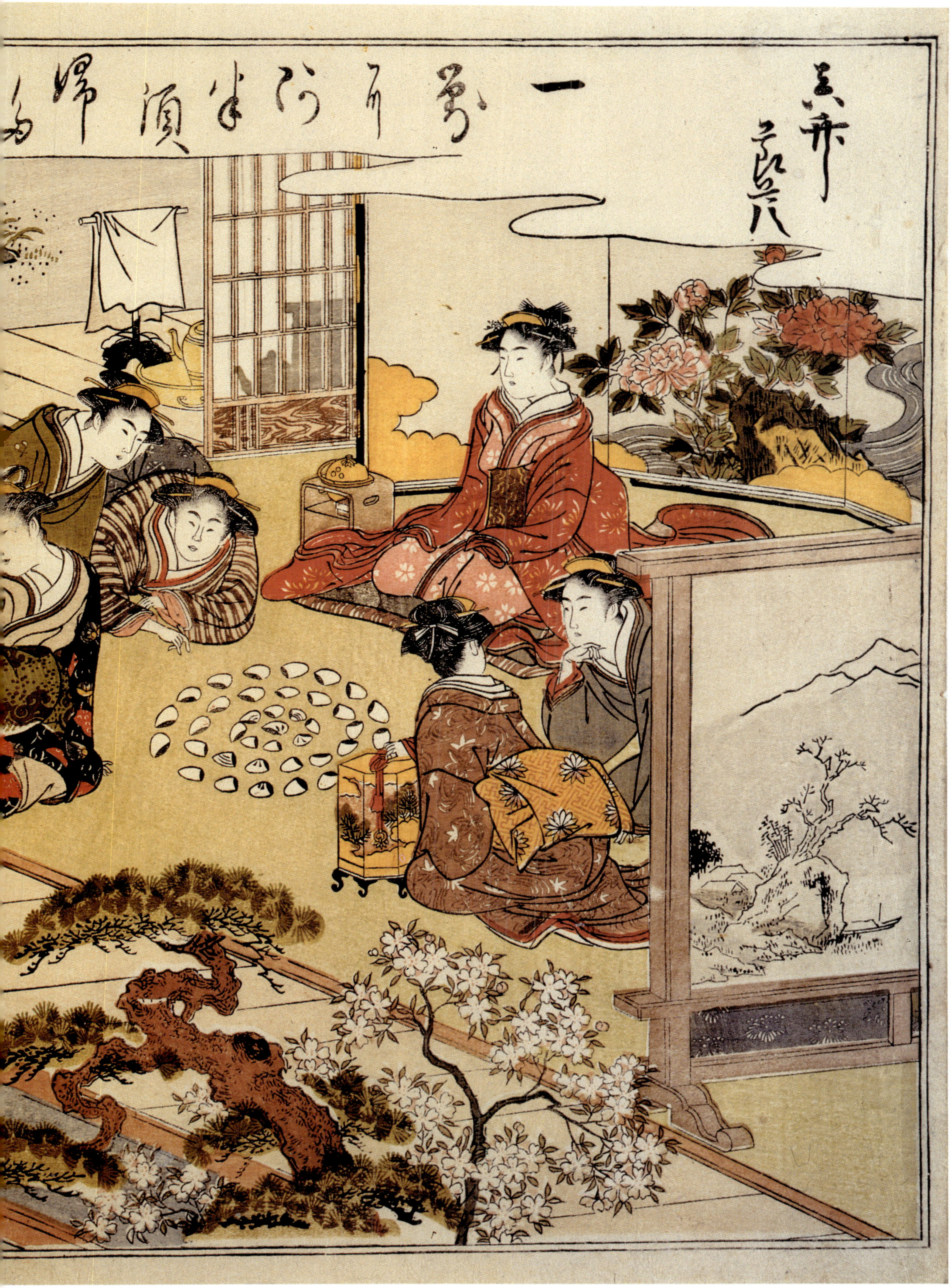

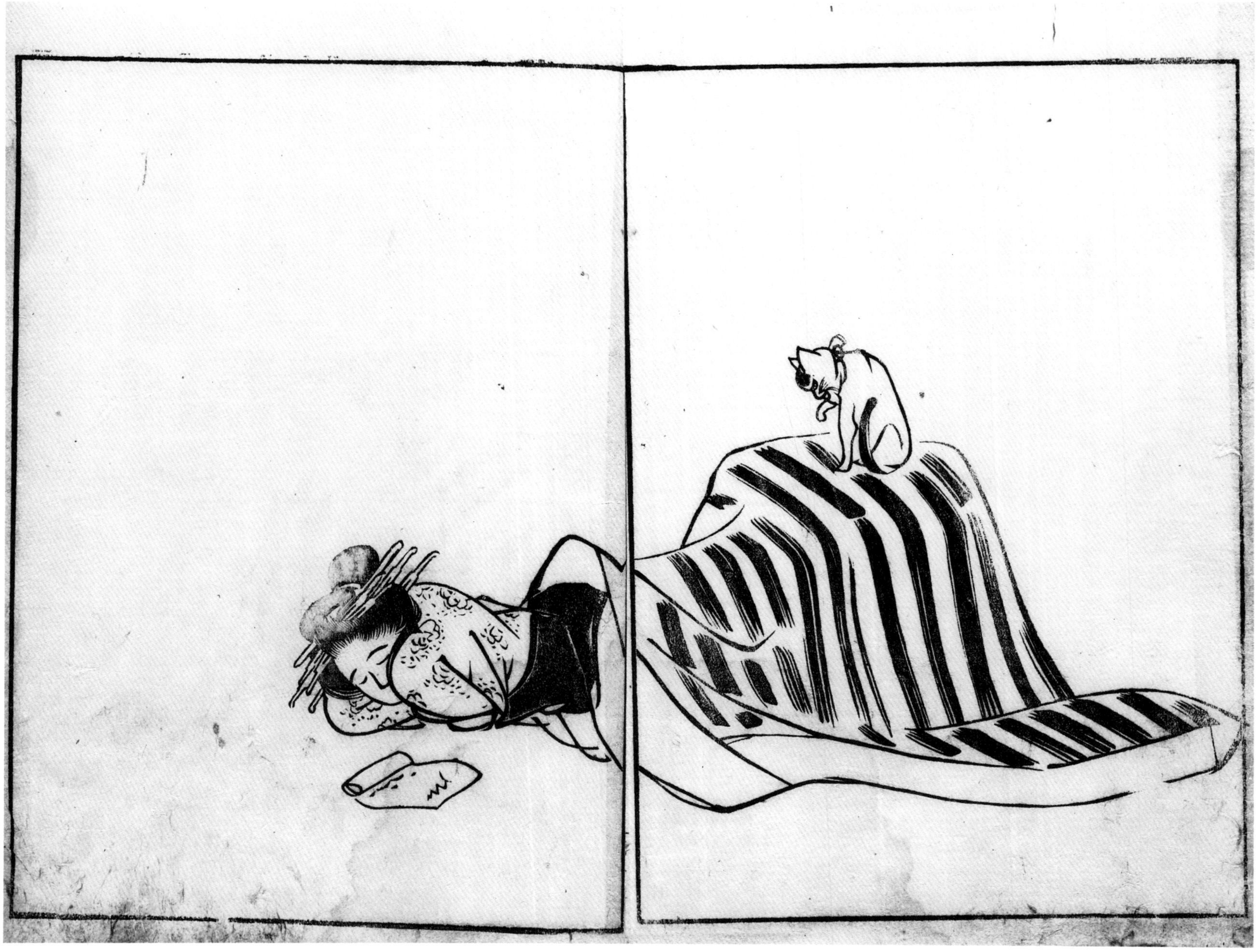

Above: Yamaguchi Soken (1759-1818) 'Arm Pillow' from 'A Book of Pictures of the Japanese People' (*Yamato jinbutsu gafu*), 1800, 3 vols. Courtesy of the Trustees of the British Museum, London.

Previous pages: Kitagawa Utamaro (1753-1806) 'Women Playing the Shell game,' from 'Gift of the Ebb Tide' (*Shioi no tsuto*), c. 1790. Courtesy of the Trustees of the British Museum, London.

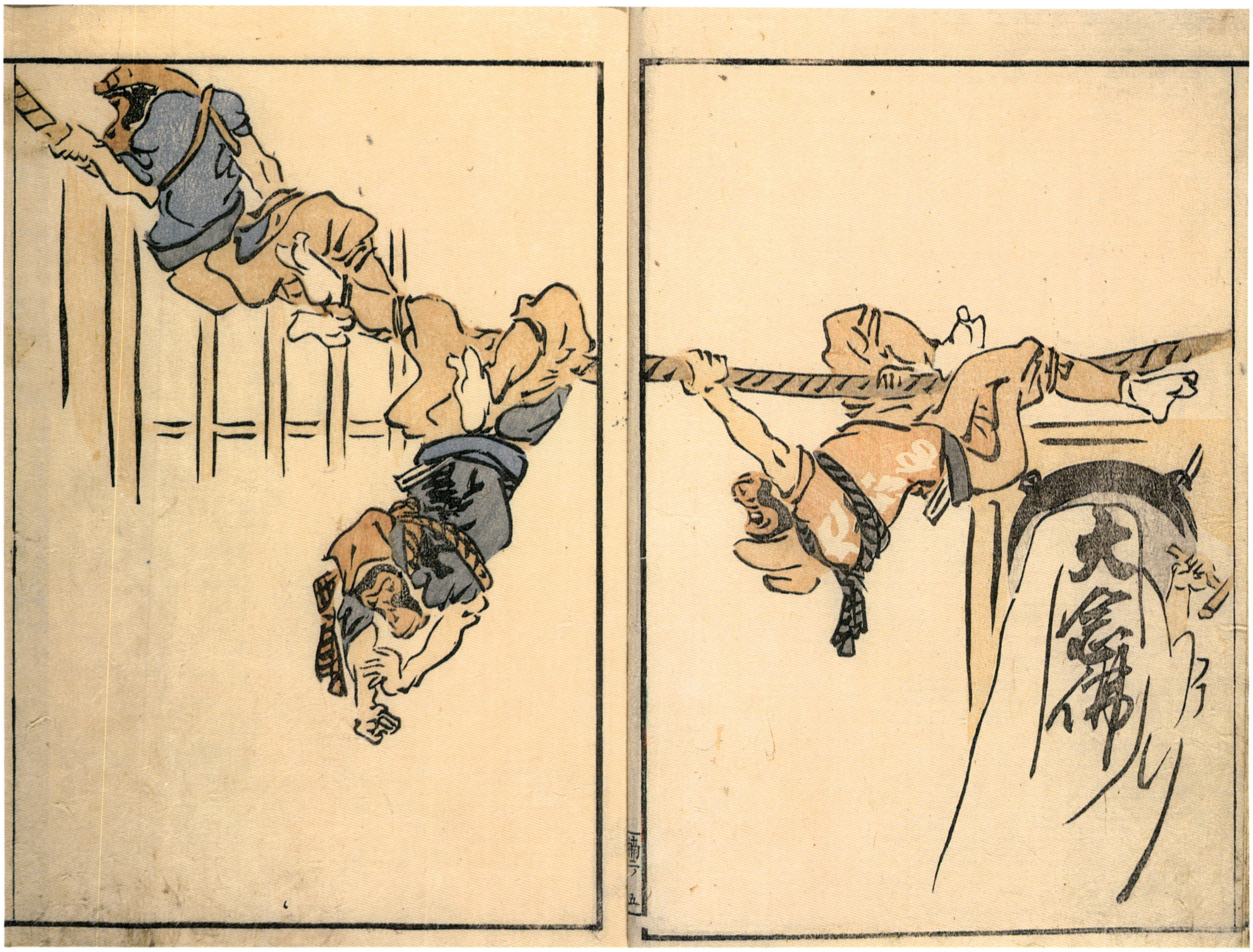

Above: Nishimura Nantei (1755-1834)
'Monkeys on a Rope' from 'A Book of Pictures by Nantei' (*Nantei gafu*), 1804, 3 vols. Courtesy of the Trustees of the British Museum, London.

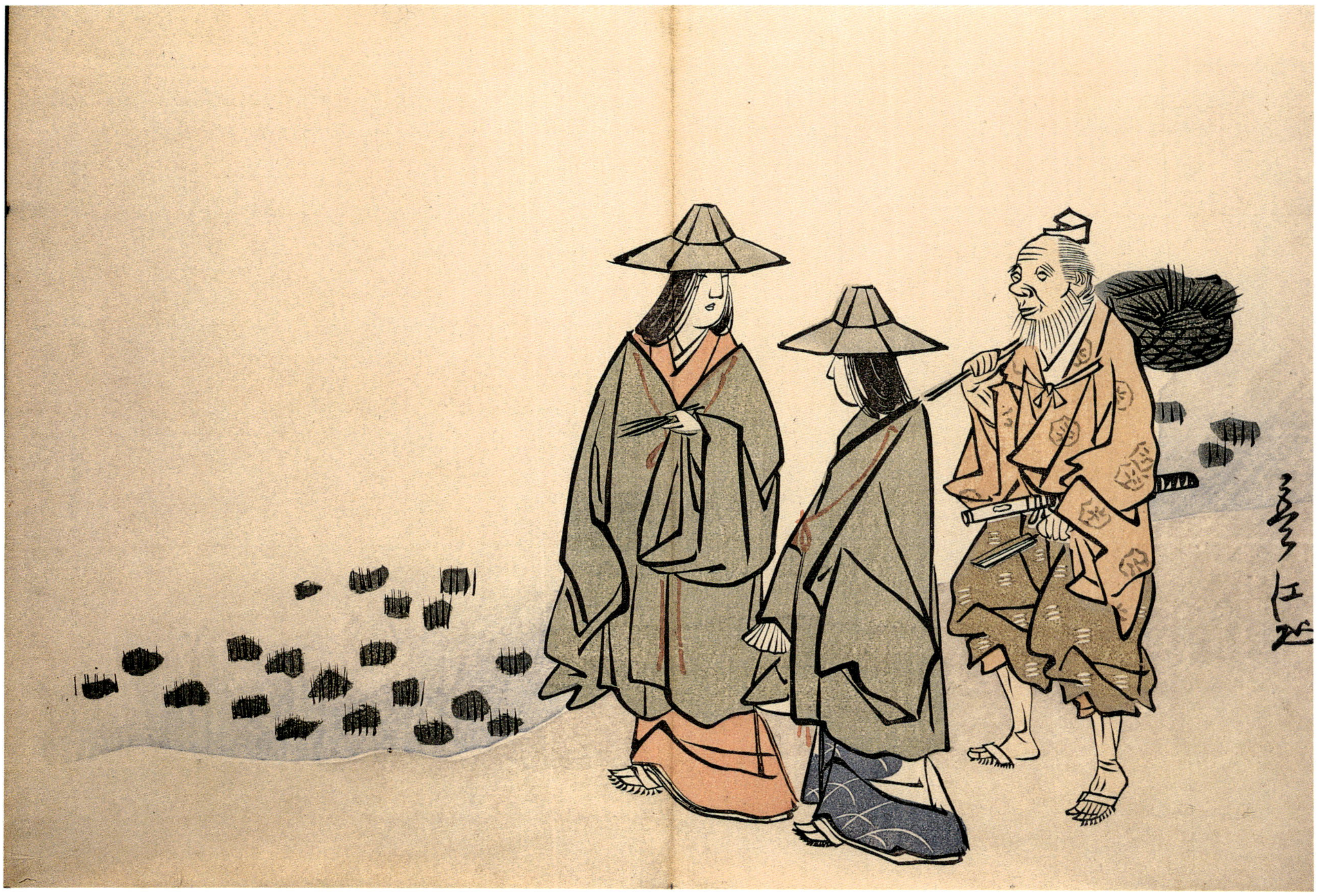

Above: Rankō Nakei (1766-1880) 'A Man Travelling with Two Women' from 'The Album of the Phoenix Bird' (*Rampōjō*), folding album, by various artists, 1806. Courtesy of the Trustees of the British Museum, London.

Right: Oku Bummei (d. 1813) '*Maiko*' (dancer) from 'A Gathering of Beauties' (*Bijin awase*) by various artists, 1807, 1 vol. Courtesy of the Trustees of the British Museum, London.

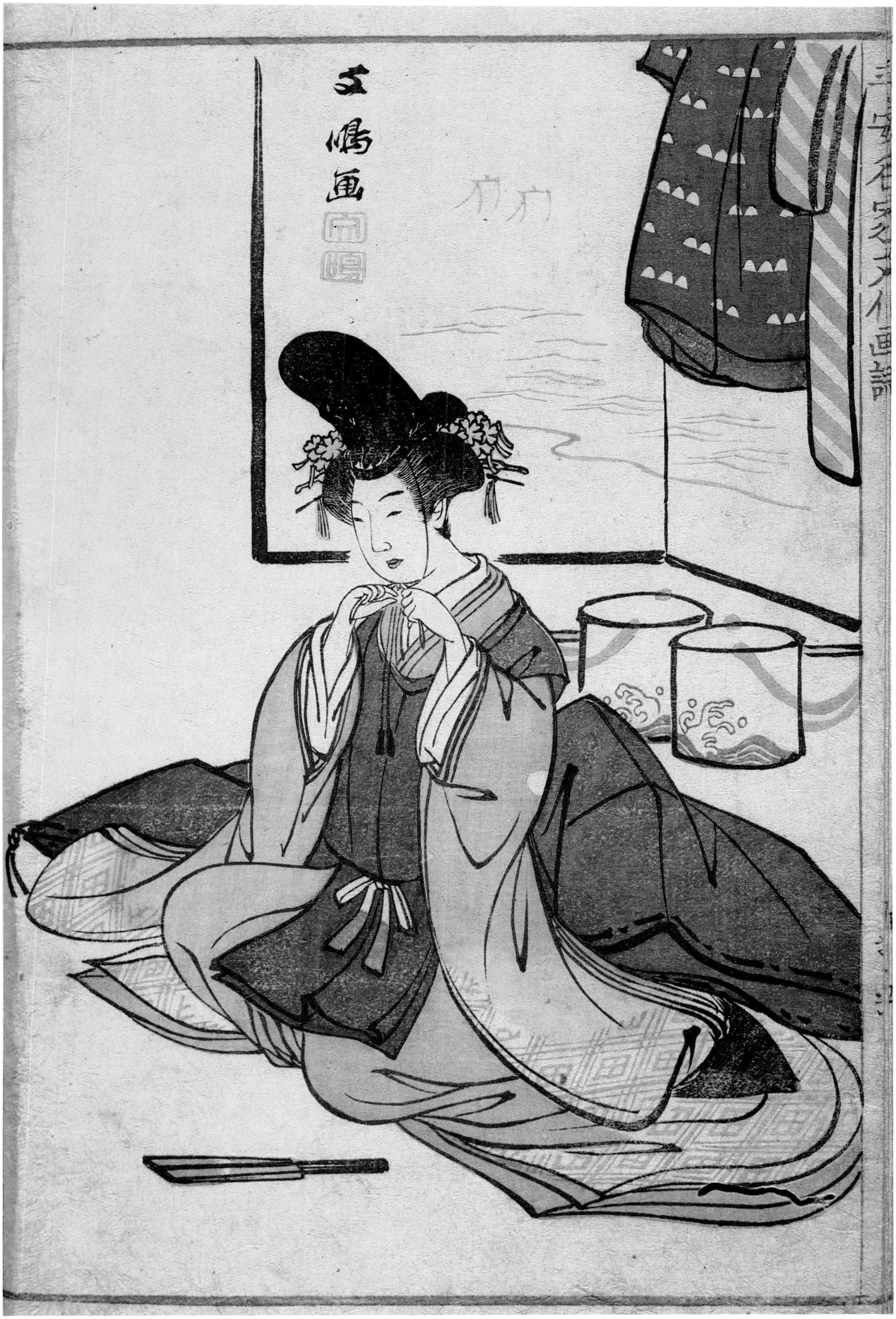
文鳴画

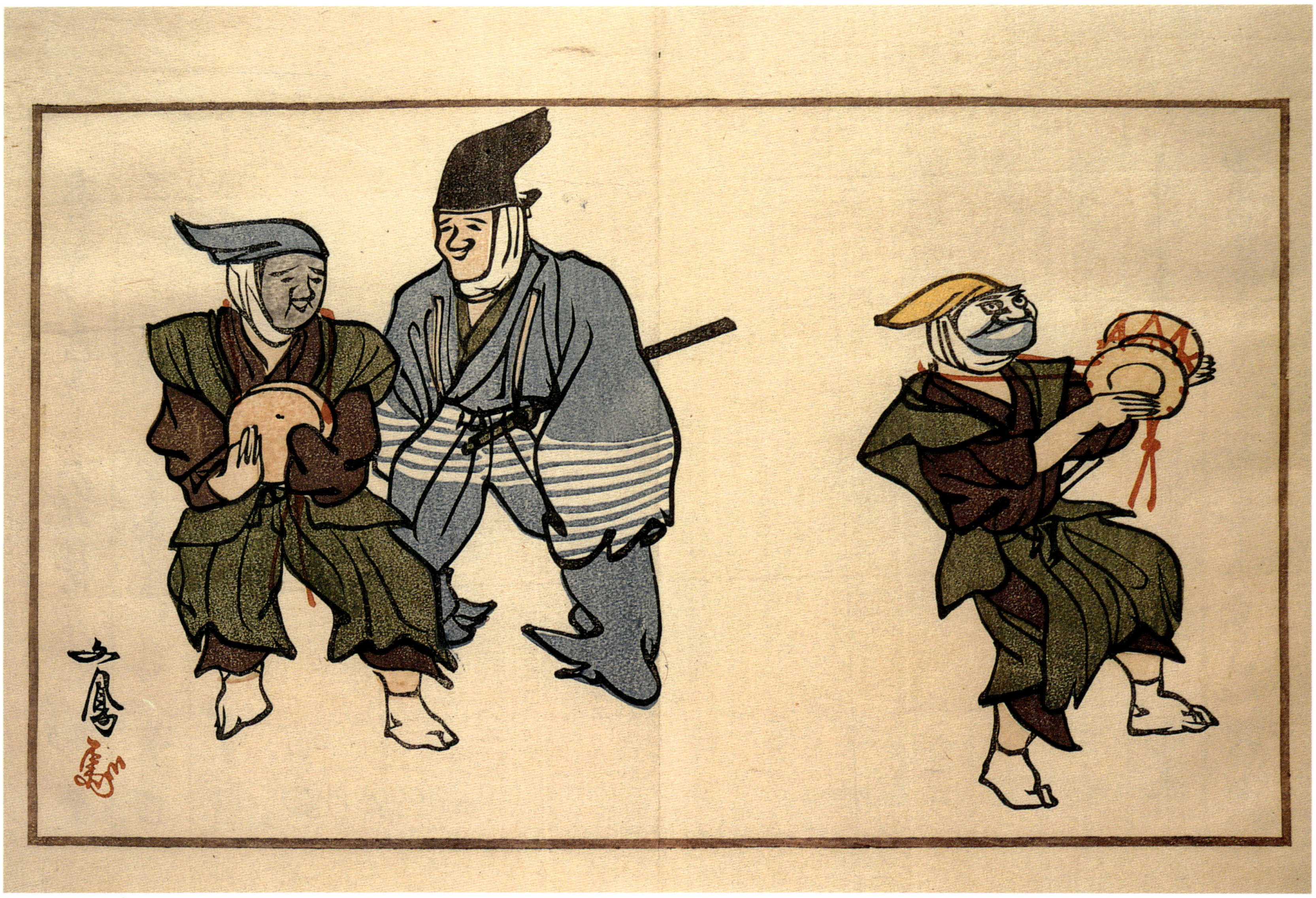

Above: Kawamura Bunpō (1779-1821) 'Tsutsumi Players' from 'The Album of the Capital' (*Tōkaijō*), by various artists, 1803, one *orihon* album. Courtesy of the Trustees of the British Museum, London.

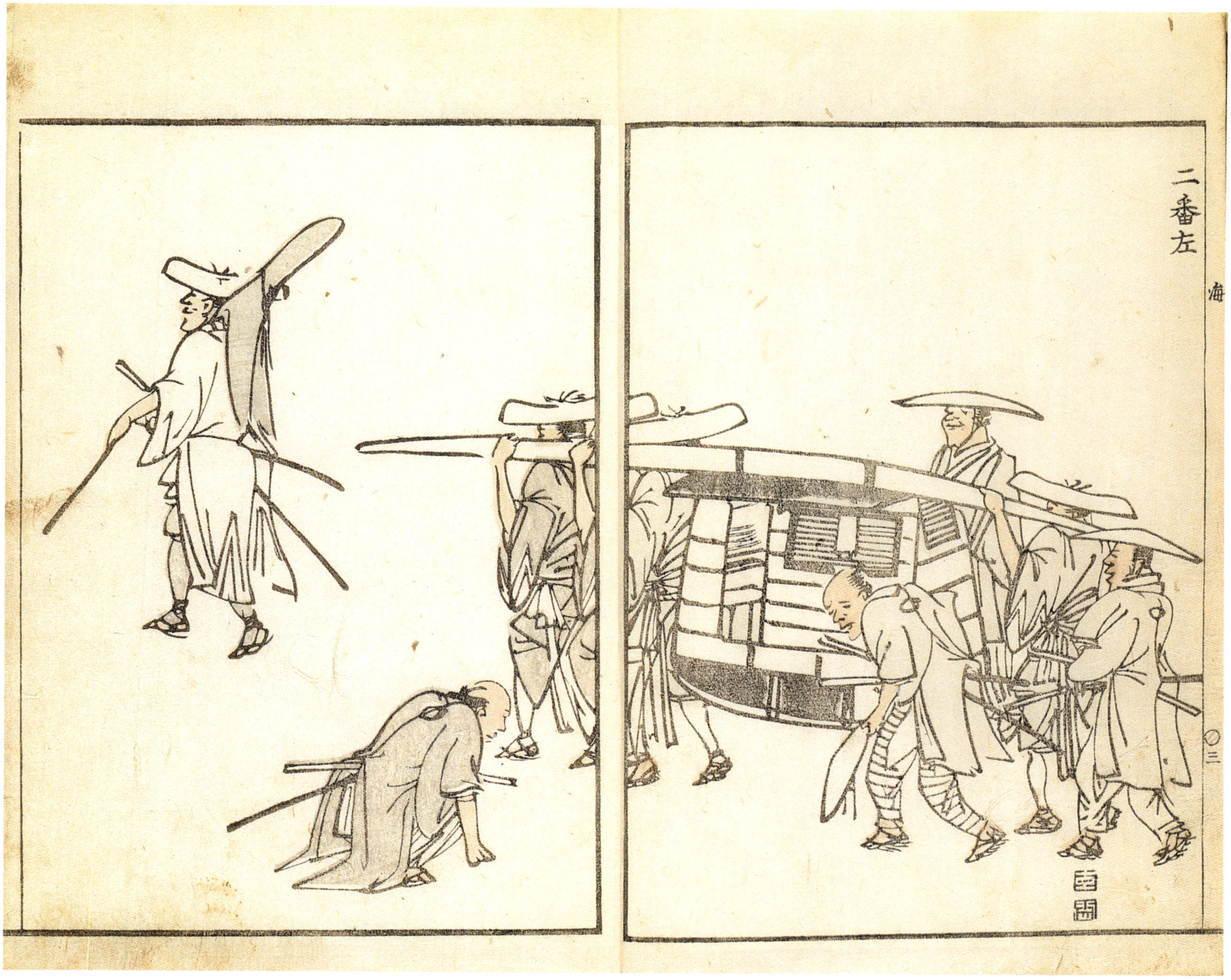

Above: Kawamura Bunpō (1779-1821) and Watanabe Nangaku (1763-1813) 'Travelers' from 'A Comparison of *kyōka* on the Highway' (*Kaidō kyōka awase*), 1811, 1 vol. Courtesy of the Trustees of the British Museum, London.

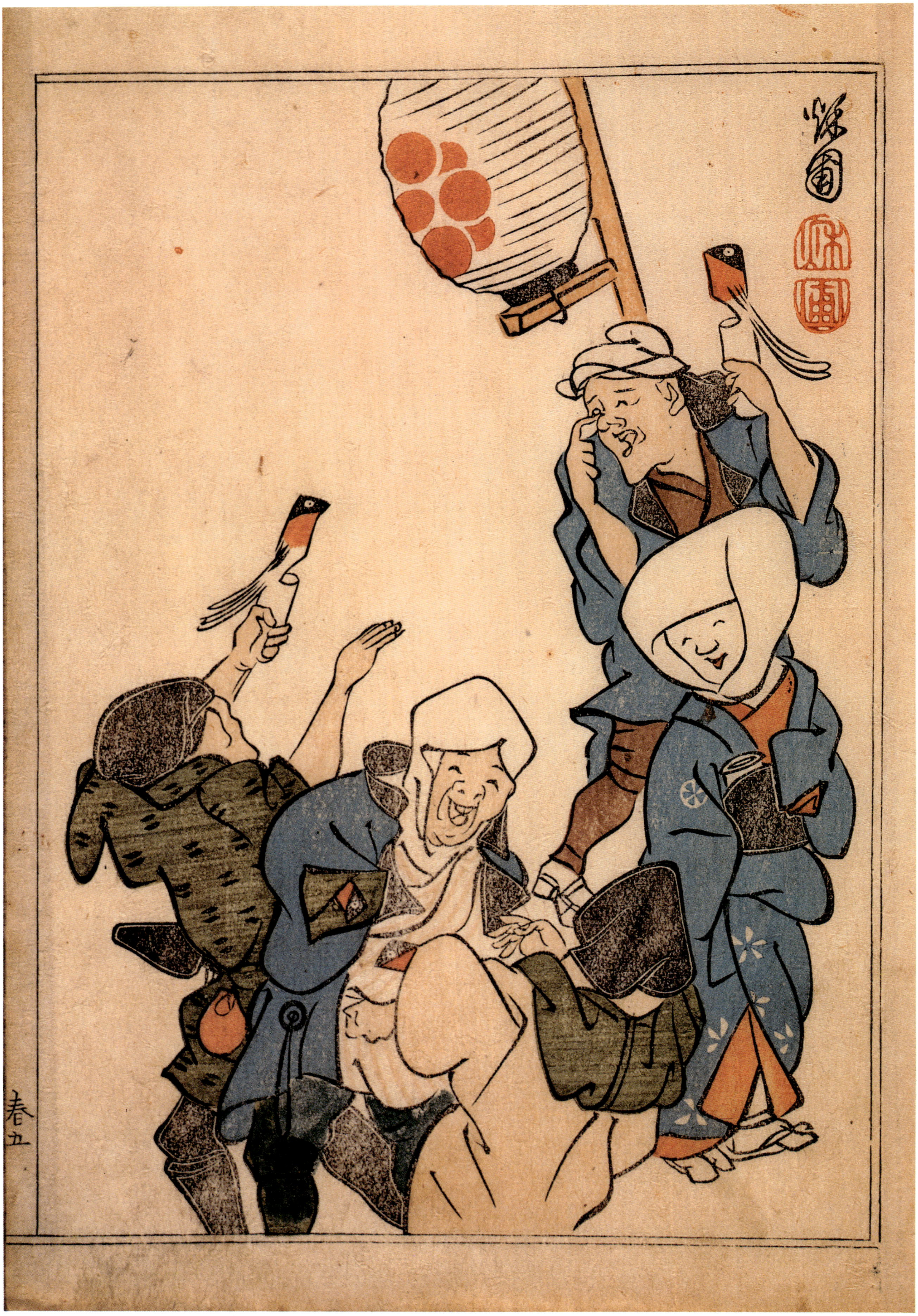
春五

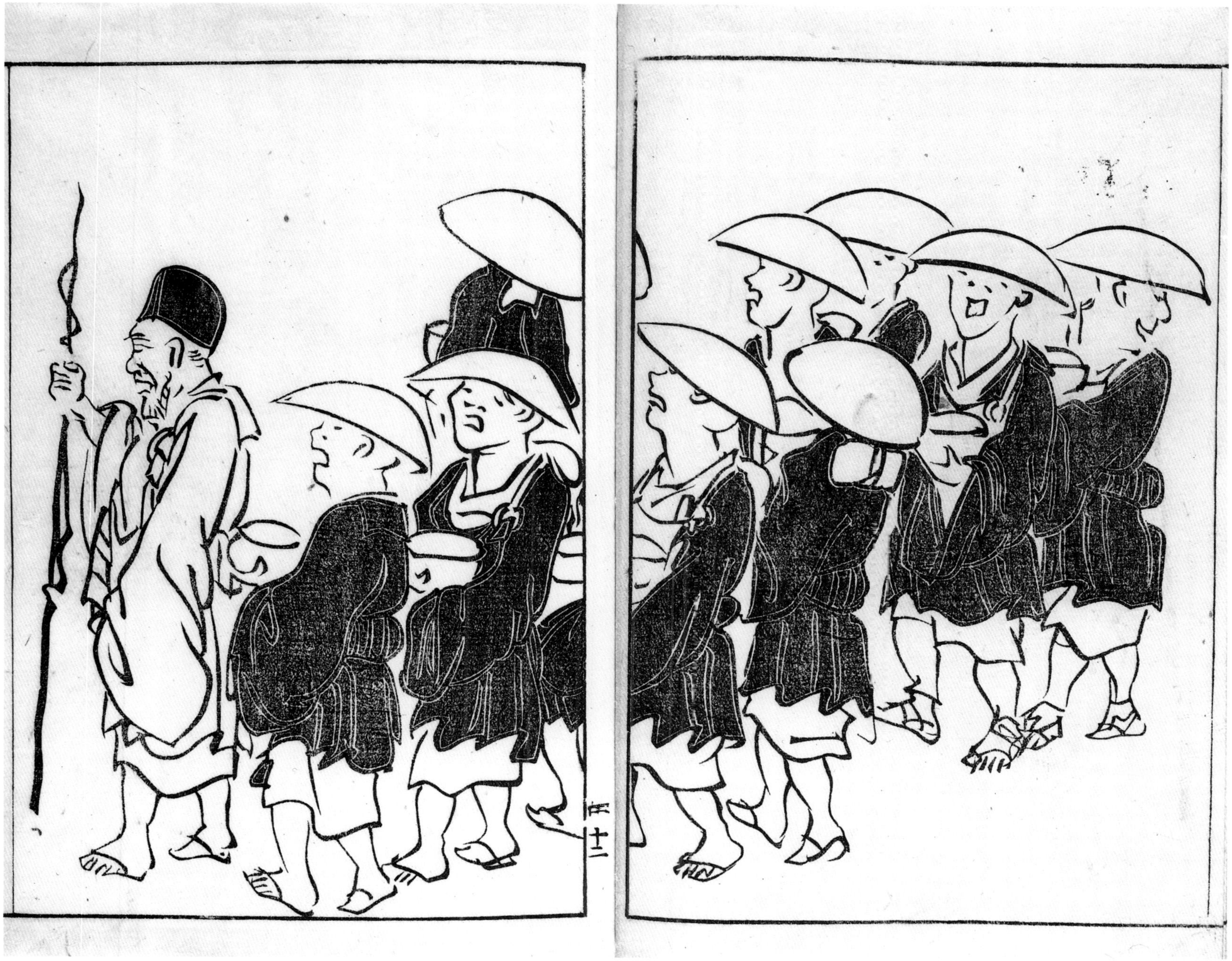

Above: Nishimura Nantei (1755-1834) 'Procession of Monks' from 'An Album of Pictures by Nantei' (*Nantei gafu*), 1804, 3 vols. Courtesy of the Trustees of the British Museum, London.

Left: Saitō Shuho (1769-1859 'Image of New Year Festivities with Bullfinches' from 'The Day Lily' (*Wasuregusa*) by various artists, 1810-15, 4 vols. Courtesy of the Trustees of the British Museum, London.

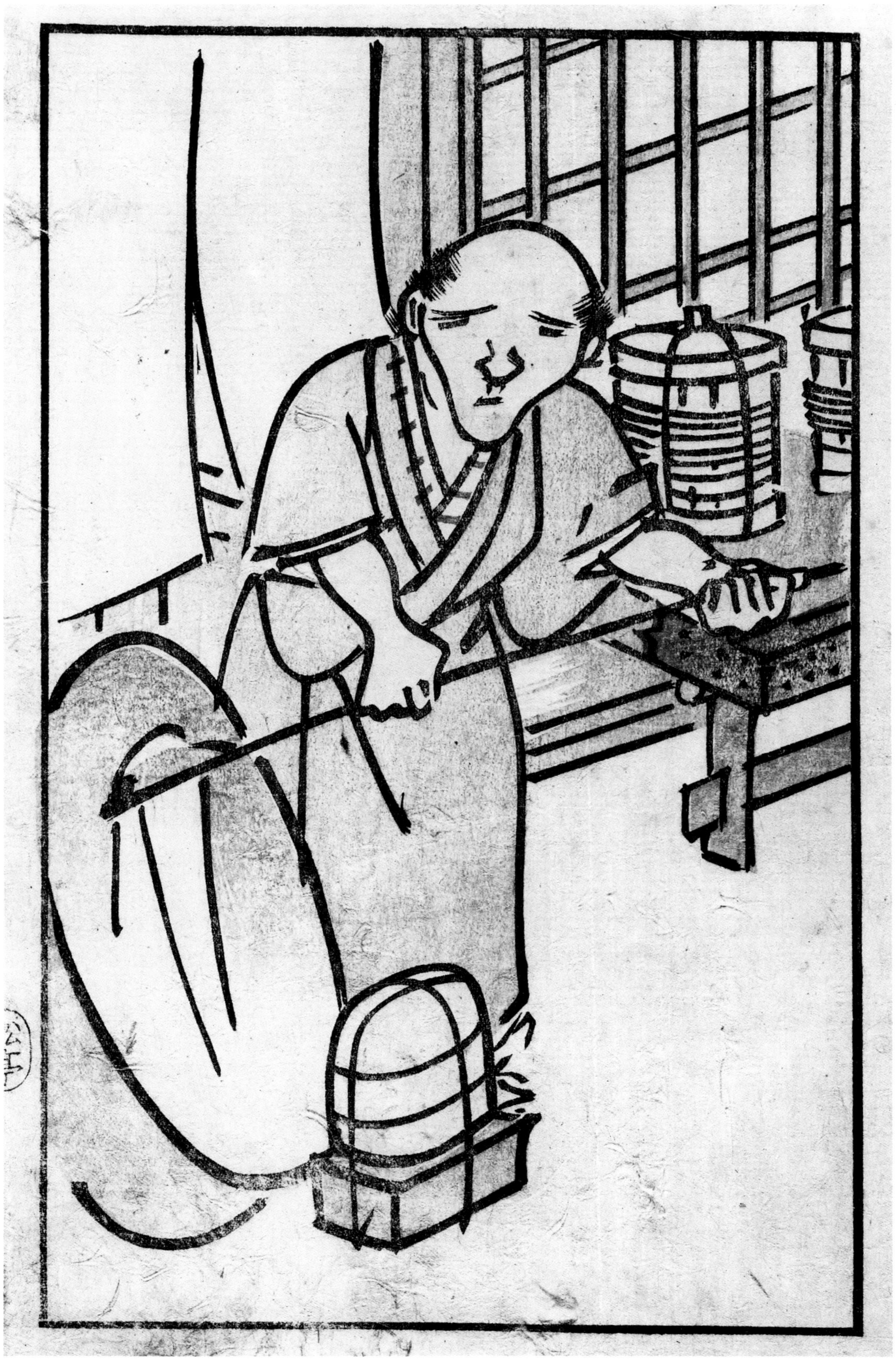

Above: Satō Suiseki (*fl* early nineteenth century) 'Image of Lanternmaker' from 'A Book of Pictures by Suiseki' (*Suiseki gafu*), 1814, 1 vol. Courtesy of the Trustees of the British Museum, London.

Right: Ōnishi Chinnen (1792-1851) 'Images of Turtles' from 'A Book of Pictures by Sonan' (*Sonan gafu*), 1834, 1 vol. Courtesy of the Trustees of the British Museum, London.

Above right: Ōnishi Chinnen (1792-1851) 'Cranes in Flight' from 'A Book of Pictures by Sonan' (*Sonan gafu*), 1834, 1 vol. Courtesy of the Trustees of the British Museum, London.

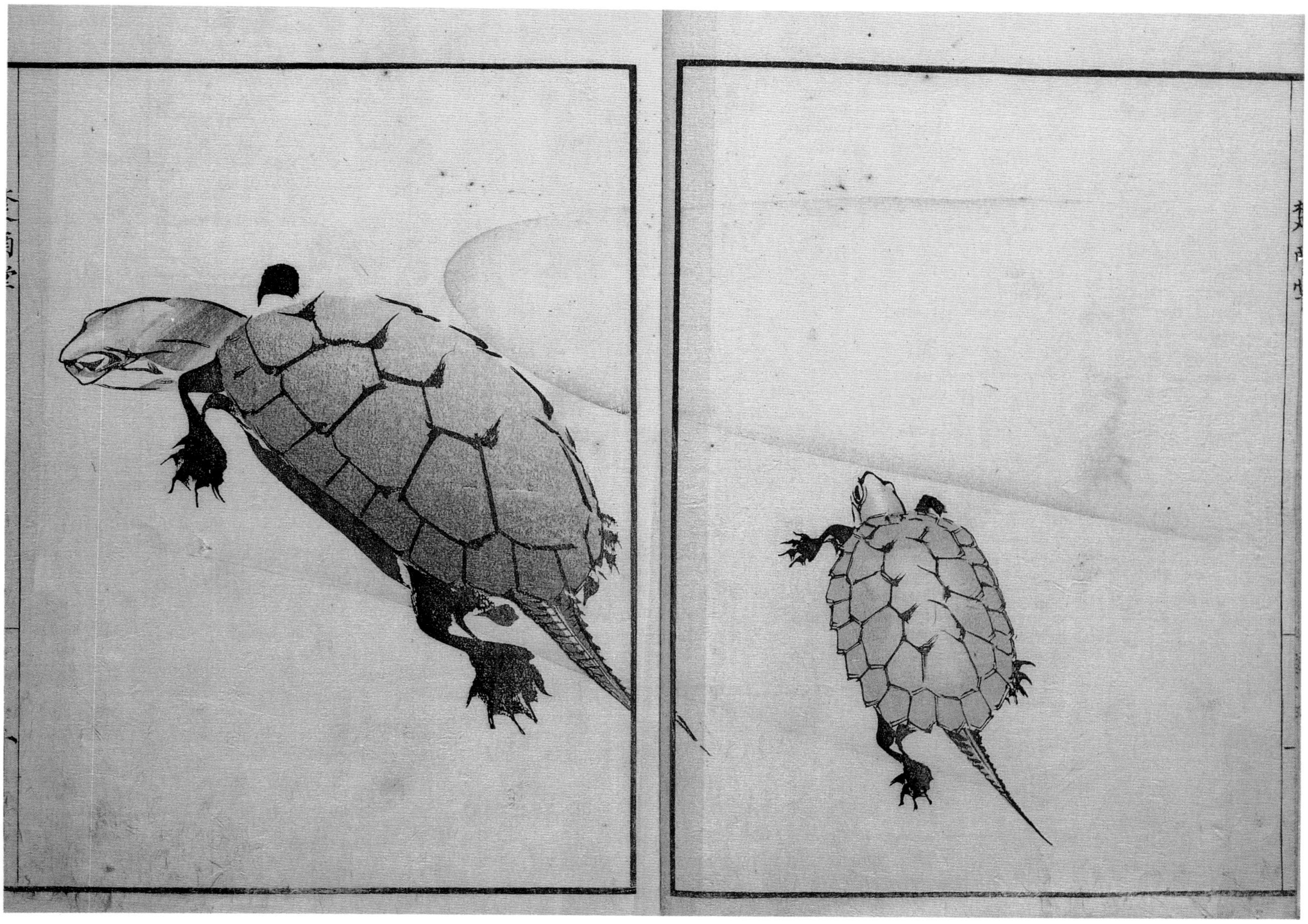

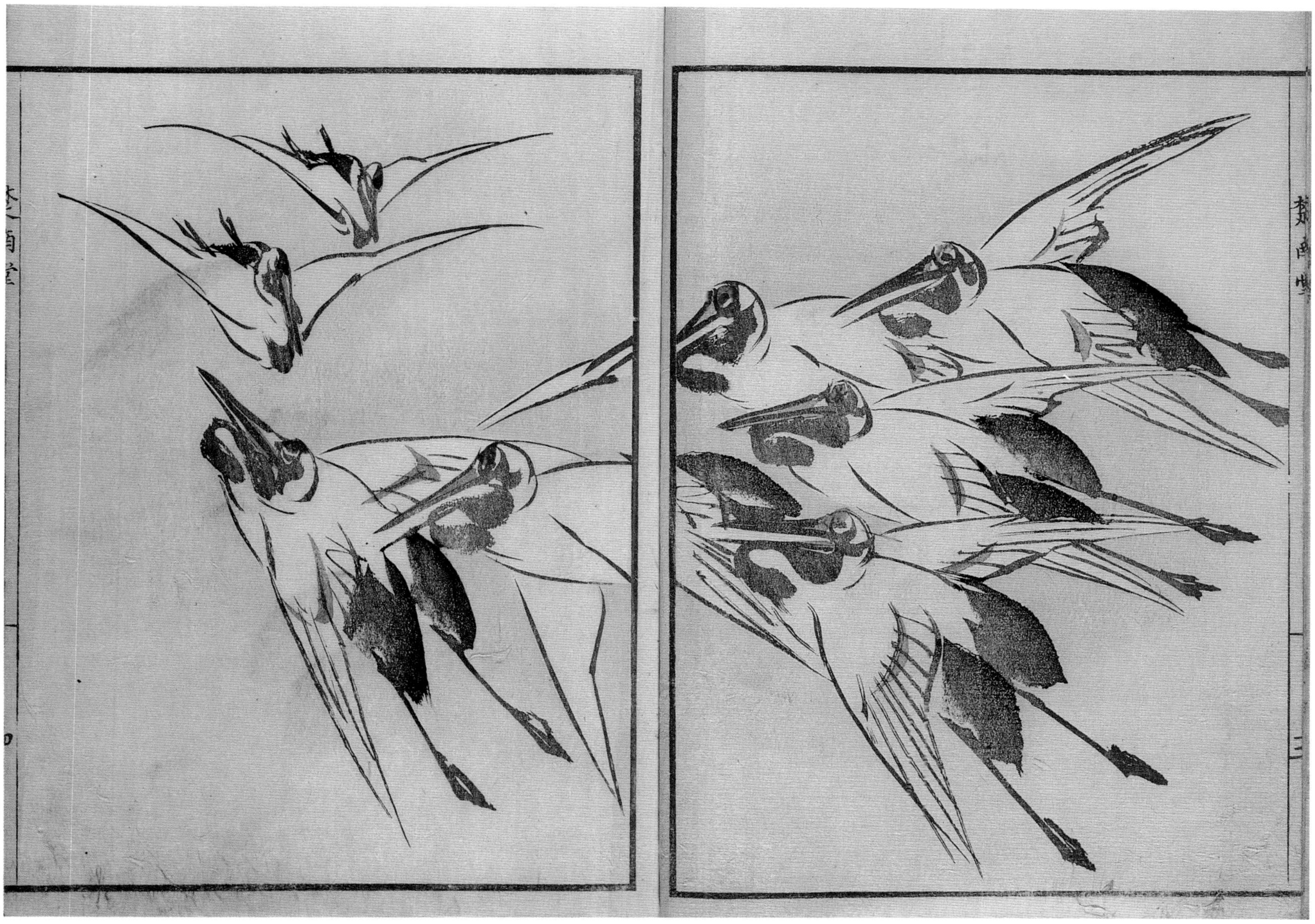

Right: Matsumura Keibun (1779–1843) 'Swallow in Flight' from 'An Album of Pictures by Kyoto Artists' (*Keijō gaen*), 1814. Courtesy of the Trustees of the British Museum, London.

Far right: Matsumoto Hōji (n.d.) 'Frog' from 'A Book of Pictures by Famous Artists' (*Meika gafu*), 1814, 3 vols. Courtesy of the Trustees of the British Museum, London.

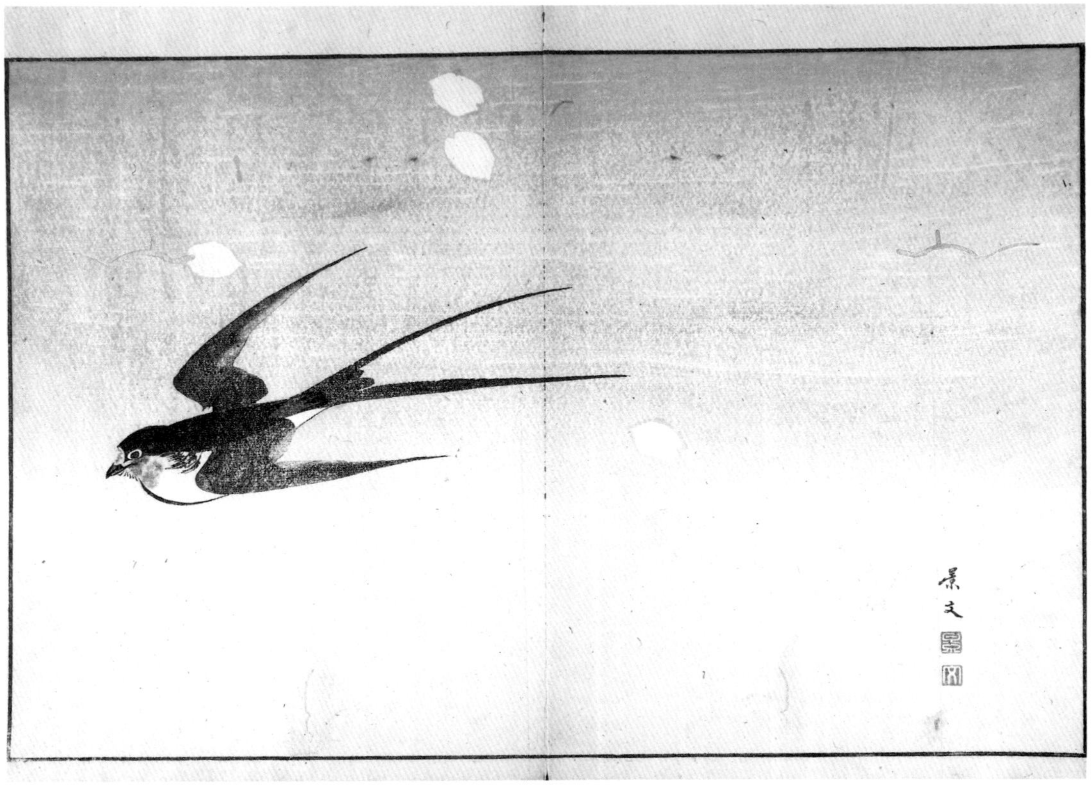

Below: Matsumura Goshun (1752–1811) 'Monk with Gong (after Buson)' from 'New Flowering Picking' (*Shin hanatsumi*), 1784, 1 vol. Courtesy of the Trustees of the British Museum, London.

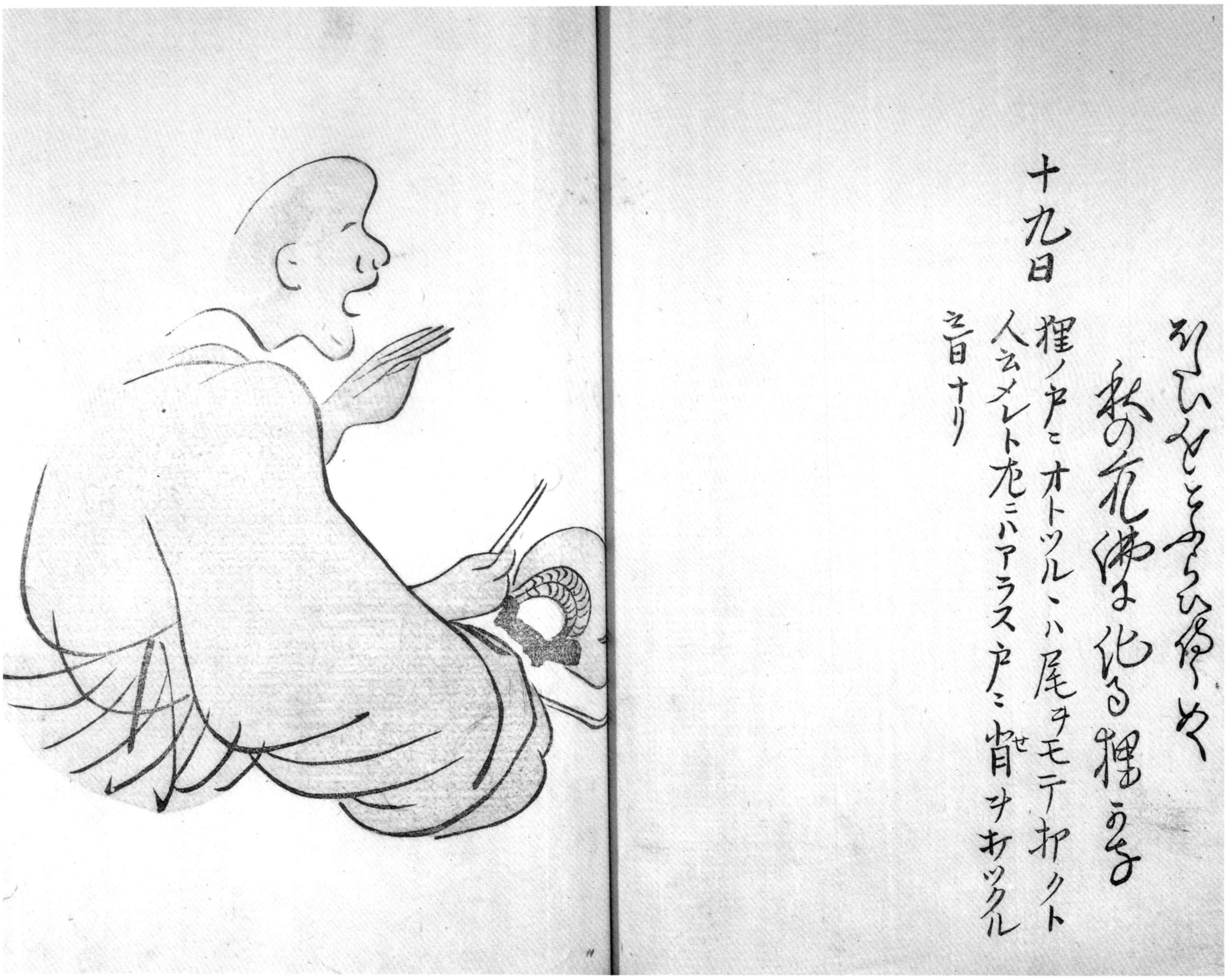

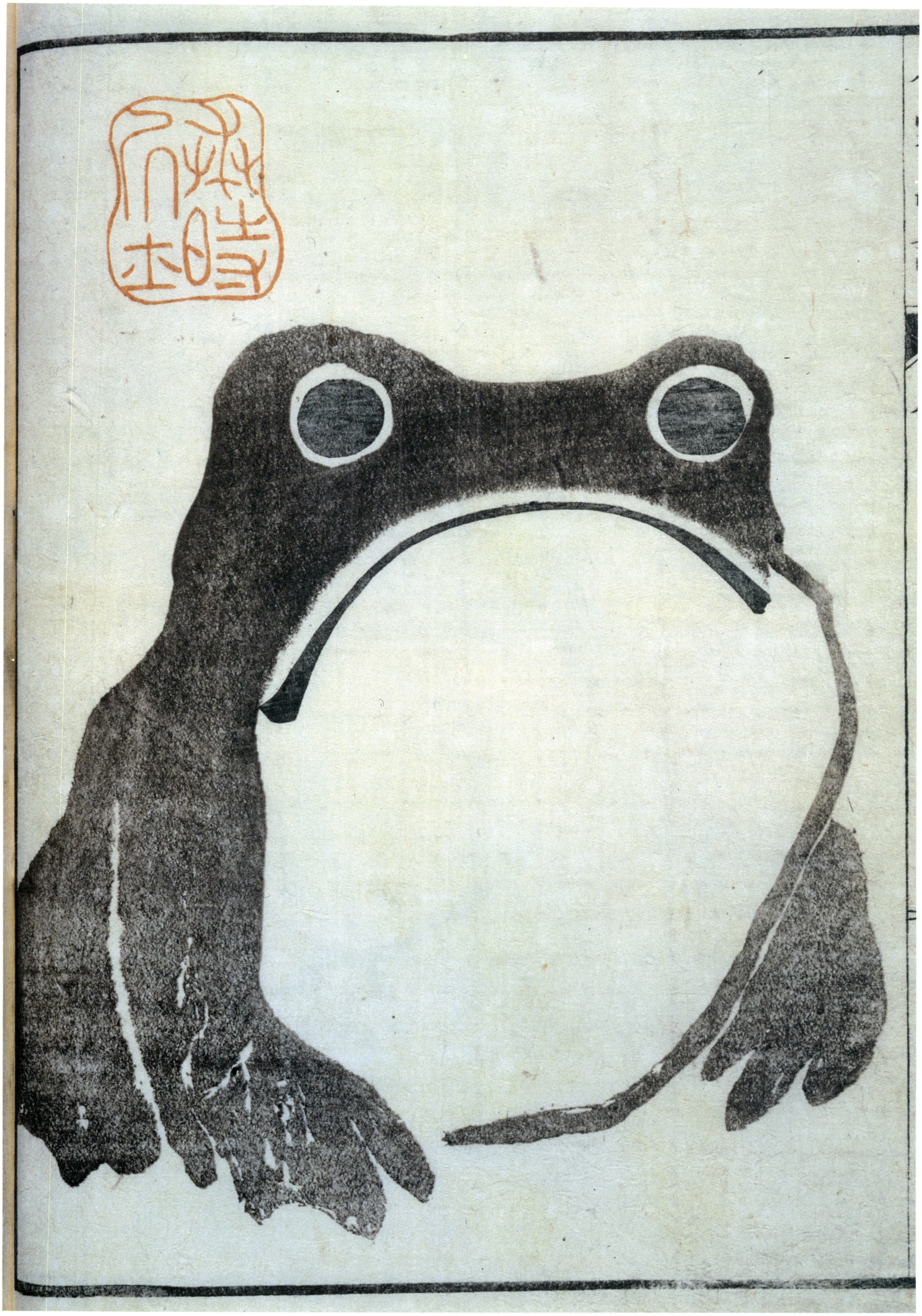

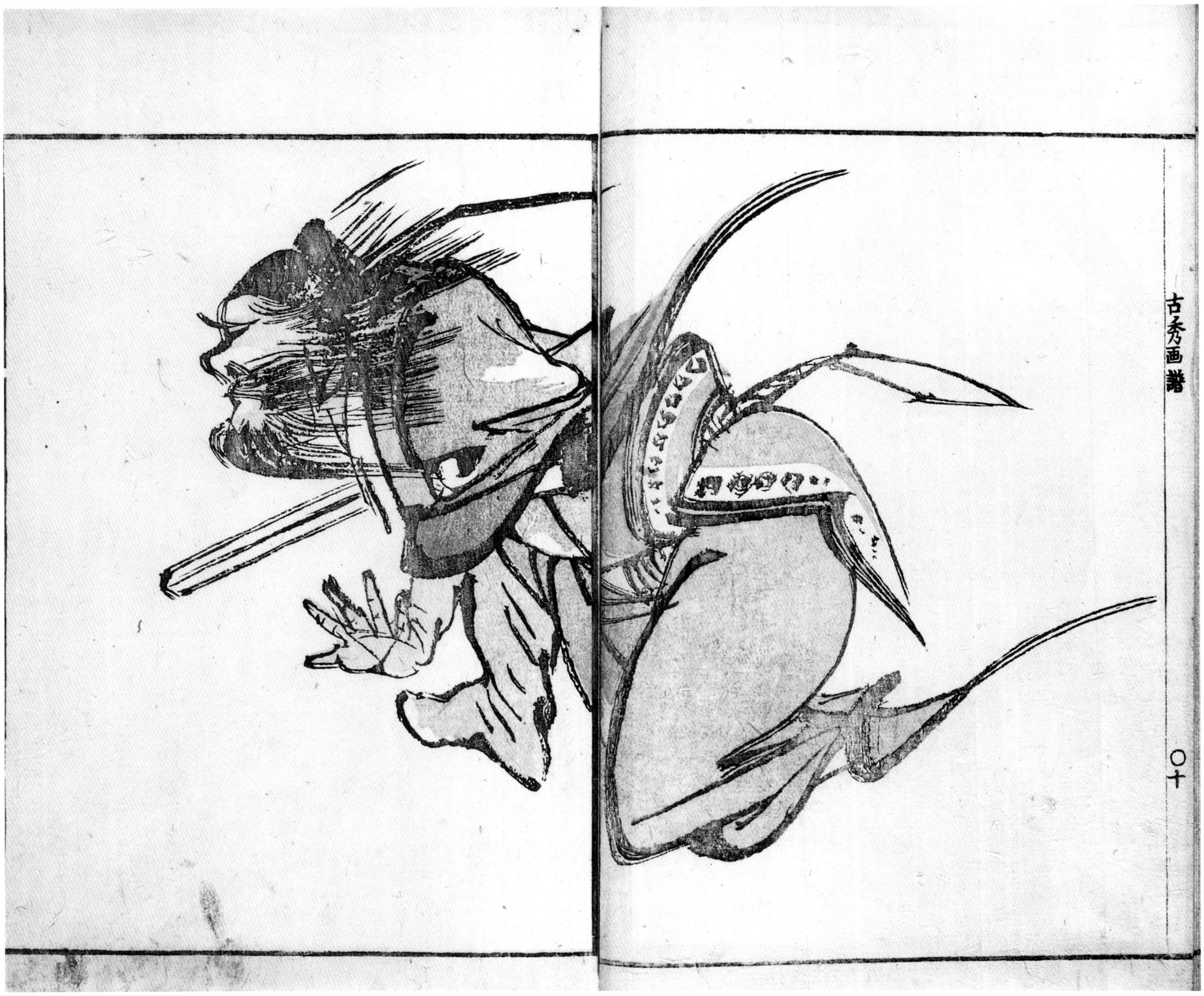

Above: Hatta Koshū (1760–1822) 'Shōki, the Demon Queller' frp, 'A Book of Pictures by Koshū' (*Koshū gafu*), 1812, 1 vol. Courtesy of the Trustees of the British Museum, London.

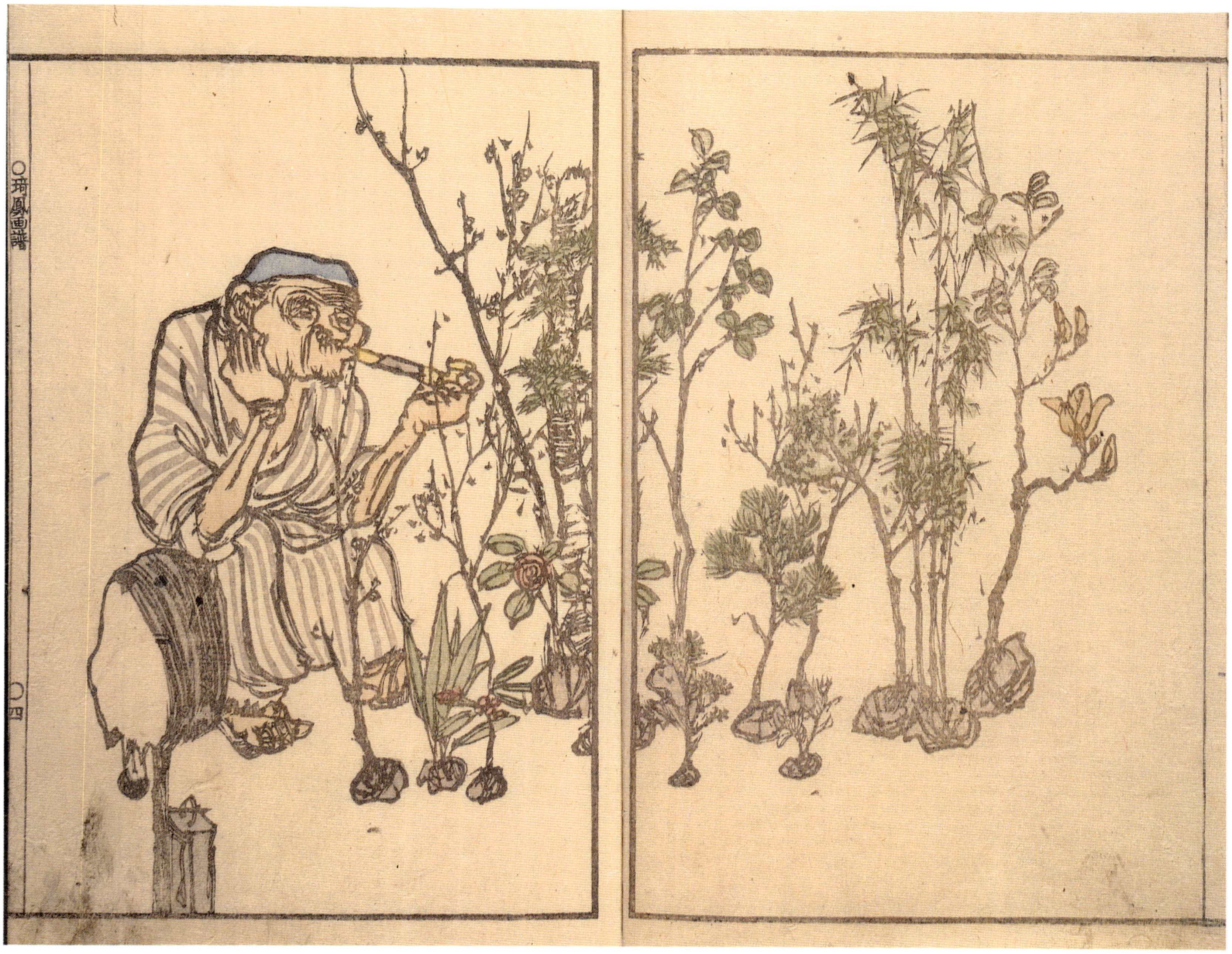

Above: Kawamura Kihō (1778-1852) 'A Monkey Smoking a Pipe' from 'A Book of Pictures by Kihō (*Kihō gafu*), 1827, 1 vol. Courtesy of the Trustees of the British Museum, London.

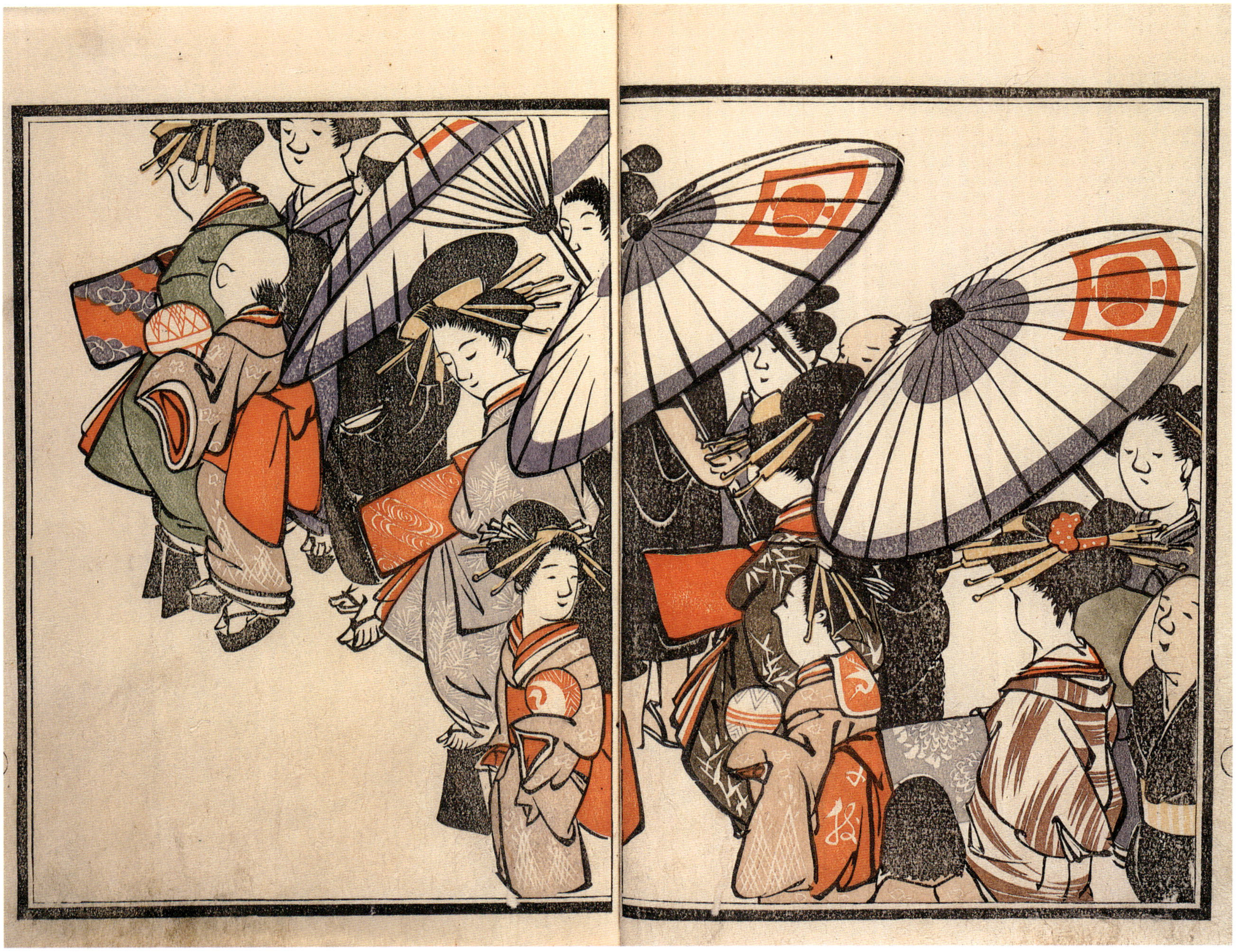

Above: Aoi Sōkyū (Saitō Shūho) (1769-1859) 'Festive Procession' from 'Mr Aoi's Chronicle of Charm' (*Kishi empu*), 1803, 1 vol. Courtesy of the Trustees of the British Museum, London.

Above right: Shibata Zeshin (1807-91) 'Gourd-vine and Fan' from 'The Straight Way to Dreams' (*Yume no tadaji*), 1839. Courtesy of the Trustees of the British Museum, London.

Right: Tanaka Nikka (d. 1845) 'Fish and Weeds' from 'A Book of Pictures by Kyūhōdō' (*Kyūhōdō gafu*) 1856. Courtesy of the Trustees of the British Museum, London.

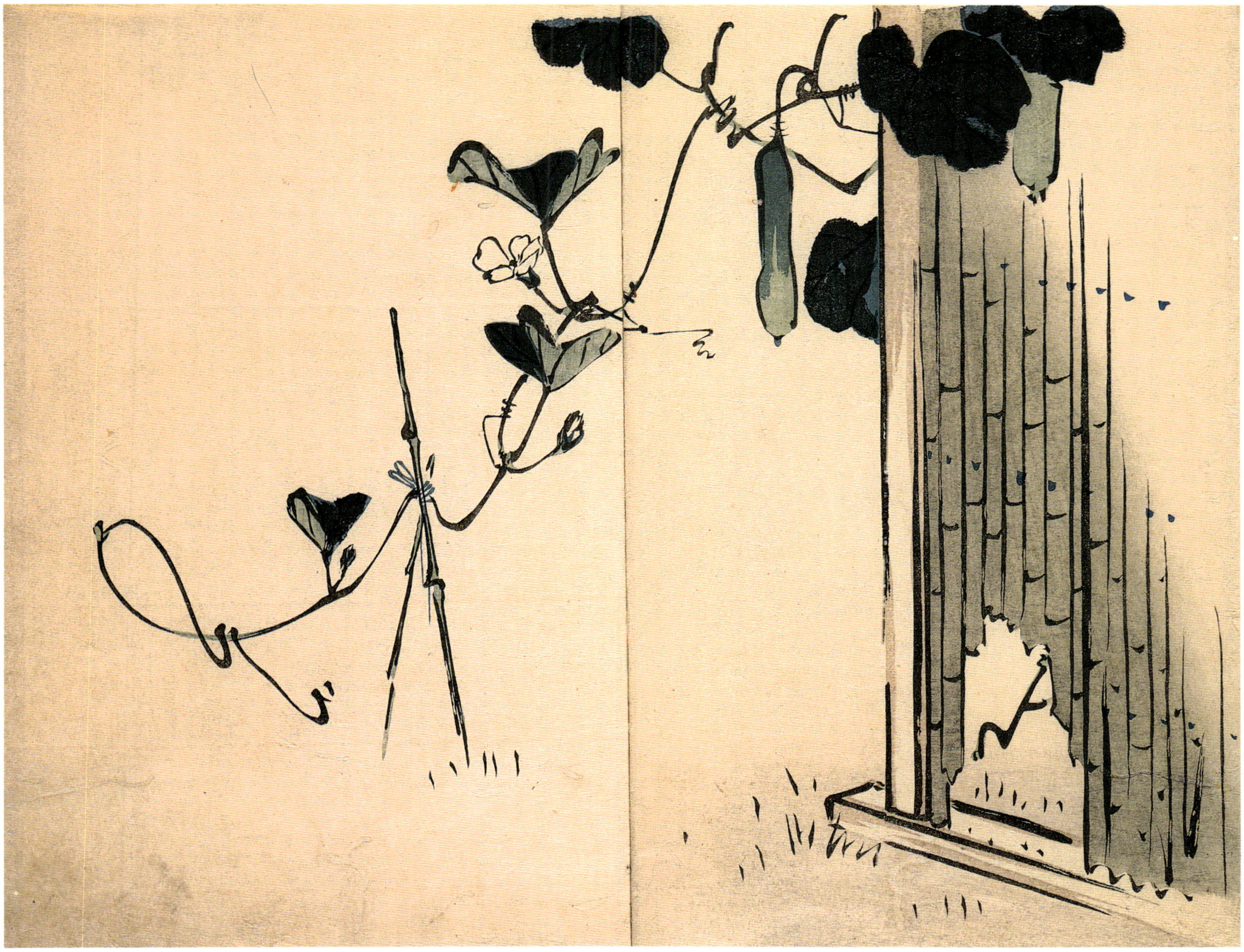

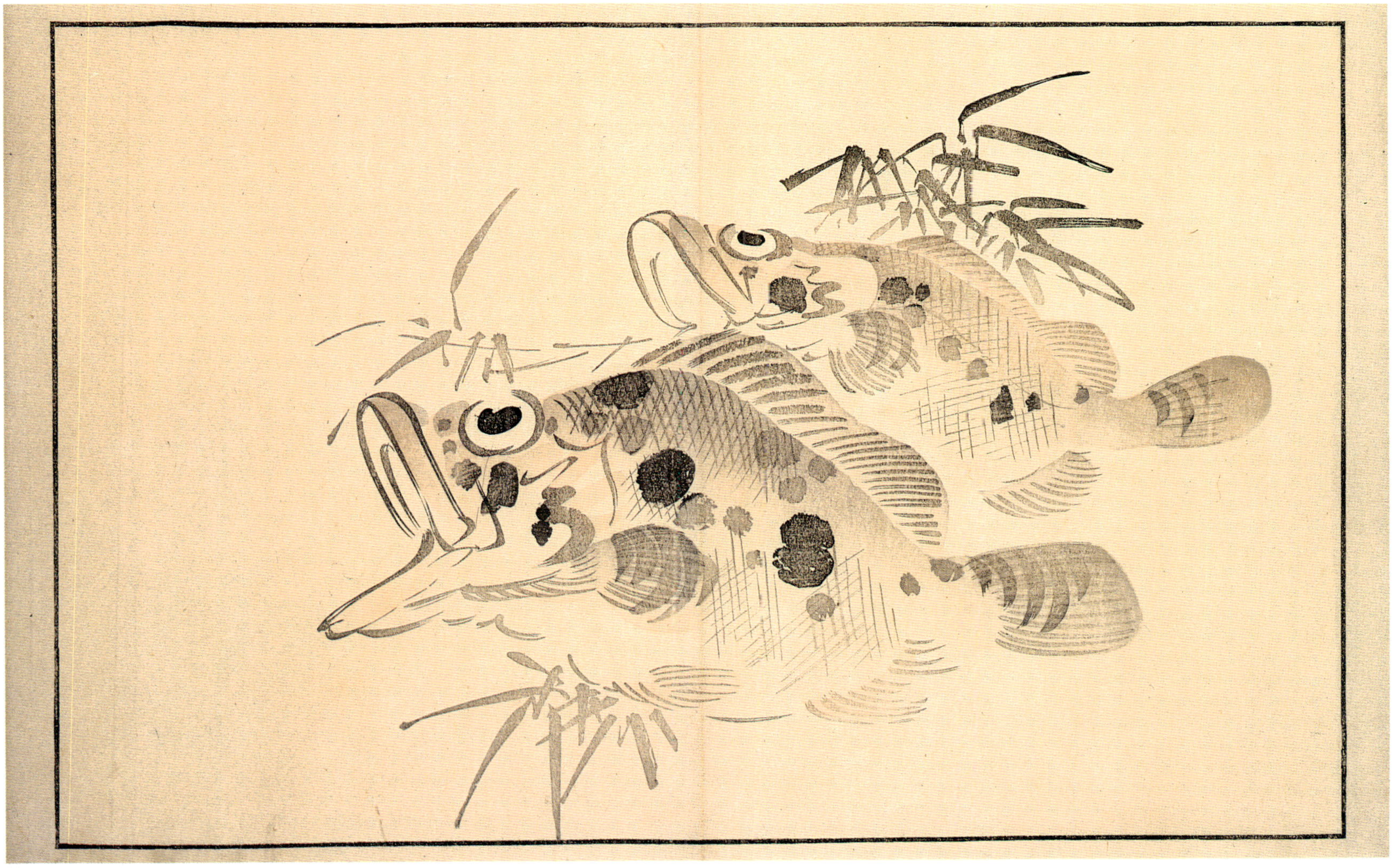

Glossary

Abuna-e (Risqué pictures). *Ukiyo-e* which illustrate gently erotic scenes.
Aiban. A print size between *chūban* and *ōban*; 13½×8¾ inches (34×22 cm).
Aizuri-e (Blue printed pictures). Prints done in shades of blue and which were seen in the prints of the late 1820s to 1840s.
Baren. A circular pad that was wrapped in a sheath of bamboo fiber and which was used in the woodblock printing process.
Beni-e (Red [beni] pictures). Prints in which *beni* (red) was applied by hand to a black and white print.
Benizuri-e (Pink printed pictures). Prints using pale pastel shades; they are principally found in prints of 1790.
Benigirai-e (red-hating picture). A print with no red (pink) pigments.
Bijin (beautiful women). *Bijinga* were pictures of beautiful women.
Bunten. Abbreviation for *Monbushō bijutsu tenrankai* (Ministry of Education Art Exhibition).
Chūban. A medium print size: 10×7½ inches (26×19 cm).
Chōnin (Townsmen). The term included the artisan and merchant class who lived in the urban centers of the Edo period.
E-goyomi. A pictorial calendar with concealed numbers denoting the long and short months.
Ehon (Picture books). Books in which a greater emphasis has been placed on pictures than text.
Gō. Pen or artist's name.
Hashira-e (Pillar prints). A narrow print size: 27½-29½×4¾-6 inches (70-75×12-15 cm).
Hosoban A narrow print size: 13×5⅝ inches (33×14.5 cm).
Kachōga (Flower and bird painting). A term used to designate a genre in prints and painting with bird-and-flower themes.
Kakemono-e (Hanging scroll picture). A vertical *ōban* diptych: 30×9 inches (76.5×23 cm).
Kamuro (Page). An young attendant to a high-ranking courtesan.
Kentō. Registration marks cut at the edges of the woodblocks.
Koban. A format used for smaller print sizes: it was frequently half the *aiban* or *chūban* sizes.
Kōbu bijutsu gakkō (Technical Art School). An official school established on the campus of the Imperial College in 1876 with the purpose of providing instruction in the Western arts. It closed in 1883.
Kanō school An official school of painters that worked in a style based in the Chinese ink painting tradition of *kanga*.
Kyōka ('mad poem'). A comic light verse based on the form of classical waka poem of 31 syllables. The first poet to be completely devoted to *kyoka* was Nagata Teiryu (1654-1734).
Kyōgō (Proofs).
Maruyama/Shijō. School of naturalistic painting of the Edo period, led by the Kyoto painter Maruyama Ōkyo (1733-95). Matsamura Goshun (1752-1811) is best known as the founder of another school of naturalistic painting called Shijō. Jointly this style is known as Maruyama/Shijō.
Meisho-ki (Records of Famous Places). Illustrated guides of famous places published for travelers and pilgrims.
Mie. A dramatic pose in *aragoto* style Kabuki.
Mitate. A parody of respected themes.
Mon (Family crest).
Musha-e (Warrior picture).
Nagasaki-e (Nagasaki pictures). Souvenir prints made at Nagasaki which primarily represent foreigners.
Nanga (or *bunjinga*). A style of painting drawn from the literati tradition in China.
Nengō (Era name). Japanese system of dating. *Nengō gyōji* are annual rites and ceremonies.
Nihonga (Japanese-style painting). A Meiji-period and later style based in traditional Japanese painting which employed ink and watercolor on silk and paper.
Nihon bijutsuin (Japan Art Institute).
Nishiki-e (Brocade pictures). Prints which employ multiple color blocks.
Nitten. Abbreviation for *Nihon bijutsu tenrankai* (Japanese Art Exhibition).
Nureba. ('tear-jerker'). Soppy romantic scenes in Kabuki.
Ōban. A large print size measuring 15×10¼ inches (38×26 cm).
Oiran (see tayū).
Ōkubi-e (large-head pictures).
Onnagata. A male actor impersonating a woman in the Kabuki theater.
Orihon (Folding book). Concertina or accordian book.
Seirō (Green Houses). Houses of courtesans.
Shibaraku (Wait a Moment!). Classic interlude in Kabuki that was invented by Danjuro I for a theatrical piece in 1697.
Shikishiban. A print size: 8×7¼ inches (20.5×18.5 cm).
Shinzo ('Newly constructed'). A young girl of about 13 or 14 years of age who is apprenticed to become a courtesan.
Shin hanga (New prints). A print movement begun by the publisher Watanabe Shōzaburō in the early twentieth century that was based on the *ukiyo-e* tradition.
Shunga (Spring pictures). *Ukiyo-e* prints illustrating erotic subject matter.
Sōsaku hanga (Creative prints). A print movement begun in the early twentieth century that advocated the artist's involvement in the creative process.
Sumizuri-e (Black and white pictures).
Surimono (Printed things). Prints that were intended to be privately distributed and were consequently often printed for special occasions.
Tan-e (Red lead pictures). Prints hand-colored with *tan* and other pigments. They were popular from 1670 to 1720.
Tanroku-bon (Pink and green books). Printed books from the early part of the seventeenth century that were hand-colored with *tan* (pink) and *roku* (green). Yellow and purple were also used.
Tanzaku. Half *ōban* size; the sizes included the *ō-tanzaku* (15×6¾ inches: 38×17 cm) and *chū-tanzaku* (15×5 inches: 38×13 cm).
Tayū. The highest ranking courtesan and a popular subject in *ukiyo-e*.
Teiten. Abbreviation for *Teikoku bijutsu tenrankai* (Imperial Art Exhibition).
Uki-e (Floating pictures). Perspective prints.
Ukiyo-zōshi (Stories of the Floating World). A type of popular fiction of the period 1683-1783.
Urushi-e (Lacquer picture). *Beni-e* with the addition of glue to the pigments to give a lustrous finish, often sprinkled with metallic dust or mica.
Yakusha-e (Actor pictures).
Yamato-e (Pictures of Yamato). Classical school of Japanese painting.
Yōga (Western-style painting). A style based on European painting which used oil paints on canvas.
Yoko-e (Horizontal picture; also called *yokoban*). Prints with a horizontal format.
Yokohama-e (Yokohama pictures). Late style of *ukiyo-e* which was popular between 1860 and 1880 and which illustrated scenes of Yokohama in the late Edo and the early Meiji.

Bibliography

Aitken, Genevieve and Delafond, Marianne *La Collection d'Estampes Japonaises de Claude Monet à Giverny* (Paris, 1983)

Avitabile, Gunhild *Die Fruhen Meister: Japanische Holzschnitte von 1680 bis 1750* (Frankfurt, 1988)

Bledsoe, Jane K, ed *Hirosada: Osaka Printmaker* (Long Beach, CA, 1984)

Brandt, Klaus J *Hosoda Eishi 1756-1829: Der Japanische Maler und Holzschnittmeister und seine Schuler.* (Stuttgart, 1977)

Chaikin, Nathan *The Sino-Japanese War (1894-1895).* (Switzerland, 1983)

Chibbett, David *The History of Japanese Prints and Book Illustration* (Tokyo, New York and San Francisco, 1977)

Dailey, Merlin C (introduction) *Utagawa Kuniyoshi: An Exhibition . . . based on the Raymond A. Bidwell Collection* (Springfield, 1980)

Evans, Tom and Mary Anne *Shunga: The Art of Love in Japan* (New York, 1979)

Fagioli, Marco *Shunga, Images du printemps: L'erotisme dans l'estampe japonaise* (Ixelles, 1989)

Forrer, Matthi *Eirakuya Tōshirō, Publisher at Nagoya: A Contribution to the History of Publishing in 19th-Century Japan* (Amsterdam, 1985)

Forrer, Matthi et al *Hokusai and his School: Paintings, Drawings and Illustrated Books* (Haarlem, 1982)

French, Calvin L *Shiba Kōkan. Artist, Innovator, and Pioneer in the Westernization of Japan* (New York and Tokyo, 1974)

Fujii, Hisae *Shiko Munakata* (Tokyo, 1985)

Gookin, F.W. *Katsukawa Shunshō (1726-1793): A Review of His Life and Works* (unpublished typescript)

Gulik, Willem van & Fred Orton *Japanese Prints Collected by Vincent van Gogh* (Amsterdam, 1978)

Hillier, Jack Ronald *Hokusai: Paintings, Drawings and Woodcuts* (London, 1955)

Hillier, Jack Ronald *Utamaro: Colour Prints and Paintings* (London, 1961)

Hillier, Jack Ronald *Japanese Colour Prints* (London, 1966)

Hillier, Jack Ronald *Suzuki Harunobu: An Exhibition of his Colour Prints and Illustrated Books* (Philadelphia, 1970)

Hillier, Jack Ronald *The Japanese Print: A New Approach* (Rutland, 1975)

Hirano, Chie *Kiyonaga: A Study of His Life and Works* (Boston, 1939)

Keyes, Roger *Courage and Silence: A Study of the Life and Color Woodblock Prints of. Tsukioka Yoshitoshi: 1839-1892* (Ann Arbor, 1982)

Keyes, Roger S *The Art of Surimono* (London, 1985)

Keyes, Roger S. and Mizushima Keiko *The Theatrical World of Osaka Prints. A Collection of 18th and 19th Century Woodblock Prints* (Boston, 1973)

Kozyreff, Chantal *Estampes Japonaises: Collection des Musées Royaux d'Art et d'Histoire* (Brussels, 1989)

Lane, Richard *Images from the Floating World: The Japanese Print* (Oxford, 1978)

Link, Howard A *Primitive Ukiyo-e: From the James A. Michener Collection in the Honolulu Academy of Arts* (Honolulu, 1980)

Link, Howard A *The Theatrical Prints of the Torii Masters: A Selection of Seventeenth and Eighteenth-Century Ukiyo-e* (Honolulu, 1977)

Meech-Pekarik, Julia *The World of the Meiji Print: Impressions of a New Civilization* (New York, 1986)

Ogura Tadao et al *The Complete Woodblock Prints of Yoshida Hiroshi* (Tokyo, 1987)

Ota Memorial Museum of Art *Katsukawa Shunshō to sono ichimon ten (Exhibition of Katsukawa Shunshō and his pupils; Tokyo, 1983)*

Poster, Amy G and Smith, Henry D Hiroshige: One Hundred Famous Views of Edo (London, 1986)

Rappard-Boon, C van *The Age of Harunobu: Early Japanese Prints, c.1700-1780. (Catalogue of the Collection of Japanese Prints, Part I;* Rijksprentenkabinet, Rijksmuseum, Amsterdam, 1977)

Rappard-Boon, Charlotte van *The Age of Yoshitoshi: Catalogue of the Collection of Japanese Prints V* (Amsterdam, 1990)

Riccar Art Museum *Kikugawa Eizan bijinga Kessaku ten (Exhibition of Ukiyo-e beauties by Kikugawa Eizan)* (Tokyo, 1985)

Robinson, Basil William, *Kuniyoshi: The Warrior-Prints* (Oxford, 1982)

Robinson, B W, intro *Kunisada: An Artist in the Kabuki Theatre: The Japanese Prints in the Antell Collection* (Helsinki, 1985)

Schwaab, Dean J *Osaka Prints* (London, 1989)

Self, James and Nobuku Hirose: *Japanese Art Signatures. A Handbook and Practical Guide* (London, 1987)

Shibui, Kiyoshi: *Ukiyoe zuten 13: Utamaro* (Tokyo, 1964)

Shōzaburō Watanabe *Memorial Exhibition for Hiroshige* (Tokyo, 1917)

Smith, Lawrence *The Japanese Print Since 1900: Old Dreams and New Visions* (London, 1983)

Strange, Edward Fairbrother *The Colour-Prints of Hiroshige* (London, 1925)

Suzuki Juzō and Isaburō Oka: *The Decadents* (Tokyo, 1975)

Tamba, Tsuneo *Yokohama Ukiyo-e: reflection of the Cultures of Yokohama in Days of the Port Opening* (Tokyo, 1962)

Tokuriki, Tomikichirō *Wood-block Print Primer* (Tokyo, 1970)

Tokyo National Museum *Ukiyo-e Prints: Illustrated Catalogues of Tokyo National Museum* (Tokyo, 1960)

Ukiyoe Encyclopedia Committee *Genshoku ukiyo-e daihyakka jiten* (Encyclopedia in Color on Ukiyo-e 11 vols; Tokyo, 1980-82)

Ukiyo-e Society of America *Life and Customs of Edo As Portrayed in Woodblock Prints of the 17th through 19th Centuries* (New York, 1978)

Ukiyo-e taikei [Great Collection of Woodblock Prints] 17 vols. Tokyo, 1974-76)

Vever Collection: *Highly Important Japanese Prints, Illustrated Books and Drawings: From the Henri Vever Collection, Part I-IV* (London, 1974-78)

Volker, Tye *Ukiyoe Quartet: Publisher, Designer, Engraver and Printer* (Leiden, 1949)

Walters Art Gallery: *Japan and the West in Japanese Prints* (Baltimore, 1982)

Waterhouse, D B *Harunobu and His Age* Trustees of the British Museum, London, 1964)

Waterhouse, David *Images of Eighteenth-Century Japan: Ukiyo-e Prints from the Sir Edmund Walker Collection* (Royal Ontario Museum, Toronto, 1975)

Waterhouse, David 'New Light on the Life and Work of Suzuki Harunobu,' *Impressions (Official Publication of the Ukiyo-e Society of America, Inc.)*, 5 (Spring 1981), pp. 1-6

Waterhouse, David *The Harunobu Decade: A Catalogue of Woodcuts by Suzuki Harunobu and His Followers in the Museum of Fine Arts, Boston* (in preparation)

Yoshida Teruji *Utamaro Zenshū.* (The Complete Works of Utamaro; Tokyo, 1941)

Index

Figures in *italics* refer to illustrations

Acknowledgments

The publisher would like to thank Martin Bristow who designed this book, Pat Coward, who indexed it, Maria Costantino, the picture researcher, Pete Brealey at SX Composing, Veronica Price, the production controller, and Aileen Reid, the co-ordinating editor, who worked together to produce this book under the severest of time pressures. For the same reason we were unable to obtain some of the illustrations to chapters 6 and 7, and references have been inserted in the text to aid identification. We would also like to thank the following agencies, individuals and institutions for permission to reproduced the illustrations:

Courtesy Abe Publishing Co Ltd, Gallery Kabutoya, Pallas Inc.: 190, 203, 204, 207, 212, 214, 215, 216, 217, 218, 219, 220, 221(both), 222, 223 (both), 224 (both), 225, 226 (both), 227 (both)
Art Institute of Chicago, Clarence Buckingham Collection: 67 (1925.2540), 66-69 (1925.2143 & 1925.2144), 75 (1925.2217), 80 (1938.498), 81 (1925.2361)
Courtesy of Bamboo Publishing: 26
Bickford Collection: 122 (both), 123 (all 3)
Courtesy of the Trustees of the British Museum, London: 19 (below), 24 (top), 50 (top), 57, 59 (left, Oscar Raphael Bequest), 76, 82, 84, 85, 86 (below), 87, 88-89, 90-91, 92 (top), 93, 94, 95, 96, 97, 98 (both), 99, 100, 101, 102, 104 (both), 106, 107, 109, 110 (both), 111, 112, 113, 114-115, 117, 147, 154, 155, 156, 157, 158, 159, 160-161, 170, 171, 172, 228, 230-231, 232-233, 234, 235, 236, 237, 238, 239, 240, 241, 242, 243 (both), 244 (both), 245, 246, 247, 248, 249 (both)
Chester Beatty Library, Dublin: 61
Courtesy of Christie's, New York: 13
Collection J Asselbergs, Netherlands: 21
Collection P Beeten, Netherlands: 19(top)
Collection Hotei, Netherlands: 7, 10, 11, 12, 14, 16, 17, 18, 20, 27
Collection R Schaap, Netherlands: 8, 9, 22, 24 (below), 25
The Fine Arts Museums of San Francisco: 79 (The Achenbach Foundation for Graphic Arts Purchase)
Honolulu Academy of Arts; James A Michener Collection: 52, 58
Kruml Collection, London: 28, 29, 30 (both), 31 33 (both), 34 (both), 35 (both), 36 (both), 37, 38 (both), 40 (both), 41 (all 3), 42 (both), 43 (both), 44 (both), 45 (both)
Metropolitan Museum of Art, New York: 74 (The Henry L Phillips Collection, Bequest of Henry L Phillips, 1940), 77 (Rogers Fund, 1927), 196 (below) (Gift of Lincoln Kirstein, 1959)
Minneapolis Institute of Arts: 62
Courtesy of the Museum of Fine Arts, Boston: 63 (Bigelow Collection), Spaulding Collection: 64, 65, 66, 70, 73
Philadelphia Museum of Art: 195, 198-199 (Given by Mr Peter Benoliel [Funds Contributed])
Courtesy of the Portland Art Museum, Oregon Art Institute: 209 (The Vivian and Gordon Gilkey Graphic Arts Collection)
Private Collection: 47, 48, 49 (both), 50 (below), 54, 55, 56, 59 (right), 60
Rijksmuseum, Amsterdam: 32 (both), 39 (top), 51, 72, 120
R O Müller Collection/Photography by Phillip Galgiani: 15, 23, 185, 186, 187, 189, 191, 192, 193, 194 (both), 196 (top), 197, 200, 201, 203
Courtesy of the Royal Ontario Museum, Toronto, Canada: 53
Courtesy of the Trustees of the Victoria and Albert Museum, London: 1, 43 (below left), 86 (top), 92 (below), 103, 105, 108, 116, 118, 119, 121, 124, 126, 127, 132, 134, 135, 136, 137, 138, 139, 140-141, 143, 144, 145 (both), 146, 148-149, 150, 151, 162, 163, 164, 165, 166, 168, 169, 173, 176, 177, 178-179, 180, 181, 182 (all 3), 183 (all 3)
Whitworth Art Gallery, University of Manchester: 2-3, 6, 125, 128, 129, 130-131, 133, 152-153, 167, 174, 175
Worcester Art Museum, Worcester, Massachusetts: 71

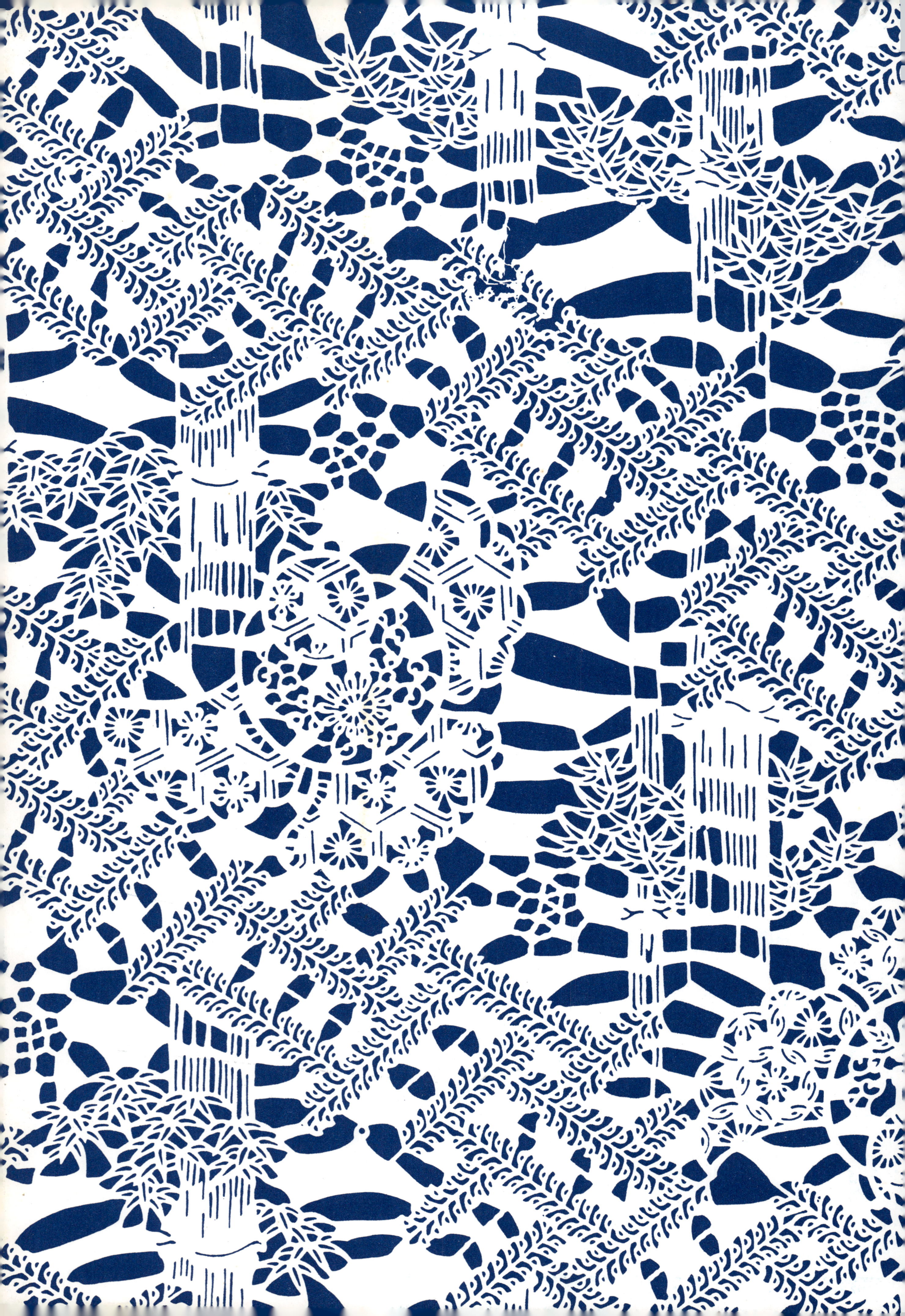